W9-CAB-390

MAGILL'S LITERARY ANNUAL 1989

MAGILL'S LITERARY ANNUAL 1989

Essay-Reviews of 200 Outstanding Books Published in the United States during 1988

With an Annotated Categories Index

Volume One

A-Lib

Edited by

FRANK N. MAGILL

SALEM PRESS

Pasadena, California **Englewood Cliffs, New Jersey**

∞ The paper used in these volumes conforms to the American National Standard for Permanence of Paper for Printed Library Materials, Z39.48-1984.

Library of Congress Catalog Card No. 77-99209

ISBN 0-89356-289-0

FIRST PRINTING

PRINTED IN THE UNITED STATES OF AMERICA

PUBLISHER'S NOTE

Magill's Literary Annual, 1989, is the thirty-fourth publication in a series that began in 1954. The philosophy behind the annual has been to evaluate critically each year a given number of major examples of serious literature published during the previous year. Our continuous effort is to provide coverage for works that are likely to be of more than passing general interest and that will stand up to the test of time. Individual critical articles for the first twenty-two years were collected and published in *Survey of Contemporary Literature* in 1977.

For the reader new to the Magill reference format, the following brief explanation should serve to facilitate the research process. The two hundred works represented in this year's annual are drawn from the following categories: fiction; poetry; literary criticism and literary history; essays; biography; autobiography, memoirs, diaries, and letters; history; current affairs and social science; science; and miscellaneous. The articles are arranged alphabetically by book title in the two-volume set; a complete list of the titles included can be found at the beginning of volume 1. Following a list of titles are the titles arranged by category in an annotated listing. This list provides the reader with the title, author, page number, and a brief one-sentence description of the particular work. The names of all contributing reviewers for the literary annual are listed alphabetically in the front of the book as well as at the end of their reviews. At the end of volume 2, there are two indexes: an index of Biographical Works by Subject and the Cumulative Author Index. The index of biographical works covers the years 1977 to 1989, and it is arranged by subject rather than by author or title. Thus, readers will be able to locate easily a review of any biographical work published in the Magill annuals since 1977 (including memoirs, diaries, and letters—as well as biographies and autobiographies) by looking up the name of the person. Following the index of Biographical Works by Subject is the Cumulative Author Index. Beneath each author's name appear the titles of all of his or her works reviewed in the Magill annuals since 1977. Next to each title, in parentheses, is the year of the annual in which the review appeared, followed by the page number.

Each article begins with a block of top matter that indicates the title, author, publisher, and price of the work. When possible, the year of the author's birth is also provided. The top matter also includes the number of pages of the book, the type of work, and, when appropriate, the time period and locale represented in the text. Next, there is the same capsulized description of the work that appears in the annotated list of titles. When pertinent, a list of principal characters or of personages introduces the review.

The articles themselves are approximately two thousand words in length. They are original essay-reviews that analyze and present the focus, intent, and relative success of the author, as well as the makeup and point of view of the work under discussion. To assist the reader further, the articles are supplemented by a list of additional reviews for further study in a bibliographic format.

As mentioned above, history-oriented books are once again included in *Magill's Literary Annual*, as they were prior to 1983. Readers who are especially interested in biography, history, and current affairs are invited to consult the twelve-volume *Great Events from History* and the *Great Lives from History*, which covers significant historical figures.

LIST OF TITLES

LIST OF TITLES

LIST OF TITLES

LIST OF TITLES

TITLES BY CATEGORY

ANNOTATED

TITLES BY CATEGORY

page

TITLES BY CATEGORY

POETRY

LITERARY CRITICISM
LITERARY HISTORY

page

TITLES BY CATEGORY

ESSAYS

LITERARY BIOGRAPHY

TITLES BY CATEGORY

AUTOBIOGRAPHY
MEMOIRS
DIARIES
LETTERS

page

BIOGRAPHY

page

page

HISTORY

TITLES BY CATEGORY

CURRENT AFFAIRS
SOCIAL SCIENCE

MISCELLANEOUS

CONTRIBUTING REVIEWERS FOR 1989 ANNUAL

Michael Adams
Wagner College

Kerry Ahearn
Oregon State University

Andrew J. Angyal
Elon College

Stanley Archer
Texas A&M University

Edwin T. Arnold
Appalachian State University

Tony Arthur
California State University, Northridge

Jean Ashton
New York Historical Society

Bryan Aubrey
Maharishi International University

Dean Baldwin
Behrend College, Pennsylvania State University

Dan Barnett
Butte College

Robert A. Bascom
Claremont Graduate School

Carolyn Wilkerson Bell
Randolph-Macon Woman's College

Gordon N. Bergquist
Creighton University

Dale B. Billingsley
University of Louisville

Harold Branam
Temple University

Gerhard Brand
California State University, Los Angeles

Peter Brier
California State University, Los Angeles

Jeanie R. Brink
Arizona State University

J. R. Broadus
University of North Carolina at Chapel Hill

Keith H. Brower
Dickinson College

Rebecca R. Butler
Dalton College

David A. Carpenter
Eastern Illinois University

John R. Carpenter
University of Michigan

Patricia Clark
University of Tennessee, Knoxville

Norman S. Cohen
Occidental College

Frank Day
Clemson University

Bill Delaney
Independent Scholar

Carol Clark D'Lugo
Clark University

Marvin D'Lugo
Clark University

Leon V. Driskell
University of Louisville

Bruce L. Edwards
Bowling Green State University

William U. Eiland
University of Georgia

Robert P. Ellis
Worcester State College

Thomas Erskine
Salisbury State University

Audrey A. Fisch
Rutgers University

David Marc Fischer
Independent Scholar

Bruce E. Fleming
United States Naval Academy

Robert J. Forman
Saint John's University, New York

Leslie E. Gerber
Appalachian State University

Dana Gerhardt
Independent Scholar

Kenneth Gibbs
Worcester State College

Richard Glatzer
Independent Scholar

Lois Gordon
Fairleigh Dickinson University

Daniel L. Guillory
Millikan University

Terry Heller
Coe College

Jane Hill
Peachtree Publishers

Ronald Howard
Mississippi College

Philip K. Jason
United States Naval Academy

Shakuntala Jayaswal
University of New Haven

Jane Anderson Jones
Manatee Community College

Carola M. Kaplan
California State Polytechnic University

Steven G. Kellman
University of Texas at San Antonio

Karen A. Kildahl
South Dakota State University

Charles Kraszewski
Pennsylvania State University-University Park

James B. Lane
Indiana University, Northwest

Leon Lewis
Appalachian State University

Janet E. Lorenz
Independent Scholar

Judith N. McArthur
University of Texas at Austin

Steven A. McCarver
Auburn University at Montgomery

Mark McCloskey
Glendale College
Occidental College
University of Southern California

Ric S. Machuga
Butte College

Charles E. May
California State University, Long Beach

Laurence W. Mazzeno
United States Naval Academy

Sally Mitchell
Temple University

Leslie B. Mittleman
California State University, Long Beach

Robert A. Morace
Daemen College

Robert E. Morsberger
California State Polytechnic University

Daniel Peter Murphy
Hanover College

John M. Muste
Ohio State University

Stella Nesanovich
McNeese University

George O'Brien
Georgetown University

Patrick O'Donnell
University of Arizona

Rosanne Osborne
Louisiana College

Robert Otten
Assumption College

Lisa Paddock
Independent Scholar

Robert J. Paradowski
Rochester Institute of Technology

Thomas R. Peake
King College

David Peck
California State University, Long Beach

Thomas Rankin
Independent Scholar

CONTRIBUTING REVIEWERS FOR 1989 ANNUAL

John D. Raymer
Indiana Technical Vocational College

Rosemary M. Canfield Reisman
Troy State University

Martin Ridge
The Huntington Library, Art Collections, and Botanical Gardens

Carl Rollyson
Bernard M. Baruch College
City University of New York

Joseph Rosenblum
University of North Carolina at Greensboro

Marc Rothenberg
Smithsonian Institution

Edward B. St. John
Loyola Law School, Los Angeles

Francis Michael Sharp
University of the Pacific

T. A. Shippey
University of Leeds

R. Baird Shuman
University of Illinois at Urbana

Anne W. Sienkewicz
Independent Scholar

Marjorie Smelstor
Ball State University

D. P. Smith
United States Naval Academy

Ira Smolensky
Monmouth College

Michael Sprinker
State University of New York at Stony Brook

Leon Stein
Roosevelt University

Jean T. Strandness
North Dakota State University

Ann Struthers
Coe College

James Sullivan
California State University, Los Angeles

David Sundstrand
Citrus College

Daniel Taylor
Bethel College

Henry Taylor
American University

William Urban
Monmouth College

Kenneth E. Walker
Frederick County Public Schools

Ronald G. Walker
Western Illinois University

Allen Wells
Bowdoin College

Bruce Wiebe
Independent Scholar

Barbara Wiedemann
University of Florida

John Wilson
Independent Scholar

Michael Witkoski
South Carolina House of Representatives

Paula P. Yow
Kennesaw College

MAGILL'S
LITERARY ANNUAL
1989

THE ACHIEVEMENT OF CORMAC McCARTHY

Author: Vereen M. Bell (1934-)
Publisher: Louisiana State University Press (Baton Rouge). 140 pp. $22.50
Type of work: Literary criticism

This examination of the five novels written by the Southern author Cormac McCarthy is the first book-length study of a difficult, little-known, but extremely important writer

Cormac McCarthy is the author of five novels: *The Orchard Keeper* (1965), *Outer Dark* (1968), *Child of God* (1973), *Suttree* (1979), and *Blood Meridian: Or, The Evening Redness in the West* (1985). All were published by Random House, but none has achieved very much public notice. Indeed, according to Vereen M. Bell in his groundbreaking study of McCarthy, these novels have sold in the neighborhood of only fifteen thousand copies altogether in their hardback editions. Yet Random House has continued to publish him, and his books are also available in paperback (*Suttree* in a Vintage edition; the other four novels from Ecco Press). Bell describes McCarthy's present position as follows:

> Cormac McCarthy is as elusive in life as life is in his fictions. He is a relatively young man, born in 1933, and little is known of him. His novels are scarcely read, even in Tennessee, his more-or-less native state. But both labor and obscurity seem to agree with him. He is a meticulous, unhurried craftsman and yet declines flatly to promote his own work, and he indirectly gives offense by disdaining academic patronage. . . . [McCarthy] remains committed to writing well and therefore patiently, aided intermittently by foundation support, including a substantial grant from the MacArthur Foundation. . . . He is a major writer in all of the conventional senses of the word, our best unknown major writer by many measures.

This is rather a romantic image Bell presents of the dedicated artist, but in McCarthy's case it seems to be the truth. Certainly it is true that McCarthy has in no way sought fame or fortune through his writing, refusing to give interviews, to publicize his works, to make personal tours. His books have remained difficult and challenging, in both their style and their subject matter. His stories are always marked with incredible violence rendered in an unflinching manner. As Bell puts it, McCarthy celebrates "life beyond the pale."

One need only look at the books to find how unappeasing McCarthy can be. His first novel, *The Orchard Keeper*, focuses on three characters: a young boy, John Wesley Rattner; a moonshiner, Marion Sylder; and an old man, an isolate named Arthur Ownby. The story is told alternately from each character's point of view. The boy's father has been killed by Sylder and his body placed in an insecticide-spray tank at the orchard "kept" by Ownby. Ownby tends to the body, keeping watch over it as the years pass. Both Ownby and Sylder become surrogate fathers to John Wesley, but it is a strange relationship McCarthy describes. In *Outer Dark*, he weaves a dark tale of a brother and sister living in the mountains of Tennessee. When the sister gives birth to their child, the brother abandons it in the woods, where it is found by a tinker. The sister-mother Rinthy goes in search of the baby, and the brother Culla follows. Their journeys are marked by threat and fear; Culla especially is stalked by three terrible figures, murderers and graverobbers both, who finally come to possess the now-deformed child themselves. *Child of God* is a horror story of madness and necrophilia in which the protagonist, Lester Ballard, murders his victims and takes away the women's corpses for companionship. *Suttree* is set in the slums of Knoxville in the early 1950's and reiterates scenes of degradation and disgust. *Blood Meridian* recounts the exploits of a band of renegade scalphunters who kill for bounty and for the pleasure of massacre. Although all these works have elements of humor (often very bizarre, but sometimes extremely funny nevertheless) and even moments of pity, they generally offer appalling examples of man's apparently innate capacity for inhumanity.

It is not subject matter alone, however, that distinguishes McCarthy from most of his contemporaries, and that has kept his work from receiving the blessing of literary tastemakers. After all, a penchant for the grotesque, the violent, and the depraved is one of the distinguishing features of much postwar fiction (and drama, too). Neither does the problem lie with McCarthy's difficulty per se, for some of the widely studied contemporary novelists are fashioners of intricately complex texts. Rather, the problem is that McCarthy's fiction eludes the categories favored by contemporary criticism—and that which cannot be classified is treated as if it did not exist.

There is no metafictional play in McCarthy's fiction, nor is there an allusive texture such as has prompted the publication of a half-dozen book-length guides annotating Thomas Pynchon's *Gravity's Rainbow* (1973). Instead, McCarthy tells stories—yet he cannot be grouped with the many contemporary novelists who, in reaction against modernism, hark back to the nineteenth century for their models. As Bell observes, in McCarthy's fiction "plots in the conventional sense, complicated stories with appropriate resolutions or outcomes, do not prevail." McCarthy's narratives are episodic, anecdotal, sometimes with a flavor of the picaresque; they are also uncompromisingly enigmatic. McCarthy refrains from offering final answers. In one sense, he declines to judge; in another, he declines to let his reader off the hook.

McCarthy's distinctive narrative strategy is wedded to his masterful and highly idiosyncratic prose style. He employs a vivid, extravagant, and often-arcane vocabulary. "Even labored and latinate passages . . . are, when analyzed, cleanly referential and descriptive," Bell contends. McCarthy's language risks extravagance in order to avoid reductionism. His "portentous" passages, Bell says, "keep a dreamlike, almost symbolist, pressure of meaning, or meaningfulness, alive in the text without providing easy or even perceptible means of release." Thus, McCarthy's world is concrete yet opaque, freighted with mystery.

It is Bell's difficult task to convince a largely unappreciative audience that reading this very challenging writer is worthwhile. This is a problem that he acknowledges in his preface, confessing a degree of embarrassment for having used straightforward prose to explicate and make accessible this writer whose great virtue is his dazzling, bewildering use of language. Yet because McCarthy refuses "to meet his readers halfway," Bell's enterprise is a necessary one. It is a measure of Bell's success that any peruser of his book will surely be drawn to make the effort and reap the rewards of reading McCarthy himself.

Bell's approach is straightforward. He begins his study with a brief introduction titled "The Mystery of Being," in which he sets up his basic theses. He then devotes each of the following five chapters to discussions of the separate novels, taken in order of publication. Although Bell sees each novel as an individual work, he also draws them together in his discussions to demonstrate the interrelationships he finds among them. He clearly means for his study to be a beginning, certainly not the final word on McCarthy, and there are many questions he leaves unanswered, many possibilities he forgoes for others to follow. Bell forcefully argues for McCarthy's importance as a major writer. He compares him to William Faulkner, T. S. Eliot, Joseph Conrad, Flannery O'Connor, even Dante and William Shakespeare, and such comparisons are effectively made. He maps out the broad issues in McCarthy's work in the same way that Cleanth Brooks did for Faulkner.

Bell gives careful attention to McCarthy's religious philosophy, demonstrating the prevalence of human evil throughout the novels and suggesting that McCarthy considers that such evil "has taken an irreversible form." It is also true, however, that McCarthy comes again and again to the basic questions of Christian theology, his symbolism often derived from his Catholic background. Although his vision is dark and violent and despairing, he continues to ponder the possibility of man's salvation. The book *Suttree* (which Bell considers to be McCarthy's strongest work) ends on such a note of grace, although it in no way mitigates the frightful nature of sin or the horrible reality of suffering in the world. Bell emphasizes the nihilism he finds in the books, but to do so perhaps fails to give proper credence to McCarthy's moments of faith. It can be argued that McCarthy is, like O'Connor and Eliot, a religious writer of the first rank, and it seems likely that future criticism will more directly address this possibility.

At the present time, however, McCarthy remains little known. Like Faulkner at a similar stage in his career, McCarthy has not yet found his audience. It may be that studies such as *The Achievement of Cormac McCarthy* will help to bring him before the serious reading public he most definitely deserves.

Edwin T. Arnold

Source for Further Study

Choice. XXVI, March, 1989, p. 1152.

ADAM, EVE, AND THE SERPENT

Author: Elaine Pagels
Publisher: Random House (New York). 189 pp. $17.95
Type of work: History of religion

A theologian argues that contemporary ideas of moral freedom and sexual morality took shape in the fourth century, when Christianity became the official religion of the Roman Empire

Elaine Pagels, professor of religion at Princeton University, asks, "When did key Christian concepts about gender, sex, and suffering take shape?" In *Adam, Eve, and the Serpent*, she points to the fourth century as the key period. Surveying three hundred years of theological controversy and polemic, Pagels concludes that Christian ideas about marriage, sex, virginity, divorce, sin, nature, and individual moral responsibility became rooted about the same time that Christianity replaced polytheism as the official religion of the Roman Empire. Pagels identifies Saint Augustine of Hippo as the theologian whose expression of these ideas became identified with the true faith. Augustine's theology triumphed, she asserts, because it fit the needs of an institutionalized religion and because it justified to believers God's ways of painfully limiting human existence.

Pagels is one of many prominent scholars in religion, philosophy, and history recently attracted to studying the first four centuries of the Christian era. This attraction was prompted by midcentury discoveries in archaeology and by a new historical methodology. The most important discovery of ancient texts was the finding of the Nag Hammadi manuscripts: apocryphal gospels, epistles, and treatises referred to in surviving works but thought lost. The new methodology comes from the *annales* school, which writes history not by chronicling wars and governments but by reconstructing daily life. Studying ordinary artifacts, routine correspondence, architecture, landscape, and even weather patterns, *annales* historians see human history as the experience of many individuals, not only the famous.

Thus, new sources of information, considered through a new perspective, enable scholars to study the first four hundred years of Christianity outside traditional polarities. These centuries witnessed an astounding transformation: What began as a small Jewish sectarian movement became the official religion of the Greco-Roman world. Finding an explanation for this phenomenon has always been a challenge for Western thinkers; by the early twentieth century two competing viewpoints had reached a stalemate. One was the medieval Christian view: the triumph of the True Faith over paganism was a clear sign of God's providential plan, a watershed in salvation history. During the theological controversies of the Reformation, these centuries were further idealized as the period of the Church's purity: That earliest Christian age possessed liturgy, life-style, and doctrine directly from the Apostles. The skeptical Enlightenment view, on the other hand, saw the decline of the Roman Empire as the fall of sophisticated, secular civilization. From this perspective, the rise of Christianity was the triumph of zealotry; tales of martyrs and miracles were exaggerations, legends, or lies. Little verifiable history of these centuries was possible, according to the skeptics; the most cynical doubted even the historicity of Jesus. Recent scholarship has broken through this dichotomy to rethink or reconceptualize the events of Christianity's early history.

One important reconceptualization concerns the relationship between orthodox and heretical Christians. The orthodox view themselves as maintaining an unbroken succession from the Apostles. They oppose heretics, who, motivated by ambition or pride or jealousy, attempt to lead the faithful astray. Like the clever serpent in Eden, the heretic woos the believer from the path of truth by deceitful double-talk. Pagels' research into the Nag Hammadi manuscripts and other nonorthodox documents challenges this view of heresy. These documents reveal a world of Christianities during the first two centuries after Christ in which a variety of texts, traditions, and practices prevailed. These Christianities complemented rather than challenged one another; though differing in belief, they stood united against Roman polytheism. Thus, the great "heresies" of the third and fourth century—Pelagianism and Donatism—can be interpreted simply as old Christian traditions that resisted change, merger, or incorporation. The Christian viewpoint that eventually took hold and triumphed called itself orthodox and labeled its defeated rivals heresies. This view of doctrinal development raises fascinating questions. What factors enable one view to survive while another perishes? How does the larger community come to value one view over another?

To answer these questions, Pagels focuses on competing responses to the Creation story in the first three chapters of the Book of Genesis. For Pagels, the interpretations of Adam's fall and the expulsion from Eden divided Christian from Jew and Christian from Christian. In a chronological treatment, Pagels traces the evolution of the debate over the theological lessons of Genesis.

Rabbinical exegesis emphasized the lessons in sexual morality that the Creation story teaches: abhorrence of nakedness and bestiality, the centrality of procreation in marriage. Early Christians, especially those influenced by the preaching of Saint Paul, invoked the story to show man's subordination to divinity and woman's subordination to man.

For second century Christians, Genesis' teaching of man's subordination to God meant that men were not subordinate to the state. The philosopher Justin Martyr used Genesis to justify a Christian's refusal to pay homage to the Roman gods and his acceptance of martyrdom. Clement of Alexandria extended Justin's insight: If God made man in His own image, all men are equal. The hierarchy of Roman society, headed by a semidivine emperor, must be evil in Christian eyes. Consequently, Christians stressed that Genesis made men responsible moral agents, with the freedom to choose between a true sovereign and a false one.

Reliance upon Genesis as a central text, however, is problematic. Its first three chapters offer several paradoxes: They present two conflicting accounts of Creation, they image God in human terms as walking and talking in the Garden, and they present the morally ambiguous figure of the serpent, both tempter and truth-teller.

These chapters also raise disturbing philosophical questions: If God created the world as good, why is it so filled with suffering? One group of Christians (called Gnostics) responded by interpreting Genesis symbolically. Since the story seemed foolish on its face, Gnostics read for a deeper, hidden logic. Gnosticism's esoteric readings worried other Christians, who were concerned that believers might surrender the concept of moral freedom in exchange for initiation into supposed mysteries. Eventually, Gnostic Christians were expelled from the community of believers.

During the second and third centuries, Christianity made converts among all levels of Roman society. At the same time, it passionately embraced the concept of celibacy. The celibate became the exemplar of moral freedom; the man or woman who remained chaste kept free of the demands of the flesh, the demands of marriage, the demands of family, and ultimately the demands of society. Freed from all human bonds, the celibate concentrated on the one bond that mattered: obedience to God's will. Those who committed themselves to the ascetic life by vows of chastity and poverty began to take preeminence in the Church over those who did not make such vows.

As the Christian community gained in numbers, it increasingly became an accepted religion, whose adherents were no longer subject to persecution. When Emperor Constantine the Great converted in 313, Christianity became the official religion of the Empire. As the official religion, it participated in the secular life of the empire: taxation, judicial proceedings, national defense. Pagels points out that it was under these circumstances that Augustine of Hippo offered a new reading of Genesis. Emphasizing the concept of original sin as the central theological lesson of Genesis—a sin that afflicted not only Adam and Eve but also all of their descendants—Augustine deemphasized the first chapters of Genesis as a story of moral freedom. The concept of universal original sin implied that humans beings need government to control their sinful natures. Augustine's concept also had comforting psychological implications. It explained the presence of suffering and death in the world, as the consequence of the First Parents' sin. Evil and mortality were not in God's plan for the world, nor are they the responsibility of individuals.

Pagels' chapter, which pits Augustine's theology against the positive outlook of Julian, Bishop of Eclanum, is riveting. Pagels skillfully juxtaposes the thoughts of each debater to build an incremental structure of point and counterpoint, assertion and rebuttal. With the dizzying philosophical sweep of Fyodor Dostoevski's "The Legend of the Grand Inquisitor," Pagels' combatants clash over numerous issues, from the purpose of painful childbirth to God's plan of salvation. The discussion is compelling because Augustine and Julian treat questions for which modern Christians have some answers but no sure resolution.

Pagels' thesis, judgments, and method of presentation are open to criticism and debate. Though she presents her conclusions modestly and speaks frankly of her fascination with Christianity's early history, some readers will respond that her explanation of theological development is reductionistic. While crediting the weight she gives to political factors and psychological appeal as causes for Augustine's triumph, objectors will stress that she ignores other important factors. For example, Christians in the mid-fourth century were highly concerned with defining sacramental and liturgical issues about individual guilt; Augustine's appeal must be read against this background of debate about baptism and penance. Similarly, some will protest that Pagels' explanation is completely naturalistic, ignoring a fundamental tenet of faith: that God continues to unfold the plan of salvation.

Pagels' portrayal of Augustine will also stir controversy. Her analysis of his theological development stresses the lasting effects of his youthful libertinism and instinctive Manichaeanism. She depicts Augustine's writings as a response to temperament and times. Her account raises the implicit question: Is theology ultimately biography? Can any theologian carry out biblical exegesis without reading himself or his experience into his conclusions? If Augustine had been a different personality, would his theology—and subsequent Western thought—have been much different? Pagels clearly sympathizes with the Gnostics, Bishop Pelagius, and Julian, whom orthodoxy brands as heretics. *Adam, Eve, and the Serpent* is not, however, a nostalgic brief for the rightness of these causes; rather, it demonstrates toward these Christians the compassion of a scholar who fully understands both sides of the historical debate.

Finally, the form of *Adam, Eve, and the Serpent* is not entirely satisfactory. Its six chapters are rewritten and linked versions of six technical articles; they rework for a general audience individual pieces prepared for scholars. Whether Pagels has successfully integrated these six themes into a whole is debatable. She chooses as her unifying device Christian responses to chapters 1 to 3 of Genesis, yet her discussion travels far beyond the confines of the Creation accounts. In fact, the issues debated by the early Christians were shaped by a reading of many biblical texts in addition to Genesis. The book's catchy title, alluding to Western history's most infamous *ménage à trois*, seems most likely to be the publisher's effort to reach a mass market. The title hints at gender issues that are currently prominent in popular culture, yet those issues actually play only a small part in Pagels' book. Adam, Eve, and the serpent actually receive comparatively short shrift in the discussion: The index lists ten references to Adam, seven to Eve, and two to the serpent.

Some readers may well begin the book thinking it concerns patriarchy, feminism, and Satanism, but they will find theological history made relevant, presented dramatically, and cared for passionately.

Robert Otten

Sources for Further Study

Booklist. LXXXIV, June 1, 1988, p. 1630.
The Christian Science Monitor. September 14, 1988, p. 18.

Kirkus Reviews. LVI, April 15, 1988, p. 602.
Library Journal. CXIII, June 15, 1988, p. 63.
Maclean's. CI, August 15, 1988, p. 52.
The New Republic. CXCIX, August 8, 1988, p. 38.
The New York Review of Books. XXXV, June 30, 1988, p. 27.
The New York Times Book Review. XCIII, August 21, 1988, p. 15.
Publishers Weekly. CCXXXIII, April 29, 1988, p. 60.
The Spectator. CCLXI, September 24, 1988, p. 28.

AFTER THE LOST WAR
A Narrative

Author: Andrew Hudgins (1951-)
Publisher: Houghton Mifflin (Boston). 134 pp. $12.50
Type of work: Narrative poetry
Time: The 1860's to the 1880's
Locale: The American South

Andrew Hudgins assumes the persona of the nineteenth century poet Sidney Lanier and uses the details of Lanier's life to explore universal themes: war, death, nature, God, family life, and work

Principal characters:
SIDNEY LANIER, a Georgia-born poet and flute player who served as a Confederate soldier during the Civil War
MARY DAY LANIER, his wife
CLIFFORD LANIER, his brother, who fought beside him in the Civil War

Literary movements often proceed by dialectic: A new mode of expression emerges in rebellion against the dominant and shopworn convention of the day; the new form is explored, refined, popularized and reproduced, until it too becomes exhausted and trite, necessitating a swing back to the form against which it originally sprang in opposition. Yet this harking back is never a simple return to the previous form, but a new creation representing a new synthesis. Thus, literary expression is constantly renewing itself. In the twentieth century, the dominant mode of poetic expression has been the lyric, wherein the poet subjectively sings of his own feelings and imaginative longings. As the century approaches its close, many poets have reacted against the lyric impulse and returned to the more objective narrative form, using plot, characterization, and setting to tell the stories of lives other than their own. Andrew Hudgins—whose first book, *Saints and Strangers* (1985), includes a striking narrative sequence as well as a number of short lyrics—is among the poets who have returned to the narrative and are rewriting its rules (hence, they are often called "neonarrative poets"). It is interesting that one of Hudgins' greatest contributions to the narrative tradition with *After the Lost War: A Narrative* is his success in blending narrative force with the beauty and grace of lyric expression.

After the Lost War is the story in verse of the Georgia-born poet and musician Sidney Lanier. The book is divided into four chronologically arranged sections, beginning with the years after the Civil War, when Lanier, a Confederate soldier, returns home. The story continues with Lanier's marriage to Mary Day and the years spent rearing a family, trying to earn a meager income as a musician and poet while struggling with ill health from injuries sustained in the war. The book concludes with Lanier's early death from tuberculosis in 1881. Each section is introduced with a few prose paragraphs that outline the major events of Lanier's life during the period. The poems within each section (from nine to fourteen in number) are not arranged chronologically, but proceed according to a more intuitive logic, by a plot of emotion and theme rather than dramatically linked events. With the compressed language of poetry, the poems succeed, often by focusing on small events and feelings, putting flesh and blood on the bare prose skeleton of events in Lanier's life, seemingly evoking more of the sweep of Lanier's life than a three-hundred-page biography might have done.

The poems are all in the first-person voice of the central character, Lanier himself; in form, they are very much like poems one would call lyrics, each capable of standing on its own without necessarily being linked to the larger movements of the story. In fact, the traditional distinction between lyric and narrative—the one a personal expression of the poet and the other a story about characters—is blurred here. In the book's preface Hudgins writes, "I'd like to thank Lanier for allowing me to use the facts of his life . . . to see how I might have lived it if it had been mine." Hudgins cautions the reader not to confuse his Lanier with the historical one; his work is not a biography, or if it is, it is a highly subjective biography, with the writer allowing himself to merge somewhat with his subject.

If the book does not really concern the historical Sidney Lanier, then what is its true subject? The answer is in the book's title. "After the lost war" describes both a time and a place—the South in the years following its defeat. Lanier's story tells many stories, showing how a number of Southerners might have felt as they worked to reconstruct their lives on new terms. Lanier's health was never quite the same after the war, and his struggle with death becomes emblematic of the South itself. In fact "with the younger generation of the South/ after the lost war, pretty much/ the whole of life has been not dying." Further levels of meaning turn on the two most significant words in the title, "lost" and "war." The narrative explores various nuances of the word "lost"—beyond merely not having been on the winning side—as in losing possessions or intangibles such as ideals, or losing direction and being confused. These themes extend the subject of Hudgins' narrative to more universal dimensions, beyond the particular time and place of its setting. The narrative also explores the larger implications of the word "war," as meaning not only soldiers locked in combat but also any two opposing sides that will not be reconciled. This is a book about struggles—between right and wrong, between nature and man, between life and death. Like a good novel, *After the Lost War* is a multilayered story with universal themes; it concerns both one man and every man.

Though a Confederate soldier, Hudgins' Lanier admits to caring little for the cause he was supposedly defending. In "The Cult of the Lost Cause," a poem addressed to his brother, he says "Forgive me, I am glad we lost." This statement is not political but moral, for he believes that it was not only the South that lost the war; rather, everyone lost. Images of war, its death and destruction, run like a stain throughout the book. In the poem titled "After the Lost War," even after the truce has been declared the stench and howl of battle still bleed into the landscape: "[E]ven in this pastoral land/ the green is mixed with battle cries/ and phantom groans," and "the flowers stank of sulphur and/ their blooms were flecked with human blood." The senseless consequences of battle are driven home by "Around the Campfire." In this poem, Lanier describes his "fond memories" of nights around the campfire, singing and playing music with his fellows, while cannons boomed and, in the occasional silences, the sounds of Yankees singing could be heard. A Texas boy had made a banjo, and though he knew he could not play it well, he took great delight in trying; this, too, Lanier calls a "fond instructive memory." One night while he was drinking whiskey with his banjo-playing friend, some cannon fire came close; when the smoke cleared he looked at his friend: "I saw/ him sitting, looking for his cup/ and for the hand he'd held it in." With powerful understatement Lanier says, "From this, I didn't learn a thing." With small moments such as this one, Hudgins brings the nightmare of war into sharp focus.

Just as clearly, Hudgins chronicles the haunting, long-term effect war has on the consciousness of its survivors. In some respects it is as though *After the Lost War* picks up where Stephen Crane's *The Red Badge of Courage: An Episode of the American Civil War* (1895) leaves off, as though Crane's young soldier has in Lanier grown up and matured and is now more fully digesting the American experience of the Civil War. Again, it is often the small details that tell the most, as in Lanier's observation that

Each spring
another woman in the town
gets up the nerve and gives to charity

her husband's or her son's old clothes.

Hudgins' Lanier can never fully get the war out of his head. Making love to his wife on their first anniversary, "I smelled the horse-sweat smell of war/ drawn from the blanket by our body heat./ It wouldn't scrub out of the heavy wool." He numbers among the war's losses not only tangibles such as life and limbs but also intangibles such as values, a sense of pride in oneself. In "Memories of Lookout Prison," Lanier recounts the time he tried to nurse a fellow prisoner back to health; when the man would not eat his bowl of corn, he thought of stealing it for himself. Lanier did not take the corn, but the sin of imagining it grieves him as much as if he had. "In the war I thought to lose an arm/ or leg. Not what I lost. Not that."

Though in some respects Hudgins can be accused of confusing centuries—that is, of putting twentieth century antiwar sentiments into his nineteenth century central character—it should be made clear that there is more to *After the Lost War* than its powerful antiwar theme. Throughout the narrative, the brutality of the Civil War is placed against a larger backdrop of activity that includes the same cruelties and losses—scenes from nature and from childhood. Though Lanier shudders at the common practice of stealing clothes off a dead man's body, he already knew a selfish lack of compassion at eight years old. In "The Hornets' Nest," he remembers as a child viciously attacking a hornets' nest with his friends. Running away, one of his friends was caught and badly stung; he was in bed for weeks. Though

Lanier did "the proper things," such as visiting his friend and writing him letters, what he really thought, Lanier confesses, was only that "*I'm glad/ it's him. I'm glad it's not me*." This poem, after "Around the Campfire," with its stunned compassion for the banjo player's loss of his hand, takes the narrative to a deeper layer of meaning. There is no simple way to divide good people from bad, or even good actions from the bad. Life is made up of both, often mixed in the same moment, as in the image of the buzzards that, after the war, the soldiers soak in kerosene and then set ablaze; their death flight is both hideous and beautiful, terrible yet somehow comforting. War does not make a man any better or worse than he really is; it merely exposes his soul, like a raw nerve.

As he is dying, in a feverish dream Lanier sees an image that seems to make clear once and for all man's paradoxical nature: "It was that all men draw from earth/ a spark of fire and a spike of cold/ that ought to cancel one another." Yet when he wakes in the morning his insight dissolves: "I don't understand my understanding." Finding meaning and then losing it is the poet's life; he wakes to try and find it again. Actually, *After the Lost War* is more about the poet's vocation than it is the soldier's. With each poem Hudgins' Lanier tries to make sense of what is before him, whether it is the war, the flight of birds, poverty, his wife's loss of sexual desire, the true nature of God, or his own approaching death. He is a keen and probing observer, forever trying to put a name to life's curious reconciliation of opposites. The final image in "Appetite for Poison" is emblematic of the poet's work. When a martin collides with a dragonfly, the dragonfly's delicate wings slowly flicker to the ground; Lanier's wife finds them and quietly presses them in her locket. So Lanier/Hudgins finds something delicate and beautiful in the collisions of life, pressing them for safekeeping in his poems.

That Hudgins achieves the depth and range a novelist could, yet with so few pages, results from the selection of powerful details that is the essence of good poetry, but it also results partly from the conversation of imagery that Hudgins engineers between the poems. Rarely does an image first appear without sometime later being echoed in yet another poem, whether it is a pair of shoes, the drone of bees, a turtle's shell, a hawk in flight, or Lanier's wife working in her garden. With each new context the image is seen from a different, even opposite angle; in this way the text, though spare, grows deep. For example, in "The World of Turtles" Lanier befriends a dead turtle washed up on the beach and contemplates his own mortality, but in "A Father on the Marsh" he takes an ax to a live turtle, to make some soup for his boys. One cannot read the one poem without thinking of the other. Like stones dropped in pools of water, Hudgins' images radiate ever-widening circles of meaning, making *After the Lost War* definitely worthy of more than one reading.

Dana Gerhardt

Sources for Further Study

Atlanta Journal-Constitution. March 20, 1988, p. J8.
Booklist. LXXXIV, January 15, 1988, p. 823.
Choice. XXV, May, 1988, p. 1401.
The Hudson Review. XLI, Summer, 1988, p. 393.
Library Journal. CXIII, January, 1988, p. 88.
Los Angeles Times Book Review. January 31, 1988, p. 10.
Poetry. CXLIII, October, 1988, p. 41.
Publishers Weekly. CCXXXII, December 18, 1987, p. 46.
Southern Living. XXIII, October, 1988, p. 88.
The Wall Street Journal. CCX, March 21, 1988, p. 16.

THE AGE OF EMPIRE
1875-1914

Author: Eric Hobsbawm (1917-)
Publisher: Pantheon Books (New York). Illustrated. 404 pp. $22.95
Type of work: History
Time: 1875-1914
Locale: Europe

An examination of the various forces—social, economic, religious, political, artistic, and military—that shaped the period from 1875 through 1914, ending the old European order and laying the foundation for the world of today

It is one of the great ironies of history that the very period which witnessed the triumph of the European imperial nations (the "Great Powers") was precisely the same period which saw the growth of those forces that would result in the cataclysm of World War I and its aftermath, with which we yet live. How it was that one society, Europe, came to dominate the world, but could not resolve its own internal contradictions, is the theme of Eric Hobsbawm's *The Age of Empire: 1875-1914*, the culminating volume of a trilogy begun with *The Age of Revolution: 1789-1848* (1962) and continued with *The Age of Capital: 1848-1875* (1975).

That it was an imperial age can scarcely be doubted. During this period at least one-quarter of the globe was parceled out to a very few nations, all of them European except for the United States, Japan, and the transcontinental colossus of the Russian Empire. At no other time in world history have there been so many rulers who could legitimately claim the title of "Emperor." On the surface, there seemed little reason that this situation could not endure indefinitely: The imperial nations appeared to be so strong militarily, economically, and even culturally, that nothing could prevent or upset their continued dominance of the earth. To some it seemed that the Western nations had assumed their rightful role in history: "manifest destiny," as it was termed in the United States; "the white man's burden," as Rudyard Kipling phrased it. The Age of Empire, then, was an age of both promise and achievement. Yet as Hobsbawm reminds the reader, the very same Kipling ("the greatest—perhaps the only—poet of imperialism") used the occasion of Queen Victoria's Diamond Jubilee in 1897 to compose a poem warning of the instability and impermanence of empires. They were fragile things, all too soon "one with Nineveh and Tyre." Kipling's brooding pessimism was shared by many during this period. Indeed, as Hobsbawm points out, there was widespread belief that certain disaster lurked ahead; most simply did not foresee it so soon.

Why should this be? Why should there be, linked almost inextricably, the sense of nearly unlimited power and inevitable decline? To answer those questions, Hobsbawm asks some of his own: What sort of world was this during the Age of Empire? How did its people live? What did they do, how did they live and dress, how did they amuse themselves, and what did they believe? These may seem to be simple, almost naïve questions, but they are the most difficult for the historian to answer, for they require the patient reconstruction of strata and substrata of past lives often lost during the course of time. Fortunately, the records for so recent a period are relatively untouched, and just as fortunately, Hobsbawm shows both imagination and sympathy in reconstructing the past. While many of his answers may not be new, his approaches are often novel and his insights revealing.

It is clear that the Age of Empire might equally be termed the Age of Uncertainty, for beneath the glittering trappings of imperial splendor there was the gnawing suspicion that Europe was heading toward some inevitable catastrophe and was dragging the rest of the world with it. This uncertainty was displayed in a thousand facets, from economics to politics, from science to the arts. Some embraced, even rejoiced in, novelty and uncertainty. It was the great period for the avant-garde in the arts, the time of Pablo Picasso, the Vienna Secession, and the Futurists. It was the era of transformation in the written arts—in English alone, one merely need think of Ezra Pound, James Joyce, or T. S. Eliot. And then, there were the movies.

Motion pictures were truly a new art form (at least in technology, if not in content), one which transformed popular culture. The fledgling cinema spread with extraordinary rapidity, helped in large part by a technological limitation: Unable to reproduce sound, early films developed a universal grammar of image, a purely pictorial presentation that made the product easily accessible throughout the world. The cinema was the true beginning of modern popular culture. To many, particularly in Europe, the advent of motion pictures signaled the end of real culture—that is, culture that could be appreciated and enjoyed only by the privileged few, or the serious, hardworking, and therefore deserving bourgeoisie. Regardless of whether these fears were justified, the development of the cinema was a sign of profound change.

There were other indications of changes in the world and how people perceived it, and Hobsbawm elucidates them clearly and concisely. He traces the wrenching shifts which took place in religion and philosophy, the social changes brought about by the emergence of the "New Woman," and the radical reordering of perceptions of reality that followed the discoveries of scientists such as Max Planck, Niels Bohr, and Albert Einstein. Above all, however, this period was most notable for its increased economic and military tension. If this was the Age of Uncertainty, the greatest fears revolved around economics and politics, which most thinking persons realized were closely bound together, and which, along with military growth, seemed to be evolving toward a dangerous future.

One need not be a Marxist, as Hobsbawm is, to recognize that unrestrained capitalism carries with it certain inescapable contradictions. The moguls, bankers, traders, and entrepreneurs who prospered during this period were certainly not socialists, but they worried—and worried publicly—about the growing strains the system placed upon the world's markets. There was both a widening and a concentration of the world economy during this time. It widened as empires expanded, bringing in new sources of raw materials and potential new markets for products and goods. This expansion in itself was enough to ensure increased competition between the major industrial powers, and since they were the major military powers as well, it brought a double danger.

The world economy contracted as wealth flowed to the developed nations, especially Western Europe (particularly Great Britain), and was concentrated there. The wealth was not in actual currency but in foreign investments. In other words, Europe held most of the world's other nations in its debt. The prosperity of Argentina, Egypt, or even Russia depended upon the decisions made in London or Paris or Amsterdam. In this way the world's economy narrowed dramatically. According to Hobsbawm, in 1914, Western Europe and the United States had 56 percent of the world's overseas investments, and Great Britain alone had 44 percent.

The result was a world economy that grew weaker and stronger at the same time. It was the sort of contradiction predicted by Karl Marx. The more a nation's economy expanded, the more it had to keep expanding in order to stave off massive unemployment and internal unrest, even collapse. The more investments a European country made in a less advanced nation, the more it became at the risk of that country's volatile economy, and the more colonial territory was gobbled up, the more frantically the European powers struggled over what remained.

This economic chaos led to two results, one generally limited to the West, though transcending national borders, and the second external, and finally devastating. The first result was the rise of labor, a phenomenon which Hobsbawm traces in its wider content, not merely as the growth of socialism or trade unionism. He inspects the vaster and much more interesting and important pattern of how the "working classes" became the "working class," and how the various distinct trades and occupations discovered that there was more to unite them than to separate them—how they became, in short, the "Workers of the World." This development was a momentous event in Western history, and it was recognized as such at the time. Some thought it would lead inevitably to revolution, anarchy, and the destruction of civilization—at least, of the comfortable bourgeois civilization enjoyed by many who were not of the working class. Others saw the rise in labor as the last, best hope to avoid the disaster of all-out war or massive, devastating economic depression.

As it turns out, neither the prophets of gloom nor the optimists had the final say, for the second result of growing economic contradictions was international military rivalry, the factor which both fatally increased the self-doubt and mistrust that pervaded the world order and allowed the heavily armed European nations to plunge, almost as sleepwalkers, into World War I. Much as the growth of empires demanded their continued expansion for economic necessity, so the increase in territories, made possible by great power, required even greater power to maintain them. Increasingly, the threats perceived by the imperial powers were not from the conquered peoples, for nationalism was hardly a concept and was dismissed as of little account rather than being recognized as the titanic force it would soon become—yet one more irony from this Age of Empire. Rather, the great powers engaged in ever-increasing growth of armaments, often preparing for encounters that logically had no purpose and which might never have happened, had they not become self-fulfilling prophecies.

An excellent case is that of the Anglo-German naval rivalry. Hobsbawm includes some revealing statistics in his work, and one of the most telling is the comparison of British and German naval strength between 1900 and 1914. In 1900, the Royal Navy had forty-nine battleships; no other single fleet came close, and indeed, the combined fleets of the other great European powers barely surpassed this total. In 1900, Germany had a mere fourteen battleships. By 1914, the British fleet floated sixty-four battleships, while the Germany navy had risen to forty. The obvious question is why.

It is fairly easy to account for Britain's large navy. Historically the British have depended upon the sea for both defense and trade. Great Britain is, after all, an island nation, and the oceans were the lifeline between its imperial possessions and its home island. At the same time, as Hobsbawm points out, the growth of Great Britain's empire meant a paradoxical decline in its self-sufficiency, as its internal production of foodstuffs and other staples declined. As it became more profitable and easier for Britain to import rather than produce nonmanufactured goods, so it became more important for Britain to guard the sea lanes which allowed it to survive. Even the hint of a threat, real or not, was intolerable. In a literal sense, economics had brought about the condition that Britannia had to rule the waves, or Britons would indeed become slaves to forces beyond their control. Perhaps they already had.

Imperial Germany, on the other hand, had no such pressing need for a powerful fleet. Its colonies were relatively poor and certainly nonessential to the homeland. They had been gained largely for prestige, and that was the reason for the existence of the German fleet. It was there to demonstrate that Germany was a Great Power. Therefore, according to this flawed but inexorable logic, the greater the fleet, the greater the power. Once Germany embarked upon the raising of a mighty navy, it could not back down, nor could Britain fail to meet the presumed challenge. It was a paradigm of the trap in which the European powers entwined themselves during this glorious, yet ultimately disastrous, Age of Empire.

There might be parallels here for many readers of today, but Eric Hobsbawm is not writing a history that compares "then" and "now." Indeed, as he states early in this wide-ranging and well-researched work, it is his contention that the Age of Empire is still with us, that it forms, in fact, the foundation of our contemporary world. Although much has changed dramatically since the period of 1875 to 1914, these changes were made possible, and were given shape and direction, by a period not yet out of sight over the historical horizon.

Michael Witkoski

Sources for Further Study

Booklist. LXXXIV, February 15, 1988, p. 968.
History Today. XXXVIII, May, 1988, p. 54.
London Review of Books. X, July 7, 1988, p. 12.
Los Angeles Times Book Review. February 28, 1988, p. 1.
The Nation. CCXLVI, February 20, 1988, p. 238.
The New York Review of Books. XXXV, April 14, 1988, p. 3.
The New York Times Book Review. XCIII, February 21, 1988, p. 15.
Publishers Weekly. CCXXXII, December 25, 1987, p. 66.
The Times Literary Supplement. February 12, 1988, p. 153.
The Wall Street Journal. CCXI, March 14, 1988, p. 24.
The Washington Post Book World. XVIII, February 14, 1988, p. 9.

ANCESTORS
Nine Hundred Years in the Life of a Chinese Family

Author: Frank Ching (1940-)
Publisher: William Morrow (New York). Illustrated. 528 pp. $22.95
Type of work: Historical biography
Time: The 1040's to the 1980's
Locale: Wuxi, Shanghai, and several nearby towns; Peking; and Hong Kong

A smooth blend of family, cultural, and political history of China, documenting a Chinese-American journalist's search for his family origins

Principal personages:
FRANK CHING, a Chinese-American journalist
QIN GUOJUN, his grandfather, a district magistrate
QIN LIANKUI, his father, a lawyer
ZHAOHUA, his mother
QIN JIAJUN, his stepbrother, a Communist martyr
QIN GUAN, a poet of the Song Dynasty (960-1279)
QIN KUI, the chief councillor to a Song emperor
QIN YUBO, a fourteenth century administrator
QIN WEIZHENG, a hermit scholar and artist
QIN XU, a hermit poet of the fifteenth century
QIN JIN, a scholar/official of the sixteenth century
QIN LIANG, also a government official, sixteenth century
QIN YAO, an official, praised for actions during drought
QIN YONG, a seventeenth century philosopher
QIN DEZAO, a common ancestor to the author's parents
QIN SONGLING, an imperial ghostwriter
QIN DAORAN, the tutor to a Chinese prince
QIN HUITIAN, a distinguished official, eighteenth century
QIN ZHENJUN, a heroic official, eighteenth century
QIN YING, a pirate-fighter and judge
QIN XIANGYE, a minor official, essayist, and publisher

To have been brought up in Hong Kong in the latter half of the twentieth century is to have been both blessed and cursed. A tiny territory, thriving on a free enterprise system that attracts people from all over the world, ruled by the British but living under the giant shadow of the Communist mainland to which it will revert at the end of the century, Hong Kong is the insecure home of more than four million people. Many fled inimical governments, uprooting centuries-old family traditions, to live there; those who can afford to leave are ready to move again and make a life elsewhere; some have already left.

Frank Ching, a Chinese-American journalist, is one who returned to Hong Kong to search for his family origins and to live, one of a band of progressive reformers. His father, a prominent lawyer who helped draft the constitution of the Republic of China, left China in disillusionment. The author consequently was born in Hong Kong in 1940 and was named for President Franklin D. Roosevelt, whom his mother admired. The family returned to China temporarily in 1942 when the Japanese attacked and occupied the city. After the war, the Ching family returned to Hong Kong, where the author lived until he moved to the United States at age nineteen. Benefiting from the renewal of relations between the United States and China in 1971, Ching started his search in 1973, when he was in his early thirties. *Ancestors: Nine Hundred Years in the Life of a Chinese Family* is the remarkable result of his patient research, travels, and good fortune for more than a decade.

One of the most interesting chapters in the book is the prologue, in which the author briefly describes the search process. His experience finding a hotel room illustrates the paradox of his voyage of discovery and, more generally, of China's relationship with the West. Having already encountered difficulty in obtaining a visa because of his job as a foreign correspondent for *The New York Times*, Ching had argued for his right to visit China as a Hong Kong-born compatriot. On the mainland, however, that status could not get him a room. Only when he produced his American identification did the hotel clerk offer him a selection of rooms.

Once past the official bureaucracy, however, Ching found that many people, strangers and relatives alike, were willing to help him, proving that the Chinese tradition of honoring one's ancestors had survived the upheavals of the Cultural Revolution. Indeed, more effectively than a lengthy sociological or political disquisition could, tiny details reveal the stubborn power of the Chinese people to endure political turmoil. In one incident, the peasants in the Wuxi area, the ancestral seat of the Qin family, hearing that the Red Guards were digging up the graves of those once considered to be feudal overlords, cunningly plastered over the names on the gravestones, so they could not be identified.

The fanatical zeal to sweep away the old did result in considerable destruction which could have made Ching's task futile. Many families, fearing the wrath of the youthful Red Guards, destroyed precious legacies of family history. Luckily, Ching discovered, Western bibliographers had managed to collect many of these family records, now housed at several major American universities. Amazingly, his own father had held on to a fragile volume, printed on rice paper and held together with thread, containing the names of all of their ancestors for nine hundred years, starting with the ancestor common to both the father's and mother's lineages, Qin Guan, a prominent poet of the eleventh century, and covering thirty-three generations on his father's side and thirty-four on his mother's. The dynasty name "Qin," pronounced "Chin," thus gave the country its Western name.

Taking his cue from this genealogical record, Ching organizes his book into twenty-eight chapters, covering twenty figures, including his father, mother, and stepbrother, with two chapters on several particularly distinguished ancestors. Though overtly simple and straightforward, the overall chronological organization is much more complex in the execution because—and this becomes the theme of the book—even outstanding individuals cannot be separated completely from the context of the clan, the era, or the nation. Because the Qin clan was a prominent one, boasting several high-level government officials, poets, and scholars, the fortunes of the clan were inextricably linked to the political vicissitudes of the nation. Interestingly, a twentieth century commentator noted that the decline of the Qin family paralleled the historical decline of feudalistic society in China. From this personal quest for the history of a family emerges the history of a nation.

To enliven the narrative, Ching sometimes begins with a reference to his twentieth century discovery—of a manuscript or a gravesite—which was instrumental in recovering a particular ancestor, and includes a variety of primary sources: poems, letters, official records. Keeping a Western-educated audience in mind, he provides helpful landmarks from European history as anchors, noting, for example, that the period of Qin Guan corresponded to the reign of William the Conqueror in England. Ching wisely provides illuminating digressions into Chinese history and social customs. For example, an understanding of the lyrical nature of Chinese poetry and its close association with popular tunes plus its importance in civil service examinations explains how an accomplished poet could achieve both popular and professional success.

It quickly becomes clear in Ching's account that history as a concept in China is almost a living thing, capable of changing as often as the rulers changed, open to seemingly endless revision. On an individual level, a person could, as Ching's earliest known ancestor Qin Guan did, change his name to indicate stages of personal growth. In addition to the name chosen by his parents, a scholar would choose a courtesy or style name which symbolized his ambitions and philosophy. Qin Guan's initial choice was Tai Xu, meaning "Great Void," from the Taoist philosophy that a great void is suffused with energy and purpose. When he had failed twice to pass the government examinations which were crucial to public success, he returned home for a period of soul-searching. After forty-nine days, he chose the name of a minor poet, Ma Shaoyou, meaning "roamed when young," to indicate his renunciation of the affairs of the world, though oddly enough, he subsequently passed the examinations and had a checkered public and private life.

With these intricately intertwined family and national stories, *Ancestors* is absorbing. If one were to cavil at this breathtaking blend of family, cultural, and political history, it would be about a flaw that is endemic to biographies in general, particularly to one such as this, which began, as Ching explains, as "a consuming passion" to respond to the call of his ancestors. It is impossible not to share in the delight of the author when he recounts the serendipitous ways that information concerning the lives of people so long dead came to him. As a conscientious reporter, Ching cannot be faulted for his selection and inclusion of hard-won information. Occasionally, however, the objectivity with which he accumulates detail—the facts, the dates, the anecdotes—becomes tedious. Perhaps, following the long line of poets in his family, he might have risked a more creative and personal interpretation of some of his findings. For example, in one chapter with the promising title "Qin Xu: The Blue Mountain and the Bamboo Stove Story," the story proves to be a rather dry account of the fate of a small stove for preparing tea, over a period of four centuries. Designed by a monk and produced by a bamboo artisan, it seems to have achieved widespread fame because its frame was of bamboo, which, the author explains, symbolizes purity and lofty ideals; its composition is not sufficient, however, to explain why it was an object of great admiration, inspiring countless poems, some even from the emperor, and paintings. By the time the reader has sorted out the connections between the stove, the fate of the temple in which it was stored, the Blue Mountain Poetry Society, and the Qins, the point of the story is lost in the details. Still, these are minor flaws in an otherwise praiseworthy achievement.

The author says in his preface that "one of the most scathing comments one Chinese can make of another is that he has *wang ben*, or 'forgotten his origins.'" With this monument to the Qin clan, Frank Ching not only has written a book that serves as a private record of one Chinese family but also has performed a public service in conveying to Western readers the rich history of an ancient and fascinating culture.

Shakuntala Jayaswal

Sources for Further Study

Booklist. LXXXIV, February 15, 1988, p. 968.
Chicago Tribune. April 5, 1988, V, p. 3.
Kirkus Reviews. LVI, February 1, 1988, p. 174.
Library Journal. CXIII, March 1, 1988, p. 65.
Los Angeles Times Book Review. April 3, 1988, p. 1.
The New York Times Book Review. XCIII, April 3, 1988, p. 3.
Publishers Weekly. CCXXXIII, January 29, 1988, p. 418.
The Wall Street Journal. April 27, 1988, p. 24.
The Washington Post Book World. XVIII, March 20, 1988, p. 1.

ANNA FREUD
A Biography

Author: Elisabeth Young-Bruehl (1946-)
Publisher: Summit Books (New York). Illustrated. 527 pp. $24.95
Type of work: Biography
Time: 1895-1982
Locale: Vienna and London

This biography of Sigmund Freud's youngest daughter traces Anna Freud's complex relationship with her father and considers how she both defended his conception of psychoanalysis and developed it in her own work with children

Principal personages:
ANNA FREUD, a psychoanalyst
SIGMUND FREUD, the founder of modern psychoanalysis, her father
MARTHA BERNAYS FREUD, her mother
MINNA BERNAYS, her aunt
LOU ANDREAS-SALOMÉ, a friend of the Freud family, a Russian-born writer trained in analysis by Sigmund Freud
DOROTHY TIFFANY BURLINGHAM, Anna Freud's lifetime companion and professional associate
PRINCESS MARIE BONAPARTE, a patron of Anna Freud's work
AUGUST AICHHORN, a Viennese psychoanalyst and social worker
ERNEST JONES, a British psychoanalyst, an associate and biographer of Sigmund Freud
MELANIE KLEIN, a psychoanalyst who is known for her theory of child aggression

Sigmund Freud, the founder of modern psychoanalysis, most popularly known for his theory of the Oedipus complex, required an Antigone to guide him in his declining years. After his death in 1939, his work needed a Vestal to safeguard it from misinterpretation and misrepresentation. Anna Freud became her father's "Vestal Antigone." The awkwardness of the mixed metaphor adequately describes the difficulties she faced in both her personal and her professional life. It was she and not her mother, Martha Bernays Freud, who attended her father throughout his eleven-year struggle with the cancer which eventually took his life. She sat with him after each of the painful jaw operations he underwent, performed all the disagreeable tasks of a practical nurse, and did so with the greatest possible love. When he had to travel for professional reasons, she traveled with him, acted as his personal secretary, and cheered him through his periodic depressions. When the Nazis annexed Austria in 1938, she saw to it that he escaped; she parried the interrogations of the Gestapo to spare him, and she was at his bedside when he died in London the following year.

Freud's death, coupled with the outbreak of the war, left a void of leadership in the field of psychoanalysis which no prospective successor could fill entirely satisfactorily. Some, such as Carl Gustav Jung and Otto Rank, had deserted the fold years earlier and were not trusted by more traditional Freudians. Others, such as

Ernest Jones, though remaining true in name, departed in spirit from Freudian precepts. Still others were both temperamentally unsuited and geographically unsuitable, such as August Aichhorn, who remained in Vienna throughout the war. Thus it fell to Freud's youngest daughter, who had trained in psychoanalysis, quite literally, by her father's side (though she had never earned a university degree) to "tend the flame" and keep psychoanalysis grounded in Freudian principles after its founder's death. It is in this sense that she was a "vestal virgin," though it is also the case that she never married and, as Elisabeth Young-Bruehl's study well and patiently argues, had no overtly sexual relationships at all, neither heterosexual nor homosexual.

Most readers of Young-Bruehl's book will likely find its first half of great interest, for it is here that the author reconstructs, based on all varieties of documentation, Freud's incredibly complex relationship with her father. Perhaps because she was the youngest daughter, bookish from childhood and neither as beautiful as Sophie nor as socially inclined as Mathilde, her elder sisters, Freud considered both her mother and her aunt, Minna Bernays, towering and loveless figures of authority. Perhaps this was also why she sought companionship in older women: Josephine (the *Kinderfrau* or nursemaid of the house); later, Lou Andreas-Salomé, the flamboyant and somewhat notorious Russian-born writer; and still later, Dorothy Tiffany Burlingham (daughter of American artist Louis Tiffany), who would cofound both the Jackson Nursery and the Hampstead Child Therapy Clinic and would work closely with Freud throughout her long career in child analysis. Even Freud's patron, the Princess Marie Bonaparte, who was influential in obtaining exit visas from Austria for the Freud family and their safe-conduct through France en route to England, was five years her senior. Bonaparte remained a source of funding for Freud's Hampstead projects well into the 1950's.

Life was neither easy nor entirely rewarding for Freud. Like all children of famous parents, she had to deal with the overwhelming problem of making her own way in an enormous shadow, cast in this instance by her father's formidable achievements. In a sense, she dealt with the problem by choosing not to deal with it, by, in effect, making herself her father's vicar and devoting herself to his memory. When Freud's daughter propounds her own theory of "altruistic surrender," the need to subsume oneself in that which is greater, it is clear that she is drawing upon her own life's experience. Still, she writes of "Etwas-Haben-Wollen" (wanting to have something), using capital letters and hyphens as though to indicate the importance and immediate need for such personal gratification. For Freud, this "something" was the children with whom she worked, the child patients she treated.

Beginning a second professional life as a Viennese Jewish émigré in wartime England, not to mention as a woman and without university credentials, clearly would have been impossible without the Freud surname. Freud knew this, and while she did use the special status her name afforded to reestablish the clinical practice she had begun in her native Vienna, few could challenge the success she achieved in work with war-traumatized children at Hampstead War Nursery, which she founded. The Hampstead Index, arranged by psychoses and cross-referenced with case histories, originated here and was extended in the postwar Hampstead Child Therapy Clinic, the only continuous empirical study of psychic disorders in children. It remains the most complete record of its kind. Considering that it was begun at a time innocent of computers, the Hampstead Index alone is an achievement in which Freud could have lodged her reputation.

In fact, however, England appreciated Freud relatively little. From her arrival, she found herself under attack by members of the Royal Society of Medicine who inveighed against analysis practiced by those without professional credentials. In this group Freud, without any university training, was certainly included. Even former associates of her father such as Ernest Jones remained cool to her, though not challenging her openly. Young-Bruehl's research has unearthed Jones's compromising correspondence with Freud's persistent nemesis Melanie Klein, in which he writes either pejoratively or condescendingly of Freud's work with children and appears to favor Klein's aggression theories. More perverse, Jones's letters to Freud written during the same period (immediately after World War II), appear to take precisely the opposite position and to support her work as alone representing the tradition of her father. Freud sensed Jones's betrayal from the start, believed that he was interested only in advancing his own reputation, and ultimately agreed to his writing the official biography of her father merely because he seemed the least distasteful alternative among those suggested.

The biography itself was more pleasing to Freud. Those familiar with it will agree with her that it does nothing to malign the Freud name or misrepresent his work. Oddly, though, it also does nothing to establish, discuss, or interpret the strong relationship of father and daughter Freud. Anna Freud's constant attendance on her father is not even mentioned. Here again is reason to be grateful for the information Young-Bruehl provides. Young-Bruehl suggests (with tongue in cheek?) that Jones himself found an outlet for "altruistic surrender" in writing what remains the standard biography of the founder of modern psychoanalysis, that Jones became so convinced of his subject's greatness while writing that he was content to see his own career in terms of his mentor's legacy. This is a moot point, though it is a fact that Jones, when he himself was dying of cancer, often compared his sufferings to those of his master.

The Hampstead Training Program, much to Anna Freud's regret, never received the full sanction of the Royal Society of Medicine. This endorsement would have assured consistent sources of funding and would have created an institution certain to survive its creator. During her lifetime, Freud relied upon miscellaneous and fortuitous sources to maintain her projects. Most of these sources were American, not British: the National Institute of Mental Health, the Yale Child Study Center (affiliated with Yale University), department-store magnate Nieman Marcus, and (poignantly, in view of her own unhappy childhood), the estate of Marilyn Monroe (bequeathed through her analyst, Marianne Rie Kris).

Part 2 of Young-Bruehl's study is less successful than its first half, primarily because she does not sufficiently examine what Freud did at Hampstead either to treat children or to train analysts. This is the period of Freud's career during which she achieved her greatest independence; her work at this time was pioneering and innovative, but it remains little known to those unfamiliar with the technical literature or not directly associated with the Hampstead Child Therapy Clinic and Training Program. Young-Bruehl's postscript attempts to discern a pattern in a changed understanding of Freudian analysis which Freud herself influenced. Still, once Young-Bruehl reaches the third and fourth generation, the survey bewilders rather than clarifies, for, as Young-Bruehl herself must realize, contemporary psychoanalysis has reached the stage at which the designations "Freudian" and "Jungian" have ceased to have clear signification. Indeed, few contemporary psychoanalysts (aside from those within the Freud and Jung institutes) burden themselves with either label.

Freud's daughter recognized the likelihood of departures from classical Freudian theory long before her death in 1982, and she struggled valiantly to keep Freudian analysis free of what she called "mysticism." By this she meant both the mythos of Jungian archetypes and what she herself perceived as heterodox to the Freudian canon. Even she came to recognize in her final years, however, that the word "Freudian" had passed from the proper to the common domain. She could stop neither John Huston's fanciful film on Freud's life nor the vagaries of French structuralists such as Jacques Lacan, who considered themselves the true Freudians.

Young-Bruehl says too little about this French schism and next to nothing about the more serious Jung controversy, beyond a brief reference to attempts by the Freud family to reconcile international copyright agreements for publication of the Freud-Jung correspondence. The prevailing mood of the book's last third is gloomy, recording with dutiful, nervous fatalism, and in painful detail, the illnesses and deaths of Freudians old and young, climaxing with the deaths of Aichhorn (Freud's dearest friend from her Vienna days, who loved her but never told her so until old age was upon them both), of Burlingham, in whom she found unquestioned loyalty and affection, and finally Freud herself, wracked by pernicious anemia and a series of strokes which ultimately sapped her energy and deprived her of movement and speech.

Robert J. Forman

Sources for Further Study

Booklist. LXXXV, September 15, 1988, p. 109.
Boston Globe. October 16, 1988, p. 106.
Chicago Tribune. October 26, 1988, V, p. 3.
Interview. XVIII, December, 1988, p. 199.
Kirkus Reviews. LVI, August 1, 1988, p. 1141.

Library Journal. CXIII, October 1, 1988, p. 84.
Los Angeles Times Book Review. November 6, 1988, p. 10.
The New York Times Book Review. XCIII, October 16, 1988, p. 7.
Publishers Weekly. CCXXXIV, November 11, 1988, p. 38.
USA Today. November 9, 1988, p. D8.
Vogue. CLXXVIII, October, 1988, p. 294.

ANTHILLS OF THE SAVANNAH

Author: Chinua Achebe (1930-)
First published: Anthills of the Savannah, 1987, in Great Britain
Publisher: Doubleday/Anchor Press (New York). 216 pp. $16.95
Type of work: Novel
Time: The late 1980's
Locale: The fictional African state of Kangan

Focusing on the personal fates of top-level officials, Achebe narrates the final stages of a military government in contemporary Africa

Principal characters:
SAM, His Excellency, the military chief of state
CHRIS ORIKO, the Minister of Information
IKEM OSODI, a poet, social critic, and editor of the national newspaper
BEATRICE OKOH, Chris's lover
ELEWA, Ikem's lover

With the publication of *Anthills of the Savannah*, the Nigerian writer Chinua Achebe ended his silence as a novelist, which began just after *A Man of the People* (1966) appeared more than twenty years previously. During this interim, he published poetry, short stories, essays, juvenile literature, and a critical treatise on Nigeria and taught on university campuses both in Africa and in the United States. Author of probably the most widely read African novel ever written (*Things Fall Apart*, 1958), Achebe has been mentioned as a candidate to follow in the footsteps of his fellow countryman, Wole Soyinka, who received the Nobel Prize in Literature in 1986.

Achebe's novels have always focused on the impact of British colonialism on the native cultures of Africa. Particularly in his earlier works, he attempted to correct the Western image of precolonial Africa as the "heart of darkness"; he has repeatedly underlined his role as educator in his essays: "I would be quite satisfied if my novels . . . did no more than teach my readers that their past—with all its imperfections—was not one long night of savagery from which the first Europeans acting on God's behalf delivered them." The setting of *Anthills of the Savannah* is the Westernized, postcolonial African state of Kangan. Yet the aura of Africa's past dignity and wisdom is incarnate in the leader of a delegation from the province of Abazon who has come to Bassa, the capital city, to plead for help for his drought-ridden land. He supplies the central motif and title for a speech later given by one of the main characters to a group of university students. In the relationship between this Anglicized African and the tribal elder, Achebe illustrates that truth is not the exclusive possession of one civilization. As the tribal elder expresses it, "What is true comes in different robes."

Shortly after *A Man of the People* was published in early 1966, a group of Nigerian army officers turned the vision of the novel into reality by wresting control of the state away from the civilian politicians. *Anthills of the Savannah* is a fictional reflection of the next tragic act in this political drama. At the outset of the novel, the government of a military strongman has already entered into a critical stage. Rumors of corruption run rampant, and the chief of the secret police and the army chief of staff have become the chief of state's most trusted advisers—an access enjoyed earlier by Chris Oriko, the Minister of Information, and Ikem Osodi, a poet, political thinker, and editor of the national newspaper. The friendship of the latter two men with His Excellency, or "Sam," as they knew him earlier in their lives, reaches back to their days as schoolmates in an English preparatory school. All subsequently received their higher education in Great Britain. After a military coup thrust Sam into the position of head of state, Chris returned to help him form a new government in Kangan. While Chris has since continued to advise his old friend on matters of state according to his own convictions, Sam has become increasingly autocratic and dependent on advisers anxious only to reflect his fears and suspicions. Ikem has stubbornly refused to betray his own social conscience in his editorials; finally, he becomes an unbearable thorn in the side of the fragile tyranny. Most important, neither Chris nor Ikem had given Sam their support in a postcoup plebescite held prior to the events of the novel and designed to elect him President for Life. This lack of support triggers the mistrust in Sam's mind and brings the events of the novel proper in its wake.

At the outset of the novel, Achebe plunges the reader directly into an argument between Chris and Sam taking place at a cabinet meeting of government ministers. Only gradually during the course of the first few chapters does he fill in the background information necessary to comprehend all the implications of this initial scene. This exposition of past events occurs in a skillfully orchestrated variety of modes—through first- as well as third-person narration, dialogue, and the inner monologue of memory and reminiscence. By giving each of the four figures a share in narrating the situation from a personal vantage point, Achebe achieves what Ikem calls at one point "the very stuff of life," a richly complex fictional reality filled with the ambiguities and contradictions inherent in everyday reality. For Achebe and his alter ego in the novel, who calls on Walt Whitman as a poet-witness to the multitude of perspectives even within the individual, orthodoxy or lack of contradiction is anathema to political thought and art.

Sam's rule over Kangan is fatally flawed precisely because it demands confirmation and forbids contradiction. His training as a military officer at Sandhurst has blinded him to compromise and taught him to perceive in the absolute terms of a tyrant. In his mind, the longtime loyalty of his two friends seems to be evolving into treason. A native son of Abazon—the only province unsupportive of Sam's campaign for the title President for Life—Ikem appears particularly suspect when a noisy delegation from the province appears outside the council chamber. Fearing the beginnings of an insurrection, Sam leaves the chamber and seeks private council from the obsequious Professor Okong. Depicted as an opportunist and clown, Okong nevertheless possesses the acute sensitivity of the court lackey for saying what may be only at an unconscious level in the mind of his superior. With great subtlety, he alludes to Abazon as rebellious and to the danger of even greater disaffection being fomented by Ikem and Chris.

His suspicions raised to a conscious level, Sam next calls in his Attorney General to confirm them. An even greater master of sycophancy than Okong, the Attorney General expertly reflects and embellishes His Excellency's state of mind. A man whose reasoning powers were formed by an inherited inferiority complex toward the white man, he rationalizes the social difference between him and His Excellency:

> You went to Lord Lugard College where half of your teachers were Englishmen. Do you know, the nearest white men I saw in my school were an Indian and two Pakistanis. Do you know, Your Excellency, that I was never taught by a real white man until I went to read law at Exeter in my old age as it were.

Long after the British have abandoned Africa, psychic remnants of colonialism still exercise control over the Attorney General's attitudes. In parodying these attitudes, Achebe seeks to contribute to their extirpation.

Yet such figures as the Attorney General, Achebe makes clear, are not the main culprits in prolonging the African inferiority complex toward the white man: The leaders of postcolonial states themselves imported the British sense of class discrimination along with their education and training. Sam's major flaw, in Ikem's eyes, was always a foolish admiration for the customs of well-to-do Englishmen. Yet, as a practical politician, Ikem recognizes that the British have long been an anachronism on the stage of world affairs. The lingering psychological effects of being for so long the "white man's burden" still have to be swept away, but the imminent dangers to postcolonial African states are posed by the economic power of the United States as well as the psychopathological aberrations of rulers such as Idi Amin and Jean Bedel Bokassa. Moreover, economic exploitation of black by black in the state of Kangan, Ikem maintains, has replaced the racial exploitation of colonialism, and Sam's government has failed to reestablish the vital links from the top to the bottom of the societal pyramid.

Despite his radical social analysis, Ikem is not a revolutionary or utopian thinker. He stubbornly and somewhat naïvely clings to the hope that he and Chris can penetrate the wall of lackeys surrounding Sam before it is too late. In a last speech to university students after his suspension from the newspaper, Ikem chides his audience for blaming the ills of their state on imperialism and international capitalism. The real causes lie closer to home among the self-satisfied civil servants and urban population of the middle class, whose lack of productivity ensures that rural villages will long remain without the benefits of modernization. Students too, he insists, live as parasites on the body of the state and belong to the retarding rather than to the progressive forces of their society. While Ikem is murdered, after his last speech is twisted into treason and during the struggles of the state to maintain a hold on the reins of power, Chris perishes almost accidentally in the chaotic circumstances once these reins have been lost. Too rigid and insulated to be capable of reform, Sam's government is finally overtaken by the fate of its predecessors.

Of the four major figures, only Beatrice, Chris's lover, remains alive at the end of the novel. Although reared by a sternly Christian father, she received an African name at birth, Nwanyibuife, which translated means: "A female is also something." A brilliant student with an honors degree in English from London University, Beatrice had rejected the sexism of her family at an early age. She rebukes Ikem for giving women no clear role in his political thought apart from the traditional one of serving as a last, stopgap measure. Consistently opposed to orthodoxy and universal solutions, he replies by challenging her to find the particular role suitable to the oppression of her society. While free people are united globally in their freedom, he argues, each oppressed people has its own kind of oppression to which it must find a unique response.

In the native myth of creation which he inserts into the flow of the mundane events of the novel, Achebe sketches the archetypal outlines of a more active role for women in Beatrice's society, a role grown dormant in colonial times. The Almighty, observing the unchecked rampages of Power in his creation, sends his daughter Idemili to Earth "to bear witness to the moral nature of authority by wrapping around Power's rude waist a loincloth of peace and modesty." Empowered with metaphysical authority, Idemili's task is to exercise moral restraint on all earthly powers by controlling aggressiveness and pride. Although Beatrice has grown up in a world apart from the myths and legends of her ancestors, Achebe suggests that the role has found her through the inherited collective wisdom of her people. Vaguely aware at times of a sense of being two people, Beatrice unconsciously practices the civilizing task for which her African heritage has prepared her. She represents for Achebe the best hope of a people's survival and continuity in a country in which violence and vainglory have become commonplace. Following the bloody end of the old regime and the ascension of yet another to the seat of power, she poses the author's anguished yet undespairing question: "What must a people do to appease an embittered history?"

During the months after the *coup d'état*, the minor characters of the novel meet regularly at Beatrice's flat and coalesce into a nucleus of survivors, drawing strength from one another and nurturing the restorative elements of the tragedy. In the bond of love between Ikem and Elewa, the girl from the common people who has born his child, a link has been established between the past and future of Kangan. The living symbol of this link is their infant daughter. At the naming ceremony celebrated in the final pages of the novel, Beatrice assumes the task of the absent father in giving the baby the name "AMAECHINA: *May-the-path-never-close*," a boy's name signifying the eternal renewal of hope. Elewa's mother and uncle arrive at the ceremony after the name has been given and are at first stunned by what they take to be a breach of custom. The uncle bursts into laughter when Beatrice claims parenthood of the child for all those gathered in the room. Only gradually does he agree to her metaphor and declares in a ritual prayer of consecration to his own god: "When I asked who named her they told me All of Us. May this child be the daughter of all of us." Like other figures from the common people in Achebe's novels, the uncle combines a rough exterior with an innate capacity for peaceful resolution of conflicts and a willingness to adapt to change, even if it entails a submisson of the individual will to the will of the group.

Achebe uses the speech of such minor figures, their Pidgin English and colorful use of proverbs and parables, to indicate that the African past has survived into the present. In general, however, the characterization of individuals has less significance for him than the depiction of the movement of society as a whole. More than any of the others, Beatrice gains an inner life of her own in *Anthills of the Savannah*. She is a multifaceted figure, at once brilliant, perceptive, sensual, and charitable. The social critic in Ikem outweighs the poet in his personality, and Chris at times seems only a voice. The main characters of the novel serve primarily as narrators of an episode of political intrigue from the epic of a modern African society. Much like Achebe's own, this society is caught up in the struggle to come to grips with its history and its position in the modern world. The epic appears to have no end in sight, and, like the writer Ikem, Achebe has no "prescriptions" to offer, only "headaches."

Francis Michael Sharp

Sources for Further Study

The Atlantic. CCLXI, April, 1988, p. 78.
Booklist. LXXXIV, February 15, 1988, p. 969.
Commonweal. CXV, May 20, 1988, p. 310.
Library Journal. CXIII, February 15, 1988, p. 177.
London Review of Books. IX, October 15, 1987, p. 24.
Los Angeles Times Book Review. February 28, 1988, p. 3.
The Nation. CCXLVI, April 16, 1988, p. 540.
New Statesman. CXIV, November 27, 1987, p. 32.
The New York Review of Books. XXXV, March 3, 1988, p. 3.
The New York Times. CXXXVII, February 16, 1988, p. 23.
The New York Times Book Review. XCIII, February 21, 1988, p. 1.
Publishers Weekly. CCXXXII, December 18, 1987, p. 55.
The Times Literary Supplement. October 9, 1987, p. 1106.

ANYTHING FOR BILLY

Author: Larry McMurtry (1936-)
Publisher: Simon & Schuster (New York). 382 pp. $18.95
Type of work: Novel
Time: The 1880's
Locale: West Texas and the New Mexico Territory

A writer of dime novels goes West, meets Billy the Kid and other characters, accompanies Billy on his adventures, and tells the "true" story of Billy's life and death

Principal characters:
BILLY BONE, a young gunman and occasional cowboy
BEN SIPPY, a rich Philadelphian, reader and writer of dime novels about the West, and follower of Billy
JOE LOVELADY, a cowboy, Billy's only friend
WILL "OLD WHISKEY" ISINGLASS, the owner of a three-million-acre ranch and ruler of a huge Western territory
KATIE GARZA, Will Isinglass' daughter, who is in love with Billy
LADY CECILY SNOW, an English botanical artist, lover of Ben Sippy and then Billy
MESTY-WOOLAH, a gigantic African, a killer for Isinglass
BLOODY FEATHERS, Isinglass' half-Apache son

Larry McMurtry continues to shift from the Old West to modern-day Texas and back again for the subjects of his novels. His great success in *Lonesome Dove* (1985), a novel of frontier days, was followed by the comic but less successful novel of Texas in the 1980's, *Texasville* (1987). In *Anything for Billy* he returns to the frontier days of the Wild West and the story of one of its most famous characters, Billy the Kid, but his approach is humorous. *Lonesome Dove* was an epic novel with a tragic ending, an impressive attempt to re-create the early days of the frontier West on a grand scale. *Anything for Billy* takes the materials of myth and treats them as comic, up to and including the inevitable death of its main character. It is on a much smaller scale than *Lonesome Dove* and takes itself and its subject much less seriously.

The voice for McMurtry's telling of Billy the Kid's story is that of Ben Sippy, a wealthy Philadelphian who read dime novels by the hundreds, became tired of waiting for new ones to be published, and began writing his own, with great success. Married and the father of nine girls, Ben leaves his indifferent wife and daughters when the wife has a trash collector haul away his huge trove of dime novels. He decides to see the West for himself, boards a ship for Galveston, and eventually, sheltering himself from a sandstorm in Apache country, runs into Billy Bone. The younger man has already built a reputation as a gunfighter, although it develops that he has never shot anyone and has only once killed a man, and then with a knife in an accident. Ben is accepted by Billy and his friend, Joe Lovelady, and the three of them begin the travels that set the plot in motion.

Anything for Billy is as full of violent incidents as any dime novel, but there is nothing heroic about any of them. One of the more subtle jokes of the novel is the fact that most of the violence is done by other men and women, even though Billy is blamed for some of the shooting. More than half the novel goes by, in fact, before Billy kills anyone.

The first two sections are a leisurely exposition of the situation. Brief chapters about Ben's meeting with Billy and Joe alternate with equally brief chapters explaining Ben's life as a reader and writer and his adventures on the way to his accidental meeting with Billy. Once the three men join, McMurtry teases the reader with descriptions of the life of gunmen and out-of-work buffalo hunters who gather together in a small West Texas hamlet called Greasy Corners and hang out in the China Pond saloon waiting for something to happen.

A great many things do happen. There are shootings. Katie Garza, daughter of the rich rancher Will Isinglass, rides into town with her Mexican bandits, challenges a famous marshal and marksman to a shooting contest and beats him, thereby destroying him, and then takes up with Billy. There are more shootings. Isinglass, known as Old Whiskey for his habit of taking a jar of whiskey with him when he goes out for a day's ride, rides into town with his entourage. A berserk cowboy challenges them and is disemboweled by Mesty-Woolah, an African in Isinglass' employ. Katie takes Billy across the river into Mexico, and Ben goes along, the only observer of the early days of their romance. In McMurtry's telling, it is all very lighthearted.

Billy himself is passive through all this activity, including his affair with Katie, which he seems not really to believe. A thin, undistinguished young man, he suffers from debilitating headaches and uncertainty about himself. He is stupid but somehow winning, alternating between foolish self-confidence and sudden doubts. It is, in Ben's telling, a kind of boyish innocence that gives him a certain charm. Despite the pleasures of Katie's attentions, he grows bored with the easy life and rides off with Ben and Joe, supposedly to track down Texans who are killing innocent men.

On the trail, they meet two riders, and for no reason Billy shoots at them, accidentally hitting and killing one of them, but missing the other with four shots at close range. Billy is no marksman. He has killed an innocent horse-trader, Joe's friend; despite the "look of cold satisfaction on his face," Billy has made a mistake. "Something had gone wrong. Luck had brought him what seemed to be a legitimate chance to become the killer everyone fancied him to be. But there was a dark side to the luck. He had killed his friend's friend, and an innocent man at that." He has also precipitated a range war that will end with Joe's death.

Billy's entire career, brief as it is, has this accidental quality. He enjoys killing, but there is nothing heroic or even meaningful about his actions, and in fact he seems to be something of a coward. In one episode, soon after his first shooting, he stands by while Isinglass' half-Apache son Bloody Feathers rides into a town and, in a dispute over an Apache girl, picks up an Italian gunslinger by one ear, holding him in the air. Billy simply watches. Later, blamed by the other gunman, he seems embarrassed and says only that he has no obligation to intervene when somebody else gets in trouble.

Anything for Billy has a very modern quality in its juxtaposition of the comic and the bloodily tragic. Ben escapes with his life after the range war because he is recognized as a dime novelist by one of Isinglass' men who has read his writings. There is a long episode in which Billy is forgotten while Ben has an affair with Lady Cecily Snow, a guest of Isinglass' who intends to kill her host and in the meantime amuses herself with Ben and her artistic studies of botanical specimens. At the end of this interlude, however, the reader finds that Joe has been followed by Mesty-Woolah in an epic chase:

> The cowboy and the African had raced one another halfway across the West—up the Pecos, across the Jicarilla country, around the great Shiprock butte, north of the Navaho canyon, south from the desert of monuments: days of hiding, nights of racing, until the cowhorse at last drew up lame and the camel was shot with Joe Lovelady's last bullet as the race finally ended, somewhere on the Mogollon Rim.

The two men return together, exhausted, to Isinglass' home ranch, where Mesty-Woolah decapitates the cowboy with one slash of his sword. Joe, the most heroic character in the novel, is dispatched in two lines, and Billy the Kid has no part in any of this action.

Virtually all the action, in one way or another, debunks the myth of Billy the Kid as a brave man and a gunfighter who killed many men. Billy is ruthless, temperamental, and indifferent to the lives of others, but in McMurtry's portrayal he is also foolish and the recipient of the credit or blame for killings in which he had no part. His involvement with Lady Cecily is an example. Having become bored with Ben, Lady Cecily seduces Billy the Kid. Katie may be his great love, but Cecily is nearer. As it turns out, Lady Cecily has an ulterior motive. She uses Billy as a screen in her continuing feud with Isinglass; she shoots Mesty-Woolah with her rifle while in Billy's company, knowing that the famous gunslinger will be blamed. She also convinces Billy that he must kill Isinglass' other children, her half-brothers. As she has explained to Ben, Isinglass robbed her father and took her mother as his lover.

McMurtry has fun with a number of different stories in *Anything for Billy*. The episodes with Lady Cecily parody romantic fiction about titled English women; she is as unromantic as she can be, propositioning Ben crudely and commenting disparagingly on his sexual performance. At another point, Ben is involved in a parody of *The Thousand and One Nights*; Isinglass plans to hang him, but promises not to if Ben can act like Scheherazade and tell him a tale every night that will keep him awake until he digests his dinner. This leads to a parody of the murder mystery, since Ben is eventually told that Isinglass' indigestion results from ground glass which Lady Cecily and his servants, all of whom hate him, introduce into his food at dinner.

The chief object of McMurtry's parody is the Western novel, in which men such as Billy the Kid have been made heroes in defiance of the facts. Several of Billy's victims are helpless boys killed without warning. Others are equally defenseless. He is finally arrested in Lincoln, New Mexico, after shooting an unarmed banker and a cattleman. Myths are made of this; Ben observes that some people believe that the banker and cattleman were rivals of Isinglass and that Billy had killed them for the old man, but like so much about Billy and his life, this rumor is pure fantasy.

The most persistent myths McMurtry attacks, through Ben, are those having to do with the death of Billy the Kid. As Ben observes, everyone who knew Billy tries to claim credit for having killed him. McMurtry arranges matters so that this seems possible. Hurt while Katie stages a jailbreak and takes him to Mexico, Billy partially recovers and decides to leave Katie to return across the border for a rendezvous with Lady Cecily. Accompanied by Ben, he meets her at Greasy Corners, where he kills one of the old buffalo hunters, thereby emptying the town of its usual denizens. Everyone with a grudge against Billy arrives at once: Isinglass and his new hired gun, Long Dog Hawkins; Bloody Feathers; and the sheriff from whom Billy had escaped in Lincoln, Tully Roebuck. Katie, however, arrives from Mexico and shoots her lover before any of the others can get to him. Annoyed by Long Dog's complaints that he had not been given the first shot, Katie shoots him, too.

In the aftermath, Ben reviews all the myths and speculations about Billy's death, pointing out that even Billy had asked Katie to give credit for his shooting to Tully, apparently on the theory that it would look bad if history recorded that he had been killed by a woman. Tully, he tells her, has a political career to think of. Thus, according to Ben, history has given Katie credit for a later career as a Mexican revolutionary but has denied the fact of her killing her lover. The unwritten jest is that Pat Garrett, credited by myth and many historians with shooting Billy, is never mentioned.

McMurtry's best joke is that in debunking the myths about Billy the Kid he has created his own myths: Will Isinglass and Mesty-Woolah are larger than life, as is Katie Garza; Joe Lovelady is a genuine if previously unsung hero; and Lady Cecily Snow, with her unabashed sexuality and her cool hatred for Isinglass, is a legend in her own right. In creating these characters, McMurtry pays tribute to the power of the myth. A worn-out myth can be discarded, but another must take its place.

John M. Muste

Sources for Further Study

Kirkus Reviews. LVI, August 1, 1988, p. 1088.
Library Journal. CXIII, October 15, 1988, p. 104.
Los Angeles Times Book Review. October 30, 1988, p. 1.
The New York Times Book Review. XCIII, October 16, 1988, p. 3.
Newsweek. CXII, September 26, 1988, p. 76.
Publishers Weekly. CCXXXIV, August 19, 1988, p. 59.
Time. CXXXII, October 24, 1988, p. 92.
The Wall Street Journal. CCXI, October 6, 1988, p. A16.

ARABESQUES
A Novel

Author: Anton Shammas (1950-)
First published: *'Arabeskot*, 1986, in Israel
Translated from the Hebrew by Vivian Eden
Publisher: Harper & Row (New York). 263 pp. $16.95
Type of work: Novel
Time: 1936 to 1982, with flashbacks to earlier periods
Locale: Israel, Paris, and Iowa City

An autobiographical fiction depicting the lives and stories of the inhabitants of Fassuta, a small village in Israeli-occupied lands

Principal characters:
ANTON SHAMMAS, the author, who pieces together recollections of his childhood and travels in France and the United States
UNCLE YUSEF, his mentor and a master storyteller who conveys to the author a sense of the past
SURRAYAH SA'ID (née LAYLAH KHOURY), a former inhabitant of Fassuta and a Muslim convert who lives on the West Bank and is married to an imprisoned PLO officer
MICHAEL ABYAD, a spokesman for the Palestinian movement and possibly the author's long-lost cousin and double, also named Anton Shammas
YEHOSHUA BAR-ON, a Israeli writer

According to common wisdom, most first novels are autobiographies in disguise. *Arabesques*, however, the first novel of Anton Shammas, a Christian Arab reared in Israeli-occupied Palestine, goes against the grain, for it is clearly a fiction—a patchwork quilt of legend, fact, fantasy, and history—which proclaims its heterogeneous status as both autobiography and novel. As its punning title indicates, *Arabesques* is a labyrinthine design that weaves together the disparate, somewhat inchoate stories and memories of the inhabitants of Fassuta, a village "built on the ruins of the Crusader castle of Fassove, which was built on the ruins of Mifshata, the Jewish village that had been settled after the destruction of the Second Temple by the Harim, a group of deviant priests." The mixed origins of Fassuta are reflected in the lives of its people, especially that of the author, who, by recounting his personal past and the more comprehensive legendary past of the village, is attempting to construct an identity in a world where national boundaries and political affiliations constrain selfhood to a singular, geopolitical dimension.

In a form of resistance to that singularity, Shammas constructs *Arabesques* as a pastiche of stories and styles that defies easy classification, just as the "self" which he discovers through writing defies identification. The novel may be viewed variously as a family romance, an example of magical realism, a mystery story, an autobiography, an oral history, or a reflection upon the act of storytelling itself. Indeed, the mode of storytelling that the author learns from his Uncle Yusef and employs in this novel delineates a way of knowing that lies somewhere between empirical fact and the fantastic extrapolations of legend:

> His stories were plaited into one another, embracing and parting, twisting and twining in the infinite arabesque of memory. . . . All of them . . . flowed around him in a swirling current of illusion that linked beginnings to endings, the inner to the external, the reality to the tale.

Thus, weaving, spinning, and quilting become the metaphors Shammas uses to explain the ways in which he reconstructs the past, not by representing it as a linear story containing sequential events and operating upon the principles of cause and effect, but by conceiving it as a repository of fragmentary memories, events, and bits of story which the narrator pieces together, almost by accident.

Yet what may appear to be a life and story guided solely by the capriciousness of the storyteller's imagination and the accidents of fate becomes, as the novel progresses, an "arabesque," a perceptible design which conveys its own kind of order in its interlacings, exfoliations, and repetitions. For example, there is the story of a treasure buried in a cave sealed beneath a huge, mysterious boulder that reflects moonlight. The cave is guarded by the mythical Ar-Rasad, a demonic rooster that the narrator compares to the cock that the Apostle Peter heard after he had thrice denied Christ. The image of Ar-Rasad standing watch over the treasure recurs frequently in the novel; the buried object becomes a figure for the narrator's own concealed identity and his attempt to liberate it by digging up the past. In the end, the boulder is dynamited by a Jewish engineer to make way for Uncle Yusef's grandson's new house. The debris of the explosion include no treasure, but in the sky a crowd observes "a crimson feather, turn[ing] round and round." Similar repetitions of image and event—the memory of Anton's father shaving the face of an Arab rebel in his barbershop, an amulet which supposedly contains the secret to the buried treasure, a deep cistern into which the author has been lowered as a child—transform the shards and loose threads of the narrative into a skein of interconnected stories, images, and relationships. In this sense, *Arabesques* is a symbolic novel that conveys the sense, if not the fact, of the author's successful reconstruction of the past.

As with any story about buried treasure, at the heart of this novel there is a mystery, and the narrator anxiously pursues its solution with the knowledge that whatever he discovers will provide the key to his identity as a storyteller and a historical being living at the intersection of political crossroads. Throughout the novel, twinnings and doublings recur with almost as much frequency as tales of lost children. Surrayah Sa'id is the mother of twin deaf-mutes; Ablah, the village madwoman, bears a child who disappears shortly after birth and whose fate is unknown; two soldiers, twins, who look "like two halves of a lentil," are killed on a strange road; Amneen, the author's cousin, suddenly disappears from the village for twenty-five years and just as suddenly returns.

The conflation of the motifs of doubling and loss occur in the story of Michael Abyad, a mysterious figure closely associated with the Palestine Liberation Organization (PLO) and a spokesman for Palestinian rights. In his disentangling of labyrinthine relationships and buried secrets, the author, Anton Shammas, discovers that Abyad may in fact be his cousin, also named Anton Shammas and presumed to have died in infancy. The dead Anton is supposedly the child of Jiryes and Almaza Shammas, the author's uncle and aunt, but it may be that Almaza has secretly given her child to the Abyads, a rich Beirut couple for whom she works as a maid. It is also hinted that Michael Abyad is possibly the son of Ablah, smuggled away from his insane mother and adopted by the Abyads. The key to Michael Abyad's identity seems to lie with Surrayah Sa'id, who has been a servant in the Abyad household and who therefore exists as the link between the village of Fassuta and the city of Beirut. The author seeks out Surrayah to hear her story and to discover, perhaps, his hidden, politically active "secret self," but in the two different versions of their meeting, the significance of Michael Abyad's revealed identity seems equally oblique. In the latter version, the author is allowed to see and touch Surrayah's once-beautiful naked body, smelling of "narcissus and cyclamen" and "the ancient odor of the stones and the dark scent of the silt rising from the bottom of the cistern," as if he has come into contact with the primal elements of his own past and those of his homeland. The amulet around Surrayah's neck, however, which purportedly contains part of the charm that will open the cave of Ar-Rasad, remains sealed, exactly as the "meaning" of his double's identity—even after a face-to-face meeting at a writer's conference in Iowa City—remains hidden.

Within the indeterminate arabesque of doubled identities and half-revealed secrets lie the significances of Shammas' evocative, strangely evasive novel. This design weds past to present and art to life, even as the quest for identity is only partially achieved, ever part of the endlessly digressive, infinitely interwoven progression of stories already told and remaining to be told. It is possible, for example, to regard Michael Abyad as the author's "other": While Anton Shammas seeks to forge his identity through the artifice of storytelling and the quest for origins, the "other" Anton Shammas seeks, in the geopolitical jargon, self-determination through political action. In these dual quests, the search for a personal and national identity are brought together. Parabolically, *Arabesques* suggests that the reformation of a people and a culture caused by political struggle rests as much upon a recognition and narration of the past as it does upon the enactment of present ideologies or the projection of future utopias. That is not to say, however, that Shammas invests everything in his art or his ability to retell and reconfigure stories. When he describes his participation in an international writer's conference in the United States, it become clear that "art," cut off from politics and removed from site of memory and event, becomes impotent and petulant. The author's quarrels with Bar-On, a Jewish writer, the pettiness of the relationships among the writers, and the insularity they experience all reflect ironically upon the notion that art is produced in isolation. Only when he returns to his conflicted native land and picks up the thread of his stories does Shammas' narrative regain its life and power.

To focus upon the question of identity—the positioning of the self in the world of story and fact—is to concentrate on but one of the novel's many digressive concerns, though, arguably, the major one. *Arabesques* is a miscellany of sorts, in which the reader can find stories of broken romances, political intrigues and betrayals, gothic commemorations of love and death in a Parisian cemetery, and reflections upon the tragic history of those displaced people whom the world has come to refer to as "the Palestinians." The most compelling aspect of Shammas' novel is that which makes the connection between autobiography and history, between the personal past of the author and the larger, mosaic-like past of his people who, like the author, seek an identity. In this respect, *Arabesques* is comparable to Gabriel García Márquez's *Cien años de soledad* (1967; *One Hundred Years of Solitude*, 1970) or Günter Grass's *Die Blechtrommel* (1959; *The Tin Drum*, 1961), which might be called "histories-in-process," that is, novels which seek to imagine the history of a displaced, repressed, or abandoned people by returning to the "past" of story and myth and fusing it with the actualities of the present.

Shammas provides the reader with a representation of a people and culture little understood in the West—not the culture of Israel in its present state of ascendancy, but that of the "other" Israel, of a people whose recent history should make them brothers of the Israelites rather than enemies of the state. Yet, here lies the paradox of *Arabesques*: The attempt to represent a people and a culture assumes that they exist in some unified or identifiable manner. Shammas' novel, however, makes it clear that a "representation" of the Palestinians must necessarily be fragmentary, for, as a people, they are dispersed, their culture shattered and, perhaps, doomed to disappear save for the efforts of a few storytellers who may recall, in their tales, bits and pieces of the past.

This last point gives to *Arabesques* an aura of gloominess and a sense of urgency that is only briefly assuaged by the charm, humor, and wisdom of Uncle Yusef's stories and Anton's childhood recollections. In this extraordinary first novel, Shammas provides the reader with a vision of an "arabesque" Palestinian life that, in the end, does confer an identity upon both the author and the people of a small village in the Galilee. This identity, *Arabesques* makes clear, is ordained neither through the sheer movements of history nor the impositions of the author, but within and between "stories," scandalous and broken though they may be.

Patrick O'Donnell

Sources for Further Study

Kirkus Reviews. LVI, February 15, 1988, p. 239.

The New Republic. CXCVIII, May 2, 1988, p. 28.

The New York Review of Books. XXXV, April 14, 1988, p. 5.

The New York Times Book Review. XCIII, April 17, 1988, p. 1.

Publishers Weekly. CCXXXIII, March 18, 1988, p. 71.

ARCHAEOLOGY AND LANGUAGE
The Puzzle of Indo-European Origins

Author: Colin Renfrew (1937-)
First published: 1987, in Great Britain
Publisher: Cambridge University Press (New York). Illustrated. 346 pp. $29.95
Type of work: Cultural and linguistic history
Time: From prehistory to the twentieth century
Locale: Europe and Asia

This work starts from the accepted relationship of many living and dead languages of Europe and Asia and goes on to consider what historical realities can have formed such relationships and what bearing these findings may have on current models of ethnicity

In this work, Colin Renfrew confronts issues at once deeply academic and extremely sensitive. On the one hand, it can be assumed that very few people will ever bring themselves to care deeply about the fact that Tocharian, an extinct language of Central Asia, appears to belong to the *centum* group of languages rather than the *satem* group. On the other hand, it should be remembered that considerations of very much this type—Norwegian is a "Germanic" language, but Polish is not—affected decisions during World War II as to which populations should be exterminated, enslaved, or gently treated, and that the ideology used to validate these decisions was to some extent formed in quiet university libraries all over Europe during the nineteenth and twentieth centuries.

The initiating agent of this comparative study of languages was the proclamation made to the Bengal Society in 1786 by Sir William Jones that Latin and Greek—which Jones had learned at school like every self-respecting English contemporary—were too close to Sanskrit, the ancient religious language of India, for the similarity to be a coincidence: They must have had a common source. The statement must have come as rather a shock to many of Jones's listeners. Latin and Greek were "respectable" languages of high prestige; Sanskrit was known only to their "colored" subjects. Jones was in effect asking these scholars to discard strongly entrenched views on race. The evidence Jones gave was absolutely incontrovertible. His revelation was followed up by a century of intense linguistic research, and the conviction eventually took hold that not only Sanskrit and the classical languages of antiquity were related but also nearly all European languages—Slavic, Celtic, Germanic and others—together with many languages of Persia, India, the Near East, and Central Asia.

One might have thought that this discovery would work against racist sentiments. If brown, white, and (perhaps) yellow races all shared some kind of common linguistic ancestry, then surely it must be deduced that language and culture could be shared, created, passed on interracially. In a curious way, though, racist sentiments prevailed over the linguistic theory. European scholars had very little difficulty in accepting that European languages were related. In a way, they had known this all along, since people can still see almost at a glance that French, Spanish, and

Italian all derive from a common source, and the common source itself, Latin, is still well-known. The "Indo-European" theory of languages only extended this model to less obvious cases. The problem was principally with the Indian languages, now closely relatable to European ones but spoken by people who looked different. What emerged from the conflict between evidence and ingrained prejudice was, in a way, an imperialist theory. The original speakers of Sanskrit, it was suggested, must have been white, because they spoke a language related to Latin or to English. They must have been invaders, imperialists, a military elite (strangely like the British in India), only they had made the mistake (not like the British in India—or not like them in official theory) of mixing racially with their dark-skinned subjects, at the same time that they imposed on them the language of the white conquerors.

From this belief arose the use of the word "Aryan"—a word which the early composers of Sanskrit hymns had applied to themselves—along with the notion of "Aryanism," the belief that "Aryans" were destined to rule the world, and the self-image of Nazi Germany as a nation that was only repeating the career of conquest its ancestors had long pursued. Even those scholars who in no way shared the beliefs of Nazi Germany, and those nations who fought desperately against them, nevertheless often had at the back of their minds the deep-seated belief that at some time in the dawn of history the ancestors of the European race had swept out of an unknown center in the East to conquer Europe, Iran, and India, and there slowly to develop differences in what had at one time been a single language. Whole grammars, it should be said, have been written of this "single language," Jones's "common source," usually labeled "Proto-Indo-European"—though not a single word of it has ever been recorded.

What was the unknown center? When did all of this happen? Did it in fact happen? And must one accept the model of conquest and military dominance? These are the questions asked in Renfrew's book, questions (as has been said already) which engage specialists in linguistics and archaeology yet which are charged with implications that extend far beyond the boundaries of these academic disciplines. The answers offered by Renfrew frequently challenge the deep self-images of Europeans and Americans alike, striking at the roots of ethnicity.

To take first the questions of where and when: Till recently, a rather reassuring interpretation had been generally accepted. It had been realized, for example, that Indo-European languages tended to have shared words for, say, cow, horse, wolf, bear, oak, beech, snow, salmon. They tended to have different words for iron, gold, and silver, and though there is a widely distributed word that resembles "ore"—Latin *aes*, Sanskrit *ayas*—it means indifferently "metal, copper, brass, bronze." These facts seem to indicate that the languages split apart before iron was known (but perhaps after copper was known), probably then in the late Neolithic period; furthermore, the homeland of the original language must have been somewhere in Northern Europe, where one could indeed find salmon, snow, and beech trees.

Does this theory hold water? It has been pointed out, for example, that on this sort of reasoning the original Indo-Europeans must have known about snow (same word), but never experienced rain (different words), and that since all Romance languages have the same word for coffee, coffee must have been drunk in Imperial Rome (what actually happened was that all the languages of Europe borrowed the word at much the same time from Turkish, or from one another). Study of the "protolexicon" is thus interesting but methodologically dubious; the same goes for "glottochronology" and especially for language-derived models of military dominance.

Take, for example, the *centum-satem* division, or the problem of "P and Q Celts." The former refers to the fact that western Indo-European languages tend to have a *k* (Germanic *h*) in the word for "hundred" (Latin *centum*). The eastern ones have an *s* instead, and this fact appears to form the basis for a neat east-west division, going back perhaps to dialect differences in the original language in the original home. This pattern was, however, destroyed when evidence of an extinct language, Tocharian, was discovered in a secret chamber in an oasis town in Central Asia—an Indo-European language, but one which (far to the east even of Sanskrit) said *kante* for "hundred."

In rather the same way, the Celtic languages have long been divided into the "P-group" (Welsh, Cornish, Breton) and the "Q-group" (Irish, Gaelic, Manx) on the basis of their word for "four" (Welsh *pedwar*, Irish *ciathar*). To this classification has been added a model of successive invasion and dominance: The "P" speakers were thought to have dislodged and driven out the "Q" speakers, only in their turn to have been invaded and dislodged by successive waves of Saxons, Vikings, and Normans. Yet there is some sign of "Q" Celtic speakers (now extinct) in Spain as well. Were they, like the Tocharians, somehow driven thousands of miles off course? Or would it not be simpler to suggest that there was no invasion at all, no sequence of dislodgments? Instead, there were simply changes of fashion in speech which started near the center of "Celticity," or of "Indo-Europeanness," but never reached the fringes, such as Ireland, Spain, and the oases of Central Asia.

Renfrew challenges, in short, the "Aryan" or "military dominance" model of language change, as well as the image of the family tree of languages. He suggests that what is required is a "processual" approach, considering both language and archaeology and taking into account the large body of information that is now known about how languages (such as English) actually spread, gain adoption, and change. The conclusions to which he comes are, broadly, as follows.

Renfrew suggests that the true home of the ancestral Indo-Europeans was not South Russia and the steppeland, as has been generally proposed, with concomitant beliefs about the importance to "Aryans" of horses, chariots, and military technology. Rather, it was in the central areas of Anatolia, in what is now Turkey, from which language could spread both east and west, as well as staying in the same place—these "stay-at-homes" creating the languages associated with Hittite, which Renfrew again rescues from the common model of invasion and military dominance. As for the time when this movement began, Renfew argues for a much earlier date than is commonly given, somewhere around 6500 B.C.

This early date allows a further question to be answered—that is, why should the Indo-Europeans have spread from one center at all? The standard explanation has suggested restlessness, population pressure, and military success, as if the Indo-Europeans had been early Vikings or conquistadores. Yet why should there have been any special population pressure from the steppe? Renfrew proposes instead that the earliest Indo-Europeans were associated with the development of agriculture, a technology which even in its simplest forms can allow a population density some fifty times as high as that of hunter-gatherer cultures. In this view, the people speaking Indo-European languages spread through Europe and Asia not in military columns pursuing loot but in small bands looking for unexploited land and taking many centuries to cross and fill up continents. They did, in fact, something like what the Amerian colonists did to the Midwest (and to the American Indians), only much more slowly. As for the hunter-gatherer populations inhabiting post-Ice Age Europe, Renfrew suggests that many of them did survive, individually and linguistically, in those areas where Estonian or Basque is now spoken, or where (in Scotland) the non-Celtic language of Pictish was employed.

Military activity no doubt accompanied some of these movements. Dealing with the difficult question of Sanskrit and the fall of the Indus Valley city civilizations, Renfrew casts doubt on the too ready assumption that this fall was caused by barbarian "Aryan" invasion. He offers two models to explain the evidence, one agricultural and pacific, the other rather closer to the "steppe-invasion" theory (the force of which, it should be said, is enhanced by the Hindu system of caste, clearly a codification of some form of color prejudice dating to a time long before the English or other modern Europeans ever set foot in India). Renfrew's overall model can in fact be adapted to fit many interpretations of evidence without being disproved or destroyed.

What Renfrew's book does primarily, though, is to lay bare the unconscious racial stereotyping behind much linguistic argument in the past. It also points out how archaeologists and linguists have tended to rely on one another, thus creating circular arguments. And it casts a certain scorn on the popular idea of uncovering basic or essential myths of social order across all the Indo-European areas from Ireland to India, while ignoring both the enormous differences between those areas and the clear similarities found in non-Indo-European societies such as Japan. Renfrew's book challenges many notions of ethnicity. Not only the Anglo-Germanic, or "WASP," idea of natural dominance but also the Hellenic self-image of culture-initiation and the Irish-Celtic one of exuberant intrinsic vitality come, at different times, under a skeptical eye. Few Europeans or Americans will be able to read it and remain entirely unaffected.

T. A. Shippey

Sources for Further Study

British Book News. September, 1987, p. 602.
The Guardian. CXXXVIII, March 6, 1988, p. 27.
Nature. CCCXXXI, January 28, 1988, p. 311.
New Scientist. CXVII, January 28, 1988, p. 64.
The Observer. December 13, 1987, p. 23.
The Times Educational Supplement. November 27, 1987, p. 23.
The Times Literary Supplement. June 24, 1988, p. 714.

ARGUFYING
Essays on Literature and Culture

Author: William Empson (1906-1984)
First published: 1987, in Great Britain
Edited, with an introduction, by John Haffenden
Publisher: University of Iowa Press (Iowa City). 657 pp. $45.00; paperback $19.95
Type of work: Literary and cultural criticism

A comprehensive edition of previously uncollected essays by one of the century's foremost literary critics

The late William Empson is probably still best known for one of his early books, *Seven Types of Ambiguity: A Study of Its Effects on English Verse* (1930), a classic of literary criticism. Empson was a self-described practitioner of verbal analysis. As another of his titles, *The Structure of Complex Words* (1951), suggests, what mattered to him most was the meanings of words and the contexts in which words are interpreted. He has sometimes been accused of being too ingenious in his interpretations of words, of finding too much significance in a writer's word selection. He was a feisty, argumentative critic who gave little ground to his adversaries.

A title such as *Seven Types of Ambiguity* suggests that there is a very clear way of demarcating different uses of ambiguity. In practice, however, Empson is not quite as systematic as the title may suggest. Indeed, he is chary of enunciating a literary theory that would provide an authoritative approach to each literary work. On the contrary, by choosing the term "ambiguity" he stresses how the complex meanings of works of literature subtly shift in significance. Language is fluid and changeable, and the critic, in his view, has to be supple enough to follow the poet's inventive, unstable use of language.

John Haffenden, Empson's authorized biographer, has brought together a very wide-ranging group of essays, articles, and reviews, written between 1928 and 1980. Empson's favorite subjects are the moderns (T. S. Eliot, William Butler Yeats, W. H. Auden, Dylan Thomas) and the English Renaissance poets (Henry Vaughn, George Herbert, Andrew Marvell). The bulk of Empson's writing is about poetry, although there are also sections titled "Fiction and Narrative," "Cultural Perspectives," "Literary Interpretation," and "I. A. Richards and Basic English." Empson is at home in all English literature, so it is not surprising to find essays on Romantic poets and on Victorian novelists as well. He seems to have had little interest in American literature.

I. A. Richards was Empson's teacher and mentor, whose own *Principles of Literary Criticism* (1924) and other writings helped to shape the foundations of modern criticism. Richards argued that in modern life poetry may very well play the role that religion had in earlier ages—that is, to foster, in Haffenden's words, "mental and moral health." Poetry has to do with the creation of values. As such, it is to be taken with the utmost seriousness and to be appreciated for its fullness and richness.

Given this "theory of value" dictum that Richards applied to modern poetry, it is no wonder that Empson believed that he had to do battle with literary critics who wanted to separate literary works from their sources. For example, one of his favorite targets was the so-called New Criticism, whose proponents in the 1930's and afterward contended that a work of literature should be interpreted only in its own terms, with no reference to the writer's biography, to what the writer may have said about the work, or to the writer's cultural background. Empson seems to have taken special pleasure in attacking W. K. Wimsatt, who argues that a work of literature should never be interpreted in terms of the writer's intentions. How can one recover intentionality? Wimsatt asks. It is impossible to get into the mind of the writer, and all subsequent expressions of intention are thus suspect. Better to treat the work of literature itself as an autonomous object. To counter Wimsatt, Empson points out that the determination of intention has been practiced in courts of law for generations. Scholarly editors frequently examine multiple drafts of literary works in order to ascertain a writer's intentions. Granting that no writer's intentions can ever be proved beyond all doubt, Empson still thinks that it is foolish to demand that the concept of intentionality be thrown out altogether.

What is striking about Empson is not only his arguments but also the personality that is palpably present in his judgments and assertions. Here, for example, is his reaction to a book by Wimsatt:

> I have long felt uneasy about Mr. Wimsatt's drive against what he calls the Fallacy of Intentionalism . . . and I am not reassured by the photograph he has put on the dustcover of this collection. He looks like a mastodon rising with dripping fangs from a primeval swamp.

This is an argument ad hominem, perhaps cruel, but the image is deliberately chosen. To Empson, there is something antediluvian about Wimsatt's insistence on rejecting obvious sources of information such as what the biography of a writer might have to tell about his writing. There is something very ugly about willfully ignoring a part of the process of creation that occurs outside the poem. Empson's strategy is to use every source that helps, whether that source is inside or outside the poem, so long as the work of literature remains the primary focus of interpretation.

A case in point for Empson is James Joyce's *Ulysses* (1922). Commenting on Richard Ellmann's "grand biography" of Joyce (1959), Empson remarks:

> You need to know what Joyce was feeling because otherwise it is often hard to tell whether a passage in the novels was meant to jeer. The speech at the party in "The Dead," where the conventional hero in his dismal style praises the unique hospitality of the Irish with applause, has struck me as an undeserved bit of satire by Joyce on his homeland; but it turns out that, after finding how much he disliked working in Rome, a great change from Trieste, he decided that his picture in *Dubliners* had left out a real virtue of the place which justice required him to include.

As much as he reveres literature, Empson does not make a fetish of it. He is willing to concede that even the greatest works of literature—such as Joyce's—might be elucidated by biography, that the critic could be better schooled in literature by knowing as much as possible about its origins in life.

Empson was a confirmed secularist, although he was greatly interested in religion. He intensely disliked Christianity, finding it primitive and morally offensive; particularly repugnant to him was the emphasis that Christianity places on God's sacrifice of His only begotten son. There is a kind of bloodthirstiness in it that he repudiates. Throughout his career, he opposed the influence of T. S. Eliot and other critics who, in his view, try to twist the meanings of modern literary works to conform with Christian doctrine. Empson had enormous respect for Buddhism and taught for some years in the Far East.

Haffenden's introduction provides a shrewd and careful outline of Empson's critical thinking. At strategic points, Haffenden quotes from key essays in the volume and then supplements this evidence by supplying revealing extracts from many of Empson's letters to colleagues and friends. Empson loved to argue, though he did not always get the best of the argument—as Haffenden points out. Or, to use Empson's term, he liked to "argufy":

> Argufying is the kind of arguing we do in ordinary life, usually to get our own way; I do not mean nagging by it, but just a not specially dignified sort of arguing.

Empson was not afraid to appear undignified in his essays or to mount—as he did with Wimsatt—a personal attack. There is something truly refreshing about his attitude—which is less that of the highly mannered professional academic than that of a down-to-earth person who cares deeply about showing why he is right and others are wrong. His essays read beautifully because they are virtually jargon-free. His language is not exactly colloquial, but it is informal. These pieces remind the reader of letters. There is a kind of naturalness in Empson's prose, communicating a sense that he is dealing directly with works of literature, with his own ideas, not merely with the literature on the subject.

It is nearly impossible to find this kind of language in academic journals today, for the norm is abstruse language and a detached approach to one's subject. Empson was aware of this failing; in a letter quoted by Haffenden, Empson mentions a professor/critic he admires, noting regretfully that he has become "Yaled for life." To be a literary theorist these days is to be especially honored, whereas straightforward explication of texts is regarded as passé. Empson tried to understand the new methodology, but he was always suspicious of literary theory. Whatever the theory, there is always the difficulty of applying it to specific works, and the application of theory is never perfect. "It is hard to feel that an adequate theory of literary criticism, if obtained, would be much more than a device for stopping inadequate theories from getting in your way," he concluded. The way Empson dismisses Jacques Derrida and other French deconstructionists is priceless: "They use enormously fussy language, always pretending to be plumbing the very depths, and never putting your toe into the water." He was quite willing to be proved wrong, but got very little out of reading "those horrible Frenchmen."

What Empson would have made of the present collection Haffenden cannot be sure. He cites Empson's approval of authors who collect their prose and publish it, and Empson announced plans to do so himself. Nevertheless, he never did come close to assembling his diverse essays, and Haffenden is surely right in surmising that Empson would have discarded some of the work in the present collection. Even though the work varies in quality, however, there is variety sufficient to keep a serious reader stimulated and entertained throughout the volume. There is also something to be said for a historical overview of Empson such as this collection provides. Since Haffenden has also written a learned introduction that emphasizes Empson's most important pieces, there is little room for complaint.

As Empson suggests in several of his essays, he is the kind of critic who is interested in how literature works. Great literature is often difficult to interpret, and the critic must not shirk his or her duty to help readers understand the intricacies of complex art. Empson finds the machinery of writing—the author's techniques—fascinating. In response to the argument that he is too little concerned with the value and the quality of art, Empson counters that the very act of choosing certain works and not others is an implicit judgment of value. Besides, no critic's appraisal of a work of literature will remain unchallenged or unaffected by the passage of time, he points out, and each new work of literature changes the critic's ideas about the possibilities of art. Not of a mind ever to apologize for his methods, Empson is a critic who faces squarely the problem of meaning in literature. There is meaning there—in the text—and he holds that it is the critic's first responsibility to find and to discuss that meaning. Finally, he knows that there is no accounting for a critic's taste, and no literary theory (not even a partial one) can get very far without acknowledging this subjective aspect of criticism. It is to Empson's credit that he was confident of and comfortable with his own methods while conceding the partiality of his approach.

Carl Rollyson

Sources for Further Study

British Book News. August, 1987, p. 519.
Library Journal. CXIII, March 1, 1988, p. 66.
London Review of Books. X, February 4, 1988, p. 6.
The Spectator. CCLIX, November 28, 1987, p. 34.
The Times Educational Supplement. January 1, 1988, p. 24.
The Times Literary Supplement. February 26, 1988, p. 211.

ARMADA
A Celebration of the Four Hundredth Anniversary of the Defeat of the Spanish Armada, 1588-1988

Author: Peter Padfield (1924-)
Publisher: Naval Institute Press (Annapolis, Maryland). Illustrated. 208 pp. $24.95
Type of work: History
Time: The 1580's
Locale: Western Europe, the English Channel, and England

A description of the historical surroundings and conditions that led to the naval encounter between England and Spain, the reasons for the battle, and the significance of the defeat of the Spanish forces

Principal personages:
ELIZABETH I, Queen of England, 1558-1603
SIR FRANCIS DRAKE and
SIR JOHN HAWKINS, the two most famous of the "Sea Rovers" in the employ of Elizabeth I
CHARLES HOWARD, SECOND BARON HOWARD OF EFFINGHAM, Lord High Admiral and the commander of the English forces in the Armada battle
PHILIP II, King of Spain, 1556-1598
DON ALONZO PÉREZ DE GUZMÁN, seventh Duke of Medina Sidonia, the commander of the Spanish naval forces in the battle
ALEXANDER FARNESE, DUKE OF PARMA, governor General of the Netherlands (under the control of Spain), 1578-1586

Any historical event is an impossibly complex topic; assessing the forces that "produce" a specific occurrence is largely a matter of exclusion as much as inclusion. When the scope of the event is enormously large itself, when the import of the occurrence is such that it holds a place in almost every historical survey offered to students from elementary school through college, the event tends to take on a life, and its effects a standardized assessment, of its own.

Such is the case with the defeat, in the year 1588, of the Spanish Armada. Excepting 1492 and 1776, perhaps no date is memorized as often by American students as that of this battle. The popular "facts" of the encounter between the English and Spanish naval forces have become institutionalized: An agressive queen defeated a complacent king; the stakes were control of the New World; the destiny of English-speaking peoples hinged upon the outcome of a raging sea battle; the Spanish lost what control of the world's oceans they had; the English demonstrated an ability to control the seas through massed naval power, a control that was to last for nearly four hundred years.

Peter Padfield does an elegant and erudite job of separating those assumptions from the facts and of offering, in a very convincing argument, some ideas to replace those assumptions that he considers inaccurate. His contentions are as much a product of his approach to history—his decisions regarding what to include and what to exclude—as they result from a set of facts or a collection of evidence. This approach is evident, and clearly presented, as early as the book's table of contents, which lists as chapter titles the components of the event: the king and queen concerned, the English rovers, the Spanish commander, the English admiral, the ships, crews and armaments, and the course of the battle itself. Early in the book, the reader realizes that in Padfield's judgment, the defeat of the Spanish was determined by the national ambiences of the two countries, the personalities of their naval commanders, the technology available to each side, and the tactics each force employed.

The effect of Padfield's approach is twofold. First, the opening emphasis on the people who caused this event personalizes the narrative. The author concentrates on their ability and inclination to make decisions and their reliance on subordinates, and makes some impressive observations about their individual and idiosyncratic ways of viewing the world. While contemporary historians are increasingly employing statistical methods, Padfield's narrative endorses the conventional wisdom that history is people. If history is also the assessment of great events, then considering the people who made an event is not only an appropriate place to start but may in fact be the only beginning that allows an understanding of the event. Starting the book this way also has, as a benefit to the reader, the effect of moving from the accessible (people) to the barely comprehendible (a large sea battle).

The second aspect of Padfield's approach is the presentation of the technology of the two fleets. Padfield ably demonstrates his experience here. He was a crew member of the *Mayflower II*, a sailing ship that reenacted the Pilgrims' voyage from England to America. He has written previously about the history of naval gunnery and the importance of naval battles. His discussion of the armaments, construction, and capabilities of the ships involved in the battle strikes exactly the right note, between the arcane and the simplistic. He avoids descriptions that are too laden with the unique vocabulary of the sea and ships; at the same time, he does not resort to simplistic explanations that do not contribute to the reader's understanding of the effects of technology on the battle.

In particular, the discussion of the armament of the ships is presented in such a way that the effects on the battle of the weapons' capabilities is clear, apparent, and understandable. Similarly, the section devoted to the capabilities of the ships themselves is not exclusively an informative exercise; the ships' ability to maneuver, their sailing characteristics, speeds, quirks, and peculiarities all have an importance that resonates when Padfield begins to describe the battle itself.

That description is well over half of the book, as the reader might expect. What comes as a pleasant surprise is the effort Padfield has made to make his account as inclusive as possible. Just as his preparation in the early chapters is wide in scope, offering what amounts to a worldview of the conditions on the historical eve of the battle, his chapters devoted to the actual fighting do not assume that the defeat of the Armada took place in a vacuum.

There is detail enough in the writing to ensure the satisfaction of even the most ardent follower of sailing-ship tactics. At the same time, Padfield never lets the reader forget that the battle was fought on the stage of the world. Not exclusively a naval concern, the point of the Spanish effort was as much the transportation of men and material in an amphibious exercise as it was the defeat of the English naval forces. In this regard Padfield sees a fundamental difference between the two navies.

England's forces were more capable of naval encounters, battles between ships for control of the sea itself. The Spanish forces were devoted to naval warfare as a method of transport, with reliance ultimately on the soldier, not the sailor. Beyond the general capabilities and intentions of the ships, the advantage went to the English in maneuverability; this advantage is central to Padfield's description of the long battle that took place up the English Channel.

Even though the battle was often intense and the carnage almost indescribable, in the long view Padfield convinces his reader that the English prevailed because of position (upwind), tactics (strike briefly and retire), and perseverance. He does not state these positions as arguable contentions; rather, he allows the reader to conclude them through the process of absorbing the narrative. Arguably, this method is not rigorous history, but popular history. So be it. Padfield's narrative is engaging, clear, and well-situated in the context of the times. It also leads the reader to understand the position of the combatants after the battle was over.

That position is the case Padfield ultimately makes for the effects of the defeat of the Spanish Armada. He is properly cautious:

> It is more useful to regard the results of naval battles as defining existing economic, technological and geographical boundaries. The Armada campaign did just that. It changed nothing in the situation that made it necessary in the first place.

Padfield's concluding chapter closes the lives of the people who led the forces, but opens the story of the Dutch rise to economic power. He does not necessarily see the popular concept of the effects of the battle as wrong, only inaccurate; he argues that economic reality finally defeated the Spanish. The defeat of the Armada of 1588 must be seen as a component of a cycle, as a contributory, assisting cause of an important shift in economic power. The Dutch persistence in fighting the Spanish for the next fifty years allowed the expansion of English power; the English did not gain the ability to colonize and conduct business at sunset on the day the Armada of 1588 was routed.

It is ironic, but fitting, that Padfield stresses the participation and personalities of individuals in his account, only to conclude that economic forces beyond the control, indeed beyond the understanding, of those people were the fundamentally important aspects of the generation and the results of the battle. If this is a Marxist view of history, it is Marxism with a human face. Our tendency to see what we desire to see in a particular historical event has rarely been corrected with as much skill and gentleness as Peter Padfield uses in *Armada: A Celebration of the Four Hundredth Anniversary of the Defeat of the Spanish Armada, 1588-1988*.

D. P. Smith

Sources for Further Study

Booklist. LXXXV, September 1, 1988, p. 33.
Chicago Tribune. February 23, 1988, V, p. 3.
The Christian Science Monitor. March 11, 1988, p. 20.
Library Journal. CXIII, September 1, 1988, p. 168.
London Review of Books. X, July 7, 1988, p. 3.
Punch. CCXCIV, May 6, 1988, p. 49.
The Spectator. CCLX, June 25, 1988, p. 36.
The Times Literary Supplement. December 2, 1988, p. 1346.
The Wall Street Journal. CCXI, July 21, 1988, p. 14.
The Washington Post Book World. XVIII, August 14, 1988, p. 1.

THE ART OF THE NOVEL

Author: Milan Kundera (1929-)
First published: L'Art du roman, 1986, in France
Translated from the French by Linda Asher
Publisher: Grove Press (New York). 165 pp. $16.95
Type of work: Literary criticism

A collection of essays which examine the history of the novel, its position in contemporary society, and Kundera's contribution to the genre

In *The Art of the Novel*, Milan Kundera considers the state of the genre. As a well-respected novelist, he is in a position to do so. Czech-born, Kundera began his career as a poet and dramatist, publishing in 1967 his first novel *Žert*, later translated and published as *The Joke* (1969, 1982). This novel, with its anti-Communist thrust, was seen as heralding a political thaw in Czechoslovakia. Other novels followed: *La Vie est ailleurs* (1973; *Life Is Elsewhere*, 1974) is the chronicle of a Communist poet with little talent and *La Valse aux adieux* (1976; *The Farewell Party*, 1976) is a farce about a health spa that claimed to cure infertility.

Although a member of the Communist Party, Kundera joined a group of intellectuals who encouraged the loosening of restrictions which culminated in a period of increasing freedom known as the Prague Spring. In 1968, however, the Russians invaded Czechoslovakia and suppressed the liberalization. Because of his activities, Kundera was censured. He lost his position teaching film studies at the Academy of Music and Dramatic Arts, his books were banned, and his work was no longer published in Czechoslovakia. In 1975, he moved to Paris, accepted a position at the University of Rennes teaching comparative literature, and continued to write novels: *Le Livre du rire et de l'oubli* (1979; *The Book of Laughter and Forgetting*, 1980), a discussion of forgetting that can be read as a comment on the deathlike state of Communist Czechoslovakia, and *L'Insoutenable légèreté de l'être* (1984; *The Unbearable Lightness of Being*, 1984), a love story set in the Russian-dominated country. His novels are known for their political nature, in particular the study of the effect of totalitarianism on the individual; for their experimental form; and for their emphasis on ideas, especially the examination of the nature of existence.

Although Kundera in the preface to *The Art of the Novel* writes, "I have tried to express here the idea of the novel that is inherent in my own novels," the book is not restricted to his own work but rather addresses broader questions concerning the genre, such as the uniqueness of the form, its vitality, and its future. Divided into seven chapters, the book appears to be fragmented because of the different forms (essay, dialogue, public address, and dictionary entries) employed and the disjointed style that resulted from the pieces being written over a period of several years and published in various journals and newspapers. Kundera insists, however, that the sections were conceived of as a book. As one reads, certain themes and ideas recur and complement one another. Thus, although initially the chapters seem unrelated in form and content, a whole emerges.

The opening essay, "The Depreciated Legacy of Cervantes"—first published in 1984 in *The New York Review of Books* under the title of "The Novel and Europe"—outlines the history of the European novel. Kundera traces the adaptations that the novel has made over the four centuries, changes made in response to an evolving society. Paraphrasing Edmund Husserl, Kundera argues that the modern age began when Galileo Galilei and René Descartes elevated the importance of that which can be measured, resulting in a degradation of those things that were not scientific or technical. As the sciences became more and more specialized and exclusive, the world became more and more fragmented. Man could not hope to comprehend the world and as a result could not even comprehend himself. In *Don Quixote de la Mancha*, Miguel de Cervantes opposed this trend toward measurement and focused on the forgotten self. Indeed, it is the novel which illuminates, and recovers from the oppressiveness of science, various aspects of man's existence.

The great novelists throughout history have modified the novel to accommodate changes in society. Cervantes encountered a world that had lost its sense of certainty. God no longer retained the supreme position that He had held in the Middle Ages. As a result, Cervantes focused on the ambiguity that confronts man as he realizes that there are no absolutes and therefore finds himself faced with unrestrained freedom. Thus, the world of Don Quixote is one of adventure: Anything is possible. A hundred years later, Samuel Richardson examined the interior life of the individual. In the nineteenth century, Gustave Flaubert faced a world bounded by institutions and government; he chronicled the trivial events of daily existence. In the twentieth century, Marcel Proust explored the effect of the past on the individual, and James Joyce questioned the ability to know the present. Kundera argues that soon all accepted value systems will be discredited and abolished, resulting in the dominance of irrationality. Modern novelists, including Franz Kafka, Robert Musil, and Hermann Broch, have already addressed this situation. Of all the genres, only the novel has been able to reflect the changes in perception that have accompanied the emergence of modern man.

The future of the novel lies in its continuing ability to evolve. Because of the novel's inclusiveness and adaptability, the death of the novel cannot be foreseen. Although declared dead or at least dying by various avant-garde groups, such as the Surrealists and Futurists, and by some academicians, the novel is strong. Arguing that in a sense only censorship can destroy the novel, Kundera links the health of the genre to the vitality of Western culture.

As maintained by Kundera, Broch and Kafka are two writers who have brought the novel into the modern age, which Kundera defines as "the bridge between the reign of irrational faith and the reign of the irrational in a world without faith." Part 3, "Notes Inspired by 'The Sleepwalkers,'" focuses on the often-neglected Broch. In his trilogy *Die Schlafwandler* (1931-1932; *The Sleepwalkers*, 1932), Broch examines the effect of the loss of values on modern man. Each novel in the trilogy presents one possibility of coping with the situation. One character clings to the old values (in the form of an old uniform); another sees the world as divided between good and evil which are indistinguishable; and the third considers only himself. Broch's characters cannot deal directly with reality but instead react to, and are governed by, symbols, which belong to an irrational system. Broch's importance lies in the fact that he introduced the irrational into twentieth century fiction.

Kundera opens part 5, a discussion of Kafka's novels, with a few lines from the Czech poet Jan Skacel:

> Poets don't invent poems
> The poem is somewhere behind
> It's been there for a long time
> The poet merely discovers it.

Kundera, through Skacel, is suggesting that great writers state universal truths, truths that have always existed but that need an artist to articulate them. Kafka is such an artist. His fictive world represents a possible existence, one in which the individual is overwhelmed by external forces and trapped with no possibility of escaping. In this oppressive environment, faceless institutions control every aspect of the individual's life. In the Kafkan scheme, events in daily life are often comic because of their absurdity. Yet the comic does not offer any relief; instead, it destroys the tragic element, thus minimalizing the stature of the victim.

Kafka presented a possibility of human existence which, unforeseen by him, has become the reality in totalitarian societies. Kundera likens the last years he spent in Prague to the world envisioned by Kafka. Kundera argues that any totalitarian state necessarily becomes Kafkan. The "concentration of power," "bureaucratization," and "depersonalization of the individual" create functionaries out of the citizens. As described by Kafka, these functionaries obey, perform mechanical and seemingly meaningless tasks, and deal with reports and files but not directly with people. This is the situation that Kundera saw in Prague. Kafka wrote about this possible existence, but he did not create it; the possibility was there for "a long long time," as Skacel observed.

In part 2, "Dialogue on the Art of the Novel," Kundera discusses his work and his aesthetics. As all novels must do, his novels explore the meaning of existence, which he defines as "the realm of human possibilities." Unlike Cervantes, who found man's being through action, or Richardson, who found the self in the interior life, Kundera uses an examination of an existential problem to discover the self. For example, in *The Unbearable Lightness of Being*, the problem— "The lightness of existence in a world where there is no eternal return"—controls the direction and development of the novel. A Kundera character represents one possible existence among many. His characters should be viewed as experimental selves, not real but imaginary. Breaking with the emphasis on realism or verisimilitude, Kundera offers the reader little in the way of character description. Instead, his characters can be reduced to a list of words that represent a code to their essence. Thus, Tereza in *The Unbearable Lightness of Being* is defined by vertigo and weakness.

Certain words and terms figure strongly in Kundera's novels. These words are discussed and defined in his novels, in his essays, and in "Sixty-three Words," a section in *The Art of the Novel*. One group of terms relates to the political thrust of his novels. Central Europe is defined as a "laboratory of twilight." "Czechoslovakia" is a word he avoids, because, created in 1918, it is too new and "frail." Kundera prefers the term "Bohemia" instead. Forgetting is seen partly as a totalitarian device to rewrite history. Other words such as "irony," "lyricism," "comic," and "repetition" relate to the form and structure of the novel. Others are relevant to an understanding of Kundera's concerns: being, lightness, nonthought, and kitsch. His definitions are themselves poetic: "Kitsch is the translation of the stupidity of received ideas into the language of beauty and feeling." Since Kundera usually writes in Czech without a Czech audience, he must rely on translations to reach his readers; this explains his concern that the terms be properly defined so that they accurately reflect his meaning.

Kundera's novels are often read as a criticism of Communist society and of totalitarian states in general. He rejects this interpretation, arguing, "The novelist is neither historian nor prophet: he is an explorer of existence." Kundera does not want to be labeled a dissident writer because "in lending himself to the role of public figure, the novelist endangers his work." Nevertheless, his novels are often situated in the history of Czechoslovakia. While he is not concerned with history as such, he recognizes the impossibility of ever divorcing the individual from the culture. In his novels, historical events are used as metaphors for the characters. In *The Unbearable Lightness of Being*, Tereza's weakness is illuminated by the capitulation of the Czech leader Alexander Dubček to the Russian leaders in 1968.

In part 4, "Dialogue on the Art of Composition," Kundera continues to discuss his aesthetics. He suggests that a novel should be brief. Otherwise, the limits of the reader's memory weaken the effectiveness of the book and destroy its "architectonic clarity." Therefore, everything nonessential should be deleted. In Kundera's novels, one finds few descriptive passages. In his opinion, the novel's theme or "existential inquiry" is of utmost importance. After the plot is sketched, he concentrates on the theme. As it develops, certain words are repeated and emphasized, thus becoming significant. It is these words that are being examined in the novel.

Kundera's novels are clearly constructed fictions. The reader is frequently reminded that the work is fiction, that it stems from the author's imagination, and that it is not intended to mirror reality. The characters are born from an idea and represent only one possibility among many. He uses his novels to explore man's being and to study the possibilities of existence. As he notes, "The novel is a meditation on existence as seen through the medium of imaginary characters." The author must rely on "imagination, freed from the control of reason and from concern for verisimilitude, [in order to venture] into landscapes inaccessible to rational thought." Kundera's novels are not tied to realism but incorporate dreamlike passages. Unlike Kafka, who blended dream into his novels so that there was no distinction between dream and reality, Kundera includes identifiable dream sequences.

The structure of Kundera's novels is strongly influenced by music. Perhaps because his father was a musicologist and his own first interest was music and music composition, he sees the sections of his books as resembling the divisions in a symphony. The large segments (parts) correspond to movements. Each chapter within a part corresponds to a measure. He likens the pace of his novels to the tempo of music, describing chapters using musical terms such as "moderato," "allegro," and "adagio." The pace or tempo then corresponds to a particular mood or emotion. Nevertheless, the seven-part structure that is found in *The Art of the Novel* and in all of his novels except *The Farewell Party* arises not out of his musical background but instead is a compulsion: As Kundera explains it, it belongs to "a deep, unconscious, incomprehensible drive."

Another aspect of music that Kundera has adapted to his novels is polyphony, an occurrence in which more than two voices or melodies are blended but each retains its identity, as in a fugue or canon. Kundera credits Broch with introducing polyphony into the novel by integrating various genres such as poetry, essay, and journalism into his books. As Kundera observes, however, in Broch's work, the pieces are not balanced and unified. Kundera, grappling with the issue, believes that he has been more successful. In part 3 of *The Book of Laughter and Forgetting*, Kundera blends autobiography, essay, fable, and narration. These sections are unified by the question "What is an angel?" Similarly, in part 6 of *The Unbearable Lightness of Being*, a combination of essay, narration, and meditation is unified by a discussion of kitsch.

Exiled and living in France, Kundera is an important novelist for the Western world. He represents, so to speak, a voice from the other side. His novels have been successful, rightly or wrongly, for their presentation of Communist society. More important, Kundera's experimentation with the boundaries of the novel have strengthened the genre. In *The Art of the Novel*, he has established himself as an important theorist by his attempt to clarify the novel's purpose and position.

Barbara Wiedemann

Sources for Further Study

Chicago Tribune. April 3, 1988, XIV, p. 4.
Kirkus Reviews. LVI, January 15, 1988, p. 105.
Los Angeles Times Book Review. March 6, 1988, p. 3.
The New Leader. LXXI, May 16, 1988, p. 5.
The New Republic. CXCVIII, March 21, 1988, p. 36.
The New York Times Book Review. XCIII, April 10, 1988, p. 13.
The New Yorker. LXIV, May 16, 1988, p. 110.
Publishers Weekly. CCXXXIII, February 5, 1988, p. 77.
The Times Literary Supplement. June 24, 1988, p. 695.
The Village Voice. XXXIII, March 29, 1988, p. 70.
The Washington Post Book World. XVIII, March 27, 1988, p. 4.

AT HOME
Essays 1982-1988

Author: Gore Vidal (1925-)
Publisher: Random House (New York). 303 pp. $18.95
Type of work: Essays

A collection of essays on politics and literature by an eloquent and controversial author who has been described as "America's finest essayist"

The essay as a literary form was introduced in the sixteenth century by the French aristocrat Michel Eyquem de Montaigne. He used the word *essai* (an attempt) to describe the essential nature of his loosely structured pieces: as Gore Vidal expresses it, "an attempt to order one's impressions and reflections on a given subject." Over the centuries the essay has had many distinguished practitioners in Europe and the United States. Names such as William Hazlitt, Charles Lamb, Virginia Woolf, T. S. Eliot, Mark Twain, James Thurber, and E. B. White immediately come to mind. In the late twentieth century, however, the essay, like its kissing cousin the short story, has fallen on hard times. The essay's problem is contained in its definition: The modern reader wants hard facts from experts and wants them quickly; he has little patience with the uncredentialed layman who is merely attempting to order his impressions and reflections or attempting to do anything else. Why waste time on somebody's attempt to arrive at the truth when there is so much documented, quantified, and electronically retrievable information going begging? The modern reader is like the man who told the lifeguard, "Don't give my wife artificial respiration! I want her to have the real thing."

In order to survive at all, the once-aristocratic essay has had to adopt various disguises, just as the French aristocrats disguised themselves to escape the Reign of Terror. The essay may appear as a magazine article, buttressed with quotations from authoritative people such as Abraham Lincoln, Albert Einstein, and Ralph Waldo Emerson, who can usually be relied upon to have said something that is applicable to just about anything. The essay appears as a newspaper column, although the author generally adopts a humorous tone to show he knows that he is merely a poor journalist who gets to work at home. Most frequently the essay appears under the guise of a book review, using some other hapless author's creation as a springboard to dive into the uncharted seas of the reviewer's own mind.

In fact, more than half of the essays in Vidal's essay collection originally appeared in *The New York Review of Books*, a prestigious periodical whose contributors have made a fine art of subordinating the ostensible subject of the review to their own purposes. Many of Vidal's essays could be used as models for a piece on "How to Write a Review for *The New York Review of Books*," along the lines of Edgar Allan Poe's "How to Write a *Blackwood* Article." The primary rule for authors in *The New York Review of Books* would seem to be: Keep the title of the work you are covering and the name of the author in the distant background. Ideally, they should be mentioned in passing, in parentheses or in a footnote. A companion rule would be that it is perfectly all right to help oneself to enormous chunks of information out of the book under review so long as one tosses them out offhandedly as if they had just come to mind.

Vidal quotes himself far more than he quotes anyone else. He is his own expert authority. This practice, however, is not to be censured in a modern essayist; if Vidal were less of an egotist he might not be an essayist at all, and he would be missed. He is an interesting writer, although it is hard to remember much of what he says. He is not for the ages but for our time. He appears almost too frequently on television, and this electronic medium, which goes on and off with the touch of a button and rarely contains anything of great significance, seems made to order for a personality such as Vidal's. His gossipy nature has made him a favorite with the American public, who are looking not for intellectual stimulation but for recreation and amusement. Although intelligent, articulate, and always original, Vidal seems, like Charles Swann and the rest of the Guermanteses in Marcel Proust's *À la recherche du temps perdu* (1913-1927; *Remembrance of Things Past*, 1922-1931, 1981), to prefer to discuss the ephemeral and the superficial, perhaps because he considers such a preference a sign of good breeding.

Vidal affects the insufferable manner of an aristocrat. His favorite put-down is the upper-class sneer. Here is an example from an essay published in *The New York Review of Books* in 1976: "Mr. Dardis' approach to his writers and to the movies is that of a deeply serious and highly concerned lowbrow, a type now heavily tenured in American Academe." Vidal's photograph on the dust jacket of *At Home: Essays 1982-1988* makes him look like one of the signers of the Declaration of Independence. His pose is strongly reminiscent of Oscar Wilde, an author of similar tastes of whom he writes quite sensitively in an essay titled "Oscar Wilde: On the Skids Again." Vidal's ancestors came to America in the seventeenth century, and this fact means much to him, if not to anyone else. It helps explain the interest in American history which has led him to write historical novels. It also helps explain his passion for politics.

There is a contradiction in his character which is constantly revealing itself in his essays. He longs for the past and hates the vulgar present, yet he makes his living in the present and some of it in that capital of vulgarity, Hollywood, California. Vidal's attitude is not uncommon among authors who harbor fears that they have not lived up to their own highest standards, who suspect that they may have sold out. In order to maintain the standard of living to which he was conditioned in early life, Vidal has had to become a showman, a self-publicist, a name-dropper, an attitudinizer; he has made a considerable amount of money doing hack work for television and motion pictures. He has also turned out a series of commercial mystery novels under the silly pseudonym Edgar Box. Is it his contemporaries he despises or himself?

His financial success has enabled him to maintain two residences. He is a man with only half a country—or with two halves that do not match. He is at home in Hollywood and at home in a flat in a two-thousand-year-old neighborhood in

Rome. He commutes between the past and present geographically and in spirit. In "At home in a Roman Street" he writes about the old buildings, the quaint shops, and the longtime residents with an absence of irony which is in striking contrast with the tone of most of the other essays in this collection. Vidal is not a writer the reader would ever expect to know intimately, or perhaps even want to know intimately, but there are times when he seems nearly human. One senses that although he may be at home in Europe and on both coasts of the United States, his well-known sexual orientation condemns him to being alone and homeless everywhere. Like Proust's Baron de Charlus, he has the prickly pride of a man who thinks that people may be laughing at him behind his back; and, as with Charlus, there is a gentle, sensitive, one might almost say feminine side to his nature which he rarely allows to peep through the mask. His anger often seems like the impotent rage of the outsider. He would like to turn the whole world around so that he is the insider and everyone else—with a few exceptions—is on the outside looking in; yet this is a hopeless, not to say self-destructive, ambition even for a writer with his talents.

At Home is the sixth collection of Vidal's essays to be published in book form. (His fifth, *The Second American Revolution*, won the 1982 National Book Critics Circle Award for criticism.) As always, the essays in the present collection show a narrow range of interests, confined mainly to politics, literature, and himself. In the preface he states: "I shall never write a formal memoir (I have never been my own subject, a sign of truly sickening narcissism)." He is being ironic, as usual. After trumpeting himself for so many years with such conspicuous success, there would be precious little left to memorialize. The only thing wrong with a book of Gore Vidal's essays is that there is too much Gore Vidal. When he writes about the United States' decline as an empire builder, he seems to enjoy saying "I told you so." He reminds one of Nero fiddling while Rome burned. In "The Bookchat of Henry James," he manages to work in an anecdote about how he spent a pleasant hour with the French author André Gide during which they briefly discussed the reasons for Henry James's popularity.

Some old-fashioned English teachers still tell their students that the first person should be eschewed in expository writing. Vidal, one of the leading figures of the New Journalism, does not go along with this schoolmarm's injunction. His "I's" finally become like the Chinese water torture. These essays were originally published separately and with time intervals; when they are compressed into one volume they create an effect comparable to the cocktail-party syndrome. His egotism and carping manner finally wear the reader down. The two authors he most resembles are Wilde and H. L. Mencken, but neither of these cynics affects the nerves the way Vidal can. Wilde and Mencken lived in more relaxed times with no acid rain, no ozone depletion, no population explosion, no killer bees, no Acquired Immune Deficiency Syndrome. The older writers must have believed that things could be improved, whereas Vidal is both a cynic and a pessimist. He hates the present and expects the future to be worse. If there were a time machine on the market, Vidal would set the dial for the eighteenth century and never be seen again.

Musing on a conversation he had with another narcissistic writer, Norman Mailer (which Vidal adroitly manages to insert into an essay ostensibly about a book on militant Christian evangelists), he asserts that human life is totally meaningless:

> There is no cosmic point to the life that each of us perceives on this distant bit of dust at galaxy's edge, all the more reason for us to maintain in proper balance what we have here. Because there is nothing else. No thing. This is it.

With all of his faults, Vidal is usually amusing, informative, and thought-provoking. He has the courage of his convictions. He has been called "America's finest essayist," and it is hard to think of anyone with a better claim to that title.

Bill Delaney

Sources for Further Study

Booklist. LXXXV, November 15, 1988, p. 533.
Interview. XVIII, December, 1988, p. 141.
Kirkus Reviews. LVI, October 15, 1988, p. 1520.
Library Journal. CXIII, November 15, 1988, p. 75.
Los Angeles Times Book Review. January 8, 1989, p. 4.
The New York Times. CXXXVIII, November 14, 1988, p. C16.
Publishers Weekly. CCXXXIV, September 30, 1988, p. 53.
Time. CXXXII, November 21, 1988, p. 40.
The Washington Post Book World. XVIII, November 20, 1988, p. 3.

AVAILABLE LIGHT

Author: Marge Piercy (1936-   )
Publisher: Alfred A. Knopf (New York). 129 pp. $16.95
Type of work: Poetry

A rich and diverse collection of poems written at midlife and infused with mature understanding

Marge Piercy began her career as a poet by cutting all ties to the academic world, which she believed was stifling her poetic talent and exploiting her as a person. She gave up graduate work at Northwestern University to "learn her craft" in "a condemned building in Chicago." Her social activism led her to condemn the jungle of cities, social injustice, and pollution, but soon she gravitated toward two of her favorite themes: sexuality and feminism. These became linked in a strange kind of lover's quarrel; one seemed to be pitted against the other. In an early poem, "The Friend," the lover invites the woman's passion but rejects her expression of it:

> I love you, I said.
> that's very nice, he said
> I like to be loved,
> that makes me happy.
> Have you cut off your hands yet?

The need to love and the frustration caused by the lover's selfishness and coldness awakened in Piercy a sense of injustice that went beyond politics. She attacked what she came to believe was the idea of women that men carried around in their heads—an idea that not only exploited women but also kept them from inheriting their sexual rights and joys:

> The token woman arrives like a milkbottle
> on the stoop
> coming full and departing emptied . . . .
> The token woman . . . will teach freshman English
> for a decade . . . .
> Your department orders her from a taxidermist's
> catalog
> and she comes luxuriously stuffed with goosedown
> able to double as sleeping
> or punching bag.

Available Light is Piercy's eleventh book of poems. In this volume, passion and anger are transcended; the poet is still informed by the same strong emotions and responds to the glories of nature with an even richer imagination, but indignation gives way to compassion and vulnerability is no longer so devastating. The "available light" of these poems is Piercy's metaphor for the feeling and perception that come with maturity.

Perhaps the clearest indication of mellowness is the poet's ability to laugh at herself, to see in her woman's body the stuff of humor:

> My friend Penny at twelve, being handed a napkin
> the size of an ironing board cover, cried out
> Do I have to do this from now till I die?
> No, said her mother, it stops in middle age.
> Good, said Penny, there's something to look foward to.

The poet can laugh at menstruation, and she has learned to take her own ideological pronouncements with more than just a grain of salt: "My face came off on motel room towels./ My poems were written by an impostor: me./ If I turn my eyes inward, cold fog swirls."

Nevertheless, Piercy remains a poet of strong convictions, and her social criticism can be as biting as it was twenty years before. In 1968, she attacked the Vietnam War; in 1988, she attacks the indifference of a corporate society:

> We die of the bottom line. We die
> of stockholders' dividends and a big bonus
> for top executives and more perks. Cancer
> is the white radioactive shadow of profit
> falling across, withering the dumb flesh.

The victims of the "bottom line," deprived of possibility, rekindle Piercy's youthful activism. The world poised to prey on a girl of the slums is etched in imagery meant to scratch out the reader's eyes:

> a hungry tiger crouching
> belly low to begin
> a sensuous creep
> toward fresh food.

Finally, however, this kind of anger yields to the wisdom of experience in a poem praising two aged women, union organizers, who evoke cries of derision from young toughs: "Whenever we weep, if we understand/ we may grow like a stalactite longer, stronger."

Piercy has always been known and admired as a "nature poet," an artist so tuned to the sensuous and sensual world that she can draw on it for powerful metaphors to embody her social and political themes. In this mature collection of poems, nature seems to come into its own, and Piercy finds herself in its embracing power. Yet, just as was true of William Wordsworth, who launched English poetry on its discovery of the connections between the experience of nature and the growth of the self, Piercy has finally accepted the inevitable revelation: that nature is there for us because we have imagined it in the context of our own being. Although she understands that the moors of Dartmoor are foreign to her own cultural origins, she feels at home among them: "I dream from something deep under my feet."

The deeper Piercy descends into her sense of nature, the more integrated her sensibility. In the great caves of the Perigord region in France, where ancient men lined the walls with their art, Piercy identifies with the female deer painted there: "When the sacred is sexual and the sexual/ sacred, in all joining. . . ."

The sacredness of the sexual pervades an entire section of poems in *Available Light*, "Country Pleasures." In "Implications of One Plus One," the poet celebrates the many different ways she and her lover make love: "Sometimes you open wide as cathedral doors/ and yank me inside." The poet has come a long way from "The Friend" (1969), where the lover kept asking the woman to "cut off her hands." Indeed, in one poem Piercy calls herself "filled with love/ like a melon." The ritualistic completion, the wholeness of the experience of loving and its rounding of a life into self-discovery is also reflected in a haunting poem about animals in winter and their sacramental need for nourishment, a need so powerful it transcends all fears and differences:

> . . . feed us now or we starve.
> A light thatching of snow:
> every grass blade prickles.
> This low light hardens the black
> in every twig to precision.

The strength Piercy derives from nature is the ultimate source of her reconciliation with memories that she had never been able to join to consciousness: "Those with whom we are truly intimate . . ./ we shape ourselves to hold them." Just as she shaped herself to hold her lover and her child in the womb, Piercy now manages to shape herself to hold the memory of her father. In "Burial by Salt," perhaps the key poem of the entire volume, Piercy recounts her troubled relationship in childhood with a father who never seemed reconciled to the fact that she was not a son. "Lonely" in "the ice caves" of his "sometime favor," Piercy insisted on a relationship: "I kept trying to start a fire or conversation." The father hurt her into poetry, much as W. H. Auden wrote of William Butler Yeats: "Mad Ireland hurt you into poetry." In Piercy's case it was not a nation or culture, but a man. Her poetic answer was at first primarily "fire," her early poetry; the answer in *Available Light* is "conversation."

That conversation ultimately takes a religious and cultural turn. Piercy's Jewish grandmother is the Vergilian guide her father never was. "Grandmother Hannah comes to me at Pesach/ and when I am lighting the sabbath candles."

"The Ram's Horn" is the last section of *Available Light*. Here Piercy rounds out the mature vision of conversation with men, with society, with nature, with her own life and death in the context of a religious commitment:

> A woman and a Jew, sometimes more
> of a contradiction than I can sweat out,
> yet finally the intersection that is both
> collision and fusion, stone and seed.

Her Judaism inspires her to re-create the moment of God's creation of the world, on her own beach at Wellfleet:

> Here on this piney sandspit, the Shekinah
> comes on the short strong winds of the seaside
> sparrow raising her song and bringing
> down the fresh clean night.

Peter Brier

Sources for Further Study

Booklist. LXXXIV, April 1, 1988, p. 1306.
Library Journal. CXIII, March 15, 1988, p. 60.
Publishers Weekly. CCXXXIII, February 5, 1988, p. 81.
San Francisco Chronicle. June 5, 1988, p. REV5.
Women's Review of Books. V, July, 1988, p. 7.

BATTLE CRY OF FREEDOM
The Civil War Era

Author: James M. McPherson (1936-)
Publisher: Oxford University Press (New York). Illustrated. 904 pp. $35.00
Type of work: Military and political history
Time: 1848-1865
Locale: The United States

A historical overview of the United States during the period of sectional conflict and the Civil War

With fifty thousand books already published on the Civil War, the task of the writer who attempts a synthesis of the period would seem to be overwhelming, but James M. McPherson has managed it with a scholar's skill and a good writer's gift for telling an absorbing story. Winner of the Putlitzer Prize for history, this volume in The Oxford History of the United States begins with a sketch of the country at midcentury, 25 percent larger as a result of the southwestern territory acquired at the conclusion of the Mexican War in 1848 and confronting long-simmering tensions over the westward expansion of slavery that were now rising toward the boiling point. Integrating social, political, and military history into one almost seamless fabric, McPherson covers the sectional conflict of the 1850's, the "crisis of the Union" that culminated in the secession of the southern states, and the war itself, from Bull Run to Robert E. Lee's surrender at Appomattox.

A work of such vast scope necessarily emphasizes synthesis at the expense of theme. If there is a unifying idea in the book, it is McPherson's acknowledged emphasis on "the multiple meanings of slavery and freedom, and how they dissolved and reformed into new patterns in the crucible of war." In spite of the existence of a growing class of urban workers and a burgeoning immigrant population, McPherson finds that "the greatest danger to American survival midcentury . . . was neither class tension nor ethnic division. Rather it was sectional conflict between North and South over the future of slavery." He thus implicitly dismisses the idea advanced by some historians that conflicts over tariff policy and states' rights were more central to the political tensions of the 1850's than the South's "peculiar institution." McPherson emphasizes that "by the 1850s Americans on both sides of the line separating freedom from slavery came to emphasize more their differences than similarities."

Under such circumstances, the Compromise of 1850 was an attempt to brace a government ready to split apart with a few political two-by-fours: It gave the South a deferred decision on the question of slavery in New Mexico and Utah in return for a stronger fugitive slave law and the admission of California to the union as a free state. A mere four years later, however, the Kansas-Nebraska Act shattered this uneasy peace by repealing the Missouri Compromise line of 1820, which had banned slavery in the northern territories, and substituting the deliberately ambiguous doctrine of popular sovereignty, which left room for violent disagreement among the territorial settlers. The Kansas-Nebraska Act completed the destruction of the divided Whig Party and gave rise to the new, entirely Northern, Republican Party, whose stated objective was to prevent the spread of slavery. Although not all Republicans were motivated by sympathy for the Negro—indeed many were deeply antipathetic toward blacks and opposed slavery only in the economic interest of working-class whites—and although the party was pledged not to disturb slavery where it already existed, Southerners regarded it as a threat. The election of Republican Abraham Lincoln in the "revolution of 1860" precipitated the "counterrevolution of 1861," the secession of the lower South and, after the firing of shots at Fort Sumter, of the upper South as well.

In stressing the formation of the Confederacy as a "preemptive counterrevolution," McPherson follows the model of historian Arno Meyer, who applied it to twentieth century Europe. Such a counterrevolution does not attempt to restore the old order, it strikes first—preempts revolution—in order to protect the status quo before revolution can erupt. The secessionists magnified the potential threat posed by Lincoln's election, arguing that waiting for an "overt act" against Southern rights was comparable to waiting for a coiled rattlesnake to strike. The time to act was before the North decided to move against slavery, as the Southern radicals believed the "Black Republicans" ultimately would.

McPherson's other important theme is that the Civil War was a political war, fought by citizens rather than by professional armies; as a consequence, political leadership and public opinion directly affected military strategy, and events on the battlefield reverberated on the home front and especially in Washington, D.C. For this reason he chose a narrative rather than a thematic format, integrating political and military events to emphasize complex patterns of cause and effect. Thus, he emphasizes that the failure of the Army of the Potomac to reach Richmond during the Seven Days' Battle in the spring of 1862 changed Union policy from the limited goal of restoring the Union into one of total war to destroy the Old South and consequently gave rise to the Copperhead faction of antiwar Democrats in the North. Antietam was a major turning point not only because Lee's Army of Northern Virginia was driven back across the Potomac, but also because it ended Confederate hopes for European recognition and military assistance, and gave Lincoln the military victory he had been waiting for as a backdrop for his Emancipation Proclamation.

Especially in the North, where the two-party system still operated and the Republican position on slavery was still evolving and far from unified, Union military success or failure had far-reaching effects. The defeats at Bull Run and Ball's Bluff led Congress to establish the Joint Committee on the Conduct of the War, and the Union failure at Fredericksburg gave Secretary of the Treasury Salmon P. Chase, who aspired to replace Lincoln as the Republican nominee in 1864, an opportunity to encourage a senatorial investigation of the cabinet. Public morale in the North rose after the victory at Stones River and temporarily blunted the Copperhead offensive against Lincoln's war policy; it plummeted again after the Confederate triumph at Chancellorsville on May 2-3, 1863, and Lincoln exclaimed in despair: "My God! my God! What will the country say?"

McPherson gives military outcomes the central place in his explanation of Northern victory and Southern defeat; he is critical of theories that undervalue events on the battlefield. In his concluding chapter he reviews the various explanations that historians have advanced for the South's ultimate defeat, analyzing the weaknesses in each. Although the North was superior in manpower by two to one and had even greater economic resources, revisionist historians have denied that the South fought against odds so great as to make defeat inevitable; they have pointed out the number of small countries that won independence against even greater odds, not the least of which was colonial America against Great Britain. Such historians have argued instead that internal divisions—the states' rights governors who refused to cooperate with the central government, the disaffection of nonslaveholders, libertarian resentment of conscription and the restriction of civil liberties—fatally weakened the South's morale and destroyed its will to fight. McPherson discounts this argument, as well as the alternative interpretation that stresses the gradual development of superior Northern military and political leadership that was evident by 1863, because both commit "the fallacy of reversibility": If the outcome had been reversed, the same factors could be cited to explain a Southern victory. He particularly faults the loss-of-morale thesis, most recently advanced by Richard E. Beringer, Herman Hattaway, Archer Jones, and William N. Still, Jr., in *Why the South Lost the Civil War* (1986), for "putting the cart before the horse"; defeat was the cause of Southern demoralization and loss of will, McPherson argues, not the consequence.

McPherson faults most explanations of Southern defeat for failing to take into account the factor of contingency, the realization that at various turning points the war might have taken an entirely different turn. He identifies four critical turning points that shaped the final outcome. The first was in the summer of 1862, when Stonewall Jackson and Lee in Virginia and Braxton Bragg and Edmund Kirby-Smith in the West launched counteroffensives that prevented the Union armies from claiming what had appeared to be certain victory. This rally by the South meant that the war would be prolonged and intensified, and Southern success seemed assured before each of three successive turning points toward Northern victory. First, Union triumphs at Antietam and Perryville in the fall of 1862 turned back Confederate invasions and killed the hope of European recognition for the Confederacy; they may also have prevented a Democratic victory in the 1862 elections, which would have hampered the Lincoln government's ability to prosecute the war, and certainly permitted the president to make his Emancipation Proclamation from a position of political and military strength.

The next critical time was during the summer of 1863, when success at Gettysburg, Vicksburg, and Chattanooga turned the North toward eventual military victory. The last one came in the summer of 1864, when enormous Union casualties of the spring campaign in Virginia—three-fifths as many battle deaths as in the previous three years of fighting—combined with the seeming lack of progress forced the North in the direction of peace negotiations and nearly resulted in the election of a Democratic president. William Tecumseh Sherman's capture of Atlanta and Philip Henry Sheridan's destruction of Jubal Early's army in the Shenandoah Valley made Union victory inevitable; only then, after the military situation became impossible, McPherson contends, did the South lose its will to fight.

Several important long-term consequences of the Northern victory emerge in McPherson's analysis. Slavery and secession were killed forever, and the word "United States" became a singular instead of a plural noun; the "union" of states, as in "the United States are a republic" became a nation and an indivisible entity. Replacing the old federal government with which the average citizen rarely came in contact, except at the post office, was a new "centralized polity." This national government levied direct taxes and collected them through an internal revenue service that it created itself, drafted citizens into a national army, imposed a national banking system, and instituted numerous other innovations. Eleven of the first twelve amendments to the Constitution, McPherson points out, had restricted the authority of the national government; beginning in 1865 with the Thirteenth Amendment, which abolished slavery, six of the next seven amendments greatly increased federal power at state expense.

Finally, the balance of political power shifted from the South, which had controlled the presidency for two-thirds of the years since the founding of the republic, and had predominated in the selection of the House Speakers, presidents pro tem of the Senate, and Supreme Court justices. For fifty years after the Civil War no Southerner was elected to the presidency, none of the House Speakers or Senate presidents came from the old Confederacy, and only one-fifth of the Supreme Court justices were appointed from the South. McPherson contends that despite the South's appearance of being different from the rest of the United States, the argument can easily be made that until the Civil War it was actually the rapidly changing North that was out of step with the rest of the world. Although slavery had been largely abolished, most societies had an unfree or only semifree labor force. Most of the world was rural, agricultural, and traditional; only the northern United States and a few countries in northwestern Europe were speeding toward industrial capitalism. Thus, Southerners were both sincere and correct when they claimed to be fighting to preserve the republic of the founding fathers: limited government that protected property rights and served an independent gentry and white yeomanry in an agrarian society. The South's preemptive counterrevolution attempted to preserve this tradition, but Union victory in the Civil War ensured the dominance of the Northern vision of America.

Judith N. McArthur

Sources for Further Study

Booklist. LXXXIV, January 15, 1988, p. 826.
Chicago Tribune. March 20, 1988, XIV, p. 3.
Choice. XXV, July, 1988, p. 1745.
Kirkus Reviews. LVI, January 1, 1988, p. 42.
Library Journal. CXIII, March 1, 1988, p. 65.
Los Angeles Times Book Review. March 20, 1988, p. 10.
The New York Review of Books. XXXV, June 2, 1988, p. 9.
The New York Times Book Review. XCIII, February 14, 1988, p. 1.
Newsweek. CXI, April 11, 1988, p. 77.
The Washington Post Book World. XVIII, March 13, 1988, p. 1.

THE BEAN TREES

Author: Barbara Kingsolver (1955-   )
Publisher: Harper & Row (New York). 232 pp. $16.95
Type of work: Novel
Time: The 1980's
Locale: Kentucky, Tucson, and land owned by the Cherokee

Escaping Kentucky for Tucson, a tough and warmhearted woman acquires a child, a community, and a connection to important issues

Principal characters:
TAYLOR (MARIETTA) GREER, the narrator, who leaves Kentucky in her mid-twenties in a three-hundred-dollar Volkswagen
LOU ANN RUIZ, who is deserted by her husband when she is seven months pregnant
TURTLE, an abused child of three
MATTIE, who runs a used-tire shop and a sanctuary for Central American refugees
ESTEVAN, formerly a teacher in Guatemala City
ESPERANZA, his wife, who mourns the loss of their child

Opening mid-anecdote, with the direct voice and assured eye for humorously specific details that have become a hallmark of the new generation of local color writers, *The Bean Trees* makes an immediate impact. One slows down to savor the rich invention and pointed observations and to appreciate the narrator's spunky, down-to-earth self-awareness. Better yet, before long one comes to appreciate that this first novel by Barbara Kingsolver has a project more ambitious—and ultimately more compelling—than simply to create bits of life that would fit neatly into semiconnected short stories. The characters grow, change, and are worth caring about. The themes—introduced without preaching—are both important and resonant. By book's end, one is full of admiration for the careful construction which brings together assorted threads and leads the plot to a breathtaking and touching conclusion.

The first-person narrator, Marietta Greer, was reared fatherless and poor in Kentucky. She plugs away in high school when the other girls are dropping out pregnant. "This is not to say that I was unfamiliar with the back seat of a Chevrolet," she reports, but those experiences had not "inspired me to get hogtied to a future as a tobacco farmer's wife." After five years of doing laboratory work in a county hospital, she buys an old Volkswagen and heads west with two plans: She will take a new name wherever the gas tank runs dry, and when the car itself gives out she will stop to settle while she still has a grubstake. She is not, however, the passive fatalist that these decisions might seem to imply. After a close call in Homer, Illinois, she coasts into Taylorville on momentum and gasoline fumes and becomes Taylor Greer, but the rocker arm goes in the middle of a treeless piece of Oklahoma owned by the Cherokees. Despite her possible claim to "head rights" in the Cherokee nation (Taylor's mother had a grandfather who was full-blooded), she uses half of her remaining money to get the car fixed so she can go on.

In the dark outside a roadside café, an Indian woman thrusts a child into the car and insists that Taylor take it. "If I wanted a baby, I would have stayed in Kentucky," Taylor says, but the woman climbs into a truck and disappears. The child is a girl, abused, undersized, silent, and slow. Taylor calls her Turtle. She presses on into Arizona, where her money and her tires are finally exhausted, and comes to a halt at Jesus Is Lord Used Tires in a run-down neighborhood of Tucson.

Alternating chapters in the early part of the book introduce another Kentucky woman, Lou Ann Ruiz, who had married a rodeo rider, gone west with him, and been abandoned just before the birth of their son. Taylor connects with her while answering ads for housing to share and takes a job at the used-tire shop. It is run by Mattie, a forthright, competent, gray-haired mechanic who needs a helper so that she can take unannounced trips from time to time. Upstairs are silent, brown-skinned visitors who come and go in the night.

With these materials in place, the story passes permanently to Taylor's first-person narration and to working out a plot of discovery, strength, and tenderness. Taylor and Lou Ann are two ordinary working women with small children, scraping by through the practical sharing of space and responsibilities and working out ways to get along with each other. When Taylor first hears Mattie mention the word "sanctuary," she thinks only of the places for birds that are pictured on the road maps published by various state tourist bureaus.

The most refreshing quality of Kingsolver's characters is their genius for taking the right actions instead of examining their feelings or conducting intellectual arguments. The novel is grounded in an awareness of the range of issues that are women's issues and demonstrates the profoundly woman-centered nature of much working-class life. When Lou Ann's Kentucky relatives visit, women fill the house in a way that men cannot. Marginal and relatively uneducated women take significant actions because they are in touch with practical reality.

This is not to say that Kingsolver herself is unaware of feminist theory. The author's intellectual understanding fuels concrete examples of issues such as the importance of naming. Taylor Greer's original name of Marietta is distinctively female and (secondarily) regional. In Kentucky, her friends called her Missy, a name inspired by her first childish attempt to break out of the class into which she was born. At three she had demanded that her mother call her "*Miss* Marietta," as she "had to call all the people including children in the houses where she worked Miss this or Mister that." This early passage lays the groundwork for understanding Taylor's adult decision to rename herself and makes clear the significance of replacing the infantilizing "Missy" and the localizing, female "Marietta" with the neutral "Taylor." The transmutation of names, indeed, becomes a thread—now humorous, now touching—that weaves throughout the story.

The book's artful construction supplies many such threads: Kingsolver's apparently effortless style sets up a background that is virtually unnoticed until suddenly convergences and revelations occur. Turtle's fascination with planting seeds in the garden extends also to toy trucks and dollies—and each time the action reappears it accumulates resonance and extends meaning. Kingsolver is also splendid with the scene, the look of vegetation, the feel of earth, the smell of rain in the desert. The snappy tone of Taylor Greer's narrative voice supplies instantly recognizable characterizations; Newt Hardbine, for example, was "one of the big boys who had failed every grade at least once and so was practically going on twenty in the sixth grade, sitting in the back and flicking little wads of chewed paper into my hair."

The only really dislikable people in *The Bean Trees* are self-involved, like the potential housemates who are "into" sensitivity, nutrition, and self-expression. With women whose common ground is reality and survival, however, Taylor makes instant connection. Sandi at the Burger Derby tips her off about thrift shops and the mall where a child can be left all day in the supervised playroom as long as the mother pretends to be shopping. At an Oklahoma motel, Mrs. Hoge urges Taylor to stay and earn money during the Christmas season. The two elderly women who live next door to Lou Ann baby-sit Turtle (and, in their own relationship, provide a fascinating and poignant surprise). Even the social worker with high-heeled pumps and a big desk finds a way to provide out-of-channels help when the state of Arizona threatens to put Turtle into foster care or a children's home.

The threat to Turtle also brings out unexpected determination in Lou Ann. Although the two Kentucky women become instant friends—as well as housemates—in the relief of hearing each other's "down home" voices in Tucson, their natures are sharply different. Taylor's spunk and self-assertion are the gift of a mother who gave her unconditional love and praise, taught her to ask for what she wants, and had a ready supply of observations, drawn from her work as a cleaning woman, to prick inflated images of the rich or self-important. Lou Ann, on the other hand, was reared in the shadow of fundamentalist religion and by a mother unable to rule in her own house. She is afraid of almost everything, collects stories of unexpected disasters, is obsessed with the idea that she is ugly and that if she speaks her mind she will drive her friends away, and has an overly developed sense of responsibility that makes her feel guilty for even thinking about anything that would make someone else unhappy. When events that seem truly out of control nudge Taylor toward depression, however, Lou Ann responds with strength and determination that prove infectious.

The plot, like the characters, engages specific individual actions that speak to larger issues. Despite the poverty of her childhood, Taylor's strength and self-confidence have protected her from recognizing the extent to which people can be helpless and victimized. As Estevan says to her, Americans "believe that if something terrible happens to someone, they must have deserved it." She is jolted by finding evidence of the abuse that Turtle suffered and numbed when she learns about the political realities of Central America—and the complicity of the United States government that supports repressive regimes and refuses asylum to endangered refugees.

Kingsolver does not preach; there are no embedded lectures or passages of political rhetoric. Yet she has created a novel full of old-fashioned meaning. Taylor Greer encounters political realities by seeing what has happened to real people, and she does what is required for both practical and moral survival. The threads of the plot are resolved convincingly with a breathtaking climax that is—all at the same time—comical, surprising, moving, and ultimately gratifying.

Sally Mitchell

Sources for Further Study

Booklist. LXXXIV, March 1, 1988, p. 1095.
Cosmopolitan. CCIV, March, 1988, p. 51.
Glamour. LXXXVI, March, 1988, p. 258.
Kirkus Reviews. LV, December 15, 1987, p. 1693.
Library Journal. CXIII, February 1, 1988, p. 76.
Los Angeles Times. April 4, 1988, V, p. 4.
Ms. XVI, April, 1988, p. 28.
The New York Times Book Review. XCIII, April 10, 1988, p. 15.
Publishers Weekly. CCXXXIII, January 15, 1988, p. 78.
Women's Review of Books. V, May, 1988, p. 1.

THE BEAUTIFUL ROOM IS EMPTY

Author: Edmund White (1940-)
Publisher: Alfred A. Knopf (New York). 228 pp. $17.95
Type of work: Novel
Time: The late 1950's and the 1960's
Locale: Michigan, Chicago, and New York City

This autobiographical novel concerns not only the coming of age of a single protagonist, but also the awakening of an entire gay culture

Principal characters:
THE NARRATOR, a first-person witness to and participant in the birth of gay liberation
MARIA, his enduring friend, an artist who first declares herself a Communist, then a lesbian
DR. O'REILLY, his cross-addicted psychiatrist
ANNIE SCHROEDER, a self-destructive, bulimic girl whom he meets through Dr. O'Reilly
WILLIAM EVERETT HUNTON, a homosexual law student with an adopted name and an artificial persona
LOU, a drug addict and ad man who acts as his guiding spirit
SEAN, an ambivalent, unstable boy who is his first true love

The Beautiful Room Is Empty is an autobiographical novel about growing up gay in America. It was preceded, in 1982, by Edmund White's *A Boy's Own Story*—a prequel featuring the same narrator—and it is clear from the author's own comments and from the conclusion of *The Beautiful Room Is Empty* that this story of a cultural evolution is not finished. *The Beautiful Room Is Empty*, which covers the 1960's, the great era of sexual liberation for American society at large, could easily have been a joyous narrative. Instead, it is a halting, doubting story of self-discovery that seems haunted by the specter of acquired immune deficiency syndrome (AIDS), which would later come to change the gay world irrevocably.

AIDS does not make an appearance in the novel—mention of the disease would be anachronistic. The novel is often characterized by a somber mood, however, which its very title introduces. White opens his book with an epigraph from Anatole France that equates the state of being human with sensual awareness. There is another epigraph, however, the one from which the book's title is taken, that comes from a letter Franz Kafka wrote to Milena Jesenska. This second epigraph is far more equivocal, filled with a sense of the impossibility of acceptance, integration, or love:

> Sometimes I have the feeling that we're in one room with two opposite doors and each of us holds the handle of one door, one of us flicks an eyelash and the other is already behind his door, and now the first one has but to utter a word and immediately the second one has closed his door behind him and can no longer be seen. He's sure to open the door again for it's a room which perhaps one cannot leave. If only the first one were not precisely like the second, if he were calm, if he would only pretend not to look at the other, if he would slowly set the room in order as

> though it were a room like any other; but instead he does exactly the same as the other at his door, sometimes even both are behind the doors and the beautiful room is empty.

This passage conjures up a marvelously evocative scenario, and the scenes from the novel it brings to mind most immediately are those depicting the furtive lavatory and subway encounters where the narrator compulsively pursues both love and anonymous sex. These scenes are certainly among the most powerful in the novel, and although the narrator emerges from such episodes with a sense of unfulfilledness, the author makes no apologies for their intensity. The alternative world, the world of "big baggy grown-ups," provides little sustenance for a young, hungry soul. Yet, the larger culture exerts a profound pressure to conform (most of the young men in the novel, including the protagonist, cherish the illusion that they will someday go "straight"), which inevitably results in conflicted identities.

Many of the characters peopling the world of this novel are more than conflicted: The narrator's analyst is a drug addict, as is the narrator's mentor, the advertising executive, Lou. There is nothing especially schematic about the manner in which White develops his themes, but it does seem that those individuals who achieve the greatest measure of peace are those who learn to embrace their unorthodox sexual orientations. Marriage does not save Lou from his addictions any more than a wished-for-homosexuality saves Sean, the narrator's first true love, from insanity. On the other hand, Maria remains the narrator's lodestar, a woman who—regardless of her shifting allegiances—always retains a certain dignity which is bound to her self-accepting lesbianism.

The narrator's method of coping with his compulsions and consequent guilt is to embrace a singular version of Buddhism, whose outer manifestations are his devotion to the study of Chinese and his capitulation to corpulence, both symptomatic of a truer, internalized Buddhist characteristic: self-denial. The persistence of gay homophobia has become a truism, but most of the time White manages to convey his vision of this oxymoronic tension gracefully, as in this exchange between Sean and the narrator:

> One night as we were lying in bed, Sean said that that afternoon he had used a public toilet and walked in on an orgy.
>
> "Oh, how awful," I said.
>
> "What are they doing there?" he asked.
>
> "What do you mean?"
>
> "Of course I know they're there for sex, but how can they do it? It's really subhuman."
>
> "Totally subhuman," I said.

In its irony and understatement, this passage has the ring of truth. When White is trying to demonstrate his narrator's qualifications as Everyman, he lapses into excess and sentimentality: "Then he was gone. I put my lips where his had been on the coffee cup. I felt elated, because that was all I'd ever wanted, to be loved, and nobody ever had."

Other attempts to place his hero in the mainstream of American life—such as references to the deaths of John F. Kennedy and Marilyn Monroe—also seem strained. The same technique, however, that of making the protagonist a presence by giving him a historical context, works well when applied to a milestone in the origins of gay politics, the riot outside the Stonewall Inn, a gay bar in New York City:

> I stayed over at Lou's. We hugged each other in bed like brothers, but we were too excited to sleep. We rushed down to buy the morning papers to see how the Stonewall Uprising had been described. "It's really our Bastille Day," Lou said. But we couldn't find a single mention in the press of the turning point of our lives.

The young narrator believes that he is alone with his sexuality not merely because his partners are nameless, faceless bathroom johns, but because such loneliness—which, like most emotions, seems more profoundly experienced during youth—is part of the human condition. White, however, is at his best when he allows his narrator to relate the texture of his sexuality—his promiscuity, the very shallowness of his encounters—without reflection. The true interest of *The Beautiful Room Is Empty* lies in its direct depiction of the otherness of gay life, with all its immediacy and intensity.

One negative aspect of the book's prime virtue is that the narrative tends to break up into a series of discrete episodes, each focusing on a particular sexual experience. To be sure, the episodic form is a literary tradition long wed to the story of a young man's progress. In part, the discontinuity of *The Beautiful Room Is Empty* adds to the reader's sense of the protagonist's uncertain identity. The hero does undergo some radical changes from the opening of the novel, when he is a repressed prep school boy, until the end of the book, when he participates in the Stonewall Uprising. How curious—especially in view of White's choice of a first-person narrative—that one comes away from the novel without any real notion of an internal evolution.

White is careful not to allow his protagonist to take too active a part in the life around him (outside the Stonewall, he stands *beside* someone shouting "Gay is good!"). As a result of this strategy, White's hero seems never really to change from that younger self who yearningly confesses, "Perhaps because I hated my sexuality and believed it could be redirected, I'd come to see every aspect of my being as vague and shifting, and in that very cloudiness had lain my definition: I was the boy who hadn't started living yet." Finally, one suspects that the protagonist remains alienated not merely from the greater society, but even from the gay subculture.

This sense of alienation is underscored by the fact that the world the narrator comes increasingly to inhabit is peopled with eccentrics, grotesques, and outlaws, individuals with whom he seemingly has little in common. Along the way, he encounters personages such as the addicted and incompetent analyst, Dr. O'Reilly, the bulimic, suicidal Annie Schroeder, and the arch sadist, William Everett Hunton. Finally, the narrator meets Lou, the hero to whom he devotes nearly half his narrative, but whom he calls a pervert. Never does the narrator forgo his longing for the average or "normal." As an undergraduate indulging in nightly cruising on the streets of Ann Arbor, Michigan, he remarks:

> The thrill came when one bagged not another old fruit but a hot young college kid, for although I myself was at least young and in college, I already saw myself as vampire-cold, turned prematurely old as a punishment for vice, and not nearly enviable enough to be that exciting thing, a "college kid." I'd learned to feel nostalgia for my own youth while I was living it.

One is left, in the end, with a sense that White's protagonist still has not found a place where he can feel at home in the world. The novel's discontinuous form surely is in part a result of a not altogether successful attempt to splice together autobiography and a political agenda ("my plots are all scrapbooks," the narrator confesses). Partly, however, it is a vehicle deliberately shaped to convey the still-unresolved dilemma confronting gays, the conflicting—and sometimes equally powerful—attractions of homoeroticism and social conformity. At times, in an attempt to make his readers share his experience, White's technique awkwardly draws attention to itself: "Come with me, then, up the concrete steps to the toilet door, ..." Most of the time, however, he succeeds admirably in communicating the bittersweet growth into self-awareness of a sensitive young man, whose experience, filled with minute particulars, speaks to the singularity of each person's life.

Lisa Paddock

Sources for Further Study

Booklist. LXIV, March 1, 1988, p. 1096.
Kirkus Reviews. LVI, January 15, 1988, p. 86.
Library Journal. CXIII, March 1, 1988, p. 79.
London Review of Books. X, March 3, 1988, p. 11.
The Nation. CCXLVI, April 9, 1988, p. 503.
New Statesman. CXV, January 29, 1988, p. 29.
The New York Times Book Review. XCIII, March 20, 1988, p. 7.
Publishers Weekly. CCXXXIII, January 22, 1988, p. 102.
Time. CXXXI, April 11, 1988, p. 74.
The Times Literary Supplement. January 22, 1988, p. 82.

BEING AND RACE
Black Writing Since 1970

Author: Charles Johnson (1948-)
Publisher: Indiana University Press (Bloomington and Indianapolis). 132 pp. $15.95
Type of work: Literary criticism

This volume offers an analysis of major black writers who have been publishing since about 1970

The epigraph to *Being and Race: Black Writing Since 1970* is a statement by French dramatist and playwright Prosper Mérimée that highlights the relationship between theory and practice: "In fiction there must be a theoretical basis to the most minute details. Even a single glove must have its theory." Charles Johnson demonstrates his belief in this idea by applying what he calls "the method of 'phenomenology'" to fiction written by black writers since about 1970. Acknowledging that the term "phenomenology" is often misunderstood, Johnson describes, rather than defines, his use of the word as a reliance upon a "philosophy of experience" in which people "bracket," or set aside, previous models for explaining phenomena and thereby rely upon intuition to illuminate the reality investigated. While this notion is derived from Edmund Husserl, the creator of phenomenology, it has been modified by later thinkers such as Martin Heidegger, Jean-Paul Sartre, Maurice Merleau-Ponty, and Michel Dufrenne—all of whom have influenced the author in his effort to use a phenomenological mode to understand black American fiction.

In the first half of *Being and Race*, Johnson focuses upon the theoretical glove by examining race, fiction, and form as they are related to the philosophical question of being. The first chapter is both a personal statement of Johnson's literary odyssey and a historical overview of black literature, beginning with its earliest developments and tracing its more recent examples in the black arts movement. Throughout this evolution, Johnson states, black writers have been concerned with making meaning of the black world, with creating various racial ideologies for the African experience.

This ideological thrust is fundamentally antiphenomenological, according to Johnson, for it eliminates a free investigation of phenomena by reducing the black experience to a one-sided acceptance of otherness. In this ideological reductionism, the black body is viewed as stained, a notion eliciting thoughts of guilt, sin, punishment, ostracism, and the need to be purified or cleansed. Given this one-dimensional view of the black experience, two options are available to the black writer: accepting this state and assuming a kind of "invisibility," or reversing the negative meaning of the black stain and assuming a kind of "black is beautiful" posture. Johnson argues that both options restrict genuine, creative work, and he calls for a suspension of this ideological approach.

The second chapter, "Being and Fiction," examines the ways in which a less ideological and more phenomenological approach can enrich the literary productivity of black writers. Johnson explores what he calls a middle ground between two views of fiction, one articulated by William Gass and the other summarized by John Gardner. In Gass's view, literature is not related to the world of real men, real women, or real events. A literary work, according to Gass, "is filled with only one thing—words and how they work and how they connect." By contrast, John Gardner sees fiction as "moral" and life-affirming, similar to Leo Tolstoy in his work *Chtoe takoye iskusstvo* (1898; *What Is Art?*, 1898) and William Faulkner in his Nobel Prize acceptance speech (1949), both of whom emphasized art as a human, not merely linguistic, activity.

The middle ground between these two views is what Johnson describes as "the presence of others in language." This notion rejects the position that language is a neutral medium for expressing things and also rejects the opposite position, that art is simply a way to express human emotion. In this middle ground, both language and fiction are viewed as transcendent, reinforcing what Johnson describes as "the old saw that great writers are sexless, raceless, and have no historical moment circumscribing their imagination and curiosity." Unfortunately, according to the author, this vision of transcendence has not been seen or communicated by many black fiction writers.

In the final chapter of this section on philosophy, Johnson looks at "Being and Form," asserting that most current fiction has a "depressing sameness, a formal one-dimensionality." Just as he calls for an elimination of ideology and a reliance upon transcendence in the first two chapters, so Johnson makes another call in the third chapter, this time for technical virtuosity that comes from experimenting with forms used by earlier writers. This experimentation will allow writers to move among genres and to play with various styles, thus using the tradition of literature to create new artistic worlds.

Given this theoretical discussion, it is not surprising that Johnson chooses to examine and praise black fiction writers who demonstrate a nonideological, transcendent, experimental virtuosity. The second half of the book identifies the men and the women, a chapter for each, whom Johnson believes are the exemplars of his views on race, fiction, and form.

In the chapter titled "The Men," Johnson surveys writers whom he describes as pioneers because of their experimental efforts: Clarence Major, Ishmael Reed, Samuel Delany, William Melvin Kelley, Al Young, John McCluskey, Jr., Leon Forrest, John Edgar Wideman, James Alan McPherson, David Bradley, John A. Williams, Cyrus Colter, John Oliver Killens, and Cecil Brown. In his survey, Johnson has special praise for John A. Williams, describing him as "a model who has borne the brunt of discrimination and continued doggedly to deliver solid works of literary achievement and to discharge his manly duties." Williams' book, *The Man Who Cried I Am* (1967), receives superlatives for its powerful message about racism and is compared to Richard Wright's *Native Son* (1940) as well as Ralph Ellison's *Invisible Man* (1952). If Williams is singled out for his contributions to black literary history, James Baldwin is omitted for his contributions to the genre Johnson calls "the 'protest novel' oriented toward race politics." Rejecting protest literature for aesthetic reasons, though acknowledging his early reliance upon that genre, Johnson consistently focuses upon male black writers who, in his estimation, advance black writing both technically and thematically.

The final chapter, "The Women," asserts the phenomenological importance of literature written by black women and the questions raised by feminists. Johnson points out that "the modern emergence of a 'woman's perspective'" has irreversibly changed the way the world is viewed, thus sensitizing readers to seeing phenomena in new and revolutionary ways. Among these new visions is the ongoing process of self-definition experienced by black women and described by Toni Morrison as the sense that the black woman "had nothing to fall back on: not maleness, not whiteness, not ladyhood, not anything. And out of the profound desolation of her reality she may very well have invented herself." As he does with the male writers, Johnson surveys the writing of black women and includes the following writers in his catalog: Gayl Jones, Toni Morrison, Alice Walker, Ntozake Shange, Paule Marshall, Toni Cade Bambara, Gloria Naylor, Kristin Hunter, Ellease Southerland, Jamaica Kincaid, and Octavia E. Butler. The book which receives the author's greatest attention is Walker's *The Color Purple* (1982), which Johnson describes as standing "at the crest of black women's fiction in the 1980s," as "the publishing phenomenon of this decade," and as "a cultural event." Predictably, given his concern with aesthetic standards, Johnson does not offer unqualified praise to a book which he views as having greater cultural significance than it does literary merit; he concludes that *The Color Purple* "is not fully realized as a work of art." He offers a similar evaluation in summarizing the contributions of black female writers, assuming what might be construed as a patronizing stance when he praises the women for having a better eye for details than their male counterparts but being limited in their abilities to manipulate plot and to demonstrate formal virtuosity. The aesthetic dimension, Johnson contends, seems to be of little interest to most black female writers, a contention that many theoreticians and practitioners will certainly question, if not deny.

In his final section, Charles Johnson explicitly addresses the question he implicitly considers throughout his study: Has the fiction written by black men and women plowed new racial and social ground and suggested new phenomena for investigation? In his negative answer, Johnson asserts that the bulk of black writing continues to be marred by a monotony of technique and content. He mentions some exceptions, but points out that black fiction continues to be a kind of genre writing in which writers fail to demonstrate the seriousness and skill necessary to forge new paths, experiment with new forms, examine new ways of viewing phenomena.

Despite this less than positive evaluation of contemporary black fiction, Johnson concludes on a hopeful note. He speaks of the challenge beckoning black writers to discover an art that

> can be dangerous and wickedly diverse, enslaved to no single idea of Being, capable if necessary of unraveling, like Penelope, all that was spun the night before and creating from entirely new social and scientific premises if need be, or adjusting the seminal work of the past to address issues relevant to this age.

On the horizon, according to Johnson, is a fiction that enables both black writers and their culture "to move from narrow complaint to broad celebration." In this clarion call to black writers, Johnson combines his two roles of creative writer and critical theorist. He is a man perhaps best known as a fiction writer—his collection of short stories, *The Sorcerer's Apprentice*, was a PEN/Faulkner nominee in 1987—and director of the Creative Writing Program at the University of Washington. In combining those credentials with his insights into literary criticism, he echoes the epigraph of *Being and Race*: Fiction and theory are brought together in this analysis of black writing since 1970.

Marjorie Smelstor

Sources for Further Study

Booklist. LXXXIV, February 15, 1988, p. 966.

The Washington Post Book World. XVIII, July 24, 1988, p. 8.

BERNARD SHAW
Collected Letters, 1926-1950

Author: George Bernard Shaw (1856-1950)
Edited, with an introduction, by Dan H. Laurence
Publisher: Viking Press (New York). Illustrated. 946 pp. $45.00
Type of work: Letters
Time: 1926-1950
Locale: Primarily England

The fourth and last volume of George Bernard Shaw's selected correspondence, this text includes 740 letters and postcards written by one of the world's wittiest writers

Dan H. Laurence, an actor and director as well as drama scholar, has devoted twenty-seven years to editing and annotating a quartet of volumes drawing on George Bernard Shaw's Himalayan range of correspondence, choosing about twenty-five hundred letters and postcards from what may constitute a total production of 250,000. Earlier volumes covered the years from 1874 to 1897 (1965), 1898 to 1910 (1972), and 1911 to 1925 (1985). All have been edited with tactful erudition and illuminative clarity. Laurence deserves grateful admiration for having brilliantly accomplished an enormously taxing enterprise. As in the previous volumes, he has dispensed with conventional footnotes and substituted concisely written headnotes containing an immense amount of background information. Two-thirds of these pieces of correspondence have not been previously published; many others were issued only in extracts. The editor has departed from his practices in the preceding texts in two ways: He has deleted some sensitive passages in deference to Shaw's testamentary wish and has restored, inside square brackets, occasionally missing words or letters omitted by Shaw's aging fingers when he handwrote or typed.

On his ninety-third birthday, Shaw wrote a letter to one of his oldest friends, St. John Ervine, which begins: "May I respectfully remind you that when Lincoln was shot . . . my age was 9 years, and my views on the subject so little in demand that I did not take the trouble to form any." Readers will have difficulty imagining any event or subject subsequent to 1865 on which Shaw failed to form views and express them originally, provocatively, and wittily. He was the supreme commentator on all public (and many private) issues during the first half of the twentieth century. His Methuselah-length life stretched from the last year of the Crimean War to the first year of the Korean War. This final volume of his collected letters covers a span when, with the possible exception of Charlie Chaplin, he may have been the most famous person in the world—certainly the most celebrated author in history, with his comments frequently front-page news.

Shaw was engrossed in virtually everything—except the formation of a Shaw society, whose existence he only gruffly tolerated during his last nine years: "Don't bother me about it. I am old, deaf, and dotty." This book shows him becoming seriously interested in the cinema, playing a vigorous role in the filming of his plays *Pygmalion*, (1913; film 1938), *Major Barbara* (1905; film 1941), and *Caesar and*

Cleopatra (1901; film 1946), as well as being involved in eventually aborted projects to bring *Arms and the Man* (1894), *The Devil's Disciple* (1897), and *Saint Joan* (1923) to the screen as well. He saw his once-controversial plays become established classics, although this did not prevent critics from attacking such late dramas as *Too True to Be Good* (1932), *The Simpleton of the Unexpected Isles* (1935), *Geneva* (1938), and *Buoyant Billions* (1947). Shaw also published a religious/ethical fable, *The Adventures of the Black Girl in Her Search for God* (1932), and two significant texts on politics: *The Intelligent Woman's Guide to Socialism and Capitalism* (1928) and *Everybody's Political What's What* (1944). The best plays of his final period are generally thought to be *The Apple Cart* (1929) and *The Millionairess* (1936).

His energy was often exuberant, never restrained. This collection shows him concerned with some lifelong preoccupations: music, phonetics, shorthand, education, eugenics, domestic and international politics, and as always, the theater. It also reveals his interest in taxation, love, grief, marriage, health, religion, boxing, painting, Albert Einstein's theories of physics, nudism, homosexuality, beekeeping, and—inevitably—dying and death.

The most dismaying portions of this correspondence deal with Shaw's attitude toward the twentieth century's leading dictators, Benito Mussolini, Adolf Hitler, and Joseph Stalin: He admired them. Shaw joined these totalitarians in a deep contempt for parliamentary democracy, regarding it as bumbling and corrupt, with the incompetent few representing the unqualified many. Influenced by the ideas of Plato, Thomas Carlyle, and Friedrich Nietzsche, he preferred a disciplined state ruled by a Man of Destiny, a benignly autocratic master spirit resembling his stage rulers, from Caesar to Magnus to Undershaft to Good King Charles. All of these are powerful, intelligent, aristocratic, and charismatic personages, decisive managers of the public weal, impervious to the caprices of the masses.

With regard to Mussolini, Shaw failed his first moral test by refusing to condemn the 1924 murder of Giacomo Matteoti, secretary-general of Italy's Socialist Party, after he had denounced the Fascists. In a 1927 letter, Shaw argues that the means a new regime uses to attain power have no significant bearing on the regime's worth once it is in charge. Rather, "some of the things Mussolini has done . . . go further in the direction of Socialism than the English Labor Party could yet venture if they were in power." Shaw hails Mussolini as a farsighted, responsible socialist, and even excuses the Italian aggression against Abyssinia (now Ethiopia) in 1936:

> In the conflict between Danakil savage and civilized Italian you must, as a civilized man, be on the Italian side. In the face of the scalp hunting North American Indian . . . and the testicle hunting Danakil, European civilization must stand solid.

After the 1938 Munich Conference, Shaw finally admitted, in his last significant word on Mussolini, "Musso let me down completely by going anti-Semite on me."

Sadly, Shaw's infatuation with Hitler was to last longer. In the 1930's Shaw considered him a messianic man of action, hailing Hitler's repudiation of the Treaty of Versailles and withdrawal from the League of Nations, welcoming the annexation of Austria in 1938, applauding Hitler as late as March, 1940, for having lifted Germany out of the gutter and made it the most dreaded power in Europe. In many letters to his Jewish-born European agent, Siegfried Trebitsch, Shaw puts the most favorable interpretations possible on Hitler's domestic policies, even calls him a great statesman—only his anti-Semitism is "stark raving nonsense: he is mad on that subject."

To his credit, Shaw was one of the earliest English commentators to denounce Hitler's Judophobia. Performances of his plays in Germany were consequently often interrupted by Nazi shouts of "Jew Shaw!" Yet in September, 1945, having read about the deaths of forty thousand prisoners in the Bergen-Belsen concentration camp, Shaw is capable of this appalling response:

> Belsen was obviously produced by the incompetence and breakdown of the military command. The concentration camps are always left to the refuse of officers' messes, for whom the job of feeding and sanitating the deluge of prisoners is too much. The result is always the same more or less.

Shaw's misunderstanding of Stalin's conduct was, if possible, even more naïve. The Soviet Union consistently had Shaw's virtually uncritical and often-enthusiastic allegiance. Though himself never a member of the Communist Party, he flatly declares, in 1934, "There is no public man in England more completely committed to Communism, and in particular to the support of the Russian system, than I." His head was turned for the rest of his life by his visit to the Soviet Union in the summer of 1931. In Moscow, thousands of residents welcomed him at the railway station with shouts of "Hail Shaw"; he was wildly cheered everywhere he went; his seventy-fifth birthday, on July 26, was celebrated by adulatory speeches from Soviet commissars; Stalin granted him a two-and-a-half-hour interview. Buoyed by his visit, Shaw advised his lifelong friend, the wealthy capitalist Nancy Astor, to "preach The Revolution." He remained infatuated with Stalin to his dying day, ignoring reports of the gulags and ranking him the world's ablest statesman, with "Roosevelt second, and the rest nowhere."

How is one to account for such blindness to the evils of despotism, such worship of strong leaders, no matter how cruel? The explanation most Shavian scholars adopt is his incurably Victorian disposition. After all, Shaw was already forty-four when the nineteenth century expired; his mental landscape had long been charted. He therefore misread modern dictators as essentially elitist and paternalistic fathers to their folk—peers of William Ewart Gladstone, Benjamin Disraeli, and Queen Victoria herself. A minority of Shavians are less kind, regarding his worship of political ruthlessness as the transfer to the arena of statecraft of the intolerant dogmatism and occasional terrorism he practiced in his literary and theatrical crafts.

The same Victorianism that misled Shaw in politics also led him honorably to a life of fair dealing, decency, good humor, kindness, and generosity. This collection demonstrates as much. Shaw may have been a public misanthrope, but privately, like his fellow Irish writer Jonathan Swift, he found it impossible to hate the Johns,

Peters, Thomases, and others who often plagued him. He advises one correspondent that the world's real problem is not to unite people in superficial and temporary love, but "to hammer it into them that their dislikes do not give them the smallest right to be unjust or uncivil to [one another]."

Amazingly, Shaw suffered many fools, if not always gladly. He was consistently generous to the editor/biographer Frank Harris, even though Harris filled his biography of Shaw with falsehoods and offended the puritanical Mrs. Shaw with his scatological, also largely invented autobiography. He forgave G. S. Viereck's publication of two "interviews" which never occurred, then granted him one, only to be forced to disclaim its publication as a grotesque misrepresentation. He permitted two would-be literary executors, John Wardrop and Fritz Loewenstein, privileged use of his papers, which both abused. He supported two distant aunts and provided for the education of several children only remotely related to him. When Beatrice Webb's illness and the depressed state of the market drained the Webbs' finances, Shaw in 1934 instructed his banker to pay one thousand pounds—at that time a princely sum—into Sidney Webb's account. He permitted publication of his romantic correspondence with the actress Ellen Terry, so her daughter could establish a memorial institute with the profits.

One sequence of letters is particularly appealing. It is addressed to Sister Margaret McLachlan, later Dame Laurentia, who became the abbess of Stanbrook Abbey. In 1931 he sent her a four-thousand-word description of his tour of the Holy Land. In 1933 the devout nun and the cheerful atheist sparred about a Voltairean story Shaw had written in 1932, eventually published as *The Adventures of the Black Girl in Her Search for God*. She urged him to scrap the work as profane; he half-decided to heed her, then changed his mind, had it issued, and charmingly asked her to pray for his heathen soul. They debated their religious views in letters which movingly exhibit their warm friendship despite their differing sentiments. In 1934 he misconceived the message on a souvenir card celebrating her gold jubilee as a nun as a notice of her death, wrote a poignant letter of condolence to the ladies of her order, was informed by Dame Laurentia that she remained among the living, and replied:

> Laurentia! Alive!!
> Well!!!!!
> Is this a way to trifle with a man's most sacred feelings?
> I cannot express myself. I renounce all the beliefs I have left. I thought you were in heaven, happy and blessed. And you were only laughing at me. It is your revenge for that Black Girl.
> Oh, Laurentia, Laurentia, Laurentia, how *could* you.
> I weep tears of blood.
>
> Poor Brother Bernard

Shaw was deeply devoted to his wife, Charlotte. In 1939 she contracted osteitis deformans, commonly called Paget's disease, which badly crippled her until she died in September, 1943. In a letter to H. G. Wells, Shaw wondrously describes how, a day or so before her death, "her furrows and wrinkles smoothed out. Forty years fell off her like a garment. She had thirty hours of happiness and heaven."

Between 1944 and 1950 Shaw kept remarkably busy despite his ripe age, contributing more than four hundred articles, messages, letters, and self-drafted interviews to newspapers and periodicals, as well as maintaining a strenuous correspondence. On September 10, 1950, he lost his balance while gardening, tumbled, and fractured his left thigh. When nurses tried to wash him twice in one day, he admonished them, "Too much washing is not good for antiques." He developed a kidney problem, for which he had surgery on September 21. On November 1, he serenely announced, "I am going to die." The next day he did. His ashes, mingled with his wife's, were consigned to the garden of his home in Ayot St. Lawrence, which is owned by England's National Trust and therefore open to the public.

Gerhard Brand

Sources for Further Study

Booklist. LXXXIV, May 1, 1988, p. 1472.
The Christian Science Monitor. July 20, 1988, p. 17.
Library Journal. CXIII, May 1, 1988, p. 81.
Los Angeles Times. June 16, 1988, V, p. 20.
The New Republic. CXCIX, August 8, 1988, p. 30.
The New York Times Book Review. XCIII, June 19, 1988, p. 12.
The Observer. June 5, 1988, p. 42.
Publishers Weekly. CCXXXIII, April 1, 1988, p. 68.
Smithsonian. XIX, September, 1988, p. 172.
Time. CXXXI, June 6, 1988, p. 87.

BERNARD SHAW
Volume I: 1856-1898, The Search for Love

Author: Michael Holroyd (1935-)
Publisher: Random House (New York). Illustrated. 486 pp. $24.95
Type of work: Literary biography
Time: 1856-1898
Locale: Ireland and England

This is the first of three volumes constituting a meticulous and comprehensive critical biography of one of the modern age's most celebrated and controversial literary figures

Principal personages:
GEORGE BERNARD SHAW, a playwright, essayist, novelist, critic, pundit, social reformer, and showman
CHARLOTTE PAYNE-TOWNSHEND, the wealthy Irish heiress who became his wife
GEORGE CARR SHAW, his alcoholic father
LUCINDA "BESSIE" GURLY SHAW, his cold mother
LUCY SHAW, his sister
VANDELEUR LEE, Lucinda Shaw's music teacher and friend
SIDNEY WEBB and
BEATRICE WEBB, a husband-wife team who helped lay the basis for the British welfare state
WILLIAM ARCHER, a critic who became one of Shaw's best friends
JENNY PATTERSON, the first woman with whom Shaw had an affair
ELLEN TERRY, a distinguished actress with whom Shaw conducted a romantic correspondence

In the early 1970's, George Bernard Shaw's British publisher, Max Reinhardt, invited Michael Holroyd to undertake the first comprehensive biography of Shaw since 1956, the centenary of the writer's birth. The Shaw estate's legatees wanted a biographer who had not known the playwright. Presumably they chose Holroyd because his biographies of two other distinguished British artists, Lytton Strachey (1968) and Augustus John (1974), had both been acclaimed, and because he had the age and energy to devote many years (fifteen preceding the publication of this first volume) to so herculean a project. This volume is incisive, compressed yet immensely informative, occasionally bold in judgment and consistently elegant in expression. On the strength of his performance and promise, Holroyd may in time complete one of the twentieth century's greatest literary biographies, to be ranked alongside Richard Ellmann's lives of James Joyce and Oscar Wilde, Leon Edel's life of Henry James, and Joseph Frank's ongoing biography of Fyodor Dostoevski.

One of Holroyd's scholarly choices may prove controversial: Aware of considerable current activity by Shavian researchers, he has decided to delay publication of his sources until after the issue of his third volume—presumably in a separate, fourth text. Shaw addicts who do not expect to live that long may find at least partial satisfaction in the four tomes of selected Shaw letters, scrupulously edited by

Dan H. Laurence, which have been issued in, respectively, 1965, 1972, 1985, and 1988 (reviewed in this volume), covering altogether seventy-six of Shaw's ninety-four years.

Holroyd takes pains to reveal the traumatic insecurity and mistrust of intimacy behind the artfully contrived persona of the publicly swaggering, cheerful, arrogantly self-confident phenomenon known to the world as G. B. S. His father, George Carr Shaw, was descended from the Protestant landed gentry which ruled Ireland from the late seventeenth to the late nineteenth century. George Bernard Shaw's paternal grandfather died bankrupt, however, and his father, along with two uncles and an aunt, became a chronic alcoholic; another uncle turned mentally ill. Shaw's mother, Lucinda Elizabeth Gurly, called Bessie, had a bullying father; her mother died when she was nine; she was then largely reared by a loathsome aunt. Having married George Carr Shaw to escape her hateful family, Bessie discovered herself bound to a befuddled ne'er-do-well who could not keep any position. She became an embittered hoarder of hurts who taught her son, nicknamed Sonny, to imitate his father in reverse—as an antimodel. Sadly, she also largely ignored Sonny. In a rarely self-revealing letter, Shaw was to write the actress Ellen Terry, many years later, of his "devil of a childhood . . . rich only in dreams, frightful and loveless in realities." With typically paradoxical defensiveness, Shaw was to claim that his parents' indifference to his welfare inculcated him with the useful virtues of self-reliance and self-sufficiency.

Bessie Shaw turned from her weak husband to a mesmeric music master, George John Lee, who later took the first name of Vandeleur. George Bernard Shaw never knew when the two had first met, but he certainly came to know that his mother found Lee an inspirational voice teacher and that the family and Lee moved into one house, with the musician's income largely sustaining them. Could Sonny have been Lee's natural son? Beatrice Webb, for one, asserted that their facial expressions were similar. The boy—surely the later man—must have indulged in logical speculation about such a parentage; however, Shaw took care not to do so on paper. Holroyd remarks throughout his book on the considerable number of triangular relationships in which Shaw was to involve himself, usually with Shaw playing the asexual friend to the married woman. He interprets Eliza Doolittle's separation from Professor Higgins to marry Freddy Eynsford-Hill in *Pygmalion* (1913) as Shaw's dramatization of Bessie's attachment to Lee. Moreover, since his father and Lee shared the first name of George, G. B. S. came to detest his first name and never used it professionally, employing either "Bernard" or "G. B. S."

Sonny was sent to the Central Model Boys' School in Dublin; he hated it as a shabby institution filled with incompetent teachers. He found his senses coming alive, however, by wide reading of his own choice and by teaching himself to comprehend musical notation and play the piano. In the spring of 1873, Lee left for London to promote his career; several days later, Bessie Shaw followed him with her daughter Agnes, leaving her son and other daughter, Lucy, behind. Sonny abandoned school to join a real-estate firm, rising from errand boy to cashier and rent collector even though he hated business. At the age of twenty, he left Dublin to seek his fortune in London, delighted to escape his native city's cultural as well as economic blight.

Shaw's mother received him with, as usual, little affection. Nevertheless, he was to share one flat or another with her for twenty-two years, until his marriage in 1898. In one of his novels, *Love Among the Artists* (1887-1888), he gave a son a speech which, according to Holroyd, directly reflects Shaw's feelings toward his mother:

> Can you understand that a mother and son may be so different in their disposition that neither can sympathize with the other? It is my great misfortune to be such a son. . . . She had no idea how much her indifference tortured me, because she had no idea of any keener sensitiveness than her own. . . . She taught me to do without her consideration; and I learned the lesson.

When Bernard Shaw reached London, his mother had already grown disenchanted with Vandeleur Lee. He had shifted his affections from Bessie to her daughter Lucy, who had a magnificent voice, and whom he pushed into taking principal roles in a musical society he had founded. The Shaws abandoned Lee, with Bessie setting herself up as a private singing teacher. Giving up a brief career of ghostwriting weekly musical articles for Lee, Shaw began what was essentially a program of self-tutelage, reading and writing with prodigious energy yet no tangible financial rewards. England's economic depression in the late 1870's and early 1880's made employment extremely difficult to obtain for a young man without regular education or influential connections. Shaw sent many articles on the arts and politics to newspapers and periodicals; they were rejected. From 1879 to 1885 he wrote five novels; none found a publisher. In 1880, he approached the editor of the *Pall Mall Gazette* with sample articles and asked him whether he had the makings of a music or drama critic; he was advised to forget about a journalistic career.

Shaw did find a home more congenial than his own in the British Museum's Reading Room. For eight years he worked there daily, doing his writing, borrowing more than three hundred books per year. Reading about vegetarianism, he became a fervent convert; eating never amounted to more than a troublesome necessity to him. Dreading contamination of any sort, he avoided not only meat but alcohol, tobacco, tea, coffee, vaccinations—and, whenever he could, sex. Holroyd graphically describes Shaw as a young man about London resembling a scarecrow, "in broken boots, . . . cuffs whose margins had been refined with his mother's scissors, trousers whose holes were hidden by a tailed coat fading from black to green. He was an example of poverty." Afflicted by smallpox in 1881, he thereafter grew a beard to hide a scar on his right cheek. It became his famous facial signature: a forked, aggressive bush. "Few people who had their attention arrested by this flagwaving at the head of the Shavian talking-machine would have known that Shaw was publicly concealing something."

Shy and self-conscious, yet tireless and ambitious, Shaw turned from a society that rejected him to socialist societies, which welcomed him. His reading of Henry

George's then-popular book *Progress and Poverty* (1879) led him to Karl Marx's *Das Kapital* (1867) and a lifelong commitment to socialism. In May, 1884, Shaw joined the recently formed Fabian Society. It included a galaxy of brilliant intellectuals dedicated to reforming English society thoroughly although gradually, in the spirit of their Roman namesake, Fabius Maximus. The Fabian Society was dominated by the brilliant husband-wife team of Sidney and Beatrice Webb, whose idyllic partnership Shaw admired and envied.

In 1885, Shaw met William Archer, already an established theater critic; they soon became the firmest of friends. It was Archer who obtained for Shaw his first journalistic job, as art reviewer for *The World*. In 1889, Shaw became a music critic, under the name Corno di Bassetto (basset horn), and filled that role with masterly distinction in several journals for a decade. His brilliant monograph on the Ring Cycle, *The Perfect Wagnerite* (1898), falls just beyond the bounds of Holroyd's first volume. From 1895 to 1898, he was also the highly influential drama critic for Frank Harris' *Saturday Review*, signing his articles G. B. S. By this time he had begun writing plays, so his standing as a critic-dramatist was complex and potentially conflicting, except that no one ever doubted Shaw's incorruptible integrity.

Holroyd lucidly discusses the seven plays Shaw wrote before 1898, starting with *Widowers' Houses* (1892), an unqualified disaster that was followed by such fine achievements as *Arms and the Man* (1894), *Candida: A Mystery* (1897), and *The Devil's Disciple* (1897).

What distinguishes Holroyd's approach from those of previous biographers is his interpretation of Shaw's relations with women. Holroyd insists that they mattered more to him than earlier writers have granted—hence the book's subtitle. As a dazzling lecturer and adroit debater, Shaw fluttered the hearts of many radical young women. He also occasionally philandered with the wives of friends, and—though rarely—consummated an affair with a divorced or separated woman. Holroyd describes three couples—the Beattys, the Avelings, and the Blands—in which the husband was both a friend of Shaw's and a notorious womanizer; in each case, the neglected wife made explicit sexual overtures to Shaw, but he resolutely avoided them. The nonaffair with Edith Bland, whose husband had recruited Shaw for the Fabian Society, was particularly farcical. She would struggle to keep him in her house, hoping to lure him to her bed; he would do his best to persuade her to go walking in the safe outdoors. After months of such frustrations she finally protested to him: "You had no right to write the Preface if you were not going to write the book."

Was G. B. S. wholly asexual? impotent? homosexual? Not at all. Holroyd offers this intriguing explanation:

> Debarred by his childhood from being able to form close emotional attachments, he gave his passionate allegiance to ideas—but saw women as vehicles for those ideas. . . . Revolution came from men, evolution through women. Shaw took the body away from women and addressed their minds. His own mind was astonishingly fast, but emotionally he was lame. The result was that women found themselves continually out of step with him.

When he was twenty-nine, a highly sexed widow finally relieved Shaw of his virginity. Jane Patterson, who preferred the name Jenny, was a singing student of his mother, fifteen years older than he and therefore closer in age to Bessie than to Bernard Shaw. Once initiated into the power of sexuality, he found it frightening: It undermined his hard-won independence and Puritan dedication to work. While the liaison with Patterson was to last eight years, it gave Shaw far more pain than pleasure, particularly when she became jealously possessive and embarrassed him in his friendships—most but not all platonic—with other women. On a February night in 1893, Patterson burst in on Shaw and the actress Florence Farr as he was visiting the latter's house, and had to be restrained from assaulting Farr. This incident gave Shaw the will to make his final break with Patterson; she never forgave him.

In the autumn of 1895, Beatrice Webb introduced Shaw to a wealthy Irish heiress, Charlotte Payne-Townshend, who impressed him as clever, placid, self-possessed, bookish, and not at all romantic. Payne-Townshend had remained single largely to vex her bullying mother, who had been determined that she should marry. Now the mother was dead, and Payne-Townshend was a free spirit. While she and Shaw did have sex, they were careful to subordinate its place in their relationship. They played a perverse push-pull game with each other: When either felt too attracted to the other, he or she fled via either work (Shaw) or travel (Payne-Townshend). In May, 1898, Shaw dislocated some toe joints and came down with a serious case of necrosis in his left foot. He was operated on and had to be nursed for months. Unable to escape Payne-Townshend, he surrendered, and they agreed to marry. Who proposed to whom? The question was never plainly answered. What is clear is that, with Shaw immobilized, Payne-Townshend had to buy the wedding license and ring—but only after the proud Shaw had insisted that their unequal income be kept in separate accounts, so he could not be accused of fortune hunting. They were wed June 1, 1898, and enjoyed happiness with each other the rest of their lives.

Gerhard Brand

Sources for Further Study

The Atlantic. CCLXII, October, 1988, p. 91.
Chicago Tribune. September 25, 1988, XIV, p. 7.
Library Journal. CXIII, October 1, 1988, p. 88.
Los Angeles Times Book Review. October 9, 1988, p. 3.
The New Republic. CXCIX, November 14, 1988, p. 38.
The New York Review of Books. XXXV, November 24, 1988, p. 3.
The New York Times Book Review. XCIII, October 30, 1988, p. 1.
Newsweek. CXII, October 24, 1988, p. 75.
Publishers Weekly. CCXXXIV, August 19, 1988, p. 62.
Time. CXXXII, October 10, 1988, p. 94.
The Times Literary Supplement. September 16, 1988, p. 1007.

BINSTEAD'S SAFARI

Author: Rachel Ingalls (1940-   )
First published: 1983, in Great Britain
Publisher: Simon & Schuster (New York). 224 pp. $6.95
Type of work: Novel
Time: The 1980's
Locale: London and Africa

An analysis of the spiritual changes resulting from a failed marriage

Principal characters:
MILLIE BINSTEAD, an American housewife
STAN BINSTEAD, her professor husband
HENRY LEWIS, her lover, a big-game hunter

Though the main characters in Rachel Ingalls' *Binstead's Safari* are American, the novel is set in England (London) and Africa. Millie and Stan Binstead, in fact, are like some of Henry James's characters in that they are the victims of assumptions which change when they encounter people and locales foreign to them. This kind of situation seems natural to Ingalls, an American expatriate who, like James before her, lives in England, where she settled in 1964 and where *Binstead's Safari* was first published in 1983. Her publishing career, indeed, has followed her taking up residence in England; *The Pearlkillers* appeared in 1964, followed by *Theft* (1970), *Mediterranean Cruise* (1973), *The Man Who Was Left Behind and Other Stories* (1974), *Mrs. Caliban* (1982), and, after *Binstead's Safari*, *Something to Write Home About: Stories* (1988). *Binstead's Safari* itself records the emotional recovery of a woman trapped and debased by her marriage. It also traces how her husband comes to love her again and to understand himself for the first time.

Millie Binstead has spent most of her marriage feeling worthless. Her husband Stan, a professor, has done little if anything to help her. In fact, the more passive and enervated Millie has become, the more Stan has despised her. Moreover, Stan has found out that he is not impotent and Millie that she is not barren, but neither has told the other; as a result, each thinks the other is to blame for their not having children. Unfortunately, neither really wants to have a child by the other. In effect, they have become strangers to each other; boredom has led Stan to other women, and self-pity has led Millie to the resentful pretense that she can do nothing on her own.

This grim state of affairs begins to change when the Binsteads travel to London, then to Africa. Stan has gotten a grant to research what he believes to be an unusual lion cult in Africa. Surprisingly Millie insists on going along, though Stan wants to leave her behind. In London, while Stan spends his time with various colleagues, including Jack, an old friend who sets him up with a woman, Millie goes exploring on her own. She visits museums and attends the ballet, her curiosity and energy no longer dormant.

During the early (town) phase of their stay in Africa, Stan pays Ian Foster and his younger partner Nicholas Fairchild, veteran big-game hunters and longtime residents of the area, to guide the Binsteads on a safari into lion country. Millie, meanwhile, meets and has an affair with Henry Lewis, a legendary local hunter and an expert on lions.

Stan has trouble pinning down the lion cult he has come to Africa to research. His London friend Jack thinks that it is a provincial extortion racket, and locals such as Ian Foster seem to know little if anything about the cult. Protocol and the language barrier also prevent Stan from learning much in the villages he visits on the safari.

Millie, meanwhile, blossoms in the earthy environment in which she finds herself. Lewis has ignited her sexual and romantic feelings, and she exchanges love letters with him through intermediaries. She discovers, from Alistair James, a young doctor who occasionally visits the camp, that she is pregnant. Despite this, she does not tell Stan about her affair with Lewis.

Stan is intensely affected by the environment, as well as by Millie. Under Foster's tutelage, he takes well to the role of hunter. He also has nightmares, mostly about his brother, which cause him to recognize the jealousy he has felt about his brother's becoming a hero by dying in the Vietnam War. In addition, Stan is amazed by the change in Millie. She seems younger now, beautiful, and he falls in love with her again. Yet she adds to his overall frustration by refusing to sleep with him and by telling him that she wants a divorce. Her success puzzles him, too, for everyone connected with the safari is taken with her, and she shows genuine talent as a primitive painter, going out most days on the safari to paint with Foster's wife, Pippa.

News arrives that ivory poachers have murdered Lewis. Shortly after this, a magnificent lion begins to visit the camp at dawn, apparently to see Millie. A local village, in the midst of a mysterious celebration, tries to include her in it, attracted by the necklace that Lewis gave her. Finally, Stan, Foster, and Fairchild, accompanied by Millie, track the lion, which kills Millie when she rushes between it and Stan.

In his grief, Stan seeks revenge. He hallucinates the lion (seeing it on Millie's grave), Lewis, and Millie. As he and Nicholas are hunting the lion, the poachers who seem to have murdered Lewis ambush them. Stan shoots one, fatally wounding him, and the other dies when his jeep mysteriously catches fire. By this time Stan thinks that the lion is Lewis himself, and the reader is led to believe that the lion has maneuvered the poachers to their deaths and Stan into a confrontation with the animal part of his own nature. This is where the novel leaves Stan: stripped of his academic remoteness in a setting which demands that one kill or be killed. The novel suggests that the cult which Stan has been trying to uncover is best understood through experience, not study.

As it progresses, the novel clarifies the corollary to this point: Romantic love has no place in nature. It is a human invention, and it distracts those who indulge in it from the real dangers and needs of life. The image for this kind of love in the novel is language, in the form of rumors, gossip, and letters. These things are tentative and unfulfilling. Because of rumor, the young balloonists who float over the landscape in the story are displayed in a love triangle remote and complex. Gossip tries to put Alistair James in the arms of Elsie, the woman in the triangle, and gossip underscores the anxiety Nicholas Fairchild feels over the mental illness of his wife, Jill—an anxiety that blurs his concentration on his work, which includes heading a safari similar to that of the Binsteads. This is the Whiteacre safari, and again gossip presents the chaotic mate-switching of the rich Whiteacres and their companions. Even Millie's and Henry Lewis' love letters describe their desires rather than their realities. Indeed, it is the romantic nature of their tie that moves Millie to throw herself into the jaws of the lion and thus lose her unborn child—this one sensible effect of her affair.

As Stan ultimately discovers about romantic feelings, "Family ties prevail over such trivialities. Family ties depend on blood." In nature, communities are at stake, not individuals, and cults make sense as a community's effort to survive, not as subjects for scholarly articles. Moreover, infatuation corrupts this effort, for it is based on ego, which misrepresents nature.

Ingalls dramatizes the feel of the lion country in the novel clearly enough for the reader to imagine being in it. Her characters are astutely drawn, and the points she makes through them are important in a time in which the disorders of civilization conflict with the priorities of nature.

There are flaws in the novel, however, which make it less than moving: The plot is dampened by chitchat, commentary, and summarized action. Clearly, Ingalls wants to show the distance between thinking about something and doing it. Nevertheless, the strategy limits the novel's suspense (except toward the end) to such questions as, "Will Millie tell Stan about her affair?" and "Will Dr. James get together with Elsie?" and "Will Millie leave Stan after all?" and "Will Nicholas and Jill Fairchild find happiness?" These questions are not meaningless, but they tend to crowd out the intensity the story might derive from its dangerous setting.

Mark McCloskey

Sources for Further Study

The Atlantic. CCLXI, March, 1988, p. 100.
Booklist. LXXXIV, February 1, 1988, p. 903.
Chicago Tribune. February 14, 1988, XIV, p. 4.
Kirkus Reviews. LV, December 15, 1987, p. 1692.
Library Journal. CXIII, February 1, 1988, p. 75.
Los Angeles Times. March 29, 1988, V, p. 1.
The New York Times Book Review. XCIII, April 17, 1988, p. 42.

Publishers Weekly. CCXXXII, December 18, 1987, p. 55.
Time. CXXXI, April 11, 1988, p. 74.
The Wall Street Journal. March 15, 1988, p. 32.
The Washington Post Book World. XVIII, March 6, 1988, p. 9.

BODY BLOWS

Author: Robert Bagg (1935-   )
Publisher: University of Massachusetts Press (Amherst). 117 pp. $17.50; paperback $7.95
Type of work: Poetry

This volume is a collection of poems, some presented here for the first time, by Robert Bagg

Robert Bagg is a translator of Greek, a professor of English, and a poet, it seems, in both languages. The first poem in his collection *Body Blows* is a "free translation," as he calls it, of one by Sappho. It is a lyrically beautiful translation in which the poet prefers death to the lonely despair she feels upon desertion by her lover. Parting provokes Sappho to ask her errant lover, "why not leave radiant/ as if you remembered the/ honey of it?" She calls forth the memories of "how lazy and sensual" the two had been, of the scents and the feel of lovemaking. The poem is, at once, joyful in memory and melancholy in loss—a tone to be found often in the works which follow it. In fact, Bagg chooses wisely this touching fragment to introduce his own work with its themes of time and memory, love and loss, even birth and death.

Body Blows is a collection of poetry written over some three decades, most of which has been previously published in Bagg's four earlier volumes of verse. Bagg presented his first collection, *Madonna of the Cello*, in 1961, only three years after he was graduated from Amherst College. That book aroused Ralph J. Mills, Jr., to pen a particularly virulent criticism for the pages of *Poetry*; he essentially called young Bagg's work sophomoric and suburban. In the same issue, however, the poet James Merrill leaped to Bagg's defense; he found the works revelatory and pronounced the young poet a man of talent and promise. Most critics seemed to agree with the latter view, though not without reservations.

Three other volumes followed: *The Scrawny Sonnets and Other Narratives* in 1973, *The Worst Kiss* in 1985, and *Special Occasions* in 1986. For the present collection, Bagg has chosen the best of the poems from his four earlier volumes; most have undergone minor changes, he notes, and several have been revised substantially. In addition, he has included several heretofore uncollected works. This judicious selection demonstrates his mastery of several forms, most notably the elegy, the long narrative, the sonnet, and the meditation.

If any force can be said to unify these poems, it is the power of memory to erase distance and time and to allow the poet to roam freely over those experiences which gave him his voice. In those poems where place is emphasized, it is never incidental, never trivial, never "occasional." Rather, these wanderings are most often trips through time—the poet's childhood, his visits to France and to Greece, the year in Italy when he won the Prix de Rome (1958-1959). For example, the casino in Juan-les-Pins is a metaphor for the gamble he makes when he spins the roulette wheel of a telephone dial on the chance he may reconnect a love affair gone awry. "Trompe l'âme" also has for its setting the French Riviera, where casual cosmopolitanism so quickly seduces as well as deceives the soul.

The road to Epidauros evokes the timeless grandeur of the Greek landscape while it allows the poet to meditate on the power of myth to explain and to subdue its natural savagery:

> Pasiphae at last
> braces her feet as she swells to the boneless
> murder of the bull's orgasm
> its mythical rage now a soft pulse   her
> hysterical delicacy lost on him

Rather jarringly, "the movie star McQueen" (as an icon of modernity?) has overtaken the poet on this road, and his intrusion, "his body vibrating from/ power he sits astride," is as foreign to the theater at Epidauros as Pasiphae's delicacy is to the bull.

A return visit by the poet to the American Academy at Rome in 1980 calls forth a meditation on just how "eternal" the city can be, menaced as it is by terrorism, by class struggle, and by nuclear annihilation. Under the specter of such modern calamities, the city's ability to inspire the poet is distorted; the comforting voice he seeks in its majesty and history is mute, stilled by fear and danger. It is a singularly disturbing vision, but one which captures the complexity and liveliness of the great city.

> Rome's sunny markets, great domes, satyrs and martyrs
> whose thought and impulse well
> imperiously to their eyes;
> lovers, mad traffic, skittish aristocrats
> whose speech dances from one language to the next
> like feeding sparrows—all of that is still there,
> but often at gunpoint, and so worth preserving
> someone will want it soon to explode.

Memory, for those without lyrical gifts, is itself a kind of elegy, but in the hands of the poet this particular lament becomes profoundly moving. "The Eighteenth Book" is Bagg's elegy for Martin Kligerman. It recounts a moment in his life when he asked a young woman if he might rest his head in her lap. Memory of the man is distilled in that one glorious "while" years before at a hillside picnic when

> Just that once his buried wrath
> demanded of her who knew   how much life
> how much life   the gods
> would let him have

In "Death at Pocono Lake Preserve," a boy drowns, and while a lifeguard attempts to resuscitate him, the onlookers marvel at the boldness of death, at how quickly and inexorably it pursues even the young and strong-limbed. Later, as the body of the dead boy "floated face down" on the poet's dreams, he awakens to the insistent sting of mosquitoes and realizes that the hungry insects are interested in him "alone with all this life." Yet the evanescent glitter of another insect, the firefly, will forever spark memory of his dead friend, for in those memories the boy will remain "live and aloof as stars," which had "blinked in the inquisition of his eyes" as he held the phosphorescent insects in his hands.

Death with all of its attendant mystery figures prominently in two of the narratives about adolescence. In "The Sewer Dare," a pair of boys, attracted by danger, crawl through a storm drain, where they are confronted with mortality at an age when the fear of death incongruously becomes "the biggest swindle" of their lives. Victims of the risky dares life proposes—here in the shape of the taunting adolescent Reichert—the two emerge unscathed physically, but angry and somehow more aware:

> "Those beauties don't even know they're alive,"
> he trumpeted—and for weeks after the word
> *Death* seeped into our foreheads, then dried out
> in sunlight and breezes of a day like this.

The experience leaves the poet sullen and vengeful; he "gets even" not only with Reichert but with his fear as well in this candid, wry exploration of an indelible memory.

In "Paolo and Francesca," Bagg rejects the Franciscan who performs the last rites for two young lovers killed in a motorcycle accident. In fact, he names the unfortunate pair for the legendary lovers; the unknown boy and girl, separated by the "brute force" of death, enter the poet's private mythography, where he will see them

> forever relying on
> the pressure on his pulse
> of her expectant eyes,
> as gasoline—
> buoyant thighs close on the body's
> acceleration into blood.

Bagg's voice, as powerful as it is when confronted with the themes of death, can become a sensual whisper when it speaks of erotic love. "Soft Answers" is a lovely, evocative celebration of love play in which the imagery glides as unerringly as the hand of the poet to his lover's breast. In "Madonna of the Cello," conception and gestation are likened to the composition and performance of music. Just as the mother "draws out the reticent sad girl in the strings" as she plays her cello, the poet envisions the unborn child in her womb as her lover strokes her body:

> Silence, after music, awakens the child.
> Her lover opens his palm
> over her turbulent belly, where the child

troubles it with his footprints, turning
against her flesh.

The varieties of love and desire for Bagg seem to be as numerous as there are individual lovers, or, to be more precise, as numerous as there are women to be admired and courted. While *la Donna* may be scrawny or full-bosomed, she is ever *mobile*. She is both Nicole Diver and Zelda Fitzgerald, as in "The Living Sweetness"; she is the heartless but desirable Claudine, whose tossed-off "Tu penses" so enflames the poet's blood; she is one of Pablo Picasso's women in "Je demande la vie éternelle," Janus-faced, with the myriad facets of youth and age, childhood and maturity, as she asks to live forever in the poet's memory. She is also William Shakespeare's Viola, a "mermaid in Skye tweed," or she is an aged Muse who can callously erase a Rembrandt drawing and scatter its dust through her drawing room. She is, in short, poetry, the bestower of the "Worst Kiss," the best kiss, and even the last kiss.

Bagg's voice can be startlingly direct in the best of these poems and maddeningly elliptical in others. Some of the sonnets in particular are so subjective in spirit that the reader could justifiably ask for a guide to Bagg's poetic cosmos before he ventures therein. Is the "faery child" of "Staying" meant to recall Edmund Spenser's immature queen, Bagg's own elusive but "principled tease" in his sonnet sequence "The Tandem Ride," or both, in a vague, ironic bow to his own erudition? Bagg is a clever, witty poet who has the skill to scatter allusions—to William Butler Yeats, to Andrew Marvell, to John Keats, to Ernest Hemingway, even to Oswald Spengler—throughout his poetry. Richard Wilbur and Dylan Thomas find echoes in Bagg's work, and he shows himself capable of borrowing one of Shakespeare's puns for his long poem "The Tandem Ride." He is most eloquent, however, when he speaks clearly to and of his forebears, as he does in "Rembrandt's Dust":

Milton, when Blake shakes him awake,
looks through humanity for his lost wives,
his lost poems, and comes to them
sighing—they are profoundedly loved
by angels with phalloi sensitive as wings,
their minds sweet as the wind from Ooololon.

Here, as occasionally elsewhere in this collection, the poet sings his homage in magical language.

It is in the use of the colloquial that Bagg often falls short, both with words and with rhythm. Some puns are obvious and leaden, such as the gratuitous "Genghis Khock" in the title poem, a narrative of male camaraderie which falters along its way before it finally arrives at its robust and original conclusion. Inadvertently, Bagg may have chosen the title poem as truly representative of the collection. Intensely personal, at times even opaque, it becomes more and more vital as its protagonists make their way through the Roman streets to the Piazza Navona:

as
nightwater greets our plunging faces—
spouting and drinking and shaking
the chill off among the other
wet and battered beasts and gods.

Some of the poems in *Body Blows* are wise and subtle; others are ecstatic with the pleasures of living or colored with the melancholy of suffering. Though all are not equally successful, all employ strikingly provocative imagery. At his most lyrical, Bagg overwhelms with the richness and variety of his skill. In "Metaphor," the figure of speech becomes itself—a metaphor for poetry, which, in turn, stands for the very mystery of life:

Metaphor
gives every discipline its drama:
turns sorrow into wisdom,
reptiles into birds,
makes Proteus a foul old seal,
energy mass, and dreams deeds;
drives all the savage things we hunt
passionately through our lives
to capture them as magic words.

In the second part of this poem, the Shroud of Turin is Bagg's symbol for that spirituality, that Platonic or religious ideal—the very face of God—where metaphor, or poetry, dwells. Fortunately for his readers, this poet embraces that shroud.

William U. Eiland

Sources for Further Study

No sources available.

THE BOOK AND THE BROTHERHOOD

Author: Iris Murdoch (1919-)
First published: 1987, in Great Britain
Publisher: Viking (New York). 607 pp. $19.95
Type of work: Novel
Time: The 1980's
Locale: London

A group of bored, self-indulgent quasi intellectuals enable a former member of their group to produce a book of radical politics which calls for their own destruction

Principal characters:
GERARD HERNSHAW, a prematurely retired civil servant, the center of the brotherhood
ROSE CURTLAND, a woman who is in love with Gerard
JENKIN RIDERHOOD, a saintly schoolmaster
DAVID CRIMOND, a radical Marxist philosopher/writer
DUNCAN CAMBUS, a civil servant and cuckolded husband
JEAN KOWITZ CAMBUS, Duncan's wife and Crimond's lover

Reading Iris Murdoch, one is reminded of Sir James Jeans's observation about the universe, that it is not only stranger than we imagine but also stranger than we *can* imagine. So it frequently seems with the characters and events that make up Murdoch's fictional universe: They are not only strange, but stranger than many readers can imagine. When asked in an interview about the perplexing improbabilities which have become almost a hallmark of her fiction, Murdoch replied that a novelist is a "privileged person, who can see into the soul and know the secret thoughts." A novelist may be accused of exaggeration, but she believes that "you'd be surprised if you could know what other people are thinking and suffering. Of course, there is a surface of ordinary social life. All the deep and extraordinary and grotesque things are concealed."

It is perhaps Murdoch's interest in and her fascinating fictional dramatizations of the deep, the extraordinary, and the grotesque which have made her one of the most discussed major contemporary novelists. Her work has been the focus of intense critical scrutiny, at least some of which has been occasioned by what some readers see as violations of realism: sudden, melodramatic turns of plot; stereotyped and/or unbelievably eccentric upper-middle-class intellectuals who behave in bizarre ways; a discursive, at times almost rambling narrative style which seems designed to tax a modern reader's patience; conclusions which do not seem satisfactorily to conclude. Yet Murdoch denies that she writes fantasy or gothic romance or metafiction of magic realism. She steadfastly places herself within the tradition of the realist novel, and expects her novels to be read as realism, however strange they initially may seem. *The Book and the Brotherhood*, Murdoch's twenty-third novel, is still another of her complex fictional amalgamations (the metaphysical, the psychological, the moral, the social) which inevitably will challenge but perhaps also may enlarge her reader's sense of reality.

The novel, as the title suggests, is about a book, but it is also most centrally about a "brotherhood," a clique of middle-aged intellectual men and women who have been friends since their student days at Oxford. Gerard Hernshaw, a complacently shallow but handsome well-to-do bachelor, is the center of this elite circle, and Rose Curtland is his chief worshiper. At Oxford, it seems that everyone was in love with Gerard, including Rose's brother Sinclair, who was killed in an accident while still a student. During the intense grief that followed Sinclair's death, Gerard and Rose were briefly lovers. Since then, Rose, a well-connected woman of independent means, has spent her life hoping that Gerard will again be interested in her. Instead of the passion she dimly desires, she finds only the camaraderie of the brotherhood and its concern with their memorial to Sinclair: a political and philosophical book supposedly being written by another member of the group, the brilliant Scottish fanatic David Crimond. Many years earlier, the group had pledged financial support to Crimond to free him to write "the book that the age requires," but in the meantime their sense of what the age requires has changed. Crimond has persisted in a youthful Marxist radicalism which the group now finds embarrassingly inconsistent with their own middle-aged bourgeois views, but they nevertheless feel honor-bound to continue subsidizing him, even after Crimond twice seduces Jean Cambus, the wife of a member of the group, and even though there is growing doubt about whether the estranged Crimond is even writing a book. Afraid to confront him, the group finds it easier to go on paying the stipend, at the same time thus cheaply purchasing self-esteem as participants in the intellectual life of their time. As Murdoch makes clear, however, except for the schoolmaster Jenkin Riderhood, they are pseudointellectuals, bookish rather than learned, unable to think of ideas as real.

Crimond is the most enigmatic character in the novel, the only one whose consciousness is never directly conveyed. He is also the most charismatic, possibly because he is so remote but also because he embodies an attractive if demoniac energy. He seems more alive than the others. At the Oxford Ball, the red-haired Crimond wearing a kilt as he dances a Scottish reel with Jean seems almost like a god, "like Shiva." Soon after, he throws Duncan Cambus, Jean's husband, into the river and leaves with Jean, who for the second time goes to live with him. Crimond's peculiar power is revealed by the fascinated way in which others react to him. Jean, who seems to be a person of discernment and judgment, is hypnotized by Crimond and only narrowly escapes from a double-suicide pact. Lily Boyne's self-abasing passion for him is both absurd and an impetus to her own intellectual and emotional growth. Rose nearly succumbs to his dangerous charm, and in the end, contemplating an unexciting future as Gerard's live-in literary assistant, half regrets that she did not. Duncan, the cuckolded husband, is powerless to refuse Crimond's irrational summons, which results in death to the innocent Jenkin Riderhood, whose moral integrity distinguishes him from the rest of the group.

Crimond appears to be one of Murdoch's enchanters, one of the many mythic figures in her fiction—such as Mischa Fox in *The Flight from the Enchanter* (1956) or Honor Klein in *A Severed Head* (1961)—who derive their power from primarily passive people, people so sunk in their subjective fantasies and so lost in their delusions that they are ripe for "enchantment," ready to be led by a strong, self-possessed personality. Such a person does not achieve power so much as have power thrust upon him, attributed to him, by weaker people. It is clear that Crimond plays such a role, but what is less clear is Murdoch's attitude toward Crimond. In interviews, Murdoch has stated that for her, a novel is a way of explaining; it is an examination of characters and their motives, and further, a novelist reveals her own morality in judging the characters. Murdoch's judgment of the "brotherhood" seems evident; except for Jenkin, they are hollow to the core, mainly shallow egotists, preferring hedonism to work and romantic self-delusion to reality, chasing after selfish fantasies they have about one another, oblivious to any larger vision of themselves or the world. They are, to use T. S. Eliot's damning phrase, "decent godless people."

The attitude toward Crimond seems much more equivocal. Murdoch allows Crimond to make the trenchant criticisms of Gerard and his group:

> There's something called history . . . a deep strong relentless process of social change. *That* is what you simply refuse to notice. You think reality is ultimately good, and as you think you're good too you feel safe. You value yourselves because you're English. You live on books and conversation and mutual admiration and drink—you're all alcoholics—and sentimental ideas of virtue. You have no energy, you are lazy people.

Even though Crimond is a somewhat selfish, destructive person whose political ideology calls for total revolution, he also represents self-discipline, creative energy, and passionate commitment. Whatever else he is, Crimond is not one of the hollow men; he has a center, a core, and out of it he writes the long-awaited book, the book which attempts "to see the whole of our civilised past in relation to the present *and the future*."

Gerard, jolted out of his solipsism by reading the manuscript of Crimond's book, comes to the stunning realization that Crimond is right about many things, and that Crimond is more the daring visionary and less the doctrinaire Marxist than was previously thought. Gerard resolves to write his own book in response to Crimond's, and regardless of whether Gerard ever writes a word, it is significant that he thinks of abandoning his parasitic existence and venturing on serious work and thought for the first time in his life. Jenkin, the only working member of the group, observes that Crimond has gone on thinking about social problems and possibilities while the rest of them have stopped thinking altogether, telling themselves that they have become "conservative." Crimond, though a seriously flawed human being, is still admirable in that he has gone on working, trying to make sense of an increasingly chaotic world, trying to "make some sort of synthesis."

Although readers learn little about what precisely is in Crimond's book, there is much to ponder in *The Book and the Brotherhood*. Many of the themes will be familiar to readers of Murdoch's other novels: conflict as the opportunity for growth; the human preference for beautiful illusion over messy reality; the deforming, distorting fantasies about self and others that blind people to the truth; the difficulty of love, which Murdoch defines as the realization that something other than the self is real. The difficulty of love and the necessity of love—these at bottom seem to be her two major themes: love defined as the ability to apprehend the distinct being of other people, the ability to accept and appreciate the essential strangeness of other people, their otherness, which can lead to that humble, disciplined respect for reality which Iris Murdoch shows is so necessary but frequently, so disastrously absent from people's lives.

Karen A. Kildahl

Sources for Further Study

The Atlantic. CCLXI, March, 1988, p. 100.
Booklist. LXXXIV, November 1, 1987, p. 417.
Library Journal. CXII, December, 1987, p. 128.
London Review of Books. IX, October 1, 1987, p. 8.
Los Angeles Times Book Review. February 21, 1988, p. 3.
The New York Review of Books. XXXV, March 31, 1988, p. 36.
The New York Times Book Review. XCIII, January 31, 1988, p. 1.
The Observer. September 13, 1987, p. 27.
Publishers Weekly. CCXXXII, December 4, 1987, p. 64.
The Spectator. CCLIX, September 12, 1987, p. 34.
Time. CXXXI, February 8, 1988, p. 73.
The Times Literary Supplement. September 4, 1987, p. 947.

BORN BROTHERS

Author: Larry Woiwode (1941-   )
Publisher: Farrar, Straus & Giroux (New York). 611 pp. $19.95
Type of work: Novel
Time: The 1940's through the 1980's
Locale: North Dakota, Illinois, and New York City

The continuing story of the Neumiller family, first introduced in Beyond the Bedroom Wall *(1975), focusing on the lives of the brothers Charles and Jerome*

Principal characters:
CHARLES NEUMILLER, the narrator of more than forty years' worth of memories
JEROME NEUMILLER, his older brother
ALPHA NEUMILLER, his mother
MARTIN NEUMILLER, his father

In a review praising John Gardner's *Mickelsson's Ghosts* (1982), Larry Woiwode faults contemporary novelists for their minimalist tendencies. Fiction is in a sad state of affairs, he says, when a writer may turn to the reader and explain that a character's room will not be described because it is uninteresting. For a reader finishing Woiwode's 611-page excursion through the mind and life of Charles Neumiller, *Born Brothers* may well seem a massive rescue job done on that neglected world, a world which treats the main character badly enough to engender the cynical reticence Woiwode gracefully criticizes in his fellow writers' work.

Late in *Born Brothers*, Charles Neumiller stands on the plains of North Dakota, which he has recently reclaimed as home after decades of exile, and, in the midst of a most evocative meditation, thinks: "The more age permits my imagination to extend under this sky, the more details register and lead me to understand that imagination is, indeed, memory—*what* is more profound than any fantasy." This Charles, a radio personality, will not spurn the rooms in which he has lived. The story of his life, *Born Brothers*, is generated in form and content by memory, a rampant river, flowing between his ears, of events and voices. Amid all the matter dredged up by this memory—scooters, bicycles, parents, automobiles, girlfriends, immunizations—the rooms into and out of which Charles finds himself moving serve as symbols of persistent restlessness, isolation, and loneliness. The trapped note is sounded in the narrators' first sentence, "I'm back on my back in that room in the Chesro . . ." (a run-down New York hotel where the feverished Charles awaits his brother's visit), and reverberates in the final words of failed-suicide Charles at novel's end: "And then all doors slam shut on us in the consuming light of our end."

Readers of *Beyond the Bedroom Wall* (1975) are acquainted with Charles Neumiller, but that book also encompassed nearly every Neumiller who had drawn breath in the last one hundred years. With similar comprehensiveness, *Born Brothers* tangles with individual selfhood. This self, Charles, has a brother a year and a half his senior, who unites from childhood with Charles's sense of himself, as twins are said to do. This union, like a perpetually incomplete cell division, exists in a flux of events and places which the brother, Jerome, survives to become a physician, but which Charles is fated to remember and remember. His native gifts as a raconteur seem to promise him a future as a storyteller and actor. Charles is blessed with a remarkable voice and an equally remarkable ear, capable of winning for him a statewide high school speaking competition. Yet he also has an internal chorus which he cannot successfully command, though he does claim to have learned to pause when questioned, to censor or admit the passing of the words which rush to his tongue. He is strange indeed, a fact which he has known from the beginning of his life.

Woiwode's way with this self is never humorous or comic, as the above might suggest he could be. A light treatment would admit fantasy, such as in Charles's own invention of the mad German scientist in one of his early monologues. "Accept this person," Woiwode seems to say, "with the seriousness with which you would welcome me if I entered the room to speak to you of myself." Walt Whitman asked for no less, and baby Charles, sitting alone on a North Dakota lawn, inaugurates the theme: "My white shoes on the grass beyond, on its spears and sheaves, are lumps of truth." These are the shoes that everyone has seen—the shoes a mother saves and sometimes sends out to be preserved in bronze. Woiwode's novel seems intent on the same type of preservation for Charles's memories, while taking up the challenge of another writer concerned with the life of families, James Agee, who wonders, in the preface to *A Death in the Family* (1957), "who shall ever tell the sorrow of being on this earth."

Charles's father, Martin Neumiller, struggles with his own case of never-arriving. His series of occupations—teacher, salesman, carpenter, teacher—includes in its oblivious sweep a number of different houses which are abandoned just as the family seems to have settled in. After one such move, Alpha's difficult pregnancy is complicated by congenital anemia. The baby dies, the mother dies, and the boys remain with their father in a former gasoline station that is being remodeled as a home. The lived-in-while-being-built unsettledness of the place wore out the mother as much as her other ailments, and this unsettledness foresees the contours of Charles's future life. As he ages, Charles is much preoccupied with fixing things up—polishing doorknobs after scraping off layers of paint, refinishing a ceiling while his daughter watches, barricading himself properly behind a door when working at his lastest recording project. Whenever fixing is being done in the novel, as in the conversion of the gutted gasoline station, a concomitant destruction is afoot, whether the bulldozing of a neighbor's house or the blowing up of a service station the brothers visit for something cold to drink.

Are things ever contained properly, the novelist asks, whether the fumes which ignite to transform a peaceful day in Illinois into an apocalyptic scene, or the members of a family who willingly pursue the ideal of union through time? The Neumillers' center was a mother, Alpha, whose bedtime stories read aloud to her sons are remembered by Charles as a togetherness as sweetly intimate as could be desired: "Then I'm gone, a speck outside myself, circulating in the currents spreading from her throat, near her source, until I feel her gather for the end. . . ." (Woiwode entrusts the narrative voice throughout the novel to the first-person present tense, bent on capturing the immediacy of sensations from past years in a network of the eternally firing presentness which is Charles's living mind.) Most present are the mysterious impingements of other selves upon Charles, especially the maternal, as above, the fraternal (Jerome), and the paternal. Charles's memory filed a father whose cigar smoke entered a bedridden Charles like God's breath into a somewhat reluctant Adam ("Daddy blew blue smoke into my ear in a way that opened up inside rooms"). The smoky breath comes from a father much concerned to comfort a sick four-year-old Charles. Alpha, ending the bedtime story, "reaches out and drops darkness down and the door shines around her in beams that travel through the windows of my days." Again, here is that pervasive imagery of rooms. The presences of loving others enter the room that Charles finds himself to be. Alpha stands in a doorway, or works at an ironing board, or is heard speaking from the other room, or is suspected of performing behind closed doors with her husband the mystery which brought Charles himself to life. When the narrator pulls out from these past interiors, it is only to land in another framed world where intersubjectivity is again a condition of walls: "Now when I pace this house and turn at angles that seem to parallel other angles, I know that I'm describing angles inside the broader ones that have been placed out far beyond me, long before, by my father."

What is this life on earth, Woiwode asks, that places a single life within the context of other single lives—a family—and assaults the whole from without and within, striking pain from the very intimacy which unifies those lives? Alpha's sons are too much on her mind, Woiwode suggests, and drive her silly with constant demands on her vigilance. Charles, tending to life-threatening falls and other injuries, pushes Alpha into a mode of irritated estrangement—the responsible dealer of punishment. Charles's birthday present to her, crafted with a dash of cheap perfume, elicits as much rebuke as gratitude. Intimacy for Alpha is daily invasion. When Charles experiments with matches, inhaling the smoke from a boxful lit consecutively in a dizzying indulgence prefiguring his later use of alcohol, Alpha burns his fingers with more matches. A cynical writer would exploit this scene for proof of adult monstrousness. Woiwode's presentation, instead, communicates purest affection for that much-loved mother who is just out of reach, subject to the winds of her own gropings for order. Woiwode's depiction of Alpha, a woman suited by temperament and intelligence for a better life but destined to forlorn anxiousness and all the shocks the flesh inherits (Charles remembers the moment her hand is drawn into the washing machine's wringers), is characterized by devout sympathy.

The trouble Charles causes himself, as well as his worrying mother, comes from his desire to know things but also from the minefield life seems to be for a growing child. Brother Jerome he comes to know through physical opposition: Jerome hits him and he hits back. They cooperate as well as brothers ever will in the use of the scooter or bicycle the father brings them. Such gifts can turn and bite Charles as well, getting broken or lost, or—as with a pet turtle—dying. All closeness, all sharing, all peace are constantly subject to hazard. Woiwode's arrangement of the text, a series of juxtapositions from all periods in Charles's life, makes this condition one that the reader must also feel. A description of young Charles playing with Lincoln Logs on the kitchen's new linoleum is followed without transition by one of the grown Charles groping in a medicine chest for the razor blade he uses on his wrists. This succession seems not a cheap trick of narration, a grisly memento mori popping suddenly from the innocent music of a jack-in-the-box, but a depiction of the whole condition of the present narrator's mind—where is *he*, exactly? What he chanced to live through still holds him at its mercy in all of its urgent replays.

"History is death," Martin tells the teenage Charles, in his despair of keeping on as a single father. In the next segment of text, Charles is in his forties with his own son, a boy in whose lineaments Jerome's are recycled. From other segments the reader pieces together the events that separate these patches of the story—events that are mostly painful and might provide an excuse for Charles if he said things to his boy which his father had spoken to him. Instead, he tells the boy how precious he is, how much his father loves being with him, watching him. Charles is now a protector, a God-fearing protector. The reader will wonder: How did the suicidal maniac become this new creature? By implication from the history that Woiwode supplies, the change resulted from long, unbearable, yet borne suffering, so that betrayals of all kinds and their endurance become the accomplishment of a lifetime. Furthermore, the interdependency of selves, living and dead, is shown to be a rich pasture in which to feed. One's place in this interdependence is a lifetime's revelation, and a comforting antidote to the isolation that typified Charles's sensibility in his twenties, during the 1960's, when he believed that "no single system or . . . God . . . can contain anybody's personal truth." Twenty years later, Charles turns that belief on its head and affirms that the only proof for God existing "is God's existence in you for eternity."

This proclamation is implicit throughout the novel. In his worst agonies of isolation, Charles is still filtering the beings of those he knows, especially his brother Jerome. The walls which Woiwode uses to embody the play of subjectivity are eminently permeable—are, he contests, made that way by a Creator. Charles, waiting for the promised visit of Jerome to his New York room, a visit he craves almost physically, feels the presence of his brother even before he arrives: "There's nothing about him I can contain, as he leaps and crosses and enters the places he already populates with an authority only he can claim." In order to live, to know himself as living, Charles has depended upon Jerome, into whose gaze he has looked for confirmation. When younger they fought furiously, using fists or whatever object came to hand for throwing. Yet this too was a kind of embrace, an infuriated attempt to control and contain the person who most was able to slice across the grain of Charles's ego. Moreover, Jerome is the *older* brother, with all the assumptions of superior ethical judgment that position brings. In the poem that ends the novel, Charles pleads with Jerome to share again all those memories of playing together in their North Dakota boyhood, "remember these small beginnings," for if the memories are not mutual "I might have invented our love."

Born Brothers stands as a powerful affirmation of life. Woiwode's profound detailing of a life's moments will charge the willing reader's brain until his own life's commonplaces stand in such relief that it may well seem he reads his own life story. The author's gift of words rises up against a lifetime's chaos, pain, and death and claims the moments of joy. When Charles's leg is shattered in a car wreck during his high school years, while his father lies in a hospital nearly dead after a too long postponed appendectomy, a surgeon threads the fragments of the boy's shattered femur on a steel rod. That rod stands as well as anything for the power of Woiwode's inward and backward gaze to affirm a life which Charles had often supposed, after his mother's death, to be not worth living.

With its original, nonchronological depiction of a living mind caught in the grip of memory, *Born Brothers* should be received as a classic realization for anyone who grew up in the decades immediately following World War II. The American experience of place—the Midwest in this instance—of persons, of the automobile age, of a time when high school still encouraged intellectual development, of families which did not dissolve under the excuse that one of the spouses needed space or "to find himself"—all of this is contained in the novel. The reader wakes up from the book to find that that world is now gone: What could Charles and Jerome possibly do, a contemporary adolescent might wonder, without video games, and what is this washing-machine attachment that eats hands?

Bruce Wiebe

Sources for Further Study

Booklist. LXXXIV, May 15, 1988, p. 1554.

Chicago Tribune. July 24, 1988, XIV, p. 1.

Kirkus Reviews. LVI, June 1, 1988, p. 789.

Library Journal. CXIII, August, 1988, p. 177.

Los Angeles Times Book Review. August 7, 1988, p. 6.

The New Republic. CXCIX, September 12, 1988, p. 47.

The New York Times Book Review. XCIII, August 14, 1988, p. 13.

Publishers Weekly. CCXXXIII, June 10, 1988, p. 68.

BORROWED TIME
An AIDS Memoir

Author: Paul Monette (1945-   )
Publisher: Harcourt Brace Jovanovich (New York). 342 pp. $18.95
Type of work: Memoir and cultural criticism
Time: 1981-1986
Locale: Los Angeles

This memoir follows the lovers Paul Monette and Roger Horwitz as they, their friends, their families, and the doctors and nurses whom they befriend try to battle the AIDS virus with love and hope

Principal personages:
PAUL MONETTE, the narrator, a writer
ROGER HORWITZ, his lover, a lawyer
SAM, their psychiatrist
CESAR, their friend, who contracts AIDS
DENNIS COPE, a doctor who specializes in treating patients with Acquired Immune Deficiency Syndrome (AIDS)

Paul Monette's *Borrowed Time: An AIDS Memoir* is one of the first books of its kind about the Acquired Immune Deficiency Syndrome (AIDS) virus: a personal narrative that puts the disease in the context of everyday life. Such an account, while fully acknowledging the suffering and anger and loss of AIDS victims and their loved ones, helps to demystify the disease. Indeed, because of the dearth of information about AIDS and the urgent need for a forum to disseminate that information, *Borrowed Time* contains a relatively full discussion of statistics, drug information, symptomatology, doctors, and clinics. In this sense, as a book crammed with vital information about AIDS, *Borrowed Time* belongs in a category with several other groundbreaking AIDS-related texts, such as Randy Shilts's *And the Band Played On: Politics, People, and the AIDS Epidemic* (1987), Larry Kramer's *The Normal Heart* (1985), William M. Hoffman's *As Is* (1985), Emmanuel Dreuilhe's *Mortal Embrace: Living with AIDS* (1988), and George Whitmore's *Someone Was Here* (1988). *Borrowed Time* must be understood within the context of art from what Dreuilhe would call the front line.

Borrowed Time, like many early AIDS-related texts, has its moments of stridency and bitterness. It contains shocking evidence of the flagrant homophobia that has surrounded every aspect of responses to the disease—from the terrifying lack of government funding of research for the disease and care for the ill to the internalization of hatred of homosexuals by gay men themselves. As well, it records Monette and Roger Horwitz's day-by-day battle with the virus, through pneumonia, near blindness, blindness, diarrhea, fevers, sweats, weakness, and moments of mental disorientation. It describes the battle for new drugs such as suramin and azidothymidine (AZT), a battle which involves drug smuggling from Mexico as well as ingenuity, connections, sheer willpower, and massive amounts of money.

Untested, unapproved, and unfinished as they are, some drugs do more damage than good. Others, however, buy for Roger precious borrowed time.

It may very well be the case that thousands of AIDS victims have needlessly died because of the red tape, competition, homophobia, and politics that have plagued the disease's victims nearly as badly as the virus has itself. "It made us crazy," Monette writes, "to think the FDA or the NIH hadn't made funds available so that thousands could be on the drug"; he adds that the "deterministic smugness, whereby we were only getting what we deserved, was so widespread in the upper chambers of the government that the AIDS issue probably never darkened the threshold of the Oval Office."

For all of its requisite bitterness and anger, however, the book is not about the unfairness of the way the Oval Office or the drug industry has responded to AIDS. Instead, *Borrowed Time* deals on a more personal level with the unfairness that AIDS should be able to destroy a love, a love like Monette and Horwitz's.

From the front line of persons with AIDS, *Borrowed Time* is Monette's narrative from the time just before Horwitz, his lover, was diagnosed with AIDS to the time just after Roger died. The Monette shown within the pages of the book is a neurotic, manic, melodramatic hypochondriac as well as a charming and successful novelist, poet, and screenwriter (best known for *Taking Care of Mrs. Carroll*, 1978). Monette says, for example, of a parade during Gay Pride Week, "I worried about the germs and wouldn't let us buy any streetside food." He celebrates the fact that in the hospital "the tenth floor is terrific if you want a lot of food. You can *à la carte* the high-caloric stuff till it fills the tray, and they'll whip up a milk shake on five minutes' notice." The threat of germs and the danger of immense weight loss to AIDS patients make Monette's overzealous concerns understandable. At the same time, the Monette who recounts his frenzied attempts to help Horwitz is smart, witty, and self-conscious. When friends toast his enormous courage, he admits, "It's not that I'm so wonderful. These very friends have seen the wall-paper curl from my overwrought opinions. I am nice to old ladies and dogs, but otherwise I might say anything at all, often about as subtle as a pipe bomb." He goes on to ponder the motives these same friends have for celebrating him, as a way of denying the immense pain of the situation. Monette is well aware that his care for Horwitz is tainted by the displacement of his own fears about AIDS—"I was turning denial [that I had AIDS] into a state of continuous tantrum"—and of his own guilt about being healthy—"at some level I felt relief that I wasn't the one with AIDS."

Horwitz, the man whose fight with AIDS is scrupulously documented through the pages of the book, is less self-consciously portrayed. A Jew from Chicago who had worked his way up in the world, accumulating a doctorate in comparative literature as well as a law degree from Harvard University, Horwitz had made it as an independent lawyer, finally able to work on the cases that mattered to him. The integrity of his commitment to his work is impressive; every return from the hospital is marked by his renewed attempts to work, even after he is beset with blindness. Losing his ability to work, for Horwitz, was "the beginning of the end";

Monette recounts the painful moment when Horwitz's office must finally be closed down and he asks, "fighting back tears, 'But what about all my files?' " Still, heroic as Monette would like to make him out to be, Horwitz has his problems as well. Both see Sam, a psychiatrist, who helps "sort out the feelings behind my [Monette's] rage at minor things and Roger's corresponding sullenness and withdrawal." Recounting how the lovers began reading Plato, near the end of Horwitz's life, in order to learn "how a man of honor faces death without any lies," Monette compares Horwitz to Socrates. In the next sentence, however, Monette sheepishly admits that his lover "would have groaned with distress to hear such an outrageous exaggeration. . . . Roger would always murmur, 'Divide by three.' "

Before AIDS, these two men had each other, and they had everything else. Monette was then at work on the screenplay of *The Manicurist*, the film that was to launch Whoopi Goldberg into stardom, and Horwitz was advancing his practice nicely. The two shared a beautiful Los Angeles house with a pool, drove a Datsun and a black Jaguar, and had friends and family who loved them. They were nearly monogamous, and they had a dog named Puck.

The AIDS scare affected Monette and Horwitz very little at first. Los Angeles, they assured themselves, was different from the fast tracks of New York and San Francisco, where the disease first did its ravaging. Like many gay men, they were able to convince themselves that AIDS would not come home to them. In September, 1983, however, Cesar, their close friend, was diagnosed with AIDS. By March, 1985, Horwitz was also diagnosed. After a great battle with the virus—a battle of will, experimental drugs, hope, and love—Horwitz died, on October 22, 1986.

Borrowed Time, however, is not simply an account of what it is like to struggle with AIDS; it is also a poignant love story. To describe the book in such terms is not to suggest that *Borrowed Time* is corny, sentimental, or bathetic. On the contrary, *Borrowed Time* manages to talk about love (something perhaps even more difficult to talk about than AIDS, in its way) without falling into the traps of conventional rhetoric and bad writing. Monette recounts, for example, how, after Horwitz has lost nearly all of his vision, the two buy "a pair of wraparound shades to cut the glare. 'Do I look like *Miami Vice*?' Roger asked me, deadpan. . . . [The glasses] advanced his vision, and equally our morale." It is always "our" morale in this book, just as it is "we" who "had to learn to walk blind." When Horwitz asks, "What happened to our happy life?" Monette answers, "It's here, Rog, it's right here. Because *we* are."

The story of Monette and Horwitz is enormously moving and convincing. If one reads it as a quite straightforward love story, the questions whether homosexuality is right or wrong and whether AIDS is a just punishment from God are thrown to the wayside. With these encumbrances removed, the tragedy that emerges is of a great love destroyed.

An argument could be made, perhaps, about the dangers of presenting such a Hollywood peaches-and-cream version of the homosexual couple faced with AIDS. Monette himself is aware of the distortions of his and Roger's story, the distortions of "the American AIDS of the first half-decade, before it began to burgeon in the black and brown communities." He bemoans that it is "very difficult to accept that men of our tribe succeeded in obtaining these elixirs [the newest in AIDS drugs], however worthless, while the rest on the moon were clamoring." Roger gets the best and the newest of everything—medical specialists, medicine, technology, service—and these privileges are won by money, connections, charm, and sheer will. Still, the blessings are not unmixed. The suramin nearly kills Roger, because it is too poisonous a drug for the body to take, while the AZT succeeds in winning for him some borrowed time. It is the ugliness of AIDS that *Borrowed Time* only touches on. It tells only in passing of the men diagnosed with AIDS whose lovers leave them. It tells little of the men and women who are too poor to afford the extremely high cost of medicines or care, too poor to afford any borrowed time. It tells only a little of the families who cannot face their sons' homosexuality, the families who take the sick men away from their lovers and nurse them to death with Fundamentalist lectures and accusations.

Borrowed Time does not seek to make people feel guilty about AIDS or about homophobia; it does not lay blame, it only records remorse. It is a book that is charming in its surprising innocence. The love story at the heart of this book gives it a universal appeal. Perhaps its greatest achievement will be its ability to educate the ignorant or prejudiced reader about homosexuality, AIDS, homophobia, and love, without alienating that same reader. This account of Monette and Horwitz's love promises to provide the average American, even the average homophobic and ignorant American, with a well-needed reason to rethink his or her prejudices and open his or her horizons. AIDS threatens a greater and greater number of Americans, but so does the sickness of homophobia. *Borrowed Time* may well provide a medicine for the latter.

Audrey A. Fisch

Sources for Further Study

Booklist. LXXXIV, June 1, 1988, p. 1634.

Kirkus Reviews. LVI, April 15, 1988, p. 599.

Library Journal. CXIII, August, 1988, p. 154.

Los Angeles Times Book Review. June 5, 1988, p. 4.

The New York Times Book Review. XCIII, September 11, 1988, p. 3.

Newsweek. CXI, March 21, 1988, p. 73.

Publishers Weekly. CCXXXIII, April 29, 1988, p. 60.

San Francisco Chronicle. July 17, 1988, p. REV7.

Time. CXXXII, July 18, 1988, p. 68.

The Washington Post Book World. XVIII, June 12, 1988, p. 3.

BREATHING LESSONS

Author: Anne Tyler (1941-)
Publisher: Alfred A. Knopf (New York). 327 pp. $18.95
Type of work: Novel
Time: The mid-1980's
Locale: Deer Lick and Cartwheel, Pennsylvania, and Baltimore, Maryland

A humorous story of a twenty-eight-year marriage told via flashbacks during a trip to and from a funeral

Principal chararacters:
MAGGIE MORAN, the novel's zany middle-aged heroine
IRA MORAN, her taciturn husband
SERENA PALERMO GILL, Maggie's best friend of forty-two years
JESSE MORAN, Maggie and Ira's son, a rock singer
FIONA MORAN, Jesse's former wife
LEROY MORAN, Fiona and Jesse's daughter, Maggie and Ira's only grandchild

In her tenth novel, *The Accidental Tourist* (1985), Anne Tyler depicted the dissolution of a twenty-year marriage following the violent death of a couple's son. In *Breathing Lessons*, her eleventh book, she presents the reverse, the duration of a marriage for twenty-eight years despite the countless grievances and compromises that come with any enduring relationship. Winner of the Pulitzer Prize for fiction, *Breathing Lessons* is the story of Maggie and Ira Moran's long-standing love and tolerance for each other. Told primarily through flashbacks as the two journey to the funeral of Max Gill, the husband of Maggie's girlhood friend Serena, the novel covers nearly thirty years in one September day and contrasts the Morans' courtship and marriage with the relationship of their son, Jesse, and his now former wife, Fiona. Because Fiona and her daughter, Leroy, the Morans' only grandchild, live near the town of Deer Lick, Pennsylvania, where the funeral occurs, Maggie, the novel's heroine, uses this proximity to convince her husband to visit Fiona and Leroy. Indeed, from its beginning, *Breathing Lessons* concerns not only Ira and Maggie's bickering and adjustments to change but also Maggie's sole struggle to reconcile Jesse and Fiona and bring Fiona and Leroy "home at last."

Set in Deer Lick and Cartwheel, Pennsylvania, where Fiona lives, and in Baltimore, the Morans', home, *Breathing Lessons* has three principal divisions, each told from a limited third-person point of view. The first and third sections focus on Maggie's consciousness, while the middle section, which constitutes something of an interlude, centers on Ira's thoughts. The first section consists of the journey from Baltimore to Deer Lick; the funeral itself, with vividly described and hilariously funny repeat performances of love songs sung at Serena and Max's wedding nearly thirty years earlier; and the gathering of old friends, all alumni of the same high school, at Serena's house following the memorial service. Somewhat reminiscent of the film *The Big Chill* (1983), this first section is witty and satiric in its depiction of 1950's music and mores. More significant, it introduces the motif of life and growth as a journey through time and demonstrates Tyler's skillful use of flashbacks to provide exposition. Here the device of a home movie of Serena's wedding serves as a trigger for Maggie's memories of her initial involvement with Ira. The second part of the novel depicts a side trip during which Maggie and Ira become temporarily involved with an elderly black man, Daniel Otis, who has left his wife of fifty-plus years and spends his days traveling the Pennsylvania country roads. Since it is centered on Ira's thoughts, this section provides his responses to his wife's and children's behavior, including his son's marriage, as well as Ira's only family history and motivation. As in the first section, Tyler reveals a masterful handling of exposition and conflicts through internal thought sequences and flashbacks. This section also introduces a minor story of considerable human interest, that of Otis, offering thereby a parallel commentary on the squabbles and adjustments that characterize enduring marriages. The novel's third section, which introduces the characters of Fiona and Leroy and Fiona's mother, Mrs. Stuckey, focuses again on Maggie's thoughts, but this time the center of attention is her memories of Fiona and Jesse's relationship. Indeed, a lengthy flashback traces the entire history of that relationship from the earliest dates through marriage and eventual divorce. The visit to Cartwheel and the return to Baltimore with Fiona and Leroy complete this section. Tyler depicts the cyclical nature of experience, a central theme of the novel, when Fiona and Leroy explosively depart yet a second time from the Morans' house.

As this plot summary and structural analysis suggest, there are four marital relationships presented in *Breathing Lessons*, two in much greater detail than the others: the long-standing marriages of the Otises, the Gills, and the Morans, and one of short duration, Fiona and Jesse's. From *Searching for Caleb* (1975) to the present work, Tyler's novels have skillfully balanced a lighthearted, humorous view of human nature with a depth of insight into the darker side of marital experience. With a sharp eye, she captures the amicable surface of Max and Serena Gill's marriage, their joking manner of calling each other by their last names, Gill and Palermo, while also recording Serena's pain at Max's lack of financial dependability and, ultimately, his passive suffering and death from cancer. Maggie and Ira's marriage, while superficially a sound balance of two contrasting personalities who can bicker and then reconcile, has its dark side: a "helpless, angry, confined feeling" Maggie experiences "from time to time." Ira too must accept the "unvaryingness" of his marriage and life. Although he objects to Jesse's reference to marriage as the "same old song and dance," the phrase haunts Ira for it reveals a bitter truth. Marriage does involve the

> same old arguments, same recriminations. The same jokes and affectionate passwords, yes, and abiding loyalty and gestures of support and consolations no one else knew how to offer; but also the same old resentments dragged up year after year. . . .

For Ira, who has abandoned his dreams of college and medical school, first to support his father and sisters, then his children, this thought carries particularly heavy weight and a recognition of failure. Moreover, although Tyler's major themes in *Breathing Lessons* include the tolerance and compromise—and love—which familial life demands, she also depicts the staleness and repetitiveness of human relationships. As Maggie recognizes, "There was no such thing on this earth as real change. You change husbands, but not the situation. You could change *who*, but not *what*."

There is wisdom and truth in this view of human relationships, a wisdom Tyler has consistently developed through each of her skillfully written novels. It is the wisdom suggested by the title of this eleventh novel, *Breathing Lessons*. The allusion is not only to Maggie's instructions to Fiona about enduring childbirth but also to the lessons one needs in how to live. As Maggie tells Fiona,

> . . . you're given all these lessons for the unimportant things—piano-playing, typing. You're given years and years of lessons in how to balance equations, which Lord knows you will never have to do in normal life. But how about parenthood? Or marriage, either, come to think of it. Before you can drive a car you need a state-approved course of instruction, but driving a car is nothing, nothing, compared to living day in and day out with a husband and raising up a new human being.

The joyful side of Tyler's fiction is her fondness for zany, unpredictable characters, her keen eye for idiosyncratic human behavior, which she observes with amused detachment, and her finely tuned ear for human speech. *Breathing Lessons* offers many examples, beginning with the zesty, slightly trashy names of her characters: Serena, Fiona, Duluth (Daniel Otis' wife). Serena and her unwed cocktail-waitress mother are both sources of amusement and vivid detail. Serena's mother talks nonstop the morning of her daughter's wedding, despite the cigarettes that dangle consistently from her mouth. Nervous about being the one to escort her daughter down the church aisle, she rambles on in a hilarious manner, running sentences together and confusing words; "scrutinizing," for example, becomes "scrupulizing." Serena herself is equally colorful. She wears a red chiffon dress with a rhinestone sunburst to her husband's funeral and insists on a rerun of her wedding, complete with Maggie's struggling to sing "Love Is a Many-Splendored Thing," this time without Ira's accompaniment. Other former classmates also must struggle to intone "My Prayer," "True Love," "I Want You, I Need You, I Love You," and other 1950's songs in froggy voices half a century old. In many places Tyler exaggerates not only for humorous effect but also to suggest a dowdy, lower-class appearance to her characters. Mrs. Stuckey, for example, wears "a fuchsia corduroy pantsuit and a corsage as big as her head" to her daughter Fiona's wedding. She too is talkative, though her conversation centers on the deceased Mr. Stuckey and her theory of ghosts. Other details serve to add humor to the novel. A shampoo coupon used at the funeral to scribble love lyrics for one of the songs Serena insists on later proves an embarrassment for Maggie when she tries to cash in the coupon at a grocery store, only to have the young male cashier read the scribbling and hand back the coupon with a polite "thank you."

Ira and Maggie are the focus of Tyler's amused observations. Despite his taciturn nature, Ira displays a delightful trait of always whistling. Over twenty-eight years of marriage, Maggie has become adept at identifying the songs he whistles. Remembering the lyrics, she can respond to Ira's thoughts, often to his complete surprise. Ira's idiosyncrasies also entail a complicated form of solitaire, which he plays almost anytime and anywhere, including in church immediately before Max Gill's funeral. Although he feels tired and lonely and something of a failure with his children, Ira is not immune to Maggie's whimsy. At one point he consents to quick lovemaking in Serena's bedroom, a scene that ends disastrously when the hostess discovers the two lovers.

Maggie herself belongs to a long line of lively, unpredictable Tyler heroines—most expert caretakers—beginning with Granny Hawkes in *If Morning Ever Comes* (1964), Tyler's first novel. Though she is not the eccentric dresser that either Serena or Granny Hawkes is, Maggie has her quirks. She is forever on a diet to lose the same ten pounds and is addicted to salty junk food. Moreover, her ability to involve herself almost instantly with strangers, her cheerful obstinacy that masquerades as enthusiasm, and her willingness to forgive herself and others for ineptness and wrongs make her one of the most likable of Tyler heroines. Her romance with Ira dates from the time she mistakenly believed him dead and sent his father a sympathy note that included an exaggerated statement of Ira's importance to her. Able to live with that error, Maggie becomes dauntless. She can diverge from one path to the next without much thought and can confront almost anyone: the unwed, frightened, pregnant Fiona, her argumentative sister, the dignified elderly Maggie tends at the Silver Threads Nursing home, and the picketers outside an abortion clinic. Indeed, unlike her husband, Maggie invades the private world of others, observing gestures they are unaware of or have forgotten. Her greatest weakness, in fact, is, as Ira pinpoints, that "she believes it's all right to alter people's lives. She thinks the people she loves are better than they really are, and so then she starts changing things around to suit her view of them." In fact, in both her acute observations and the more serious flaw Ira describes, Maggie most resembles that idiosyncratic person, the fiction writer and artist who engineers lives to suit his story.

Breathing Lessons is a novel rich in vivid, realistic details of action and character. Through the years Tyler's novels have become increasingly witty, amusing, and opulent in detail, while at the same time painting a portrait of the losses and lessons life carries. Indeed, in many ways, this eleventh novel is a work filled with quarrels, a book about family feuding over insignificant things and the touchiness that sometimes strikes certain family members. Yet it is also a novel about that most valuable of "breathing lessons": enjoyment. As Otis says, perhaps "the whole point of things," of life itself, is to "spill it! Spill it all . . . ! No way *not* to spill it. [Then] . . . just look at the times we had." *Breathing Lessons* reminds the reader to do just that.

Stella Nesanovich

Sources for Further Study

Booklist. LXXXIV, July, 1988, p. 1756.
Kirkus Reviews. LVI, July 1, 1988, p. 931.
Library Journal. CXIII, September 1, 1988, p. 184.
Los Angeles Times Book Review. September 11, 1988, p. 3.
Ms. XVII, September, 1988, p. 86.
The Nation. CCXLVII, November 7, 1988, p. 464.
The New York Times. CXXXVIII, September 3, 1988, p. 13.
The New York Times Book Review. XCIII, September 11, 1988, p. 1.
The New Yorker. LXIV, November 28, 1988, p. 121.
Newsweek. CXII, September 26, 1988, p. 73.
Publishers Weekly. CCXXXIV, July 1, 1988, p. 67.
Time. CXXXII, September 5, 1988, p. 75.

A BRIEF HISTORY OF TIME
From the Big Bang to Black Holes

Author: Stephen W. Hawking (1942-   )
Introduction by Carl Sagan
Publisher: Bantam Books (New York). Illustrated. 198 pp. $18.95
Type of work: Science

One of the leading figures in modern theoretical physics presents his view of the struggle to develop a unified theory of the universe and what success in this endeavor would mean to the human race

Two of twentieth century physics' greatest achievements are the general theory of relativity and the theory of quantum mechanics. The former, conceived by Albert Einstein, explains the force of gravity in terms of the curvature of four-dimensional space-time and deals with the large-scale structure of the universe. The latter is based on the concept of energy as bundles or quanta and Werner Heisenberg's uncertainty principle and is concerned with phenomena on the subatomic level. Both theories have been enormously successful in explaining phenomena at their respective scales. Physicists have also developed grand unified theories which have unified three of the four forces in the universe: the electromagnetic, which holds atoms together; the strong, which binds the components of the nucleus of the atom; and the weak, which is involved in radioactive decay. They have failed, however, to reconcile general relativity with quantum mechanics or to unify the force of gravity with the other three fundamental forces. There is no place in general relativity for the uncertainty principle. Physicists are seeking a new theory which will successfully integrate general relativity and quantum mechanics into a quantum theory of gravitation.

The search for that unified theory of relativity and quantum mechanics is the primary theme of *A Brief History of Time: From the Big Bang to Black Holes*. This is a challenging, qualitative examination of historical and contemporary views on the nature of time and the universe (as opposed to a literal history of time) by one of the major figures in theoretical physics in the 1970's and 1980's. Stephen W. Hawking, Lucasian Professor of Mathematics at Cambridge University, the chair once held by Sir Isaac Newton, is a victim of amyotrophic lateral sclerosis (Lou Gehrig's disease); he has been slowly losing control over his physical faculties, but his mental abilities have remained unimpaired. In this, his first effort at writing for a nontechnical audience, Hawking provides brief excursions into a number of areas of modern physics, but his real concern is cosmology. Using but one equation, he traces the changing concepts of the size, structure, history, and nature of the universe from the work of ancient Greeks, through that of Galileo, Newton, and Einstein, to his own work. He presents clear but sophisticated and demanding descriptions of such phenomena as black holes and the arrow of time.

Hawking has organized the book into thematic chapters, with the discussion within each chapter arranged chronologically. He begins with a review of the many cosmologies that have appeared in Western civilization. The second chapter examines the changing views of space and time, culminating in Einstein's theory of general relativity. Then comes a discussion of the concept of an expanding universe. The next two chapters, on the uncertainty principle and the fundamental particles and forces, complete the background discussion. Two chapters on black holes are followed by one presenting Hawking's views on the origin and future of the universe. The penultimate chapter discusses arrows of time, devices which distinguish the past from the future, providing a direction for the passage of time. In the final chapter, Hawking considers what a unified theory might look like. Included in the book are biographical sketches of Einstein, Galileo, and Newton, as well as a glossary of scientific terms.

There are three decisions that every author of a nontechnical work on cosmology or other aspects of modern physics must make. The first is one of presentation. The language of theoretical physics is mathematics. How will the popularizer replace the equations which are the basis of the science? The alternatives include extensive use of analogies, illustrations, or colorful and poetic language. Second, the author must decide the extent to which he or she will simplify complex concepts in order to make them understandable to a general readership. In particular, does the author risk oversimplification for the sake of readability? The question of presentation is closely linked to that of simplification. The indicators most useful in evaluating a simplification of complex scientific theories and experiments are the analogies used by the author to illuminate esoteric facts and theories, especially facts and theories which either are not easily grasped intuitively or contradict everyday experience, and the type of illustrations used. How frequent or outrageous are the analogies? Are inexact analogies used? Are the illustrations useful and meaningful or simply cute? Third, the author must decide how intrusive he or she will be. The book can either offer a consensus view of the state of science or an idiosyncratic one. It can be written to appear neutral or in obvious support of an author's personal scientific agenda.

Hawking decided not to make this a facile book to read. Although he discarded his usual mathematical manipulations, he has made few other concessions to his readers. The concepts about which he is writing are not easy to understand, but he refuses to risk oversimplification. His analogies are relatively infrequent. He does not overindulge, for example, in sports analogies, a common problem among oversimplifiers. The illustrations serve the book well. There are none of the cartoons commonly found in nontechnical books. Instead, he relies on numerous graphs or graphic drawings to make his points.

This is also a very personal and particular explanation of cosmology. Integrated into Hawking's exposition of scientific theories and experiments are personal asides, autobiographical details, and commentaries. *A Brief History of Time* serves as Hawking's intellectual memoir. Historians of science and some of his colleagues will object to the way in which he distributes credit for scientific discoveries. They will also find the account highly subjective. The history of physics, as opposed to the history of the universe, presented in these pages reflects Hawking's personal reading of the significance of particular scientific theories and experiments. It does not always match up with the scholarly consensus. His habit of carefully identifying those scientists who disagreed with his views and were later obliged to change their own opinions comes across as egotistical intellectual strutting. This book should not be approached as an objective record of the efforts of scientists to understand nature. It is most valuable if it is viewed as one scientist's account of his struggle. Hawking supplies tremendous insight into his own thought processes and his interpretations of the work of others but relatively little into those of his fellow physicists.

It would be a mistake to think of this book simply as a nontechnical discussion of modern cosmology, because Hawking has tried to convey much more than merely the state of cosmology in the 1980's. There is another dimension to it which will strike some readers as the most interesting and others as very disturbing. He goes beyond what many readers might think to be the legitimate boundaries of science, asking questions not frequently found in science books. He is not content to limit himself to understanding what happens, nor is he satisfied with the ability to reduce events to mathematical equations. He wants to know why events occur in the way they do. Interwoven in his popular scientific exposition is a philosophical tract raising fundamental metaphysical and theological questions. Hawking asks, without providing any final answers, Why does the universe exist? Is there a creator of the universe? If so, who created the creator? Is there a master plan for the universe, and if so, what is it? What he is doing is examining the place and nature of God in the universe. He sees science as a search for understanding God's will.

In raising such, in some minds, unscientific questions, Hawking reveals his discomfort with the boundaries that divide contemporary realms of knowledge. Distinctions between the scientist and the philosopher—their differing modes of inquiry and their differing intellectual objectives—bother him. He is a throwback to an earlier age, the eighteenth and nineteenth centuries, when physicists were known as "natural philosophers," an astronomer could see evidence for the existence of God in the intricacies of the equations which describe the orbit of a planet and publicly proclaim it without risking his professional reputation, and the boundaries between philosophy and science were artificial and easily crossed, as evidenced by the contributions of such outstanding American philosophers as Charles Sanders Peirce and William James to both science and philosophy. Back then, science, philosophy, and theology were places on a continuum of human knowledge about the universe, not isolated and self-contained fiefdoms.

A Brief History of Time is not especially significant as a nontechnical exposition of science. The presentation will probably prove too terse and difficult for its intended audience. As an illumination of Hawking's mind, however, it is invaluable. Its greatest reward will be for those readers concerned with the conflict between science and religion, the gulf between the humanists and the scientists, and the segmentation of human knowledge. Hawking has issued a plea for the restoration of the unity of knowledge in the guise of a description of the search for a unified field theory. It is a plea worthy of thoughtful consideration.

Marc Rothenberg

Sources for Further Study

The Christian Century. CV, May 18, 1988, p. 513.
The Christian Science Monitor. April 22, 1988, p. 19.
The Economist. CCCVII, June 25, 1988, p. 91.
Kirkus Reviews. LVI, February 15, 1988, p. 258.
Library Journal. CXIII, April 15, 1988, p. 87.
Los Angeles Times. April 8, 1988, V, p. 14.
Nature. CCCXXII, April 21, 1988, p. 742.
The New York Review of Books. XXXV, June 16, 1988, p. 17.
The New York Times Book Review. XCIII, April 3, 1988, p. 10.
The New Yorker. LXIV, June 6, 1988, p. 117.
Publishers Weekly. CCXXXIII, February 19, 1988, p. 66.

A BRIGHT SHINING LIE
John Paul Vann and America in Vietnam

Author: Neil Sheehan (1936-   )
Publisher: Random House (New York). Illustrated. 861 pp. $24.95
Type of work: Biography
Time: 1962-1972
Locale: South Vietnam and Washington, D.C.

A critique of the American war effort in Vietnam as exemplified in the career of John Paul Vann

Principal personages:
JOHN PAUL VANN, a military adviser and pacification director during the Vietnam War
NGO DINH DIEM, President of South Vietnam, 1955-1963
DANIEL ELLSBERG, a war planner and an antiwar critic
DAVID HALBERSTAM, a correspondent for *The New York Times* in Vietnam
ROBERT KOMER, the head of the CORDS pacification program
EDWARD LANSDALE, an operative for the Central Intelligence Agency
PAUL HARKINS, the head of Military Assistance Command Vietnam during the Kennedy Administration

"He personified the strongest endeavor and, as it was to prove, the tragic limits, of his country's experience in Asia." The parallels between Joseph Stilwell (of whom Barbara Tuchman wrote these words) and John Paul Vann are haunting. Both were military men sent to Asia as advisers to help achieve global objectives—in one case, defeating the Japanese in World War II; in the other, stopping the spread of communism. Runty in appearance, yet possessing tremendous stamina and undaunting courage, both believed that the United States could be a worldwide force for positive social change. Their power and influence over events were momentous, yet, in the end, ephemeral. They failed in their respective missions because of the unmalleable bonds of the indigenous societies to which they were sent. There could be no American solution to the revolutionary whirlwind of twentieth century Asia.

Neil Sheehan covered the Vietnam War as a journalist and later obtained the so-called Pentagon Papers for *The New York Times* from former Defense Department official Daniel Ellsberg. In one sense, *A Bright Shining Lie: John Paul Vann and America in Vietnam*, winner of the Pulitzer Prize for general nonfiction and the National Book Award for nonfiction, is a very personal saga of the author's loss of illusions regarding the justness of America's containment policy in Asia. Sixteen years in the making, the book is carefully factual, but its tone is one of muted anger at the needless destruction that resulted from flawed policies. As the title indicates, there was a dark underside to postwar American foreign policy, just as there was an element of duplicity to the character of John Paul Vann.

When Vann first arrived in Vietnam in March of 1962, the war seemed an adventure, a chance for old veterans to get back in action and young officers to prove their mettle: "The frequent presence of danger and the occasional shooting created the tension and zest of war without the unpleasantness of dying." Like most American advisers, Vann knew little about Vietnamese history or culture. If the peasants sympathized with the enemy, Vann attributed it to their political naïveté or to pragmatic necessity. He confidently expected that they could be won over through a combination of paternalism and military aggressiveness.

By the time of Vann's second tour of duty in 1965, the conflict had become a war of attrition. Vann had become a caustic critic of American military strategy but accepted almost as an article of faith the goal of preventing a Communist regime from coming to power in South Vietnam. He "could not abide defeat," writes Sheehan, and remained unshaken in his vision and faith "in an ever-innocent America."

Book 1 opens with Lieutenant Colonel Vann reporting for duty at the Saigon headquarters of MACV, the Military Assistance Command Vietnam. In an effort to shore up the autocratic regime of Ngo Dinh Diem, President John F. Kennedy had ordered a buildup of military advisers that reached 11,300 by Christmas of 1962 and 16,000 a year later. The hope was that they would train, lead, and inspire the army of South Vietnam (ARVN) into becoming an efficient fighting machine. Sent to the Mekong Delta, Vann became adviser to Colonel Huynh Van Cao, commander of the Seventh Division. A Catholic from Diem's home town of Hue, Cao had sided with the French during the first war of liberation and was more interested in remaining in readiness to support the Saigon regime against a possible coup than in searching out and killing the Viet Cong. Cao's troops often alienated the local populace by acts of thievery and brutality. Vann complained, but to no avail.

Vann tried to use flattery to goad Cao into being more aggressive. When he did risk troops in combat, however, Cao got into trouble with Diem. As Sheehan concludes, Ngo Dinh Diem and his family "never learned anything, they never forgot anything, and they fervently believed that whatever they desired was innately correct and virtuous."

In book 2, Sheehan concludes that America's postwar containment policy was a blend of national self-interest, idealistic rhetoric, and subconscious condescension toward Asians. With the United States' reimposition of French colonial rule, an opportunity was lost for creating a united Vietnam that could have been a check against Chinese expansion. That, after all, had been the original rationale for the quixotic experiment in nation-building that followed the fall of Dien Bien Phu and the (supposedly temporary) partition of Vietnam at the Geneva Conference of 1954.

Viewing themselves as liberators rather than counterrevolutionaries, American policymakers hoped that South Vietnam would go the way of the Philippines, where a Communist insurgency had been defeated. Even had the South Vietnamese been inclined to resist amalgamation, however, Diem's oppressive policies made the South, in Sheehan's words, "ripe for revolution." Diem balked at meaningful land reform and instituted a Denunciation of Communists campaign which victimized tens of thousands of innocent people. His Strategic Hamlets program and assaults on the Buddhist majority were the culmination, not the cause, of his downfall.

The Battle of Ap Bac, a turning point of the Vietnam War, is the central focus of book 3. Prior to Ap Bac, the Viet Cong were viewed with contempt by most of Vann's superiors. The conventional wisdom was that they could be annihilated if lured into a fight. At Ap Bac some 350 guerrillas defeated a well-armed unit four times their size, killing eighty ARVN soldiers and three American advisers and downing five helicopters.

This battle put Vietnam on the front pages of newspapers and on the evening television news. In its aftermath, Diem and General Paul Harkins worried more about the loss of face than coming to grips with the ramifications of the debacle. Vann took to leaking stories to the press contingent and became especially close to David Halberstam of *The New York Times*. Outlining his pessimistic conclusions in a written memorandum, Vann vainly sought to educate a succession of touring dignitaries, including Pentagon emissary Victor "Brute" Krulak and White House adviser Maxwell Taylor. When an alarmed Harkins asked his intelligence chief to gather rebuttal evidence, the officer was forced to admit that "the only thing wrong with what he wrote is that all of it is true."

Returning to Washington, D.C., in April of 1963, Vann hoped to brief the Joint Chiefs of Staff on the futility of the counterinsurgency effort, but his enemies caused the cancellation of his formal presentation at the last moment. Meanwhile, the Diem regime was unraveling. In fact, Ambassador Henry Cabot Lodge helped orchestrate the coup that toppled him. In one sense Vann was vindicated, but the succeeding regimes proved even less stable. In the wake of Diem's ouster, the Viet Cong made gains in the Mekong Delta which erased whatever progress Vann had made there.

By the time Lyndon B. Johnson became commander-in-chief, Vann had retired from the army to work for a Denver-based aerospace company. Reporters saw his resignation as a protest, an act of moral herosim. The real reason Vann left, however, was a black mark on his record that made improbable his promotion to the rank of general. Years earlier, while stationed at Fort Leavenworth, Kansas, Vann had seduced a fifteen-year-old family babysitter. Facing court-martial for statutory rape, Vann had managed to beat the charges but could not get them expunged from his file.

That incident is but one aspect of Vann's secret life which Sheehan explores in book 5, "Antecedents to the Man." Born to unwed parents in 1924, the offspring of a narcissistic, alcoholic mother, Vann grew up in Norfolk, Virginia. He was befriended by a Methodist minister who turned out to be a pedophile. The man helped get Vann into Ferrum Training School and Junior College. Four years later he enlisted in the army, hoping to become a pilot, but he missed combat in World War II. He was married in 1945 to a young woman from a respectable family in Rochester, New York. A compulsive womanizer and indifferent parent, he filled his daily routine with petty deceptions. He commanded a Ranger unit in Korea but later fabricated a story about personally fending off a Chinese human-wave attack.

Out of the service in 1964, Vann became despondent. By year's end he was making inquiries into how he might get back to Vietnam. He finally obtained a position with the Agency for International Development as regional director of pacification in the Mekong Delta.

Book 6, "A Second Time Around," highlights Vann's pacification work against the backdrop of the escalating war. At the time of Vann's return in March of 1965, Saigon was engulfed in rumors of yet another coup, and things were so unstable that the American embassy was bombed ten minutes after Vann left. Sent to Hau Nghia Province (Vann called it a Siberian assignment), Vann supervised the building of schools, the raising of hogs, the distribution of relief, and—unofficially—the gathering of intelligence.

Vann welcomed the American troop buildup but believed in a defensive posture except where there were large enemy forces and few civilians. Still the acerbic critic, he put together a position paper entitled "Harnessing the Revolution in South Vietnam" which recommended the virtual takeover of the war effort by Americans.

In October of 1965 Vann was sent to Camp Vung Tau where he trained Vietnamese pacification teams. The teams were used by the Central Intelligence Agency (CIA) to identify and eliminate Viet Cong agents. When Vann feuded with the CIA, he was "promoted" to pacification director of III Corps. In June of 1967 came another promotion to deputy director of pacification. His boss, Robert Komer, was using computer studies to extol the pacification effort. Vann, however, responded with gallows humor to Walt Rostow, who asked in December of 1967 whether the worst would be over in six months: "Oh hell no, Mr. Rostow. I'm a born optimist. I think we can hold out longer than that."

In book 7, "John Vann Stays," Sheehan traces the events leading up to the 1968 Tet Offensive and Vann's subsequent role as a key implementer of Richard M. Nixon's policies of Vietnamization. Even though Tet seemed to prove the validity of Vann's warnings, Vann himself could not accept the handwriting on the wall. He liked being in Vietnam: the danger, the opportunities for sex (he had two Vietnamese wives and many casual liaisons), the status, the invitations to visit the White House on his yearly returns home. It was so intoxicating that, in Sheehan's opinion, he "finally bent the truth about the war as he had bent other and lesser truths in the past."

With the Viet Cong infrastructure having been devastated during Tet, Vann deluded himself into believing that pacification efforts would yield better results, especially if the debacle shocked the Thieu government into instituting long-needed reforms. Where once he had bemoaned excessive civilian casualties, he came to rely on B-52 bombing raids and helped set up the nefarious Phoenix program, which "neutralized" an estimated twenty thousand people. By 1972 he was in command of all United States forces, both civilian and military, operating in the strategically important Central Highlands and Central Coast.

Obtaining the general's stars that had eluded him for so long (though technically a civilian), Vann played a crucial role in blunting the North Vietnamese Army's 1972 offensive. After Binh Dinh and Tan Canh were abandoned without even a fight, the roads were swollen with refugees and fleeing soldiers. The ARVN commander wanted to abandon Kontun, but Vann seized control and at great personal risk coordinated its defense. His feat only delayed the inevitable; after Vann died in a helicopter crash, President Nixon parlayed the victory of Kontun into a bargaining chip at the Paris peace talks.

It was only fitting, Sheehan concludes, that Vann did not live to see the end of the American phase of the war or the subsequent fall of Saigon. John Vann, Sheehan wrote, "was not meant to flee to a ship at sea, and he did not miss his exit. He died believing he had won his war."

In the 1980's it became fashionable in some revisionist circles to suggest that the United States could have won the Vietnam War if only the military had been given free rein. Sheehan shows how impossible was the task of pacifying the countryside or creating a viable non-Communist government in Saigon. In the absence of popular support, all military victories would have rested on quicksand.

A Bright Shining Lie shows not only that Vietnam was an impractical misadventure but also that what the United States did was shameful. In 1964, Vann had predicted that the United States could pour its entire armed forces into Vietnam and still not accomplish anything worthwhile. In his unwillingness to accept the logic of his own findings, Vann epitomized a nation blinded by hubris and incapable of thinking creatively or wisely. Therein lies the central thread uniting this biography of a flawed man and history of a quagmire war.

James B. Lane

Sources for Further Study

The New Republic. CXCIX, October 24, 1988, p. 32.
The New York Times Book Review. XCIII, September 25, 1988, p. 1.
Newsweek. CXII, October 10, 1988, p. 72.
Time. CXXXII, October 17, 1988, p. 80.

BRITISH WRITERS OF THE THIRTIES

Author: Valentine Cunningham
First published: 1987, in Great Britain
Publisher: Oxford University Press (New York). 544 pp. $64.00
Type of work: Literary history
Time: The 1930's
Locale: Great Britain

An analysis of the social and political interests of British writers in the 1930's, as reflected in their writings and lives

The 1930's in Great Britain were a time of strained seriousness and sophomoric frivolity, of Marxism and fascism, of fads and traditionalism. In *British Writers of the Thirties*, Valentine Cunningham looks at the decade's social and political issues as seen in the lives and works of its major and minor poets, novelists, playwrights, essayists, and critics. Cunningham, a fellow and tutor in English literature at Corpus Christi College, University of Oxford, is an expert in political literature, having written *Everywhere Spoken Against: Dissent in the Victorian Novel* (1975) and edited *Spanish Front: Writers on the Civil War* (1986). He is sympathetic toward the goals of the leftist writers of the 1930's but is less than impressed by their political achievements. Sorting through facts and fictions about the period and such figures as W. H. Auden, T. E. Lawrence, and Wyndham Lewis, he uncovers compromises, lies, hypocrisy, back-stabbing, Old-Boyism, and decadence on both sides of the political spectrum.

Cunningham acknowledges that his approach to literary criticism is unfashionable but claims that deconstructionists have only "half an argument" because they ignore the context in which literature is created. By connecting historical events, the private lives of writers, and literary works, he attempts to reveal "whole ranges of sets of meanings rippling outwards into the dense textures of the wider literature and history of the period." Believing that history has an enormous impact upon intellectual activities, Cunningham tries to make connections that are not readily obvious without straining for effect, admitting that there is no single correct way of reading the 1930's. He could be faulted for implying a clear-cut Right-Left division on almost everything—even cricket and soccer—but he does perceive a blurring of issues in several instances.

Although the majority of British writers in the 1930's professed left-of-center political views, conservatives held their own since they included "the period's biggest literary guns": T. S. Eliot, William Butler Yeats, Wyndham Lewis, and Evelyn Waugh, among others. Eliot made *The Criterion* a house journal for many spokesmen for rightist issues, especially the virtues of and dangers posed to British ruralism. Right-wingers saw what Eliot called "the *urbanization of mind*" as a major threat to the country-house, small-village way of life they favored. Conservatives were hostile not only to industrializied cities but also to suburbs, resulting in John Betjeman's famous plea, "Come, friendly bombs, and fall on Slough." Right-ists such as Laura Riding and F. R. Leavis were upset that the 1930's became a period of mass movements. Cunningham says that these conservatives "couldn't bear the idea of their fellow man grouped in the large heeded numbers of the modern democratic world." Such attitudes led to a romance with the fascism of Sir Oswald Mosley and Adolf Hitler. Lewis expressed his admiration for the latter in *Hitler* (1931), and Henry Williamson, in *Goodbye, West Country* (1937), went so far as to claim that the air of Germany was fresher than that of his native land.

Cunningham expects perverse logic and silliness from the Right but is constantly disappointed in the same from the Left. He accuses Stephen Spender of "the wish-fulfilment that continually infected the writing of '30s Leftists: who tended to slip easily from what was, to what they wished were the case, an elision eased by their confused rhetoric of a future always coming into being." Spender, Auden, Christopher Isherwood, and their friends professed sympathy and admiration for the working class but had little real contact with ordinary people. When George Orwell, who did have such contact, objected, in *The Road to Wigan Pier* (1937), to the odor of workers, the literary Left was embarrassed and outraged. Even Orwell remained merely a visitor to the poverty of the working class. Among all the leftists of the 1930's, only Christopher Caudwell (formerly Christopher St. John Sprigg) decided to live and work among the proletarians, in the East End of London. By contrast, Isherwood's contribution to understanding the worker's problems involved eating sweets to try to ruin his good bourgeois teeth.

If the intellectuals of the Left could not deal directly with the proletariat, they could at least try "to capture the mass-audience for good writing and art, to discover their own mass-appealing subject-matter and . . . seek to transform bourgeois art and aesthetics in the process, creating new, non-bourgeois kinds of art for the awakened masses." Unfortunately, according to Cunningham, the Left never determined how to make the working class an effective subject of art. The bourgeois writers did not understand this subject well enough, and Cunningham considers Lewis Grassic Gibbon (James Leslie Mitchell), best known for his trilogy *A Scots Quair* (1932-1934), the only proletarian writer to have created truly lasting work. Cunningham still praises lesser novelists, tied to the conventions of strict realism, for revealing working-class life and putting "working-class regions of Britain, the humble parts of cities, and their ordinary denizens, very firmly on to the twentieth-century novel's map." In general, the fiction of the 1930's did little in presenting the hardships of proletarians that had not already been done much better by Elizabeth Gaskell, Charles Dickens, and D. H. Lawrence.

Many bourgeois writers on the Left became less involved with politics toward the end of the decade. Communists and fellow travelers were disillusioned by the Hitler-Stalin Pact; Spender and C. Day Lewis concluded that their writing suffered from too much time spent on committees and rallies; Auden and Isherwood retreated "from commitment and politics" by leaving for the United States.

Cunningham sneers at bourgeois writers of all political persuasions for constantly snuggling into the cozy comforts of their class, hiding from harsh realities among those with shared educational backgrounds, experiences, and assumptions. These writers dedicated their books to others like themselves and praised one another's writings in public. As a result of these incestuous relationships, much of the British literature of the decade became "an enormous private joke, a huge private box or royal enclosure whose entrance fee was membership of the bourgeois cousinhood." Cunningham condemns these writers for having "been shaped by the same sort of nursery reading which they hadn't . . . grown out of and which they allowed to go on defining for them the shape of the adult world."

Appropriately, the 1930's was a decade of what Cunningham calls child prodigies of letters. Many prominent writers such as Auden, Isherwood, and Spender were young, and youth was worshiped then as it would be again in the 1960's. Many writers' favorite subject was their school experiences; they found ways of working their school days into "every imaginable and unimaginable literary corner." Auden and Isherwood never moved beyond "seeing life in terms of playing-field heroics and the taking of exams." Cunningham credits, for once, Wyndham Lewis for being the first to attack his country for having become a giant nursery peopled by Peter Pans.

Cunningham relates their infatuation with youth to the homosexuality of many of the period's major figures. Literary homosexuals stuck together, puffing one another's work extravagantly, often at the expense of their supposedly high critical standards. Cunningham also connects the leftist views of these writers to lust for large proletarians. One of the results of the homosexuality of many writers was a neglect of family life in the decade's literature: "A whole generation of writers refused to countenance the normal family in their work, as they refused in their lives to acquire wives and become fathers."

The British writers of the time were as fascinated by violence as by youth, in part because of the impact of the horrors of the Great War on more than one generation. Cunningham considers a key phrase of the period to be "the destructive element," coined by I. A. Richards, describing the chaos of the war and the ensuing uncertainty that persisted into the 1930's. Many writers, he says, felt that they inhabited a dream of violence and were constantly threatened by destruction. Cunningham finds numerous examples of sadism in the decade's life and letters, especially among conservative writers such as Charles Williams, C. S. Lewis, and J. R. R. Tolkien. The destructive element was even responsible for the period's fascination with detective fiction. These fictional detectives "always grant answers to the prayer for meaning in an otherwise absurd, murderously contingent universe. Small wonder, then, that the detective becomes for the '30s the type of all solution seekers and perceivers of order."

Heroism in literature and real life was another major concern for many writers obsessed by airmen, motorcyclists, mountaineers, leaders of all types:

> The '30s mind and imagination are . . . continually measuring, sizing up, wondering who is big enough to cope, who big enough to admire, and what makes a person, an ideology, a political system imposingly grand enough to compel the public to look up to it.

The dominant hero, ironically for both Left and Right, was T. E. Lawrence. As intellectual, writer, and man of action, Lawrence of Arabia was a role model for such armchair activists as Auden:

> Some consolation was to be derived . . . from the notion that if the manifestly small, boyish, homosexual, neurotically self-conscious man could become as 'big,' as 'Truly Strong' as T. E. Lawrence continued to be, there might be some personal redemption possible

for others like him. Cunningham, however, is disturbed by the need for leaders such as Lawrence, Vladimir Ilich Lenin, Joseph Stalin, Hitler, and Mosley, who were concerned primarily with power over people. He is suspicious of "the treacherously romantic egotism" of Lawrence but interprets this hero's life as emblematic of the ideals, self-delusions, and destructive element of the decade.

A motif running throughout the lives and literature of the 1930's that touches upon all the previous concerns in some way is travel: "The islanded writer was given to dreaming of happier isles elsewhere, holiday islands, enclosures over the water that might prove happier places than the oppressively islanded home." Writers such as Auden, borrowing from Henry James, considered travel a quest for the Great Good Place. Cunningham sees the 1930's, despite the decade's political concerns, as an age of escapism, resulting from the need to shut one's eyes to a chaotic universe. Evelyn Waugh typifies one kind of literary traveler: "He's on the look-out simply for freakish experience snappily to record in order to jazz up his prose into best-selling stuff. He will be distantly satirical, toughly unmoved, egregiously superior to what he goes through." At the other extreme is the Graham Greene of *Journey Without Maps: A Travel Book* (1936), which portrays the traveler as a "delver into the self," a "psychoanalytic explorer," a "seeker after truth."

The major event of the decade for those concerned with politics, violence, heroism, and travel was the Spanish Civil War, which offered young British writers the chance to rectify their guilt over having missed the Great War. It also seemingly provided escape from the restraints of class and the romance of adventure flavored with political commitment. The war presented those on the Left with the opportunity to meet the "challenge to take sides, to go over to the side of the workers of the world, and in a strikingly personal way." Nevertheless, while George Orwell was wounded and Christopher Caudwell killed, such instances were rare. More common was the experience of Auden, who saw only enough of the fighting to realize that it was not for him. Isherwood spent years longing for such a test of his courage and convictions, only to pass up the chance. On the Right, poet Roy Campbell fled the conflict, only to become a heroic killing machine in his writings.

Cunningham spices this intellectual history with frequently lively writing. He describes Campbell as

> the biffing bronco who preferred poets who came stinking of horses and sweaty from football, who liked punching people and knocking their teeth out and breaking their dentures and specs, who loudly despised the pansy Leftists who wouldn't step outside and fight and who wore underpants.

Cunningham presents Auden's poetry as displaying a "gluttony for the oddest concatenations of things. . . . He loves grabbing this and that, here and there, like a greedy child or a crazed cleric amok at a church jumble sale." Cunningham's study is also enlivened by his frequent anger at literary sins, as with James Joyce's *Finnegans Wake* (1939): "The exercise appears as a selfish retreat into the hermetics of linguisticity that is not only destructive of traditional fiction's ways with the world, people, and reference generally, but also destructive of readers."

Despite the title of his book, Cunningham can be criticized for ignoring those writers who do not illustrate his theses. Such figures as Noel Coward, Jean Rhys, Edith Sitwell, and P. G. Wodehouse are barely mentioned. Minor writers such as Geoffrey Grigson, Tom Harrisson, John Lehmann, Charles Madge, Ruthven Todd, and Edward Upward receive as much attention as do Elizabeth Bowen, Henry Green, Aldous Huxley, Anthony Powell, and Virginia Woolf. Women writers are not prominent in his study, Cunningham explains, because they were essentially left out of a world dominated by the Old Boy sensibility.

British Writers of the Thirties is nevertheless an insightful, carefully researched, stimulating account of a complex, contradictory decade. Cunningham finds his subject somewhat disappointing, as writer after writer turns out to be less than he should have been as artist and person. The 1930's offered so many opportunities that went unrealized because too many writers were in love with the comforts of their class.

Michael Adams

Sources for Further Study

British Book News. October, 1987, p. 700.
Encounter. LXX, April, 1988, p. 62.
The Guardian Weekly. CXXXVIII, February 21, 1988, p. 28.
Library Journal. CXIII, January, 1988, p. 87.
London Review of Books. X, June 23, 1988, p. 12.
The Observer. February 7, 1988, p. 24.
Punch. CCXCIV, March 4, 1988, p. 48.
Quill and Quire. LIV, May, 1988, p. 29.
The Spectator. CCLX, February 6, 1988, p. 26.
The Times Educational Supplement. February 12, 1988, p. 25.
The Times Literary Supplement. June 10, 1988, p. 651.

CAPOTE
A Biography

Author: Gerald Clarke (1937-   )
Publisher: Random House (New York). Illustrated. 632 pp. $22.95
Type of work: Literary biography
Time: 1924-1984
Locale: Primarily New York City and Long Island; also Europe, California, Kansas, and Alabama

Clarke's critical biography, twelve years in the making, is the most comprehensive extant work on Truman Capote, the controversial, often outrageous Southern author and self-proclaimed inventor of the nonfiction novel

Principal personages:
TRUMAN STRECKFUS PERSONS (TRUMAN GARCIA CAPOTE), an American author
LILLIE MAE FAULK PERSONS CAPOTE (NINA CAPOTE), his mother
ARCH PERSONS, his father
JOE CAPOTE, his stepfather
NELLE HARPER LEE, an American novelist, his next-door neighbor during his childhood
RICHARD HICKOCK and
PERRY SMITH, murderers whom he used as protagonists in *In Cold Blood*
CARSON MCCULLERS, an American writer, his antagonist
NEWTON ARVIN, an American literary critic and scholar
JACK DUNPHY, his longtime lover

If, as Truman Capote (originally Truman Streckfus Persons) alleged, he invented the nonfiction novel, Gerald Clarke's enormous, meticulously researched *Capote: A Biography* exemplifies the genre, the actual origins of which some literary scholars dispute. Clarke's book, clearly a documented nonfiction account, reads like a novel, perhaps because Capote's life unfolds like an intricately contrived fiction. Even its duller periods, for which Capote manufactured events and stories to gloss over the banalities, sparkle with the sheer invention of Capote's gnomish mind at work.

Capote's formative years were tailor-made to produce the complex personality who gained instant public recognition when a photograph of him in a houndstooth waistcoat reclining on an Empire divan dominated the back dust jacket of his first novel, *Other Voices, Other Rooms* (1948). Wispy blond bangs fell over his forehead, beguiling eyes stared from the book jacket at a mystified, titillated book-buying public, and provocative, pouting lips suggested the homosexuality with which Capote quickly became identified.

The drama of the picture eclipsed the controlled artistry of this first novel by an unknown writer not yet twenty-four. The book fast became a cult item, as much for the photograph as for the finely crafted prose and sharp imagery that lay between its covers. For whatever reasons—most likely because of the early instinct for self-promotion that made him adamant about which picture of him would grace the book—Truman Capote had been noticed, and, through continued self-promotion, he would alternately enjoy and painfully endure celebrity until his death.

Marrying an amiable con man, Arch Persons, had provided Capote's mother, Lillie Mae Faulk (later Nina Capote), with an instant perspicacity: Within days of the wedding, Lillie Mae knew that she had made a dreadful mistake. Within days of that discovery, she made an additional discovery: She was about to become a mother. She did what she could to arrange an immediate abortion, a more daunting task in the 1920's than in later years. Arch, with whom Lillie Mae never really lived in any conventional connubial situation before Truman was born, glowed at the prospect of his approaching fatherhood. He sweet-talked Lillie Mae into going with him on a vacation to Colorado, after which her pregnancy was too far along for her to risk an abortion.

Lillie Mae returned to her comfortably fixed family in Monroeville, Alabama, to begin her countdown. As the day of reckoning approached, however, her guardian, hard-nosed Cousin Jennie Faulk, shipped Lillie Mae off to her husband in New Orleans, where the reluctant mother-to-be waited out the rest of her confinement in a commodious suite at the Monteleone Hotel.

On September 30, 1924, the unwelcomed event occurred. Lillie Mae was taken to Touro Infirmary, where, at three o'clock in the afternoon, she was delivered of a boy whose father named him Truman after an old school chum and Streckfus after the family for whom he then worked.

Although their ill-starred union lasted officially for seven years, Lillie Mae took a procession of lovers—by Arch's perhaps conservative count, at least twenty-nine, including prizefighter Jack Dempsey. Arch had grandiose schemes that usually failed and that occasionally landed him in jail. Truman, from his earliest recollection, had cause to fear what psychologists think children fear most: abandonment by one or both parents. Lillie Mae often left him in the care of relatives. When she looked after him herself, she saw no need to shield him from knowledge of her recurring sexual intimacies with various lovers.

As Lillie Mae found it increasingly difficult to be a full-time mother, she entrusted Truman more or less permanently to relatives. The boy spent much of his first seven years in Monroeville with two maiden aunts and a bachelor uncle. His only real friend was a next-door neighbor a couple of years younger than he, Nelle Harper Lee (later author of *To Kill a Mockingbird*, 1960), who remained a lifelong friend. Because Truman was perceived locally as a sissy, most parents forbade their children to play with him.

Lillie Mae, divorced from Arch in 1931, soon was married to a successful Cuban businessman, Joe Capote, and lived comfortably with him in New York. Aspiring to a new social elegance, she changed the Southern-sounding "Lillie Mae" to the more sophisticated "Nina." When Truman came to live with his mother and Joe Capote, who adopted the boy and had his name legally changed to Truman Garcia Capote, Nina disapproved openly of her son's effeminacy. Because her feelings toward him were always ambivalent, Truman's life with her in New York intensified the love-hate relationship that was to outlast even Nina's suicide in 1953.

Nina finally sent Truman to St. John's Military Academy in Ossining, New York, where he spent a miserable nine months. He then resumed his studies at Trinity School, and he began tenth grade at Greenwich High School when the family moved to Connecticut. By this time, having realized that he wanted to be a writer, Truman had little tolerance for any studies that would not lead to this end.

Clarke emphasizes Capote's formative years to explain the writer, who was Clarke's neighbor at Sagaponack, Long Island, and—to the extent that Capote could permit friendship—his friend for two decades. Lillie Mae's early promiscuity, details of which Truman claimed to remember from age two, became ingrained in Capote's personality. He knew early that he was homosexual and frankly discussed his orientation with some family members. Sexual promiscuity seemed a part of his orientation, as it was of his mother's.

The pattern of some of Capote's friendships in later life is understandable in the light of his upbringing. The adult Capote, five feet, three inches tall, balding, formed close associations with married couples, often celebrity couples such as Bill and Barbara ("Babe") Paley. He related to them essentially as a son would relate to his parents. Yet Capote, as Clarke skillfully documents, became the spoiler in these relationships, irresponsibly starting rumors, sometimes baseless, calculated to derail the marriage.

In such situations, Capote was always more than a casual friend or acquaintance. He loved the people involved, and they loved him. These friendships usually had lasted for years. That was exactly what Capote required. He could then take revenge on the couple as parent figures by destroying their relationship if not their marriage, usually also scuttling his relationship with them, as in the case of the Paleys.

Clarke relates this side of Capote's intriguing, eerie personality to his interest in the Clutter murder in Kansas, which is the subject of *In Cold Blood* (1966). As soon as he read about the mass murder of the Herbert Clutter family, something fell into place in Capote's subconscious. The apprehension, trial, conviction, and sentencing to death for murder of Richard Hickock and Perry Smith provided Capote with the ingredients for his nonfiction novel. He bribed his way onto death row to interview the condemned men and gained continuing access to them through visits and twice-weekly letters to and from each of them.

The nature of *In Cold Blood* required that it have a definitive ending, the most artistically desirable of which would be the execution of the two convicted men. The book could not be finished until the case was. As court after court worked through appeals and granted stays of execution, Capote, who was forming a personal relationship with the two, particularly with Perry, who himself aspired to be a writer, reacted in ways so psychologically complex as to defy full understanding.

On the one hand, Capote needed the two dead so that his book could end on a decisive note. On the other hand, he had become for both men their tie with the world outside death row. They trusted him; they needed him. In their last days, it was to him they turned, but he denied them, lied by telling them that he was not allowed into the prison, delaying his visit to them until an hour before their executions. Psychologically, Capote, who in his later years increasingly engaged in character assassination, was as much a murderer as Dick and Perry. The only difference was that he killed in more subtle ways, a point that could hardly have been lost on someone of Capote's sensitivity.

Capote, who was close to Clarke as this book was being written, told its author that he would lose respect for him if he did not tell the whole truth. To do so is to expose an intriguing creative artist whose inherent viciousness caused him to lose virtually all of his friends before he died on August 25, 1984, at the age of fifty-nine, by which time he had lost his desire to live. The portrait that emerges from Clarke's biography is of a man whose heredity and environment conspired overwhelmingly against his living an untroubled life.

The Truman Capote constructed by Clarke's extensive portrayal is a person who could never accept life as real. Rather, life was a play in rehearsal. One tried things out; if they did not work, one rearranged them. The great shock to which Capote suddenly awakened after the publication of "La Côte Basque" (1975), his scurrilous *Esquire* exposé of America's major jet-setting socialites, who had for years welcomed him eagerly into their circle as a charming and interesting companion, was that life is real and that the scenes in which damage is done cannot be rewritten and replayed to minimize that damage.

His article resulted in or at least hastened the suicide of Ann Woodward and caused sufficient embarrassment among the rest of his socially prominent companions that most of them dropped Capote completely. The social butterfly lionized by everyone who counted had suddenly become a social pariah, whose only outlet was to spew forth vitriol on television talk shows, sometimes eliciting libel suits.

In several ways, Clarke's composition of this book presents an interesting parallel to Capote's composition of *In Cold Blood*. Clarke was close to his subject, although as Capote's life played out, it became increasingly difficult for Clarke or anyone else to deal with him. Just as *In Cold Blood* could not be completed until the final outcome had been decided, so it would have been difficult for Clarke to publish *Capote* during its subject's lifetime.

The story Clarke recounts so accurately and objectively is a Dorian Gray narrative. Whereas Dorian Gray did not age physically, however, Capote never let himself mature emotionally into a genuine adulthood. He kept the voice his fourth-grade schoolteacher recognized when she heard it decades later, preserving the faint lisp and Southern accent of the towheaded boy who played with the girl next door in Monroeville, Alabama, in those innocent days of the late 1920's.

Clarke's psychological presentation of Capote is tantalizing, if incomplete. The attempt to understand a psychopathology as complex as Capote's would baffle a battery of psychologists. The important fact with which Clarke leaves his readers is that out of this psychopathology grew a literature of intense interest and artistry, created by a writer who died many times before he died.

R. Baird Shuman

Sources for Further Study

Booklist. LXXXIV, April 15, 1988, p. 1369.
The Economist. CCCVIII, August 27, 1988, p. 78.
Kirkus Reviews. LVI, April 1, 1988, p. 508.
Library Journal. CXIII, June 15, 1988, p. 60.
Los Angeles Times Book Review. June 12, 1988, p. 3.
The New York Times Book Review. XCIII, June 12, 1988, p. 1.
Newsweek. CXI, May 30, 1988, p. 62.
Publishers Weekly. CCXXXIII, May 13, 1988, p. 258.
Time. CXXXI, May 30, 1988, p. 60.
Vogue. CLXXVIII, June, 1988, p. 86.
The Wall Street Journal. June 2, 1988, p. 20.

THE CAPTAIN AND THE ENEMY

Author: Graham Greene (1904-)
Publisher: Viking Press (New York). 189 pp. $17.95
Type of work: Novel
Time: Approximately 1967-1977
Locale: London and Panama

An elliptical and ironic tale about a young man's inability to experience love and to understand its functioning in personal relations or its expression in political actions

Principal characters:
VICTOR BAXTER, also known as JIM, the narrator and protagonist
THE CAPTAIN, variously known as ROGER BROWN, J. VICTOR, COLONEL CLARIDGE, CARVER, and SEÑOR SMITH, a confidence man and surrogate father for Jim
LIZA, the Captain's beloved and Jim's surrogate mother
BAXTER, known as THE DEVIL, Jim's aloof father
AUNT MURIEL, Jim's dead mother's sister, his guardian
CYRIL "FRED" QUIGLEY, a Central Intelligence Agency operative in Panama
PABLO, Jim's Panamanian bodyguard
COLONEL MARTÍNEZ, the head of the Panamanian National Guard

In his autobiographical volume *Ways of Escape* (1980), Graham Greene observed that since the 1960's his work has steadily moved from the tragic intensities of his "Catholic novels" (written between 1938 and 1961) toward what he called the "tragicomic region of La Mancha where I expect to stay." In the works of this "late" phase of Greene's career, theological issues were no longer so centrally focused as they had been in earlier novels such as *The Power and the Glory* (1940) and *The Heart of the Matter* (1948). Politics, particularly involving the revolutionary struggles of Third World nations, moved to center stage. In mode these novels were more realistic and less rigidly schematic than the theological thrillers of Greene's middle years. Novels such as *The Comedians* (1966) and *Travels with My Aunt* (1969) involved a larger and more varied canvas, with comic characters in particular given more latitude. There was accordingly a certain allowance given to eccentricity, to farcical adventures, with a prevailing authorial tolerance of the bittersweet human spectacle. In short, notwithstanding Greene's growing concern with political engagement, the world of these novels—and the narrative structures used to represent it—tended toward the diffuse, the inclusive, and the picaresque.

One of the insights suggested by *The Captain and the Enemy*, Greene's twenty-sixth novel in a career spanning six decades, is that he may have moved beyond La Mancha after all. Although a few of its characters and themes are reminiscent of the novels of the 1960's and 1970's, *The Captain and the Enemy* exemplifies a new style in being terse and elliptical, its settings and its characterization unusually sketchy, and offering more than a few hints that it may be read as a sort of parable of human evil. In all these respects the novel resembles other works Greene has published in the 1980's such as *Doctor Fischer of Geneva: Or, the Bomb Party* (1980), *Monsignor Quixote* (1982), and even *The Tenth Man* (published in 1985, though originally composed in the 1940's). These relatively slender volumes have been seen by some critics as evidence of the diminished powers of a novelist in his middle eighties. Perhaps it would be fairer to say that Greene has discovered a form that will more readily distill his vision of humanity.

In *The Captain and the Enemy* this vision is embodied in the juxtaposition of opposed worlds. Superficially these worlds may be associated with the two major settings in the novel, England and Panama. More fundamentally, Greene is positing two sets of opposed values: the pragmatic and realistic on one hand and the imaginative and romantic on the other. The novel opens in a public school obviously modeled on Berkhamsted, where Greene underwent an adolescent crisis about which he has written incisively in *A Sort of Life* (1971). The protagonist and narrator, Victor Baxter, is abducted from the school by a man identified as the Captain, who claims to have "won" the boy from his father in a game of backgammon. Soon the Captain has installed the twelve-year-old Victor, whom he has unaccountably renamed Jim, in a London basement flat, where he will spend most of the next ten years under the watchful eye of the Captain's lady friend, Liza. Meanwhile, the Captain is involved in a series of mysterious schemes both in England and abroad, periodically reappearing before the boy and Liza in different guises to escape detection by the police. Eventually the Captain lands in Panama, where he believes he will make his fortune by smuggling arms to, among others, the rebel Sandinistas of nearby Nicaragua during the last days of the Somoza regime in the late 1970's. His plan is to send for Liza and Jim to join him once he strikes it rich. Much of the novel consists in the boy's waiting for the reappearance of the Captain or for news of his colorful adventures in the world of crime and intrigue. Otherwise Victor/Jim's life is tedious. Moreover, Liza's passive existence, as seen by Jim, epitomizes the drabness of ordinary life. He longs for escape from this life, just as he had welcomed escape from the school. To him the Captain represents a sort of gypsy ideal which engages and shapes his imagination:

> He was an adventurer, he belonged to that world of Valparaiso which I had dreamt about as a child, and like most boys I had responded, I suppose, to the attraction of mystery, uncertainty, the absence of monotony, the worst feature of family life.

The Captain's activities are all the more romantic to Jim because they are never fully explained. The mystery, however, only further stimulates his curiosity, and the Captain remains for him "an eternal question-mark never to be answered, like the existence of God." That this is more than a casual analogy is clear from the fact that the Captain's antagonist at the outset is Jim's real father, referred to throughout as "the Devil." He it was who so willingly went along with Jim's removal from the school and his home (Jim's mother having died years before), and in years past he had been Liza's lover, eventually forcing her to undergo an unwelcome and dangerous abortion. Further, "the Devil" tries repeatedly to undermine Jim's confidence in the Captain, discrediting the latter's adventures as no more than the fabrications of a con artist. The first embodiment of the "enemy" of the title, he plants the seed of doubt and distrust in Jim's mind regarding his surrogate parents.

Despite its brevity, *The Captain and the Enemy* is more complex and playful than most other Greene novels in its narrative point of view. Told mostly in the first person (itself a form rarely found in Greene) by the twenty-two-year-old Jim, looking back on his adolescence, the tale involves the familiar theme of lost innocence. The loss does not occur during a single shattering event, however, but unfolds gradually over time, as it does in real life. Innocence in this case amounts to spontaneous feeling, the capacity to care for and with others. One of the most noticeable things about Jim is his inability to feel anything approaching love. The very word makes him shudder. Yet he spends much of his time trying to fathom the subtle bond between the Captain and Liza. Whatever it is, it encompasses kindness and basic loyalty, and it endures recurrent separation and suffering. For Jim, however, it remains as elusive as the Captain's identity itself. Out of frustration with his inability to understand—and his incapacity to feel—love, he categorically denies its validity. Instead, Jim can feel only jealousy and hatred of those who love. Eventually, he comes to despise the Captain for regularly abandoning Liza and for imprisoning both her and himself in false hopes of permanent reunion. Yet when Liza suddenly dies Jim feels nothing, not even gratitude for her years of nurturing, and he cruelly withholds the news of her death from the Captain until it will bring the most pain possible. Hence, Jim is a sort of moral cripple, one whose perceptions, especially of anything as complex as human relations, are scarcely to be trusted. A measure of Greene's artistry is that despite Jim's shortcomings as an observer the reader gradually becomes aware of the delicacy and the underlying strength of the feelings shared (though seldom verbalized) by the Captain and Liza.

The complexity of viewpoint in this case involves more than the use of an ironic narrator. Jim is not only an observer but a would-be writer, whose reflections on his craft echo some of Greene's well-known pronouncements. Jim's imagination took shape, like Greene's, from boyhood reading (Rider Haggard was a favorite of both) and fantasies about exotic lands; both endured an adolescent crisis at school and an extended separation from home and parents (in Greene's case, six months of psychoanalysis in London); both suffered from chronic boredom and dreamed of escape; both turned first to journalism, then to imaginative literature as "ways of escape." Indeed, *The Captain and the Enemy*, the reader learns at the beginning of part 2, is Jim's manuscript-in-progress, at times retrospective, at times virtually cotemporal with his ongoing experiences. In the book's brief epilogue, the point of view shifts abruptly to the third person, as other characters read and interpret (or misinterpret) Jim's narrative and mention events occurring after he discarded it in a wastebasket. Jim himself expresses doubts whether he is faithfully recording remembered events or embroidering them with fiction, just as the Captain had been accused of fabricating his life in narrating it to Jim and Liza. At one point, Jim even confesses a sense of guilt, not because of his inability to love the Captain and Liza but because "I had taken them quite coldbloodedly as fictional characters to satisfy this passionate desire of mine to write." In such passages Greene hints at reservations about his own vocation, lamenting the "coldblooded" isolation imposed on the writer by his calling. In this condition of detachment from human ties and commitments, the artist in effect consorts with "the enemy," eventually internalizing it.

It is instructive to compare the section of the novel set in Panama with *Getting to Know the General: The Story of an Involvement* (1984), Greene's memoir of his travels to Central America during the 1970's and of his friendship with General Omar Torrijos, the charismatic leader of Panama during the period leading up to the treaty guaranteeing the return of the Canal Zone by the United States to Panama. The memoir is many things—travel book, personal tribute to Torrijos, political diatribe against American regional hegemony, declaration of faith in the Marxist opponents of corporate capitalism—but it is clearly no novel. Indeed, it describes the conception of Greene's ill-fated plans for a novel that was to be called "On the Way Back," set in Panama, drawing on his acquaintances and experiences there. The plans proved abortive because his characters "had emerged from life and not from the unconscious and for that reason they stood motionless like statues in my mind. . . . They were real people and they could have no life independent of me in the imagination." As Greene declared in *A Sort of Life*,

> All that we can easily recognize as our experience in a novel is mere reporting: it has a place, but an unimportant one. . . . Perhaps a novelist has a greater ability to forget than other men—he has to forget or become sterile. What he forgets is the compost of the imagination.

Although some of the superficial details and peripheral characters in the Panama section of *The Captain and the Enemy* were adapted from Greene's own travels there, the main action is purely imaginary. The pace here abruptly shifts into the more headlong urgency of the thriller, a form of which Greene has long been one of the masters. A new character, "Fred" Quigly, is introduced and quickly assumes prominence. Possessor of a British passport and a vaguely American accent, calling himself both a financial counselor and a freelance news correspondent, Quigly is a marvelously elusive and ambiguous character, whom Jim instinctively distrusts and yet to whom he is inexorably drawn. The simplest interpretation of Quigly is that he is an agent of the Central Intelligence Agency (CIA) trying to prevent the Captain, now called Señor Smith, from creating an embarrassing incident that might upset the treaty negotiations. As the Captain's antagonist, he is another embodiment of the "enemy," which explains his influence upon Jim. Jim's ignorance of the human heart is equaled by his ignorance of all Central American politics, so that he is as unable to fathom the significance of the Captain's activities in smuggling arms to the Sandinistas as he is their basic motive—the desire to provide for his "family," that is, Liza and Jim. Although not an ideologue, the Captain sees intuitively a continuity between service to loved ones and commitment to a more just and humane society. He emerges in the end a genuine hero, though a quixotic one, whose stature is measured in terms of his benevolent motives rather than his success—his last attempt to defeat the "enemy" (now identified in part with Anastasio Somoza and the Americans who supported him) has failed, but failed gloriously.

During this process, Jim assists the "enemy," acting in utterly bad faith by deceiving the Captain about Liza's death and betraying him with Quigly. Yet in the short coda presented in the third person, consisting of an interview between Quigly and Colonel Martínez, head of the Panamanian National Guard, it is suggested that Jim may have had a change of heart at the end. Rejecting Quigly's offer of a job as a stringer, and abandoning his manuscript, Jim finally regrets his lies to the Captain and sets off to pursue his own destiny in Valparaíso, only to meet with a fatal accident en route. That this climactic event occurs, as it were, offstage and is merely reported after the fact by Colonel Martínez (who speculates that it may not after all have been an accident), is indicative of Greene's avoidance of a melodramatic conclusion. Instead, he ends with Martínez's cryptic suggestion that "the son has followed the father," underscoring the ambiguous meanings of this modern parable.

If *The Captain and the Enemy* lacks the power and amplitude of Greene's greatest fiction, it is nevertheless an important work that demonstrates the author's attempts to continue developing narrative forms sufficient to express his vision of the world. Its metafictional elements and elliptical structure, its tantalizing yet elusive parabolic pattern, might even be said to represent gestures toward post-modernism. However that may be, the novel offers a salutary reminder of how difficult it is to place Graham Greene confidently in any category more confining than at the forefront of English novelists of the twentieth century.

Ronald G. Walker

Sources for Further Study

Booklist. LXXXIV, July, 1988, p. 1754.
The Economist. CCCVIII, September 17, 1988, p. 106.
Kirkus Reviews. LVI, August 1, 1988, p. 1085.
New Statesman and Society. I, September 16, 1988, p. 38.
The New York Times. CXXXVIII, October 17, 1988, p. C22.
The New York Times Book Review. XCIII, October 23, 1988, p. 11.
Publishers Weekly. CCXXXIV, August 5, 1988, p. 72.
Time. CXXXII, October 31, 1988, p. 88.
The Times Literary Supplement. September 16, 1988, p. 1013.
The Wall Street Journal. CCXI, October 18, 1988, p. A28.
The Washington Post Book World. XVIII, August 28, 1988, p. 1.

CHARLOTTE MEW AND HER FRIENDS
With a Selection of Her Poems

Author: Penelope Fitzgerald (1916-   )
Introduction by Brad Leithauser
First published: Charlotte Mew and Her Friends, in Great Britain, in 1984
Publisher: Addison-Wesley (Reading, Massachusetts). Illustrated. 290 pp. $17.95
Type of work: Literary biography
Time: The mid-1860's to 1928
Locale: London

This biography of Charlotte Mew suggests the repressed emotions that may account for both the power of her verse and the limited nature of her poetic output and reputation

Principal personages:
CHARLOTTE MARY "LOTTI" MEW, a poet
ANNE MEW, her sister, a painter
HAROLD MONRO, a poet, a publisher, and the proprietor of the Poetry Bookshop
ALIDA MONRO, who promoted Charlotte Mew's poetry
ELLA D'ARCY, an emancipated woman of the 1890's who helped edit *The Yellow Book*
AMY DAWSON SCOTT, a literary patron and founder of the International Association of Poets, Playwrights, Editors, Essayists, and Novelists (PEN)
MAY SINCLAIR, a novelist and suffragist

Charlotte Mary Mew (1869-1928)—a poet now in the process of rediscovery—is one of those perplexing figures: a writer of great promise who produced a disappointingly small body of work. Her first published story appeared in 1894 in the second issue of *The Yellow Book*, at that time the most avant-garde journal for new writers and New Women of the 1890's. A small collection of her poetry was printed as a Poetry Bookshop chapbook in 1916. Yet although Mew's work was admired by such contemporaries as Walter de la Mare, John Masefield, Virginia Woolf, and Thomas Hardy, and although other *Yellow Book* and Poetry Bookshop writers became significant figures in their respective generations, Mew published very little of significance aside from these two brilliant beginnings. Penelope Fitzgerald's *Charlotte Mew and Her Friends: With a Selection of Her Poems*, working from biographical materials limited by Mew's reticence and by the sometimes contradictory memoirs written by people she knew, presents what is known of her life and provides the data from which one can make guesses about Mew's inability to bring forth a major body of work.

Tillie Olsen, in *Silences* (1978), movingly identified factors which cause the unnatural thwarting of creative powers: Writers may be silenced because they are born in the wrong class or sex, denied education, have unacceptable visions, are numbed by economic struggle, distracted by nurturing, muffled by censorship, or paralyzed by personal circumstances and the anguish of failing belief in the self. In the case of Charlotte Mew, the causes would seem to lie in the strong contradictions which marked a generation of women in transition between the Victorian and modern worlds and caused her to repress and conceal (perhaps even from herself) the subjects and emotions that struggled for expression in her verse.

Mew's family background, with which the book begins, was typical of the upwardly mobile mid-Victorian generations. Her father, Fred Mew, a farmer's son, went to London to be trained as an architect. He took a job with H. E. Kendall, Jr., a distinguished and gentlemanly specialist in the design of houses, ultimately becoming a junior partner in the firm and the husband of Kendall's daughter, Anna Maria. Although Charlotte Mew's parents were reasonably well-off, her childhood was marked by the hidden economies that were needed in order to maintain a social standing that was just slightly beyond reach. After Kendall's death, Fred Mew proved unable to sustain the business. The available assets were invested to produce an annuity which provided an income barely sufficient to maintain middle-class status during the lifetime of Anna Maria Mew, Charlotte's mother. Although by the 1890's some young women of middle-class and even upper-class backgrounds were living in flats, holding jobs, and proclaiming that careers did not compromise their gentility, Charlotte Mew and her sister Anne remained at home and clung to traditional respectability.

Writing had long been one of the accepted ways for a woman to earn necessary income—yet the placement of Mew's first published story in the second number of *The Yellow Book* reveals the other side of her nature. The journal proclaimed that it would "have the courage of its modernness, and not tremble at the frown of Mrs. Grundy." Mew's story, "Passed," impressed the editor at once, and Mew, in turn, was exhilarated by her entry into the world of New Women who wrote for the magazine, women with cropped hair who wore tailored suits, smoked cigarettes, and ranged London without chaperons in pursuit of their professional lives. It would seem that such a debut should have led Mew into the literary and personal relationships that could have secured for her a place among the innovative writers of turn-of-the-century fiction. Mew, however, never again published a story in a periodical with comparable intellectual and artistic repute.

Fitzgerald suggests (although it is not clear on what evidence) that Mew's internalization of respectable Victorianism caused her retreat from *The Yellow Book* in the summer after Oscar Wilde's arrest for homosexual offenses. Although Wilde had not contributed to the magazine, its coeditor, Aubrey Beardsley, was tainted by association because he had illustrated the English edition of Wilde's *Salome* (1893). Moral questions, however, need not be the whole story. *The Yellow Book* had rejected the second story which Mew submitted, and, in any event, its payments to contributors were extremely modest. Fred Mew's death in 1898 left the Mew sisters and their mother in financial straits. They made genteel arrangements for taking in a lodger (planning the rooms and hours so that visitors would be unaware of her presence). Anne, who had studied painting at the Female School of Art, undertook small commissions for decorative work which she could execute in her room at home. Charlotte pursued a salable but undemanding style that let her place stories and essays in *Temple Bar*, a popular mass magazine of the 1860's which was by 1900 in the last stages of its descent into stodginess and extinction. It did, nevertheless, pay its contributors.

A full generation after her story had appeared in *The Yellow Book*, Mew once again attracted attention from the literary avant-garde, this time as a poet. Ezra Pound published one of her poems in *The Egoist* and forwarded copies to *Poetry* in Chicago. "The Farmer's Bride," printed in *The Nation* in 1912, attracted the attention of literary patron Amy Dawson Scott and of novelist May Sinclair (who sent copies of Mew's work to H. D., Rebecca West, Edward Garnett, and other influential reviewers). Alida Monro sought out Mew's address and persuaded her to join in readings at the fabled Poetry Bookshop, which in those days sold from its shelves all poetry in print by living English poets and was the recognized haven for young writers to find company, exchange ideas, and talk about their craft. Harold Monro published a collection of Mew's work under the title *The Farmer's Bride* (1916). Sydney Cockerell, director of the Fitzwilliam Museum at Cambridge, recommended the book to T. E. Lawrence and brought Siegfried Sassoon to have tea with Mew. The aging Thomas Hardy invited her down to visit him at Max Gate.

Despite the powerful impression Mew's verse made on those who had it called to their attention—and particularly those who heard the readings she could sometimes be persuaded to give—it achieved little in the way of general recognition, and Mew published very few new poems after the 1916 collection. To an extent the masculinist assumptions of the poetry establishment can be blamed; the work of only one woman poet, for example, was printed in the four *Georgian Poetry* anthologies which were intended to define the period's new voices. Yet Mew's retreat from her own success is also apparent and demands biographical explanation.

Charlotte Mew and Her Friends is the work of an accomplished biographer working in traditional fashion. The book's vocabulary and approach are suited to general readers, the endnotes provide limited documentation, and although Fitzgerald expresses opinions, she does not invent dialogue or speculate at length on Mew's thoughts and emotions. The available sources include Mew's published work, a very few of her letters (some still in private hands), and scrappy mentions in the writings of and about people whom she knew. Indeed, as the phrase "and her friends" indicates, the book is filled out by the inclusion of several chapters describing people who were at one time or another important to Mew.

The picture that emerges is therefore also scrappy and sometimes tangential. Mew's letters adopt tones appropriate to their recipients, and she seems to have projected different personalities for the various acquaintances who wrote about her. The poetry—which Fitzgerald cites primarily when it can be elucidated by biographical reference—is enigmatic, perplexing, and moving. Like Emily Brontë (whose verse Mew greatly admired) or Robert Frost, Mew generally writes in the voice of a persona whose words expose fragments of a concealed narrative. The poems express moments of emotion which are all the more intensely felt because of the ambiguity and frustration which both feed the emotion and impede its expression.

The repressed emotional content that accounts for the power of Mew's verse and may also explain her intermittent silencing must be inferred from the slender biographical materials. Aside from the inhibitions imposed by upbringing, family, and class, Fitzgerald suggests two subjects which were for Mew both extremely significant and too dangerous to express. One is the question of real (not romanticized) insanity, the other the nature of her own romantic or erotic desires.

Among Mew's friends, even those who pitied the way in which the sisters and their mother struggled against poverty did not realize that the heaviest drain on their narrow income was the need to provide support for a brother and another sister who were confined to mental asylums. Henry, who had been a promising young assistant in his father's architectural office, experienced a breakdown in his early twenties; Freda, the youngest Mew sister, was hospitalized from her mid-teens. Furthermore, two of Mrs. Mew's siblings were also mentally incompetent. Aside from the feelings of shame that lead people to conceal insanity in the family, the eugenics movement, which had grown strong by the 1890's, suggested that those with "defective" families had a moral duty not to reproduce. Charlotte and Anne Mew came to the conclusion that they had no right to marry.

For Charlotte, at least, the decision may have been a convenient relief. Although there is no direct evidence that she recognized or understood her sexual orientation, the topic is introduced early in the book in the chapter titled "Love Between Women." While attending Gower Street School, Mew (like many another schoolgirl) suffered an adolescent passion for her teacher, Lucy Harrison. When Harrison left the school for a rest, Mew was so distressed that she began to bang her head against the wall. Harrison herself subsequently fell in love with another teacher, Amy Greener, with whom she was to live for nearly thirty years. After Harrison and Greener departed for a school in Yorkshire, Mew, at sixteen, decided that school had nothing more to offer her and refused to undertake any further education.

There appear to have been at least two other strong passions in her life. In 1902, she made an unexpected trip to Paris, hoping that she could help and look after Ella D'Arcy, who had also been associated with *The Yellow Book* women. Ten years later, she fell in love with the novelist and suffragist May Sinclair (although the story that she pursued Sinclair around her bedroom rests only on a secondhand report set down in a letter long after the fact). It is not at all clear whether Mew herself knew that her love for women had an erotic content and a name. Although Paris by the turn of the century had a lesbian subculture with recognized meeting places, and although the manuals of the Federation of Working Girls' Clubs (for which Mew did volunteer social work) warned that girls should not be allowed to form close attachments to their leaders, the changing climate of opinion which made romantic friendships between women suspect was not widespread in England until after World War I. Mew was often described as looking like a young boy. She was very small and (like many professional women of the period) wore man-tailored jackets with her skirts; she smoked cigarettes and was boyishly awkward in her walk and gestures. In her essay on Brontë's poetry, Mew energetically denies the element of masculinity which critics often found in Brontë. Brontë's genius, Mew argued, was wholly "spiritual" and "freed from any accident of sex." Like many critical appreciations, Mew's words may reveal more about her own self-image than about her subject. It seems possible that the boyish persona gave her a way to refuse the conventions of stereotypical femininity while protecting her from conscious awareness of the erotic desires which a man—rather than a boy—would feel toward women.

An edition of Mew's collected poetry and prose was published by Virago Press in association with Carcanet Press in 1981, and scholarly articles and dissertations that consider her work have appeared since then. Poems by Mew have been included in the 1973 *Oxford Book of Twentieth Century English Verse* and the 1985 *Norton Anthology of Literature by Women: The Tradition in English*. In its American edition, *Charlotte Mew and Her Friends* combines Fitzgerald's biography with a selection of Mew's poems and an introduction by Brad Leithauser which discusses her literary qualities and poetic techniques. The recognition is overdue, for although Charlotte Mew did not produce a major body of work, the poems that she did publish reveal a distinctive and profoundly troubling voice.

Sally Mitchell

Sources for Further Study

The Atlantic. CCLXII, August, 1988, p. 80.
Booklist. LXXXIV, May 1, 1988, p. 1471.
Kirkus Reviews. LVI, April 1, 1988, p. 511.
Library Journal. CXIII, May 15, 1988, p. 83.
Los Angeles Times. May 26, 1988, V, p. 16.
The New Leader. LXXI, August 8, 1988, p. 17.
The New Republic. CXCIX, August 22, 1988, p. 36.
The New York Times Book Review. XCIII, August 7, 1988, p. 15.
Publishers Weekly. CCXXXIII, April 8, 1988, p. 82.
The Washington Post Book World. XVIII, June 26, 1988, p. 9.

CHATTERTON

Author: Peter Ackroyd (1949-)
First published: 1987, in Great Britain
Publisher: Grove Press (New York). 234 pp. $17.95
Type of work: Novel
Time: The 1980's, 1752-1770, and 1856
Locale: England, primarily London

Past and present more than meet in this brilliantly parodic novel addressing the relationship between originality and imitation, art and copy

Principal characters:
CHARLES WYCHWOOD, a poet, the discoverer of the Chatterton secret
VIVIEN WYCHWOOD, his wife
EDWARD, their son
PHILIP SLACK, a librarian, friend of Charles Wychwood
HARRIET SCROPE, a popular novelist
STEWART MERK, an art forger
THOMAS CHATTERTON, a poet, literary forger, and type of the tragic poet as conceived by the English Romantics
HENRY WALLIS, a nineteenth century painter
GEORGE MEREDITH, a nineteenth century writer and the model for Wallis' *Chatterton*

In his well-known essay "Tradition and the Individual Talent," the subject of one of Peter Ackroyd's four previous books, *T. S. Eliot: A Life* (1984), sets forth the two central obsessions of the literary modernists: the impersonalism (or impersonations) of the writer and the interdependence and interpenetration of past and present, or more specifically, the ways in which the past influences the present and the present influences the past. These same obsessions figure prominently in Ackroyd's third and most emphatically postmodern novel, *Chatterton*, as they do in his two earlier ones, *The Last Testament of Oscar Wilde* (1983) and the archly parodic *Hawksmoor* (1985). The impersonation that plays so important a role in T. S. Eliot's theory—and, according to Ackroyd, in Eliot's life—plays an equally important role in Ackroyd's *Dressing Up, Transvestism and Drag: The History of an Obsession* (1979). *Chatterton* is itself a literary impersonation, a kind of transvestite novel: a mystery novel, a literary biography, and an English comedy, at once wildly comical and deadly serious, light yet obsessive. In its own highly readable way, it manages to raise virtually all the twentieth century's most problematic and insistent literary questions—the existence of the text as object or mirror or sign, and the writer as authority and presence or as that absence or void that the reader is expected to fill. In the guise of a very old-fashioned work ostensibly about the eighteenth century poet Thomas Chatterton, Ackroyd's novel proves decidedly contemporary.

The event which starts the novel in motion is Charles Wychwood's acquisition of a mysterious painting and his subsequent "discovery" that, contrary to received literary history, Thomas Chatterton did not die in 1770, a suicide at age eighteen.

Instead, he lived on long after faking his own death, writing many of the finest poems of the late eighteenth and early nineteenth centuries. Attributed to William Blake, William Wordsworth, and others, these works were in fact composed by Chatterton, master forger and Romantic genius. The fact that Charles is a poet manqué—author of a book of photocopied sheets that he and his wife Vivien have stapled together and left with local booksellers—complicates the matter insofar as it turns his literary sleuthing into a kind of comic psychodrama, starring himself as Chatterton. Charles's obsession first with the painting and then with Chatterton may indicate his having uncovered something important, in effect the literary coup of the century. Then again, it may simply reflect his desire to procrastinate in the writing of the long poem on which he was supposed to be working, with the encouragement and financial support of his too-maternal wife. Is Charles fooling himself? Is he a case of arrested development, a true believer in the Romantic myth which Chatterton represents even though he lives in the age of postmodernist irony? Are his intimations of immortality the real thing or are they delusions, and if they are delusions do they derive from his own Romantic aspirations or from the undiagnosed brain tumor that will soon kill him? If, as Charles likes to say, "there are no rules," then "everything is possible," including Charles's genius, Chatterton's unrivaled greatness, and Ackroyd's novel.

Charles's capacity for self-deception may be no greater than the reader's own gullibility, which Ackroyd both encourages and undermines. When the popular novelist Harriet Scrope attributes to Charles words she knows come from a book review, "that reality is the invention of unimaginative people," Charles, hired to ghostwrite her memoirs, is duly flattered, which is to say duped. Yet her words are in a way his, for they do accurately represent his own view. If "everyone needs stories," as Charles says to his wife, and if "everything is made up," as Harriet claims, and if history is, as Harriet believes, "the one thing we have to make up for ourselves," then the proliferation of truths, interpretations, and stories which *Chatterton* at once encourages and questions may prove the most necessary of human activities. Furthermore, the storyteller, the novelist, may be the most representative man insofar as the need to indulge in stories is coupled with the need to resist them, or rather to resist the finality of any one story, of any one interpretation.

Wiping the mysterious painting with a damp cloth, Charles seems to complete it, but his act is, unknown to himself, a paradoxical one, for what Charles does is to complete the painting by restoring it to its original state, freed of dirt and grime. Yet even this act is ironic. His act restores only the topmost image of a painting that much later is discovered to be less a portrait than a palimpsest, as well as a mirror which reflects the viewer's own image. The novel's title is a sign of its own interpretive multiplicity. It signifies the historical figure Thomas Chatterton, or more specifically the myth and mystery he represents. *Chatterton* is also, however, the title of another painting, completed by Henry Wallis in 1856, one which hangs in London's Tate Gallery and which figures prominently in the imaginations of Charles, his son Edward, and the reader, (for whom the painting is conveniently reproduced on the novel's dust jacket). Wallis' painting exists in the novel (as it does on the dust jacket) in reproduction—reproduced by the printer and by Ackroyd's words and in Charles's and the reader's imaginative interpretations of it and of the man whom the painted figure is presumed to represent. This figure is not the man as he actually was (this being irrecoverable) but the man as he came to be understood, or represented—first by the Romantics, then by Wallis, and finally by Charles and the reader, each adding interpretive layer to interpretive layer in a work that continues to appear merely and naïvely itself: picture rather than sign.

"A great Genius can affect anything, and I understood their Passions as soon as I imployed their Styles: it was not some cold Burlesque but rather—". Read first by Charles and the reader as Thomas Chatterton's own words from a recovered but presumably fragmentary manuscript, these lines are later exposed as having themselves been forged sometime after Chatterton's death by his publisher, Samuel Joynson. Joynson, so the novel has it, turned against Chatterton after the posthumous publication of certain letters in which Chatterton spoke bitterly of Joynson. The publisher devised a plan to discredit Chatterton by forging the manuscript quoted above, in which Chatterton acknowledges having forged his own death. Rather than clearing up a mystery, however, this explanation further complicates matters, for what the novel implies (though nowhere states) is the possibility that the letters upon which Joynson based his decision to discredit Chatterton may have themselves been forged by the rival bookseller who published them, perhaps in order to discredit Joynson. In other words, Charles is right: Everything is possible.

If one of the questions raised by *Chatterton*, as well as by Chatterton, is "What is true?" then another, equally important and equally vexing, is "What is art?" or "What is the artist?" How is art to be distinguished from forgery and the artist from the forger? The modern debate over the political and ideological assumptions implicit within any given literary canon (recognized classics of world literature, for example, are for the most part written by white, male, Western authors) is not far removed from Ackroyd's novel. The same may be said of other issues drawn from the critical debates of the 1960's, 1970's, and 1980's: Harold Bloom's "anxiety of influence" theory, structuralist and poststructuralist skepticism as to the existence of any individual talent whatsoever, and the problematic status of much contemporary art, including literary art, which increasingly takes the form of an "anxious object"—tentative, polyphonic, essentially and perhaps even entirely parodic. It is an art of forgery made in Chatterton's own image. Speaking of Joseph Seymour, another of the novel's many artists, the supposedly knowledgeable Sarah Tilt claims, "He's such a recognisable artist. . . . Each work is unmistakably his." Seymour's late works, the ones Sarah likes most, were, however, all forged by Seymour's assistant, after arthritis had left the "real" artist incapacitated. Following the success of her first novel, Harriet Scrope suffered a mental rather than physical paralysis, from which she escaped by plagiarizing the work of another novelist; borrowing his plots liberated her imagination.

Chatterton is, in fact, filled with stalled, baffled writers and artists: Charles (his poem), Harriet (first her novels, now her memoirs), Seymour (his paintings), Sarah (her *Art of Death*, already six years in the making), and even the nineteenth century writer George Meredith, the model for Wallis' Chatterton, whose own stalled career was (in Ackroyd's version) at least partly responsible for his wife's running off with Wallis. The aesthetic crisis extends further, however. As yet another writer, Andrew Flint (currently writing a biography of Meredith) complains, there no longer seem to be any "standards to encourage permanence—only novelty." Flint's complaint is clearly something of a permanent feature in the world of art and literature, but in *Chatterton* the situation appears to have grown more critical as the gap between style and truth, mimesis and invention, widens, and the one between original and forgery narrows. Here, art and literature take on a self-referential life of their own, which, however obliquely, does manage to reconnect with a "real world" that, as it now seems, the reader must "forge" for himself.

Ackroyd's method is, as Chatterton's was, one of pastiche. Pastiche has become a dominant mode in the twentieth century, yet despite its rise it remains suspect, for it insists not only on its own derivativeness but indeed on the derivativeness of all art and on the seeming triumph of imitative technique over "imaginative exploration." As Mrs. Meredith's friend, Miss Slimmer, says of Chatterton's poetry, "It is all *pasticcio*," meaning that it is only pastiche and therefore merely parasitic. Unlike Charles, who literally devours the pages of the books he reads, the self-conscious Borgesian postmodernist pasticheur knows what he is doing and knows too the limitations as well as the very real possibilities of his chosen mode. He escapes the Romantics' obsession with originality by practicing the art of bricolage. He does not complain, as Meredith does, "I never know what is mine any more," for he understands, as the novel's Chatterton does (at least according to what one old pamphlet says about him), that "original genius consists in forming new and happy combinations, rather than in searching after thoughts and ideas which had never occurred before."

The reader finds himself in much the same position, splicing together a workable and wholly provisional interpretation from the multiplicity of sources, stories, and parallels which the novel provides so overgenerously, including its own system of narrative causality. Following a brief biographical sketch of Thomas Chatterton, which in effect invites the reader to confuse fiction with history, the novel's first part traces Charles's acquisition of the painting, his discovery of the represented figure's identity, and his subsequently solving the mystery surrounding Chatterton's death. In the second section, the past—Chatterton's as well as Wallis' and Meredith's—repeatedly interrupts the narrative present, and in the third section the two worlds and times intertwine, so much so that not only does the past seem to be relived in the present but the present is foreseen in the past as well. As the novel progresses, the comic elements become less noticeable, the supernatural and psychological more pronounced, until the reader takes over the role that death has forced Charles to abandon: that of the literary sleuth whose solution to the mystery comes to supplant or at least vie with history, accounting for Wallis' *Chatterton* in new and unusual ways (Chatterton's death, for example, was not a suicide but the result of a botched attempt to cure himself of the clap).

Two additional surprises remain—two additional mysteries to be solved. One is Ackroyd's ability to evoke so much interest in and sympathy for pastiche characters whose delusions, actions, and even names (Merk, Slack, Slimmer, Scrope) suggest humorous condescension. The other is that Philip comes to take his friend Charles's place both as Vivien's husband and Edward's father and as a writer. He now believes that he will be able to write his own novel in his own style, one that will deal with Charles's Chatterton theory. As Philip comes to understand, although the painting and papers were fakes, the feelings they evoked in Charles were nevertheless real. Still, right as Philip may be, he seems no more so than Harriet Scrope, who chooses just as wisely to free herself of the mystery, preferring as she says, "to stay with the living for as long as possible." Like novels by J. M. Coetzee (*Foe*, 1986) and Philip Roth (*The Counterlife*, 1986), *Chatterton* offers the reader a multiplicity of what must finally be read as irreconcilable stories. Chatterton concludes—appropriately enough—provisionally, with what Frank Kermode has termed "a sense of an ending," leaving the reader precariously but necessarily balanced between belief and "clerkly skepticism," sure of Ackroyd's skill but perhaps doubtful whether his brilliant novel is to be taken seriously. That, one may conclude, is its art and its achievement.

Robert A. Morace

Sources for Further Study

The Atlantic. CCLXI, February, 1988, p. 86.
British Book News. August, 1987, p. 523.
Contemporary Review. CCLI, October, 1987, p. 213.
History Today. XXXVIII, January, 1988, p. 53.
Illustrated London News. CCLXXV, November, 1987, p. 91.
Library Journal. CXIII, January, 1988, p. 96.
London Review of Books. IX, September 3, 1987, p. 17.
Los Angeles Times Book Review. February 14, 1988, p. 3.
The New York Review of Books. XXXV, April 14, 1988, p. 15.
The New York Times. CXXXVII, December 31, 1987, p. 17.
The New York Times Book Review. XCIII, January 17, 1988, p. 1.
The New Yorker. LXIII, February 8, 1988, p. 100.
Time. CXXXI, January 18, 1988, p. 65.
The Times Literary Supplement. September 11, 1987, p. 976.
Tribune Books. January 17, 1988, p. 6.
The Wall Street Journal. CCXII, January 19, 1988, p. 26.

CHEKHOV
A Spirit Set Free

Author: V. S. Pritchett (1900-)
Publisher: Random House (New York). 235 pp. $17.95
Type of work: Literary biography and criticism
Time: 1860-1904
Locale: Primarily Russia; occasionally France, Germany, and Italy

Using Anton Chekhov's life as a narrative frame, V. S. Pritchett studies that master's major literary works, showing the development of his art and proposing that Chekhov's genius is to be found much more in his stories than in his plays

Principal personages:
ANTON CHEKHOV, a physician and writer
PAVEL CHEKHOV, his father
ALEKSEY SUVORIN, a millionaire publisher, his supporter
OLGA KNIPPER, an actress, his wife

V. S. Pritchett begins his biographical and critical study with an emphasis—fortunately, free from the jargon of psychoanalysis—upon the influence on Anton Chekhov of his father, Pavel, an intolerant and sometimes violent patriarch about whom Pritchett has this insight: He "had much in common with the classic self-made Victorian puritan . . . a fierce believer in Self-Help and the work ethic, a despot in the family." The miracle of Chekhov's life, and the reference of Pritchett's subtitle, *A Spirit Set Free*, is that Pavel's violence—engendered and justified, he said, by the fact that he had grown up the son of a serf and had himself been treated harshly—fixed in his youngest son, Anton, not a similar callousness but rather a sensitivity to human suffering. Chekhov always sided with his mother's cause and later in life was drawn by this instinct to the causes of peasants and others displaced or neglected by the bureaucratic indifference and the new industrialism that transformed Russia during his lifetime. It is remarkable that Chekhov's accomplishments as a doctor, civic volunteer, traveler, and writer could have been done by a consumptive who died at age forty-four.

Chekhov's sensitivity to human needs and his sharp eye for the subtle and sometimes unflattering structures of human interaction interest Pritchett most of all, because they are the foundation of Chekhov's art. In Pritchett's view, Chekhov's genius, the product of his sympathy and his cool, scientific observation, shows itself best of all in the short stories, from which the plays are only derivative. Tracing the growth of the artist in his stories is Pritchett's central concern: "Chekhov's stories are, in this sense, his life, tunes that his Russia has put into his head."

Accordingly, this volume is as much a study of the art as it is of the life. Its strengths are excellent, detailed analyses of particular works and masterful character sketches of Chekhov and those around him. Pritchett acknowledges in his introduction that though he has for decades been an enthusiastic reader of Russian writers and has written an admirable volume on Ivan Turgenev (*The Gentle Barbarian: The Life and Work of Turgenev*, 1977), he speaks no Russian and has never traveled to the Soviet Union. *Chekhov: A Spirit Set Free* reveals nothing quantitatively new about its human subject, but is rather an interpretation of the life as researched by others and the works as translations: the standard biographical and critical studies of Chekhov he names at the outset, such as D. S. Mirsky's *A History of Russian Literature* (1926-1927), Ernest Simmons' biography, and Donald Rayfield's *Chekhov: The Evolution of His Art* (1975), and Chekhov's own works, especially stories in the Constance Garnett translations. Pritchett's volume is a homage to Chekhov the writer, and to the idea that writing bridges the gap between the individual and the world, encourages self-knowledge, and expands the soul. Art redeems. Chekhov's progress from the young medical student who under the pseudonym Antosha Chekhonte published comic formula fiction to the mature artist who acquired an irritating degree of fame but never enough money is the rising arc on which Pritchett rests his thesis: that though the tubercular Chekhov spat blood for almost twenty years before he died, and spent those same years acting as primary supporter of his father's family and as social conscience in an almost medieval society, his was a magnificent and victorious life.

Pritchett makes his case by showing that beginning in the mid-1880's with Chekhov's summer stays on an estate outside Moscow, his art gradually grew, not merely in technical sophistication, but also in visionary scope, away from the self and outward toward nature and humankind. Pritchett's criteria for good stories, criteria such as "serious moral insight" and a distrust of moral "trade-marks and labels," imply that the artist must find a domain somewhere between the self and society. He praises the Chekhov who was at once the "gentle skeptic" and "the greedy observer." He quotes, as many have, the Chekhovian dictum that readers should not "confuse two things: *solving a problem* and *stating a problem correctly*. It is only the second that is obligatory for the artist." Above all, Pritchett shares and practices Chekhov's belief that detachment must not waver when emotional issues, especially the artist's own, enter the story. Numerous examples grace his book, none more than on the subject of the prophetic quality of Chekhov's humanity. Defending Émile Zola on the Dreyfus case, Chekhov wrote to the conservative Aleksey Suvorin that

> a brew has been gradually concocted on the basis of anti-Semitism, a principle reeking of the slaughterhouse. When something is wrong with us we seek the cause outside ourselves . . . capitalism, the Masons, the Syndicate, the Jesuits—all phantoms, but how they do relieve our anxieties!

For his narrative frame, Pritchett uses Chekhov's life, but without any desire to offer a complete or continuous chronology. Rather, his emphasis is upon several important themes that influenced the art. The first of such subjects is the isolation of the self. Chekhov, frequently beaten by his father and then left in Taganrog as hostage by his bankrupted family, was by nature a self-protective person, always sensitive to the predatory in human relationships and yet throughout his life the victim of intrusions, especially from what he referred to as his "abnormal family." Pritchett shows that Chekhov's decision to write serious fiction is concurrent with his preoccupation with finding convictions but avoiding labels such as "liberal" and "conservative." Pritchett cites "On the Road" as an example of Chekhov's reservations: Like the play *Ivanov* (1887; English translation, 1912), which is derived from it, the story portrays "the disastrous history of an educated man's search for 'convictions.'" Pritchett also shows that Chekhov found no easy solution to his dilemma. Years later, after the death of his tubercular brother Nikolay had given him the feeling that "there's not a kopeck's worth of poetry left in life," he purged his grief by writing "A Dreary Story," a powerful, self-accusing, and moralizing tale of an educated man who recognizes that his life is characterized by the "lack of a central idea." The most he can believe is "that science is the most essential thing in the life of man; that it always has been and will be the highest manifestation of love. . . . This faith is perhaps naïve and may rest on false assumptions, but it is not my fault that I believe that and nothing else." This character's education and his habits of detachment merely screen an immense egotism. Chekhov solves one problem by creating him terminally ill ("We see people die," Chekhov had once said, "but do not think of our own death"), yet his own problem remains, and Pritchett joins other critics in pointing to this time as the great impasse in Chekhov's life: "He has isolated himself." Writing alone will not save him.

Pritchett regards Chekhov's journey in 1890 across Russia to the penal colony on Sakhalin Island as the rebirth of the "nomad" in him, as the payment of his "debt to medicine," and as the beginning of his escape from the impasse of solitude and self-absorption. The pains of the journey and the human degradation on display at Sakhalin resulted in an intensely imaginative period, and Pritchett sees Chekhov's greatest problem as the attempt to balance his efforts at literature with those in "what had become social medicine." He calls this the "clinical" period of Chekhov's life, from which come stories such as "The Black Monk" and the classic "Ward 6" (which Vladimir Ilich Lenin claimed turned him into a revolutionary). Pritchett takes pains to show that Chekhov is still haunted by the moralizing qualities of Leo Tolstoy he had consciously sought to leave behind, and that he still cannot allow an intimate relationship into his life, fending off his female admirers with a mixture of self-mockery and condescension: "Dear Lika," he wrote to a persistent young woman, "when you become a great singer and are paid a handsome salary, then be charitable to me, marry me, keep me at your expense, that I may be free to do nothing." Despite Pritchett's assertion that the stories are the life, such moments provide glimpses of an important aspect of Chekhov's personality not hinted at by his mature fiction.

Pritchett's account emphasizes the mid-1890's as a crucial period in Chekhov's growth as an artist because of the appearance of new subjects in his fiction, one representing the future and the other the past. The former is the factory theme, appearing at first as a concern for the wives and daughters of the ruthless men of industry who were arriving from the cities to displace the lazy landowners. Stories such as "A Doctor's Visit," "A Woman's Kingdom," and "Three Years" portray a world of military-style organization among the owners, squalid conditions for the workers, and industrial dust over all nature. Peasants made for Chekhov the theme from the past, and stories such as "The Peasants" and "In the Ravine" illustrate his social consciousness. The Russian landscape so dear to Chekhov comes to be portrayed more from the point of view of those who work on it: Its immensity and indifference to humankind are ultimately destructive, for Chekhov could not shake the suspicion that the backbreaking toil needed to battle nature negated all the philanthropists' and social engineers' attempts to enlighten the peasants through schools and libraries.

Pritchett's balance between exposition of the stories and summary of the life works well to this point, but it becomes clear in the last third of the volume that the union has been at least as much convenient as inevitable, for Pritchett offers no biographical explanation for the outpouring of superb stories such as "On Official Duty," "The Lady with the Little Dog," "The Darling," "The Betrothed," and "The Bishop," or the greatest plays, *Tri sestry* (1901; *Three Sisters*, 1920) and *Vishnyovy sad* (1904; *The Cherry Orchard*, 1908). Pritchett here deemphasizes his parallel between art and circumstance and provides some of the book's best analysis and commentary. A good example of the biographical is Chekhov's courtship of and marriage to the actress Olga Knipper. An especially good example of the literary is the seven-page discussion of "The Lady with the Little Dog." In addition, Pritchett makes judicious general commentary, pointing out for example that Chekhov's best stories are not framed, but rather open; the very best involve journeys. He creates here some of the book's most memorable vignettes, and they have nothing to do with the fiction except that they offer yet more testimony to Chekhov's supreme subtlety and intelligence. One is Chekhov's 1895 visit with Tolstoy, when he is immensely impressed by the "fanatical faith" of Tolstoy's daughters ("a man can deceive his fiancée or his mistress," but "daughters are like sparrows: you don't catch them with empty chaff"). Another describes the silent, unanswerable look Chekhov gave his sister after she had fallen in love and asked his opinion about her marrying: "It is extraordinary to see Chekhov become as ruthless as the woman teacher who destroys the love affair of her pretty sister in 'The House with the Mezzanine.'" Yet another scene, which itself reads like a consummate Chekhov story, is Pritchett's account of the great man's death at a German spa:

> A few hours later he was gasping for breath. They were going to send for oxygen but Chekhov said he would be dead before it came, so a bottle of champagne was brought. . . . Then he said in Russian, "I am dying," then in German, "Ich sterbe," and died at once. . . . Very strangely, [Olga] had not expected him to die.

Pritchett creates his book out of a nice balance between the facts of Chekhov's life and the art it produced. Recognizing that his emphasis upon literary analysis will demand considerable knowledge of the stories and plays, he is compelled to spend a significant amount of time summarizing them. That strategy is the book's one drawback. Still, the insights of one masterful short-fiction writer about another are not to be missed: Pritchett makes Chekhov come alive as a writer and a man because he possesses sympathy and intelligence comparable to Chekhov's own.

Kerry Ahearn

Sources for Further Study

Boston Globe. September 27, 1988, p. 26.
Chicago Tribune. October 16, 1988, XIV, p. 9.
Kirkus Reviews. LVI, August 1, 1988, p. 1134.
Library Journal. CXIII, October 1, 1988, p. 88.
The New York Review of Books. XXXV, December 22, 1988, p. 25.
The New York Times Book Review. XCIII, November 27, 1988, p. 3.
Publishers Weekly. CCXXXIV, August 5, 1988, p. 75.
The Wall Street Journal. CCXI, September 20, 1988, p. 36.
The Washington Post Book World. XVIII, October 23, 1988, p. 1.

CITIES OF SALT

Author: Abdelrahman Munif (c. 1933-)
First published: Mudun al-milh: al-Tīh, in 1984, in Lebanon
Translated from the Arabic by Peter Theroux
Publisher: Random House (New York) 627 pp. $18.95; paperback $12.95
Type of work: Novel
Time: The 1930's
Locale: Wadi al-Uyoun and Harran, parts of an imaginary Arabian kingdom

In an unnamed Persian Gulf country in the 1930's, desert life is transformed forever by the arrival of Americans searching for oil

Principal characters:

MITEB AL-HATHAL, a leader in the wadi who first recognizes what the coming of the American oil explorers will mean
IBN RASHED, who opposes Miteb and becomes an important liaison to the Americans
DABBASI, who later competes against Ibn Rashed for leadership of the Harrani people
EMIR KHALED AL-MISHARI, the representative of the government and the official political leader in Harran
AKOUB and
RAJI, two drivers on the Ujra-Harran road
SUBHI AL-MAHMILJI, who comes to Harran, opens a successful medical business, and befriends the emir

Cities of Salt has been banned in several Middle Eastern countries (including Saudi Arabia) since its first publication in Beirut in 1984, and it is easy to understand why. Abdelrahman Munif, a Jordanian living in Paris, has written a novel which dates modern Persian Gulf history from the coming of American oil explorers in the 1930's and the consequent exploitation of this oil-rich desert region. Those characters in the novel who fight the Americans die or are driven out; those who help them become rich and powerful themselves. In the culture clash that follows the arrival of the Americans and their technology, Bedouin ways are lost forever, and what rises in their place erases Arabic history. As the first volume of a trilogy, *Cities of Salt* describes powerfully this transformation of culture in a crucial center of the modern world.

The story in such a long novel is actually quite simple. *Cities of Salt* opens in Wadi al-Uyoun, and its first quarter describes the destruction of the wadi, as American bulldozers level the oasis to make way for the exploration for and eventual production of oil. Only Miteb al-Hathal, who "sensed that something terrible was about to happen," stands up in protest, but few heed his dire predictions. (It is not just that the Americans "had terribly odd habits and smelled peculiar"; Miteb senses also that they are "devils" who cannot be trusted.) Miteb watches the "butchery" of the wadi, but all he can say is, "I'm sorry, Wadi al-Uyoun . . . I'm sorry!"

> This was the final, insane, accursed proclamation that everything had come to an end. For anyone who remembers those long-ago days, when a place called Wadi al-Uyoun used to exist, and a man named Miteb al-Hathal, and a brook, and trees, and a community of people used to exist, the three things that still break his heart in recalling those days are the tractors which attacked the orchards like ravenous wolves, tearing up the trees and throwing them to the earth one after another, and leveled all the orchards between the brook and the fields.

The wadi, this "earthly paradise," has been destroyed. Miteb disappears, to become a ghost, but his spirit haunts the rest of the novel, and his predictions become a forecast of what will eventually happen, his name a call to the inevitable revolution.

The last three quarters of the novel take place in the small Bedouin village of Harran, which is quickly transformed by the Americans into a major oil depot and shipping center. Actually, two cities spring up here: an American Harran, complete with swimming pools, air conditioners, and other amenities for the American managers who work here; and an Arab Harran, which is cheap and poor and barely capable of sustaining Arab ways. Eventually, over the years of the novel, working conditions worsen, Arabic leaders become unresponsive to the people's needs, and worker unrest grows.

> They felt afraid, but still dared to say things they would never have said had they not been so consumed with sorrow and anger. Why did they have to live like this, while the Americans lived so differently? Why were they barred from going near an American house, even from looking at the swimming pool or standing for a moment in the shade of one of their trees? Why did the Americans shout at them, telling them to move, to leave the place immediately, expelling them like dogs? . . . Why did the Americans make them perform tasks that they themselves would never dream of doing? Although the workers held their peace and showed nothing but contentment, the Americans were never satisfied by anything but constant work.

The novel ends with no final resolution, but with the first strike against American oil exploitation. Only the future, Munif implies, holds the answer to this conflict between opposing ways of life. The two remaining volumes of the trilogy will take readers closer to that future.

If there is a literary category for *Cities of Salt*, it would be "Arabic proletarian novel," and many of its features may be unfamiliar to Western readers. The novel certainly has an old-fashioned, nineteenth century narrative style that fits perfectly the story it is telling, but which may seem slow-moving to contemporary readers. (Almost the whole first chapter, for example, is given over to describing the wadi.) This leisurely pace is matched by the novel's point of view, which maintains a certain distance from the characters and lacks the psychological intensity or inner focus that modern novels often display. Yet it is this detached point of view—describing events from a vaguely Arabic perspective—that most effectively reveals the cultural clashes throughout the novel. For example, Munif describes how puzzled the inhabitants of the wadi are by the Americans' "morning prayers"—which turn out to be their athletic exercises. The Arabs also cannot figure out why these alien people are digging into the arid sand, and Munif allows readers to deduce on their own, over many pages, that the Americans are seeking oil.

Munif's narration (in Peter Theroux's strong and sensitive translation) portrays starkly the passing of the Bedouin way of life. Here is a sample passage, a description of the area surrounding the wadi:

> Al-Hadra and its surrounding areas a few days' ride in every direction had not changed since God created the earth. Since the life of the people was marked by extraordinary difficulty and harshness because of the lack of rain, the scarcity of caravans and the consequently high prices they paid for flour, sugar and cloth, they were used to it and never expected anything better. If the earth became too crowded, something had to give. It was usually death that solved the problem, in the form of raids and feuds, frequently the results of disputes over grazing and water, or as the result of diseases that struck men and animals. Death was the regulator that made them capable of living and enduring, and when the men got tired of death and were no longer able or willing to continue killing one another, or when caravans arrived, they felt the powerful lure of travel, unprepared as they were and having given it no previous thought. When they did leave, there was more room for the others, who kept on living.

There is something oblique about this style of narration that may be unfamiliar to American readers. Contemporary novels in English usually have a linear development: They move from point *a* to point *b* with a certain logical progression. Munif—like the Bedouin caravans that traverse his novel—takes a more circuitous route. The first quarter of *Cities of Salt*, for example, takes place in Wadi al-Uyoun; the action then moves to Harran, and Wadi is almost forgotten. Similarly, new characters are introduced late in the novel, and earlier characters are dropped almost completely. Short stories are told along the way, almost as eddies in a narrative stream, but their relation to the structure of the larger novel is at best indirect. Finally, dialogue in the novel reflects this circuitous quality: Characters rarely gain information from one another directly; rather, it is given by implication or parable.

There is another side to this use of language, however, and that is its wonderfully figurative quality. Characters talk to one another in riddles and metaphors: "The jackal is a lion in his own country," a Bedouin worker says when asked why he will not go to the United States for training. "Pull your thorns with your own hands," the emir responds to a request for assistance. "Beware of your enemy once, but of your friend beware a thousand times," Ibn Rashed warns regarding Dabbasi. This rich, delicate language confirms the novel's understated qualities.

At the center of *Cities of Salt* is the clash between two cultures: the modern, technological American and the primitive, Bedouin Arabic. The mysterious "black boxes" that the Americans are always turning on are tape recorders; the generators in Wadi frighten its inhabitants terribly; the emir falls in love with his telescope. The childish reaction to the first radio reveals the primitive background of these people: "How could this box speak and make music? Who was playing the instruments? Where did he sit? How could he eat and sleep, and how did that tiny space hold him?" Ironically, it is through this technological wonder (and thanks to the news from the British Broadcasting Corporation) that the people of Harran learn of the Americans' plans to turn their area into a gigantic oil center. Yet it is not only the technology that is different; beneath the surface there are deeper differences. Americans interview Bedouin workers and offend them with their questions about religion. They bring prostitutes to Harran and the people are horrified—and fascinated. (The Harrani baker falls in love with one of the women from a distance and ultimately loses his mind.) Americans drink "devil's piss" (alcohol), go on vacations when the summer gets too hot, and treat their workers as prisoners. In those rare passages when Munif gives the American perspective, it only confirms the gap: "These people are strange—they seem so mysterious," one American comments. "You never know whether they're sad or happy. Everything about them is wrapped up, layers upon layers, just like the desert under their feet!" "They're like animals," another answers, "jostling each other and moving around in this primitive way to express their happiness. Imagine!"

In some ways, this is a 1980's *Grapes of Wrath:* a 1930's novel about the clash between the haves and the have-nots. (The bulldozers leveling the wadi may remind readers of John Steinbeck's description of the same machinery pushing the Okies off their land.) Moreover, for English-speaking readers unfamiliar with it, the novel is an introduction to a contemporary Arabic literature of richness and subtlety. *Cities of Salt* speaks of a part of the world that American readers have ignored for too long, even though, as the novel makes clear, Americans have been part of Arabic history, and American and Arabic futures are of necessity intertwined.

David Peck

Sources for Further Study

Chicago Tribune. August 14, 1988, XIV, p. 5.
The Christian Science Monitor. September 2, 1988, p. B6.
Kirkus Reviews. LV, December 1, 1987, p. 1645.
Los Angeles Times Book Review. May 29, 1988, p. 3.
Publishers Weekly. CCXXXII, December 11, 1987, p. 58.

CITIZEN COHN

Author: Nicholas von Hoffman (1929-)
Publisher: Doubleday (New York). 483 pp. $19.95
Type of work: Biography
Time: 1927-1986
Locale: New York and Washington, D.C.

Roy Cohn was widely known as counsel to Senator Joseph R. McCarthy's infamous committee, but for most of his life, he was a highly successful New York attorney, much admired and much hated

Principal personages:

ROY MARCUS COHN, a successful New York attorney
AL COHN, his father, a politician and judge in the Bronx
DORA MARCUS COHN, his mother, with whom he lived until her death
SENATOR JOSEPH R. MCCARTHY, the leader of a highly publicized search for subversives in government during the early 1950's, Cohn's employer and defender
JOSEPH WELCH, the counsel for the army during the so-called Army-McCarthy hearings in 1954
ROBERT F. KENNEDY, an enemy and rival of Cohn, later attorney general
ROBERT MORGENTHAU, the attorney who indicted Cohn on charges of bribery and conspiracy
BARBARA WALTERS, a television newsperson who was a friend of Cohn
PETER FRASER, Cohn's longtime lover

Roy Cohn was internationally known during a period of eighteen months, during 1953-1954, when he served as chief counsel to the Government Operations Committee of the Senate, chaired by Senator Joseph R. McCarthy. McCarthy and Cohn made numerous charges about the presence of subversives and security risks in various government agencies, and Cohn and another young man, G. David Schine, made a highly publicized tour of United States Information Services libraries in Europe, announcing that they found in these libraries many works by authors they deemed subversive. When McCarthy's popularity dropped drastically as a result of the so-called Army-McCarthy hearings in the summer of 1954, Cohn resigned and returned to his career as an attorney in New York City.

Before and after his period of national notoriety, Cohn was a highly successful advocate for his clients, chiefly because of his skill in using the network of contacts in the New York political world which he had inherited from his father and developed in the course of his career. Those in his circle of friends and acquaintances stretched from such gangland figures as Carmine Galante and Fat Tony Salerno to J. Edgar Hoover, William F. Buckley, Jr., and New York's powerful Cardinal Spellman. It also included George Steinbrenner, Ronald and Nancy Reagan, Donald Trump, and such media figures as Rupert Murdoch, Sam and Si Newhouse of the Newhouse chain of newspapers, and Barbara Walters. Cohn made himself useful to many of these people, and some of them helped shield him from criminal charges brought against him at various times at the urging of Robert Kennedy and Robert

Morgenthau. From his early entrance into the legal world (he had to wait until his twenty-first birthday to pass the bar examination), he made use of his father's contacts and his own. Prior to his association with McCarthy, he had been an assistant United States attorney in New York, with precocious skill at drawing the attention of the news media. In that office, he had participated in the prosecution of accused spies Julius and Ethel Rosenberg. His public life was colorful and well publicized.

His private life, equally colorful but not much publicized, until it became known that he had died of Acquired Immune Deficiency Syndrome (AIDS), was kept separate from his public activities, at least as long as his mother was alive. Dora Marcus Cohn was evidently unhappy in her marriage to Al Cohn, a minor politician and judge in the Bronx County Democratic machine from the 1920's through the 1950's. She married late and, as a member of the once-powerful Marcus family, considered that Al Cohn was socially beneath her. She therefore devoted all of her attention to her only child; relatives report that for as long as she lived, she acted as if he needed the care and attention due to a small boy. During her lifetime, she shared Roy's living quarters and supervised his life. For as long as she lived, he was seen frequently in public in the company of women, and he took care to plant stories in gossip columns mentioning the possibility of his marrying. Once Dora Cohn was dead, he was more open about his homosexual relationships, although he continued to deny that he was homosexual. Stricken with AIDS, he claimed until the very end of his life that he was dying of liver cancer.

Cohn's public and private lives are described in detail in Nicholas von Hoffman's *Citizen Cohn*. It might seem improbable that a person known for his liberal views as a newspaperman and author would take the trouble to write a biography of Roy Cohn or that he would be evenhanded in doing so, but von Hoffman has done both. He was both fascinated and repelled by Cohn, a divided attitude which seems to have characterized many of those who knew the lawyer. Von Hoffman is clearly repelled by many of Cohn's actions but argues that Cohn's anti-Communism (unlike that of his mentor, McCarthy) was sincere and not simply a means of furthering a political career. He is also fascinated by the contradictions and mysteries of Cohn's life.

The person von Hoffman describes was complex and difficult: Skillful in representing his clients in negotiations, Roy Cohn failed to prepare for courtroom appearances, relying on his skills in argument to cover up his sometimes scant knowledge of the case in which he was involved. He knew judges and attorneys, but he seems not to have known or cared much about the law. He could be, and often was, charming, but he could also be careless and cruel in his dealings with others. He was generous with friends, but he was equally generous with himself; he spent money on such luxuries as yachts, townhouses, holidays, but he was careless with his possessions, allowing them to decay, and he never accounted for the money that flowed through his hands. He was never convicted of a criminal offense, but at the end of his life, he was disbarred for lying about a loan he had taken from a client that he swore had been part of a fee.

What is most impressive, in the picture von Hoffman draws, is the seemingly boundless energy that drove Cohn. He would work a long day, traveling to various parts of New York or to Washington, D.C., then spend long hours in nightclubs entertaining friends and clients while conducting business by telephone, and still have energy left for one or more of his lovers. The next day, he might be off for a vacation in some distant watering spot, but even there, he was constantly on the telephone to colleagues and highly placed officials. Until he contracted the disease that would kill him, he seemed never to tire.

One problem von Hoffman faced in researching and writing this biography was the reluctance of many of the people who knew Cohn to talk about him. Much of what von Hoffman reports about Cohn's childhood and family life is based on interviews with those still living, but there are unresolved contradictions in statements about Dora Cohn and her role in her son's life, and Al Cohn is a shadowy character in this book. With regard to Roy Cohn's private life, there was an understandable reluctance among some to discuss his sexual preferences and behavior, although von Hoffman is able to quote extensively from some of Cohn's closest associates. Many of the people who knew Cohn, perhaps believing that von Hoffman would attempt to do a hatchet job on Cohn, declined to talk to the author. Barbara Walters, for example, was not interviewed. In the face of these difficulties, von Hoffman has clearly tried to include statements defending Cohn as well as attacks by Cohn's enemies and tried to show his subject's virtues as well as his vices.

This evenhandedness, however, is not necessarily a virtue in *Citizen Cohn*. For one thing, it is clear from von Hoffman's point of view that Cohn was a man who did more harm than good. This fact can operate to make the attempted evenhandedness seem more a rhetorical strategy than an attempt to be fair: If the author is so careful to treat his subject fairly, it could be objected, how much worse must that subject's deeds have been? However impartial von Hoffman may have tried to be, his judgments cast doubt on his methods. Directly or implicitly, *Citizen Cohn* makes judgments such as the following: If Cohn's motives in his days with McCarthy were good, his persecution of those whose views he attacked was cruel and careless. If Cohn was successful in defending clients, he was careless in choosing those clients, and his success was a matter of shady deals and influential friends more than legal skill. Some clients, in fact, were badly served by his careless methods. He did favors for many people, including judges, and when the time came, he was able to exact favors in return; in his view, it was the way the system had always worked, and he could boast of his skill in using the system. To von Hoffman, Cohn was a hypocrite, a homosexual who publicly claimed to abhor sexual deviation, a victim of AIDS who used his powerful contacts to get treatment for himself but who declined to use those contacts or his place in the public eye to encourage government support for AIDS research; he was, according to von Hoffman, despised by many in the gay community.

Much about Cohn remains hidden, at least from von Hoffman. This is true of the lawyer's legal dealings. Many of the cases with which he was involved ended in unusual ways, but there is no substantial evidence that crooked deals had been worked out. Some reasons for the close relationship between Cohn, J. Edgar Hoover, and Francis Cardinal Spellman are clear—they all despised Communism—but von Hoffman hints at deeper reasons without being able to define them. The style in which Cohn lived suggests strongly that very large amounts of money went through his hands. It seems clear that many legal fees were paid directly to him, never passing through the books of his law firm, so that no credible account of his earnings can be made. He made sure that the building he lived and practiced in, his yacht, and his Rolls-Royces were owned by the firm, not by him. When he died, according to one source quoted by von Hoffman, the Internal Revenue Service believed that Cohn owed $7 million in back taxes.

The compulsion to be evenhanded is one problem in *Citizen Cohn*, and the problem of reliable sources is another. Perhaps the most serious one, however, is the fact that von Hoffman has been most effective in earlier books and articles when he has allowed his satirical wit free play, and he does not do so in this book. He seems to have believed that the horror of Cohn's death and the fascination he exerted while alive would have made humor and ridicule inappropriate and cruel; thus, there is a strong sense, in *Citizen Cohn*, that punches are being pulled. The odyssey of Cohn and Schine, searching for doubtful books in European libraries and incurring the scorn of the press and European government officials, is shown to have been ridiculous, and von Hoffman adds to it a little-known story about reporter Art Buchwald and a nonfunctioning wire recorder. For the most part, however, von Hoffman seems to have been figuratively biting his tongue, refraining from making his subject's actions the object of satiric wit. Opportunities for this are not lacking, including many which would not make Cohn the goat. There was, for example, the heavy-handedness of Senator John McClellan's questions, which seemed to hint at a homosexual relationship among Cohn, McCarthy, and Schine; von Hoffman makes little of this opportunity for satire, or of many others. It is as if he had decided that he could fend off accusations of unfairness to his subject by making his book solemn. Unfortunately, solemnity here leads to clumsiness in the writing, and the book is not helped by careless editing, which leaves intact errors and infelicities of various kinds.

Despite its imperfections, *Citizen Cohn* is an important book about a significant figure in recent history. Sidney Zion's "authorized" biography includes more information provided by Cohn himself, but von Hoffman's book has an important point of view. Von Hoffman has demonstrated convincingly the roots of Roy Cohn's attitudes toward people and power, and he has created an impressive portrait of a complex man. Cohn helped shape the world we live in, for better or for worse, and von Hoffman has helped to show how he was able to do this and some of the results of his actions.

John M. Muste

Sources for Further Study

ABA Journal. LXXIV, June 1, 1988, p. 112.
Booklist. LXXXIV, May 1, 1988, p. 1290.
Library Journal. CXIII, June 1, 1988, p. 108.
Los Angeles Times Book Review. April 10, 1988, p. 1.
The Nation. CCXLVI, May 21, 1988, p. 719.
National Review. XL, June 24, 1988, p. 44.
New York. XXI, April 18, 1988, p. 88.
The New York Times Book Review. XCIII, April 3, 1988, p. 1.
Newsweek. CXI, April 4, 1988, p. 68.
Publishers Weekly. CCXXXIII, April 1, 1988, p. 49.
Time. CXXXI, April 4, 1988, p. 82.
The Times Literary Supplement. June 24, 1988, p. 701.

A COHERENT SPLENDOR
The American Poetic Renaissance, 1910-1950

Author: Albert Gelpi (1931-   )
Publisher: Cambridge University Press (New York). 482 pp. $34.50
Type of work: Literary history and criticism

An extremely erudite examination of the most prominent American poets of the Modernist generation, combining thorough biographical and critical considerations with incisive commentary on many poems

One of the distinguishing strengths of great poetry is the singular voice of the individual poet. This daunting originality, however, often carries with it a sustaining conviction that only that poet's approach to his work represents a valid vision of artistic excellence. To be sure, the poet frequently needs reassurance that his strategies for production are successful, yet when this understandably self-protective stance is combined with a critic's instinctive tendency to establish patterns of consequence in any cultural era, a superficial depiction of literary history begins to develop in which differences are exaggerated and similarities are oversimplified.

In an exceptionally knowledgeable and wide-ranging study, Albert Gelpi has attempted to go beyond the limits of any previous grouping to include ten poets he regards as the creators of an "American poetic renaissance" in the years during and just after World War II, a time when the "great imaginative enterprise" (As Hugh Kenner describes Modernism) of the twentieth century was at its most energetic and vital. To include John Crowe Ransom and H. D. (Hilda Doolittle) in the same angle of vision requires a kind of confidence that stems from an acute understanding and familiarity with a vast body of material—cultural, political, philosophical, and historical as well as literary. Gelpi has the requisite background in the main currents of Western thought to be able to see unexpected patterns of connection and reflection among ideas and developments in various disciplines. It is clear, too, that in addition to the poetry of his subjects he has also read most of the comments which the poets themselves have made about their own work, and one of his basic techniques is to arrange a poet's words into an illustration of his or her intentions. This method casts Gelpi's theoretical propositions in the form of discoveries of extant patterns that were previously not quite clear rather than impositions of order upon a mass of chaotic data.

To justify his inclusion of these ten writers—all white, educated, and bourgeois but radically different in more significant categories of measurement—within his survey, Gelpi offers in his introduction a compact presentation of his view of modern poetry. Gelpi sees Modernism as a product of the "twinned generative strains" of Symbolism and Imagism, and presents as the goal of Modernist art "the imaginative fashioning of the unruly and resistant materials of experience through the expressive resources of the medium—paint, stone, language—into an autotelic work of coherent splendor." His basic proposition is that Modernism and Romanticism, two supposedly opposing ideologies, have a "subtler continuity" that is more interesting and deeper than their points of dissonance. Gelpi sees American poets—Ralph Waldo Emerson and Wallace Stevens, Walt Whitman and Ezra Pound—making what he calls "Janus-faces, Romantic and Modernist, looking in opposite directions." Then, however, in a pattern which operates throughout his work as the most fundamental aspect of his critical approach, he reverses directions, proclaiming that Modernists "longed for and adopted positions that are unmistakably, though sometimes covertly, Romantic."

The concept of contradiction operates as one of Gelpi's most basic aesthetic and philosophical instruments, and he uses it to define the Modernist stance and, by eventual extension, to define what he regards as the most crucial components of twentieth century American poetry. His title, *A Coherent Splendor*—taken from Pound's translation of a passage from Sophocles in which Heracles exults, "what SPLENDOUR,/ IT ALL COHERES"—embodies all the implications of ultimate contradiction: Pound knew that coherence would always be an unreachable goal for the artist in the modern world, but that he must act as if it were attainable. The splendor is in the act, something akin to the action of Albert Camus' Sisyphus, who also knew the futility of his efforts but continued them as the only way to create meaning. As Camus observes, "One must imagine Sisyphus happy." Similarly, for Gelpi, the Modernist poets were "happy" within the action of their poetry, a Romantic notion, while acknowledging that their artistic vision was unlikely to disclose a "happy" state of existence beyond the art itself, a notably paradoxical Modernist inclination.

The opening chapter, on the "pre-Modernist" Ransom and Robert Frost, exhibits many of the characteristics of Gelpi's general approach. Because Gelpi relies on a rigorous presentation of abstract ideas for much of his basic argument, he provides substantial biographical information as a humanizing balance, showing the relationships among the poets under discussion. Between Frost (the "woodsman") and Ransom (the "chevalier") there was not much direct contact, but they were aware of each other's work and generally respectful of it (in contrast to the much more ambivalent relationship between William Carlos Williams and Stevens, which Gelpi examines next). This preliminary material is followed by a close reading of poems that Gelpi considers to be among the poet's most representative. Gelpi is looking for the enduring in the work of writers overvalued by a blindly sentimental public and undervalued by hypercerebral post-Modernist critics, and his discussion is more restorative than revisionist, a consolidation of assumptions.

Gelpi stresses Ransom's ideas more than his poetry because of Ransom's meager output and also because he uses Ransom to relate the history of the New Critics. The concentration on ideas works much better in the chapter on Stevens, because Stevens' poetry is so much more interesting than Ransom's and because Steven's theories are at the heart of the controversy concerning the two elemental modes of Modernism, the imagination and the object. By introducing Williams here (in anticipation of the chapter on Williams) and by reading Stevens and Williams against each other, Gelpi is able to consider the "crucial debates of the Modernist aesthetic," including the origins of creativity, the function of the poet's personality, the relationship of Romantic ideas to Modernist thought, and the role of subjective psychological states. He appropriately recognizes language as a dominant factor in Stevens' poetics, observing that the problem of a particular poem is "resolved not at the level of argument but at the level of language" (citing "Sunday Morning") and that Stevens transferred "sensed objects into a fictive linguistic world" which he called the "*mundo* of the imagination." Connecting Stevens to the Symbolist poets (Arthur Rimbaud, Paul Verlaine, Stéphane Mallarmé) to account for the "essential gaudiness" that is an aspect of Stevens' rhetorical spell, Gelpi states that one of the conflicts of Modernist art, the oscillation between imagination and reality in the process of creation, is brought toward resolution in Stevens' poems through the use of metaphor. The concept of rhetorical devices is expanded to include metaphor as a manifestation of "the power of the mind over the possibilities of things." In keeping with his plan to conclude each chapter with a summary phrase, he calls Stevens a "sceptical Platonist," offering a variant on a word he had previously applied to Frost.

In the next three sections, the heart of the book, Gelpi's consistently intelligent and logical discussion reaches another dimension as his passionate appreciation for T. S. Eliot, Pound, and H. D. further energizes his writing. The importance of his subject has never been in question, but here an extra inspirational factor works to draw him closer to the poems, so that his own fervor matches the "high energy construct" (as Charles Olson phrased it) of the poetry. The deployment of irony by Ransom, Frost, and Stevens may have controlled Gelpi's position in discussing them, but while his later chapter headings continue to suggest contradiction and paradox, he has subtly shifted to the subjective side of the pole. In addition to the vivacity of his style, Gelpi unleashes a swarm of ideas that resonate beyond the ones he chooses for the coordinating points of his discussion. In regard to Eliot, especially, the density of insight proscribes summary, but the mixture of biographical information and poetic development underscores the emotional core of Eliot's work that pressed against the shaping forces of his mind.

In conjunction with the 1988 publication of Eliot's letters, Gelpi's argument that there is "no Beatrice" in his poetry seems particularly apt. An obsession with the feminine in terms of "neurotic misogynist fears" is the starting point for Eliot's poetry in Gelpi's view; this obsession leads to a dialectic between mind and body, between Prufrock and Sweeney, who Gelpi finds "impossibly twinned" so that the famous objective correlative is seen as "a desire to engage and a fear of engaging the feminine aspects of the self and the world." Tracing Eliot's apprehension of the sensual from his Calvinist conviction of original sin through his inclination toward the unified sensibility of the seventeenth century with its holistic religious sense of the cosmos, Gelpi shows how the multivoiced arrangement of *The Waste Land* (1922) evolves toward the projection of the poet's own voice in *Four Quartets* (1943). Through close readings of most of Eliot's major poems, as well as his verse drama, Gelpi clarifies references, establishes connections, highlights Eliot's skills as a craftsman of language, and moves toward an understanding of Eliot as a poet and critic who eventually arrived at a classical Christian position, discerning "the immanence of grace in flawed nature."

The section on Pound is equally impressive. Starting with key incidents and decisions in Pound's life, Gelpi then tackles the *Cantos*. For sixty-five pages, Gelpi moves through Pound's life-epic in an exceptionally lucid, meticulously organized, and uncommonly perceptive investigation of a poem that has generally intimidated readers with its esoteric references, encyclopedic learning, multilingual composition, and apparent lack of structure. Gelpi functions here like Dante's Vergil, providing guidance through a fascinating nether realm and removing the obstacles that have prevented a more widespread public reading of the poem. Mixing biographical material, personal recollections of Pound's acquaintances, and excerpts from Pound's extensive literary theorizing, Gelpi puts together a picture of the mind that made the poem, showing how Pound's obsessions emerged and were organized into the *Cantos*. Gelpi then recapitulates the progress of Pound's poetics, covering his pronouncements and experiments with Imagism, vorticism, and Futurism to show how Pound's techniques developed. He notes the various literary traditions that interested Pound—Emerson and Whitman in American literature, the Chinese ideogram, and troubador songs, among others—to clarify the historical influences. As the cantos themselves are discussed, with Pound's own uncertainties measured to account for areas of confusion, all Pound's methods are examined through a close reading of their actions and effects, with crucial references explained and passages not in English either translated or explained. Gelpi's handling of the first fifty cantos offers erudition with no self-consciousness, making the poem available by dispelling the arcane aura that has always loomed over it.

The second part of the discussion of the *Cantos* shows how Pound worked to reintegrate a shattered sense of the self after his periods of incarceration, first in Italy and then in St. Elizabeths Hospital in the United States. Here, Pound was forced to recognize his personal failures, reevaluate his actions, and tentatively begin to recover his mind so that he might try to write the promised "Paradiso" which was the goal of his life's work. Gelpi shows how Pound dealt with his realization of his own mistakes, and then how he struggled toward a much less arrogant and ultimately Romantic vision in the *Drafts and Fragments of Cantos CX-CXVII* (1969) that concludes the *Cantos*. Gelpi's view that Pound found paradise in nature, with the human mind able to perceive only the "inherent organic character of its process" recalls and supports his ongoing contention that Modernism and Romanticism are parts of a Janus-faced image. By illustrating the problems Pound faced trying to compensate for (if not atone for) his political and social barbarism, Gelpi enables even a reader who detests some of the things Pound did to see the loveliness of the last cantos, their evanescent, redemptive, modest beauty.

The section on H. D. is the most brilliantly original in the book. Known more by reputation and anecdote than for work, H. D. is presented from a psychobiographical perspective based on Gelpi's familiarity with Sigmund Freud, H. D.'s own contact with Freud, and a typically thorough and illuminating reading of H. D.'s poetry. In a brief discussion of Marianne Moore and Amy Lowell, the concept of the woman writer as a "double-bearing" artist (bearing children, bearing poems) is developed in terms of Adrienne Rich's distinction between the lesser "feminine" (illustrative or decorative) and the more significant "female" (constitutive of moral exploration) modes of expression. Gelpi then shows how autobiographical elements have been imaginatively transformed in H.D.'s work into a mythic vision of a continuously creative existence. Gelpi argues that the posthumous *Trilogy* (1973) ranks with *Four Quartets* and *The Pisan Cantos* (1948) as one of the major poems of World War II; furthermore, he concludes that *Helen in Egypt* (1961) is "the most ambitious and successful long poem by a woman in English." He suggests that the *Trilogy* is distinctive as a transformation of "a man's war epic into a woman's love lyric" and that the "final illuminations" of *Helen in Egypt* are akin to the ancient wisdom proclaimed in Frost's "Directive," Williams' "Sparrow," and Eliot's *Four Quartets*.

The last quarter of the book remains consistently interesting but not quite as exciting as the central part, since Gelpi's sense of exploring great art is diminished by his attitude toward his subjects. His consideration of Williams' long poem *Paterson* (1946-1958) is solid, as is his examination of that poet's attitude toward the central issues of Modernism, and his relationships with various painters and other poets. The special urgency of the sections on Pound, Eliot, and H. D. is largely absent, though, and this lack makes the chapter merely excellent rather than extraordinary. Similarly, the chapter on Allen Tate and Hart Crane is something of a digression, since Tate is important as a critic much more than as a poet, and Crane is as much a case unto himself as any of the poets the book mentions. Gelpi uses Crane's ties to Romanticism as an entry into his poetry and provides a powerful analysis of *The Bridge* (1930), Crane's major accomplishment. In the last part of the book, correctly designated a "coda," Gelpi reflects his thoughts on Modernism through a consideration of two poets, Ivor Winters and Robinson Jeffers, who saw themselves as aggressively anti-Modernist in approach. Gelpi may have been drawn to these men because of his own involvement with the psychic landscape of California, but his remarks on Winter's maverick vehemence and Jeffers' self-possessed aloofness operate as a "critique of the Modernist tradition" from a radical standpoint. Even though the last chapters are not quite as compelling as the central ones, they have enough solid material to make a book in themselves for a man of lesser ambition, and they are certainly connected to the primary concerns of Gelpi's study.

A Coherent Splendor is a book which no student or teacher of American literature would want to overlook. Its richness and insight make each of the separate sections valuable, able to stand alone as an introduction to the poet covered. As John Dryden said of Geoffrey Chaucer in his oft-quoted remark, "Here is God's plenty."

Leon Lewis

Sources for Further Study

American Literature. LX, December, 1988, p. 688.
Choice. XXVI, September, 1988, p. 113.
The Christian Century. CV, August 17, 1988, p. 745.

THE COLLECTED LETTERS OF JOSEPH CONRAD
Volume III, 1903-1907

Author: Joseph Conrad (1857-1924)
Edited, with an introduction, by Frederick R. Karl and Laurence Davies
Publisher: Cambridge University Press (New York). Illustrated. 532 pp. $49.50
Type of work: Letters
Time: 1903-1907
Locale: England; Capri, Italy; Montpellier, France; and Geneva, Switzerland

The third of eight projected volumes of the collected letters of a major British writer

Principal personages:
JOSEPH CONRAD, a Polish-born seaman-turned-writer
JESSIE CONRAD, his wife
BORYS CONRAD, his older son
JOHN CONRAD, his newborn son
H. G. WELLS, a novelist, his friend
JOHN GALSWORTHY, a novelist, his friend and benefactor
FORD MADOX FORD, a novelist with whom he collaborated
JAMES BRAND PINKER, his literary agent
EDWARD GARNETT, a writer and publisher's reader, who early in Conrad's career encouraged him in his work
ROBERT BONTINE CUNNINGHAME GRAHAM, a Socialist writer, his close, enduring friend
WILLIAM ROTHENSTEIN, a portrait painter, his friend
HENRY-DURAND DAVRAY, a translator into French of some of his works

Seaman and writer, public figure and family man, native of Poland and adopted son of England, Joseph Conrad, in a letter to a fellow émigré, aptly described himself as "homo duplex." As the third volume in his collected letters reveals, this complex dualism tormented his life while it enriched his writings. During this period, from 1903 to 1907, Conrad's letters show him struggling with the difficulties of considering himself always an outsider while coming to appreciate the advantages of his unique double angle of vision. These letters, always interesting but sometimes enigmatic, are made to shed much light on their author through the superb scholarship of the editors, Frederick R. Karl and Laurence Davies, who provide many helpful tools, including full and excellent annotation, a fine introduction, an alphabetical list and description of all Conrad's correspondents, and a chronology of these years of Conrad's life.

Conrad's acute awareness of his dual allegiance to Poland and England largely accounts for the odd defensiveness, even touchiness, which he exhibits in many of these letters. On the one hand, he attempts to answer the generally unvoiced accusation of disloyalty to his country of origin. In a letter to a fellow Polish émigré, he asserts, "During the course of all my travels round the world I never, in mind and heart, separated myself from my country"; he therefore urges, "I may surely be accepted there as a compatriot, in spite of my writing in English." In the same vein, he maintains, "Both at sea and on land my point of view is English, from which the conclusion should not be drawn that I have become an Englishman. That is not the case." On another occasion, he amplifies this point when he states: "I feel the laziness common to all Poles. I'd rather dream a novel than write it. . . . And then, English is still for me a foreign language whose handling demands a fearful effort." With the same self-consciousness of the outsider, he worries that in leveling any criticism against his adoptive country, he will be misunderstood: "I don't think my word will have any weight at all. I've been so cried up of late as a sort of freak, an amazing bloody foreigner writing in English . . . that anything I say will be discounted on that ground by the public."

Yet it is this very difference or foreignness which initially helped to establish Conrad's unique place among his literary contemporaries. As his friend Edward Garnett notes, "It is good for us English to have Mr. Conrad in our midst visualising for us aspects of life we are constitutionally unable to perceive." Nor was Conrad himself averse to capitalizing upon his foreignness or exotic background to promote his works. In fact, it was he who suggested to his agent, J. B. Pinker, that they package *The Mirror of the Sea* (1906), his reminiscences of his life as a seaman, together in a single volume with his writings on literature (which he proposed to call "The Mirror of Life"), because Conrad believed that the rarity of the combination would help to sell the volume.

Despite Conrad's touchiness on the subject, it was during this period that Conrad came to a sharpened sense of his distinctiveness as a writer, so that he describes *Nostromo* (1904) as "a very genuine Conrad." With this same cool awareness, he writes to Pinker, "One may read everybody and yet in the end want to read me. . . . For I don't resemble anybody. . . . There is nothing in me but a turn of mind which whether valuable or worthless can not be imitated."

As unusual a component in Conrad's work as his Polish origin is his twenty years' experience as a merchant seaman, which, as this volume of letters reveals, provided him not only with a vast quantity of material throughout his literary career but also with the attributes he valued in himself and in his characters. He states that he takes equal pride in having his friend Robert Bontine Cunninghame Graham dedicate his book to him as he took in "that long ago moment, in another existence" when he was praised by his commanding officer as a seaman for "sobriety and trustworthiness." Repeatedly he describes his circumstances as a writer by using metaphors of his previous career: "I will have to pump till the handle breaks or the ship goes down under me." Perhaps, too, it is Conrad's equal valuation of his experiences at sea with his work as a writer that accounts for his puzzling overestimation of the literary achievement of *The Mirror of the Sea*, a work that modern critics consider much slighter than his fiction of this period.

Perhaps the most interesting duality of Conrad's life appears in this volume in the twin personages of Conrad the public figure and Conrad the private man. Seldom does he fully let down his guard, even with fellow writers and intimate friends. Accordingly, the Conrad who appears in most of this correspondence is extremely polite, even courtly; punctilious to observe good form; tactful and generous with praise in response to the works of fellow writers; and extremely reticent in discussing his individual writings and his own artistic methods. This characteristic guardedness points up all the more strongly the occasional letter in which he drops his public mask—or what he calls "my polite 'letter writer' which expresses itself with great force & elegance"—to reveal the private self.

The accounts of the activities of the public man in these letters reveals this to be a productive, if troubled, period in Conrad's life. As a writer, he was—and knew himself to be—at the height of his powers. During this period, he wrote two of his major novels, *Nostromo* and *The Secret Agent* (1907), as well as a number of fine stories, including "The Brute," "The Duel," "The Informer," and "Il Conde." He began the short story "Razumov," which would evolve into the major novel *Under Western Eyes* (1910). He completed two fictional collaborations with Ford Madox Ford, *Romance* (1903) and *The Nature of a Crime* (1909). He assisted in translating a number of his works into French. He also wrote a number of important nonfiction pieces, including the autobiographical reminiscences *The Mirror of the Sea* and the essay "Autocracy and War." His brain was teeming with ideas, many of which never bore fruit, such as his ideas for a Mediterranean novel and for a further collaboration with Ford on a novel about an artist, and his plans to write popular plays (only a single one-act play was written and produced during this period). Other of these ideas were later transmuted into works much different from their original conceptions, such as the idea for a story about "a dynamite ship," which evolved into the novel *Chance* (1913).

As earlier in his life, Conrad was troubled during these years by a constant shortage of money and by bouts of serious illness. He suffered from dental problems, nervous crises, and many severe episodes of gout, during which he was bedridden. In addition, during this time, his wife suffered a fall in which she injured both her knees; despite various treatments and an operation, this accident left her partially crippled. In addition, their son Borys, always a delicate child, was beset by a succession of life-threatening ailments, including scarlet fever, pleurisy, rheumatism, whooping cough, and pneumonia. An additional responsibility entered Conrad's life with the birth of a second son, John. During this time, his money worries were partially alleviated by a grant of five hundred pounds from the government, in recognition of his achievements, a sum which enabled him to pay off his most pressing debts.

The responses of the private man to these occurrences in his life are most revealing. The letters show Conrad to have been a solicitous and tender husband and father, staying up at night to attend a gravely ill Borys while attempting to finish *The Secret Agent*; jocularly informing his friend John Galsworthy of his pleasure at the birth of John, whom he describes as "a quiet, unassuming extremely ugly but upon the whole a rather sympathetic young man"; complaining of Borys, "That boy is not a reader"; and sacrificing comforts to give Borys riding lessons to restore him to health.

The letters also show Conrad's fastidiousness about his work, even under extreme financial pressure: his meticulousness in revision, his fury at unauthorized editing, particularly at the shortening of his works, and his bristling at the suggestion that he is improvident with money or at the thought that others consider him irresponsible. For example, he takes as a personal insult the standard stipulation that the grant of five hundred pounds be administered in installments.

Upon occasion, Conrad doffs his ceremonial garment of wholehearted admiration in his role as unquestioning appreciator of the works of his fellow writers to reveal a shrewd and severe critic. He does so in considering a play by his ally and early publisher Garnett. Although Conrad attempts to couch his criticism in tactful terms, they reveal the play to be hopelessly muddled and psychologically obtuse. Garnett is wounded and huffy in reply, a response that no doubt reinforced Conrad's general reluctance to offer candid criticism to a fellow writer.

Perhaps the greatest disappointment in this volume of letters is in Conrad's silence about his own concerns and practices as a writer, especially during the writing of two of his most important works, *Nostromo* and *The Secret Agent*. Readers familiar with the previous two volumes of letters and with Conrad's peculiarly private and suspicious temperament already know that as an artist he was always loath to discuss the work in hand, except generally to disparage it. He articulates this revulsion in a letter of 1903: "I would just as soon think of laying bare . . . my method of home life—which, I trust is based on nothing less than the sincerity of domestic affections—as my method of work which is based on truth too, of not a very different order." Yet even these readers will be unprepared for Conrad's almost total silence on the subject of *Nostromo*, which took him almost a year to write. Although Conrad describes the finished book as "no mean feat" and notes, "I've never written anything with so much *action* in it," his final assessment is the enigmatic statement: "What the book is like I don't know. . . . It is something—but not *the* thing I tried for."

On the subject of *The Secret Agent* he is, although not expansive, considerably more enlightening. Declaring it "a work of some mark," Conrad describes it as "a sustained effort in ironical treatment of a melodramatic subject." He adds,

> I don't think that I've been satirizing the revolutionary world. All these people are not revolutionaries—they are shams. . . . By Jove! If I had the necessary talent I would like to go for the true anarchist—which is the millionaire. Then you would see the venom flow. But it's too big a job."

Less directly but just as revealingly, Conrad's letters of this period offer a fascinating glimpse into an aspect of his life in which the public man and the private man coalesce: in his responses to some of the critical issues of his day. In this vein, he protests Belgian exploitation in the Congo State, "where ruthless, systematic cruelty towards the blacks is the basis of administration," a concern that looks back to *The Heart of Darkness* (1899) and ahead to the exploitation of native labor in the silver mines of Costaguana in *Nostromo*. He rages at an incident in which the Russian navy's Baltic fleet opened fire on British fishing boats, supposedly mistaking these peaceful vessels for Japanese torpedo boats. Conrad's indignation at

Russian suspicion and reckless disregard for human life anticipates his scathing attack on Russia in *Under Western Eyes*. Most telling of all is Conrad's lengthy public outcry, published in the *Daily Mail*, against the British censor of plays, an official arbiter of public morality who in fact had prevented the staging of works by Henrik Ibsen, Maurice Maeterlinck, and George Bernard Shaw. Unlike some of his fellow writers such as Garnett, who were willing to compromise and accept some more enlightened official in this role, Conrad emphatically declared, "My conviction is that the Censor should *not be at all*": "His office flourishes in the shade, not in the rustic shade beloved of the violet, but in the muddled twilight of men's imperfect apprehension, where tyranny of every sort flourishes."

In protesting such tyranny, Conrad drew on his double heritage—on the England that in the past "had in her keeping the conscience of Europe," that would "take up cudgels for humanity, decency and justice," and on the Poland which got him "used to go to battle without illusions . . . to be knocked on the head only." This is the double inheritance of "homo duplex"—Conrad the man and Conrad the writer. Out of this double legacy comes the dual enterprise of all Conrad's works: to expose tyranny and to reveal truth.

Carola M. Kaplan

Sources for Further Study

The Economist. CCCVI, March 19, 1988, p. 96.
London Review of Books. X, September 15, 1988, p. 9.
The New York Times. July 26, 1988, p. C17.
The Times Literary Supplement. September 2, 1988, p. 954.

COLLECTED POEMS

Author: Louis Simpson (1923-   )
Publisher: Paragon House (New York). 385 pp. $24.95
Type of work: Poetry

Louis Simpson, winner of the 1964 Pulitzer Prize in Poetry, here offers generous selections from the ten books he published between 1949 and 1983

At the head of this wonderful book's table of contents, Louis Simpson tells the reader, "These are not all my poems—they are the poems I would like to be remembered by." Fortunately, however, Simpson has been more generous here in selecting from his early work than he was in his previous retrospective collections, *Selected Poems* (1965) and *People Live Here: Selected Poems 1949-1983* (1983). *Collected Poems* contains 179 poems that not only provide ample evidence of the poet's changing concerns and ways of doing things but also give more pleasure, poem by poem, than do most lifetime collections. Even a reader who has read Simpson steadily and admiringly for years may be surprised at the swiftness with which any sense of duty—that vague feeling, compounded of obligation and self-conscious virtue, which often accompanies the approach to a large book of poems—simply evaporates.

In addition to the two selected volumes, Simpson published eight books of poems before the present collection. According to certain milestones of a poetic career, they fall into two groups of four. Simpson was born in Jamaica, in the British West Indies, and came to the United States when he was seventeen. He did not become an American citizen until he had been through several major engagements as an American soldier during World War II. The discovery of America, then, is a theme which recurs frequently in Simpson's poetry; the treatments of that theme become increasingly complex and rewarding as the poet himself becomes more thoroughly American.

Simpson's first three books displayed an ease with the more or less traditional forms which characterized one strain of American poetry in the 1950's and 1960's; in his fourth, *At the End of the Open Road* (1963), there is a relatively sudden shift to poems in more relaxed and open forms. For various reasons, most of them private, a number of other poets of roughly the same generation—James Wright, W. S. Merwin, Galway Kinnell, and Adrienne Rich, for example—were making similar shifts at about the same time. The various cultural forces that contributed to this phenomenon need not be considered here, especially since the work of each of these poets provides, in itself, specific reasons for that poet's having sought a new way of working and specific instances of formal continuity.

According to the preface of this collection, Simpson's first book, *The Arrivistes* (1949), was published in Paris at his own expense. It contains poems about the landscape of Jamaica, about the oddity and emptiness that can characterize life in New York, and about episodes recalled from the war. These are all matters which have often engaged the poet since; even some relatively minor images have a noticeable persistence in his work. In *The Arrivistes*, for example, there is this stanza, from "Lazarus Convalescent":

> The water laps, the seagulls plunge and squawk
> And lovers lock in wind that makes him shiver.
> "I'll have to learn to use a knife and fork
> Again. Look there above us!
> Spry's for Baking . . . starry spectacle.
> For Frying. More, a miracle."

In *The Best Hour of the Night* (1983), the most recent of the individual collections, the blinking advertisement for Spry turns up again, in "Periodontics." This is a four-page poem in which the speaker's thoughts make apparently casual leaps of association, which the poet has been careful to link with consummate subtlety. Trying to ignore the pain of having his teeth cleaned, the speaker studies the initials on the dental unit; they are also those of Paula Chapman, a high school sweetheart who lived across the street from the Spry sign. A recollection of their humiliating night at the prom ends with the speaker "drinking quantities/ of pink lemonade out of paper cups." On the next page, back in the present and the dentist's chair, he accepts from the hygienist "a paper cup/ with the liquid that's bright red/ and bitter." The poem ends with an account of a brief and unsatisfactory reunion between Paula and the speaker; after twenty years,

> The magic, as they say, was gone,
> like a song that used to be on the hit parade.
>
> But there is always a new song,
> and some things never change.
> Not long ago, visiting a friend
> who lives on Riverside Drive
> I saw that the sign for Spry
> is still there, shining away.
>
> "Spry for Baking." It blinks off
> and on again . . . "For Frying."
> Then the lights run around in a circle.

The absence of regular rhyme and meter in Simpson's later work is certainly noticeable, but it is not total. Throughout *The Best Hour of the Night* there are brief passages, like the third and fourth lines above, in which something like common measure makes a fleeting but effective appearance. In conversation once, Simpson appeared surprised and doubtful that this is so; one reason for his surprise may be that in his early work the meter of the ballad is often an occasion for slightly archaic or literary diction, which almost never appears in his later poems.

One of Simpson's most famous poems in the ballad rhythm is also among his earliest. "Carentan O Carentan" is a bitter recollection of the young soldier's introduction to battle; the form lends a haunting wistfulness to the gruesome narrative details:

> There is a whistling in the leaves
> And it is not the wind,
> The twigs are falling from the knives
> That cut men to the ground.

The war, the poetry of young love, and the mastery of strict form run like a current from *The Arrivistes* through *Good News of Death and Other Poems* (1955) and *A Dream of Governors* (1959). In his third book, Simpson handles these elements with an authority that seems to lift the best of his poems out of time, as in "To the Western World," a poem of fifteen lines which recapitulates the discovery of America by European explorers and, later, by immigrants. The third stanza memorably characterizes an age and a way of life:

> The treasures of Cathay were never found.
> In this America, this wilderness
> Where the axe echoes with a lonely sound,
> The generations labor to possess
> And grave by grave we civilize the ground.

In *At the End of the Open Road*, for which Simpson was awarded the Pulitzer Prize, there are few examples of this mode. "My Father in the Night Commanding No" and "The Riders Held Back" are both fine poems in four-line rhymed stanzas, though in the context of the whole collection they at first seem a bit overdressed. Yet their presence gives the reader a chance to hear both the early voice and the new voice in one volume, thereby demonstrating the strength with which Simpson handles a more open style and form.

Five of the poems Simpson has collected from *At the End of the Open Road* refer to Walt Whitman, or address him directly. Whitman's assertions—about poetry, people, and America—are tested in poems which acknowledge their indebtedness to him without echoing his voice. In "Lines Written near San Francisco," Simpson presents a landscape that seems to have skipped some of the history behind other civilizations. This country seems to have gone from the promise of wilderness directly into late decline:

> While we were waiting for the land
> They'd finished it—with gas drums
> On the hilltops, cheap housing in the valleys
>
> Where lives are mean and wretched.
> . . . .
> Whitman was wrong about the People,
> But right about himself. The land is within.
> At the end of the open road we come to ourselves.

Whitman reminded his readers that writing poetry was not always a matter of keeping a sharp eye out for the extraneous and then excising it; he demonstrated, and preached, that poems could be inclusive in difficult, ill-mannered ways. From this notion Simpson fashioned a six-line poem which has perhaps been more often quoted than any other poem in *At the End of the Open Road*. "American Poetry" must be able to digest all kinds of things, and "it must swim for miles through the desert/ Uttering cries that are almost human."

For Simpson, the suburbs seemed at that time a useful analogy to the desert. "In the Suburbs," another well-known six-line poem, seems hopeless enough:

> There's no way out.
> You were born to waste your life.
> You were born to this middleclass life
>
> As others before you
> Were born to walk in procession
> To the temple, singing.

The preface to *Collected Poems* ends with a few words about making poems in an unpoetic age:

> In recent years I have written about occurrences, sometimes very ordinary ones, in which there is a meaning hidden beneath the surface. Bringing out such meanings, it seems to me, is a road poetry can take in a world that, as it grows more industrial, seems less beautiful in the old sense. The more banal and "anti-poetic" the material, the more there is for the poet to do. For this work a sense of humor is as necessary as an awareness of the drama, the terror and beauty of life.

Simpson has always made occasional use of an odd, surrealistic humor; it is not absent from *At the End of the Open Road*, the most baleful of his collections, but he is right to note that it becomes more useful in the four books which followed his prize-winner.

Two of the themes that most often recur in Simpson's later work are the triviality and despair of much suburban life and the mystery of a lost, imagined past. Simpson's mother, he explains in the preface, was born in Russia and told him stories of that land. These Simpson has remembered and has used to shape an imaginary Russia, populated with his relatives and with characters created by such writers as Leo Tolstoy and Anton Chekhov. Most of the poems about Russia appear in *Adventures of the Letter I* (1971), though there are a few in both *Searching for the Ox* (1976) and *Caviare at the Funeral* (1980). In these, anecdote and character, the need for a story, seem central—so much so, in fact, that the "actual" and "fictional" characters are equally alive, just as Huckleberry Finn and Abraham Lincoln are equally "real" in most American imaginations.

The poems about suburbia range from the despairing through the wickedly satirical to the hopeful. Simpson includes himself, or a character who must be seen as standing in for him, in many of these poems. "Sacred Objects," from *Adventures of the Letter I*, begins with a mildly zany self-deprecation:

> I am taking part in a great experiment—
> whether writers can live peacefully in the suburbs
> and not be bored to death.
>
> As Whitman said, an American muse
> installed amid the kitchen ware.

This passage makes it hard to take seriously the notion of the "great experiment," but in fact a large number of Simpson's later poems represent its amazingly successful results. Mundane activities such as putting out the garbage, paying bills, riding the commuter train, and stripping paint from woodwork would seem to put a poet in danger of stultifying repetitiveness, but the equipment which Simpson has been selecting and honing for more than forty years continues to stand him in good stead. These poems are astonishing not only for the daring banality of their surfaces but even more for the range of their tones and the depth of their emotional resonances.

On the one hand, there is the sharp satire of "The Unwritten Poem," which characterizes "a life beginning with 'Hi!' and ending with 'So long!'" On the other, there is the extraordinary complexity of "The Previous Tenant," a fourteen-page poem presenting more people and events than are described in many novels. It winds confidently among various attitudes, from regret through affection to contempt, toward characters at least one of whom seems roughly equivalent to the author. Writing, and the reactions of one's neighbors to one's being a writer, come in for a fair drubbing in a few of these poems, though the effect is never to suggest that the writer should do anything but what he does. Simpson sometimes seems to wonder how he can go on, but the work itself provides all the necessary answers to that question.

Henry Taylor

Sources for Further Study

Library Journal. CXIII, December, 1988, p. 116.

The New York Times Book Review. XCIII, November 13, 1988, p. 32.

THE COLLECTED POEMS 1931-1987

Author: Czesław Miłosz (1911-   )
Translated from the Polish by various hands
Publisher: Ecco Press (New York). 511 pp. $30.00
Type of work: Poetry

This selection of poems written over more than a half century attests the extraordinary aesthetic and moral power of Miłosz's poetry and his preeminence among twentieth century poets

Were there still any doubt concerning the preeminence among poets of Czesław Miłosz, winner of the 1980 Nobel Prize in Literature and the man many have called Poland's greatest living writer, *The Collected Poems: 1931-1987* will surely put that doubt to rest. Slightly more than five hundred pages long (yet still not "complete"), this volume bears witness to its author's power, compassion, and moral commitment. The poems appear nakedly, as it were, accompanied only by a short preface, a handful of notes, and an index. In the preface, Miłosz points out that the collection was not his idea but that of Daniel Halpern, director of Ecco Press, and that the poems are neither solely nor uniquely his. Rather, as translations, they are the result of a cooperative effort, a vast collaboration. (His assertions here are typical of Miłosz's style: blunt, open assaults on the reader's complacency.) "The existence of this body of poetry in a language different from the one in which it was written," Miłosz notes, "is for me the occasion of constant wonder." That Miłosz is fluent in English and has in fact translated a number of his own poems and helped in the translation of others seems to accentuate the subtle relationship that exists between the poems in Polish and the translations in English. It is a relationship involving simultaneous reflection and distortion, so that the translation both does and does not say what the Polish original sought to say. The original work exists (in this edition, which is not bilingual) as an idea only—which is to say that it both declares its presence and disappears.

Not surprisingly, exile plays an important part in the works of a man who has himself lived in exile since 1950 but who continues to write in Polish, out of necessity as much as out of longing. "I muse on the meaning of being this not that," he writes. Divided from home and self by virtue of time, place, and language, he articulates in the most compelling manner possible the theme of so much twentieth century writing: that "so much disinheritance is our portion." (As the preface makes clear, these translations form part of that disinheritance; they exist as an act of dispossession, or, more optimistically, by an act of communal sharing and responsibility.) The exile inevitably becomes the wanderer, the voyager, the explorer. Born in rural Lithuania, Miłosz is Adam expelled from Eden, eternally in search of the home he has lost. His exile—his having chosen not to live under a totalitarian government in postwar Poland—is at once crushing and Catholic. It brings him both freedom and

A shame of failing to be
what I should have been.

The image of myself
grows gigantic on the wall
and against it
my miserable shadow.

In the relative Eden of California Miłosz finds less than he has hoped and searched for. The loveliness of the landscape and the year-long temperateness of the climate lull him into a nearly timeless state, where even death no longer seems to matter. Berkeley makes him physically comfortable yet morally uneasy. There he cannot believe in the power of poetry to effect change (or at least a change in the poet's and the reader's awareness), and this may be the reason he longs "to find my home in one sentence." His wandering is not, therefore, merely geographical and political; it is linguistic as well. His home is alternately Lithuania or Poland or California or the word to which he ultimately turns in triumph and despair. What saves him from that despair (and from that triumph too) is his belief in some truth, or some homeland, that lies beyond his power and his poetry: a world beyond the word and, alternately, a word beyond the comprehensible, sensuous world. His is a faith challenged at every turn by skepticism and self-doubt, which in turn combine with a typically Polish faith in the poet as national hero and savior, as in his "Confession":

Faithful mother tongue,
I have been serving you.

. . . .

You were my native land; I lacked any other.

. . . .

Now, I confess my doubt.
There are moments when it seems to me I have squandered my life.
For you are a tongue of the debased,

. . . .

But without you, who am I?

. . . .

perhaps after all it's I who must try to save you.

If the religious background of Miłosz's poetry ought not to be overlooked, neither should its historical context. History, particularly of Poland in the twentieth century, pervades Miłosz's writings in a variety of ways: as that to which Miłosz bears witness, refusing the balm of moral amnesia; as a dehumanizing force to be overcome by the assertive individuality and counter-voice of the poet; as the violence of the modern age ("breasts pierced by shrapnel"); and, finally, as the poet's own alter ego. Since Miłosz, born in 1911, and his century are nearly coeval, its history is in a sense his (and vice versa); each is incomplete without the other. What then should one make of Miłosz's decision not to play a part in postwar Poland? As he has explained in *The Captive Mind* (1953), he came to oppose communism for two reasons: He objected to its faith in history (and historical inevitability) and, corollary to this, to its annihilation of the individual, both in theory and in practice. "The true enemy of man," Miłosz writes some thirty years later, "is generalization," including and especially "so-called History . . . with its plural number." Insisting upon his own individual existence, he stands forth as survivor, as witness, and as poet. As survivor he feels as much guilt as gratitude, however, and as witness he evidences a similar ambivalence. He writes of the dead, of those whom History has destroyed, in order to save them from oblivion, which is to say from the forgetfulness which the majority of survivors seem to prefer; however, he realizes that he can save them only in words and that he offers these words to those "whom I could not save" at least in part in order to free himself from their ghostly hold on him. Yet to accomplish such an escape would put him on the side of the very forgetfulness that his poems resist so successfully.

Against History Miłosz arrays the only weapons at his disposal: compassion, poetry, memory, and the present moment. The four are by no means separable. Miłosz defines compassion, for example, as "that ache of imagination," and the present moment has meaning for Miłosz precisely because of the poet's ability to change it into memory. "The poet remembers"; he is the recording as well as the avenging angel.

> To know and not to speak.
> In that way one forgets.
> What is pronounced strengthens itself.
> What is not pronounced tends to nonexistence.

The task here is a usual one for the Polish poet, for throughout its history Poland has often existed solely in the works of its artists, writers, and composers. (This is not to say that Miłosz is not critical of a nation that "will remain what it is, the backyard of empires/ Nursing its humiliation with provincial daydreams.") Miłosz's attitude toward the past is, therefore, divided. On the one hand, he claims, "others . . . sustain me/ Anytime I think of them," and on the other he refuses to become a "ritual mourner." Unwilling to live without joy, he cannot live in Poland, where the dead cry out to have their stories told. Unwilling to live without the sustaining power of memory, he cannot live, which is to say write, except as a Pole and in his "faithful mother tongue."

Against his tenacious belief in the power of memory to offset History's annihilation of the individual, Miłosz posits the sensuous and redemptive power of the present moment. Against "so much death," he holds out life's small joys and pleasures. He invests the world, which exists in the eternity of the ever-renewing present moment, with a decidedly religious significance: "The holy word: Is." The moment contains all that is true and eternal and all that has been lost. Yet here too one detects paradox. In order to be made eternal, the moment must be recovered through an act of remembrance. Moreover, the beauty of the world can prove too great; it may overwhelm the individual or, worse, make him forget. "In splendor the earth's poor moment renews itself," but then "Memory closes down its dark waters./ And those, as if behind a glass, stare out, silent." They remain silent until Miłosz gives them voice—gives them his voice: angry and insistent, unforgiving and unforgetting.

The Collected Poems attests the doubleness of Miłosz's vision. "For me . . . everything has a double existence./ Both in time and when time shall be no more." The eternal exile, separated from home and from self, displays a special fondness for oxymoron ("alert repose") and paradox ("Life was given but unattainable"). Although he uses the "simple speech" of his poems to counter the official lies of History, his simplicity proves deceptively complex. He speaks in a variety of voices and adopts an even wider variety of poetic and extrapoetic forms, often combining two or more in a single poem: lyrics, narratives, monologues, dialogues, satires, chronicles, dreams, descriptions, albums, notes, and notebooks. In the "From the Rising Sun" sequence, for example, he mixes poetry and prose, fact and imagination, past and present, Lithuania and California to create a geography and chronology of the imagination in which present moment and eternal memory come to coexist. As for his poetic voice, no matter how personal a poem may be, Miłosz for the most part avoids lyricism in favor of contemplation and assertion. Irony and self-deprecation, however, keep the tendency toward the didactic firmly in check. Most interesting of all, his poems imply the existence of an audience; apparently, Miłosz's need to be heard, to be witnessed, is as great as his need to be the witness for his age.

Perhaps the poems betray a certain doubt in this regard only because they assume an even greater faith in the existence of an enduring world of moral values. What endures exists beyond comprehension and therefore beyond poetry as well. Whether what endures is an absolute (such as God) or "transient, fleeting forms," Miłosz cannot say, and it is this inability which comes to haunt many of the later poems fully as much as the ghosts of the dead haunt many of the earlier ones. These later works evidence Miłosz's growing sense of his own incompletion, insignificance, and inadequacy: ". . . the moment between birth and disappearance/ Is too much, I know, for the meager word." Even as the self-criticism and self-deprecation grow, however, so does the opposing voice of reconciliation. If he has failed to sustain his power and vision and if he has not been the prophet he had hoped to be, still he may find forgiveness, for he has learned to accept "what was left for smaller men like me:/ A feast of brief hopes, a rally of the proud,/ A tournament of hunchbacks, literature." Caught between joy and lamentation, gratitude and guilt, accusation and affirmation, he acknowledges this simple, painful fact: "Life's sweet, but it might be pleasant not to have to look." *The Collected Poems* attests the power of the art and vision of a man who has been condemned not only to see but also to speak.

Robert A. Morace

Sources for Further Study

The New York Review of Books. XXXV, June 2, 1988, p. 21.
The New York Times Book Review. XCIII, June 19, 1988, p. 6.
Publishers Weekly. CCXXXIII, February 26, 1988, p. 187.

THE COLLECTED POEMS OF WILLIAM CARLOS WILLIAMS
Volume II: 1939-1962

Author: William Carlos Williams (1883-1963)
Edited, with a preface, by Christopher MacGowan
Publisher: New Directions (New York). 553 pp. $37.00
Type of work: Poetry

The mature work of a master of American English which demonstrates in poem after poem that William Carlos Williams belongs among Robert Frost, T. S. Eliot, and Wallace Stevens as a great poet of the modernist era

The 1938 catalog for the New Directions Publishing Company, a fledgling operation launched by James Laughlin, announced the forthcoming publication of *The Complete Collected Poems of William Carlos Williams*. It is fitting that fifty years later, Laughlin—now recognized as a visionary pioneer in American publishing—has presented the second volume of the collected poems of a man who has been gradually acknowledged as one of America's greatest poets during the years New Directions issued his work. As recently as 1950, the revised edition of an 843-page anthology called *A Little Treasury of Modern Poetry, English and American* carried ten poems by its editor, Oscar Williams, and only two by William Carlos Williams, while *Time* identified him as "a New Jersey pediatrician who versifies between cases." This sort of ignorance was offset by acute observations by fellow poets such as David Ignatow, who spoke for many others when he said, "Without him, American poetry was impoverished for me." By 1983, Paul Mariani could claim in a critical biography that he was "the single most important American poet of the twentieth century." While Mariani's opinion is hardly a majority view, it suggests the importance of the second volume of what New Directions describes as "a complete and authoritative record of the development and achievement of one of America's major poets." This edition includes not only those poems published in other collections but also many uncollected poems, arranged chronologically, which had been previously available only in the magazines where they originally appeared. This is a book designed for a wide audience.

Readers who wish to learn about the life of an author understandably recoil from scholarly studies in which poems are surrounded with arcane references, minutiae, and jargon. Christopher MacGowan, who coedited the first volume of Williams' poems (which included his writing prior to 1939), has avoided the forbidding qualities of academic journals in this collection. This second volume includes all the work Williams did until he stopped writing in 1962, the year before his death, with the exception of the *Paterson* sequence, which will make up a third book. MacGowan's intention (and surely Laughlin's as well) has been to gather and organize a great mass of relevant material so as to present not only the poems but also a lucid, detailed account of a poetic life.

MacGowan's approach is clearly expressed in the preface and in the first appendix, in which he addresses the reader to explain the decisions he has made. The tone he chooses establishes a feeling of cordiality, so that an invitation is extended rather than a lecture threatened. As MacGowan explains how he determined the location within Williams' work of a poem first published many years after it was written, the logic of his argument is sufficient to satisfy the scholar's demand for precision as well as the amateur's concern for clarity. The authority that MacGowan earns enables him to offer interpretive comments about the circumstances of a particular poem's origins when speculation is required. His explanations of references within the poems that are not immediately apparent are directive and economical. By the time MacGowan explains the principle behind editorial adjustments ("I have corrected a number of verbal, spacing and lineation errors"), he has already satisfied questions about his capability in this crucial task by his discussion of less important decisions. The overall effect of his explanations is to suggest that he has the sensitivity to the poetry required for an accurate interpretation of Williams' wishes in matters of editing, as well as the degree of accuracy demanded to organize material from many sources. When he uses the language of the technician—for example, "the printers included a square bracketed catchword at the bottom of the page keyed"— he further supports the impression that he is at home with every aspect of his material.

Backing up all of his decisions is the thoroughness and care that is the foundation of all solid scholarship. MacGowan demonstrates his mastery of the details of Williams' publishing history in many instances, such as his comment that one of Williams' editors failed to send him page proofs of *The Desert Music and Other Poems* (1954), and although Williams prepared "a page full of changes and corrections to be incorporated into subsequent prints," errors continued until the present edition. This kind of information substantiates MacGowan's actions, while at the same time indicating how flaws occur in the publishing process even when well-intentioned professionals are involved. In another instance, MacGowan relates how Williams, after suffering a series of strokes, threw a set of galleys into the garbage in frustration at his physical limitations. In addition to accounting for further editorial problems, MacGowan's anecdote connects the poet's physical being directly to the process of creation, leading to a discussion of his decisions concerning the line breaks in those poems in which Williams composed three-step lines both as a form of organization and as a means of handling diminished dexterity.

The basic principle upon which MacGowan operates, to "confirm authorial sanction for all changes" between editions, and then to "accept all changes in *Collected Later Poems* that appear consistent with Williams' practice, is especially important in terms of Williams' use of the triadic or three-step line in *The Desert Music and Other Poems*. In relation to the poem "Some Simple Measures in the American Idiom and the Variable Foot," Williams discussed his desire to develop a rhythmic measure that would accurately correspond to what he considered the unique pulse and flow of American speech and thought. Even those critics who regard Williams' "variable foot" as an ambiguous concept recognize the integrity of the arrangements he made. When design constraints led to revisions in Williams' original manuscripts, the weight of emphasis was altered so as to undermine the rhythms he was developing. MacGowan mentions that in his deliberations concerning the form of poems with triadic lines, he consulted many Williams scholars. He found that some favored printing all run-over lines as extensions of the line above, some considered that individual decisions must govern each instance, while some held that these lines were deliberate variations on the three-step motif. MacGowan's decision offered as suggestive, not definitive, was to "leave the additional lines exactly as they appeared." His argument is that any choice would be interpretive. Once again, the weight of his discussion supports his authority. On the other hand, with characteristic reasonableness, he leaves open the possibility of another reader's making an equally appropriate decision based on careful consideration of the evidence. In this way, MacGowan's text is a close approximation of Williams' wishes, but open in areas of dispute. This seems to be in the spirit of Williams' own devotion to craft combined with a reluctance to force opinions on others, even when he was relatively sure of his position. In all matters of editorial judgment, MacGowan seems to have drawn his own sensibility into close approximation of Williams' mind and instincts.

The notes that follow MacGowan's explanation continue the merger of the poems into the life of the poet. The operating principle here is that the more one knows about the circumstances of composition, the more one will be able to respond to the full range of the poet's work. This approach involves not a substitution of biography for a careful reading of the poems but an exchange of data. Since there have been some solid critical examinations of the poems, MacGowan rarely offers interpretation or analysis, instead providing complementary annotation that makes analysis easier. In many cases, the note might simply clarify or explain an obscure allusion—the traditional function of the footnote—but in some cases the notes include selections from Williams' prose notes "that provide a sense of Williams' thinking" or from letters that accompanied a poem submitted to a magazine (revealingly followed frequently by MacGowan's observation that "the poem was not accepted"). In a series of translations from Iwan Goll's autobiographical sequence *La Chanson de Jean sans Terre* (1936), extensive explanatory notes concern the people involved in the work and also indicate how Williams became interested. Other notes include Williams' reflections on the origins of a poem or letters to Laughlin concerning the proper dedication of a book. Interspersed amid all this material are occasional observations from Williams not necessarily directly linked to a particular poem but reflective of his attitudes at that time in his life. These quotations add further flavor to what is actually an implicit autobiographical portrait that grows through the notes. Williams' comment on a *Books Abroad* poll in 1939, to determine the "most distinguished book or group of books" by a living author, that Ezra Pound's work would place him far ahead "until his recent imbecilities," his evaluation of French Surrealist poets ("a crappy and ignorant crew of something out of a dog's stomach") and his letter of praise to Kenneth Burke ("I particularly liked your manner of explanation when you lowered your voice and spoke quietly of the elementals that interest us both") contribute to the portrait of the artist as poet. While MacGowan generally remains out of the picture, his shaping influence is apparent when he gently corrects the poet. For example, MacGowan notes that in the original picture *The Kermess* by Pieter Bruegel the Elder that inspired the poem "The Dance," the bagpiper "has no 'bugle and fiddle' to accompany him," and he comments that the manuscript of "The End of the Rope" was nibbled by a mouse, "devouring the 'Williams' of WCW's signature, and possibly the final word of the poem (soon?). I have printed the poem from the nibbled manuscript."

All the apparatus that MacGowan has compiled and arranged works toward the goal of the first volume, "the aim of presenting Williams' development and achievement in as clear a way as possible." As is the case with all collections, the intent is to see a life's work whole and to try to help the reader see its patterns of organization and its richness. In this volume, the full ripening of Williams' talents is focused in what Cid Corman calls the "poetry of a man defending himself against the encroachment of death." The poetry of love—love for the things of the world, love for the endless variety of life, love for his wife—has a darkened poignancy, growing out of the later years of a life Mariani calls one of "complex tragedy and brilliance." Well-known poems such as the extraordinary "Of Asphodel, That Greeny Flower"—which Robert Lowell praises as delivering "to us what was impossible, something that was poetry and beyond poetry"—and the ten poems based on Bruegel's paintings are as impressive as they were at the time of their publication. If anything, the changes in perception concerning the nature of poetry itself wrought over decades by the effect of Williams' work makes them seem even more outstanding.

"The Province" demonstrates Williams' clarity of vision in seeing the world, "The Gentle Rejoinder" his calmness and lucidity in shifting nuances of mood, "The Lesson" his genius with words as he describes the metaphysics of the mind's process of perception. Throughout *Journey to Love* (first published in 1955), Williams explores the sorrows of love redeemed through the beauty of expression, proving that the consolation of language is possible when that language is sufficiently inventive and incisive.

Although Williams is known as a poet of modern America, his sensitivity to the weight of tradition is reflected in the lyrical imagery of his translation of Rene Char's "To Friend-Tree of Counted Days" and in his version of a medieval chanson, "Bird Song." The poems in which Williams explores the ordinary aspects of American life are almost startlingly fresh because of the often-copied but still singular style he developed and because of his immersion in the energy flow of American thought and expression. The foundation for his use of the American language, however, was his command of the ancient, time-honed craft of poetry developed through centuries of British writing. The continuing life of poetry in the English language is a part of Williams' achievement, as is his indispensable contribution to the nascent American language. All of that is apparent in this volume, along with the sharp eye, great heart, tough mind, and true ear of a good man and a great poet.

Leon Lewis

Sources for Further Study

Booklist. LXXXIV, July, 1988, p. 1778.
Chicago Tribune. August 28, 1988, XIV, p. 6.
Library Journal. CXIII, July, 1988, p. 83.
The New Criterion. VII, September, 1988, p. 14.

THE COLLECTED POETRY OF ROBINSON JEFFERS
Volume I: 1920-1928

Author: Robinson Jeffers (1887-1962)
Edited, with an introduction, by Tim Hunt
Publisher: Stanford University Press (Stanford, California). 549 pp. $60.00
Type of work: Poetry

This initial volume of a projected four-volume complete works of Robinson Jeffers covers the first decade of his mature work, in which he creates a bold and original alternative to the modernist direction in poetry

The Collected Poetry of Robinson Jeffers: 1920-1928, edited with an introduction by Tim Hunt, is the first volume of a projected four-volume chronological edition of Jeffers' work; it does not, however, present the poetry with strict chronology, for the apprentice works *Flagons and Apples* (1912) and *Californians* (1916) are reserved for volume 4. Meticulously researched and carefully edited, set in a handsome typeface with ample space given to the poems on the page, this volume contains the complete poems from those seminal publications between 1920 and 1928 that constitute the central pillars upon which Jeffers' reputation rests: *Tamar and Other Poems* (1924), *Roan Stallion, Tamar, and Other Poems* (1925), *The Women at Point Sur* (1927), and *Cawdor and Other Poems* (1928).

A scholarly collection of Robinson Jeffers' poetry was certainly timely fifty years after *The Selected Poetry of Robinson Jeffers* was published in 1938. Sufficient time has elapsed for the wide swings in Jeffers' reputation—from the effusive praise of the 1920's and 1930's to the abrupt dismissal of his work by the New Critics in the 1950's—to have been damped sufficiently to permit a more balanced assessment of his poetry. Just previous to the publication of the volume under discussion, Robert Hass edited and introduced *Rock and Hawk* (1987), a collection of Jeffers' short poems. By omitting the long narrative poems, however, Hass deflects attention from Jeffers' unique contribution to twentieth century poetry. Although few critics have expressed unalloyed admiration for the long narrative poems, these poems contain the essence of Jeffers' original poetic vision. No final assessment of his achievement can neglect the great verse narratives from the decade covered by the first volume of *The Collected Poetry of Robinson Jeffers*: "Tamar," "Roan Stallion," "The Women at Point Sur," "The Tower Beyond Tragedy," and "Cawdor."

Jeffers has always been a poet difficult to fit into the literary conventions of the twentieth century, for he chose to follow a path eschewed by the modernist tradition. In his foreword to *The Selected Poetry of Robinson Jeffers*, published at the height of his popularity, Jeffers stated that it had been his plan from 1920 on to write narrative poetry that would "present aspects of life that modern poetry had generally avoided." Not only did Jeffers choose subject matter rejected by the poets of his generation, but he also developed an extremely long poetic line, reminiscent of that of Walt Whitman but rhythmically flatter, devoid of the techniques of irony, compression, and ambiguity so admired by both modernists and New Critics. His long verse fictions—set in the Monterey Peninsula area of California and inhabited by ordinary people motivated by unusually strong and perverse emotions—were written with a narrative and metaphorical directness more characteristic of the prose of the late nineteenth century American novel than of the imagistic condensation and conversational tone associated with, for example, Ezra Pound, T. S. Eliot, and William Carlos Williams, all publishing major works during the period covered by the volume under discussion.

The long narrative poem "Tamar" initiated Jeffers' individualistic poetic plan. Covering seventy-three pages in *The Collected Poetry of Robinson Jeffers*, this poem announces the major themes found in Jeffers' poetry: a preoccupation with sexual deviance prompted by personal obsessions as well as a wide reading in the works of Sigmund Freud and Carl Gustav Jung, a focus on ritual acts of violence influenced by the patterns of ancient myths and the classical dramas of ancient Greece, a fascination with Friedrich Nietzsche's doctrine of the will to power, and an aloof pessimism suggestive of Arthur Schopenhauer's. To summarize "Tamar" briefly, Lee and Tamar Cauldwell, children of California rancher David Cauldwell, repeat the pattern of incest begun earlier by David and his sister Helen. In order to legitimize her pregnancy, Tamar seduces Will Andrews, son of a neighboring rancher. At the end, Tamar collects Will, David, and Lee—all three men under the control of her sexual power—into one room of the house. Set on fire by her half-witted Aunt Jenny, the burning house consumes all as the floor of the room "turned like a wheel." The floor's turning, suggestive of grand natural cycles or perhaps the fiery wheel upon which the mythical Ixion is bound, is only one mythic allusion among many in this poem. Like many writers contemporary with him, Jeffers used mythic patterns to structure his artistic vision. What differentiates Jeffers from his contemporaries, however, is the directness with which he combines myth with realistic violence and sexual perversion.

"Tamar" is a shocking poem, full of outlaw passion and lurid details wrapped in a rhetoric of such gusto that the embers of forbidden passion and insanity are fanned into searing flame. The rank incest that is the focus of the poem and seems at first reading to be so outrageous to the average reader's sensibility accomplishes three thematic objectives. First, incest locates the motivation of the characters in a matrix of fundamental psychological forces described by Freud as the Oedipus complex, a frequent substructure of literature from Sophocles' *Oedipus Rex* and William Shakespeare's *Hamlet* to D. H. Lawrence's *Sons and Lovers*. Second, incest lends a mythopoetic depth to the narrative, since this forbidden act forms a central part of classical myth (the Titans, for example, spring from multiple incest) and classical drama (*Oedipus Rex* and Aeschylus' *Oresteia* for example). Both of these thematic employments of incest establish the action of the poem among elemental passions perennial in art, myth, and religion, demonstrating "that life is always an old story, repeating itself always like the leaves of a tree." The third function of incest is singularly related to Jeffers' art. Jeffers celebrates amoral, or perhaps more accurately premoral, individuals who storm the wall of custom and through the breach reveal a reality undreamed of by human consciousness except in the outer reaches of nightmare. Uncovered by the violent rupture of society's most powerful moral restraints, a reality becomes visible that cannot be tamed by the anthropomorphic tendency of human knowledge. This new reality, this Ur nature that defies conventional human understanding, exists outside human events and is therefore an inhuman nature.

"Roan Stallion," more compact and less muddled than "Tamar," defines the structure of the inhuman nature that informs humankind's severely limited understanding. In this narrative poem, California, the wife of a dissolute rancher named Johnny, develops a sexual passion for a noble red stallion that Johnny has won at cards. After a hallucinatory sexual interlude with the stallion, she allows the stallion to trample Johnny, and she reluctantly kills the horse afterward. Jeffers, as narrator, announces, "Humanity is the mould to break away from, the crust to break through, the coal to break into fire" and opts for "tragedy that breaks man's face and a white fire flies out of it; vision that fools him/ Out of his limits, desire that fools him out of his limits, unnatural crime, inhuman science,/ Slit eyes in the mask; wild loves that leap over the walls of nature."

The above quotation reveals that Jeffers is not an unquestioning disciple of either Freud or Nietzsche but an explorer of new territory. Like Nietzsche, Jeffers desires a break from the inhibiting mold of conventional humanity and esteems the will to power, but the new result of that break will not be a superman, a transvaluation of what it means to be human, but nature created by a god "not in a man's shape," a transvaluation of the cosmos itself. In Jeffers' aesthetic system, that which humanity considers unnatural leads to an apprehension of a deeper, truer nature that does not enter into the human domain until wild love or tragedy shatters the human-centered perspective of conventional culture. Rather than being a regression to an infantile libidinous state, Jeffers' use of incest and zooerasty opens the doors of perception onto vistas of the underlying structure of phenomena, in a manner similar to Jung's description of incest as a symbolic act that prefigures an aesthetic revision of the world.

The human tragedy that pervades Jeffers' poetry results from the inability of many of his characters to deal objectively with the influx of energy from the inhuman universe. Most are like Tamar, who, feeling the upsurge of powerful passion from fundamental nature, egotistically assumes, "I am the fountain." Yet human beings are not the source, the fountain, of the power that wells up from inhuman nature. Because they are women and therefore biologically participate in the fundamental generating force of nature, Tamar and other female characters in Jeffers' narratives present natural conduits for elementary energy, but the profound source of this power, the original mother, is, as Jeffers states in "Continent's End," older than art, older than the primordial sea: "Mother, though my song's measure is like your surf-beat's ancient rhythm I never learned it of you. Before there was any water there were tides of fire, both our tones flow from the older fountain."

Jeffers' poetic journey to the mouth of this "older fountain" is further defined in

"The Tower Beyond Tragedy," a free adaptation of Aeschylus' *Oresteia*. In his verse drama, Jeffers essentially retells the events of the *Oresteia*, but Jeffers' drama ends with Orestes repudiating both his murder of Clytemnestra, a matricide presented with incestual overtones, and the sexual advances of his sister Electra, an incestuous act that would establish his political power in Mycenae. After committing matricide, Orestes flees to the forest, where he enters the "motionless and timeless centre" and "the pure flame and the white, fierier than any passion; no time but spheral eternity." The pure source itself contains no human passion, though fierce emotions may present pale analogies to its "pure flame." When human beings tap this source and misinterpret or misuse its power, then tragic events and excessive passion occur. As Orestes explains to Electra, "It is all turned inward, all your desires incestuous, the woman the serpent, the man the rose-red cavern." Only when turned outward, freed from human love and ingrown sexuality, can the older fountain of nature spend its power without causing human tragedy. This radical detachment from human love and emotions Jeffers later called Inhumanism.

Jeffers wrote of the divine beauty of this world from a vantage point beyond human values and emotions. Rather than following the paths blazed by poets and novelists in the modernist tradition, he traveled an artistic path opened by the realists and naturalists that preceded him. Like Theodore Dreiser, Stephen Crane, and other naturalistic writers, Jeffers wove his themes out of a combination of pessimistic philosophy, the violation of taboos, the primacy of sexuality in human action, and the indifference of nature. He, however, took these themes to the limit, achieving a detachment far above human values from which to describe a nature created by an inhuman god. It is upon the success or failure of his stark vision in his long poetic fiction that Jeffers' reputation rises or falls.

Kenneth Gibbs

Sources for Further Study

The American Poetry Review. XVI, November/December, 1987, p. 33.
Choice. XXVI, December, 1988, p. 646.
Library Journal. CXIII, April 15, 1988, p. 83.
The New Yorker. LXIV, December 26, 1988, p. 91.

COMING OF AGE IN THE MILKY WAY

Author: Timothy Ferris (1944-)
Publisher: William Morrow (New York). 495 pp. $19.95
Type of work: History of science

A lucid and eloquent exploration of humankind's efforts to comprehend the enormities of cosmic space and time

Something of a challenger to Carl Sagan's position as the leading American science journalist, Timothy Ferris, who teaches journalism and astronomy at the University of California at Berkeley, has written an unusually polished and elegant history of our ideas of the universe and Earth's position in it. He comes to this book with an authority and assurance demonstrated in many articles and essays on science in a variety of journals, ranging from *Harper's* to *Reader's Digest*, from *The New York Times* to *Rolling Stone*. The range of readers reached by these magazines reveals something of Ferris' ability to make his message understandable. He is a great bridger of the gap that many still experience between the "two cultures," the sciences and the humanities, a gulf that C. P. Snow tried to cross in the late 1950's and early 1960's with his famous novels and essays (for example, *The New Men*, 1954, and *Science and Government*, 1961). If the chasm has begun to narrow, much of the credit must go to writers such as Sagan and Ferris who have taken science to the people. Ferris is at home in broadcasting as well as print. He wrote and narrated the award-winning ninety-minute PBS special "The Creation of the Universe," and he has agreed to serve as science correspondent for *The MacNeil/Lehrer Newshour.*

Ferris' ability to write in an engaging way on difficult concepts in astronomy and physics does not mean that he sacrifices breadth and depth. There is much carefully documented historical exposition in *Coming of Age in the Milky Way*, because Ferris knows that the majority of his readers will have a surer grasp of the developments in philosophy and intellectual history than of the evolution of scientific theory. He is also convinced that the layman will be more open to learning about science if he can be persuaded that there is more of the artist in the scientist than is usually believed. Ferris manages to establish these ideas early in his book, in a clever and highly insightful discussion of Aristotle's contribution to the mapping of space. The very qualities that are always singled out as being Aristotle's greatest strengths—his close observation of phenomena and powers of classification—are seen by Ferris as obstacles; they actually interfered with the philosopher's effectiveness as a scientist. His addiction to description and explanation made Aristotle "intolerant of ambiguity," a quality "not salutary in science"; his "cast of mind . . . propelled him to the extremities of empty categorizing." The result was occasional illumination, but he also left whatever he touched "anesthetized." It was Plato, says Ferris, from whom science inherited a profound skepticism "about the ability of the human mind to comprehend nature by studying objects and events." Science cannot succumb to the temptation of settling for perfect descriptive models of the universe. Were it to do so, says Ferris, science itself would come to a stop.

Although beautifully constructed, Ferris' own book avoids the pitfall of too schematic an appearance by concentrating on the history of our way of thinking about the universe rather than on the history of the universe itself. Ferris does this by dividing his book into three sections: "Space," "Time," and "Creation." These sections trace the historical and theoretical understanding of how mankind moved from mapping space to grasping the age of the universe and finally to struggling with the problem of genesis: the universe and its origins.

Nicolaus Copernicus asserted the existence of a heliocentric universe, but his descriptive model retained many of the epicycles and misleading spheres of the Aristotelian and Ptolemaic maps. Despite the sun's replacing Earth at the center of things, science still had a very misleading map of the cosmos. When Sir Isaac Newton "created a mathematically quantified account of gravitation that embraced terrestrial and celestial phenomena alike," however, the map sparkled. Through Newton's insight astronomy accepted not only the concept of a sun-centered planetary system but also the idea of a universe far more extensive than ever imagined. In the following century, the concept of galaxies took hold. Stars that seemed fixed were discovered to be actually moving in systems made up of countless suns of their own. Albert Einstein extended Newton's domain of the stars and planets to the geometry of the cosmos as a whole. Einstein's general theory of relativity led him to the disturbing discovery that the universe, since it could not be static, must be either expanding or contracting. Ferris demonstrates that late twentieth century opinion and research supports the notion of expansion and thereby reaffirms the importance of time to a full understanding of the cosmos. "Natural laws themselves may prove to have a mutable past."

It took a long time before time was seen objectively by man. The ancients had cyclical notions of time, and until the nineteenth century the creation was still seen as a fixed moment in time from which all things in the universe, animate and inanimate, originated: All species had been created at the same time, and each had its place in the Great Chain of Being. As fossil evidence accumulated, however, it became impossible to insist that all the species on Earth today had always been there. This was a mind-stretching discovery. Suddenly Earth was no longer some five or six thousand years old as the biblical calendar would have it; instead, time rushed over man in enormous waves, and the age of Earth itself became an antediluvian mystery.

If this was true of Earth, what about space? From the vast stretches of geological and biological time clocked by Charles Lyell and Charles Darwin in the nineteenth century and the first discoveries of radiometric dating by Ernest Rutherford in the twentieth, science brought together two strongly linked secrets of the universe: its immense age and the enormity of energy locked in its tiniest particles—atoms. The key to understanding the energy of the stars of an expanding universe became the exploration of the structure of the atom.

After Max Planck's quantum theory (1900) had established the unprecedented hypothesis that energy comes in discrete units or intermittent spurts rather than being emitted continuously, classical physics was never the same. The decisive break with Newtonian thinking came in 1927, when the young German physicist Werner Heisenberg arrived at the indeterminacy principle: One can learn either the exact position of a given particle (such as a proton) or its exact trajectory, *but not both*. "The more closely physicists examined the subatomic world," writes Ferris, "the larger indeterminacy loomed." The main reason for this indeterminacy lay in the fact that the very act of observation itself, the scientist's inquiry, influences the qualities that subatomic particles present.

With this discovery, the observer of the cosmos is caught in an intellectual paradox. The more he knows about the physics of the universe, the less he can observe, identify, and map. Like the philosophical Idealist, he is forced to rely on his imagination, on the suggestions of symmetry deep in his own consciousness, in order to discover the "deeper symmetry hidden beneath the extant broken symmetry" of the cosmos. It may be our function as human beings to carry within our heads the specter of that "primordial symmetry" which sustains the universe itself but which *it* has forsaken. Ferris suggests that the universe has given up "the perfection of nonbeing for the welter of being." Its abandonment of perfection has made it possible for us, imperfect creatures that we are, to exist. We are part of the universe's constantly expanding being. We are scattered in time and space. We are here because we are part of an imperfection that has not forgotten its Platonic origins. Ferris closes his brilliant meditation on man's place in the universe by stressing an essential duality, a contradictory embrace of light and dark, Eros and Thanatos. Science is finally amoral, but man has no finer instrument by which to measure the stage of his own drama.

Peter Brier

Sources for Further Study

Booklist. LXXXIV, July, 1988, p. 1768.
Boston Globe. July 31, 1988, p. 96.
Chicago Tribune. August 10, 1988, V, p. 3.
The Christian Science Monitor. July 13, 1988, p. 17.
Kirkus Reviews. LVI, June 15, 1988, p. 872.
Los Angeles Times. July 15, 1988, V, p. 8.
The New York Times Book Review. XCIII, July 17, 1988, p. 1.
Publishers Weekly. CCXXXIII, June 10, 1988, p. 62.
Vogue. CLXXVIII, July, 1988, p. 70.

THE COMPANY WE KEEP
An Ethics of Fiction

Author: Wayne C. Booth (1921-)
Publisher: University of California Press (Berkeley). 555 pp. $24.95
Type of work: Literary criticism

A provocative volume of literary theory by a well-known and well-regarded literary critic and rhetorician that attempts the audacious task of revitalizing ethical criticism in a time of widespread skepticism about the possibility of defining literary values

Prominent critics of the late twentieth century have taken turns announcing the death of ethical criticism; in this new book, Wayne Booth dares to declare its rebirth—as well affirming its centrality to the very act of reading and interpreting literature. Despite the daunting task Booth has set for himself in this learned, weighty treatise, he is clearly more than equal to it. During his illustrious academic career, Booth has published a number of important, well-received books on literary theory as well as more than a hundred articles, essays, and reviews on various rhetorical and other literary topics, including the teaching of writing. Since Booth has also served as the coeditor of *Critical Inquiry*, a preeminent journal of literary theory and criticism, it is not surprising that this current volume should merge two of the reigning interests reflected in his published work: exploring the processes of literacy—how and why writers and readers do what they do—and ascertaining the sources of the value placed on reading literature.

Just as Booth's first work, *The Rhetoric of Fiction* (1961), almost single-handedly revived the rhetorical study of fiction, *The Company We Keep: An Ethics of Fiction* offers the prospect of rehabilitating the notion of evaluative criticism—that is, of assaying the responsibilities authors and readers have to one another and to the texts that bring them together. Booth continues his stabilizing influence in contemporary criticism by mediating between extremes in warring critical camps and establishing moderating boundaries for a responsible pluralism in contemporary criticism. Refusing to align himself with any one critical camp, Booth attempts to articulate a wholeness and balance in the critical response to literary texts. This new work specifically addresses the question of how personal or corporate values within a culture can influence the creation, understanding, and interpretation of texts and how every reader is licensed to enter the "conversation" about their literary merit.

The Company We Keep in many ways exemplifies the rhetorical strategies characteristic of Booth's other principal works: challenging orthodoxies while at the same time calling for the restoration of neglected or forgotten notions and modes of inquiry. Here, too, his prose is at once playful and profound, comprising both witty conversation and determined polemic. He regards his reader as an interested and interesting friend. One is never lectured or cajoled, and Booth plays the game according to the rules he tries to articulate in this work. At its best, *The Company We Keep* engages readers on many levels. While concentrating on "literary" issues,

Booth still manages to educate the attentive reader broadly with wide, quite breathtaking surveys of what such disciplines as philosophy of science, psychology, sociology, linguistics, and physics might contribute to one's understanding of the theory and practice of ethical criticism. Even Booth's frequently expansive footnotes are instructive—even indispensable—often rivaling in informative value the main texts of less talented contemporary critics and theorists. Any given page from this book seems not so much to contain information as to overflow with it, the product of the fertile argumentation of a writer whose early reputation as a master rhetorician is consistently upheld. Yet nothing here is gratuitous or obscurantist; eschewing the opacity and sleight of hand embraced by other practitioners within literary theory, Booth makes every argument count, each one fitting into the elaborate foundation he has designed to undergird his apologia for ethical criticism.

Booth divides his book into three parts: "Relocating Ethical Criticism," an attempt to explain why "ethical criticism fell on hard times" and how it might be revived; "Criticism as Ethical Culture," where Booth delineates how authors, readers, and texts ingratiate themselves as lively components within a reading community, and then how each proceeds both to reflect and to challenge received notions about what constitutes an ethical act; and "Doctrinal Criticism," a final elucidation of how specifically ideological criticism—feminist criticism is the prototype here—often operates to affirm and, unwittingly, to undermine the program of depoliticizing discourse. A comprehensive bibliography of ethical criticism and related works adds to the usefulness of the book and underscores the comprehensiveness of Booth's achievement in this book.

Booth begins his rehabilitation of ethical criticism with an anecdote recalling his uneasiness twenty-five years earlier when a young black colleague at the University of Chicago denounced Mark Twain's *The Adventures of Huckleberry Finn* (1884) as a racist work for its demeaning depiction of blacks and refused to teach it. Booth suggests that he and his fellow teachers at the time regarded this response simply as naïve or uninformed. Upon later reflection, Booth declares that he has come to realize that what this black professor had in fact uncovered is the illegitimate but unacknowledged tendency in modern academic criticism to divorce oneself blithely from the moral implications of a text—to focus instead on its supposedly neutral and extractable "aesthetic" qualities and to leave evaluation of its themes or characterization to the vagaries of personal taste and individual values. Yet, Booth argues, one ultimately cannot avoid moral judgments of the texts one reads even though one may attempt to call this ethical criticism by some other name. Booth thus introduces *The Company We Keep* as a belated, extended apology to his black colleague and as an evolving inquiry framed as a challenge to his fellow critics to take seriously the role all readers must inevitably play in the assigning of value to or the privileging of certain texts—or readings of texts—above others.

Booth moves next to a convincing explanation of why ethical criticism faded from the critical scene (the threat of censorship; the widespread skepticism that clearly defined values could be derived from reading a literary work; the triumph of abstract theories of art over practical criticism) and then to a meditation on what elements could rightly constitute an ethical criticism. It is here that Booth provides what is perhaps his most original contribution to the project of reclaiming ethical criticism. Arguing that the traditional "fact/value split"—the belief that one cannot derive values from facts—must be overcome in interpreting and judging literature, Booth offers a new mode of inquiry he calls "coduction." Readers arrive at their judgment of value in narratives, Booth believes, the same way they arrive at their judgment of the values of other persons: namely, by experiencing them in a variety of contexts that are both like and unlike their previous encounters. That is to say, in any new encounter with someone or something new, one immediately interprets that person or thing against the background of one's own and others' reported encounters with persons and situations. It is at once a personal, intuitive process and a communal process, for the experience of other persons with this new thing influences one's response to it. Booth succinctly explains the import of this notion for literary critics and readers:

> Coduction will be what we do whenever we say to the world (or prepare ourselves to say): "Of the works of this general kind that I have experienced, *comparing my experience with other more or less qualified observers*, this one seems to me among the better (or weaker) ones, or the best (or worst). Here are my reasons." Every such statement implicitly calls for continuing conversation: "How does my coduction compare with yours?"

The explicit benefit of coduction, according to Booth, is that it helps collapse the unwarranted distinction between how one arrives at a judgment of value and how it is to be defended. A reader-critic is no longer in the unenviable position of arbitrarily separating inquiry and discovery from explanation and proof. Freed to articulate the impact of a work on his or her psyche *as* the explanation or proof of its value or lack thereof, the critic is therefore immediately involved in a conversation with other readers about the text's ethical frame and is not forced to mount a predictably defensive diatribe that tries vainly to fix attention on "the work itself." In the realm of coductive argument, the work itself, so Booth says, agreeing with many of his contemporaries, becomes less available for cannon fodder among critics fond of retreating to pure aesthetics in their literary discussions.

The rest of *The Company We Keep* emerges as a compelling defense of coduction and as an exemplification of its methodology in extended readings of well-chosen narratives. Its lucidity is matched by its nearly exhaustive demonstration of how coductive argument can resolve or at least supplant much anxiety about rendering ethical judgments of texts. Booth's first task is to turn aside the charge that coduction is simply a neologism that disguises plain old subjectivism. Coduction is not merely or especially subjectivism in new dress, Booth posits, because there are built-in boundaries to its application. In its very nature, coduction is communal—that is, it operates within a fixed community of readers' evaluations; it calls forth dialogue and debate, the terms of which are never completely arbitrary or relative. Coduction simply acknowledges the consensual nature of knowledge and judgment;

there are no purely private judgments, just as there is no ultimately private language. One judges and expresses one's judgment publicly and thus subjects it to potential correction or refinement. This is, in fact, a reiteration of a theme Booth championed in his earlier work, *Critical Understanding: The Powers and Limits of Pluralism* (1979): the value of critical pluralism. Booth believes that questions about the validity of individual interpretations—like questions about the validity of individual value judgments—always rest upon values that are outside the literary enterprise as such and are built through the rhetorical process of consensus building.

When reader-critics attempt to grope toward or adopt shared notions of authorial intent, reader expectation, textual determinacy, and the inhabitability of a narrative's evoked worlds, they can talk to one another ("coduce") and understand the sources of their agreement and disagreement through this rhetorical process. The same process informs the disentangling of claims and counterclaims about the alleged values of particular works. Coming to a final, fixed assessment of a work is less important to Booth than is the process itself. The alternative critical stance to this coductive pluralism is either an idiosyncratic, interpretive autonomy that undermines the validity of all critical discourse and breeds anarchy or a highly structured, hyperobjectivist position that demands a univocal interpretation and value judgment to which all perceptive readers are expected to subscribe.

Booth rejects both extremes; his metacritical position finds a nurturing middle that encourages critics to evaluate works while understanding that no one assessment can be exhaustively true or final, since different readers will bring different expectations, experiences, and worldviews to the work at hand. There remains, nevertheless, a range of plausible value judgments—a pluralism that is limited by the kinds of readings a text can evoke in a given reading community—that welcomes variant readings and assessments but refuses the utterly or inescapably tendentious readings that can have no demonstrable basis in the text, authorial intention, reader, or reading community.

In many ways, *The Company We Keep* is a final eulogy to the excesses of New Criticism and its prohibitions of the intentional and affective fallacies. Simply put, New Critics argued that authorial intention was irrelevant at best and impossible to discern at worst and that a reader's response to a text was not equivalent to its meaning; this approach led the reader to substitute his own paraphrases for the impact of the work as a whole. Booth's work specifically calls in question the cogency of these injunctions and attempts in this work to describe painstakingly the rhetoric, or series of relationships, an author or reader could present or discern in a text intentionally to guide moral responses to its perspectives and meanings. This rhetorical view of literary criticism that Booth posits specifically embraces the maligned "fallacies" and calls into question the very usefulness of reading and interpreting if the author and reader are denied the normal relations that any speaker and hearer might enjoy.

The Company We Keep thus represents a major contribution to the understanding of textuality. It extends, in Booth's words, his "criticism of criticisms," an attempt to provide the means by which critical methods can be debated and evaluated. "The company we keep," that is, the books and authors we read, shape our reading environments, but, more important, they shape our day-to-day experiences of the world outside texts, thus altering our moral responses. This fact does not, however, lead Booth to some final, arbitrary formula for determining what should be read: "We must both open ourselves to 'others' that look initially dangerous or worthless, and yet prepare ourselves to cast them off whenever, after keeping company with them, we must conclude that they are potentially harmful." Booth's eclecticism allows him to be gracious and forbearing, extracting valuable reading strategies from otherwise mutually exclusive points of view and modes of inquiry. *The Company We Keep* admirably supplies a centrist output among extremes in critical theory at the end of the twentieth century; Booth's pluralism of limits continues to make literary conversation possible even where literary unanimity is an unreachable goal.

Bruce L. Edwards

Sources for Further Study

Kirkus Reviews. LVI, September 15, 1988, p. 1372.
Library Journal. CXIII, November 15, 1988, p. 74.
Los Angeles Times Book Review. December 18, 1988, p. 3.
The New York Times Book Review. XCIV, January 22, 1989, p. 3.
The Times Literary Supplement. December 16, 1988, p. 1399.

CONRAD AIKEN
Poet of White Horse Vale

Author: Edward Butscher (1938-   )
Publisher: University of Georgia Press (Athens). Illustrated. 518 pp. $34.95
Type of work: Literary biography
Time: 1889-1925
Locale: Savannah, Georgia; New Bedford and Cambridge, Massachusetts; and London and East Sussex, England

This first volume of a projected two-volume biography of American man of letters Conrad Aiken takes a psychoanalytic approach to Aiken's life, from the tragedy of his childhood through his early struggles to establish himself as a writer

Principal personages:
CONRAD AIKEN, an American author
WILLIAM FORD AIKEN, his father
ANNA AIKEN, his mother
JANE DELANO KEMPTON, his great-grandaunt
T. S. ELIOT, his Harvard classmate and friend
JESSIE MCDONALD AIKEN, his first wife

Biographer Edward Butscher seems drawn to subjects whose lives are marked by trauma and who therefore are appropriate material for his psychoanalytical approach. His first biography was a controversial psychoanalytical study of American writer Sylvia Plath, whose tortured life ended in suicide; the present work, his second biography, is a Freudian study of Conrad Aiken, whose life was tragically marred when he was only eleven by the murder-suicide of his mother and father.

Butscher makes no apologies for his highly "interpretative" approach, prefacing volume 1 of this life of Aiken by asserting his belief that a biographer would be remiss to ignore the insights of modern psychology. Butscher also affirms that since this is a literary biography which attempts to study the influences that shaped an artist's work, his discursive, impressionistic technique is justified because he is exploring the dynamics of human creativity. The technique often leads Butscher, however, to make highly problematical judgments about Aiken's psychic development as if they were unquestionable facts. For example, in describing the eight-year-old Aiken's pity for a kitten abandoned in the streets, Butscher says that it is easy to see that this response is a psychic expansion of the self-pity created by his father's neurotic behavior and his mother's lack of interest; such an empathic response to "lower forms of sentience," says Butscher, reflects Aiken's own feelings of insecurity.

A biographer has a wide range of options in approaching his or her subject—from a straightforward, objective account of external, documented events to a theoretically determined interpretive analysis of the motivations that characterize the subject's mental life. Butscher's biography of Aiken is quite definitely of the latter sort. Every page is conditioned by psychoanalytic assumptions and heavily loaded with a stiff, almost nineteenth century prose style. Nothing is simple or straightforward here; everything is grist for the Freudian mill.

Only one powerful event dominates the early life of Aiken, argues Butscher—the death of his parents. Indeed, Aiken himself, in his own quasi-autobiographical essay *Ushant* (1952), makes much of that horrifying occasion when he discovered the two bodies and thus "found himself possessed of them forever." In making *Ushant* his single most important source and in drawing so liberally and unquestioningly upon the book, however, Butscher makes the mistake of taking the work to be a strict autobiography rather than an impressionistic and thus novelistic fiction. This is not to say that Aiken falsifies events in *Ushant* but rather that his response to them is the artist's response, not the response of the individual personality; thus, *Ushant* is organized and expressed in terms of the artist's structural and aesthetic need, not necessarily his personal needs.

Butscher might just as well have drawn his conclusions about the mental life of Conrad Aiken from such novels as *Blue Voyage* (1927) or *Great Circle* (1933), both of which make use of the same basic structure and some of the same images as *Ushant* does. Indeed, without admitting that Aiken is writing fiction in these works instead of autobiography, Butscher quotes from them as if he were reporting factual events. He very often notes that Aiken "records" a certain conversation or event from his life in one of his novels, and then goes on to comment on the passage as if it were a historical account of real people rather than a fictional account of a created character.

Butscher explicitly scorns the traditional form of biography. Noting that Joseph Killorin, Aiken's friend and confidant, is busy working on an authoritative life of the writer, Butscher suggests that it will only be an account of the poet's voyage through a "vale of cancelled checks." Instead, Butscher opts not only for taking *Ushant* to be autobiography but for trying to compensate as well for what he considers to be Aiken's failure in that work by providing the analysis which he says Aiken was unable to muster. Clearly, the fact that Aiken was one of the first American writers to make explicit use of Freudian insights in his poetry and fiction makes Butscher's approach seem a viable, even an inevitable, one. Yet Butscher seems to ignore the difference between an artist's use of psychological insights to create the inner life of a fictional character and a biographer's assumption that he can penetrate the inner life of a real-life subject by analyzing fictional characters.

Butscher insists that Aiken was neurotic, obsessively concerned with his own sexual adventures. As one reads this biography, however, it is not clear who is sex-obsessed—the subject or the biographer. Butscher very frequently makes it quite clear that on strictly moral grounds he disapproves of what he calls Aiken's Don Juan neurosis, which led to what he sees as Aiken's compulsive marital infidelity.

Throughout the crucial first chapter of the book, which deals with Aiken's childhood, Butscher constantly refers to *Ushant*, but never does he admit that the book may be fictional in any way. Instead, in his Freudian analysis, he seems determined to outdo Aiken's own amateurish psychoanalytic efforts. The tragic central reality of

Aiken's inner growth, says Butscher, is that he was never able to make the transition from self-pity to genuine love. Instead, he remained frozen in a narcissistic phase, locked within his own childish self and permanently unable to be sensitive to others.

As a result of his father's crime of killing his mother, says Butscher, Aiken developed a permanent sexualization of his feelings into an appetite for women as little more than meat. Connected with this impulse was Aiken's drive to marry chaste maternal substitutes while feeding his sexual hungers in a never-ending series of affairs.

One can be grateful that not all of Butscher's treatment focuses on his guesses about Aiken's sexual life; the chapters on Aiken's years as a student at Harvard University deal with the many distinguished faculty members there who influenced Aiken's intellectual development and, more important, the significance of his early friendship with fellow student T. S. Eliot. In spite of the importance of Aiken's intellectual and aesthetic development, these areas are not as fruitful to a strictly Freudian analysis as sexuality. Consequently, Butscher watches Aiken carefully as he tries to lose his virginity, for, the biographer argues, it is only after this much-desired loss that Aiken was able to attain a more balanced relationship with people.

After Aiken's graduation from Harvard and first marriage, the major thrust of Butscher's biography focuses on the aspiring young poet's efforts to establish himself as a writer and as an important part of the new modernism, in which his friend Eliot was destined to play a much larger role than Aiken himself. Much of this middle section of the book deals with Aiken's battles with Amy Lowell and the Imagist movement. Yet even these initiatives, says Butscher, served to buttress Aiken's psychic defenses and reflected his bourgeois orientation—an orientation also expressed, Butscher cannot resist noting, by the contradiction between his "unbridled lust" and his puritan dislike of modern bathing suits and the new music and dance of the time.

Throughout the biography, Butscher comes back again and again to what he perceives as a mother complex that sexualized and embittered Aiken's feelings toward all women. Even his discussions of Aiken's poetry, from which he quotes quite liberally, are conditioned by what Butscher perceives as "subtexts" of incest, Oedipal threats, and the relationship between sex and death. Although in its discussion of Aiken's work this is indeed a "critical biography," it is only critically valid if one accepts its Freudian assumptions.

According to Butscher, Aiken's poetry and fiction project a juvenile sexual identity. The basic factors are Aiken's Don Juan drive to seduce an unending stream of women and his efforts to save fallen women. Furthermore, Butscher argues that if one were to take Aiken's relationships with women further (which indeed Butscher does), one would find the mirror image of the mother and finally Aiken's own female self, or Jungian anima.

Aiken's relationship with Eliot also is seen by Butscher from the Freudian point of view. In commenting on Aiken's review of Eliot's influential collection of essays

The Sacred Wood (1920), he says that the review is a venting of Aiken's repressed hostility toward the oppressive talents of an older brother. Although Aiken did not admit this hostility, Butscher says, it damages the review. Yet Aiken's comment that Eliot is often cryptic and unclear in the essays reflected the consensus of reviewers at the time. When Eliot published his epoch-making poem *The Waste Land* (1922), it had a powerful impact on Aiken's self-image, continues Butscher, for his old friend and competitor had outdone him. In fact, says Butscher, considering Eliot's rise to prominence, it is a wonder that Aiken continued writing at all. It is typical of Butscher's approach that if Aiken's professional efforts were unaffected by Eliot's success that it must mean that it is a "wonder," for it does not fit his theories.

Butscher recounts Aiken's efforts to establish his credentials as a poet and a man of letters, discussing his poetry in *Earth Triumphant and Other Tales in Verse* (1914), *The Jig of Forslin* (1916), *Senlin: A Biography and Other Poems* (1918), and *The House of Dust* (1920), as well as his reviews, which were published as a collection, *Skepticisms: Notes on Contemporary Poetry*, in 1919. Much of the discussion focuses on Aiken's attempts to use his poetry to come to terms with his own conflicts and inner tensions by creating various masks or personas, for Butscher is much more interested in Aiken's personal uses of his poetry than he is in its aesthetic value.

This first volume of Butscher's projected two-volume study ends with a discussion of Aiken's poem "Changing Mind," which, Butscher argues (as critics before him have), marks a turning point or new direction in Aiken's poetry, a movement toward a more direct confrontation with the ghosts of the past that haunted him. According to Butscher, with this poem, Aiken, a sickly and rapidly aging poet, announces an "ideational maturation" of his poetic life. With it, Aiken begins a voyage of discovery that leaves the obsessions of childhood even as it rediscovers childhood as the substance of future art.

Since this book only covers Aiken's life up to his mid-thirties, before he had written the works that have since assured his permanent place as an important poet and short-story writer, one can only imagine that the second volume, which will take the story of Aiken up to his death in his mid-eighties, will be even more highly detailed with Butscher's brand of psychoanalytic insights, for if volume 1 begins with the trauma of the death of Aiken's parents, volume 2 will surely begin with Aiken's unearthing and coming to terms with that memory and beginning an exploration of the self that will generate the remainder of his life's work.

Charles E. May

Sources for Further Study

Kirkus Reviews. LVI, June 15, 1988, p. 869.
Library Journal. CXIII, August, 1988, p. 160.

The New York Review of Books. XXXV, December 22, 1988, p. 45.
The New York Times Book Review. XCIII, November 27, 1988, p. 33.
The New Yorker. LXIV, September 19, 1988, p. 116.
Publishers Weekly. CCXXXIV, July 1, 1988, p. 62.

DALVA

Author: Jim Harrison (1937-   )
Publisher: E. P. Dutton/Seymour Lawrence (New York). 324 pp. $18.95
Type of work: Novel
Time: 1986, with flashbacks
Locale: Nebraska, other parts of the Midwest, and California

Spanning five generations of a pioneering Midwestern family, this novel focuses on a woman's search for her son and on the troubles of the Sioux Indians in the nineteenth century, as seen through the eyes of the woman's great-grandfather

Principal characters:
DALVA, the narrator and protagonist, a middle-aged Midwestern woman from a wealthy farming family
MICHAEL, a history professor at Stanford University, her lover
DUANE STONE HORSE, a half-Sioux farmhand, her first lover and her husband
RUTH, her sister
NAOMI, her mother
PAUL, her uncle
J. W. NORTHRIDGE, her great-grandfather, a naturalist and missionary

Many of the elements which have established Jim Harrison's reputation as a poet and novelist are present in *Dalva*. These include an outdoor, Midwest setting marked by an appreciation of the natural world possessed only by those who have been reared close to it (Harrison is from rural northern Michigan) and an earthy, unsentimental approach to his story and his characters. Yet *Dalva* does not have the same degree of violence, cruelty, and nihilistic despair that characterize the work for which Harrison is best known: the three novellas in *Legends of the Fall* (1979). *Dalva* is indeed a story of loss and suffering, but it includes other elements: enduring love, compassion, strength, and family loyalty. It is also in parts very humorous.

The novel is divided into three parts. The heroine, Dalva, a beautiful, forty-five-year-old woman from Nebraska, is the narrator of parts 1 and 3. Part 2 is narrated by her current boyfriend, a brilliant, clumsy, self-centered, alcoholic professor named Michael. The narrative is initially set in 1986, but there are extensive flashbacks to Dalva's childhood and adolescence, to other periods in her life, and to the life of her great-grandfather, J. W. Northridge. The latter was regarded by his contemporaries as an eccentric. He befriended the Sioux Indians and traveled throughout the Midwest as an agricultural missionary, helping the Sioux adjust to their unhappy transition from hunting to farming. These flashbacks are accomplished by means of extracts from Northridge's journal, which Michael is studying in the course of his scholarly research on the Indian question and the advent of farming in Nebraska.

Harrison uses as epigraph an old saying, unattributed, which sets the tone and one of the main themes of *Dalva*: "We loved the earth but could not stay." In this novel, everything passes; only the earth endures. Yet the melancholy regret for the transience of things is accompanied by the search for continuity and the longing for permanence. It is no coincidence that all Dalva's family are diary writers; it is "as if they thought they'd disappear if they didn't put themselves on paper." Although they remember and mourn their losses, they must eventually make peace with the past and with themselves for the duration of their stay.

The concern with loss occurs in two separate strands of the novel: the personal life of Dalva and the collective life of the Sioux Indians during the latter half of the nineteeth century. Dalva is a woman destined to have the things women cherish snatched from her. Her father was killed in the Korean War, when she was nine. Her first lover, and the only one for whom she ever cared, was Duane Stone Horse, a half-Sioux boy who made love to her when she was fifteen and promptly disappeared from her life. Pregnant, she then learned that Duane was the illegitimate son of her own father, and therefore her half brother. Her grandfather tells her that Duane had offered to marry her but had fled when told it was impossible.

Dalva's third loss in life came when she was forced to give up her baby son at birth; thirty years later, she still knows nothing of his fate. As for Duane, she was briefly reunited with him fifteen years after he left, but he was dying from wounds received in Vietnam. He and Dalva married in secret, but Duane committed suicide the next day. Dalva told no one of this experience, although she still carries the pain of it thirty years later.

Thus, it is not surprising that Dalva is haunted by what she calls the "terrifying and inconsolable bitterness of life" and its inescapable fragility. It is through Dalva that the novel gains much of its melancholy, contemplative, reflective spirit. She sees her life in terms of repeated patterns, of circles and spirals. The past is always present to her, particularly when she visits old haunts, and she tends to project her feelings onto the natural world: When she hears sea lions bellowing, she supposes that they are calling out to absent partners.

Yet in spite of this, she is not morbidly preoccupied with her tragic past. On the contrary, she has realized that what is normally thought of as suffering is really only life itself making each human being "unavoidably unique." This resilient strength is epitomized by her recollection of her grandfather's words: "Each of us must live with a full measure of loneliness that is inescapable, and we must not destroy ourselves with our passion to escape this aloneness." In the end, she is rewarded; at the climax of the novel she meets her son, who has been looking for her. The reunion is a tribute to the enduring love she feels for Duane and proof that there is some continuity in life other than that of grief. She realizes that it is possible to remember the past without being suffocated by it, and she provides an answer to her boyfriend Michael's disturbing observation that time never forgives anyone a single second and his question of "whether life is long enough to get over anything" (the latter is prompted by the refusal of Dalva's mother to read Northridge's journals because they would bring her dead husband to mind, thirty-six years after he was killed).

The second occurrence of the theme of suffering and loss has a collective manifestation in the form of the Sioux Indians, whose cultural heritage, independence, and way of life were systematically destroyed by the white man. It is a poignant tale, revealed obliquely through Northridge's journals and Michael's reflections on them. Northridge was a botanist and Methodist missionary. After serving in the Civil War, digging graves and writing letters on behalf of the dying, he took up the cause of the Sioux. For twenty-five years, from 1865 to the massacre at Wounded Knee in 1890, he befriended them, lobbying on their behalf in Washington, D.C., teaching them to grow food, learning their language and dialects. Ironically, he was too sympathetic to Sioux religion and culture to be much of a missionary for Christianity. ("It is indeed difficult to convince the Sioux of the uniqueness of the Sabbath when in his beliefs every day of the week is Sabbath.") Like Dalva, Northridge experienced grievous personal loss; his young Swedish wife, Aase, died of tuberculosis shortly after their marriage. Like Naomi, who attempted to keep in touch with her dead husband, he tried to contact Aase's spirit as well as the spirits of the dead Indians he had known.

Northridge was regarded as a menace and as a lunatic by both the government and the settlers. Eventually, he became virtually an Indian himself, taking to peyote and participating in the Ghost Dance. Finally, he went mad. The climax of his story, revealed in the closing pages of the novel, came when he murdered three government soldiers and left their remains in a subbasement of his farm. The room served as a mausoleum, also containing the bodies of five Sioux warriors who had wished to have their remains, with their cherished artifacts, undisturbed by grave robbers. When Dalva inherits the property, she is guided by a note from her grandfather and finds the mausoleum. In some subtle way her discovery releases the spirits of the past, and Dalva is then quickly reunited with her son.

Although *Dalva* is a work of fiction, any reader is likely to be disturbed by the facts which are noted by Northridge and glossed by Michael. Michael compares the nineteenth century situation in the Great Plains with modern South Africa and, worse, with Nazi Germany. He comments that the American government never kept a single treaty it made with the Indians, that twenty thousand buffalo hunters destroyed between 5 and 7 million buffalo—virtually the entire buffalo population—on which the Indians depended for their subsistence, that the Indians died of diseases brought by white settlers, and that their degeneration was hastened by alcohol given to them by the settlers in exchange for their valuables. These are well-known facts perhaps, but in this fictional context they acquire fresh impact.

The character of Michael is worth comment, because the section he narrates is the most entertaining and stimulating of the novel. In fact, so successful is it that it makes Dalva's weightier but more ponderous narrative seem tedious by comparison. Certainly it sets a different mood. Michael is an assistant professor at Stanford University; his research on Northridge will help to win tenure for him. He is loquacious in the extreme and has an unintentional habit of being provocative and rude—not out of malice but because he does not realize that his wit and opinions, forcefully expressed, are likely to cause offense. (His address to the local Rotary

Club is a hilarious example.) He is, as Dalva points out, somewhat unconscious in spite of his brilliant mind, and he spends much of his time trying to extricate himself from the difficult situations his tactlessness has caused. This makes him something of a comic figure, an effect which is increased by his obsessive love of food and drink, which he indulges even though he is overweight and not in the best of health. He is completely at a loss in a rural setting, although his rather innocent and harmless lechery survives the transition; eventually, this lands him in the hospital with a broken jaw inflicted by an irate father whose sexy seventeen-year-old daughter had been the willing object of Michael's attentions.

It is through the character of Michael that the author pokes fun at the tradition of academic scholarship. Michael's doctoral dissertation won high praise even though it was littered with faked material (necessitated by the fact that he had spent much of his travel grant on high living in Chicago). The dissertation was later published by a university press, but Michael confesses that the whole thing was written in an alcoholic haze fortified by Dexedrine. Michael himself has enough self-awareness to comment satirically on his own profession: "We academics are known for creating artificial questions to which we give artificial answers, thus ensuring our continuing employment."

Many of the minor characters in this novel are well drawn. Dalva's mother Naomi has an admirable tolerance and an easygoing good sense, and Dalva's grandfather possesses an imperturbable wisdom and detachment. ("Take courage, the earth is all that lasts.") Together with Dalva's uncle, Paul, these characters provide some serenity and stability to counteract the intensity of Dalva and the eccentricity of Michael.

Although *Dalva* is an engrossing novel, powerfully told, it is not without its faults. Michael's narration in part 2 is very successful, but he disappears into the background in part 3 and his story trails off lamely. Thus, the novel has a rather disjointed quality, and one almost wishes that Michael could have been the hero of his own picaresque tale. Perhaps he is material for a future novel.

Dalva's search for her son is another disappointment. It is announced early and hovers around for most of the novel. Michael offers to trace the son, but Dalva never accepts his offer. Instead she asks a friend of her former brother-in-law to help, and he succeeds by the simple expedient of asking Dalva's uncle, Paul, whom Dalva could have asked at any time. The effect is one of anticlimax. In addition, the reunion of mother and son relies a little too much on coincidence to be satisfactory.

There are also three errors in chronology. At one point Dalva is described as being two years older than her sister Ruth, but four pages later, when Ruth is three, Dalva is "six or seven." Their father died in 1950, when Dalva was nine, in which case Ruth cannot have been only five years old "a few years after Dad died." Moreover, Dalva's father had been dead only six years, not "nearly ten," at the time of Dalva's pregnancy, since the latter occurred in 1956.

Bryan Aubrey

Sources for Further Study

Booklist. LXXXIV, March 15, 1988, p. 1220.
Chicago Tribune. March 20, 1988, XIV, p. 1.
The Christian Science Monitor. June 13, 1988, p. 19.
Kirkus Reviews. LVI, February 1, 1988, p. 146.
Library Journal. CXIII, April 1, 1988, p. 97.
Los Angeles Times Book Review. April 10, 1988, p. 12.
The New York Times Book Review. XCIII, June 12, 1988, p. 28.
Publishers Weekly. CCXXXIII, January 29, 1988, p. 41.
The Washington Post Book World. XVIII, March 6, 1988, p. 3.

DANGER AND SURVIVAL
Choices About the Bomb in the First Fifty Years

Author: McGeorge Bundy (1919-)
Publisher: Random House (New York). 735 pp. $24.95
Type of work: History
Time: The 1930's to the 1980's
Locale: The United States

An illuminating account of political decisions about nuclear weapons, written by a well-known scholar and statesman

Principal personages:
VANNEVAR BUSH, a scientific adviser to Franklin D. Roosevelt
J. ROBERT OPPENHEIMER, a scientist, the "father" of the atom bomb
FRANKLIN D. ROOSEVELT, thirty-second President of the United States, 1933-1945
SIR WINSTON CHURCHILL, Prime Minister of Great Britain, 1940-1945 and 1951-1955
HARRY S. TRUMAN, thirty-third President of the United States, 1945-1953
DWIGHT D. EISENHOWER, thirty-fourth President of the United States, 1953-1961
JOHN F. KENNEDY, thirty-fifth President of the United States, 1961-1963

McGeorge Bundy's *Danger and Survival: Choices About the Bomb in the First Fifty Years* is a fascinating and important book. This comprehensive history surveys the ways national leaders have dealt with nuclear weapons, from the beginning of the nuclear era through the Reagan Administration. Bundy's message is a comforting one: We can control and live with the bomb. Bundy acknowledges that statesmen have failed to limit the proliferation of nuclear weapons; however, he argues that far more significant is the fact that since 1945 no such weapon has ever been used. Bundy sees the danger of nuclear war declining with each passing decade. Never, he declares, has there been a serious threat of a nuclear exchange.

Bundy writes with the authority of a man of affairs as well as a scholar. He has lived close to power ever since, as a young man, he became the protégé and biographer of Colonel Henry Stimson, the secretary of war who was responsible for supervising the Manhattan Project during World War II. Whether as an academic teaching at Harvard University or New York University, or as head of the Ford Foundation, Bundy has moved in influential circles. Bundy's most notable public service was acting as national security adviser to Presidents John F. Kennedy and Lyndon B. Johnson during the years from 1961 to 1966. As such, he played a part in the Cuban Missile Crisis of 1962, when for a few days in October the world seemed to be on the brink of a nuclear conflagration.

Because of his background, Bundy's book transcends normal genre classifications. It is a history replete with all the conventional scholarly apparatus. Yet it is much more. Because Bundy is who he is, was who he was, *Danger and Survival* is also a meditation on the political management of nuclear weapons. A statesman might use it as a primer on how to deal with the bomb. Perhaps, in his heart, that is what Bundy hopes some statesman will do.

David Halberstam, in his book *The Best and the Brightest* (1972), an early and famous critique of the Kennedy and Johnson administrations, faulted Bundy and many of his colleagues for a can-do spirit that flew in the face of harsh realities around the world. Most notably in Vietnam, they rationally atttacked a problem that defied reason, sought a solution to a problem that could not be solved. The field of nuclear strategy has long seemed to many to be one of the arenas of modern life that mock rational analysis. The risks involved in using nuclear weapons are so high, and the scenarios describing the consequences of their use so frightening, that much popular discourse about nuclear weapons and strategy has resolved itself into one or the other of two alternatives: Either talk of nuclear management is mad, because these weapons could not be used short of global annihilation, or the logic of nuclear strategy is so skewed that it can only be described in terms of satire and black humor, as in the film *Dr. Strangelove, Or: How I Learned to Stop Worrying and Love the Bomb* (1964).

Bundy, a practical man, who unlike lay critics has actually dealt with the bomb, pays no heed to such attitudes. This veteran of the Cuban Missile Crisis makes no allusion to *Dr. Strangelove*, a cultural landmark inspired by that crisis. Bundy's aloofness from popular concerns is the source of the many strengths and one weakness of his book.

Bundy believes that the nuclear situation must be faced resolutely and mastered rationally. To his great credit, he does not shirk the hard task of confronting the distasteful and fearful. He possesses in full measure the virtue he calls for in his book—the courage to face up to the inevitable dangers of a nuclear world. Bundy holds out no hope of an easy escape or of a simplistic solution to the nuclear dilemma. His study of history and his personal expertise both give the lie to any dream that statesmen will suddenly lose their limitations of knowledge and vision and end the threat of nuclear war. The bomb is here to stay. The only question open is how to reduce its menace to acceptable bounds. Here there is reason for optimism, for here comes into play the other great lesson of Bundy's research and experience.

In the decades since the bombing of Hiroshima and Nagasaki, no nation has used a nuclear weapon against an enemy. A long, if grudging, peace has existed between the two superpowers. The lesser nuclear powers have also refrained from using their weapons to upset the international equilibrium. Bundy sees behind this restraint a balance of terror. His analysis of the exact nature of this balance is sophisticated, instructive, and ultimately heartening.

Bundy believes that the nuclear peace has been kept because nuclear weapons have failed to live up to the expectations of the men who first built and deployed them. Early in the nuclear era, it was widely believed that possession of the bomb would give a nation an absolute advantage in dealing with other powers. It was thought that by brandishing nuclear weapons, the leaders of a nation might intimidate a country lacking such armament or gain respect from a state similarly equipped. American leaders were not insensible to these diplomatic advantages. The Soviets never wavered in their determination to have the bomb once they learned of the American effort. The British and French, as declining imperial powers with glorious traditions and uncertain futures, resolved to have nuclear weapons in order to preserve their places as great powers. The Chinese built the bomb to check first American and then Soviet nuclear bullying. The Israelis have constructed such weapons to inspire prudence on the part of their neighbors.

Yet, according to Bundy, the historical record shows that the diplomatic advantages reaped by these powers from their hugely expensive nuclear investments have been negligible. The existence of an American bomb did nothing to deter the Soviets from swallowing Eastern Europe and challenging the free world elsewhere. In the late 1950's and early 1960's, the Soviet Union was unable to extract Western concessions on Berlin by rattling its missiles. The international position of the British and French continued to decline relative to the superpowers, and they enjoyed little more international leverage than their ally West Germany, which had no nuclear weapons program of its own. China was defended as much by its size and population as by its nuclear warheads, and Israel remains vulnerable and insecure. In fact, Bundy believes that the only successful instance of nuclear diplomacy may have been President Dwight D. Eisenhower's threat to use the bomb against the Chinese if they attacked Nationalist Chinese positions on the small islands of Quemoy and Matsu. Those islands were a disappointing return for a once-grandiose dream.

Bundy sees the reason for this nuclear inutility in the practical reality that any power will be chiefly concerned about what might happen to it and not the other nation in an exchange of nuclear weapons. The use of these weapons against a nonnuclear power would bring an international reaction no nation has yet dared to face. The use of such weapons against a nuclear power invites at least limited catastrophe. To date, no statesman has been willing to risk the loss of a city, a province, quite possibly himself, for whatever benefits might be derived from a victorious nuclear war.

Thus, Bundy demonstrates that it is nuclear danger and not, as many have believed, nuclear superiority that over the years has decided the outcome of confrontations and crises. Whenever the United States or the Soviet Union has enjoyed a temporary nuclear advantage it has availed nothing, because successive generations of American and Soviet leaders have balked at paying the price of victory. This is the reason for Bundy's startling assertion that the superpowers have never come close to nuclear war, even during the Cuban Missile Crisis. That crisis has come to be regarded as the moment of supreme danger during the nuclear age. Bundy, however, spent the crisis at the side of President Kennedy. As a result, he knows that at the worst moments of that interlude both the American and Soviet governments were determined to avoid using nuclear weapons. He makes clear that the quest for nuclear superiority is a chimerical pursuit. In the realm of nuclear weaponry, truly enough is enough.

In the course of making these observations, Bundy explodes several myths and misconceptions that have bedeviled writings about nuclear weapons. It has been widely held that the United States began its drive for an atom bomb after President Franklin D. Roosevelt received a letter from Albert Einstein in 1939, warning of the theoretical possibility of such a weapon. Bundy demonstrates that this famous letter did spark some interest, but that the crucial decision came only in October, 1941, at the behest of the British and Roosevelt's scientific adviser, Vannevar Bush. Bundy disproves the old canard that the United States dropped the atom bomb on Hiroshima and Nagasaki to intimidate the Soviets. After sifting through the evidence, Bundy argues convincingly that neither President Harry S Truman nor his advisers had this effect in mind during the final deliberations on using the atom bomb. He also dismisses the charge that American diplomats flaunted the United States' possession of the bomb during postwar negotiations with the Soviets. He casts doubt on the story, told and believed by Eisenhower, that threats of utilizing the atom bomb ended the stalemated Korean War, by scaring the Chinese to the negotiating table. Bundy concludes that the Chinese had their own reasons for wanting to bring that bloody war to an end.

If there is any weakness in Bundy's study, it is a mirror-image of its strengths. Bundy, a reasonable and pragmatic man, writes of a world in which, for all of their failings, all statesmen are more or less reasonable and pragmatic. In a foreword, Bundy begs off exploring the question of nuclear terrorism, noting that this danger, however frightening, does not hold the potential for global holocaust implicit in great power conflicts. Yet what if a man with a terrorist mentality ever gains power in a nuclear state? A major reason the United States government hastened to build the atom bomb during World War II was the fear that Adolf Hitler was working on a similar project. Will the world be spared another Hitler? Bundy does not give enough attention to the irrational element in human behavior and history.

There is much in Bundy's own evidence that, when read another way, inspires concern about irrational drives balancing the pragmatism of statesmen. Bundy criticizes the mania for secrecy that enveloped the Manhattan Project. In part, this reflected necessary security measures in wartime. Bundy notes, however, that the secrecy was so pervasive and extended so high in the government that it prevented adequate discussion of the political potential and use of the atom bomb. The bomb became a mysterious sacred cow and as such was used against Japan with remarkably little debate or reflection. This secrecy also inspired in the American leadership an exaggerated sense of the security of the American nuclear monopoly and of the dangers of international cooperation in regulating nuclear weapons. Hence, in the first years of the nuclear era, the American government, though genuinely anxious for some sort of international arrangement to control nuclear weapons, did not go as far as it might safely have gone in negotiating such an agreement. The growing hostility and inveterate suspicion of Stalinist Russia may have prevented the possibility of international nuclear regulation in any case, but the American mania for secrecy bedeviled what chance there might have been for creating a stable and cooperative international environment.

On one level, the British and French decisions to build nuclear weapons made sense in the 1950's and 1960's. Owning the bomb was a way to earn the respect of the superpowers. Yet these decisions were also very much the product of nostalgia for lost glory. They reflected the British and French leaders' understanding of what was necessary for their people's sense of self-worth. These motives might be psychologically comprehensible, but they open up varied, and disturbing, justifications for the proliferation of nuclear weapons. Such motivations complicate enormously the game of nuclear statesmanship Bundy describes so masterfully.

Perhaps Bundy is correct in downplaying the irrational in nuclear strategy. Governments must continue to play the game, regardless of the complexity of the rules. As he notes at the conclusion of his book, we must have not only courage in dealing with the future but also hope. McGeorge Bundy accomplishes what he set out to do in *Danger and Survival*. He has written a brave and bold book that illuminates the murky world of nuclear weapons for citizen and statesman alike. It is to be hoped that this will not be the last public service of a long and distinguished career.

Daniel Peter Murphy

Sources for Further Study

Los Angeles Times Book Review. December 18, 1988, p. 1.
The New York Review of Books. XXXVI, February 2, 1989, p. 28.
The New York Times. CXXXVIII, December 15, 1988, p. B2.
The New York Times Book Review. XCIII, December 18, 1988, p. 1.
Publishers Weekly. CCXXXIV, October 14, 1988, p. 60.
The Washington Post Book World. XVIII, December 11, 1988, p. 1.

THE DAY I BECAME AN AUTODIDACT
And the Advice, Adventures, and Acrimonies That Befell Me Thereafter

Author: Kendall Hailey (1966-   )
Publisher: Delacorte Press (New York). 278 pp. $15.95
Type of work: Autobiography
Time: 1981-1985
Locale: California and England

Excerpts from the diary of a precocious adolescent who at the age of fifteen decided to finish high school early and educate herself

Principal personages:
KENDALL HAILEY, the narrator
OLIVER HAILEY, her father, a playwright
ELIZABETH FORSYTHE HAILEY, her mother, a novelist
THOMAS HAILEY, her uncle, confined to a wheelchair since childhood because of polio
HAILEE MAY HAILEY ("NANNY"), her grandmother
BROOKE HAILEY, her younger sister
MATTHEW, her boyfriend

The Day I Became an Autodidact: And the Advice, Adventures, and Acrimonies that Befell Me Thereafter consists of excerpts from a young woman's diary covering a period of about four years. The thread that ties the entries together is the theme of self-education. This potentially tedious topic, however, is constantly interrupted by the ebullient author's precocious remarks about a variety of other subjects. She can only be serious for a short time, and then her naturally optimistic and irreverent personality breaks through.

If her book resembles any other well-known work, it is not the journals of professionals such as Anaïs Nin or André Gide but the diary of the ill-fated Anne Frank. Although Anne Frank was living in daily terror while Kendall Hailey has always enjoyed comfort and security, there is nevertheless a striking resemblance. Both books are mosaics of youthful feminine dreams and aspirations. Both record the frustrations of loving spirits cooped up too long with people who get on their nerves. Both authors became autodidacts at approximately the same age, though for different reasons. Both books offer the reader the voyeuristic pleasure of peeking into a young woman's diary.

Het Achterhnis (1947; *The Diary of Anne Frank*, 1953) is important as a record of the Holocaust. What importance, however, can be attributed to the diary of this privileged Californian? It would have to be found in the element of autodidacticism. According to many authorities, society is witnessing a revolution in education which is part of the overall social revolution that futurist Alvin Toffler has called "The Third Wave." The old-style school, which was shaped by the needs of the factory system, no longer fits the needs for adaptability and creativity of a post-industrial society. Many bright young people, as if unconsciously responding, are dropping out of school or rebelling in self-destructive ways. *The Day I Became an Autodidact* may be read as a record of an experiment in an alternative mode of education and as such may be one of the more significant books to appear in recent years.

Hailey has been fortunate in having two highly literate parents. Her father is a well-known playwright, her mother a best-selling novelist. Both have not only permitted but also encouraged their daughter to be a nonconformist. Seemingly as a reaction to this permissiveness, Kendall is in many ways more conservative than the majority of her peers. She has no interest in drugs and only a minimal interest in sex. Although well-meaning friends have advised her to get out on her own and experience life, she has so far been content to remain in the family bosom, sharing the kind of relationship with them that seems to be rapidly disappearing from American life.

When she announced at the age of fifteen that she was going to finish high school early and wanted to stay home for the next five years while she educated herself, her parents said, "Why not take ten?" Her family will remind the reader of the characters in Moss Hart and George S. Kaufman's *You Can't Take It With You* (1936). There is even a crochety uncle, confined to a wheelchair since childhood, who could pass for Lionel Barrymore in the film version of that famous play.

The list of illustrious autodidacts includes Abraham Lincoln, Ernest Hemingway, Virginia Woolf, Thomas Alva Edison, Joseph Conrad, Rudyard Kipling, Charles Dickens, Mark Twain, Benjamin Franklin, and George Bernard Shaw. Hailey is the kind of omnivorous young bibliophile who reads under the blankets with a flashlight after the elders have ordered lights out. Her goal at the outset of her self-education was nothing less than to read everything ever published.

She is not intimidated by venerable names such as Aristotle or Sophocles. She dives into the lengthy *À la recherche du temps perdu* (1913-1927; *Remembrance of Things Past*, 1922-1931) by Marcel Proust with the insouciance of a surfer paddling into a twenty-foot breaker. Her opinions of prestigious authors are refreshingly original and occasionally so iconoclastic that it is easy to see why she might be better off as an autodidact than sweating through some of the breadth requirements of a liberal arts curriculum. Here, for example, is her assessment of one of the world's foremost thinkers:

> I am appalled by Plato. That anyone could write a book like *Laws* (which denies free thought and places all authority with the state) and still be considered a great philosopher is shocking. He was no more than an ancient Hitler. . . . I am certainly glad I read about the old fool, so if his name ever comes up I shall not have to be quiet out of undeserved awe.

This viewpoint hardly sounds like one that would be developed in a paper for Philosophy 1A, but no doubt a great many young people would express similar opinions were it not for the chilling hand of the grade point average. College is supposed to be a place where people are encouraged to think for themselves, but all too often students realize that their opinions had better harmonize with those of their professors and section leaders; they therefore learn to psych out the teacher, and regurgitate what they have heard. Instead of being taught to think, they are conditioned to conform, then hailed on Commencement Day as "our future leaders."

Hailey expresses pity for her peers who have gone on to college. She quotes from letters describing dormitory life, cafeteria food, juvenile horseplay, smutty conversations, and the boredom of compulsory reading and lectures punctuated with periodic anxiety attacks over impending exams. In the meantime, Hailey luxuriates in her freedom from peer pressure and the pressure of authority. She begins her self-education program following an orderly plan, moving from the Greeks to the Romans and up the chronological ladder; eventually her curiosity gets the better of her, however, and she kicks over the partitions that arbitrarily separate subjects and centuries at school.

The professional educator might be expected to say, "Aha! No discipline, no rationale, no continuity, no depth. The road to anarchy." It would be hard to imagine anyone with a vested interest in institutionalized education, however, expressing any other point of view. Hailey's is a young voice, but it contains a wisdom beyond the author's years. It is strongly reminiscent of Ralph Waldo Emerson, who said,

> Trust thyself: every heart vibrates to that iron string. . . . For nonconformity the world whips you with its displeasure. . . . Man is timid and apologetic; he is no longer upright; he dares not say 'I think,' 'I am,' but quotes some saint or sage.

At the same time, it must be acknowledged that Hailey has had many unusual advantages. Both her parents are well educated and have a wide circle of talented friends. During the period covered in this book, the family travels throughout the United States and England, mostly in connection with the production of her father's plays or the promotion of her mother's new books. With her parents' advice and encouragement, Hailey tries writing plays and novels. She acts in her father's plays and contributes scenes of her own composition. Many of the world's best books are right in her family library, and she has the further advantage of a good fundamental education obtained from an expensive preparatory school. With all these advantages, she is admittedly not a neutral subject for an experiment in autodidacticism. She is not totally unique, either. As Toffler writes in *Future Shock* (1970):

> With the move toward knowledge-based industry and the increase of leisure, we can anticipate a small but significant tendency for highly educated parents to pull their children at least partway out of the public education system, offering them home instruction instead.

The Day I Became an Autodidact is loosely organized. The entries are not dated, the section divisions are arbitrary, and the reader has to do a lot of guessing because the author is talking to herself. Her book gives the impression of having been tailored down from bulkier material in order to focus on self-education. It also appears to have passed through a number of editorial hands. Other entries that have been spared in the cutting deal largely with the author's passionate interest in acting and her ambivalent feelings toward family members, including her younger sister, whom she loves and hates in the same breath: "Brooke and I find that the love and respect of a sister is almost more wonderful than getting her into trouble." This kind of witty, almost Wildean irony is characteristic of the author's style and one indication of her talent.

It is natural to speculate on what the future might have in store for this conservative young rebel. Will her self-education prove an asset or a handicap? She clearly has the potential to become a professional writer, if that is the career she chooses. In addition to intelligence, wit, originality, and a good sense of style, she has that rarer quality of being able to love people in spite of and even because of their faults. Still living at home, however, Hailey has not yet been tested. She has had little romantic experience; the one boyfriend to whom she refers constantly throughout her book is younger than she and hardly a passionate suitor. She has not experienced tragedy, although it is lurking in the wings: Her father suffers from Parkinson's disease; and her Uncle Thomas, who has been a major influence in her intellectual development, has recently had a brush with death as the result of a cerebral hemorrhage.

Whatever the outcome, the reader will wish this extremely likable young person the best of luck and probably congratulate her on escaping the procrustean bed of higher education. A. S. Neill, founder of the famous Summerhill school in England and an advocate of total freedom in education, wrote: "My own criterion of success is the *ability to work joyfully and live positively*." If Hailey manages to retain her curiosity, her integrity, and her zest for life during the ominous years of the twenty-first century, that in itself may be a strong testimonial for autodidacticism.

Bill Delaney

Sources for Further Study

Booklist. LXXXIV, April 15, 1988, p. 1375.
Chicago Tribune. March 14, 1988, V, p. 3.
Kirkus Reviews. LVI, January 15, 1988, p. 102.
Los Angeles Times. March 6, 1988, VI, p. 1.
Publishers Weekly. CCXXXIII, January 22, 1988, p. 93.
Wilson Library Bulletin. LXII, May, 1988, p. 78.

THE DAY OF CREATION

Author: J. G. Ballard (1930-   )
First published: 1987, in Great Britain
Publisher: Farrar, Straus & Giroux (New York). 254 pp. $17.95
Type of work: Novel
Time: Late twentieth century
Locale: An arid region in central Africa

A dreamlike story of a man's obsessive quest for the source of a river

Principal characters:
DR. MALLORY, a medical doctor with the World Health Organization
NOON, a young mountain girl who belongs to a guerrilla band
MISS MATSUOKA, a Japanese photographer
GENERAL HARARE, the head of a small guerrilla army
NORA WARRENDER, the widow of a Rhodesian veterinarian who had run an animal-breeding station
CAPTAIN KAGWA, police chief at Port-la-Nouvelle
PROFESSOR SANGER, a small-time producer of television documentaries about animals
MR. PAL, Sanger's Indian assistant

Most of J. G. Ballard's books are either science fiction or visionary novels. *Empire of the Sun* (1984), however, is written in a realistic mode. *The Day of Creation* is realistic in style and imagery but plunges into the realm of fantasy. In this novel, Ballard achieves a remarkable merging of realism and illusion. The real world of poverty, disease, and filth in primitive central Africa is juxtaposed to the fictional world of the television documentary, presented as an exploitative invention passing itself off as real. This juxtaposition appears to be a metaphor for the relationship between the events of the novel and the delusions of the narrator. Lucid description, characteristic of realism, reveals grimy people with decaying teeth, infection, malnutrition, and fever living in squalid, unsanitary conditions. The same type of vivid description presents the hallucinations of the narrator. In the latter, Ballard achieves effects similar to surrealist art with its realistic images of fantasies.

Although the events of the novel seem vivid and real, the reader has a sense of being caught up in a gigantic dream. This effect grows out of the mode of narration and the character of the narrator. Events of the novel unfold through the eyes of Dr. Mallory, a physician who runs a World Health Organization clinic in the small town of Port-la-Nouvelle in the parched terrain of central Africa.

Mallory's narration of events seems quite real even when he expresses confusion. Comments by others who view him as eccentric, always finding the extreme position, and obsessed with underground water, however, should raise a caution flag to the reader. General Harare, leader of a small guerrilla band, tells Mallory that, because of his obsession with underground water, his "career has suffered so much." When Mallory assures him that he will give attention to his career, the general says, "Your real career, not the one inside your head. It may be too late. . . ." Nora Warrender, the widow of a Rhodesian veterinarian who had run an animal-breeding station near the airstrip at Lake Kotto and had been shot by a deserting soldier, makes it clear that she thinks Mallory is suffering from delusions. Referring to the young mountain girl, Noon, who had been left behind when General Harare's guerrillas fled Port-la-Nouvelle upon arrival of Captain Kagwa's soldiers, Nora says to Mallory, "I'm sure she can see that you are half-way to the dream-time." Later, when Mallory tells Nora that he is sure that he really is the river, she says, "You're clearly quite mad."

Superficially, the novel has many of the trappings of an African adventure. A petty guerrilla war between Captain Kagwa, a provincial police captain with about sixty soldiers, and a small guerrilla band led by General Harare serves as a backdrop to the main events of the novel. In his quest for the source of the river, riding the stolen car ferry, the *Salammbo*, which still has Captain Kagwa's dilapidated Mercedes on board, Mallory has to engage in several duels with Captain Kagwa's helicopter. When he is not fending off Captain Kagwa, Mallory must be concerned about a possible ambush by General Harare's forces. Despite the danger the war poses for Mallory, the war does not seem to matter. It is trivial except for the death and pain it inflicts. Which side wins appears to be a matter of indifference except to the two leaders.

The theme of the novel and its central symbol is the River Mallory, a river that springs up suddenly in the desert and draws to itself teeming life and activity. The river is a symbol of life, cleansing, and maternal nourishment. At the same time, ironically, it becomes a symbol of stagnation, pollution, disease, and death. The river is a fulfillment of Mallory's "dream of a green Sahara." Within a short time after it emerges, it becomes a tropical paradise of vegetation, fish, and animals. As people cluster around, however, and dig small irrigation ditches, the water becomes stagnant and polluted.

Mallory views the river as his creation. Because most of the people have moved away from Port-la-Nouvelle and Mallory has few patients, he undertakes an irrigation project after the last engineer leaves. Studying "the underground contour lines on the survey charts that sometimes seemed to map the profiles of a nightmare slumbering inside [his] head," Mallory drills six wells in the dry bed of Lake Kotto without success. Ironically, when a soldier is returning Mallory's bulldozer after using it to extend the airstrip beside the dry lake, he casually pushes a huge oak stump and opens a small spring that soon becomes a large river.

Viewing the river as his creation, Mallory is enormously possessive of it and, at the same time, is obsessed with the desire to stifle it. He tells Captain Kagwa, "All this water has ruined my irrigation project." Unable to stifle the river where he first discovers the spring, Mallory sets out to locate the source of the river. His purpose in seeking the source is ambivalent. On the one hand, he is driven by his wish to destroy the river, with which he is in competition and on which he wants vengeance for the fear it has prompted in him. On the other hand, he identifies the river with himself and senses that it is dying, and he thinks of trying to save it. This ambivalence can be seen in Mallory's attitude toward damming the river. At one point, he says that this would be like applying a tourniquet to his own arm, which would lead to gangrene. Later, he leads in the building of a barrage knowing that the diverted waters will become stagnant and polluted. This is both a pragmatic defense against Captain Kagwa's oncoming forces and part of his compulsive need to destroy the river.

Television wildlife documentaries and television mercy missions, which Mallory views as deceptions and corrupt exploitations of the natural environment and hungry people, become an embodiment of Mallory's quest for the source of the river. Despite his contempt for Professor Sanger, the producer of documentaries and small-scale mercy missions, Mallory's quest for the source of the river is the scenario for an unfilmed television documentary. Most of the time, Mallory sees television as telling lies and does not agree with Sanger's assertion that "television doesn't tell lies, it makes up a new truth. In fact, the only truth we have left." Mallory feels a rivalry with Sanger, believing that each of them is trying to impose his own image on the River Mallory. Mallory especially resents Sanger's "cheap commentary." Mallory says, "His pseudo-scientific prattle assumes that television's flattering revision of nature was an act of creation as significant as the original invention of this great river and its abundant life." Later, however, Mallory begins to realize that he is dependent upon Sanger's presence and almost accepts that he is "appearing in a drama directed and overseen by" Sanger.

Intertwined with Mallory's quest for the source of the river is his obsession with Noon, the young mountain girl who accompanies him on the car ferry. In her undivided need to reach the source of the river and in the way she draws Mallory along, she appears to be almost a mythic character. Her presence, as well as Mallory's sense that his seeking the source of the river has some deeper meaning, makes his journey a grotesque perversion of the quest for the Holy Grail. Her waiflike traits and the mystery surrounding her make her a compelling force in Mallory's imagination.

To a greater degree, however, she is an object of desire. As he sees Noon changing from a girl into a young woman, Mallory fantasizes about possessing her and about the two of them populating a new Eden on the River Mallory. This fantasy prevails as he watches her spear fish and observes her fascination with Sanger's videotapes. It also persists as they work together to fend off Kagwa's helicopter attacks and struggle against fever and exhaustion.

The events of *The Day of Creation* constitute an adventure, but the events are subordinate to Mallory's psychological journey. Like the protagonist in Joseph Conrad's *Heart of Darkness* (1902), Mallory is exploring his inner self as he journeys toward the source of the river. There are horrors in the journey, but the intertwining of the real with delusion not only blurs distinctions but also superimposes the horrors of both worlds upon each other. Yet all is not darkness. At times, Mallory has ennobling thoughts and feelings, and rational awareness emerges from his delusion. Like the ancient mariner in Samuel Taylor Coleridge's poem, *The*

Rime of the Ancient Mariner (1798), he finally feels compassion for living things. Mallory, after having poisoned the river by damming it and diverting its waters into irrigation ditches, feels a commitment to a small monkey. He knows that the animal will perish when the land becomes desert again, and he wants to renew the flow of the river with clear water.

Even as Mallory is obsessed with his desire to destroy the river that Sanger has named for him, realism occasionally breaks through, and Mallory realizes that eventually the river will dry up of its own accord. At other times, he guesses that it is not really the river he is trying to kill but himself.

Bizarre as many of his experiences are, Mallory achieves a kind of mastery over his world. His sense of failure and lack of purpose as a physician and a person are replaced by his pride in the river. His obsession to reach the source of the river takes him on a voyage of psychological discovery. The resolution when Mallory reaches the river's source and returns leaves several unanswered questions and a sense of puzzlement about what it all means. There is, however, something heroic in Mallory's quest, and the reader is caught up in the intensity and vividness of Mallory's obsession. *The Day of Creation* thus affords the reader a vital, imaginative experience.

Ballard's characters wrestle with what is real and what is a construct of the imagination. They struggle with the challenge to remake as much as they can of the world around themselves. This struggle comes through with intensity in *The Day of Creation*. In his delusion that he has created the river and in his effort to master it, Mallory has, in a sense, created his own universe. Although Mallory seems strange to many of his associates, Sanger appears to recognize the significance of Mallory's imaginative accomplishment when he calls the River Mallory "a complete invention."

The Day of Creation is not a book one can easily lay aside. It continues to stir the imagination long after it has been read. Like the knight in John Keats's "La Belle Dame sans Merci," Mallory appears to have had a life-changing experience, out of space and time. He no longer quite belongs in the ordinary and is unsure what was real and what was imagined in his experience. He waits and longs for Noon. The vividness of Ballard's images and the intensity of the imagined world he creates draw the reader into that world with Mallory. It is a haunting but refreshing experience.

Kenneth E. Walker

Sources for Further Study

Booklist. LXXXIV, March 1, 1988, p. 1049.

Kirkus Reviews. LVI, March 1, 1988, p. 298.

Library Journal. CXIII, May 1, 1988, p. 88.

London Review of Books. IX, October 1, 1987, p. 18.
New Statesman. CXIV, September 11, 1987, p. 26.
The New York Times Book Review. XCIII, May 15, 1988, p. 28.
The Observer. September 13, 1987, p. 27.
Publishers Weekly. CCXXXIII, February 19, 1988, p. 70.
Rolling Stone. DXIII, November 19, 1987, p. 76.
Time. CXXXI, April 25, 1988, p. 99.
The Times Literary Supplement. September 11, 1987, p. 977.

THE DEATH OF METHUSELAH AND OTHER STORIES

Author: Isaac Bashevis Singer (1904-   )
Translated from the Yiddish by the author and others
Publisher: Farrar, Straus & Giroux (New York). 244 pp. $17.95
Type of work: Short stories
Time: Ancient, medieval, and modern times
Locale: Poland, New York, and antediluvian Earth

Twenty short stories that examine the imaginative links between man's tendency to explain evil in sexual terms, modern man's disappointment with his culture, and the disappointment described in Genesis that led God to destroy His creation

This volume of short stories, the tenth since *Gimpel the Fool and Other Stories* (1957), explores what Isaac Bashevis Singer calls in an author's note "modern man and his disappointment with his own culture." The stories are permeated with an irony that results from the clash between mystical explanations of life and rational ones. Ancient and modern views are juxtaposed. Many of the characters are wanderers, sojourners of some sort; many are advanced in age. A holy man, a recluse, an artist, criminals, Holocaust survivors, faithless husbands and wives, perverts, cynics, prodigies, businessmen, the poor, the simpleminded, demons, the dead, the legendary, all are witnesses to an experience of life at odds with itself. Sinners tell stories in which they complain of other sinners; convicts tell tales of bigamy and murder; a philanderer collects anecdotes of faithless women. Singer himself seems to be present in the persona of a Yiddish writer to whom many of these stories are told. *The Death of Methuselah and Other Stories* is an extraordinary collection, both in terms of its odd and mystifying subject matter and, especially, in terms of Singer's gifts. A myth unmasked by Singer, for some strange reason, remains as alive as ever.

The best introduction to the fiction of Isaac Bashevis Singer is his volume of memoirs, *Mayn Tatn's Bes-din Shtub* (1956; *In My Father's Court*, 1966). There, in chapters that read like short stories, he describes the shaping influence of both his household and his father's *beth din*, or rabbinical court, on his young mind. The two, the family and the court, were so intertwined, he writes, that it was not easy to tell where one ended and the other began. Both of his parents came from families of rabbis, but while his father's family were Hasidic, or mystical in bent, his mother's were rationalistic; while his mother advocated a rational approach to life's puzzles, his father always saw God's mysterious hand at work. The rabbinical court not only reinforced this dialectical and argumentative habit of mind but also brought strange people into the house daily, people with stories not unlike those in *The Death of Methuselah.* It is clear from his memoirs that Singer himself recognizes how this contest of outlooks was absorbed by him and developed into an ironic vision. Unlike his elder brother Israel Joshua, whose example in questioning the Jewish way of life, in moving out of the house, and in writing for Yiddish newspapers Isaac Bashevis did follow, the younger brother did not discard the old, mysterious explanations in favor of realistic ones. Instead, he kept them both, allowing the rational to call into question the irrational and showing the power of the mystical to silence reason.

The opening story from *The Death of Methuselah* establishes a traditional religious perspective, and yet it is a perspective marked by doubt. A tense and troubling story from some unspecified time in the dark and distant past, "The Jew from Babylon" pictures the last day and night of an aged miracle worker with a strange name, Kaddish ben Mazliach. Shunned by the rabbis and community leaders as a sorcerer and the subject of fearful stories told about him in and around Lublin, still he is called upon to drive out evil spirits, and he is answering such a call in the village of Tarnigrod. Even the horse that pulls the wagon seems to sense his passenger's dangerous power. Faltering and absentminded as he has become, he thinks that this may be "his last and most decisive battle with the Evil Ones. If they didn't surrender this time, how would they be driven away into the desert behind the black mountains forever?" Singer makes this first story an introduction to the imagination attuned to the demonic.

The magician, after a long day's work in the tainted house, is cursed by the local rabbi, abandoned by his wagon driver, and forced to pass the night in the empty house where he worked his incantations all day. In his sleep he is attacked by "bearded images with horns and snouts," and then he finds himself lifted by a wind, in flight, surrounded by demons in a wedding dance, himself the bridegroom of Lilith, the Queen of the Abyss: "They threw themselves at his throat, kissed him, fondled him, raped him. They gored him with their horns, licked him, drowned him in spit and foam." The final sentence resonates with an ambiguity much like that of Young Goodman Brown's dying hour, the same indefinite "they," the same dubious "as if": "In the morning they found him dead, face down on a bare spot, not far from the town. His head was buried in the sand, hands and feet spread out, as if he had fallen from a great height."

The miracle worker's vision of his world is a truly terrifying one, but it is not one common to the twentieth century—thus the irony. If the gleeful Black Wedding were not enough to suggest the author's tongue-in-cheek attitude, the double entendre "his head was buried in the sand" should be too much to ignore. On the other hand (and in Singer's world there is always another hand), are rational philosophies developed by modern man really more adequate explanations of reality? Baruch Spinoza, Immanuel Kant, G. W. F. Hegel, Arthur Schopenhauer, Sigmund Freud, all are cited as authorities in the stories that follow, but the stories themselves confirm that "primitive" explanations are every bit as valid as are modern; in the last analysis, some things are beyond explanation, and that is where fiction is most potent.

Singer documents in his memoirs how, as he was coming of age, he simultaneously yearned for the modern and lived immersed in a culture that was still medieval in important ways. Escaping the deprivations of wartime Warsaw in 1917, he traveled with his mother to her family's village of Bilgoray, where customs had not changed "for centuries." There, while being exposed to a language and history of a much earlier time, the teenager avidly read the works of Spinoza and physics texts and became acquainted with the progressive-thinking villagers. These contending forces so shaped his emerging imagination that even sixty years later their influence can be recognized. In the author's note to this collection, for example, he writes that pondering modern man's disappointment with his own culture leads him to think back to the history of creation as related by "the divine genius who wrote the Book of Genesis." When he thinks about the modern, he turns for inspiration to the ancient.

It is in keeping with Singer's creative preference, however abrupt the change may seem, that the exotic and superstitious first story be followed by a quiet conversation between two urbane men in a modern European café. "The House Friend" is a series of anecdotes about "married women with lovers tolerated by their husbands" told by the artist Max Stein to the young writer. The two sophisticates amuse themselves by discussing the peculiar marriages of people so bored with themselves that they must have a third party join them. Their attempts to explain such behavior with ideas from Schopenhauer's writings on blind will and from Freud's on sexual anomalies produce no satisfactory answers. The older artist rejects the younger man's label of "homosexual" for such people, preferring the proverbial wisdom: "What people really are they don't know themselves. The fact is that we all are searching. No one is happy with what he has."

The third story, like the second, dramatizes the experience of a threesome, but whereas in "The House Friend" the wife runs away from the two men, in "Burial at Sea" the wife is killed by one of her husbands. The sense of corruption, betrayal, and hopelessness builds to oppressive proportions in "The Trap" and "A Peephole in the Gate." A woman whose husband apparently led her into an affair with his nephew tells her story to the patient writer in the hope that he will publish it in "The Trap." The writer persona in "A Peephole in the Gate" meets a fellow Polish Jew on board an ocean liner bound for Argentina who tells the same story over and over about the perfidies of women. One theme that enters into the cumulative narrative in the first third of the collection is that of self-torment or self-destructiveness. Without recognizing it, the storytellers reveal their own complicity in their suffering. The listening writer feels moved to point this out to Sam, the man who distrusts all women in "The Peephole in the Gate": "But you demand faithfulness only from others." The writer's role becomes like that of a psychoanalyst or a rabbi as he counsels Sam: "If you don't believe in God you have to live with whores."

Thus, Singer finds that modern man is no less harassed by evil than was medieval or ancient man, that given its particular preoccupations and geography, the modern era is no less bizarre than were much earlier times, and that across the spectrum of time the individual's struggle with inner evil remains a constant. The evil is no less real whether it be called a demon, a dybbuk, Satan, ego, cynicism, lust, jealousy, or some other name. Nevertheless, there does seem to be a prevailing human tendency to link sexual knowledge with evil, a tendency at least as old as the story of Adam and Eve. No fewer than thirteen of the twenty stories in *The Death of Methuselah* have in the foreground sexual relationships—hence the reference to the "Divine genius who wrote the Book of Genesis" in the author's note, and Methuselah's dream of the she-demon Naahma.

Singer writes that "The Death of Methuselah" was not planned by him in his usual way but seemed to write itself "almost 'automatically,'" something of a revelation about "cosmic and human art." In the closing sentences of this last story, a glimpse into God's mind reveals His recognition of His creation's fatal flaws. Just before his death Methuselah is granted this knowledge:

> It became clear to Him that all punishment was in vain, since flesh and corruption were the same from the very beginning and always will remain the scum of creation, the very opposite of God's wisdom, mercy, and splendor. God had granted the sons of Adam an abundance of self-love, the precarious gift of reason, as well as the illusions of time and space, but no sense of purpose or justice. Man would manage somehow to crawl upon the surface of the earth, forward and backward, until God's covenant with him ended and man's name in the book of life was erased forever.

A somber vision, but one consistent with the proto-Judaic worldview found in the Book of Genesis by a twentieth century descendant. It is not a despairing vision, if man's creativity is not perverted: "Art must not be all rebellion and spite; it can also have the potential of building and correction. It can also in its own small way attempt to mend the mistakes of the eternal builder in whose image man was created."

As distinctive as his Yiddish heritage makes him, and as faithfully as he has reflected his people's stories, Singer belongs to the ranks of the great writers of his time. He is a modern who, like James Joyce, William Butler Yeats, William Faulkner, and Thomas Mann, lived through and found expression for the turbulence and catastrophes of this century, so much of which was rooted in the past. Like them, he was able to enter into the conflicts of his time and place, to suspend the elements of these antagonisms like grains of sand suspended in a great whirlwind, to identify and bring to life the contending values of old versus new, clean versus unclean, young versus old, man versus woman, the naïve versus the knowing, the fantastic versus the realistic. Like his experience, his fiction is one of extremes, filled with ambivalence and ambiguity.

As much as anything else, these tensions and matched opposites are explorations into the structure of the imagination. Is humanity's dualism its most fundamental limitation, or its most important strength? In "The Accuser and the Accused," a traveling Yiddish journalist claims that he recognized another Yiddish writer, from New York, walking in a long Catholic procession on Good Friday in Lima, Peru. Despite the outlandishness of this charge, even after the deaths of both men the writer-narrator remains fascinated with the "uncanny power" that suspicion evokes; he plays with the possibility that multiple personality or religious uniformity or "a woman (or two or three women)" would account for the strange sight of a Jew dressed as a Catholic priest. "So many impossible things have become possible in my lifetime," he confides, "that I've made up my mind to erase the word 'impossible' from my vocabulary."

In his youth, explanations of life's meaning were all-important. As he matured, he saw how any explanation is limited by the vision of the explainer. He also found that as desirable as rational understanding may be, gaining a higher degree of consciousness does not eliminate the need for God. Isaac Bashevis Singer possesses the rare courage and talent necessary for taking both the mystical and the rational seriously; thus, this book is an important one.

Rebecca R. Butler

Sources for Further Study

Booklist. LXXXIV, February 1, 1988, p. 889.
Chicago Tribune. April 10, 1988, XIV, p. 5.
Kirkus Reviews. LVI, March 1, 1988, p. 320.
Los Angeles Times Book Review. May 1, 1988, p. 1.
The New Leader. LXXI, June 27, 1988, p. 20.
The New York Times Book Review. XCIII, April 17, 1988, p. 3.
Publishers Weekly. CCXXXIII, March 4, 1988, p. 98.
Time. CXXXI, May 2, 1988, p. 84.

DIARY
Volume I

Author: Witold Gombrowicz (1904-1969)
Edited, with an afterword, by Jan Kott
First published: Dziennik, 1957, in France
Translated from the Polish by Lillian Vallee
Publisher: Northwestern University Press (Evanston, Ill.). 232 pp. $29.95
Type of work: Diary
Time: 1953-1956
Locale: Argentina, with many references to Poland

A distinguished Polish expatriate author's diary of his life in and reflections on Argentina during the 1950's

In the two decades following World War II, Witold Gombrowicz won international acclaim as Poland's leading novelist and dramatist, paralleling his friend Czesław Miłosz's career as a distinguished poet and essayist. Gombrowicz was born on his parents' extensive landed estate in southeastern Poland and reared in the careful customs of an old and wealthy landowning family, attending exclusive private schools. In 1923 he began studying law at the University of Warsaw, sometimes sending the butler to attend lectures in his stead. After completing his legal studies, he studied philosophy and economics in Paris for eighteen months and then started his career as an attorney in 1928, but soon he spent most of his time writing short stories. A group of these stories was published in 1933 as *Pamicętnik z okresu dojvzewania* (memoirs from adolescence).

Gombrowicz preferred associating with literary and intellectual friends in Warsaw's cafés to practicing law or otherwise conforming to the stolid values of Poland's squirearchy. In a scathing article on the novelist Henryk Sienkiewicz, appended to this volume of his *Diary*, he denounces the class of his birth and upbringing as incapable of reaching "the sources of living grace," instead remaining "satisfied with such surrogates as ceremony, honors, [and] distinctions" while guilty of "gluttony, debauchery and pride."

In 1934, Gombrowicz resigned from his position at a Warsaw municipal court, desultorily managed an apartment building belonging to his family, and devoted most of his energy to writing. In 1938, he published his first play, *Iwona, księżniczka Burgunda* (*Ivona, Princess of Burgundia*, 1969). While no theater produced this drama for twenty years, it proved a popular success in both Poland and Western Europe in the 1950's and 1960's. The plot centers on a candid princess who discomfits members of her family and court by refusing to play the established social games, thereby exposing the other characters' inauthentic existences.

In 1938, Gombrowicz established a strong reputation among avant-garde critics with his first novel, *Ferdydurke*, which became his best-known work after World War II although not receiving American publication until 1961. The story centers on a thirty-year-old man, Johnnie, whom a malicious schoolmaster-magician, Professor Pimko, metamorphoses into a schoolboy of fifteen. Such a situation enables the author to dramatize conflicts on which he would dwell in all of his works: the polarities between immaturity and adulthood, socially imposed masks and authentic feelings, culture and nature. Gombrowicz's existentialism anticipates many of Jean-Paul Sartre's notions in *L'Être et le néant* (1943; *Being and Nothingness*, 1956), particularly his conviction that in society the others define and constrain the behavior of each individual, with human beings condemned to the enactment of stereotyped roles. Patterned, mutually infectious behavior thus tends to mark the human community, even though it wars against the interior reality of people's psyches. In his *Diary*, Gombrowicz calls *Ferdydurke* his most self-revealing text, "outrageously bold and provocative, in which I, a young whippersnapper, settled accounts with all of culture!" He notes that the novel's North American appearance went virtually unnoticed, drowning in Americans' "sleepy immobility," whose juices "dissolve everything."

In August, 1939, Gombrowicz sailed to Argentina as a celebrity invited to participate in the maiden voyage of a Polish ocean liner. News of the outbreak of World War II coincided with the ship's landing in Buenos Aires. Gombrowicz faced a self-defining choice: He could return to Europe (the liner eventually sailed to England, since German troops had rapidly overrun Poland), or he could stay in Argentina. Classified as unfit for military service by the physician of the Polish embassy in Buenos Aires, he chose the second option, even though he had only two hundred dollars with him. He was to remain in Argentina for twenty-four years, leading a penurious existence.

True to his rebellious and rough-edged nature, Gombrowicz refused to assume his expected role as the impoverished and humble artist-in-exile in the community of Polish-born *estancieros* (ranchers). The only income he could earn was as a bank clerk, while his books sold hardly at all. Nevertheless, he endured his difficulties without complaint, and they are barely mentioned in the first volume of his *Diary*, which covers the years 1953 through 1956 and was first published in 1957.

Gombrowicz presents himself with immodest intimacy in the first four entries of his *Diary*:

MONDAY
Me.
TUESDAY
Me.
WEDNESDAY
Me.
THURSDAY
Me.

He thus offers himself to the reader unadorned, without mask or mystery. Or does he? After all, what most concerns Gombrowicz in his work—and presumably his life—is the myriad ways in which men create forms or molds by which they perceive themselves and are perceived by others. The reader should therefore remain wary: Gombrowicz is both his confessional self and the Writer in his roles as Intellectual, Exile, Rebel, Anarchist, Existentialist, Dialectician, and Self-Dramatist. Perhaps the myth of Proteus describes him best: He has the power, inclination, and need to take all manners of shapes.

Gombrowicz does indulge in a few confessions: He admits that, as he grew older, he became increasingly fascinated with youth as "a value in itself," though admitting it to be "a destroyer of all other values." He therefore sought solace in young men and women—usually the former—from the pangs of his poverty, loneliness, and rootlessness. Like Thomas Mann's mythic Aschenbach in *Der Tod in Venedig* (1912; *Death in Venice,* 1925), he felt himself pulled "down . . . to the lowest stratum, into the land of degradation. . . . And I, Ferdydurke, repeated the third section of my book, the story of Mientus who tries to fraternize with the stable boy." For a while, he admits, he indulged in homosexual orgies, obsessively pursuing young men (particularly sailors) in the vain hope of avoiding the ugliness of the slow death called aging.

Occasionally, Gombrowicz also admits, he would yield to the temptation to have himself paged to the phone as Conde Gombrowicz and to boast of his family's (remote) kinship with the Spanish Bourbons. He berates himself: Instead of charming Argentineans with his wit and intelligence, he offered them a trek through his genealogical forest. Why? Sheer game-playing perversity. "If only I really were a snob. But I am not. I have never even made the slightest effort to 'be in society' and 'society' bores, even disgusts, me."

These personal disclosures remain incidental, however, to the emphasis on literary and intellectual issues. Gombrowicz ruminates on two important works he composed during his Argentine stay: *Ślub* (1948; *The Marriage*, 1969), and *Trans-Atlantyk* (1953).

The former is Gombrowicz's most profound play, parodying three rituals: a wedding ceremony, a king's coronation, and a son's devotion to his father. On the literal level, the action presents the dream of a soldier, Henry, during World War II. In his nightmare, Henry returns to his aristocratic home to find his father and mother debased into drunken innkeepers and his fiancée Molly transformed into a whore. To restore his parents' dignity and Molly's virginity, Henry treats them deferentially and declares his father "king" and Molly "princess." Soon hostility breaks out between father and son. Henry dethrones his father, crowns himself king, and plans to marry Molly at a wedding ceremony where, in a godless world, he will pronounce the sacraments as his own priest. Jealous of his friend Johnny's attentions to Molly, he forces Johnny's suicide. Yet Henry sickens of his omnipotence. He decides to substitute Johnny's funeral for his own wedding, then orders his guards to imprison him so that some sort of order beyond his own caprice can regulate society.

In his *Diary* Gombrowicz immodestly declares that in this drama he was "aiming for a peak on the scale of *Hamlet* or *Faust*, a work in which I could express not only the pains of the epoch, but the new human sensibility that was being born. . . ." Earlier, he declared, "On stage, therefore, *The Marriage* should become a Mount

Sinai, a place full of mystical revelations."

Trans-Atlantyk is a difficult, unique novel whose title Gombrowicz uses to suggest a look at Poland from Argentina, across the Atlantic. It appears to be overtly autobiographical, dealing with many events during Gombrowicz's first years in Buenos Aires and having a Polish narrator who faces both East and West. Like all the author's texts, however, it is essentially parodistic, mocking many stereotypical Polish attitudes. Its style is that of the seventeenth century Polish *gaweda*, a genre imitative of spoken rather than written narratives, replete with associative remarks. Many members of the Polish colony in Argentina were offended by the book's satire. As Gombrowicz ruefully notes, "*Trans-Atlantic* is the most patriotic and most courageous thing I have ever written. Yet it is exactly this work that draws fire to me for being a coward and a bad Pole."

In the *Diary*, Gombrowicz not only settles accounts with his native culture and his status as émigré but also worries about such perplexing problems as the writer's responsibility to his readers, the overall tensions between literature and society, the nature of European as opposed to Latin American culture, Catholicism, Marxism, existentialism, and the essential duplicity of the self. "By taking you to the backstage of my being," he warns his audience, "I force myself to retreat to an even more remote depth." The self is a battlefield, he indicates in many passages, with clashing forms imposed by humanity's contradictory drives to define the world and the individual and to escape those definitions. Clearly Gombrowicz is an absurdist, yet he is also an iconoclast who defies even the loosest classification. The contemporary writers with whom he most frequently locks polemical horns are Albert Camus and Jean-Paul Sartre.

In *Diary* he carefully analyzes Camus' *L'Homme révolté* (1951; *The Rebel*, 1956). He admires its humanistic ardor, idealism, and heroic vigor. Nevertheless, he strongly disagrees with Camus' exaltation of tragic individualism, instead stressing social conditioning:

> For me, conscience, the individual conscience, does not have the power that it has for him as far as saving the world. Don't we see again and again that the conscience has almost no voice in the matter? Does man kill or torture because he has come to the conclusion that he has the right to do so? He kills because others kill. He tortures because others torture. The most abhorrent deed becomes easy if the road to it has been paved, and, for example, in concentration camps the road to death was so well trodden that the bourgeois incapable of killing a fly at home exterminated people with ease.

What of some sort of Marxism, then? He admits his attraction to communism's collectivist dialectic, since he shares its conviction that the culture shapes the person and that an individual can live meaningfully only within a network of dependencies. Yet Gombrowicz turns Marxist thinking against itself to demonstrate that its critical process ceases as soon as a person commits himself to the revolution's ranks.

What, then, of Catholicism? He feels uncomfortable about Catholicism's militantly defensive posture against communism, with God being used as "the pistol with which we would like to shoot Marx." More significant, he cannot overcome his skepticism regarding Catholicism's claims to ultimate truths, considering himself a son of François Rabelais and Michel Eyquem de Montaigne.

As for existentialism, Gombrowicz crows that he played its tunes as early as 1936 and salutes it as an intellectually fertile philosophy which he finds enormously appetizing. And yet—and yet—he sadly doubts that the kind of authentic life that Søren Kierkegaard, Martin Heidegger, Sartre, and their many followers affirm is possible. He tried to live it but found it impossible: "It can't be done because that authenticity turned out to be falser than all my previous deceptions, games, and leaps taken together." He fears existentialism's drive to "penetrate me in my deepest existence, it wants to *be* my existence. Here, therefore, my life bolts and begins to kick."

Gombrowicz insists, then, on remaining a free intellectual, a genial idol smasher courageously willing to pay the price for his nonconformity in isolation and occasional depression. In the face of fashionable lures dangled by institutions or causes, he insists on the craggy dignity of remaining his own person. His often brilliant and eloquent *Diary* may be the most enduring legacy of a provocative and gifted writer whose complex work occupies a central place in the modern literary canon.

Gerhard Brand

Sources for Further Study

Chicago Tribune. March 13, 1988, XIV, p. 6.
Kirkus Reviews. LV, December 15, 1987, p. 1711.
Los Angeles Times Book Review. April 10, 1988, p. 8.
The Nation. CCXLVI, April 30, 1988, p. 611.
The New Republic. CXCVIII, June 20, 1988, p. 35.
The New York Review of Books. XXXV, April 14, 1988, p. 25.
The New York Times Book Review. XCIII, May 22, 1988, p. 14.
Publishers Weekly. CCXXXII, December 18, 1987, p. 46.

DICKENS
A Biography

Author: Fred Kaplan (1937-)
Publisher: William Morrow (New York). Illustrated. 608 pp. $24.95
Type of work: Literary biography
Time: 1812-1870
Locale: London and environs

This biography of Charles Dickens emphasizes the emotional contradictions and ambiguities that marked the novelist's personality and his fiction

Principal personages:
CHARLES DICKENS, a British novelist
JOHN DICKENS, his father
ELIZABETH BARROW DICKENS, his mother
CATHERINE HOGARTH DICKENS, his wife
ELLEN TERNAN, an actress

The early life of Charles Dickens is, for many readers, as familiar as his stories. Buffeted by a financially and emotionally insecure childhood, put to work in a factory at age twelve, rejected at twenty-one by a woman he had courted for two years (her father saw no future in marrying her to a self-educated shorthand reporter), Dickens was by his twenty-sixth birthday not only married (to someone else) and a parent but also, on the strength of his first two books, acclaimed as one of England's most important living novelists. General knowledge, however, often ends with the fragmentary schoolbook accounts of a man whose adolescent suffering fueled *David Copperfield* (1849-1850) and *Great Expectations* (1860-1861). Fred Kaplan's *Dickens: A Biography* emphasizes the continued emotional contradictions and ambiguities of the novelist's adult life.

Domestic discontent and an apparently inescapable fear of financial ruin drove Dickens to a hyperactive public life and a workaholic commitment to simultaneous projects with overlapping deadlines. He was both a crusading social reformer and an antidemocratic snob. Compulsively seeking close personal relationships, he consumed friends and turned viciously on publishers. His writing molded the sentimental nineteenth century image of childhood, yet a letter announcing the birth of a son remarks that "on the whole I could have dispensed with him." Never ceasing to blame his mother for thrusting him out to work when his father was imprisoned for debt, he sent several of his own boys off to India or Australia at sixteen and recognized that his daughter Kate married at nineteen primarily to escape from home.

Kaplan is a literary scholar, an acclaimed biographer for his 1983 study of Thomas Carlyle, and coeditor of *Dickens Studies Annual*. The book he has produced is fair, authoritative, and at the same time highly readable. It is packed with swift-moving incident and capsule portraits of the people Dickens knew. There is not, however, any new or startling information. Kaplan's access to unpublished materials in the ongoing Pilgrim Edition of Dickens' letters from Oxford University Press provides depth and personal voice but does not raise or settle any controversies. Historical context is provided by brief phrases characterizing Dickens' associates rather than through analysis of the social and intellectual movements that were powerful in nineteenth century England.

In the century since John Forster's *The Life of Charles Dickens* (1872-1874) revealed the blacking-factory episode and obfuscated the reasons for the novelist's separation from Catherine Dickens after twenty-one years of marriage, hardly a year has passed without one or more books on Dickens. The biographies have taken approaches ranging from idolatry to scandalmongering and tones from magisterial to psychiatric to banal. Edgar Johnson's 1,355-page *Charles Dickens: His Tragedy and Triumph* (1952) remains the most comprehensive source for informative detail and for critical overviews of the novels.

Kaplan's more condensed rendering provides a vivid sense of Dickens as a person driven by inner conflicts and the need for public admiration. He strives to understand Dickens' feelings and actions without becoming either a partisan or a critic. His handling of the marital separation, for example, is deliberately temperate. Yes, the middle-aged man fell in love with a young actress—but no, the ending of a marriage is seldom quite that simple. Kaplan reports Dickens' dreams of imprisonment, his romantic fantasies about a succession of young women, and his ungenerous criticisms of the dependency of a wife from whose hands he had (early in marriage) seized the management of every detail, down to the choice of names for their children. Yet he also shows the power disturbance that made sleep, work, and home life virtually impossible and the strength of Dickens' need for emotional replenishment. One can understand that a woman of nineteen who married a struggling journalist and had ten children (and more than one miscarriage) in the next fifteen years might lack the intellectual sparkle to stimulate his mind, the energy to share his public life, and the emotional resources to fill his insatiable needs. The turmoil, the negotiations over separate dwellings and financial arrangements, the self-serving public statements, and the pain on all sides are concretely revealed in twenty succinct pages.

Yet despite the apparent striving for nonpartisan treatment, Kaplan's close focus on his central character—and perhaps also his effort to keep the book's size within bounds—often leads him to see others through Dickens' eyes. Why, for example, was Catherine Dickens so accident-prone? On the 1842 trip to the United States, Dickens wrote that she "falls into, or out of, every coach or boat we enter . . . scrapes the skin off her legs; brings great sores and swellings on her feet; chips large fragments out of her ankle-bones; and makes herself blue with bruises." Kaplan quotes the passage as fact—without discussing what the words may suggest about Dickens' attitude toward his wife or whether (provided there is some grain of truth in the description) it might be worth looking for an explanation. Might Catherine have had poor eyesight? a neurological disease? an unconscious drive to resist the role in which she had been cast? Or was she simply exhausted by the frantic pace of excursions, balls, receptions, and dinners? (She had left four children behind with nurses; the oldest had just turned five.) In 1847, traveling with her husband to a literary event in Glasgow, Catherine suffered a miscarriage—she was six months pregnant—in a railway compartment. Such incidents are reported by Kaplan, but Dickens' characterization of Catherine as irresponsible and lazy, remaining in her room while others did the work of the house, is never subjected to the analysis that might suggest competing explanations.

Kaplan creates a relatively succinct and driving narrative through the use of verbs that encapsulate and evaluate Dickens' feelings. Though such judgments may be derived from the letters and other primary sources, the result is a world interpreted from Dickens' own perspective. After the early parts of *David Copperfield* had been published, for example, Dickens received a letter from Mrs. Seymour Hill, a manicurist who lived in his neighborhood and was a dwarf, expressing the distress she felt that her physical deformities had been used for the character of Miss Mowcher. Kaplan's report of the incident says that the writer of the letter "claimed to be deeply affronted." The verb "claimed," though technically accurate, casts doubt on Hill's feelings and removes the suspicion that Dickens had exhibited startling insensitivity.

To an extent, the one-sided portrait is inescapable. Dickens went to extensive effort to create a public persona that expressed the manner in which he wanted to see himself. Though his novels appear to exhibit great empathy for the downtrodden, he took pains to conceal the tenuousness of his "respectable" origins and his stint among the multitude of child laborers in Victorian England. Not only had his father been imprisoned for debt, but his maternal grandfather, Charles Barrow, also had fled to the Continent in 1810 after being caught embezzling from the naval pay office in Portsmouth, where he was employed. Nor did he talk about his Dickens grandparents, who were illiterate domestic servants, although his grandmother was remembered by the family for whom she worked during her long widowhood as a magnificent impromptu storyteller. Dickens created a further barrier to biographical objectivity by systematically destroying the letters that he received. Indeed, Kaplan's book opens with the great bonfire of September, 1860, when Dickens enlisted the aid of his children to carry basket after basket of letters from his study and feed them all to the flames—letters from his parents, his brothers and sisters, his wife and children, Ellen Ternan, and virtually all the literary men and women who were his contemporaries. His own letters, however, survive in remarkable abundance (presumably treasured by recipients who had a sense of their value). The biographer is thus forced to do without the tones, feelings, arguments, and competing visions that might have been revealed in the other half of the correspondence.

Explanations of Dickens' motives rest on Kaplan's interpretation of the psychic forces that shaped his personality. The extent to which this attribution shapes the book's texture may be seen in a passage discussing the marriage to Catherine Hogarth:

> At twenty-three, he needed to come into his patrimony. There was to be no financial inheritance. His emotional legacy was mainly an unhappy one. He needed to create his own good fortune, both material and emotional, to become father to himself. He wanted to match his emancipation with the full symbols of adult responsibility. With a strong sense of having been deprived of a familiar hearth, he used the Hogarths' as the threshold of his own. Marriage to an amiable, conventional, sweet-tempered, and domestic woman, who would cooperate with his desire to be master of his own home, to be in control of his life and work, to have compliant, contained, and unthreatening sexual relations, to have children with whom to express his own familial needs, was strongly attractive.

Although Kaplan's interpretive strategies leave room for disagreement, his familiarity with the enormous volume of Dickens scholarship (second only to that on William Shakespeare) produces a text remarkably free of demonstrable error. *Oliver Twist* (1837-1839) was, however, published serially in monthly installments, not the weekly installments suggested on page 307. Presumably the sentence means to refer to *The Old Curiosity Shop (1840-1841)* instead of *Oliver Twist*. There are some odd choices in the brief identifying phrases. Introducing George Henry Lewes in the context of amateur theatricals may make it convenient to call him "a talented, semiprofessional actor and a writer of steamy romantic novels," but even at the date in question (1847), Lewes had already completed a history of philosophy, and he would become a pioneer in the field of physiological psychology. Again, although Martha Rudd did bear three children to Wilkie Collins, she did not take "her place in his home."

Kaplan's commentaries on the novels also emphasize personal psychology. He sees in most of the books some transfiguration of the author's family history or then-current emotional climate, expressed through disguises, transferences, reversals, and new permutations of unmet needs or unresolved self-conflicts. These discussions of the novels are not, however, cast as literary criticism but as indicators of quasi-repressed feeling, and form a relatively minor part of the book.

The miseries of Dickens' childhood were not particularly unusual; many other Victorian writers had similar histories of emotional deprivation, sudden family trauma, and social or educational aspirations ruptured by economic reality. *Dickens: A Biography* convincingly emphasizes the extent to which it was Dickens' reactions—rather than the incidents themselves—that affected his life and work. Kaplan creates, in readable language, a vivid portrait of a flawed human being.

Sally Mitchell

Sources for Further Study

Library Journal. CXIII, September 1, 1988, p. 169.

The New York Times Book Review. XCIII, November 13, 1988, p. 3.

Publishers Weekly. CCXXXIV, September 2, 1988, p. 94.

DICTIONARY OF THE KHAZARS
A Lexicon Novel in 100,000 Words

Author: Milorad Pavić (1929-)
First published: Hazarski rečnik, in 1986, in Yugoslavia
Translated from the Serbo-Croatian by Christina Pribićević-Zorić
Publisher: Alfred A. Knopf (New York). Illustrated. 338 pp. $19.95
Type of work: Novel
Time: The eighth or ninth century A.D., the seventeenth century, and 1982
Locale: The region between the Black and Caspian Seas, the Balkans, and Istanbul, Turkey

Dictionary of the Khazars *assembles a history of the so-called Khazar polemic, elaborating it into a metafictional puzzle related in a fantastic style*

Principal characters:
JOANNES DAUBMANNUS, the printer of the seventeenth century dictionary from which *Dictionary of the Khazars* is supposedly reconstructed
AVRAM BRANKOVICH, a Christian scholar, an Austrian diplomat
YUSUF MASUDI, a Muslim scholar
SAMUEL COHEN, a Jewish scholar
ISAILO SUK,
ABU KABIR MUAWIA, and
DOROTHEA SCHULTZ, twentieth century scholars
YABIR IBN YAKSHANY, a satanic lute-player

The Khazars dominated the region between the Black and Caspian Seas between the seventh and tenth centuries, after which their fate becomes hard to trace. Sometime in the eighth or ninth century the Khazars converted to either Christianity, Islam, or Judaism—which one is not known—and then declined rapidly. In Milorad Pavić's telling, the Khazar ruler—the kaghan—had a dream and enlisted "a dervish, a rabbi, and a monk" to explain it. The ensuing debate over religion forms the "Khazar polemic," which still inspires scholarly controversy. This much of Pavić's tale is historical, as are the sketches of Cyril, his brother Methodius, and Judah Halevi. The seventeenth century story and its sequel in 1982 are both fantastic fictions.

Presented as a "reconstruction of the original 1691 Daubmannus edition (destroyed in 1692), including its most recent revisions," *Dictionary of the Khazars: A Lexicon Novel in 100,000 Words* is divided into three parts: "The Red Book," giving Christian sources on the Khazar question, "The Green Book" of Islamic sources, and "The Yellow Book" of Hebrew sources. These books constitute the bulk of the novel, and they are enclosed by a bogus scholarly apparatus—"Preliminary Notes" and two appendices—followed by a metafictional musing, "On the Usefulness of This Dictionary," and "List of Entries." It is all satisfyingly contrived and playful.

As the reader proceeds through *Dictionary of the Khazars*, reading each entry, he will reconstruct the stories around a series of triads. The main characters in each book have their counterparts in each of the other books. Thus, each book has a participant in the Khazar polemic (Cyril the Christian, Ibn Kora the Muslim, and Isaac Sangari the Jew), a chronicler (Methodius, Al-Bakri, and Judah Halevi), a seventeenth century student of the polemic (Avram Brankovich, Yusuf Masudi, and Samuel Cohen), a twentieth century scholar (Isailo Suk, Abu Kabir Muawia, Dorothea Schultz), and a devil from the hell of each religion (Nikon Sevast, Yabir Ibn Akshany, and Ephrosinia Lukarevich).

The complicated fate shared by Brankovich, Masudi, and Cohen dominates much of the book. Brankovich is an Austrian diplomat in Constantinople who practices his military skills and becomes absorbed in the story of the Khazars. The demonic Sevast is one of Brankovich's two scribes, and it is he who tells Brankovich's story. At one point, Brankovich consults a fortune-teller and is told, "You are dreaming of a man with a mustache, one half of which is gray. Young, with red eyes and glass fingernails, he is heading for Constantinople, and soon the two of you will meet. . . ."

The man with a mustache is Cohen, a Dubrovnik Jew, whose story is told in "The Yellow Book." Cohen shares with Brankovich the fate that each dreams the other's life and each is drawn to the other by an interest in the Khazar sources. Brankovich brings eight camel-loads of books to Constantinople to support his study of the Khazars, and is learning Hebrew to master the sources in that language. Sevast explains Brankovich's obsession:

> He is trying to cure himself of the dream that holds him captive. The Kuros of his dreams [Cohen] is also interested in the Khazar question, and Kyr Avram [Brankovich] knows this better than we do. The one and only way for Kyr Avram to free himself from his dream is to find this stranger, and only through the Khazar documents will he find him, because they are the only trail leading to him.

When Cohen is banished from Dubrovnik in 1689, he travels with the Turkish Sabljak Pasha to the Danube, where the pasha's forces encounter the Austrians and Brankovich. Cohen comes upon the sleeping Brankovich and runs a spear through his chest, but as soon as Brankovich dies, Cohen falls into a fatal coma. Since each dreams the other's life, with one always awake while the other is asleep, Cohen cannot live without Brankovich to dream him into existence.

The third scholar of the Khazar sources is the Muslim Yusuf Masudi, and his life intersects with Brankovich's and Cohen's. Masudi is a dream hunter. The dream hunters were a sect of Khazar priests who "could read other people's dreams, live and make themselves at home in them, and through the dreams hunt the game that was their prey—a human, an object, or an animal." The dream hunters were patronized by the Khazar Princess Ateh, and their knowledge was collected in the form of the original Khazar dictionary.

When Masudi, an Anatolian lute-player, learns from an old man that he has inherited the dream hunter's role, he receives from the old man an Arabic text of the original dictionary and is told, "As soon as you come upon two people who dream of each other, you have reached your goal!" The reason for this lies in "The Tale of

Adam Ruhani," a myth that the old man relates to Masudi and which is paralleled by "A Note on Adam Cadmon" that Cohen reads. The Adam Ruhani narrative describes him as one of the three original angels of the Creation, who fell to tenth place in the angelic hierarchy but keeps trying to climb back to his former position. His fate is Sisyphus-like: He alternates between rising and declining.

The dream hunters draw from people's dreams bits and pieces of the whole body of Adam Ruhani, incorporating them in the Khazar dictionaries in an effort to put together once more "the enormous body of Adam Ruhani." If a dream hunter apprehends Adam on one of his ascents toward God, great benefits can ensue from the approach to Truth, but disaster may follow if Adam is in decline. People who dream of each other, such as Cohen and Brankovich, may offer signs to indicate whether Adam is rising or falling, and it is for that reason that the old man tells Masudi that he will have reached his goal when he finds two who dream each other's existence.

Masudi then wonders, "perhaps the only way to compile a Khazar encyclopedia or dictionary on the Khazar question would be to assemble all three stories about the dream hunters and thus obtain one truth." Tracking his man through people's dreams, Masudi identifies Cohen from a remark he makes in a young girl's dream: "Your intention is good and acceptable to the Creator, but your deeds are not." Masudi knows that he has found his man because these are the same words that were spoken centuries before in the Khazar kaghan's dream that prompted the kaghan to bring together the emissaries from Christianity, Islam, and Judaism, thereby initiating the Khazar polemic.

When Masudi eventually finds Brankovich, through the help of a Greek monk, Theoctist Nikolsky, he becomes Brankovich's valet and explains that Cohen is the man Brankovich is seeking. Sevast, Brankovich's demonic scribe, accuses Masudi of lying and destroys the feedbag in which Masudi had been carrying the Arabic version of the dictionary he had received from the old man. This incident demands two glosses. First, the reason that Sevast is so angry is that in his satanic role he must be opposed to the approach to Truth represented by the reconstruction of the body of Adam Ruhani as it is put together piece by piece in the Khazar dictionaries. Sevast's role is recounted in the entry on Brankovich in "The Red Book," and his counterparts in the stories of Masudi ("The Green Book"), and Cohen ("The Yellow Book") are, respectively, Yabir Ibn Akshany and Ephrosinia Lukarevich. Second, when Sevast destroys Masudi's feedbag and its manuscripts, he does not realize that the words have already been memorized by his fellow scribe, Nikolsky. Moreover, Nikolsky has memorized the Christian sources in Brankovich's library. Thus, when Nikolsky, who is present at Brankovich's death, sees the comatose Cohen drop a bag full of manuscript pages, he picks them up and then has possession of all three versions of the Khazar dictionary. It is these manuscripts that become Daubmannus' *Dictionary* of 1691, in turn reconstructed in *Dictionary of the Khazars*. All of this is put together and clarified in Nikolsky's dying confession in appendix 1.

"The Green Book" contains a "Fragment from Basra," a scrap of text from Daubmannus that explains much. It says, in part, that

> in 1689 after Isa, Adam Ruhani is on the descending curve of his orbit and is approaching the point where the orbit of the moon crosses that of the sun, the hell of Ahriman; hence, we do not, as we might, pursue you dream hunters and readers of the imagination, who follow him and try to assemble his body in the form of a book. But when in the end of the twentieth century after Isa, he follows the ascending orbit of his wanderings, his state of dreams will approach the Creator, and then we shall have to kill you, you who recognize and collect parts of Adam's body in people's dreams and compile on earth a book of his body. For we cannot permit a book of his body to become a state.

This passage comments on the 1689 story of Brankovich, Masudi, and Cohen and clarifies what happens to Dr. Isailo Suk, Dr. Abu Kabir Muawia, and Dr. Dorothea Schultz in the Kingston Hotel in Istanbul in 1982. Suk is a historian who has studied the remains of what is thought to have been a Khazar burial site at Chelarevo by the Danube. He is staying at the Kingston Hotel while attending a conference on the cultures of the Black Sea regions, and it is at this conference that he meets Schultz. Muawia is a professor at Cairo University who was badly wounded in military combat in the 1967 Arab-Israeli war. He is a scholar of Judah Halevi, the twelfth century chronicler of the Khazar polemic, and his interests bring him to the same conference. Schultz is married to a man who was disfigured by Muawia in battle during the 1967 war. When she learns that Muawia is to be at the conference, she puts a pistol in her handbag and resolves to shoot him.

The scene in which Schultz meets Muawia is crucial. She is sitting at breakfast in the hotel garden when Muawia walks in. Sitting at a nearby table are the Belgian Van der Spaaks—father, mother, and four-year-old son. They are actually the reincarnated demons Nikon Sevast (the mother), Yabir Ibn Akshany (the father), and Ephrosinia Lukarevich (the son). This unholy trinity has a satanic mission at the Kingston Hotel: to make sure that the Khazar sources are not reassembled in the form of Adam Ruhani's body at a time when Adam is in ascent toward the Creator. The dramatic scene in the hotel garden, then, is the fulfillment of the prophecy found in the fragment from Basra.

When Muawia enters the garden, he surprises Schultz by sitting down at her table. He tells Schultz that he has discovered the "Khazar Orations" of Cyril, heretofore known only by a reference to them in Cyril's biography. Cyril's work, he explains, was quoted, but without mention of Cyril's name, by Judah Halevi. (Halevi was a real scholar who wrote an actual book of the Khazars.)

Schultz is stunned by this revelation, and at this point there occurs the fifteen-line paragraph that in one version produces the female version of *Dictionary of the Khazars* and in another the male version. (Important clues to the narrative gender crux here can be found on pages 247, 318, and 320.) Schultz immediately rises from the table and hurries to Suk's room, meeting Mr. Van der Spaak just leaving, only to find that Suk has been smothered to death with a pillow. Just as she finds Suk, she hears a pistol shot from the garden and rushes back to find Muawia dead and the

Spaaks' young son playing near the scene.

In testimony at the trial of Schultz for Muawia's murder, the hotel maid, Virginia Ateh (herself an avatar of the Khazar Princess Ateh), relates that she saw the Spaak child shoot Muawia with the pistol left on the table by Schultz. She is discredited as a witness, however, and Schultz saves herself from the serious crime of premeditated murder with political motive by maintaining that at the time Muawia was killed she was smothering Suk with his pillow. The Van der Spaaks leave the scene quite in the clear.

Dictionary of the Khazars can be described in many ways. It is a narrative puzzle with affinities to such works as *Pale Fire* (1962) by Vladimir Nabokov, *Letters* (1979) by John Barth, and the fictions of Jorge Luis Borges. It is also an exploration of the genuine historical enigma of the fate of the Khazars, worked up in a mix of history and fantasy. It is an allegory of the chaos in the Middle East, where Christians, Arabs, and Jews carry on an endless and bloody historical polemic. Furthermore, it is an overarching theodicy in its dependence on the tale of Adam. (In what might be called the Brankovich Christian version, this appears as "Note on Adam, the Brother of Christ" in Nikolsky's appended confession, in Masudi's Muslim version it becomes "The Tale of Adam Ruhani," and in Cohen's Hebrew account it is "A Note on Adam Cadmon.") As a theodicy, the story of Adam offers a cautionary word on pride, or hubris: Tracking down the secrets of the Creation and assembling them can produce knowledge that is of great benefit to man, but the misuse of these secrets can lead to great tragedy.

Frank Day

Sources for Further Study

The Atlantic. CCLXII, November, 1988, p. 100.
Booklist. LXXXV, October 15, 1988, p. 365.
Kirkus Reviews. LVI, September 15, 1988, p. 1351.
Library Journal. CXIII, November 15, 1988, p. 86.
The Nation. CCXLVII, December 5, 1988, p. 610.
The New Republic. CXCIX, December 19, 1988, p. 38.
The New York Times Book Review. XCIII, November 20, 1988, p. 15.
Publishers Weekly. CCXXXIV, August 12, 1988, p. 43.
Time. CXXXII, December 5, 1988, p. 99.
The Washington Post Book World. XVIII, November 13, 1988, p. 6.

THE DROWNED AND THE SAVED

Author: Primo Levi (1919-1987)
First published: I sommersi e i salvati, 1986
Translated from the Italian by Raymond Rosenthal
Publisher: Summit Books (New York). 203 pp. $17.95
Type of work: Memoir and historical commentary
Time: World War II to the 1980's
Locale: Poland, Italy, and the world at large

A Holocaust survivor, impelled into testimony by his experience of evil, meditates on memory and complicity

"The Lager," writes Primo Levi, referring not to beer but to the German word for concentration camp, "was a university." It was not one to which most of us would choose to apply, even if tuition were waived. Levi survived Auschwitz summa cum laude, and *The Drowned and the Saved*, his last completed book, is his brief but trenchant valedictory address.

A chemist by profession and a writer by compulsion, Levi, an assimilated middle-class Italian Jew from Turin, found himself forcibly matriculated along with Jews, Gypsies, dissidents, and other undesirables from Eastern and Central Europe. He learned a debased form of German as part of his curriculum at one of the most notorious of the death camps. He claims that the survival rate among those who understood German was higher than among those who did not. Much more crucial, however, are the lessons about human nature that this Ancient Mariner—formerly known as Prisoner Number 174517—insists on sharing with a world that has little patience for the past. Levi refused to have his tattoo erased; for forty years, he bore the victim's stigma with neither shame nor pride, but rather a sense of duty to bear witness.

What Elie Wiesel dubbed the Holocaust—a systematic attempt by the Third Reich to exterminate the Jews—is by now one of the most thoroughly documented phenomena in history. Anyone who denies that approximately six million European Jews were slaughtered between 1933 and 1945 is either a fool or a fiend. *The Drowned and the Saved* is not yet another detailed account of the hideous operations by which the Nazi death camps tried to carry out the so-called final solution. Earlier books by Levi, including *Se questo è un uomo* (1947; *If This Is a Man*, 1959, best known as *Survival in Auschwitz: The Nazi Assault on Humanity*) and *La tregua* (1963; *The Reawakening: A Liberated Prisoner's Long March Home Through East Europe*, 1965, also as *The Truce*), are important contributions to that vast library. Yet among the myriad accounts and discussions of the war against the Jews, J. M. Cameron, in *The New York Review of Books*, says of *The Drowned and the Saved*: "There will not be another more subtle, more humane."

Here, in terse, lucid prose, crisply translated from the Italian by Raymond Rosenthal, Levi provides a commentary that is oriented as much toward the future as the past. He muses over how "an entire civilized people, just issued from the fervid cultural flowering of Weimar, followed a buffoon whose figure today inspires laughter, and yet Adolf Hitler was obeyed and his praises were sung right up to the catastrophe." Why, more than forty years later, dwell on the Nazi atrocities? "It happened, therefore it can happen again" is the burden of the testimony by the tiny remnant who survived.

Memory is the explicit theme of Levi's first chapter, as it is the implicit irritant to the entire book. In a remarkably dispassionate feat of analysis, he sorts through his own recollections in an effort to understand the objective mechanisms of memory and evil themselves. Levi is fascinated by the consolatory deceptions that both villains and victims have contrived in order to put a painful past behind them. It is possible, and natural, he notes, for them to be perfectly sincere in their lies. If, as he quietly insists, "the entire history of the brief 'millennial Reich' can be reread as a war against memory, an Orwellian falsification of memory, falsification of reality, negation of reality," *The Drowned and the Saved* is a modest act of mnemonic counterinsurgency. Levi opposes the inevitable and evitable simplifications of history and notes that his book "contains more considerations than memories, lingers more willingly on the state of affairs such as it is now than on the retroactive chronicle." In fact, for all of its historical motivation, the book ruminates on the past principally in order to extract food for ahistorical thoughts about human nature. A chapter titled "Useless Violence" catalogs the varieties of degradation—nudity, excrement, tattoos, slave labor, medical experiments, and the like—in the Lager, but it does so in the clinical manner of an entomologist, to conclude that murderers dehumanize their victims in order to assuage their guilt. Levi is torn between attributing an ingeniously diabolical logic to the entire operation and characterizing it as the definitive denial of reason.

Levi, a gentle, decent man, is uncomfortable in the role of either spokesman or judge. God is absent from his moral universe, and the moral struggles of *The Drowned and the Saved* do not constitute a theodicy. Instead, the focus is on the human agents of torture and annihilation. All humans share in the perpetration of evil, he insists, though to dilute responsibility is to provide absolution. The best, claims Levi, were annihilated. He insists that mere chance enabled a few to emerge alive from the death camps and that one must resist generalizing from their anomalous experiences. Portraying the Lager world as a "gray zone" in which everyone became a functionary, inexorably implicated in the mechanism of destruction, Levi presents an indecipherable universe devoid of heroes. Its inhabitants were degraded, not sanctified. As torment was gratuitous, so was salvation arbitrary. The Lager that he depicts was a complex microcosm of the totalitarian state it served, and compassion and brutality coexisted at all levels. For all that he suffered and observed, Levi asks that the reader withhold judgment. "One is never in another's place" is a severe principle that condemns to failure his own project of witness. Communication is the process of putting someone in another's place, and if, as Levi notes elsewhere, "to refuse to communicate is a failing," inadequacy and refusal are kindred failures. He is, in any case, intent on combating the tendency to reduce everything to soothing stereotypes as well as the tendency to succumb to the temptations of amnesia.

Levi outlines the stages of acclimatization to the Lager and the hierarchies of function within it in order to demonstrate that not the least of its humiliating horrors was the eradication of innocence. For a modicum of additional nourishment, starving, exhausted prisoners eagerly accepted degrading roles as sweepers, messengers, interpreters, kettle washers, and checkers of lice and scabies. Yet he refuses to condemn these, or even the *Kapos*, those who were made chiefs of barracks and labor battalions and exercised powers of life and death over fellow prisoners. Even in his discussion of the *Sonderkommandos*, those inmates entrusted with running the crematoria, Levi writes with compassion as much as revulsion.

The case of Chaim Rumkowski, the autocrat of the Lodz ghetto who abetted the liquidation of his fellow Jews but also defied the Nazi tyrants, suggests how insidiously the Holocaust implicated even its victims. In response to the recurrent, and naïve, question of why so few inmates rebelled or escaped, Levi explains the impossibility of resistance and yet cites examples of courageous defiance. He recounts the story of Mala Zimetbaum, a Polish Jew who managed to break out of Auschwitz-Birkenau in order to alert the outside world. A stranger in a hostile land, she was soon, and inevitably, recaptured and hauled back to camp to be hanged as a public example. At the foot of the gallows, in a parting gesture of defiance, she slit her wrists with a concealed razor.

Levi notes the rarity of suicide among Lager inmates, because they lacked the leisure for the kind of reflection necessary to self-slaughter and because any personal guilt they felt was at the time already being assuaged by harsh punishment. The ineffable ordeal of Primo Levi is worlds away from the adventures of Indiana Jones, but the author describes survival in Auschwitz as "an important adventure that has profoundly modified me, given me maturity and a reason for life." Despite, or because of, everything he has suffered, Levi's is a sane, humane, and sanguine voice proclaiming that "there is no need for wars or violence, under any circumstances." He implores us to remember the Lager lest it recur in other guises elsewhere. In his litany of other carnages—the Spanish Conquest, Hiroshima and Nagasaki, the gulag, Vietnam, Cambodia, Argentina, Afghanistan—the Nazi war of extermination against the Jews, for its scale, efficiency, and malevolence, remains unique. That is his contention and his hope.

Levi's *Survival in Auschwitz* was one of the earliest accounts of the Lager written by a former inmate. First published in 1947, it made only a modest impact, but its republication a decade later transformed Levi into a public figure. "Letters From Germans," the penultimate chapter in *The Drowned and the Saved*, recounts the afterlife of the author's earlier book. In particular, it discusses the elaborate correspondence that developed between Levi and his German readers. Some use the book to fashion intricate strategies of exculpation, and most, to Levi's mind, deliberately or inadvertently misread him and history. All contribute to his own painstaking ordeal of self-examination. With sad and luminous dignity, Levi rejects arguments that Hitler invented anti-Semitism and mesmerized Europe with his mad designs or that most Germans simply did not know about the mass murders.

Within its cross section of humanity, Auschwitz housed a few intellectuals, and one chapter of *The Drowned and the Saved* questions whether they were better equipped than others to cope with adversity or whether in fact sophistication is a handicap when existence is leveled to instinct. Levi cites the example of Jean Améry, a Belgian philosopher whose experience in Auschwitz injected him with a poison that eventually, in 1978, led to his suicide. "Sweet are the uses of adversity," observed a character in William Shakespeare's *As You Like It* (c. 1599-1600). Adversity itself is rather sour, but perhaps one must believe that its uses are sweet, or else life becomes a vat of acid. "The aims of life," contends Levi, in a voice that is remarkably calm and humane, "are the best defense against death: and not only in the Lager."

In April, 1987, shortly after completing *The Drowned and the Saved*, Primo Levi died, at the age of sixty-seven, by hurling himself down a flight of stairs.

Steven G. Kellman

Sources for Further Study

The Atlantic. CCLXI, February, 1988, p. 86.
Library Journal. CXII, November 15, 1987, p. 76.
Los Angeles Times Book Review. December 27, 1987, p. 3.
The New York Review of Books. XXXV, March 17, 1988, p. 3.
The New York Times. CXXXVII, January 5, 1988, p. 21.
The New York Times Book Review. XCIII, January 10, 1988, p. 3.
The New Yorker. LXIV, May 23, 1988, p. 86.
Publishers Weekly. CCXXXII, November 27, 1987, p. 72.
Time. CXXX, December 28, 1987, p. 65.
The Times Literary Supplement. May 13, 1988, p. 520.
Washington Monthly. XX, April, 1988, p. 58.
The Washington Post Book World. XVIII, March 13, 1988, p. 11.

DUSK AND OTHER STORIES

Author: James Salter (1925-)
Publisher: North Point Press (Berkeley, Calif.). 157 pp. $14.95
Type of work: Short stories
Time: The 1980's
Locale: Tangiers, Illinois, New York, West Point, and Italy

Some terse and elegant stories that look with unflinching compassion on modern disappointment and disillusionment

James Salter has written novels that explore the dark interior of modern consciousness. Broken hopes, dashed dreams, the very taste of failure are all at the center of his art. Nevertheless, he is not a singer of dirges. The lucidity of his style, the avoidance of even a whisper of sentimentality, the sureness of his voice all lend a brilliant surface to his work. The confidence of his writing exudes a joy of its own, and this joy seems to provide sustenance to his mournful subjects. His defeated people take on the illumination of art. Even when they themselves come only to partial self-awareness, the reader receives the impression that their state stands revealed. In one story in *Dusk and Other Stories*, an alcoholic chases a thing of beauty into the night; unlike the pursuer in John Keats's famous poem, however, he must confront the terror of a nameless shadow. His wife is there to comfort him, but Salter's haunting description of the man's delusion is there to liberate the reader: "The more intently he listened, the more elusive it was." What is "elusive" to Eddie Fenn becomes the substance of what Salter manages to capture for the perceptive reader.

Nevertheless, Salter does not make things easy for the reader: Exposition seems fragmented. The reader does not always know what to do with the richly detailed but abrupt sentences which are tossed about with such assurance and yet are disconcertingly alinear, a spate of stones scattered in a seemingly irregular pattern. Slowly everything coheres. Understatement, terse dialogue, and muted climax all interlock in the effect traditionally associated with the short story.

In "Twenty Minutes," the reader finds himself pitying, with a strange and perplexing pity, a wealthy, easygoing woman whose life is slowly snuffed out in a riding accident. The horse is indifferent, as is the landscape. Only the reader is involved. "The Cinema" is a dazzling tour de force, a parody of a Fellini film in its plenitude of characters and moods, which captures the cynicism and glitter of international film production. At the end of the story, the reader is tricked into an embarrassingly pleasurable, satiated voyeurism.

"Via Negativa" appeals to the reader's wicked delight in the pain of others, what the Germans called *Schadenfreude*. Nile, a second-rate writer who takes excessive pride in the modesty of his reputation, calls on his mistress. He brags of his failure and suggests that successful writers fear him because of his obscurity. The implication is that he is too good to be as successful as they are, that they have sold out while he remains pure. Salter immolates him in his pride-in-failure by rendering him a cuckold. Jeanine, the mistress, leaves him in her apartment to attend a party, where she takes up with another writer who is flagrantly successful and extravagantly selfless: "Generosity purifies." As Jeanine is swept up by her new lover's power, Nile is reduced to the humiliation of ransacking Jeanine's apartment, reading her letters from other men, and finally running in despair to his own apartment, where he tries to console himself by playing Bach on a piano that is out of tune. The cruelty of all this seems as appropriate as the compassion of "Twenty Minutes."

The eighth story in this collection of eleven is appropriately entitled "Dusk." The last light of day mingles with the opaqueness of night. By sharing its title with the collection as a whole, this story presumes to supply the emblematic heart of Salter's book. A divorced woman's lover, a caretaker, announces that he is returning to his wife. Mrs. Chandler, the divorcée, falls into passive melancholy as though she never has expected anything else, as though she has been identified with disappointment in the very act of embracing the hope embodied in the affair. She suggests that they have one last drink; he declines. She tries to express her regret at his returning to his wife, but she cannot find the words. He comes to her aid: "You wish it hadn't happened."

It is like Salter to raise an ambiguity at so crucial a moment in the story. To what does "it" refer? Their affair or his returning to his wife, Marian? To underscore the ambiguity, Mrs. Chandler answers, "Something like that." Her lover dwindles from his vagueness to a sordid anxiety: "What are you going to do, come up to her sometime and tell her everything?" Mrs. Chandler in turn sheds her vagueness for the false security of her social superiority to the caretaker-lover: "I wouldn't do that." He shoots back, "I hope not." Everything has collapsed. Looking into her mirror after the caretaker's final departure, Mrs. Chandler fears her approaching age: "The summer with its hope and long days was gone."

It is not merely the elegiac tone of lamentation or loss that counts here, it is instead the "dusk" that follows loss, the consciousness of passing strength, of ebbing life. The setting of "Dusk" is the hunting season. Everywhere men are shooting geese. Mrs. Chandler is matched symbolically to a murdered bird: "The rain was coming down, the sea was crashing, a comrade lay dead in the whirling darkness."

"American Express," one of Salter's longest stories, extends the metaphor of dusk into a long Italian journey, a satirical twilight pastoral. Unlike the famous Italian journey of Romantic self-discovery, of which the archetype is Johann Wolfgang von Goethe's *Italienische Reise* (1816, 1817; *Travels in Italy*, 1883), the aimless drifting of Frank and Alan through Umbria, punctuated with pickups and encounters with elegant whores, leads to little more than loneliness and sordid self-destruction. Frank and Alan, who began their friendship in the glow of reckless ambition, have realized their dream: They are powerful, maverick lawyers. Yet their success is largely the result of a cynicism that they finally turn on themselves. They become victims of their own corrupted temperaments, the same temperaments which stoked the fire of their success.

Nowhere does Salter's tense dialogue and description of travel and passing encounters, not to mention male friendship, echo the work of Ernest Hemingway more closely than in "American Express." Unlike Jake Barnes and his circle in *The Sun Also Rises* (1926), Frank and Alan have no tragic wounds; their aimlessness is not the result of a social or moral malaise. Salter's antiheroes are merely spoiled college buddies whose meteoric rise to wealth has rendered them as plastic as the credit cards by which they live. The counterpart to Hemingway's Pedro Romero, the heroic and idealistic bullfighter who falls in love with Lady Brett Ashley in *The Sun Also Rises*, is the nameless Italian schoolgirl who permits Frank to seduce her and then rises from his bed with one word, "Basta."

Salter is usually kinder than "American Express" suggests. In "Lost Sons," an out-of-place West Pointer who has become a moderately successful landscape painter attends a class reunion. This most nonmilitary of men proves to be more of a soldier in spirit than most of his career soldier classmates. Finally, however, it is neither compassion nor detachment that determines Salter's tone and point of view. He is the classic Flaubertian stylist—so trusting in his craft that he can risk the pride of the gods to see and know all.

Peter Brier

Sources for Further Study

Booklist. LXXXIV, January 1, 1988, p. 750.
Chicago Tribune. April 19, 1988, V, p. 3.
Kirkus Reviews. LV, December 15, 1987, p. 1696.
Library Journal. CXIII, January, 1988, p. 100.
Los Angeles Times. February 17, 1988, V, p. 1.
New York. XXI, January 25, 1988, p. 63.
The New York Times Book Review. XCIII, February 21, 1988, p. 9.
People Weekly. XXIX, April 18, 1988, p. 17.
Publishers Weekly. CCXXXII, December 11, 1987, p. 49.
The Washington Post Book World. XVIII, March 6, 1988, p. 1.

ELIA KAZAN
A Life

Author: Elia Kazan (1909-)
Publisher: Alfred A. Knopf (New York). Illustrated. 848 pp. $24.95
Type of work: Autobiography
Time: 1907 to the 1980's
Locale: New York City and Hollywood

An outstanding autobiography—candid, self-critical, and uncompromising—by one of America's greatest film and theater directors

Principal personages:
ELIA KAZAN, one of the great directors of the stage and screen
GEORGE KAZAN, his father, a rug merchant who disliked his son's quest for an education and a career in the arts
ATHENA KAZAN, his mother, who abetted his educational and artistic ambitions
MOLLY THATCHER KAZAN, his first wife, who became her husband's best adviser and champion
BARBARA KAZAN, his mistress, later his second wife
MARLON BRANDO, an actor
HAROLD CLURMAN, one of the founders of the Group Theater
ARTHUR MILLER, a playwright
MARILYN MONROE, an actress who was Kazan's lover for a short time
CLIFFORD ODETS, the star playwright of the Group Theater
LEE STRASBERG, one of the founders of the Group Theater, later artistic director of the Actors Studio
TENNESSEE WILLIAMS, a playwright
DARRYL F. ZANUCK, a Hollywood mogul under whose supervision Kazan often worked

Elia Kazan has written a robust, intimate, and candid account of his nearly eighty years in America as an immigrant son, insecure college student, apprentice actor, famed director in New York and Hollywood, novelist, lover, and husband. It is not simply that Kazan is willing to discuss the most private matters of his life and career but the familiar tone he takes with his readers that is most beguiling. He often challenges his readers, asking them whether they consider themselves superior to him when he speaks of cheating on his wife or retaliating for slights he experienced as a Greek boy who did not fit the conventional Anglo conceptions of a handsome, successful man. Instead of merely recounting the experiences of his life, he dramatizes them, rekindling the anger and shame he felt over being excluded from proper society, the satisfaction he took from whisking women away from other successful men. As he bluntly admits, much of his behavior has been motivated by ambition and revenge.

Most autobiographies contain photographs, but few autobiographers take Kazan's tack of interpreting pictures of himself, his family, and others and of inviting readers to likewise. The early pages of *Elia Kazan: A Life* recount Kazan's mixed feelings about his harsh father, who wanted his son to go into the carpet business, who opposed his wish to go to Williams College, and who expected his son to choose a woman from his own immigrant class. The photographs do indeed bear out Kazan's depiction of a family dominated by the father but also closely knit, loving, and at ease with one another. Kazan's youthful photographs support his recollection of himself as an unformed boy: There is something empty in his face. It is, as he says, a mask, covering all sorts of doubts and desires.

When Kazan's father learned that his wife had connived to send their eldest son to college, he knocked her down. Kazan suggests that his mother was relieved. Why? She saw that she could take the punishment—that this was the worst her husband could do and that her son would not be prevented from pursuing his own career. Kazan brilliantly evokes this old world, in which the husband seemed to be absolute ruler and yet had to bend (however grudgingly) to the will of mother and son.

At Williams College, Kazan was a loner, waiting on tables, waiting in vain to be invited to join a fraternity. He did well in his classes, especially excelling in literature, but did not know what to do with himself after graduation. He tagged along with a friend who was doing postgraduate work at the Yale School of Drama. There Kazan learned what it meant to be a professional in the theater. He was handy and hardworking, learning how to put together scenery and run a play production.

Kazan's big break came when the famed directors of The Group Theater, Harold Clurman and Lee Strasberg, invited him to become one of its members. Kazan freely admits that he was not much good as an actor, even though he spent nearly all of his time studying acting and created a sensation in The Group's production of Clifford Odets' radical play, *Waiting for Lefty* (1935). Kazan made himself useful to people, performing as stage manager and technician when he could not get acting parts. Gradually he learned from Clurman and Strasberg how to direct actors and made it his ambition to become a director of plays and motion pictures.

Kazan provides many fascinating passages on his fellow professionals. He shows how he learned from them and evaluates his own strengths and weaknesses. For example, Clurman was adept at stimulating actors' enthusiasm for their parts. He could take a whole cast and instill in each member a deep emotional and intellectual feeling for his role and for the play. He was sometimes at a loss, however, when it came to translating this feeling into "stage business" and would leave it to Kazan to decide where the actors were to move. Kazan believes that as a director he had a better sense of the values of a whole production, but he could not improve upon Clurman's deft handling of actors as an ensemble.

As its name suggests, The Group Theater advocated collective creativity. It was dedicated to producing plays of social significance and to developing theater craft. Some Group members were Communists and wanted to produce plays that reflected a class analysis of American society. They saw themselves as artistic revolutionaries. For a time, Kazan fell under their influence, not surprising for a young man who had felt excluded by the ruling class and yearned for both distinction and power. Yet Kazan's politics were temperamental, and he was much too single-minded in his pursuit of his own success to remain under the discipline of any political faction.

The Group Theater followed the principles of Konstantin Stanislavsky, the great Russian teacher of acting. According to this philosophy, an actor's performance of a part must come from deep within the self. It was artificial and mechanical for actors to learn how to cry, to sigh, and to memorize gestures that conveyed certain kinds of emotions. That was how acting had been taught to Kazan at Yale, and how many professional actors pursued their craft on the New York stage. The Group Theater revolutionized acting, with Strasberg's adaptation of Stanislavsky's method becoming the reigning dogma. In vivid vignettes, Kazan portrays the formidable, authoritarian Strasberg intimidating actors, making them abandon all superficial mannerisms and habits in favor of penetrating psychological insights. In the end, he made actors much more intelligent about the parts they played. The danger of his method was that it had a certain depressing heaviness. Some actors could not take the psychological pressure he put on them. As a director, Strasberg was usually a flop—almost never managing to integrate his brilliant insights into a production that flowed gracefully and organically. Kazan acknowledges Strasberg's important role in the Group Theater but also reveals the acting teacher's vanity and self-serving ambition.

Kazan gives full credit to his first wife, Molly Thatcher, for giving him confidence as a man and as a professional. She was an Anglo to Kazan, a descendant of the Puritan founders of America. She had a sharp critical mind and helped him choose his plays, his actors, and his political positions. That she accepted him and had faith in him immeasurably improved Kazan's chances of success. Yet his desire to prove himself, to wrest from other powerful men the women who were the signs of their success, overcame him. He could not resist these alluring women, with whom he committed adultery in virtually every conceivable setting: in their husbands' beds, in Times Square hotel rooms, in theater boxes, in dressing rooms, between acts of plays—wherever and whenever he had the opportunity. Although Kazan attributes much of his sexual activity to revenge, and to a prolonged adolescence in which women seemed beyond his grasp, sex also seems to have been a part of the opportunities he associated with being successful in America. Sex itself, for an immigrant boy whose looks had held him back, was the great opportunity.

Kazan also acknowledges that he has always been more attracted to women than to men. The feminine personality appeals to him, and he has found a similar predilection in playwrights as diverse as Tennessee Williams and Arthur Miller—usually considered to be the great rivals of their age in the theater. Kazan directed both of their reputation-making plays, *A Streetcar Named Desire* (1947) and *Death of a Salesman* (1949), in an especially fruitful period that included his direction of films such as *Gentleman's Agreement* (1949) and *Pinky* (1950), which took up themes of anti-Semitism and racism. What binds together these diverse projects is Kazan's identification with outsiders and with a feminine sensitivity to male and female characters who fail to measure up to the standards of a power-driven, prejudice-ridden society.

Nearing his eightieth year, Kazan has given sharp focus to many of the intriguing personalities of his time: Clifford Odets, Arthur Miller, Marilyn Monroe, Lee Strasberg, Marlon Brando, James Dean, John Steinbeck, and many other important figures from motion pictures, the stage, and literature. New information comes to light about Monroe's early career—particularly the way her mentors abused her and made her already shaky sense of self-worth weaker. Miller is "Art," so that Kazan can show how his friendship with the playwright influenced their creative work together. Compared to Kazan, Miller appears rather naïve, making a mistake the more sexually experienced director avoided: thinking that he could rescue Monroe from the crass world of Hollywood producers and hangers-on. Kazan was too much a part of that world, too shrewd in assessing Monroe's weaknesses, to fall into the trap of trying to save her.

Kazan is unsparing about himself. He is unapologetic about his 1950's decision to identify some of his friends as Communist Party members or fellow travelers; by that time he no longer believed in communism and could not abide the air of secrecy that protected the Party. He admits that he wanted to continue his career as a film director and to avoid the blacklist. He lost friends because of his role as informer but does not regret his testimony before the House Committee on Un-American Activities (HUAC). Yet Kazan is no absolutist. What was right for him was not necessarily right for others. He believes that Odets should not have cooperated with HUAC. Doing so destroyed the playwright's integrity, his sense of himself as a radical and as a just man.

One of the most attractive qualities of this autobiography is Kazan's constant weaving together of his feelings then with his feelings now. He writes as a seventy-eight-year-old man, happily married for the third time, devoted to his family, but still moved by his past—electrified by his performance in *Waiting for Lefty*, still angry over the way he was vilified for his HUAC testimony, and still insecure about his status as a non-Anglo American. As he suggests at the beginning of his autobiography, he comes from a long line of assimilationists. His ancestors, the Anatolian Greeks, wore the fez in Turkey in order to blend in with the native population. In typical fashion, however, Kazan turns the tables on his readers by asking which one of them has not worn the fez, has not in various ways assimilated by smoothing over differences that might have gotten in the way of a secure home and career. Kazan does not claim to be exactly like everyone else. Rather, he suggests that everyone else has, to a certain extent, behaved as he did. It is a cunning argument—exactly what should be expected of a man who has always preferred to work a crowd, not confront it. As actor, director, and novelist, Kazan has been an entertainer, electing to introduce weighty social, psychological, and political issues in the context of a story. He is a self-described artist, not a philosopher, politician, or activist.

Although Kazan's autobiography can be attacked as self-serving, it is remarkable for its depth and thoroughness. It presents quite a contrast to the memoirs of his contemporaries—Lillian Hellman, for example, who preferred the sketchier form of the memoir which allowed her to dwell on only certain episodes, thus saving considerable embarrassment and explanation. What Kazan's long memoir lacks in economy is more than compensated for in its comprehensive treatment of his life.

Carl Rollyson

Sources for Further Study

American Film. XIII, July, 1988, p. 55.
Booklist. LXXXIV, March 1, 1988, p. 1050.
Chicago Tribune. April 24, 1988, XIV, p. 1.
The Christian Science Monitor. LXXX, June 23, 1988, p. 20.
Film Comment. XXIV, May, 1988, p. 11.
Los Angeles Times Book Review. April 10, 1988, p. 3.
The New Republic. CXCVIII, May 9, 1988, p. 34.
The New York Times Book Review. XCIII, May 1, 1988, p. 7.
Publishers Weekly. CCXXXIII, March 11, 1988, p. 95.
Time. CXXXI, May 9, 1988, p. 83.
Variety. CCCXXXI, June 8, 1988, p. 84.
The Village Voice. XXX, May 17, 1988, p. 58.
The Wall Street Journal. CCXI, May 2, 1988, p. 22.

ELIOT'S NEW LIFE

Author: Lyndall Gordon (1941-   )
Publisher: Farrar, Straus & Giroux (New York). 356 pp. $19.95
Type of work: Literary biography
Time: 1927-1965
Locale: Primarily England and the United States

Focusing on the second half of T. S. Eliot's life, the years from 1927 to 1965, and the connection between his art and life, Lyndall Gordon traces the poet's spiritual journey from sin and penitence to love and forgiveness

Principal personages:
T. S. Eliot, an Anglo-American poet
Vivienne Haigh-Wood, his first wife
Emily Hale, his longtime friend, an American professor
Mary Trevelyan, his friend, a music scholar
Valerie Fletcher, his secretary, later his second wife

Lyndall Gordon's *Eliot's Early Years*, published in 1977, treats the first thirty-eight years of the poet's life, from his birth on September 22, 1888, until his conversion to Anglo-Catholicism in 1927. Gordon, who lectures in English and American literature at St. Hilda's College, University of Oxford, is primarily concerned with the ties between Eliot's life and work.

Eliot was born into an affluent St. Louis family, the lonely last child of elderly parents; his father was a brick manufacturer, his mother, a poet and a religious woman. At Harvard University, his undergraduate studies included Sanskrit and metaphysics; his graduate work concentrated on the philosopher F. H. Bradley. Shortly thereafter, Eliot moved to London and cultivated a polished and meticulous British sophistication, as he aspired to the career of poet and also worked at Lloyds Bank. The tall, lanky young man, brandishing a tightly wrapped umbrella and wearing a tweed suit, cravat, spats, and proper bowler is a familiar image from this time, a period during which he also associated with the preeminent literati of the postwar period, Virginia Woolf and Ezra Pound.

Even while at Harvard, suggests Gordon, Eliot pursued the quest for salvation, indeed the quest for martyrdom: "He was struck by martyrdom and sainthood," by "a life that would pass through the ordeals of the waste and penitence towards the ultimate attainment of love." Eliot came to believe in "a God of pain, whose punishment . . . was almost the only sign of the absolute paternal care." This spiritual sojourn, which became increasingly more refined, and its major twists and turns, along with its final and perhaps ironic success, constitute the subject of Gordon's narrative in *Eliot's New Life*.

She returns to several matters taken up in the earlier book. One is Eliot's troubled marriage to the suffering Vivienne Haigh-Wood, a gentle and fragile young woman, who exacerbated her husband's deeply felt awareness of sin, yet who encouraged and was perhaps responsible (along with Pound) for his career as a poet.

Divided between the dream for salvation and the reality of his dependent and guilt-generating wife, Eliot underwent numerous stages of creative invention and spiritual development. There were three other women, however, who played major roles in his artistic and spiritual development.

Until the last eight years of his life, although the world respected him as spokesman for an era, Eliot was tormented by a sense of personal failure. Indeed, it was not until his second marriage in 1957 to his secretary Valerie Fletcher that he found inner peace and "a different pattern of redemption: not through the heights of divine communion . . . but through a more common solace." As Gordon explains, the love Eliot's wife brought him was to him a sign that he was finally blessed. Yet Gordon's subject—Eliot's journey to this state of peace and the women he befriended en route—is not a pretty story. One understands perfectly well, reading this well-documented narrative, why the poet forbade biographies during his lifetime.

Eliot's New Life exposes even further than *Eliot's Early Years* the myth of this poet's aesthetic of "impersonality." Eliot believed that the writer should be totally separated from his literary creations (William Shakespeare is neither Hamlet nor Lear), having well prepared "a face to meet the faces" of his readers. As James Joyce defined it in *A Portrait of the Artist as a Young Man* (1916), the author becomes so refined and distanced from his characters, it is as though he were standing behind his fictions, paring his fingernails. Rejecting this notion of impersonality in Eliot's work, Gordon takes as her major assumptions the following. Although Eliot led a double life (the public man was elegant and confident, but the inner man tormented and isolated), he had a clear plan regarding how to reach his goal of spiritual purification, and he manipulated both his art and his life accordingly. Unlike the more traditional writer whose art follows or reflects his life, Eliot's life complemented his work—because he consciously structured it to do so. He might externalize in poetic verse his sense of sin and need for penance, but this would then be implemented in the specifics of his daily life.

That Eliot would convert to Anglicanism, she begins, was foreshadowed in the now-famous essay "Baudelaire," in which he acknowledges that the awareness of sin alone provides the pathway to salvation; this recognition is imperative, for it permits one then to structure one's life toward the good. Indeed, Eliot's explanation provides Gordon the title for this book: "The recognition of the reality of Sin is a New Life." Damnation thus becomes an immediate form of salvation; original sin is the sign of election: "Only when we are awakened spiritually are we capable of real Good."

It was in 1910 that Eliot actually stated his plan to convert—in a little-known poem, "Silence," to which, unfortunately, Gordon makes only brief reference. Here the twenty-one year-old expresses his quest for vision, for salvation and beatitude, which she interprets as his rejection of sexuality (which disgusted him) and the crass materialism of the modern world. In so doing, she continues, he committed himself to the love of God, rather than of man or woman. Needless to say, the reader can foresee the potential complexities of any relationships that might, and certainly did, evolve.

First, there was the impulsive marriage to Vivienne, who was devoted, highly intelligent, and witty, but mentally disturbed and utterly incapable of pursuing her talent for music, writing, and dance, let alone of maintaining a stable personal relationship. Vivienne's emotional neediness tortured Eliot continuously: She threatened suicide if he were to leave her, and while he remained for several unhappy years, the marriage depleted him of any illusion regarding the comforts of human relationships. As one acquaintance put it: "Vivienne was Eliot's muse only so long as he shared her hell." There are, all the same, numerous scholars who maintain that it was Eliot's steely coolness that drove Vivienne to desperate, neurotic behavior and that theirs was a brutally symbiotic, masochistic-sadistic relationship that cultivated her mental illness as it simultaneously sharpened Eliot's misogyny and fear of sexuality and closeness. Another acquaintance (anticipating *The Waste Land*'s "Why do you never speak? . . . What are you thinking of? What thinking? What? . . .") observed their manic-depressive relationship by designating Vivienne as feverish and Eliot as languorous; she also reported that Vivienne "was terrifying. . . . I felt to myself; Poor Tom, this is enough! But she was his muse all the same."

Whatever the truth, in 1932 Eliot left Vivienne, according to Gordon, for fear that she would destroy him. He had his solicitor deliver the message that he was breaking it off. He then kept his address a secret (not only from Vivienne but also from all of his friends), and she, at one point, desperate to see him, placed an (unprinted) advertisement in *The Times*: "Will T. S. Eliot please return to his home at 68 Clarence Gate Gardens which he abandoned Sept. 17th, 1932." Another time, still desperate to see him, she dressed in a large black cape and hat and went to a public reading. He signed three books for her and left with someone else.

Eliot took a vow of celibacy in 1928; to reject the world for a life of contemplation, speculates Gordon, it became necessary that all future dealings with women relegate them to abstractions. Until now, she continues, Eliot had been frightened of women, seeing them as "inciters or prey of low desire" or madonnas.

In 1927, Eliot had renewed a relationship with a childhood friend, Emily Hale, the daughter of a Boston minister whom he had met as early as 1908. Although most of their subsequent acquaintanceship was through letters, this, and several meetings over the years, afforded him profound spiritual peace and joy. Indeed, he said that he found in her a Beatrice figure to lift his spiritual darkness toward "pristine beatitude." If life with Vivienne had been his hell, his association with Emily reactivated and cultivated his visionary powers. Emily also represented the prewar Boston of his childhood and the focus for the nostalgia he felt for his origins. Says Gordon, she stirred "a dream of beatitude through their mutual memory of pure love." He could regain his youthful "purity of feeling" and recover his dream of visionary prowess.

Needless to say, Emily fell in love with Eliot, and although he professed a deep need for her, whether he shared her kind of romantic love is uncertain. According to Gordon, he saw her primarily "as the material of religious poetry"; she, however, "wanted marriage, not immolation."

A key question is why, after Vivienne's death in 1947, Eliot did not marry Emily. Perhaps, as Gordon suggests, he remained haunted by guilt toward Vivienne; in this context, Gordon quotes *The Cocktail Party* (1949): "I cannot live with her . . . [and] cannot live without her." Elsewhere, she writes: "A new life sheds the old. The problem for Eliot was that the old life, in the form of Vivienne, refused to go away." Perhaps Eliot believed that marriage would intrude upon his spiritual quest. Most likely, writes Gordon, Eliot was still repelled by the notion of physical intimacy. She quotes one of his poems on chaste love:

> Terminate torment
> Of love unsatisfied
> The greater torment
> Of love satisfied.

In any case, Emily received Eliot's highest form of flattery—artistic embodiment in most of the last, great work. Following their visit to Burnt Norton in 1935, for example, when he felt the redemptive glimpse of beatitude, she became the "Lady of silences," his Beatrice, of *Four Quartets* (1943). She also provided the model of Celia in *The Cocktail Party* and inspired *Murder in the Cathedral* (1935) and *The Family Reunion* (1939).

Did Eliot really love Emily? After Vivienne died, Eliot's sister-in-law invited him to her house (and also invited Emily, unknown to Eliot); when the poet arrived and saw her there, he left immediately. The truth of their relationship remains unclear, although Gordon adds a few final, blunt facts. After Eliot married his secretary Valerie (again impulsively) and news of their marriage reached Emily, she was devastated. She immediately donated the thousand letters he had written to her between 1927 and 1957 to Princeton University (with the proviso they not be read until fifty years after her death), she also resigned her teaching position and suffered an emotional breakdown. (Eliot had already asked a codirector at Faber and Faber to burn all of her letters: his response to the new Princeton holdings was apparent chagrin.) Although Emily continued to write him proper and formal letters, he never answered them.

Two other women remain to be discussed, for Eliot always knew at least two, if not three, concurrently. Wartime separation from Emily, who was teaching in the United States, led him to an attachment to a British woman named Mary Trevelyan. Their relationship had nothing at all to do with his poetry or his past. A music scholar and member of the professional elite, Mary was a pragmatic, unromantic woman, "what the English call a good sort, reliable without being in the least dull." Her intelligence and wit appealed to Eliot. "What gave Mary her sense of a special friendship," writes Gordon, "was that she was permitted to witness Eliot's transformations from distant politeness to informal chatter, jokes, and eventually confidences about his family, his grandfather . . . and the trials of his marriage."

Yet here, too, Eliot withheld any deep emotional commitment. "To Mary," writes Gordon of their relationship, it "meant intimacy; to Eliot only the exchange of masks, the formal for the informal." In a word, Mary was his prop as he detached himself from Emily. Like Emily, however, Mary would have married Eliot, and despite their taking two vacations together, theirs remained an intense but chaste relationship. As Mary said, rationalizing the issue of whether he loved her, his feelings were different from those less gifted. Once again, the woman proposed marriage, but Eliot replied that he would never marry anyone. Eliot also "deflected her back from the role of lover to her customary one of guardian." Gordon muses, "One can only suggest her devastation when, a few years later, he married his secretary Valerie Fletcher and wrote her that he hoped they could remain friends."

Of this second marriage and Valerie Fletcher, Gordon writes least, although what she says is fascinating. Eliot gave up his religious zeal and self-absorption and became overtly romantic; he even wrote of a new and passionate sexuality (see "To My Wife," for example) and frequently said, "This last part of my life is the best, in excess of anything I could have deserved." As Gordon explains, everyone—even those whom he had hurt over the years—was deeply happy for the man, which leads to the major problems of this book.

Since Gordon's connections between the life and art are at best tenuous (there really is little to convince the reader that Prufrock is the young Eliot, rather than a persona), then of what possible use is this entire project, other than to provide gossip about one of the world's literary giants and inevitably to tarnish the man's image? Eliot will remain perhaps the century's most influential poet, regardless of his relationship with women. This book can leave one only with a diminished regard for the man. Regardless of Gordon's weak rationalizations throughout (for example, his indifference to his friends resulted from his own sensitivity), Eliot ultimately emerges as a selfish man who used people and sloughed them off when he was done with them. A visit to his friend Virginia Woolf after his wife was long deposited in the mental asylum prompted Woolf to write: "Mrs. Eliot has almost died at times in the last month. Tom, though infinitely considerate, is also perfectly detached." Eliot is portrayed as cold and uncaring to virtually all of his friends, even Geoffrey Faber and John Hayward in his terminal muscular dystrophy.

Gordon's chronology of Eliot's relationships and works is jumbled, and as she moves back and forth in time and focuses simultaneously on the four different women, the reader has a difficult time coordinating the work and life, presumably her main endeavor. On the other hand, when she analyzes individual works, such as *Four Quartets*, and sets aside her project to connect character with life, the discussions, while not wholly original, are interesting in the extreme. Her thesis that Eliot's life followed the pattern of *The Divine Comedy*—he was in hell with Vivienne, in purgatory in his middle years, in penance and expiation with both Emily and Mary, and in paradise with Valerie—is thought-provoking. Gordon also connects Eliot's religiosity with his American ancestors, and her evocations of

Jonathan Edwards, Cotton Mather, Nathaniel Hawthorne, and Henry James are fascinating, as are the connections she makes between the poet's life, Calvinism, and the fictional characters of Hawthorne and James. The book is also filled with wonderful odd observations, such as how kind Eliot was as an editor both at Faber and Faber and *The Criterion* and his amusing relationship with Groucho Marx.

Gordon reports that after Eliot died, Mary Trevelyan asked of herself and John Hayward, "Have John and I known and loved the real man?" While this is a question which those closest to the poet might well have asked, it is inappropriate to put before the reader, for it is surely one he cannot or ought not ask. Apart from the matter of serving curiosity, which this amply does, it will not, one would hope, in any way change readers' relationship to a poet they have loved.

Lois Gordon

Sources for Further Study

Boston Globe. September 26, 1988, p. 17.
The Economist. CCIX, October 1, 1988, p. 99.
Kirkus Reviews. LVI, July 1, 1988, p. 949.
Library Journal. CXIII, September 1, 1988, p. 168.
National Review. XL, November 7, 1988, p. 65.
The New Republic. CXCIX, December 12, 1988, p. 28.
The New York Review of Books. XXXV, November 10, 1988, p. 3.
The New York Times Book Review. XCIII, October 16, 1988, p. 1.
Publishers Weekly. CCXXXIV, July 22, 1988, p. 47.
The Times Literary Supplement. September 23, 1988, p. 1037.

EMPEROR OF THE AIR

Author: Ethan Canin (1960-)
Publisher: Houghton Mifflin (Boston). 179 pp. $15.95
Type of work: Short stories
Time: The 1980's
Locale: The United States, especially California and New England

A fine first collection of nine stories by the recipient of a Houghton Mifflin Literary Fellowship

Ethan Canin grew up in California and is a resident of Boston, where he is enrolled in the Harvard University Medical School. A graduate of the Iowa Writers Workshop, he has published widely and has amassed an impressive list of awards: the James Michener Award, the Henfield/*Transatlantic Review* Award, the Houghton Mifflin Literary Fellowship, and a $20,000 fellowship from the National Endowment for the Arts. Additionally, two of the stories in *Emperor of the Air*, Canin's first collection, appeared respectively in the 1985 and 1986 editions of *Best American Short Stories*. Canin's work has been compared to that of John Cheever, Peter Taylor, and John Updike, three masters of the short story. Few young writers can claim such prestigious accomplishments.

Emperor of the Air contains nine stories that center on moments of awareness and decision, moments of beauty, hope, and love. These crystalline moments, coupled with rich descriptive prose, grant power to Canin's stories. Yet Canin exhibits some of the young writer's tendency to limit his range. Of the nine stories here, eight have first-person narrators, only one of whom is female. Also, though his male figures are strongly delineated, many of Canin's female characters are superficially or stereotypically drawn. Too many of them are manipulative and unlikable or extraordinarily self-punishing and naïve. A writer of traditionally structured stories, Canin relies heavily on retrospection, which he handles successfully. A weakness perhaps emerges in his tendency to dwell on the struggle between parents and children.

Though it contains sections of retrospection, the title story in an exception. Its focus is the conflict, not between parent and child, but between the sixty-nine-year-old narrator and his neighbor over the continued life of the narrator's vermin-ridden elm tree. Mr. Pike, the neighbor, wants the 250-year-old elm destroyed before it crumbles into his house or its vermin infest his own young elms. The narrator, a traditionalist whose health is failing, fights to save the tree, even stooping to a scheme to infest Mr. Pike's trees. The elm is a symbol of the narrator, his childhood and ancestors, a link with the past. Like the narrator, who has suffered a heart attack, it is decaying from within, while Mr. Pike, who is linked with modern shoddiness and self-interest, remains strong and adamant. Conscientious in carrying out this characterization, Canin uses even the different types of wristwatches the two men wear to detail their differences.

The beauty of this story can be found in Canin's precise descriptions of the moments of awareness and joy the narrator experiences, moments that celebrate life. Even the insects that infest the narrator's tree are described in a way that is both scientific and poetic. The most poignant moments, however, come near the story's end. When the narrator stumbles into his neighbor's homemade bomb shelter, he realizes that Mr. Pike is after all "a hopeless man, . . . small and afraid." Moments later, the narrator, himself a childless man whose father taught him about the night sky, overhears Mr. Pike attempting to name the constellations for his son, even though "he didn't know what they were and was making up their names as he spoke." Witnessing Mr. Pike's vulnerability, the intimacy he expresses with his son, brings a moment of overwhelming joy and wonder to the narrator, a sense of rebirth.

Canin's writing peaks in these moments, but not all the stories in *Emperor of the Air* have the power of the title story. Two stories that frustrate rather than elate are "The Year of Getting to Know Us" and "Where We Are Now." Both have male narrators in their mid- to late thirties or early forties. Both have peculiarly flat tones, products of the narrators' voices. Both present unfavorable portraits of women who demand or expect too much of their husbands and their marriages. Both also involve marital difficulties, though the true conflict in "The Year of Getting to Know Us" is an unresolved one between the narrator and his father, a cold man, indifferent to his son and family life. The problem with these stories is their lack of the clarity of values and character found in Canin's "Emperor of the Air." Leonard, the narrator of "The Year of Getting to Know Us," is a cool and objective man, satisfied, he maintains, with his marriage and life, though his wife has an extramarital affair to see if she can hurt him. On the surface, Leonard is unlike his remote father, yet the story ends with a flashback that leads the reader to question that assumption. Just how much did Leonard's father influence him? What kind of man is Leonard, really? Why is he so accepting of his wife's affair? Indeed, what sort of woman would have an affair to hurt her husband, to get him to react?

"Where We Are Now" is equally frustrating. The narrator, Charlie Gordon, presents himself as a man of principle, a high-school teacher and coach who passed up a career in baseball in order to lead an authentic life. A hero in his own eyes, Gordon, like Leonard in "The Year of Getting to Know Us," displeases and disappoints his wife. In the end, he abandons his values, his strong belief in the importance of honesty, to please her. Again, the reader is left puzzled. Is Gordon as shallow and shoddy as the life reflected in the neighborhoods he and his wife, Jodi, visit? If Gordon is merely a decent man corrupted by a corrupt world, what, then, can be said of his wife's role in his corruption, for it is she who leads him to lie? Like "The Year of Getting to Know Us," "Where We Are Now" raises questions that remain unanswered, yet the two stories are successful in portraying subtle moments of awareness and isolation. For Leonard, that moment comes the morning after his father's death, when he realizes that he never knew his father. For Charlie Gordon, there are two such moments: when he realizes that he does not trust his wife and, later, when he decides to compromise his values and lie for his wife's sake. In these moments, the two stories reveal Canin's gift for capturing the subtle perceptions that alter human relationships and lives.

"Pitch Memory," "Lies," "The Carnival Dog, the Buyer of Diamonds," and "Star Food" are four stories in Canin's collection that focus on parent-child relationships. All reveal Canin's gift for characterization and his skill at capturing moments of intimacy and decision. "Pitch Memory" is the only story in *Emperor of the Air* that has a female narrator. The center of conflict is the relationship of the narrator and her mother, who sees her daughter as a failure because she is an artist and a waitress. Since the father's death, the mother has been shoplifting and has become obsessed with her daughter's success. While the narrator's sister, Tessa, is a prosperous doctor, the narrator is the family failure. The story's title refers symbolically to this failing, specifically to the family's musical talents, which the narrator does not share. Her drawing is both a substitute for and a defense against this failing.

"Pitch Memory" opens with a bitter judgment of the mother as a thief and uses imagery of shadows to mark the worsening of the parent-child relationship. It closes, however, with a moment of intimacy and warmth. Two moments of awareness unite the story. The first comes when the narrator's father found her boyfriend in her bedroom but did not condemn her. The other comes when the narrator realizes that she must pay off a department-store guard who has caught her mother shoplifting. Both are moments of loss, as is the closing scene of the story, when the narrator listens to her mother's unconscious humming as the older woman sleeps on her daughter's shoulder. "Despite all science," the narrator comments, "we will never understand the sadness of certain notes."

"Lies" is one of the strongest stories in this collection. Its focus is the relationship of the narrator, eighteen-year-old Jack, and his father, as well as that between Jack and his girlfriend, Katy. A story of decision and maturation, "Lies" is a boy-meets-girl, boy-gets-girl story with a twist. The moment of crisis is the narrator's decision to leave his dead-end motion-picture theater job and flee with Katy in her brother-in-law's Fleetwood Cadillac, an appropriately named vehicle for escape. In making his choice, the narrator alienates himself from his father at the same time that he frees himself from the control of his boss, another father figure. The voice, the tone, and the vocabulary are perfectly matched to those of a working-class Roxbury, Massachusetts, teenager and represent a triumph of Canin's skill in characterization. Only his portrait of Katy as a flirtatious and thoughtless female slips in this otherwise fine story.

"The Carnival Dog, the Buyer of Diamonds" is the only story in *Emperor of the Air* narrated in third person. It is the story of Myron Lufkin and his father, Abe, a man who worships the body and settles all issues through physical contests. Told retrospectively, the story recounts the period in Myron's life when he decided to quit medical school. A tale capturing the mythical combat between father and son, "The Carnival Dog, the Buyer of Diamonds" is humorous and lighter in tone than the other stories in this collection, yet like those other stories, it exhibits Canin's skill in character portrayal. Like Canin's other stories, moreover, "The Carnival Dog, the Buyer of Diamonds" is beautifully written, with passages of poetic prose. Medical school for Myron is "a mountain of facts, a giant granite peak full of outcroppings and hidden crevices." The moment of awareness and decision is also rendered poetically. Pinned to the icy ground by his father, Myron reaches a decision in terms that suggest a metaphor for the conflict between the insubstantial dreams of youth and the reality of death: "These are clouds above us, and below us there is ice and earth."

In "Star Food," another first-person narrative, Canin continues to explore the relationship of a young man, eighteen-year-old Dade, and his parents, especially his father, the owner of Star Foods grocery. Here the conflict is not only between Dade and his parents but also between the two parents themselves. Dade's mother is a dreamer who encourages inactivity in her son, believing that he will discover something marvelous through his idleness. His father, in contrast, is a pragmatist, who thinks that his son is bluffing in order to avoid the hard work needed to succeed in life. The unifying image and symbol for this story is the star. It is a symbol both of the father's grocery business, which the son will someday inherit, as well as of the dreams and enlightenment for which the mother hopes. Significantly, Dade spends his evenings on the grocery's roof, which houses a giant neon-lit star, looking at the sky. Like other stories in Canin's collection, "Star Food" is a tale of adolescent confusion and decision, a conflict exacerbated here by the parents' conflicting voices. The moment of choice comes for Dade when he acts independently of both parents.

Two strikingly different and equally powerful stories round out Canin's collection: "American Beauty" and "We Are Nighttime Travelers." "American Beauty" is an ironic tale of adolescent conflict, not with parents, but among siblings. The title refers to a hardware brand on a hammer with which the narrator's brother, Lawrence, threatens his sister. At the same time, the title alludes ironically to the destructiveness of the middle-American family as depicted here. Set in Point Bluff, Iowa, the story's focus is the close relationship of Edgar, the narrator, and his older brother, Lawrence, a tough, unloving figure, and the antagonism between the two brothers and Darienne, their sister. Canin captures the tension among siblings through a series of disturbing episodes that mirror Edgar's admiration and confusion about his brother. Once again, however, women are unfavorably portrayed. The seductive neighbor, Mrs. Silver, seems more a lawn ornament than a character. Edgar's mother quotes the Bible so often that the reader does not question why her husband left, and Darienne, though depicted as a talented artist and musician, is frustratingly self-punishing. A powerful story of how siblings allow only limited intimacy and deny feelings, "American Beauty" presents the difficult choice for the narrator of following his mother's sympathetic advice about his sister or imitating Lawrence's cruel treatment. Significantly, the story ends with Lawrence's bitter departure and a moment of shared sorrow between Edgar and Darienne.

A tale of romance about an aging couple who have been married for forty-six years, "We Are Nighttime Travelers" is perhaps the most poignant story in *Emperor of the Air*. His health failing, the narrator, Frank Manlius, sets out to court his wife again with a gentle and romantic passion long forgotten in their shared lives. Here Canin manages not only to create the right tone and pacing but also to capture the bewilderment of Francine, the narrator's wife, without stereotyping or condescension. Elements of setting and weather are all used successfully to portray the late-life romance of this aging couple. A delicately modulated story of subtle feelings, "We Are Nighttime Travelers" is Canin at his best, rendering moments of intimacy and rejuvenation, what the narrator calls "the feeling of a miracle."

Emperor of the Air is an impressive first collection of stories, despite some limitations and weaknesses. At their best, the stories capture subtle moments of awareness and feeling, moments that speak to the reader's heart.

Stella Nesanovich

Sources for Further Study

Chicago Tribune. March 10, 1988, V, p. 3.
The Christian Science Monitor. March 16, 1988, p. 20.
Kirkus Reviews. LV, December 15, 1987, p. 1688.
Library Journal. CXIII, February 1, 1988, p. 75.
Los Angeles Times. February 3, 1988, V, p. 6.
The New Leader. LXXI, March 21, 1988, p. 21.
New York. XXI, January 25, 1988, p. 53.
The New York Times Book Review. XCIII, February 14, 1988, p. 7.
People Weekly. XXIX, February 1, 1988, p. 13.
Publishers Weekly. CCXXXII, December 25, 1987, p. 61.
Short Story Review. V, Summer, 1988, p. 12.
The Wall Street Journal. February 16, 1988, p. 34.
The Washington Post. January 20, 1988, p. C2.

EMPIRE OF FORTUNE
Crowns, Colonies, and Tribes in the Seven Years War in America

Author: Francis Jennings (1918-)
Publisher: W. W. Norton (New York). Illustrated. 520 pp. $27.50
Type of work: History
Time: 1745-1776
Locale: Primarily Pennsylvania

The author explicates and judges the complex motives and schemes of French, English, and American imperialists, the goals of various Indian leaders and groups during the closing years of the French empire in North America, and the matrix of Indian-white relations on the eve of the American Revolution

Principal personages:
BENJAMIN FRANKLIN, a Pennsylvania politician, land speculator, and opponent of the proprietory faction
SIR WILLIAM JOHNSON, the superintendent of Indian affairs
LORD LOUDOUN, the commander of the British forces in the colonies
THOMAS PENN, the Proprietor of Pennsylvania and a foe of representative government
FRANCIS PARKMAN, a narrative historian of the French and Indian War
LAWRENCE H. GIPSON, a historian, the leader of the imperial school of scholarship

This is the third volume of a trilogy that traces the gradual expansion of English influence in America. The first two books—*The Invasion of America: Indians, Colonialism, and the Cant of Conquest* (1975) and *The Ambiguous Iroquois Empire: The Covenant Chain Confederation of Indian Tribes with English Colonies from Its Beginnings to the Lancaster Treaty of 1744* (1984)—brought Francis Jennings' analysis to roughly 1744. The significance of his work is not debatable. His major contribution, especially in this final volume, is to demonstrate that various Indian groups confronting both the English and the French had their own agendas, leaders, and strategies involving both European intruders and other tribes and that they were anything but passive or reactive pawns easily manipulated by colonial authorities. Jennings endeavors to make clear that tribal leaders were rational human beings with defined objectives who exercised power in attempting to achieve them. Jennings also explains how they were deceived by corrupt white men or were the victims of their own tribal or personal ambitions. Jennings does a fine job in delineating the conflicting interest groups within Pennsylvania and the devious role played by the proprietor, Thomas Penn. In fact, this is probably one of the best interpretive studies of Pennsylvania during the Seven Years' War.

Many of Jennings' conclusions—for example, his observation that the American Revolution had its origin in the legislative and legal experiences of the colonists before the Peace of 1763—may not be entirely new, but they are formidably buttressed with both facts and vigorous arguments. Thus, the strength of Jennings' book lies in its effort to present fresh interpretations and new material as well as to recast the history of the Anglo-American colonial experience. Jennings, who for years headed the Newberry Library Center for the History of the American Indian, seeks to replace the romantic narrative histories of Francis Parkman and to supplement the thirteen-volume, magisterial work of Lawrence Henry Gipson, *The British Empire Before the American Revolution* (1936-1970).

Both the content and style of Jennings' work make him a revisionist. He has read widely and deeply in both the published and the unpublished literature, and it is undeniable that he has turned up errors in the work of his predecessors, especially Parkman, who wrote dramatic but sometimes biased accounts and did play hob with the facts to make his narratives conform to his overarching interpretation of Anglo-French conflict. Jennings, however—who has a deeply ingrained hostility toward historical as well as political establishments—goes further: In his judgment, Parkman is a "racist" and a "liar."

From the outset, Jennings makes clear that he is eager to destroy the leading myths of this era. His book is therefore front-loaded with judgments that are themselves debatable about an earlier generation of historians, about institutions, and about human motivation. Aware of what he is about, Jennings also anticipates his critics by insisting that they show where he has erred rather than merely declare him to be controversial. As a result, Jennings writes combatively from a defensive stance.

Unfortunately, Jennings' writing is free of neither errors nor distortions. Two examples should suffice. Jennings says, "One of [the] cruelest [British] commanders was General James Wolfe who had trained at Culloden and on 'police duty' in the Scottish Highlands." He provides two citations. The first, to Gipson's work, indeed says that Wolfe was on police duty in the Highlands and comments on his courage and his almost meteoric rise in rank but says nothing of cruelty. The second citation is to the novelist-historian John Prebble's *Culloden* (1961), which has no documentation and says nothing at all about Wolfe other than that his regiment at Culloden helped stop the men of Atholl. Jennings also omits a few facts: Wolfe had been in the army twelve years before the Battle of Culloden, had led the King's Liverpool Regiment, and despite his youth was no trainee. Moreoever, Prebble later contradicts Jennings regarding Wolfe's cruelty. According to Prebble, following the battle General Henry Hawley (known as "the Hangman") "turned to one of his staff, who is thought to have been James Wolfe, and told him to pistol [shoot] the Rebel dog [young Charles Fraser]. The officer [Wolfe] refused, offering his commission instead." Prebble infers that Wolfe would rather give up his position than kill a wounded prisoner. Prebble simply does not say what Jennings uses him to substantiate. For Jennings to present Wolfe as Gipson and Prebble do would not have fit his view of the British military attitude toward Indians, a point he wants to make. Was Jennings simply careless in his citation or was he, Parkman-like, determined to make a good story of it and thus make Wolfe a party to the Culloden massacre to give his American experience a new meaning? There is abundant and conclusive evidence that Wolfe was a brutal soldier—who was not in the eighteenth century?—but that is not at issue. What is at issue is Jennings' use of evidence and citation. The reader may suspect a pattern here, and if careful checking bears it out how is he to assess Jennings when he deals with major revisionist issues?

Another example is Jennings' treatment of Major General Daniel Webb. Jennings finds Webb's behavior in the field reprehensible and refers to him as a "mental defective or a poltroon or both." Strong words—especially "mentally defective"—if carefully defined, but they are not. Later, buried in a footnote and in a different context, Jennings refers to Stanley Pargellis' essay on Webb, which says that the general had palsy. What is the reader to make of this peculiar juxtaposition? If Webb had palsy, he was probably neither mentally defective nor a poltroon; he may have been behaving well within the medical paradigm for his illness. Jennings in this instance is so given to overblown rhetoric and so eager to make pejorative judgments that he leaves the reader with a distorted image of the past. One need not be an apologist for Webb but merely a careful historian, one who looks at all the facts, to question Jennings' use of his sources in this instance.

In fact, Jennings seems to confuse judgment with interpretation. This leads him to fill his text and footnotes with negative comments about historical figures, even if the comments do not in any way relate to the issue under discussion and may confuse it. Thus, although George Washington's reputation for ordering wine is well-known, Jennings incorporates it in a footnote as if it were a remarkable discovery. Much the same can be said of his treatment of Washington and Benjamin Franklin as speculators in western lands and as avid expansionists. (Incidentally, this judgmental quality, plus Jennings' quest for pungency, produces some interesting prose, such as, "it is an even bet whether [General] Loudoun's epistolary style resembles sludge more than wind.")

Colonial historians often fare worse than their subjects: Parkman is a novelist; Pargellis has the facts but does not interpret them properly; and when Jennings cannot fault Gipson for accuracy, he condemns him for being an Anglophile, an apologist, and a mythmaker. Jennings fails to recognize that his own consistent use of Gipson's data, his repeated mention of Gipson as an authority, accompanied by his harshly judgmental comments, not only weakens his own argument but also reestablishes Gipson's credibility as a dispassionate and objective writer.

If Thomas Penn and his minions, English generals, British imperialists, American expansionists, overly zealous land jobbers, Indian agents, and establishment historians are the villains in Jennings' treatment, does any individual or group fare well? It would be unfair to assert that Jennings has a pro-Indian bias. He is basically sympathetic toward certain tribes depending on context, and certainly he is on the mark if an author wishes to make moral judgments about the dishonesty and corruption of many whites. Nevertheless, he has more in mind. What he really tries to do is point out that when whites in the past or modern historians have depicted Indians stereotypically as savages or irrational factors in history, they are wrong on both counts. He emphasizes that there was no act of savagery by the Indians that was not matched by the English and the French. He stresses too the purposefulness of some tribes, especially the Iroquois, as they sought to maintain a hegemony over Ohio and Pennsylvania tribes that was critical to their survival.

Admittedly, Jennings' sympathies lead him to almost universal disdain and criticism for white attitudes and behavior, but he struggles for fairness. For example, he concedes that not all Indian leaders were honest, that not all tribal actions were devoid of self-aggrandizement, and that not all Indian warfare was exempt from extreme brutality. He betrays his sympathies, however, when he confronts a hard and disconcerting fact. For example, tucked away in a footnote is the sentence, "I have been surprised by an account of the Iroquois practicing bacteriological warfare by corrupting with animal carcasses the drinking water of British troops." Why surprise? Even more important, why not include it in the text where there is a discussion of the English use of smallpox at Fort Pitt in 1763?

The Quakers also receive sympathetic treatment. Jennings provides one of the clearest explanations of Quaker factions and forcefully lays to rest the canard that the Quakers in the Pennsylvania legislature were unwilling to vote funds for frontier defense. Among the Quakers, Jennings' sympathies are solidly with the propeace element led by Israel Pemberton, Jr., the so-called King of the Quakers and Thomas Penn's *bête noire*. The Pemberton faction not only sought to uphold the original peaceful posture of William Penn regarding the colony's native neighbors but also confronted Thomas Penn and his dishonest henchmen on issues of civil government and frontier policy.

Pemberton may not have been as wealthy as Croesus, but along with his friends, family, and supporters he could raise enough money to attend Indian treaty conferences and seek to secure honest and peaceful agreements. In Jennings' opinion, Pemberton's honesty and integrity are beyond challenge, and he emerges as an advocate of republican government and truthfulness as well as fairness in dealing with the western tribes. Pemberton believed that only Indian-white conflict would result from repeated fraudulent dealings. To expand the area of white settlement at the expense of tribes that had no place to live once their lands had been surrendered was to court bloody frontier wars. In his quest for a peaceful solution to white expansion, Pemberton offered the Indians nurture, support, and honest dealings. According to Jennings, Pemberton, like many sincere Quakers, believed that all issues among rational men could be resolved through honest reconciliation. A cynical reader following Jennings' evidence, however, might conclude that the Quakers, Chamberlain-like, sought peace through bribes and appeasement.

Jennings is not a Quaker, and his warm endorsement of Pemberton's actions, not only in opposing Thomas Penn as a dishonest authoritarian but more especially as a peace activist, may be more revelatory of Jennings' experience and personal values than those of Pemberton, who could be almost Machiavellian. Jennings, despite the combative nature of his rhetoric, is in this book a passionate advocate of peace and a thoroughgoing skeptic when it comes to accepting established authorities, especially if they are governmental or historical apologists for conflict. His study, therefore, probably by his choice, renders an iconoclastic reconstruction of the past.

In measuring the scholarly worth of Jennings' book, a reader comes away with mixed feelings. On the one hand, there are so many probing truths that it must stand as an important piece of revisionist scholarship. On the other, there are questions of evidence, distortion, and exaggerated prose. What is one to make of the highly personal, intrusive, and often *ad hominem* judgments that weaken Jennings' analysis? Is he standing back defiantly and thumbing his nose at his professional colleagues in colonial history, or is he, like the good Quaker, scolding a tale-telling, imaginative child with the admonition, "thou little you, thee"? Most readers would prefer to believe the latter; evidence supports the former.

Martin Ridge

Sources for Further Study

Kirkus Review. LVI, January 15, 1988, p. 104.
The New York Times Book Review. XCIII, May 15, 1988, p. 20.
Publishers Weekly. CCXXXIII, January 29, 1988, p. 42.
The Washington Post Book World. XVIII, March 13, 1988, p. 1.

AN EMPIRE OF THEIR OWN
How the Jews Invented Hollywood

Author: Neal Gabler (1950-   )
Publisher: Crown (New York). Illustrated. 502 pp. $24.95
Type of work: Biography and social history
Time: The late nineteenth century to the 1980's
Locale: Hollywood, California, and New York City

A social history of the Jewish moguls who founded the studio system in Hollywood and created a popular image of an America from which they were to a large extent excluded

Principal personages:
ADOLPH ZUKOR, a Hungarian Jew, born in 1873, the head of Paramount Pictures
CARL LAEMMLE, the eldest of the Hollywood Jews, born in Laupheim, Germany, in 1867, the head of Universal Pictures
LOUIS B. MAYER, a Russian-born Jew who adopted July 4 (1885?) as his birthday, rising from his father's junkyards in Canada to become head of the greatest of the studios, Metro-Goldwyn-Mayer
HARRY WARNER, born in Poland in 1886, and
JACK WARNER, born in Canada in 1892, who with their brothers Sam and Albert founded Warner Bros.
HARRY COHN, born in 1891 in New York City, the head of Columbia Pictures

The relationship between history and biography has always been difficult to define. Society and the individual are inseparable and interrelated; there is no individual outside of society, yet society is made up of individuals. The biographer necessarily distorts history by viewing the past through the life of his or her subject. What is alien to this subject, what occurs outside the control or knowledge of the individual, is reduced in importance or omitted, while contributions, even minor ones, are magnified. Social history, on the other hand, emphasizes the role of people in groups and sees vast forces operating in society that significantly negate the agency of individual human beings. At one extreme there is the psychohistorian who examines childhood development and the unconscious to explain human actions; at the other extreme is the social historian who ignores such factors and all but obliterates the historical role of "the Great Men."

In *An Empire of Their Own: How the Jews Invented Hollywood*, Neal Gabler attempts to overcome this problem by welding prosopography—or collective biography—with social history. The resulting study of the Jews who invented Hollywood (his phrase), while failing to overcome the dualism between the individual and society, does provide a fascinating study of the growth of the film industry and the studio system.

Five of the six major studios were headed by Jews, marginal to and discriminated against by the dominant Protestant culture. Jewish lawyers, Jewish writers, Jewish agents, Jewish producers, Jewish exhibitors controlled much of the nascent film industry. Coming from similar impoverished Eastern European backgrounds at the end of the nineteenth century, they created an industry that had tremendous power to shape an idealized American culture. The images and ideas which they presented on the motion-picture screens, Gabler writes, paradoxically "colonized the American imagination": "The movies were quintessentially American while the men who made them were not." The Hollywood Jews emerged as moguls during a period of rampant xenophobia; they were outsiders longing for acceptance, looking in on the respectable gentility of the Protestant world from which they were excluded. In their drive to assimilate with that culture, they created on the screen an idealized America and in the process "reinvented the country in the image of their fiction." In the process, they rejected their own history and traditions.

The Hollywood Jews had much in common. Most of them had fathers who were financial failures and mothers who were adored; most were immigrants from Eastern Europe; very few practiced their Jewish religion, yet almost all of them depended on Jewish-controlled institutions for financing; most had family connections that aided them in their business; most had little formal education. These generalizations provide the basis for Gabler's psychologizing of non-Jews as well. Frank Capra, one of the great cinematic geniuses, maintained a "strange, symbiotic relationship" with Harry Cohn of Columbia Pictures. Capra was Italian and not Jewish, as was the founder of the Bank of Italy, Amadeo Peter Giannini. When non-Jewish-controlled banks refused loans to the new film industry, Giannini formed an alliance with the Jews of Hollywood and backed their productions. Gabler's explanation of this anomaly is that Capra and Giannini, like the Hollywood Jews, were marginal to the cultural establishment and had similar European impoverished backgrounds: outsiders united against the powerful common enemy. As for Darryl Zanuck of Warner Bros., the fact that he was not Jewish does not appear until page 349, where he is introduced as a Protestant from Wahoo, Nebraska, who had been in Hollywood so long that he "might have been called a Jewish fellow traveler, and his closest friend was a Jewish talent agent."

To be Jewish then, in Gabler's terminology, does not refer to religion. Most of the Hollywood Jews were not Jewish; indeed, there was a strong leaning toward Catholicism and Christian Science within their families. Nor is it reflected in cultural traditions: very few attended a temple or even held seders at Passover (only Carl Laemmle and Harry Warner did so). Gabler quotes "Rabbi to the Stars" Edgar Magnin as observing that film executives such as Laemmle, Harry and Jack Warner, Louis B. Mayer, William Fox, Irving Thalberg, and "dozens" of others joined his B'nai B'rith congregation not for religious observance but "to secularize religion." "Jews," then, was the name given to them by the Protestant world that excluded them.

Gabler at times seems unsure what he believes determines a person's Jewishness, other than birth. His biographical sketches portray many of the Hollywood Jews as self-effacing, even anti-Semitic. Harry Cohn is quoted as saying, "All the trouble in the world is caused by Jews and Irishmen." Adolph Zukor, the head of Paramount, kept his Judaism, along with his *t'fillin* (Jewish prayer boxes), in his closet. Mayer was so American that he adopted the Fourth of July as his birthday, was adamantly anti-Zionist, and married a non-Jew; his adoptive daughter, Suzanne, became a nun. Yet Gabler comments that one of Mayer's major characteristics was his excess: "Everything Mayer did had to be more—a relatively common affliction among Jews." Almost alone among the major figures treated in *An Empire of Their Own*, Harry Warner was a religious Jew; it is the traits of his crude, pugnacious, non-religious brother Jack, however, that Gabler describes as Jewish.

From their poor and humble beginnings, these men created Hollywood in their own images. Despite the homogeneity that Gabler finds in their life experiences, they had very different personalities—from the tyrannical Cohn to the gentle and "decent" Laemmle—and the films they produced reflected their individual taste and values. Zukor at Paramount produced films that "purred with the smooth hum of sophistication"; Laemmle, at Universal, made Westerns and horror films; Metro-Goldwyn-Mayer (MGM), the "Tiffany" of studios, made films of quality, marked by an air of unreality, morally and culturally uplifting. Cohn and Capra at Columbia produced films, mainly optimistic comedies of middle-class America, in which good overcomes the sinister forces of evil—life as Cohn "wished it to be." At Warner Bros., there were low-budget, rapidly produced tough-guy movies—"contemporary and urban"—starring James Cagney, Humphrey Bogart, Edward G. Robinson, Paul Muni, John Garfield, Bette Davis, and Joan Blondell, along with the swashbucklers of Errol Flynn.

It is the bringing together of the lives of these moguls and the films they produced that makes this book exciting. Gabler writes succinctly of the emergence of "the Jewish Prince," Irving Thalberg, the boy genius who rose from a position as lowly secretary in Laemmle's Universal Studios to become studio head at age twenty. Thalberg then moved to MGM, where he married film star Norma Shearer and made a series of wonderful films; he died at age thirty-seven. His life reads like a novel—one was actually written by F. Scott Fitzgerald, and was later made into a motion picture. Gabler demonstrates the relationship between the men and the system which gave life to Thalberg's creative powers and the films he made with such stars as his famous discovery, Greta Garbo. The world from which they, as Jews, were barred, the intellectual life to which they aspired but which was beyond them, the gentility of the haut monde which forbade them entrance—all of this could be found in their films. They might reject their Judaism, but it made no matter, they were still outsiders; only the films they made were accepted. These films, Gabler argues, created an America out of their imagination that was accepted by the public as reality itself.

With the beginning of World War II, the first generation of Jewish moguls began to die and their influence fade. Then came the shock of communism and the House Un-American Activities Committee (HUAC) investigations, which tore asunder the film industry along with the Hollywood Jews' image of self. No matter how far to the right they went, no matter how conservative their politics, no matter how much they desired to assist the committee, they were Jews and aliens; their films were not to be trusted. If there is little new in Gabler's treatment of the HUAC investigations, there is still power in the story when personalized as to its impact upon these Hollywood Jews. They tried to wrap themselves in the flag and join in the Communist witch-hunts as a means of combating anti-Semitism, but they were powerless, perhaps for the first time in their adult lives. Simultaneously, the courts struck down as monopolistic the studio system they had created. No longer could the moguls control both production and distribution; no longer could they hold their stars in contractual bondage. The era of the old Hollywood, with its magnificent empires dominated by Jewish moguls, was past.

Living in their mansions, dressed in their finery, they lived out their lives playing cards in the Hillcrest Country Club, which they built to ape their gentile neighbors, or raising horses, or gambling, in imitation of their vision of genteel sophistication. Cigar-smoking and loudmouthed, as portrayed by Gabler, they could not gain acceptance into the world to which they aspired despite their wealth and influence. Their Hollywood clergyman, Rabbi Edgar Magnin, built the Wilshire Boulevard Temple with their money and devoted his life to creating a tinseltown religion to serve his Jewish but often nonreligious Hollywood congregation. He gave them great spectacles: the conversion of Elizabeth Taylor and her marriage to Eddie Fisher before a star-packed congregation. He was there to preside over the conversion of Sammy Davis, Jr., as well. As significant, but perhaps even more suitable to Magnin's show-business approach to Judaism, was the manner in which he officiated at the deaths of the Hollywood moguls. Thousands gathered to witness Thalberg's funeral in 1936, and when Mayer died in 1957 mourners heard Rabbi Magnin eulogize Mayer's heroic struggles against "pseudo-liberals, Reds and Pinks" and Jeanette MacDonald sing "Oh, Sweet Mystery of Life."

Their sons and daughters could not replace them. The studio system was gone; so were the moguls. Paramount was taken over by Gulf and Western, Universal by the huge talent agency Music Corporation of America (MCA), Columbia by Coca-Cola, Warner Bros. by the Kinney Company, MGM by Kirk Kerkorian, a hotel magnate. "What remains," says Gabler, "is the America of our imagination and theirs." In this dream world which they created, they were themselves lost.

There have been other biographies on these men and the studio system. Lester D. Friedman has written a book, *Hollywood's Image of the Jew* (1982), that analyzes celluloid images of Jews. There have been many books on the Hollywood Red Scare, and even a film, *Almonds and Raisins* (1983), on the Yiddish film industry. Many books have examined Hollywood and its beginnings. *An Empire of Their Own*, however, is the first book to synthesize this material into an account of the life of the Hollywood Jews and their impact, via their films, on the American mind. In places, the connection between the biographical material and Gabler's thesis is remote: The relationship between a person's Jewishness and his actions may not be explained; the role of certain persons such as Samuel Goldwyn and Darryl Zanuck, is downplayed, and the two studios Radio-Keith-Orpheum (RKO) and United Artists, that were not dominated by Jews are ignored completely or in part. Yet the story of "how the Jews invented Hollywood" is one worth telling, and in Gabler the Jewish film pioneers have a sympathetic chronicler.

Norman S. Cohen

Sources for Further Study

Booklist. LXXXV, September 1, 1988, p. 23.
Chicago Tribune. September 28, 1988, V, p. 3.
Commentary. LXXXVI, December, 1988, p. 72.
Kirkus Reviews. LVI, August 1, 1988, p. 1119.
Library Journal. CXIII, November 1, 1988, p. 104.
Los Angeles Times Book Review. September 25, 1988, p. 2.
The New York Times Book Review. XCIII, October 23, 1988, p. 1.
Publishers Weekly. CCXXXIV, August 5, 1988, p. 75.
Time. CXXXII, November 21, 1988, p. 138.
Variety. CCCXXXIII, November 2, 1988, p. 84.

THE ESSAYS OF VIRGINIA WOOLF
Volume II: 1912-1918

Author: Virginia Woolf (1882-1941)
First published: The Essays of Virginia Woolf, Volume II: 1912-1918, in 1987, in England
Edited, with an introduction, by Andrew McNeillie
Publisher: Harcourt Brace Jovanovich (San Diego, California). 381 pp. $22.95
Type of work: Essays
Time: 1912-1918

These essays exemplify Virginia Woolf's transition from literary apprentice to regular reviewer, in the process of formulating the principles that would inform her own innovative novels

The Essays of Virginia Woolf, Volume II: 1912-1918 covers the years from 1912, when Virginia Stephen married Leonard Woolf, to 1918, when she was thirty-six. For much of the first half of this period, Woolf suffered from mental illness and wrote almost nothing. The first four essays date from 1912 and 1913; then, after two and a half years of enforced inactivity, she began to do literary reviews early in 1916. In addition to increasingly frequent work of this sort, she and her husband founded the Hogarth Press in their home in 1917. Among their early publications, her short stories "The Mark on the Wall" and "Kew Gardens" foreshadow her mature accomplishments in fiction. By the end of this busy period, she had also found time to complete her second novel, *Night and Day* (1919).

Of the ninety-seven essays in this volume, more than half have not seen print since they appeared in *The Times Literary Supplement*, her almost exclusive outlet for critical prose during these years. Published anonymously in accordance with editor Bruce Richmond's policy, her contributions included many reviews of ephemeral books; some notices of works by such important contemporaries as war poets Rupert Brooke and Siegfried Sassoon; occasional reviews of significant re-issues, several of them novels by Joseph Conrad; and a few miscellaneous literary essays, two of which are centennial tributes to Charlotte Brontë and Henry David Thoreau. She did not review any novels by the greatest of her contemporaries, James Joyce and D. H. Lawrence, nor, because Richmond frowned upon reviews by authors' close friends, did she satisfy her urge to write about Lytton Strachey's *Eminent Victorians: Cardinal Manning, Florence Nightingale, Dr. Arnold, General Gordon* (1918).

Although the best essays in this volume tend to be ones previously published by Leonard Woolf, this sequence complements the first volume of Anne Olivier Bell's edition of Woolf's diary in furnishing insights into her aesthetic of fiction, which was developing rapidly during the later 1910's. In one review, while discussing the creative process, a subject which fascinated her, and noting poets' frequent inability or disinclination to reveal much about their own processes, Woolf contends that "the best way of surprising their secrets is very often to read their criticism." A perusal of these essays—even her discussions of now-forgotten books—turns up a number of her own "secrets." To be sure, these critical comments do not apply particularly to *Night and Day*—which some critics and friends considered a retrogression from her first novel, *The Voyage Out* (written before her breakdown and published in 1915), for her husband and medical advisers were encouraging her to ease back into creativity with a conventional novel that would not impose too great a strain on her nervous system during her recuperation—but it is easy to spot ideas that would find embodiment in *Jacob's Room* (1922) and even more notably in *Mrs. Dalloway* (1925).

Writing about a translation of a selection of Fyodor Dostoevski's short stories in 1917, she praises his

> power of reconstructing those most swift and complicated states of mind, of rethinking the whole train of thought in all its speed, now as it flashes into light, now as it lapses into darkness; for he is able to follow not only the vivid streak of achieved thought, but to suggest the dim and populous underworld of the mind's consciousness where desires and impulses are moving blindly beneath the sod.

Any reader of these lines will mark the deftness with which she is delineating her own ambitions in the psychological novel and will realize also why Leonard Woolf did not want to rush his sensitive wife's own literary plunge into that "dim and populous underworld."

Her remarks on both major and minor Russian writers are especially revealing. Invariably, she drew contrasts between the English and Russian literary sensibilities with an eye to the latter's superiority at presenting heightened psychic and emotional states. With reference to Valery Brussof, less well-known in the West than Dostoevski, she commends his ability to investigate "the borderland between sanity and insanity"—a borderland only too familiar to her. She complained that English literature tended to relegate fantasy to a special category remote from ordinary life, while the Russians understood how it impinges upon, and can be imaginatively related to, the everyday world.

A book by the English poet Sassoon entitled *The Old Huntsman and Other Poems* (1917) reminds her that "to call back any moment of emotion is to call back with it the strangest odds and ends that have become somehow part of it." Despite the fact that a number of her contemporaries were beginning to exploit the possibilities of stream-of-consciousness fiction, poets and earlier novelists such as Dostoevski and Conrad more often provoked such observations. She had to force herself to read Joyce, whom she considered ill-bred; held at arms' length the pioneering English practitioner, Dorothy Richardson; and resisted the attractions of Marcel Proust for years despite her close friend Roger Fry's enthusiasm for *À la recherche du temps perdu* (1913-1927; *Remembrance of Things Past*, 1922-1931, 1981). The generation of Joyce, Richardson, Proust, and Woolf was absorbing, more or less independently, possibilities suggested by the same earlier writers and by the coming of age of psychology as a science, and Woolf in particular did not want to fall into any imitation of her contemporaries, instead preferring to construct her own literary edifice on the foundation provided by writers who had worked in the infancy of the psychological novel. She was determined to use nobody's "odds and ends" but her own, though in retrospect it seems unlikely that she could have made much use of those from Joyce's Dublin or Proust's Paris.

An example of a Woolfian interest akin to, but apparently quite independent of, one of Joyce's occurs in a phrase which appears often in the present volume. Whereas Joyce's word "epiphanies" derives from his religious training, Woolf's analagous "moments of vision" echoes the title of a book and poem by Thomas Hardy published in 1917. She finds these moments of vision in Conrad's *Lord Jim* (1900), which she describes as experiences emerging from and fading into darkness—the same images she uses in depicting Dostoevski's way of presenting mental experience. While she perceived the great differences in the pace and emotional intensity of the two men's work, she no doubt hoped that she would be able to fuse in her own fiction Conrad's spaciousness and richness with the Russian's energy and intuition. She uses "moments of vision" as the title of a review of Logan Pearsall Smith's *Trivia* (1917), in which she discerns

> his purpose to catch and enclose certain moments which break off from the mass, in which without bidding things come together in a combination of inexplicable significance, to arrest those thoughts which suddenly, to the thinker at least, are almost menacing with meaning.

To her, "vision" is less likely to be grounded in visual experience in the manner of Joyce's epiphanies, more likely to strike her as an aspect of the perception of time, but both writers were employing their insights into the way "things come together" to reconstruct the English novel.

Aside from their suggestions of Woolf's developing creative ambitions, the essays in this volume also illustrate her ripening critical powers. Even though she fretted that regular reviewing cut into time needed for her fiction, she obviously enjoyed writing reviews and complained to her diary when Richmond "rejected" her work—a term that often signified a desirable assignment gone to another writer. In March of 1918, for example, after her reviews had appeared in eleven straight weekly issues, she commented rather bitterly on two such rejections and envied her husband his own current reviewing tasks, but she consoled herself with the knowledge that *Night and Day* was proceeding "at an astonishing rate." Within a few years, she would reduce reviewing in favor of projects more exciting to her than this novel, but in 1918, she was thriving on her double-barreled career.

She selected none of these essays for inclusion in *The Common Reader: First Series* (1925) or *The Common Reader: Second Series* (1932), but as editor Andrew McNeillie points out in his useful introduction, she mined a 1916 essay on Charlotte Brontë and one from 1918, "The Russian View," in preparing later essays for the first of these collections. More important, the reader can see the genesis of her famous challenge to Arnold Bennett, H. G. Wells, and John Galsworthy, "Mr. Bennett and Mrs. Brown," a talk delivered in 1924, here in earlier reviews of their work. Writing on a book of Bennett's essays in 1917, she politely demurs at his generous estimate of Wells's and Galsworthy's work and begins the process of skewering Bennett: "We do not think that this is a book of first-rate criticism; but it is the book of an artist." What is her justification of this second clause? "Nobody could read one of these short little papers without feeling himself in the presence of the father of fifty volumes." Continuing in this ironic vein, she makes clear her aversion to both the principles and practice of this enormously popular and prolific writer. A few weeks later, she deemed the dogs in Galsworthy's novel *Beyond Saga* its most interesting characters. In 1918, she accused Wells of embodying the ideas of *Joan and Peter* in "crude lumps and unmodelled masses." None of these books comes close to being its author's best work, but her point, later to be developed systematically in "Mr. Bennett and Mrs. Brown," is unmistakable: These novelists were heaping up great masses of observation and detail and extending their list of literary credits without taking the time and care to create characters about whom readers could care.

It might seem that such acidulous reviews contradict her assertion in a review of an even weaker novelist that "the interest and value of the art of criticism is more than anything in the critic's ability to seize upon what is good and to expatiate upon that." She goes on, however, to insist that this practice must emanate from a carefully honed sense of the first-rate. Thus, she feels obliged to damn her unholy trinity of Bennett, Galsworthy, and Wells with faint praise, for she has in mind the standard set by writers in the great tradition of English fiction through Conrad, Hardy, and Henry James, and maintained, as she would later suggest in "Mr. Bennett and Mrs. Brown," by Lawrence, Joyce, and E. M. Forster.

Another of her well-known later essays, "How Should One Read a Book?," is variously prefigured here. In the Brontë essay, she expresses a frequent theme: "We offer merely our little hoard of observations, which other readers may like to set, for a moment, beside their own." Later, she would elevate this modest ambition into a principle: Readers must cultivate their own "hoard" before seeking the assistance of the critic. She bears witness to the importance of prior activity on the part of the unprofessional reader in a remark about a critic of Samuel Butler, admirable "when he says something so true that we have always been on the point of saying it ourselves." She was convinced that the common reader, especially one who commonly reads worthwhile books, can develop a sense of literary standards reliable enough to guide him or her in appraising and appreciating new books properly. Like other innovative writers who espoused the great tradition—one thinks of her friend T. S. Eliot—she expected that her own departures from convention would be understood by a reader thus fortified. In several of these essays, she deplores the kind of criticism that winds up a dialogue among specialists. Although she sometimes reports favorably on academic criticism, her ideal critic communicates enthusiasm and shares insights with an audience of alert, nonacademic readers. The critic, she says in an arresting phrase, must give "the sense of possessing a live and combative conception of our author." In this way, she acknowledges the inevitable disagreements among even alert readers. She would have more to say in "How

Should One Read a Book?" about the reader's duty to resist being bowled over by even the most formidable expert.

Later volumes of this edition will undoubtedly contain a higher proportion of well-known, previously reprinted essays, but none is likely to exceed this one in satisfying the desire of Woolf's admirers to watch the year-to-year unfolding of her talent. Clearly, this edition conduces better to this ambition than the dozen or so volumes of her essays previously available. One of the most useful features of McNeillie's edition is its carefully prepared index of proper names and thematic references. His annotations of individual essays are laborious and sometimes of little practical use. Many notes simply supply writers' dates, and it is irritating to come upon a superscript guarding the name of, say, Charles Dickens, turn to the note, and find merely another reiteration of the fact that he was born in 1812 and died in 1870. So august a writer as John Milton receives this treatment; only William Shakespeare, of English writers, is deemed identifiable without his dates. Most readers would be better served by translations of Woolf's quotations from a French work, fifteen lines of which are to be met in her review of a novel by Jules Romains. These defects, however, do not seriously mar a work destined to be the definitive collection of Virginia Woolf's essays.

Robert P. Ellis

Sources for Further Study

Booklist. LXXXIV, April 1, 1988, p. 1305.
British Book News. September, 1987, p. 606.
Chicago Tribune. April 17, 1988, XIV, p. 6.
Contemporary Review. CCLII, February, 1988, p. 108.
The New York Times Book Review. XCIII, March 27, 1988, p. 8.
The Observer. December 13, 1987, p. 23.
The Times Educational Supplement. January 8, 1988, p. 28.

THE FACTS
A Novelist's Autobiography

Author: Philip Roth (1933-)
Publisher: Farrar, Straus & Giroux (New York). 195 pp. $17.95
Type of work: Autobiography
Time: The 1930's to the 1970's
Locale: New Jersey, Pennsylvania, Chicago, New York, and Massachusetts

A slyly self-conscious essay in autobiography by an American Jewish novelist notorious for his personalized fictions

Principal personages:
PHILIP ROTH, a prominent American Jewish novelist
NATHAN ZUCKERMAN, his alter ego in several novels
HERMAN ROTH, his father, an insurance salesman
BOB MAURER and
CHARLOTTE MAURER, his faculty mentors at Bucknell University
POLLY BATES, his girlfriend at Bucknell
JOSIE, his tormented and tormenting wife
MAY ALDRIDGE, a wealthy, genteel woman with whom he spends five years

Though *Moby Dick* (1851) begins with the words "Call me Ishmael," only the most naïve reader would call Herman Melville by that name. A first-person narrator is as fictional—and nonfictional—as any other character that authors insert into their creations. Erica Jong's first novel, *Fear of Flying* (1974), is the bawdy story of a randy young woman named Isadora Wing who happened to have much in common with her inventor. Its sequel, *How to Save Your Own Life* (1977), portrays Isadora agonizing over the fact that almost everyone assumes that her first novel, *Candida Confesses*, is an exact transcription of her own life. Is *How to Save Your Own Life* an exact transcription of Jong's anguish over the public's failure to distinguish between exact transcription and fiction?

Throughout a productive career, Philip Roth, too, has seemed to be drawing more directly than most other novelists on the circumstances of his own life. His recurring characters Peter Tarnopol and Nathan Zuckerman are akin to each other and to their creator in being prominent American Jewish authors. Roth's first book, *Goodbye, Columbus* (1959), a scathing satire of the American Jewish middle class, was denounced from synagogue pulpits for allegedly telling secrets out of court. His most notorious novel, *Portnoy's Complaint* (1969), an epic of onanism, inspired Jacqueline Susann to declare: "Philip Roth is a good writer, but I wouldn't want to shake hands with him."

Rich, infamous, and miserable, Roth reacted to the scandal of *Portnoy's Complaint* by writing *Zuckerman Unbound* (1981), in which Zuckerman is made rich, infamous, and miserable by publishing *Carnovsky*, a novel vilified for "depicting Jews in acts of adultery, exhibitionism, masturbation, sodomy, fetishism, and whoremongery." The hapless Zuckerman is given the first and last words in *The*

Facts: A Novelist's Autobiography. It is as much a meditation on the nature and limitations of autobiography as it is a candid account of the elusive writer's life.

What induced Roth, who has guarded his privacy somewhat less than J. D. Salinger but much more than Norman Mailer, to abandon the masks of fiction and provide what he coyly calls "the facts"—as though the Muse were no longer Calliope but Sergeant Joe Friday? On the dust jacket of *The Facts* is a 1950 photograph of Roth's senior homeroom class at Weequahic High School in Newark. The future author gazes into the camera with a cherubic smile, the kind of boy of whom teachers and parents were justly proud. Yet one notes that, in the group portrait, he is standing slightly to the side of the others, as though already committed to Emily Dickinson's ambition to "tell all the Truth, but tell it slant."

In his 1961 essay "Writing American Fiction," Roth bemoaned the imagination's inability to rival the grotesque reality of contemporary American life. Why invent when the world already offers up events and characters that exceed the powers of fantasy? Roth's fictions have been a slanted tribute and challenge to that world. His new autobiography is a carefully constructed demonstration of how difficult it is not to shape "the Facts."

Despite its subtitle, *The Facts* does not attempt a complete chronology of the novelist's works and days. Instead, it is a series of five retrospective sketches, each connected to a crucial stage in the growth of a prominent American Jewish author. Roth begins with an account of his stable childhood in a lower-middle-class Newark neighborhood where almost everyone was Jewish and his principal interest was baseball. His father, a sedulous insurance salesman denied advancement because of his company's gentlemanly anti-Semitism, is presented more sympathetically than the fathers in any of Roth's fictions. The next chapter, "Joe College," is a memoir of initiation into a very different environment, the rural, goyish campus of Bucknell University, where he began to cultivate literary and amorous interests. The section's climax comes with Roth's perverse decision to break with his girlfriend Polly Bates, because their relationship seemed idyllic.

At the physical and emotional center of the book is Roth's version of a disastrous marriage to the woman he pseudonymously calls Josie, though her real name—Margaret Martinson Williams—is public knowledge. A bibulous divorcée with two abandoned children, "this wretched small-town gentile paranoid" represented a denial of everything a "nice Jewish boy" was reared to respect. Yet, for all the turbulence of their relationship, Roth credits Josie as his diabolical inspiration, "the greatest creative-writing teacher of them all, specialist par excellence in the aesthetics of extremist fiction."

"All in the Family" recounts the hostility Roth encountered among Jews when he began writing about them without flattery, and making that very hostility further fuel for his fiction. At the end of the final chapter, after the death of Josie in an automobile accident, Roth breaks with May Aldridge, the loving, loyal, and genteel antithesis to his wife. Determined to be absolutely independent, he nevertheless recognizes that wish as a chimera. As Roth's Nathan Zuckerman had already discovered in *The Counterlife* (1987), every life implies a counterlife, and the imagination is inextricably entangled in the facts.

Roth frames *The Facts* with reflexive meditations on his uncharacteristic project of writing about his own life. The book opens with a letter addressed to Zuckerman, the American Jewish novelist who, in the several Roth novels in which he appears, is something of his author's alter ego. Roth explains to Zuckerman why he has now decided to dispense with his usual artifice of fictional surrogates in order to try to represent himself directly. "Is the book any good?" Roth asks Zuckerman, and the reader. Zuckerman's response, critical of Roth for being too discreet, too genial, devoid of the furious energy that empowers his finest fictions, comes in a thirty-four-page analysis that constitutes the final chapter of *The Facts*. Yet it is hardly the last word on its prolific, obsessive author. Zuckerman's bemusement over "*the kind of stories that people turn life into, the kind of lives that people turn stories into*," a quotation from *The Counterlife*, provides a suitable epigraph to *The Facts* and to Roth's entire career.

Though Roth claims "exhaustion with masks, disguises, distortions, and lies," he nevertheless, in another of his characteristically sly exercises in imagination, has his Zuckerman note that autobiography is "probably the most manipulative of all literary forms." Written when its fifty-five-year-old author was recovering from what he refers to vaguely as surgery whose complications put him on "the edge of emotional and mental dissolution," *The Facts* presents itself as the attempt of a middle-aged author to reconcile himself at last to the ghosts of his past. For the man who gave voice to Alexander Portnoy's vociferous complaints, this is an oddly mellow evocation of the joys of Jewish family life in what are presented as the halcyon years following World War II. Even the post-football-game pogrom against the Jews of Weequahic by their rivals of Barringer High is presented almost wistfully, as a thrilling adolescent adventure. Zuckerman aptly asks his author what has become of his trademark anger. He accuses Roth of idealizing and sentimentalizing people and situations that have long ceased to threaten him, of leeching the venom from his sources of creativity. He has transformed the primal domestic household that empowered the rage behind his best-known fictions into "a serene, desirable, pastoral haven." Yet Roth also retains the services of Zuckerman to poison the treacle.

Zuckerman analyzes three themes that dominate *The Facts*: Roth's journey from Jewish Newark to the larger American society; his traumatic involvement with Josie, the woman whose tormented existence was contrapuntal to his own; and his engagement with the world beyond his parochial concerns. To that list, a critic might well add the author's continuing dialogue between manic invention and servility to "the facts."

One of the most dramatic episodes in *The Facts* is Roth's account of his shock at the fierce, overt hostility he encountered when invited to speak in 1962 at Yeshiva University. An ostensible apologia for his life, *The Facts* is Roth's attempt, at last, to come out from behind his succession of disturbing masks and proxies and to clarify his relationship to them. Yet the Philip Roth of this autobiographical essay, a man discomfited by comfort, who abandons supportive, irenic women such as May Aldridge and Polly Bates to take up with a psychotic scourge such as Josie, is as unsettling as the protagonist of any of his other books. His theme, as always, is anguished independence—from his Newark nest, from constricting relationships, from ethnic role models, and from obeisance to "the facts."

If Philip Roth had never written his distinctive fictions, few would be interested in his account of a not especially exceptional life away from books. Without the intense and widespread reaction that his stories have provoked, he certainly would never have written *The Facts*, a maligned and self-maligning author's attempt to set the record straight by shaping it to fit the category of nonfiction. Just as *Our Gang* (1971) employed grotesque caricature in order to posit truths about the Nixon Administration and *The Ghost Writer* (1979) implausibly resurrected Anne Frank in New England in order to discover universal truths about the connections among suffering, love, and art, so *The Facts* marshals verifiable data to create another of Roth's troubled narratives.

Students of Roth's career will likely be intrigued by correspondences between events in his life and episodes in his writing. In *My Life as a Man* (1974), for example, Peter Tarnopol is duped into marrying Maureen Johnson when she feigns pregnancy by borrowing the urine sample of a black woman she encounters in the park. In *The Facts*, Roth points out that the woman he calls Josie perpetrated virtually the same fraud on him. He claims that this section of *My Life as a Man* was the most directly autobiographical of his fictions, because he simply could not imagine a more dramatic scenario: "Those scenes represent one of the few occasions when I haven't spontaneously set out to improve on actuality in the interest of being more interesting."

Beyond its clues about an author's sources, *The Facts* is valuable as a documentation of Roth's continuing interest in the question, What is the stance that a novelist should adopt toward actuality—antagonism or servility? It is a product of contemporary culture's impatience with literary fabrication, the fascination with "true stories" that has accounted for the vogue of the "nonfiction novel" and for the fact that nonfiction regularly outsells fiction. Roth writes his novels with the autocensure of an instinctive witness, and he writes his autobiography with the aspirations of a novelist.

The Facts rehearses the old quarrels familiar to readers of Roth's stories and novels—with the suffocations of motherly love, with the animus of a Jewish establishment outraged at his refusal to be a communal cheerleader, with the refractory nature of women and preliterary life. *The Facts* appeared just a few months after Arthur Miller, another highly respected American Jewish writer, published his autobiographical *Timebends* (1987) and a few months before poet Karl Shapiro's retrospective *The Younger Son* (1988). Jews are no longer insurgents at the peripheries of the literary establishment. Yet Roth's autobiography is not a summation and not a celebration of his success—even at taunting success. It is a pause, a somewhat uncharacteristically diplomatic way of pursuing by other means his war with the facts.

Steven G. Kellman

Sources for Further Study

Booklist. LXXXIV, August, 1988, p. 1868.
Kirkus Reviews. LVI, August 15, 1988, p. 1225.
Library Journal. CXIII, September 1, 1988, p. 170.
The New Republic. CXCIX, November 21, 1988, p. 37.
The New York Review of Books. XXXV, October 13, 1988, p. 24.
The New York Times Book Review. XCIII, September 25, 1988, p. 3.
Newsweek. CXII, September 26, 1988, p. 72.
Publishers Weekly. CCXXXIV, July 29, 1988, p. 213.
Time. CXXXII, September 19, 1988, p. 94.
The Wall Street Journal. CCXI, August 30, 1988, p. 17.
The Washington Post Book World. XVIII, August 28, 1988, p. 1.

A FAR CRY FROM KENSINGTON

Author: Muriel Spark (1918-)
Publisher: Houghton Mifflin (New York). 189 pp. $17.95
Type of work: Novel
Time: 1954-1955
Locale: London

A witty novel about a young war widow's unusual encounters in the literary world of London, and her involvement in mysterious events surrounding her home life

Principal characters:
NANCY HAWKINS, the narrator and protagonist, a young war widow who works as an editor
HECTOR BARTLETT, a hack journalist and literary hanger-on
WANDA PODOLAK, a Polish dressmaker, Hawkins' neighbor
EMMA LOY, a well-known novelist, Bartlett's friend
MILLY SANDERS, an elderly Irish widow, Hawkins' landlady
WILLIAM TODD, a medical student, Hawkins' future husband

In Muriel Spark's eighteenth novel she returns to a setting similar to that of her *Loitering with Intent* (1981). Both novels are set in London in the years of austerity following World War II, and both feature a female first-person narrator who is involved in the literary world. Both touch on fringe religion and the occult, as well as blackmail (the latter features in almost every novel Muriel Spark writes), and both have a cast of brilliantly created, eccentric, but believable characters, who never lose their effectiveness for the reader by slipping into caricature.

Writing from the perspective of the 1980's, the narrator of *A Far Cry from Kensington*, Nancy Hawkins, recalls her ups and downs as a twenty-eight-year-old widow (her husband was killed during the war), working as an editor for a struggling, and shortly to fold, publishing house in London during the 1950's. At that time, the most immediately noticeable thing about Nancy (who was known to all of her acquaintances as Mrs. Hawkins) was her bulk: "I was massive in size, strong-muscled, huge-bosomed, with wide hips, hefty long legs, a bulging belly and fat backside." Her appearance gives her an air of matronly wisdom; others readily confide in her (although she notes that later, when she began to get thin, people no longer did so), and everyone holds her in high esteem as a "capable woman." She finds this reputation more than a little irksome, however, and her advice "to any woman who earns the reputation of being capable, is to not demonstrate her ability too much." Mrs. Hawkins herself, however, never makes a serious effort to follow this advice, and some of the pleasure of the book results from her many tips, often made directly to the reader, on topics such as how to get thin (with an accompanying tip about the nature of willpower), how to get a job, how to concentrate (acquire a cat—its tranquillity will help to soothe one's excited mind), how to deal with casual correspondence, and, the best tip of all, how to write fiction. Here is only part of her advice, offered to a writer who has something to say but little idea about how to go about it:

> You are writing a letter to a friend . . . a dear and close friend. . . . Write privately, not publicly; without fear or timidity, right to the end of the letter, as if it was never going to be published, so that your true friend will read it over and over, and then want more enchanting letters from you. . . . Before starting the letter rehearse in your mind what you are going to tell; something interesting, your story. But don't rehearse too much, the story will develop as you go along, especially if you write to a special friend, man or woman, to make them smile or laugh or cry, or anything you like so long as you know it will interest. Remember not to think of the reading public, it will put you off.

Excellent advice indeed, and there is no doubt that Mrs. Hawkins—levelheaded, sensible, calm, intelligent, and, yes, capable—is an attractive protagonist.

The plot in which she finds herself bound up has two strands. They appear at first to be separate, but later are cleverly and unobtrusively woven together. The first strand features an unpleasant, talentless hack and literary hanger-on named Hector Bartlett, who has ingratiated himself with a well-known novelist, Emma Loy. Hector—who in addition to his literary pursuits is an adept of a pseudo-science called radionics—attempts to befriend Mrs. Hawkins as well, but she has her own phrase to describe him: *pisseur de copie.* "Hector Bartlett, it seemed to me, vomited literary matter, he urinated and sweated, he excreted it." With a bluntness that is not her usual manner, she uses this epithet not only to Bartlett's face but also to anybody else whenever the subject comes up. Her remark runs like an irreverent leitmotif throughout the book, its unexpectedness and inappropriateness frequently producing a comic effect. In sticking to her self-appointed task—she thinks that it is one of the prime duties of her job to inform her colleagues that Hector Bartlett is a *pisseur de copie*—Mrs. Hawkins alienates Loy, who twice sees to it that she is fired from her job.

The second strand of the plot centers on Wanda Podolak, an excitable and neurotic Polish dressmaker, who is one of a half dozen tenants in the boardinghouse Mrs. Hawkins shares in South Kensington. Podolak receives an anonymous letter threatening to report her to the tax authorities for not filing a return. Other notes follow, varying the attack, and are followed by telephone calls. Podolak becomes fearful and paranoid, thinking that everyone in the house is conspiring against her. Eventually she drowns herself in the Thames.

As Mrs. Hawkins unravels the circumstances of Wanda's death, she learns that Hector Bartlett was the blackmailer. He had been so mortally offended by Mrs. Hawkins' taunts that he had forced Podolak into a crazy attempt to harm her by using a "radionics Box," by means of which the practitioners of this "science" purport to diagnose and cure a wide variety of ailments. Although Mrs. Hawkins regards such claims as nonsense, she correctly surmises that if followers of radionics use it (as they believe) for good, they must also believe that it has the power to do harm. (The cult of radionics as sketched by Spark bears a strong resemblance to the theories of Wilhelm Reich, with a touch of Dianetics.)

Such a terse summary can do little justice to this novel, however. There are so many comic touches, and so many engaging characters, that the sinister element never darkens the pleasing effect. Most of the main characters are fellow boarders of Mrs. Hawkins, whose recollections of them are at once sympathetic and gently satirical. Among the most memorable characters is Milly Sanders, the owner of the boardinghouse, a sixty-year-old Irish widow who is notable for her unusual beliefs—such as her conviction that a woman cannot become pregnant unless she has experienced an orgasm ("she called it 'that feeling' "), and for her tendency to dole out little snatches of folk wisdom as she serves tea ("She always mixed tea with maxims"). There is the cockney nurse, the meticulous and obsessive Kate Parker, "who was very thorough and eager in her cleaning, indeed about everybody's house-cleaning," and poor young Isobel Lederer, secretary and socialite, the empty-headed daughter of a well-off father. One of the most hilarious scenes in the novel describes Isobel, pregnant and unsure of who the father is (and apparently not very interested in finding out), sitting in her room with her father and all her fellow tenants, who counsel her about her best course of action. Oblivious to her own humiliation and to the conversation flowing around her, she merely asks one tenant, a medical student named William Todd, whether he has seen the latest theater offerings.

Given all this, the reader might be excused for thinking that *A Far Cry from Kensington* is merely a slight though delightful novel, somewhat in the manner of the works of Barbara Pym. Yet Spark's novels, although light on the surface, often yield more sophisticated themes on further examination. She is a serious and a profound writer, strongly influenced by the Roman Catholicism to which she converted in 1954. Spark once remarked that "in the broad historical sense the [Catholic] church does teach you to see things in proportion. This has a very, very releasing effect. Nothing matters very much of things that previously seemed to matter a great deal, and yet everything matters a great deal. It's a paradox." This statement gives a clue to the deeper resonances of *A Far Cry from Kensington.* Like Spark, Mrs. Hawkins is a Catholic. Hers is a quiet Catholicism which does not obtrude itself onto others. It is not superficial or bound to ritual observances. Although Mrs. Hawkins regularly recites the Angelus at noon, such habits are not the essence of her faith; in fact, she regards them as no more than superstitious holdovers. Her religion, she says, goes far beyond such surface observances, although she does not elaborate on what form it takes. Perhaps that is so because it is a deeply internalized faith, which gives her the ability to see the events of her life, and those of others, *sub specie aeternitatis*. Her ability to "see things in proportion" (to use Spark's words) is certainly one of her outstanding characteristics.

This ability can be seen in the very opening sentences of the novel, which also set an atmosphere of immense stillness: "So great was the noise during the day that I used to lie awake at night listening to the silence. Eventually, I fell asleep contented, filled with soundlessness, but while I was awake I enjoyed the experience of darkness, thought, memory, sweet anticipations." It is through this process of serene nighttime cogitation, "listening to the silence," that she has gained a sense of proportion about her life, "so that the weight of destiny no longer bore on the current problems of [her] life." This sense of equanimity, together with her ability to stand back from the immediate pressures of her day-to-day experience, is strikingly apparent when she is told that she has been fired from her job at Ullswater Press. At the very moment she hears the news, which by any normal standards would be upsetting, there is a moment of pure transcendence; her awareness floats beyond her mundane circumstances: "The late afternoon sun touched lovingly on the rooftops reminding me of time past and time to come, making light of the moment."

This sense of poise and serenity is strongly reinforced by the structure of the novel and the narrative techniques it employs, which combine to impart a kind of spiritual tranquillity. It is no coincidence that Mrs. Hawkins is looking back on events which are long past, and it is significant that she looks back on them in the silence of the night, in her hours of "sweet insomnia" (on one occasion she calls it her "beloved insomnia.") Played out once more on the silent screen of her remembering mind, events take on their proper perspective. Neither Mrs. Hawkins nor the reader is imprisoned in the present moment; there is detachment, distance, equanimity. It is the larger view. The reader is reminded of this when on occasions the narrator flashes forward to events which took place after the events of the story, or when she reminds the reader of her current circumstances: "The morning noise of the office took over. I remember it now in these sweet waking hours of the night that I still treasure so much, here far away from the scene of my life in those days, far away in time." Even the title of the book, *A Far Cry from Kensington*, suggests a sense of distance and detachment, and the title phrase acts as a kind of framing device for the whole novel. The novel begins with it, as Mrs. Hawkins observes that her present life is "a far cry" from her 1950's Kensington life, and it also ends with it, as she jumps forward thirty years to tell of a chance encounter with Hector Bartlett at a restaurant in Tuscany: "It was a far cry from Kensington, a far cry." The novel thus rounds back on itself, once more giving the reader a sense of perspective. Everything gets put in its proper place. To return to Spark's words about Catholicism: "This has a very . . . releasing effect."

Whether Spark had all this in mind, or whether she would put such thoughts only into the mind of a Hector Bartlett, is another question. *A Far Cry from Kensington* is certainly not a novel to be solemn over, but one to be enjoyed for its wit, ingenuity, and delicacy.

Bryan Aubrey

Sources for Further Study

The Atlantic. CCLXII, August, 1988, p. 80.
Chicago Tribune. July 11, 1988, V, p. 3.

Contemporary Review. CCLII, April, 1988, p. 213.
Library Journal. CXIII, July, 1988, p. 96.
Los Angeles Times. July 14, 1988, V, p. 12.
New York. XXI, August 1, 1988, p. 45.
The New York Times Book Review. XCIII, July 31, 1988, p. 1.
Newsweek. CXII, August 15, 1988, p. 60.
Publishers Weekly. CCXXXIII, May 27, 1988, p. 48.
Time. CXXXII, July 4, 1988, p. 70.
The Times Literary Supplement. March 18, 1988, p. 301.

THE FIFTH CHILD

Author: Doris Lessing (1919-)
Publisher: Alfred A. Knopf (New York). 133 pp. $16.95
Type of work: Novel
Time: 1966-1986
Locale: Near London

Lessing makes the birth of a strange child the occasion for a disturbing and ultimately pessimistic examination of injustice at both social and family levels

Principal characters:
HARRIET and DAVID LOVATT, a young couple whose dream of the perfect family turns into a nightmare
JAMES LOVATT, David's father
DOROTHY WALKER, Harriet's mother
BEN, the Lovatts' fifth child

Since the publication of her first book, *The Grass Is Singing*, in 1950, Doris Lessing has proven to be a writer as versatile as she is prolific, producing approximately thirty-three books of poems, stories, plays, essays, and, most important, novels. Even as a novelist, she has proved extraordinarily varied in her approach; the realism of her early and middle periods gave way to the mysticism and science fiction of her Canopus in Argus series, published in the 1970's and 1980's. Lessing's willingness to experiment with fiction's forms, indeed her obsessive need to do so, is best evidenced in a relatively early work, *The Golden Notebook* (1962). Here she weaves together the themes of personal and artistic crisis in a new and, for the period, wholly representative way, forming what critic and novelist David Lodge has called the "problematic novel." In it, Lessing takes as her subject the inadequacy of the conventional novel and her own hesitance about writing such a work (coupled with the writer's need to write).

Much less insistent about its own form, Lessing's most recent novel, *The Fifth Child*, is nevertheless disquieting both formally and thematically. Considerably longer than the conventional short story, it seems wanting as a novel, lacking a certain necessary scope and substance—or so the book seems at first. Moreover, this work—its length and therefore status as novel a bit uncertain—begins realistically, its satiric edge present but muted; soon, however, Lessing adds certain supernatural touches that transform her realistic fiction into gothic thriller and ultimately into a disquieting fable of considerable social, psychological, and, above all, moral depth and complexity. *The Fifth Child* is therefore the kind of novel that evokes for its reader as much pain as pleasure. It deliberately, if unselfconsciously, disrupts the reader's complacency about formal and moral matters. The complacency it disrupts, however, it in a sense fosters; the novel begins by first drawing in the reader, convincing him to take the side of David and Harriet in their determined efforts to realize their dream of happiness in England of the 1960's, where "making it"—both sexually and financially—are in, and love and family are decidedly out.

Written in a brisk, no-nonsense style, the verbal equivalent of David and Harriet's straightforward marital code, the novel drives the reader as well as its two main characters toward the catastrophe lying at the heart of the narrative.

Harriet Walker and David Lovatt meet at an office party, where each feels and clearly is out of place: old-fashioned; conservative; moral; in a word, different. They are instantly drawn to each other. Each wants the other, wants the fulfillment of their anachronistic vision of happiness, an Ozzie-and-Harriet dream of family bliss (on a larger scale than Ozzie and Harriet Nelson ever imagined). Despite the criticism of parents and siblings, they buy a huge house outside London and have four children in six years, all the while turning their home into a kind of family hotel at holiday times. This happy home is not, however, without its own weak points. These Harriet and David are more than willing to overlook: an offhand reference to the English class-system, a mere mention of the growing wave of crime, the fact that it is David's father, James, and his wealthy second wife who pay the mortgage and Harriet's mother, Dorothy, who keeps house. Frequent references to the untended garden hint that Harriet and David's idyllic family life may be partial at best, merely a middle-class pastoral.

The birth of their fifth child, Ben, brings their blissful dream to an abrupt end. Ben is a rather unusual child, and Lessing makes every effort to render him in nearly supernatural terms. In the space of only five pages, Harriet calls him a troll, a goblin, a leech, an alien, a little beast, and a nasty little brute. Physically odd if not quite deformed, he is soon perceived as a threat by the entire family—including the dog and cat, which he kills.

Ben resembles Ira Levin's character Rosemary's baby, but he is considerably more than that, as soon becomes apparent when the Lovatts, backed once again by James's money and with what Harriet's sister Sarah calls "typical upper-class ruthlessness," decide to institutionalize him. He is placed in an institution located in the wasteland of northern, industrial England—an area that has fallen victim to economic policies which have sought to save the south at the expense of the north. Angela, Harriet's other sister, tells the family, "My God! . . . Sometimes when I am with you, I understand everything about this country."

Whether Ben is understood as a devil, a reversion to some earlier evolutionary type, or a symbol of Great Britain's growing underclass—made up of disfranchised blacks, Asians, and unemployed whites—he is perhaps best approached as a latter-day version of Herman Melville's character Bartleby the Scrivener. However variously his existence can be explained, his presence is simply and finally a given; the real issue is not how to deal with him, but the fact that he must be dealt with at all.

His presence proves all too well the inadequacy of the Lovatts' love, of the British faith in their own just society, and a host of other fond illusions held in common by characters and readers. Without Ben, the Lovatts are a family; with him they are not. Their eldest child, Luke, explains matter-of-factly to his siblings, "They are sending Ben away because he isn't really one of us," but as even—or especially—the children intuit, such a rationale begs the question. If Ben can be excluded from the family so easily and finally, so then can they. The irony here is that in a very real and more than merely biological sense, Ben is one of them. He is the perfect embodiment of the obstinacy with which David and Harriet pursued their dream of a large, happy family in the face of their parents' and other relatives' strong objections and of their obstinate refusal to be like their contemporaries: sexually free, financially well-off, ultimately selfish and uncaring. Despite their efforts, David and Harriet do become selfish and uncaring when they choose to institutionalize their child; as the situation is presented, however, it is hard for the reader not to agree with them to some extent. The fact remains that, like Bartleby, Ben is intractable and not amenable to reason (or love).

Just as Bartleby stands forth his own inexorable self, so too does Ben, in his own less overtly existential, more pathologically deviant way. Nevertheless, Harriet chooses to rescue him, because he is her son. For her pains, she is forced to watch as her husband grows more distant, as three of her children leave home, and as the fourth, Paul, becomes increasingly fearful and maladjusted—all without her having significantly improved Ben's life. She rescues him from the living death he was forced to endure in the institution; in exchange, he is made to suffer a more expansive but no less insidious form of confinement: existence at the margins of society.

From childhood intractability and malevolence, Ben graduates to robbery and possibly rape, to that love of violence and general lawlessness that Anthony Burgess depicted in such frightening detail in *A Clockwork Orange* (1962). To her credit, Harriet does take Ben home. Once there, however, there is nothing she can do for him other than exact a measure of obedience by threatening to send him back to the institution. Coming to distrust the medical doctors and other professionals with whom she must deal and feeling in a very real sense abandoned by her family, Harriet turns Ben over to a local youth, John. In John's gang, Ben gains a degree of acceptance—which is to say, recognition.

To recognize, literally "to see," plays a crucial part in this deceptively simple, artfully straightforward novel. Harriet believes that she sees something the others—her husband, her doctor, "all of them"—cannot or will not: "Everyone in authority had *not* been seeing Ben ever since he was born. . . . Would people always refuse to see him, to recognize what he was?" The "what" Harriet wants them to see remains undefined: What exactly does she see? That despite appearances, Ben is indeed human? Or that he is not? What she wants for Ben may be nothing more than what she comes to want for herself, "that at last someone would use the right words, share the burden. . . . She wanted to be acknowledged, her predicament given its value." If the words Harriet wants are to come, then they will do so in the very form and complexity of the novel itself, for what Lessing accomplishes in *The Fifth Child* is nothing less than the naming—the recognizing rather than the resolving—of Harriet's (and Ben's) predicament.

On at least one level, *The Fifth Child* concerns Harriet's situation as a woman, a wife, a mother. (Much of the novel is in fact focused through her.) After bearing four children in six years, Harriet is physically as well as psychologically exhausted. Her dream of a large, happy, ordinary family becomes an intolerable burden. Pregnant with Ben, her imagination grows morbid: The child in her womb is becoming the monstrous embodiment of her own repressed hostility, of the dream turned nightmare. Thus, Dr. Gilly, the London specialist she consults, may be right: The cause of the problem may not be Ben at all but rather her unreasonable hatred of the child whose existence has consumed her every moment and every thought but who also frees her of ever having to bear another child. This view puts Harriet in the worst possible light. Seen more sympathetically, she has been made to bear too great a burden, made to feel a "criminal" first for wanting to have another child, then for having a "monster," and finally for bringing the monster child home rather than letting him die in the institution. Thus does the mother of the monster become a monster herself.

Yet this interpretation does not explain all the novel's complexity. Lessing has designed *The Fifth Child* to provoke thoughts about women, about families, about contemporary Great Britain. Whether all that the novel evokes can or even should be made consistent, reducible to some one overriding theme, is another matter altogether. The novel's realist, supernatural, sociological, and feminist perspectives do not quite jell, nor do they seem to parallel one another as neatly as some readers would like. These perspectives are bound together by a general sense of injustice and by the need to find a way to live morally in the absence of fixed moral standards. Against the backdrop of this call for moral improvisation, the novel suggests that the contemporary world stands on the verge not of solution but of apocalypse, the perhaps necessary precondition to moral change.

Robert A. Morace

Sources for Further Study

Booklist. LXXXIV, January 15, 1988, p. 809.
Kirkus Reviews. LVI, January 1, 1988, p. 10.
London Review of Books. X, April 21, 1988, p. 20.
Los Angeles Times Book Review. March 27, 1988, p. 3.
Ms. XVI, March, 1988, p. 28.
The New Republic. CXCVIII, May 16, 1988, p. 39.
The New York Review of Books. XXXV, June 30, 1988, p. 30.
The New York Times. CXXXVII, March 30, 1988, p. 20.
The New York Times Book Review. XCIII, April 3, 1988, p. 5.
Publishers Weekly. CCXXXIII, January 29, 1988, p. 413.
Time. CXXXI, March 14, 1988, p. 86.
The Times Literary Supplement. April 22, 1988, p. 452.
Tribune Books. March 20, 1988, p. 6.
The Washington Post Book World. XVIII, March 20, 1988, p. 3.

THE FIRST SALUTE
A View of the American Revolution

Author: Barbara Tuchman (1912-1989)
Publisher: Alfred A. Knopf (New York). Illustrated. 347 pp. $22.95
Type of work: History
Time: Principally 1770-1781
Locale: The American colonies, England, and the West Indies

Tuchman examines the political background, especially the rivalries among European states and the relationship of those states to the American colonies, to assess the impact of foreign involvement on the American Revolution

Principal personages:
SIR GEORGE BRYDGES RODNEY, a British admiral, commander of various naval forces during the American Revolution
GENERAL GEORGE WASHINGTON, Commander in Chief of the Continental Army
JOHANNES DE GRAAFF, the Dutch governor of the Isle of St. Eustatius in the West Indies
GENERAL CHARLES CORNWALLIS, the commander of British land forces in the southern American colonies
ADMIRAL FRANÇOIS JOSEPH PAUL DE GRASSE, the commander of the French fleet sent to aid the American revolutionaries

When one picks up a book about the American Revolution, one usually expects the action to begin in 1775, with the first encounter of American Minutemen against British forces at Lexington, Massachusetts. Perhaps the narrative will start a bit earlier, in Boston Commons, where an angry crowd confronted British soldiers who killed Crispus Attucks in the ensuing melee; or the first scene may be played out in that city's harbor, where angry colonists tossed bales of tea into the sea to protest unfair taxation. The opening paragraphs of such a study could well be set in the Virginia statehouse in Williamsburg, where Patrick Henry delivered his "Give me liberty or give me death" speech, or in Philadelphia, where anxious delegates from the various Colonies gathered to discuss ways of seeking redress for wrongs visited upon them by the mother country.

All these possibilities are, despite their inherent drama, predictable; yet none of these serves as the opening of Barbara Tuchman's study of this important event in American and world history. The first chapter takes place far from the cold of Valley Forge or the tense atmosphere of Boston under siege. Instead, the reader is taken to the West Indies, to the tiny island of St. Eustatius, where a Dutch colony was operating a profitable trade in sugar and other commodities. There, on November 16, 1776, four months after the rather foolhardy American colonials had brazenly declared their independence from England, Governor Johannes de Graaff ordered the sentry at the island's fortification to fire a salute to an American vessel entering the harbor. This gesture, Tuchman tells the reader, was the first official act by a foreign power recognizing the Colonies' right to exist as a separate nation. The unstated but subtle comparison with the somewhat smaller-caliber explosion on the green at Lexington three and a half years earlier is clear: This was, in terms of international relations, the shot heard round the world.

Readers familiar with Tuchman's previous works will not be surprised by this unusual lead for her wide-ranging analysis of the impact of America's revolution on the Western Hemisphere. Earlier books suggest that this author is at her best when probing around the edges of important events or ideas to see how little-discussed people or incidents have had significant impact on creating the world as readers know it today. Her past successes give ample evidence of that method. *A Distant Mirror: The Calamitous Fourteenth Century* (1978) presents the exciting history of fourteenth century Europe by focusing on the life of a little-known statesman, Enguerrand de Coucy, whose involvement in French and English political and social life makes him a superb mirror for the strengths and foibles of that age—a time remarkably like the twentieth century, Tuchman argues. Similarly, *The Guns of August*, her 1962 Pulitzer Prize-winning study of World War I, concentrates on causes leading to calamity rather than on events during the years of conflagration. *The March of Folly: From Troy to Vietnam* (1984) examines an unusual concept: the tendency, in Tuchman's view, of states to commit acts contradictory to their own self-interest. To prove her point, she examines four incidents ranging from the Trojan War to the American involvement in Vietnam. Throughout her career as a popular historian, Tuchman's particular signature has been her angle of vision, an uncanny ability to see important movements in history from a perspective little used by conventional academics in their study of the past.

The First Salute: A View of the American Revolution is much like its precedessors in this respect. It is not simply another study of the forming of the American nation; rather, it is a review of the way the Colonies' war with England was shaped by, and helped to shape, relationships between England and its European neighbors, especially France and the Netherlands. Tuchman shows how events unfolding in America forced the British to alter both their military strategy and their pattern of international diplomacy in the entire Western Hemisphere. The author's interests lie not in battles, primarily, but in behind-the-scenes activities that led to confrontation and especially in the personalities of those men who figured prominently in bringing about the military events that other historians examine. Early chapters reach back to the sixteenth century, tracing the roots of the economic warfare in which England and the countries of the European continent engaged, as trade with the new world became an important factor in these nations' economies. Providing readers with a sound foundation in Anglo-Dutch relations in the course of three centuries, Tuchman shows how the rivalry between England and its neighbors across the English Channel, coupled with its rise as the preeminent power on the seas, led to alliances between France and the countries of the Netherlands, which wished to thwart the British nation's growing hegemony both on the North American mainland and in the fertile islands of the Caribbean.

Without denigrating the importance of trade with the North American Colonies, Tuchman points out the dilemma England faced as it was forced to divert more and more resources to preserving that source of commodities while its European neighbors continued to mine rich lodes in the more tropical regions of the Atlantic south and east of the American shores. In much the same way that the English king and his ministers were torn between fighting in America and keeping a watchful eye on military buildup on the Continent, these same men were forced to look two ways at the trade problem: As the British expended more energy to keep the colonists in check, they ran the risk of losing the more lucrative sources of goods that were theirs for the taking on the islands of the West Indies. Hence, the recognition of the American Colonies by its European neighbors gave England serious cause for concern. British leaders could see the possibility of having to fight in two places, both on the North American continent and along the shores of the many islands in the West Indian chain, if England wished to preserve its stranglehold over trade on the North Atlantic rim. The prospect presented strategic difficulties sufficient to paralyze even the most formidable and efficient political and military organizations.

According to Tuchman, the British government under George III was neither formidable nor efficient. Poor appointments within the various ministries made governance difficult at best. Much of the best sections of *The First Salute* deal with the problems caused for the British generals and admirals by bungling politicians, who, far removed from the site of hostilities, nevertheless attempted to dictate strategy and make decisions about objectives and logistics management. Those decisions often hampered the professional soldiers and sailors in their efforts to bring the Colonies into submission. Two historical personages figure prominently in this narrative: Admiral Sir George Brydges Rodney and General Charles Cornwallis. With skill and great sensitivity, Tuchman sketches portraits of these British warriors, showing their strengths and weaknesses as leaders both in the field and in the political arena. Her depiction of Rodney is especially captivating. He was a fiery sailor whose experience had earned for him the respect of peers in the naval profession, but that same spirit did not always sit well with politicians who controlled appointments within the Admiralty. Passed over on occasion for commands that went to junior and less qualified men, Rodney struggled with his superiors to gain the necessary ships and provisions to conduct a competent blockade of the Colonies and to destroy their fledgling fleet—to no avail. His personal domestic tragedy is introduced to show that the man was not simply a martinet but rather one who cared passionately for his family, his career, and his country. There is even a hint of wistfulness in Tuchman's assessment of this would-be hero; one gets the sense that, given the proper support from home, Rodney may have made the course of history, especially American history, significantly different.

Charles, second Earl Cornwallis, also comes in for sympathetic treatment. Though a cautious man, he seems to have been right in his judgments about the strengths of the Americans, but unable to convince superiors to give him the necessary men and equipment to complete the subjugation of the southern Colonies. Tuchman is convincing in her portrayal of Cornwallis as a pawn sacrificed for political ends by statesmen and superior officers intent on saving their own reputations and preserving England's position in world trade and influence relative to its European neighbors—even if it meant losing the North American Colonies in the bargain.

Balanced against these portraits of British warriors, Tuchman sketches the activities of two heroes on the American side: French Admiral François Joseph Paul de Grasse and the Continental Army's commander in chief, George Washington. Almost a quarter of the book is devoted to the actions preparatory to the decisive battle at Yorktown. In the process of delineating the buildup of forces on both sides, Tuchman presents these two figures as men of vision and daring, committed to their causes and willing to make significant sacrifices to bring about victory for the Colonial forces. While the presentation of Washington in such a guise is not new, it is nevertheless convincing and appropriate within the context of Tuchman's narrative. Standing in contrast to Cornwallis, Washington emerges as a figure who deserves the plaudits his countrymen gave him then and continue to accord him well into the twentieth century.

In the past, Tuchman has been criticized by scholarly reviewers who have charged her with inaccuracies and distortions. To a certain extent, one may dismiss such attacks as the inevitable fate of the successful popularizer. (It should be noted, too, that many academic historians have praised Tuchman's work.) In the case of the *The First Salute*, however, scholarly criticism has been particularly harsh and detailed. The naval historian N. A. M. Rodger, for example, writing in *The Washington Post Book World*, judged that "Barbara Tuchman is unfortunately entirely ignorant of everything to do with the sea, and her attempts at explanation will be unintelligible to novice and expert alike." Rodger and other reviewers also faulted Tuchman for relying on badly outdated sources and enumerated many factual errors.

Whatever the merit of these criticisms, Tuchman knows how to tell a story. The reader is rewarded for his efforts with a sense of closeness to the events she depicts: In this book, one can feel the excitement building as the opposing forces close on the tiny spit of land on the west bank of the York River. Such narrative ability sets Tuchman apart from her contemporaries who may provide more facts, but who seldom do as well in giving readers a sense of the past and an appreciation of its importance to the present.

Laurence W. Mazzeno

Sources for Further Study

The Atlantic. CCLXII, December, 1988, p. 96.

Booklist. LXXXIV, August, 1988, p. 1868.

Boston Globe. September 25, 1988, p. 105.

Library Journal. CXIII, September 15, 1988, p. 82.
The New Republic. CXCIX, November 28, 1988, p. 32.
The New York Review of Books. XXXV, December 22, 1988, p. 56.
The New York Times. CXXXVIII, October 4, 1988, p. C21.
The New York Times Book Review. XCIII, October 16, 1988, p. 14.
Newsweek. CXII, October 10, 1988, p. 72A.
Publishers Weekly. CCXXXIV, August 12, 1988, p. 43.
Time. CXXXII, October 3, 1988, p. 88.
The Washington Post Book World. XVIII, October 2, 1988, p. 1.

THE FORGOTTEN WAR
America in Korea, 1950-1953

Author: Clay Blair
Publisher: Times Books (New York). Illustrated. 1,136 pp. $29.95
Type of work: History
Time: 1950-1953
Locale: Korea

Unquestionably the definitive account of the United States Army's long march back from near disaster to an equivocal military victory in Korea, in a war it never should have fought

Principal personages:
DEAN ACHESON, Secretary of State, 1949-1952
DOUGLAS MACARTHUR, an American general, the commander of the United Nations Forces in Korea, 1950-1951
MATTHEW B. RIDGWAY, an American general, the commander of the United Nations forces in Korea, 1951-1952
HARRY S. TRUMAN, thirty-third President of the United States, 1945-1952
JAMES A. VANFLEET, an American general, the commander of the Eighth Army, 1951-1953
WALTON WALKER, an American general, the commander of the Eighth Army, 1950-1951

In *The Manchurian Candidate* (1962), a film about an American soldier captured in Korea and programmed by the Chinese to kill the American president, Laurence Harvey plays Raymond Shaw, a soldier who is brainwashed to forget everything his masters tell him which might interfere with his mission. For the generation of Americans that has grown up since 1962, the Korean War is almost as obliterated in the American memory as it is in the consciousness of the zombielike Shaw. Is this merely because it was a national tragedy, a compound of errors and ineptitude as well as of sacrifice and heroism? So was Vietnam, the subject of so much more scholarly and popular attention, and the source of so many parallels with Korea. In both cases, American soldiers died by the thousands in an Asian civil war, and a corrupt regime was defended against ruthless, patient, and resilient northern invaders. In both wars there were prolonged negotiations during which American military strength was leashed, a president left office humiliated, and his successor vowed a quick solution. There was also public indifference to the returning veterans and congressional resolutions to stay out of foreign wars. The similarities between Korea and Vietnam are almost endless (as, it should be noted, are the differences), and to even a casual student of American politics and culture they are fascinating. For the moment, books and films about Vietnam are popular. Like Korea, however, in another ten years it too will be forgotten, as all wars are quickly forgotten, except by those who were personally involved and the hard core of military history buffs. Those who doubt this sad truth may test it by asking the next college graduate they meet the location and meaning of Bataan, the Somme, or San Juan Hill.

Certain names and incidents are full of associations for many: Frozen Chosen;

the Pusan Perimeter; the Thirty-eighth parallel; Panmunjom; the triumphal amphibious landing at Inch'ŏn and the useless one at Wŏnsan; brainwashing; the riots by the North Korean prisoners at Cheju-do; Hamburger Hill, Porkchop Hill, and Heartbreak Ridge; the fighting retreat of the Marines from the Chosin Reservoir; "bugging out," a less heroic term associated with the headlong flight of the American Eighth Army when the North Koreans attacked; General Douglas MacArthur's "old soldiers never die" speech after he was sacked by President Harry S. Truman; General Walton "Johnny" Walker's death and General William Dean's capture; and Matthew Ridgway and the second push northward. There were also the papa-sans, slickie boys, hooches, and kimchi, the cold and the heat, the stench of dead bodies; and the stink of fields fertilized with human feces. All that was long ago, however, only a few years after World War II had ended, and even for those who were in Korea during the war and after, let alone those who have been born since that war, the notoriously misnamed "police action" has become a confused montage of memories and images.

It all comes together, though, in Clay Blair's monumental narrative reconstruction of the first and most critical year: from the blitzkrieg that began on June 25, 1950, to the beginning of the sitzkrieg, about twelve months later with the truce talks, which dragged on for another two years. Some comparisons provide an index to the ferocity of that year: By the time Seoul was secured by American forces in mid-September, less than ninety days after the North Koreans attacked, total American ground casualties "stood at about 27,500, including about 6,000 dead, about 19,000 wounded, and about 2,500 captured or missing." By the signing of the armistice in July, 1953, nearly 34,000 Americans would have died in battle. It took the United States twelve years in Vietnam to lose 56,000 men. More Koreans died than could be counted, perhaps as many as 2 million.

Why was the United States there? Why did American forces fight so poorly during the first year? Was the effort worth the cost? Blair does not neglect these questions, at least not the first two. Indeed, there seems to have been little omitted from his vastly detailed book—which has been faulted for the minutiae with which he recounts not only major but also minor engagements—with thumbnail sketches of hundreds of people, especially the middle levels of the American command, who asked themselves the same questions. Briefly, Blair's explanation is that the United States became involved to fill the power vacuum left by the departure of the hated Japanese overlords at the end of World War II. The casual and peremptory division of the two Koreas, north and south, at the thirty-eighth parallel, was agreed upon in 1946 and all but forgotten by the Soviets and the Americans, neither considering the peninsula worthy of argument. South Korea provided a buffer for Japan, and North Korea provided a similar buffer for Manchuria, and thus for the Soviet Union and China.

What still remains hazy, even after all these years, is the motivation of North Korea's leader, Kim Il-Sung, in deciding to launch the attack on South Korea. Blair follows the traditional explanation—that the Truman Administration, especially

Secretary of State Dean Acheson, had inadvertently signaled the exclusion of South Korea from the zone of untouchable American protectorates such as East Berlin. Even more troubling was the American insistence on invading North Korea, after the initial invasion had been repulsed, rather than halting at the thirty-eighth parallel and returning to the prewar status. The war could have ended within a year, instead of dragging on for three years with many more casualties.

Blair is particularly good in addressing this question. He would probably disagree with the assertion, which Neil Sheehan made in *The New Yorker* (July 4, 1988), that MacArthur was primarily to blame for crossing the parallel, "wasting the lives of the thousands of men who had died for the victory and the thousands more who died subsequently in a defeat they did not deserve." Simply put, it was not in the American character to take the kind of beating the North Koreans had inflicted upon the Eighth Army without attempting revenge.

That initial thumping has worried and intrigued observers of the American military ever since. How could the same army that had recently performed so well in World War II be so humiliated? Blair is very tough on the army, but he writes from the soldier's point of view; his is a friendly, almost in-house critique which fully appreciates the difficulties the Americans had to face. Indeed, his book is on one important level a study of the corporate structure of the American military, with particular emphasis on the United States Military Academy at West Point and the role played by West Point officers in bringing the army back from disaster. It is Blair's ability to link the innumerable battlefield actions which he describes with the personalities of those who took part in them, from general officers to privates. Blair admires these professional soldiers, and, on the whole, the system which allows the best, such as Matthew Ridgway, to rise to the top, the mediocre, such as Walton Walker, to function effectively, and the weak to be rotated out of power.

He does not admire Douglas MacArthur, however, whose recommendation after World War II to commit U.S. ground troops to defend South Korea "was one of the most ill-conceived decisions in the history of the professional American military establishment." Blair does not disagree with Truman's decision to fire MacArthur for insubordination when the general insisted on trying to persuade the American public that he should be allowed to invade Manchuria. Yet the plucky little president, so fondly remembered by most today, is really the chief villain in Blair's book, not for dismissing MacArthur but for having, much earlier, decimated the postwar military to the point that it was all but helpless. The sorry performance of the army in Korea is, Blair argues, directly traceable to Truman's "frenzied and disgraceful demobilization" of the armed forces at the end of World War II and even more to his uninformed contempt for the military. Blair makes an impressive and detailed case for the prosecution of Truman as an ignorant, stubborn, and rash leader who precipitated and compounded disaster.

It is one of the ironies of history, and of what one looks for in reading about the past, that Truman is also celebrated for having in 1948 forced integration upon the military, a conservative establishment by nature and one unusually dominated by

Southerners; the particular irony here is that most of the initial reviews of Blair's book concentrated not on his detailed accounting of the war or on the military as corporation, but on the controversy over the performance of the mostly black Twenty-fourth Infantry Regiment. It is greatly to Blair's credit that he shows how both the official army history of the war and the popular magazine accounts of the Twenty-fourth's supposed cowardice and incompetence were misleading. At the same time, it should be noted that to concentrate entirely, as the reviewer for *Time* magazine did, on this intriguing sidelight of the war is to miss the sweeping overview that Blair's fine book provides.

The final question, however, remains to be answered: Was it worth the cost? "Americans paid a high price for President Truman's decision to 'draw the line' in South Korea," Blair says. He does not argue, however, as others have, that South Korea today stands as a vivid contrast and reproach to North Korea in its prosperity and vitality; that Japan would certainly be a different country than it is today with a Communist Korea as its neighbor; or that the United States demonstrated its willingness to sacrifice its life and treasure to help threatened allies. Rather, he concludes his long book with an extended and apparently fatigued account of the frustrating Panmunjom peace talks that finally, after two years of sitzkrieg, brought peace to Korea. Or is it peace?

> Ironically, the United States did not ever withdraw its military presence from South Korea. The Eighth Army, comprised of about 40,000 men, fielding one combat division, is still there, serving as a trip wire force to back up the ROK [Republic of Korea] Army at the DMZ [demilitarized zone]. It stands as a reminder of and a living memorial to America's forgotten war.

It is not yet known then, whether the Korean War was worth it, because it still, in effect, continues.

Tony Arthur

Sources for Further Study

Chicago Tribune. February 7, 1988, XIV, p. 5.

Choice. XXV, July, 1988, p. 1743.

Los Angeles Times Book Review. February 28, 1988, p. 11.

The New Republic. CXCVIII, May 2, 1988, p. 34.

The New York Times Book Review. XCIII, February 28, 1988, p. 31.

The New Yorker. LXIV, July 4, 1988, p. 48.

Publishers Weekly. CCXXXII, January 8, 1988, p. 69.

Time. CXXXI, March 14, 1988, p. 90.

The Washington Post Book World. XVIII, January 31, 1988, p. 1.

FREUD
A Life for Our Time

Author: Peter Gay (1923-)
Publisher: W. W. Norton (New York). Illustrated. 810 pp. $25.00
Type of work: Biography
Time: 1856-1939
Locale: Vienna, Austria, and London

A major biographical study of the life, work, and cultural milieu of the founder of psychoanalysis

Principal personages:
SIGMUND FREUD, influential architect of the theory and practice of psychoanalysis
MARTHA BERNAYS FREUD, his wife
ANNA FREUD, their daughter, also a psychoanalyst
CARL GUSTAV JUNG, his most important early disciple
WILHELM FLIESS, his most important early confidant
ALFRED ADLER, one of his first followers
OTTO RANK, first secretary of his psychoanalytic group
ERNEST JONES, his most influential British supporter
SÁNDOR FERENCZI, one of the closest of his inner circle
LOU ANDREAS-SALOMÉ, his close friend and supporter
PRINCESS MARIE BONAPARTE, his friend, confidante, and benefactress in his last years

This definitive new biography of Sigmund Freud, one of the most influential minds of the twentieth century, complements such previous efforts to capture the life and times of the controversial founder of psychoanalysis as *The Life and Work of Sigmund Freud* (1953-1957) by Ernest Jones and the more recent *Freud: The Man and the Cause* (1980) by Ronald W. Clark. Although Jones's study of Freud is valuable for its personal insights into the life and thought of his mentor, it is often marred by his idolizing of his subject and his jealousy of Freud's other followers. Clark's book provides additional information about Freud's personal life; it is weak and derivative, however, in its analysis of Freud's thought.

Neither of these two earlier biographies provides what Peter Gay is best at re-creating: the complex relationship between Freud's thought and his life and the cultural and historical framework from which his ideas sprang. As a graduate of the Western New England Institute for Psychoanalysis, Gay is well prepared to explicate the intricacies of Freud's thought; as a cultural historian whose first volume of his two-volume study *The Enlightenment: An Interpretation* won a National Book Award in 1967, he is eminently qualified to ground Freud in his cultural milieu. Indeed, this is the dual focus and the particular forte of *Freud: A Life for Our Time*.

The book is divided into three basic parts: "Foundations: 1856-1905," which covers Freud's life from his birth until the publication of *Drei Abhandlungen zur Sexualtheorie* (1905; *Three Essays on the Theory of Sexuality*, 1953); "Elaborations:

1902-1915," which deals with his efforts to create a broad-based psychoanalytic movement; and "Revisions: 1915-1939," which focuses on the high tide of psychoanalysis as a cultural theory, as well as on Freud's flight from Nazi persecution and his battle with cancer until his death in 1939.

An early indication that this book is more a study of the intellectual life of Freud than an account of his personal experience is the fact that "Foundations," which covers the first fifty years of Freud's life, encompasses only approximately one-fourth of Gay's text. Readers seeking anecdotal information about the childhood, adolescence, or early married life of Freud will find little here. Although Gay does comment on the poverty of Freud's early life, he is primarily interested in focusing on his brilliance as a student and on his aspirations, typical of talented Jewish boys of the time, to become an educated professional. Although he discusses Freud's love affair with Martha Bernays, citing some of his letters to her, he is mostly interested in how the letters reveal Freud's early disposition toward psychological analysis. Indeed, soon after Freud's marriage, his wife seems to disappear from this account as the young doctor begins his professional life.

That so much of Gay's biography focuses on Freud's intellectual life and so little on his personal life is appropriate for a man who from a very early age was driven by what Gay calls a "greed for knowledge." Moreover, as a product of his cultural milieu, Freud was the typical late nineteenth century Jewish patriarchal figure: His life was dominated by his professional interests; the house and the children were the responsibility of the wife and mother; and family life focused primarily on allowing Freud to do his work. Thus, much of this first section on Freud's early life deals with his relationship with his teacher, Ernst Brücke, and his first coworker, Josef Breuer; examines the influence of Jean Martin Charcot, whose use of hypnotism moved Freud away from physiology and toward psychology; and explores the importance of his friendship with Wilhelm Fliess, who, although a crank in many ways, served as a sounding board and an alter ego for some of Freud's early ideas.

Part 1 also focuses on Freud's most influential early clinical and theoretical studies, particularly his work with Breuer on hysteria and his first important case history of the talented "Anna O" (Bertha Pappenheim), who coined the term "the talking cure" for what was to become the psychoanalytic method. During this important early period Freud developed (and then abandoned) his seduction theory, which suggested that female hysteria was caused by an early sexual assault; also during this time he subjected himself to extensive self-analysis, coined the term "psychoanalysis," began using the famous couch, formulated the "Oedipus Complex," and, perhaps most important, wrote *Die Traumdeutung* (1900; *The Interpretation of Dreams*, 1953), that epoch-making study of the dream which helped usher in the twentieth century focus on the inner life of the human animal.

The second part of Gay's study, "Elaborations," is primarily concerned with Freud's energetic efforts to found a worldwide psychoanalytic movement and the resulting infighting of many of his early followers, most of them members of the first professional psychoanalytic group, the so-called Wednesday Psychological Society, which met regularly at Freud's home. Gay discusses each new Freud convert in turn—Alfred Adler, Wilhelm Stekel, Otto Rank, Sándor Ferenczi, Hanns Sachs, Abraham A. Brill, and Ernest Jones—but reserves his most extensive discussion for Carl Gustav Jung, the so-called crown prince of psychoanalysis, Freud's early favorite, the Swiss psychiatrist he groomed to take over his position as leader of the new movement. Jung, however, was destined to be one of the first of a long line of revisionists of Freud's thought and thus broke from him by developing a psychology of his own.

The "Explorations" section of the book also recounts Freud's most famous cases and case histories: the analyses of the Rat Man, Dora, Little Hans, and the Wolf Man. During this period Freud also turned his mind increasingly toward how psychoanalysis could reveal some of the secrets of art and culture; thus, Gay examines his studies of such famous artists as Leonardo da Vinci and Michelangelo as well as his more general studies of the relationship between the artist and daydreaming and the relationship between myth and the mind of man.

The final section of the book, "Revisions," begins with the cultural upheaval of World War I and focuses on the effect of the war on Freud's professional and intellectual life. Much more time, however, is spent on Freud's effort to lay out the structural framework of psychoanalysis in a series of three important postwar books: *Jenseits des Lustprinzips* (1920; *Beyond the Pleasure Principle*, 1955), *Massenpsychologie und Ich-Analyse* (1921; *Group Psychology and the Analysis of the Ego*, 1922), and *Das Ich und das Es* (1923; *The Ego and the Id*, 1961).

By the early 1920's, Freud had already contracted the mouth cancer that was to cause him great suffering and lead eventually to his death. His illness brought him closer than ever before to his youngest child, Anna, whom he recognized as a woman of great intelligence and ability. She cared for him during the last years of his life and helped him to hold together a psychoanalytic society that increasingly threatened to break apart not only because of the fear of the loss of its founder but also because of the constant revisionism of its members.

Many of Freud's psychoanalytic sons began to deviate from the main line of psychoanalysis as Freud grew weaker, including one of his most loyal early followers, Rank. Despite his cancer and his deserters, however, Freud continued in the last years of his life to explore further implications of his theories as well as to fight the incessant battles against attacks on his movement and his ideals. Partially as a result of the vehement attacks on Freud by feminists, Gay devotes a section of the last part of the book to the papers on the psychology of women which Freud wrote between 1924 and 1933. Most of that space Gay spends in apolegetics for the most controversial of Freud's theories about female sexuality—the notion of "penis envy," which has alienated feminists since Freud first proposed it.

Freud's final studies broadened psychoanalysis to encompass the nature of both religion and society. In two of his most somber and pessimistic books, *Die Zukunft einer Illusion* (1927; *The Future of an Illusion*, 1961) and *Das Unbehagen in der Kultur* (1929; *Civilization and its Discontents*, 1961), he analyzed the failure of religion and the essential compromise that makes civilization possible. As the threats of another war and the increasing seriousness of his cancer embittered his last years, Freud continued to study, to write, and to try to assure the future of psychoanalysis.

In the last chapter of the book, Gay depicts Freud's poignant final years as life became increasingly intolerable in Vienna because of the threat of Jewish persecution in Nazi Germany. In contrast to being surrounded by devoted male followers in his early career, Freud's last years seemed to revolve around three women who mothered and protected him, his daughter Anna, Princess Marie Bonaparte, and Lou Andreas-Salomé—all of whom cooperated in the rescue of Freud from the threat of the Nazis, first by taking him to France and then to London, where he lived out his life in comparative peace. Even amid the anguish of the personal cancer that was ravaging his body and the Nazi cancer that was sweeping through Europe, however, Freud seemed most concerned with his final sustained work, *Der Mann Moses und die monotheistische Religion* (1938; *Moses and Monotheism*, 1960), in which he finally tried to come to terms with his Jewishness and his professional experience by focusing on a theme central to his own life—the relationship between the leader and his followers.

Freud's last days were dominated by the increasing pain of his ulcerated mouth cancer; nevertheless, as was typical of his entire life, he disdained sedation and remained lucid, wishing to read, think, and write. When he finally accepted that there was nothing left for him but suffering, he asked his doctor to give him an overdose of morphine, which placed him into a peaceful sleep from which he did not wake. He died on September 23, 1939, at three o'clock in the morning—stoical, dignified, and unselfpitying until the end.

Gay's biography is an engrossing study of one of the most influential minds of the twentieth century. As the notes indicate, it is based on extensive and detailed research, although the foundations of the study never really get in the way of Gay's depiction of the drama of Freud's life. Yet it is a drama of a particularly intellectual kind; Freud's life was a life of the mind—a life of research, study, and writing spent dedicated to the discovery and communication of ideas. Although those searching for tidbits of personal gossip will be disappointed by Gay's book, those who are interested in the intellectual history of psychoanalysis and its effect on the modern world will find much to engage them.

What Gay has achieved here is the difficult task of placing Freud not only firmly within the context of his time but also authoritatively within the context of his ideas. The book is neither an oversimplified popularization of psychoanalysis nor an overly technical analysis of Freud's psychology; it is an intelligent and lucid introduction to a major movement of the modern world. It is a book in which the man and his mind are dynamically re-created and integrated with his age. Whether one is an adherent of Freud's thought or an enemy of his ideas, one cannot be unaffected by Gay's study; Freud is simply too much a giant of modern thought, and Gay's book is simply too much a giant of biographical analysis.

Charles E. May

Sources for Further Study

Chicago Tribune. April 10, 1988, XIV, p. 1.
Kirkus Reviews. LVI, February 1, 1988, p. 177.
Los Angeles Times Book Review. XCIII, May 8, 1988, p. 1.
Nature. CCCXXXIII, May 19, 1988, p. 217.
The New York Times Book Review. XCIII, April 24, 1988, p. 3.
Newsweek. CXI, May 2, 1988, p. 71.
Psychology Today. XXII, July, 1988, p. 68.
Publishers Weekly. CCXXXIII, March 4, 1988, p. 91.
Time. CXXXI, April 18, 1988, p. 85.
The Times Literary Supplement. May 20, 1988, p. 547.

THE GOLD COAST

Author: Kim Stanley Robinson (1952-   )
Publisher: St. Martin's Press (New York). Illustrated. 389 pp. $18.95
Type of work: Science fiction
Time: The late twenty-first century
Locale: Orange County, California

A group of affluent Californians of the future try to discover a meaningful adult life in a childish society

Principal characters:
JIM MCPHERSON, a twenty-seven-year-old aspiring poet
DENNIS MCPHERSON, his father, a trouble-shooting engineer for Laguna Space Research, a major defense contractor
LUCY MCPHERSON, his mother, an active member and employee of a Christian church
ABE BERNARD, his friend, a highway rescue-unit driver
TASHI NAKAMURA, his friend, a surfer, trying to live close to nature and avoid being part of the system
SANDY CHAPMAN, his friend, an illegal drug manufacturer and salesman

Kim Stanley Robinson's *The Gold Coast* reminds one of Charles Dickens' *Bleak House* (1853). Nineteenth century industrial London becomes twenty-first century electronic Orange County, California, but the extremely wealthy remain almost utterly unaware of the wretchedly poor. Orange County has become a multilayered "autopia," with freeways on pylons arching over and shading the old towns, with malls and mansions in the sun, with comparative slums beneath the roads, and with virtually every square inch paved. London's Chancery Court reappears as the military-industrial complex; this system also aids and destroys its servants, enemies, and casual associates with seemingly complete arbitrariness. The powers of the social and economic order in future California, as in past London, appear to be in a mad conspiracy against the happiness of all individuals. Only a slight extension of contemporary Western consumer-military culture, future Orange County encourages everyone to live in perpetual childhood. The children of the well-off are indulged, for their energy and creativity are not yet necessary to the social order.

Like Dickens, Robinson presents a large cast of characters with a variety of motives, apparently acting out their individual values and interests. Each action is shown to take place "in a network of circumstances." Jim McPherson's ambivalent struggle to escape the protecting bubble of his extended childhood leads to a tantrum that threatens either to harm or to save most of his friends and family.

Sandy Chapman works harder than any legitimate executive in the novel, but entirely in an underground economy of recreational drugs. Technically skilled, he has an almost normal middle-class marriage, though it is called an alliance, and a middle-class motive for making money, to care for his ailing father. Despite his mirroring legitimate entrepreneurs, he is kept in a state of adolescent rebellion that shows itself in his leisure life-style of constant parties, pranks, larks, and overconsumption of his own products. He is one of the progeny of Ken Kesey in Tom Wolfe's *The Electric Kool-Aid Acid Test* (1968).

Tashi Nakamura is a traditional rebel, trying in every way he can to avoid plugging into the system. He believes that the more ways one has to exchange money, the more ways one is plugged in. He also earns money illegally, reconditioning carbrains, the components that govern the new electronic automobiles. These machines drive themselves, using computer programs to follow magnetic tracks to their destinations, almost always without collision. Tashi lives in a rooftop tent and surfs at night to avoid the hordes of surfing consumers and to participate in the rhythms of the natural sea. Occasionally, he walks into the mountains to escape Orange County. When his alliance falls apart, he moves to Alaska, one place that is not yet like his home.

Only Abe Bernard, among Jim's closest friends, holds a regular, full-time job in the system. He drives a rescue vehicle for victims of malfunctioning cars. This job requires him to risk life and limb getting his ambulance through traffic. The excitement of this driving fulfills Abe, but the horror of the accident scenes, where he cuts open smashed cars to free the often dead victims, threatens to drive the sensitive young man insane. Even this job, however, is a kind of childish attempt to assert an adult self apart from his fabulously wealthy parents, with whom he lives. It is not a job he can continue, but it sets him apart from his wealth and puts him in contact with more ordinary people, such as the black medic, Xavier, his partner.

Jim, Sandy, Tashi, and Abe have been friends since their high school days, when they were on the wrestling team. Their wealth and their rebellious stance toward their society allows them to continue associating and behaving much as they did in school, prolonging, frustrating, and disguising their need to achieve adult individuality. Jim McPherson is, in some ways, more sensitive than his friends, but they all believe that their lives do not extend into the future and that the present moment, however rich in stimulation, is not adequate. The frantic social pace of their lives, with the almost continuous drugs, frequent casual sexual relations, and the constant warm bath of sensory stimuli for sale, holds them in a womblike bubble that Jim finds increasingly unsatisfying. To find the answer, Jim is constantly seeking avenues into the past, to understand the motions of history that have produced him and his moment. He intuits, but is long in comprehending, that knowing his history will help him find himself and the part he can play as a poet in shaping a more humane future.

Jim typifies his generation. He knows that he is being deprived of something essential, but he cannot tell what it is. His most likely models seem to live in a world unavailable to him. His father works for the spider in the center of the establishment web, the Pentagon, apparently contributing directly to the increasing involvement of the United States in the multipoint world war that has continued since World War II. Jim's mother believes in Christianity and gives her life to realizing the church's mission to the poor, but Jim cannot share her faith. Jim's elderly relative, Tom, tells him wonderful stories of what Orange County was like when there really were orange groves. Jim loves the stories but cannot bear to visit Tom in his care facility, because finally those stories of loss are too painful.

As Jim's frustration builds, he is attracted to industrial sabotage. He joins a supposedly loosely organized band of disaffected pacifists who use high-technology weapons to cripple defense-industry development laboratories at night when no one is present. His first reactions to these successful acts of rebellion are euphoric, but they prove to be like drugs, only temporary escapes from his malaise. He comes to notice that he is unable to maintain commitments to people, that he lets himself be distracted from his promises by the pleasures of the moment, that he has no work through which he can really express himself, and that he has no central self to commit to others. When he understands that he and his three friends are being pulled apart by the increasing complexities of their lives, he feels deeply threatened, for their friendship is as much as he has of a self.

This crisis in his relationships and his search for identity coincide with several other events, the main one being the sabotage planned for Laguna Space Research (LSR), where his father works. Responding to this complex crisis, Jim nearly destroys himself. As he looks back on that night, he begins to see more clearly the network of circumstances in which each individual acts and so begins to understand how to be an adult in his childish world.

Dennis McPherson, Jim's father, has committed himself to the ideal of producing weapons technology that will make war impossible. His life's work has repeatedly shown him that this is a near-impossible task, but he persists nevertheless. While Jim is trying to find himself, Dennis receives his golden opportunity, the chance to design a robot airplane that will dive at humanly unattainable speeds to destroy tank formations, then escape vertically to attack again. His unit successfully develops a prototype of this weapon that would make conventional, large-scale invasions impossible. Then LSR fails to gain the contract when it is learned that the whole proposal has been part of an elaborate rivalry between air force generals. It will probably never be built to function in the way Dennis had intended.

Already suffering this disillusionment, Dennis is forced by an unsympathetic boss to try to salvage another project, whose purpose is to intercept nuclear missiles in their booster phases, part of the continuing development of the Strategic Defense Initiative (SDI). This project is failing because the company falsified test results to obtain the contract and later discovered that they could not do what they had promised. Dennis faces the galling irony that the system they can actually build would work fine for destroying missiles in their silos, before they are fired, but that because the United States must build only defensive weapons, they cannot complete this system.

In two major ways, Dennis' idealism is bottled up in the realities of military-industrial policy and bureaucracy, just as his passion for engineering excellence is reined in by his ambitious boss. On the night Jim is supposed to help destroy the laboratory that is working on the failing second project at LSR, Dennis and Jim, who have been vaguely fighting for months, argue about their work. For the first time, Jim understands his father's idealism, the purpose behind choosing his place in the system. When he understands this rationale and learns from his mother something of what Dennis has endured on the two weapons projects, Jim sees that his father has made a valid choice. Jim cannot carry out the sabotage.

Ironies multiply as the net of circumstances closes. The loosely organized saboteurs are, in fact, a business, run for profit by a drug and weapons smuggler. LSR's parent company contracts to have its own laboratory hit in order to escape having to confess deception in gaining the SDI contract. When Jim steals the missiles intended for the sabotage and uses them to attack all those whom he sees as more immediate enemies, he stymies LSR's plans. The laboratories are closed and his father is fired.

Those who are threatened by Jim's tantrum, in which he attacks real estate offices, malls, and other symbols of the decay of Orange County, may find themselves better rather than worse off, but Jim does come to see how human actions are interconnected and, therefore, that what he does makes a real difference. He is not a child forever captured in a world Disneyland, as he and his friends have sometimes believed. To begin maturing, Jim has had to see the reality of world poverty—on a trip to Europe with his friends—to understand that the world is not right. He has had to see that the past does not disappear, even when it is paved over. He has had to realize that the system is inescapable and to learn, therefore, how as a writer he can become a witness of his time, producing literature that can be put to use.

When Jim learns these things, he is ready to commit himself to a woman artist he has met who seems similarly committed. Then he destroys his rather empty poetry and gathers from his writing the historical sketches of the development of Orange County that have formed some chapters of *The Gold Coast*. Finally, he completes the one chapter he has been unable to write before, the chapter on the destruction of the orange groves. He accepts loss and looks toward a future.

Robinson has said that *The Gold Coast* is the second volume of a thematic trilogy, in which he lays out three futures for Southern California. *The Wild Shore* (1984) projects a future that comes after a nuclear exchange removes the United States from the center of the world stage. *The Gold Coast* shows the opposite road to perdition, a California that becomes a center of world militarism. In a statement after completing *The Gold Coast*, Robinson explained that the third novel would be utopian, showing a better future for California. *The Gold Coast* is a rich and ambitious novel, a Dickensian panorama with well-developed characters and a complex, engaging plot.

Terry Heller

Sources for Further Study

Booklist. LXXXIV, February 15, 1988, p. 974.

Kirkus Reviews. LV, December 15, 1987, p. 1706.

Los Angeles Times Book Review. March 13, 1988, p. 1.
The New York Times Book Review. XCIII, April 24, 1988, p. 28.
Publishers Weekly. CCXXXII, January 8, 1988, p. 74.
Washington Post Book World. February 28, 1988, p. 8.
Washington Post Book World. June 26, 1988, p. 15.

GOLDWATER

Author: Barry M. Goldwater (1909-) and Jack Casserly (1927-)
Publisher: Doubleday (New York). Illustrated. 414 pp. $21.95
Type of work: Memoir
Time: The twentieth century
Locale: Arizona and Washington, D.C.

A recollection by one of America's most prominent political figures of his roots, youth, and career in public life

Principal personages:
BARRY M. GOLDWATER, a longtime conservative Republican senator and a 1964 presidential candidate
PEGGY GOLDWATER, his wife
LYNDON BAINES JOHNSON, his opponent in the 1964 election; thirty-sixth President of the United States, 1963-1969
ROBERT MCNAMARA, Secretary of Defense under Johnson
RICHARD M. NIXON, thirty-seventh President of the United States, 1969-1974
RONALD REAGAN, fortieth President of the United States, 1981-1989
SAM NUNN, a Democratic senator, Goldwater's ally in bringing about reorganization of the United States Armed Forces

This book constitutes Barry Goldwater's farewell to public life. Rambling and at times superficial, it is no literary masterpiece. Nor does it provide much in the way of raw material for historians or political scientists. The book does, however, bear Goldwater's unique stamp. In it, he reveals his strengths and weaknesses, likes and dislikes, insights and oversights. He also successfully conveys his concerns and hopes for America's future.

Goldwater opens the book in a curious manner, launching into a chapter-long sermon in which he chastises Congress, media moguls, and the United States Department of Education, to name only a few of his targets. This critique of current institutions and policies is both mercurial and familiar enough so that it does little else than remind readers (as if they needed reminding) that the author has a reputation for shooting from the hip. His personality thus established, Goldwater returns to his Arizona roots in the second chapter, proceeding more or less chronologically from that point to discuss his youth, experience in the military during World War II, and entry into politics in 1949. He then moves to his early years as a senator in Washington, D.C., the presidential race of 1964, the war in Vietnam, Watergate, the state of the American intelligence establishment, and the effort, during his last term in the Senate, to bring about reorganization of U.S. Armed Forces. He closes with a homage to his wife, to whose memory the book is dedicated, and adds some choice comments about the future of the nation, conservatism, and the Republican Party (in descending order of importance).

"Big Mike" Goldwater (originally Goldwasser), Barry's grandfather, was the first member of the family to set foot in Arizona. This took place in 1860. A Jewish political dissident, Big Mike had emigrated from his native Poland (then under the control of Russia) and arrived in San Francisco in 1852. Joined later by one of his brothers, he ultimately settled in Arizona, establishing a successful retail business. The book's account of this transition from the shtetl of Eastern Europe to respectability in the frontier West is spotty, particularly regarding the family's conversion from Judaism to Episcopalianism, certainly an enabling factor in Goldwater's political career. What does come through, however, is a definite frontier mentality, which, along with an interest in the retail business, Goldwater inherited from his ancestors.

Goldwater's political views were also influenced by his mother, Josephine (or as her family called her, "Mun"), an energetic and extraordinarily patriotic woman. According to Goldwater, it was from his mother that he learned his conservative principles, including a healthy disdain for Frank D. Roosevelt's New Deal. Goldwater also remembers his mother as loving but a strict disciplinarian when he overstepped his bounds. Nevertheless, he was not always a model youngster, and ultimately got into enough trouble so that he was sent off to military school by his father, Baron (or Barry). There he learned his lifelong love of things military, with much of the credit going to Sandy Patch, one of his instructors. With the help of his military school education, Goldwater came of age in one piece (although football injuries would limit both his military career and his mobility in later years) and without getting into serious trouble. His college career was cut short when his father died in 1929. Goldwater took over the family business and guided it successfully through the Great Depression, claiming to have done so without laying off a single employee.

Aside from tending the family business, Goldwater pursued several hobbies, the most avid of which was flying. An officer in the Army Reserve, Goldwater probably would have become an army pilot if his eyesight had been up to standard. Indeed, his preference for a military career over one in politics is made clear several times in the book. (The manpower shortage which developed during World War II did give Goldwater a chance to serve as a pilot, mostly as an instructor.) In 1934, Goldwater was married. He and his wife, Peggy, were to enjoy fifty-one years together before her death in 1985.

After the war, Goldwater moved back to Arizona, working in his family's store and starting up Arizona's Air National Guard. At the urging of friends and in the footsteps of his revered Uncle Morris (who, ironically, had founded the Democratic Party in Arizona), Goldwater entered politics in 1949 as a reform candidate for the Phoenix City Council. Quickly establishing his credentials as a legislator as well as his flair for plain speaking, Goldwater ran successfully for the United States Senate in 1952. Once again, he had entered the fray reluctantly, at the urging, this time, of fellow Republicans looking to resurrect their party's strength in the wake of the Democratic New Deal coalition which had come to power in 1932.

Washington, D.C., was a brand new world for Goldwater. It never replaced his deep attachment to Arizona, which remained his home, but it did become his life.

When Goldwater arrived in Washington, McCarthyism and other forms of Red-baiting were still fashionable. It would not be so for long. Within the first two years of Goldwater's term, Senator Joe McCarthy, head Communist-hunter, had fallen into disgrace. He would later be censured by his Senate colleagues. With the exposure of McCarthy's excesses, and with the passing from the political scene of traditional conservative leaders such as Robert Taft, right-wingers lacked a creditable national spokesman. Soon, Goldwater began to fill this vacuum, attracting the attention of influentials such as William F. Buckley, Jr., and William Rusher, editor and publisher, respectively, of *National Review*.

Ultimately, Goldwater's championship of right-wing causes put him into a position to run for the presidency in 1964. Goldwater tries to make two things abundantly clear about his presidential campaign. First, he asserts that he never had an overwhelming ambition to run, and, further, that once John F. Kennedy was assassinated, he absolutely did not wish to run for the presidency against Lyndon Baines Johnson. A campaign against Kennedy, he reasoned at the time, could evolve into a valuable debate not only on issues but also on basic political principles and ideals. With Kennedy's death, the prospect of a philosophical campaign dissolved in the light of Johnson's unscrupulousness. (Skeptics will say that what really happened was that Kennedy's death pushed the sentiments of the country firmly behind his domestic priorities and also destroyed the Goldwater campaign's Southern strategy, since Johnson was a Texan in good standing. Goldwater specifically denies that these considerations entered into his thinking.) Goldwater ran nevertheless. He claims that he did so because of the absence of an acceptable alternative within the Republican Party and also because so many conservatives placed their hopes in Goldwater's candidacy. Goldwater also claims, however, that he knew from the beginning that he had no chance of winning. His goal was to turn the Republican Party into a long-range vehicle for conservative aspirations throughout the country.

As it turned out, Goldwater's fears and hopes were both borne out, at least in his view. The Johnson campaign did, indeed, hit below the belt (Johnson aide Bill Moyers comes in for special disdain) and, with the help of media distortion, was able to paint an inaccurate portrait of Goldwater's positions on such issues as the use of tactical nuclear weapons in Vietnam and civil rights. On the other hand, the campaign served as a breeding ground for the conservative activists and middle Americans who ultimately would elect Ronald Reagan to office in 1980. This success, in turn, would restore the country's morale after the devastating effects of the Vietnam War and Watergate.

As one might expect, Johnson is also a key culprit in the book's discussion of Vietnam, mostly for his unwillingness to confront the American people with the truth about the war's ultimate human and dollar costs. It is Robert McNamara, Johnson's secretary of defense, however, who comes in for the most pointed criticism. According to Goldwater, McNamara not only lost sight of crucial, nonquantifiable human factors in his quest for statistical data as a basis for decision making (a charge going back at least as far as David Halberstam's *The Best and the Brightest*,

1972) but also usurped responsibilities properly belonging to military commanders and fell into erratic patterns of behavior which greatly hindered the war effort. Also blamed for the American failure in Vietnam is one of Goldwater's favorite targets, the mass media, for their distorted presentation of the war, especially of the Tet Offensive.

More fundamentally, Goldwater is frustrated by the limited objectives of the Vietnam War—that is, the fact that American strategists did not aim to win but instead fought a minimalist war with restrictive rules of engagement. The result, in his eyes, was the purposeless loss of American lives overseas. Goldwater criticizes Jimmy Carter for granting amnesty to Americans who evaded the draft by leaving the country. He recommends that those who openly resist the draft during wartime face a ten- or twenty-year prison term. In Goldwater's view, it is apparently not for the common soldier to reason why, only to do and die. He is much easier on the Joint Chiefs of Staff, briefly raising the question of why they stood for so self-defeating an approach to the war rather than resigning or somehow calling attention to the defects of the Vietnam policy. No convincing answer is provided, as Goldwater, uncharacteristically, treads softly here.

Goldwater's treatment of Watergate focuses on the unraveling and personal failings of Richard M. Nixon, whom Goldwater portrays as "the most dishonest individual I have ever met in my life." The isolation of the Nixon presidency at both its outset and its end is described, with Goldwater emphasizing his own role and that of Alexander Haig in getting Nixon to resign rather than put the country through the ordeal of his impeachment and trial. Consistent with his views on Carter's amnesty for Vietnam draft dodgers, Goldwater is also highly critical of Gerald Ford for his pardon of Nixon.

Despite his condemnation of Nixon, Goldwater makes it clear that he is fully supportive of broad grants of power to the executive branch with regard to the making of foreign policy in general and intelligence gathering in particular. As a result, Goldwater is highly critical of congressional behavior weakening the Central Intelligence Agency (CIA) in the aftermath of Watergate abuses. He also blames the Iran-Contra affair on Congress' interference with legitimate perogatives of the executive branch, and heaps ridicule on the televised hearings. The need for secrecy, he contends, supersedes the public's right to know, since national security is at stake. Indeed, Goldwater suggests lengthy prison terms both for those who leak and for those who print or broadcast classified information.

Goldwater closes his survey of important political events and issues by recounting his effort to bring about reorganization of the military, the goal being to obtain far greater coordination among the different branches of the armed forces (Army, Navy, Air Force, and Marines). Botched missions in Iran under Carter (the attempted rescue of the hostages) and Beirut under Reagan, as well as the highly inefficient invasion of Grenada, prove the need for such reorganization. Most notable about this account is the credit given to Democratic Senator Sam Nunn for helping to push reorganization through the Congress. In a truly bipartisan spirit, Goldwater accords Nunn the most undiluted praise of any public figure in the book.

At this point in his book, Goldwater brings his wife and four grown children onto center stage. In 1980, having promised not to run for the Senate again, Goldwater needed his family's dispensation to break his promise and squeeze in one more term. Peggy made the final decision, allowing her husband to pursue his political destiny. Goldwater ran and, overcoming illness and a lackluster campaign, won reelection. Unfortunately, Peggy died before the term was over, having never fully retrieved her husband from the rigors of public life. Despite his lack of eloquence, or perhaps because of it, Goldwater leaves no doubt about the importance of the role played by his wife in providing a dependable refuge from the public arena. Nor does he leave any doubt about his love and appreciation.

Goldwater concludes his book with some offhand comments on the state of the nation, conservatism, and the Republican Party. He is guardedly optimistic about the first two, though he has serious doubts about the absolutism of the New Right, exemplified by Jerry Falwell and others. The surge in Republican fortunes Goldwater sees as cyclical. He predicts a Democratic resurgence in twenty years or so. Clearly, principle is more important than party to Goldwater. He gives still greater importance to the welfare of the nation—though, in his scheme of things, it is very difficult to pursue the good of the nation without recourse to conservative principles.

Barry Goldwater left the Senate as one of the best-respected and best-liked men in Washington. That part of his personality also comes through in this book. Many readers will find it easy to disagree with Goldwater. They will find it much harder to dislike him.

Ira Smolensky

Sources for Further Study

Booklist. LXXXIV, August, 1988, p. 1867.
Business Week. November 14, 1988, p. 38.
Commentary. LXXXVI, November, 1988, p. 70.
The Economist. CCCIX, October 22, 1988, p. 98.
Kirkus Reviews. LVI, August 1, 1988, p. 1121.
Library Journal. CXIII, October 15, 1988, p. 93.
Los Angeles Times. September 19, 1988, VI, p. 1.
National Review. XL, November 7, 1988, p. 72.
The New Republic. CXCIX, November 28, 1988, p. 41.
The New York Times Book Review. XCIII, October 16, 1988, p. 13.
Publishers Weekly. CCXXXIV, August 19, 1988, p. 63.

THE GREENLANDERS

Author: Jane Smiley (1949-)
Publisher: Alfred A. Knopf (New York). 558 pages. $19.95
Type of work: Historical novel
Time: The fourteenth century
Locale: Greenland

A historical novel that traces the lives of medieval Scandinavian settlers in Greenland over three generations and attempts to account for the dissolution of this culture, which had entirely disappeared by the fifteenth century

Principal characters:
ASGEIR GUNNARSSON, a wealthy Greenland farmer
HELGA INGVADOTTIR, his Icelandic-born wife
MARGRET ASGEIRSDOTTIR, their daughter, born 1345
GUNNAR ASGEIRSSON, their son, born 1352
BIRGITTA LAVRANSDOTTIR, Gunnar's wife, born 1357
GUNNHILD GUNNARSDOTTIR, born 1374,
HELGA GUNNARSDOTTIR, born 1376,
ASTRID GUNNARSDOTTIR, born 1381,
MARIA GUNNARSDOTTIR, born 1384, and
JOHANNA GUNNARSDOTTIR, born 1386, daughters of Gunnar and Birgitta
KOLLGRIM GUNNARSSON, born 1378, son of Gunnar and Birgitta

In *The Greenlanders*, Jane Smiley has written a fascinating historical novel set in fourteenth century Greenland, a richly detailed account of the mysterious decline and fall of an isolated Scandinavian culture. Smiley centers her story on the experiences of a single family, tracing their fortunes over three generations. The implicit questions raised by the fate of the Greenlanders seem pertinent to our own age. How does a culture become extinct? What happens when a society becomes too inflexible to adapt to changing conditions?

After Eric the Red discovered Greenland in 982, it was colonized by Norse settlers from Iceland, who settled in two regions along the fjords called "the western and eastern settlements." For about five hundred years, these Norse settlers raised cattle and sheep, fished, hunted, and traded with Europe, until ships no longer arrived and the colony was isolated from its cultural roots. Famine, disease, and colder winters gradually decimated the small Greenland colony, which could no longer provide for itself.

Smiley's narrative evokes a clear sense of the Greenlanders. Through her portraits of farmers, herdsmen, hunters, priests, and lawgivers, through accounts of their feasts, marriages, love affairs, hunts, and feuds, Smiley brings to life an extinct culture, yet one that seems surprisingly like our own. Living in a harsh but beautiful region of tall, dark mountains, steep pastures, and deep fjords, far removed from European culture, these are a sturdy, self-reliant people accustomed to holding their own opinions and doing as they please. Gradually, they are troubled by new apprehensions: The winters seem harsher, the food supplies dwindle, the skraelings, or Eskimos, attack more frequently, the bishop from Norway never returns, there are outbreaks of lawlessness and witchcraft, trading ships no longer arrive from Europe, the colony is sacked by English pirates. Is this God's judgment for their sins? Have they been abandoned? Is this the end of the world? Are they facing the extinction of their culture? Who will tell their story? Why should they disappear after centuries of relative prosperity?

This desire to be remembered motivates Gunnar Asgeirsssson to learn how to prepare parchment, so that he may "tell all the folk of the world . . . what is really the case with us." The narrative advances by a cumulative unfolding of the intertwined stories of the Greenland community. The novel's opening is rather simple and matter-of-fact: "Asgeir Gunnarsson farmed at Gunnars Stead near Undir Hofdi church in Austfjord." It concludes just as simply: "And the children peeped out of the bedcloset, and Gunnar told his tale." In between lie 558 pages of closely woven narrative, the saga of a fictional world as rich and varied as that of any of Honoré de Balzac's historical novels. "Because a lot of the characters were historically attested," Smiley has explained in a *Publishers Weekly* interview, "they really seemed to come to me as living things outside of myself. I felt as though I were bringing to light the story of a lost people, as if I'd known those people and was finally telling their tale to the world in the ways that they deserved to have it told."

There is nothing postmodernist or minimalist about Smiley's fictional technique. Her novel is firmly rooted in her thorough knowledge of the Icelandic sagas and her meticulous historical and archaeological research, which took her to Greenland while she was writing the book. "I found the sagas fascinating as examples of absolutely pared-down narrative," Smiley remarks. "I decided that they were really about cause and effect more than anything else, because some little tiny cause would always lead to cataclysmic effects, and the saga would map out these effects, both geographically and historically." Her novel is divided into three long chapters, "Riches," "The Devil," and "Love," which serve as thematic metaphors for the three generations of Greenland life that she chronicles.

The Greenlanders is a chronicle of the events occurring within the lifetimes of Margret Asgeirsdottir, born in 1345, and her brother, Gunnar Asgeirsson, who was born in 1352. The narrative takes their family from the relatively properous years of the mid-fourteenth century through the increasing strains and tensions that faced the small Greenland settlement in the latter half of the century. Asgeir Gunnarrson had considered himself a lucky man in his marriage and his holdings, but his children do not inherit his complacent temperament. Margret is a sturdy and self-contained woman who takes after her uncle Hauk, a hunter, and like him enjoys solitary walks and rambles among the hillsides, searching for herbs and berries. Aside from one brief episode of passion for a Norwegian visitor, Skuli Gudmundsson—an adulterous affair that leads to her lover's death—Margret leads a bleak and stoical life. After she is cast off by her husband, Olaf, she becomes an itinerant servant, wandering among the homesteads, supporting herself with her weaving. Her adultery isolates her from her brother Gunnar for thirty-four years before they are finally reunited.

Gunnar is an unpromising child, slow to develop and apparently lazy, although like his sister he enjoys weaving and later learns to write on parchment, on which he laboriously chronicles the history of the settlement. A storyteller as well, Gunnar remembers the old stories of Eric the Red and serves as a living memory for his people. Gunnar, too, lives with the burden of sorrow, witnessing the burning alive of his son, Kollgrim, for witchcraft in the seduction of the Icelandic woman Steinunn Hrafnsdottir, the suicide of his wife, Birgitta, in grief for their son, the death of his daughter Helga in childbirth, and the murder of his sister Margret at the hands of the Bristol men. Indeed, the lives of the Greenlanders seem so oppressive that the old priest Sira Pall Hallvardsson is led to wonder over his prayers:

> How was it . . . that the Lord gathered these folk together in one spot for only a long enough moment so that they came to love and depend on one another, and then wrested them apart for eternity, some to perdition, some to Heaven, some to bide their time in purgatory? And how could it be that the soul should endure perpetual separation, when even the little separations between deaths were hardly bearable?

The interpolated tale of the infatuation of Kollgrim Gunnarsson and Steinunn Hrafnsdottir, wife of a prominent Icelander, is a particulary instructive example of Smiley's creative use of her source material. A ship of Icelanders, blown off course, arrived in Greenland in 1406 and the crew stayed for a few years before sailing back. Regarding their stay, an entry in the Icelandic Annals observes tersely, "Steinunn was seduced through witchcraft by a Greenlandic man and he was burned at the stake and Steinunn went crazy from the grief." Smiley expands this note into one of the climactic episodes in the novel, in chapter 3, creating a story with all the dramatic tension and suppressed emotion of an Ingmar Bergman movie. Kollgrim is something of a misfit in the colony, a loner, a hunter, like his uncle Hauk, who accidentally meets Steinunn while she is staying at St. Nikolaus Cathedral in Gardar to escape the melancholy of winter. Steinunn is frustrated and unhappy with her marriage to Thorgrim, and she is much taken with the tall, silent hunter who accompanies her on walks among the hills above Gardar; they begin to spend time together. When the two are discovered in Steinunn's room by Thorgrim and his men, the husband could take his revenge by having Kollgrim banished to the wilderness, but he chooses instead to try him for witchcraft at the annual outdoor legal assembly, or Thing, and have him burnt at the stake. Kollgrim, whose wits have been impaired by an accidental dunking in icy fjord waters, is unable to defend himself against these strange charges, and he is found guilty by the assembly. His death had been prophesied by the madman Larus as a means of expiation for the sins of the Greenlanders, but all that is accomplished is the setting in motion of a cycle of revenge that ultimately brings Gunnar to repent of his vengeful desires. Steinunn lapses into a coma after Kollgrim's death and gradually wastes away, her will to live destroyed by her grief.

After Kollgrim's death, Gunnar retreats to his parchments, a broken man, bent by grief and loss. His decline is paralleled by the gradual disintegration of the Greenlanders' society, as the farmsteads are abandoned, men no longer go on the annual seal hunts, the annual assembly is no longer held, churches are abandoned, and people take the law into their own hands. Some Greenlanders lapse into the old pagan worship of the Norse gods, and others follow the mad prophet Larus, who offers them homespun visions of the apocalypse. When two ships of Bristol pirates, blown off course late one season, land in Gardar and sack the cathedral, rape, and pillage, the Greenlanders are so demoralized that they can scarcely defend themselves. For many, it seems that the apocalypse is indeed at hand.

These forebodings are somewhat mitigated by the fact that most of the Greenlanders seem confused and unaware of what is happening to them. They lament the loss of their livestock, the disappearance of the reindeer herds and seals, the decline of skills and learning, the loss of priests and lawmakers, but even as their living conditions steadily decline, they keep hoping that things will improve. Smiley's tone is ironic as much as compassionate: The Greenlanders are confused and bewildered as much by their own limitations as by the forces of nature and history. When environmental conditions became harsher, they were unable to abandon their European customs and learn from the Eskimos, whom they feared and loathed, considering them demons and less than human. Tied to their livestock and their permanent habitations, the Greenlanders were unable to adapt a nomadic life like that of the Eskimos, to use fur clothing, live in tents, and follow the seals and the reindeer. Their virtue, perhaps even their heroism, is in their stoical acceptance of what they perceive as the inevitable.

While Smiley's novel does not solve the mystery of this remote Scandinavian settlement that so completely disappeared, it does re-create with great plausibility the events that probably led to its disappearance. There is finally a sobering realization, as applicable to our own precariously overextended, technological society as it was to the relatively primitive society of the Greenlanders, that nature does not owe humankind the favor of perpetuating its existence indefinitely.

Andrew J. Angyal

Sources for Further Study

The Atlantic. CCLXI, May, 1988, p. 94.
Booklist. LXXXIV, March 1, 1988, p. 1049.
Chicago Tribune. April 3, 1988, XIV, p. 5.
The Christian Science Monitor. September 7, 1988, p. 18.
Houston Post. May 15, 1988, p. F10.
Kirkus Reviews. LVI, February 15, 1988, p. 240.
Library Journal. CXIII, April 15, 1988, p. 96.
The New Republic. CXCVIII, May 16, 1988, p. 36.
The New York Times Book Review. XCIII, May 15, 1988, p. 11.
Publishers Weekly. CCXXXIII, March 25, 1988, p. 50.

GREY IS THE COLOR OF HOPE

Author: Irina Ratushinskaya (1954-)
Translated from the Russian by Alyona Kojevnikov
Publisher: Alfred A. Knopf (New York). 355 pp. $18.95
Type of work: Memoir
Time: 1983-1986
Locale: The "Small Zone" in a Soviet labor camp near Mordovia, three hundred miles west of Moscow

A poet and human rights activist recounts her three years in a labor camp, where with a small group of female political prisoners she struggled to survive physically and spiritually

Principal personages:
IRINA RATUSHINSKAYA, the narrator, a political prisoner
GALYA BARATS,
PANI JADVYGA,
NATASHA LAZAREVA,
PANI LIDA,
TANYA OSIPOVA,
RAYA RUDENKO,
ELENA SANNIKOVA,
TATYANA VELIKANOVA, and
TATYANA VLADIMIROVNA, other political prisoners housed in the Small Zone
LIEUTENANT PODUST, a female jailer in charge of the Small Zone

The concentration camp is one of the twentieth century's contributions to the inventory of inhumanity. Citizens of nearly every country have experienced the concentration camp to some degree. No people have known it more intimately or more fatally than Russians.

In the 1920's, Lenin and Leon Trotsky constructed numerous camps across the Soviet Union to hold—and perhaps reeducate—thousands of opponents of the October Revolution and the Bolshevik government. In the 1930's, their successor, Joseph Stalin, committed the country to a rapid industrialization which it could not afford and then converted the camp populations into pools of slave labor. Working long hours and living under primitive conditions, inmates suffered high mortality rates. To keep the camps supplied with human fodder, Stalin's secret police (NKVD) discovered that political criminals were easier to find and convict than ordinary felons. Millions who worried about socialism's future, doubted their leader's wisdom, worked with Westerners, read foreign books, or simply spent some time abroad received prison sentences of eight to twenty-five years. By the late 1940's, as many as ten million citizens representing every Soviet republic inhabited this system of camps that stretched from Finland to Kamchatka but clustered in the remote regions of Siberia and Asia. So many dotted the landscape that they resembled an archipelago; the archipelago was called the gulag, an acronym of the state agency responsible for its administration. The Communist Party repressed all public discussion of the gulag's existence.

After Stalin's death in 1953, hundreds of thousands of survivors were declared rehabilitated and set free. The archipelago remained, though the number of islands was reduced. Throughout the 1960's and 1970's, the population of the gulag swelled or shrank depending upon the Communist Party's toleration for dissent at any particular moment. As the story of the Stalin-era camps slowly became public, as the deaths of millions of innocent citizens were reluctantly admited, the Party leadership promised that such monstrous slaughter and widescale abuse would never occur again. The current state of the labor camps, no longer as widespread or as fatal, was not a topic for open debate and discussion. The outsider might well have believed that the gulag, like the state itself in Marxist theory, was withering away.

Grey Is the Color of Hope is a memoir of labor camp life in the 1980's. Irina Ratushinskaya served three years for political "crimes." Her labor was comparatively light—she made industrial gloves—and she spiritedly resisted her jailers' intimidation. Yet the arbitrariness, hardship, and cruelty of her term show that Mikhail Gorbachev's reforms have yet to touch the gulag. *Perestroika* still has not restructured the treatment of inmates, nor has *glasnost* opened prison gates for political prisoners. Ratushinskaya's book is a memorial for those who died in the camps, a reminder of those who still serve long, unjust sentences, and a plea to eradicate an evil from the soil of her country. Ratushinskaya assumes the traditional role of the Russian writer: to act as a second government when the first government abuses its own citizens.

The body of the memoir begins in March, 1983, with Ratushinskaya's departure from a State Security Committee (KGB) prison in Kiev after six months of interrogation. She is transported westward to a remote camp in Mordovia and housed in a special camp-within-a-camp for female political prisoners. She is quickly assimilated into a tightly knit band of a dozen women; united as one, they resist their captors' efforts to punish them physically or break them psychologically. For her resistance, Ratushinskaya serves several stints in solitary confinement; she preserves herself by writing and memorizing hundreds of poems. Some are smuggled out of prison and published in translation, prompting American and European writers to campaign publicly for her release. The memoir ends on the day before the Rekjavik summit in October, 1986. As a goodwill gesture toward the United States, Gorbachev orders her release.

The memoir limits itself to Ratushinskaya's three years and seven months in Mordovia. As a result it is a claustrophobic book. It brings the reader into the camp world as the *zeks* (prisoners) experience it. Just as imprisonment cuts Ratushinskaya off from husband and friends, so her narrative cuts the reader off from reminders of the world outside. Nor does the narrative maintain a normal chronological sense of time. Instead, the reader learns the rhythm by which *zeks* live: time marked by restrictions imposed, hunger strikes undertaken, prisoners' sentences begun, ended, or extended, semiannual visits by loved ones anticipated and remembered.

Grey Is the Color of Hope is also a modest book. Though Ratushinskaya is the narrator, she is not—at least in her own eyes—the heroine of this story. She is silent about the actions that led to her arrest and imprisonment; she hardly mentions the efforts she and her husband made to monitor the Soviet government's compliance with the Helsinki Accords on Human Rights. She fails to describe the samizdat (self-published) literature she circulated and the demonstrations she made in support of physicist and rights activist Andrei Sakharov. Ratushinskaya includes in the memoir perhaps half a dozen poems she wrote in prison, but she does not boast of the substantial body of verse she composed. She downplays her own suffering except when it illustrates what all prisoners suffer. Only by turning to secondary sources will a reader learn that her prison poems number in the hundreds, that more than half her sentence was served in forms of solitary confinement (*shizo* and PKT), or that she lost forty pounds on a hunger strike and experienced respiratory, cardiac, and gynecological dysfunctions simultaneously.

For Ratushinskaya, the real heroine of Mordovia is the Small Zone itself. Its dozen inhabitants, isolated from the larger prison population, receive special harassment from camp officials. If these prisoners were ordinary felons—if they had only robbed, assaulted, or defrauded their fellow human beings in the normal course of things—their jailers would understand and accept them. As political prisoners, however, they endure a harsher regimen, because the warders cannot fathom their allegiance to abstract rights, their persistence in ideals, or their confidence in human dignity. Clad in gray uniforms that distinguish them from criminal *zeks*, the women of the Small Zone are as alien to camp officials as Martians. To other Russians, however, the gray-clad politicals are the conscience of the nation. Thus is gray the color of hope.

The eleven women of the Small Zone are a fascinating group both as individuals and as children of their time. They bring to the group individual talents and distinctive personalities; their stories are a microcosm of late twentieth century Soviet history. Galya Barats, a large, cheerful woman whom no camp uniform can fit, was once a believing Marxist and loyal Party member; she and her husband received sentences for publicly offering to trade places with any Westerners who profess admiration for the Soviet Union. Pani Jadvyga, who grows vegetables in the Small Zone's sandy soil and worries where her body will be buried, is a Lithuanian, first imprisoned in 1945 when the Soviet Army conquered her native Lithuania; since then she has suffered three rounds of prison and exile for professing Christianity. Raya Rudenko, a round-cheeked, cheerful Ukrainian peasant whose portrait could illustrate a tourist brochure, works a seamstress' magic to turn scraps of cloth into underclothes, warm linings, and decorative touches; none of these comes with prison garb. Tatyana Velikanova, a human rights activist like Ratushinskaya, unhesitatingly leads the Small Zone in hoarding its few treasures and in defying authorities; her warders repay her with additional isolation, deprivation, and abuse. Tatyana Vladimirovna, a veteran inmate wise in the ways prisoners exploit one another, tries to sow dissension in the Small Zone and acts as informant.

Political prisoners need extraordinary inner strength and mutual support in order to stand firm against the tactics and techniques the jailers employ. Some methods are physically brutal; others are psychologically wearing. For serious offenses against camp discipline, political *zeks* are placed in the dreaded *shizo*, a minuscule, unheated cell of stone and wood, in which loneliness, reduced diet, and physical discomfort test the firmest resolve. Politicals are subjected to unexpected searches, interrogations, and transfers to heighten anxiety. Warders play an elaborate charade about rules, pretending that the camp is run according to public regulations but ingeniously perverting them to dispirit the prisoners. For example, the women of the Small Zone receive a certain ration of bread, but the kitchen often provides a fraction less than required. Painstakingly the prisoners weigh the ration. If it is the correct weight, they have wasted time and energy; if not, they protest, with only occasional success. The game is played not only with food but also with clothing, work quotas, letters, and personal belongings.

Against this arsenal the prisoners pit their resolve and solidarity. They hold fast to political or religious ideals: the Helsinki Accords, Christian brotherhood, the example of good men and women already suffering because of the state. They ignore the larger issues of the world and focus their attention on daily living: finding a cloth strip to patch a frayed uniform, nurturing a flower or a plant beside the barrack, keeping the latrine clean. They share memories of loved ones and expectations for the future. They exchange what gifts they can on birthdays and holidays: a poem composed in *shizo*, a scarf from variegated rags, a pot of tea from hoarded leaves. They enact the old customs of the Ukraine, of Lithuania, and of the Crimea: They sing forbidden carols at Christmas, bathe in melted snow at the New Year, and throw boots out the door to see which way the toe points—and in which direction their true love awaits.

The life, the security, the sense of identity that community provides is the memoir's most important theme. Ironically, the Small Zone depicts the ideal Communist society, where, as Karl Marx envisioned, society would receive "from each according to his talent" and provide "to each according to his need." The world around the Small Zone—the labor camp that encloses it, the Soviet state that commands it—calls itself Marxist but cannot recognize true communism in its midst. The state that professes to eliminate class and national distinctions cannot see that these women prisoners truly subordinate their ancestry and social background to their common humanity.

Grey Is the Color of Hope is clearly the work of a poet. Its narrative pace is leisurely rather than quick. Ratushinskaya is concerned with the sensation of events more than with the sequence of action and reaction. She pays attention to what people say, how they look, what they feel. She relies on adjectives, metaphors, similes, and allusion to lead the reader inside the experience of imprisonment. In most of the book her tone is controlled and restrained, remarkably objective for one who has suffered. The communal spirit of the Small Zone enables her to transcend the emotions her jailers try to create: fear, anxiety, self-doubt, surrender. She views her own situation with ironic detachment. At KGB headquarters, she decides that she must be a queen because strong-armed attendants follow her every step, the willing hands of guards open cell and courtroom doors for her, and chatty interrogators keep her from lonely silence. Through her images, the poet remakes the world around her into one she can live in and can live for.

Grey Is the Color of Hope joins a long list of major Russian literary works about the experience of prison camp: Fyodor Dostoevski's *Zapiski iz myortvogo doma* (1861-1862; *Buried Alive*, 1881, best known as *The House of the Dead*); Eugenia Ginzburg's *Krutoi marshrut* (1967-1978; *Journey into the Whirlwind*, 1967, and *Within the Whirlwind*, 1981), and Aleksandr Solzhenitsyn's *Odin den Ivana Denisovicha* (1962; *One Day in the Life of Ivan Denisovich*, 1963). Like them, it portrays the tyranny that Russians inflict upon one another in the name of ideology, monarchical or Marxist. Like them, it shows the heroism needed to resist, survive, and triumph.

Robert Otten

Sources for Further Study

Boston Globe. October 9, 1988, p. 91.
The Christian Science Monitor. October 7, 1988, p. B1.
Kirkus Reviews. LVI, August 15, 1988, p. 1223.
Library Journal. CXIII, October 15, 1988, p. 87.
Los Angeles Times Book Review. October 23, 1988, p. 1.
The New Republic. CXCIX, December 5, 1988, p. 40.
New York. XXI, October 3, 1988, p. 69.
The New York Times Book Review. XCIII, October 30, 1988, p. 11.
The Observer. June 5, 1988, p. 43.
Publishers Weekly. CCXXXIV, August 26, 1988, p. 70.
The Spectator. CCLX, June 18, 1988, p. 31.

HAING NGOR
A Cambodian Odyssey

Author: Haing Ngor, with Roger Warner
Publisher: Macmillan (New York). Illustrated. 478 pp. $19.95
Type of work: Historical autobiography
Time: 1970-1984
Locale: Cambodia, Thailand, and the United States

A harrowing and perceptive account by a Cambodian refugee doctor and now-famous actor of his experiences under the Communist Khmer Rouge regime from 1975 to 1979

Principal personages:
HAING NGOR, a Cambodian doctor and actor
CHANG MY HUOY, his wife
NORODOM SIHANOUK, former king of Cambodia, 1953-1970
LON NOL, military dictator of Cambodia, 1970-1975
POL POT, head of the Khmer Rouge and Communist dictator of Cambodia, 1975-1979
DITH PRAN, a Cambodian journalist imprisoned under the Communist regime and played by Haing Ngor in the award-winning motion picture *The Killing Fields* (1984)
JOHN CROWLEY, an American official of the Joint Voluntary Refugee Agency

Elie Wiesel, the Holocaust survivor and Nobel Prize-winner, has remarked that the twentieth century will be remembered primarily as the century of testimony. The horrors of the century have inspired many superb accounts of the Holocaust and of the Soviet purges and labor camps. *Haing Ngor: A Cambodian Odyssey* exposes the reader to a lesser-known but no less horrible and significant episode, the brutal and fanatical Khmer Rouge ("red Khmer") Communist regime of 1975-1979.

Haing Ngor is eminently suited to tell this story. He survived the hell of Cambodian genocide, understood it, and sought to communicate it powerfully and articulately in book and film. He has succeeded brilliantly, presenting a rare combination of keen description of the personal experience of daily life with a valuable understanding of historical events.

Before the Communists came to power, Ngor was a dedicated obstetrician. After his years of unspeakable suffering, he became an award-winning actor in the United States. He will always, however, think of himself as a survivor: "I am a survivor of the Cambodian holocaust. That's who I am." He has dedicated his fine work to his father, mother, and wife, who died under the Communist regime. Ngor's story begins with his childhood and youth in a seemingly tranquil country. Cambodia, a country the size of Washington state, in Southeast Asia, borders on Thailand and Vietnam. Like Vietnam, it was colonized by the French and became independent in 1953. It remained an agricultural country, Buddhist in religion, and fiercely nationalistic and proud of its traditions. Most Cambodians were peasants and dark-skinned Khmers. Other Cambodians were a combination of lighter-skinned Khmer and Chinese, or Khmer and Vietnamese. Ngor himself was a mixture of Chinese and Khmer stock and came from a fairly prosperous middle-class family.

Ngor characterizes the Cambodians as an outwardly gentle and shy people, family oriented and pleasure-loving. He sees a dangerous underside, however, to Cambodian history, society, and culture. Cambodian society contained deep problems and resentments that have smoldered for centuries. These tensions took the form of hatred between country dwellers and city dwellers, suspicion of foreigners and neighbors who have coveted Cambodia, ignorance of the outside world, and a heritage of widespread corruption and extortion of the weak by the strong. Above all, Cambodians tend to nurse long-standing grudges. Children are reared to be extremely deferential to adults and to bury their anger, while adults are supposed to save face by rigidly controlling their emotions when they are insulted. There is a terrible price to be paid for this, says Ngor. The Cambodians call it "kum," revenge, and when it explodes, it is sometimes uncontrollable. The people who carried out the Cambodian mass murders were partially motivated by revenge.

Ngor portrays himself as a rebellious, street-smart, resourceful, and tough youth. He became a Buddhist monk, then a doctor, and fell in love with a woman without obtaining his father's consent. These qualities of toughness and independence helped Ngor survive his later extreme ordeals.

In 1953, Cambodia became independent of France. King Norodom Sihanouk emerged as a popular figure who steered a neutral course between the West and the Communists. In 1970, however, the country began to fragment. When North Vietnam created sanctuaries in Cambodia, and the United States invaded Cambodia to destroy these pockets, General Lon Nol, a military dictator supported by the United States, overthrew Sihanouk. Corruption and incompetence ran riot, and civil war erupted. Communist China and North Vietnam supported the growing movement of Communist guerrillas of Cambodia, the Khmer Rouge (red Khmers). The guerrillas were increasingly supported by poor peasants and were led by Pol Pot, a Cambodian nationalist and Communist disciple of Joseph Stalin and Mao Tse-tung. In April of 1975, the Cambodian capital, Phnom Penh, fell to the Communists, and life for the Cambodians became a nightmare from which they have not yet awakened.

As soon as the Communists came to power, they embarked on a fanatical attempt to remake Cambodian society through radical social reorganization and, above all, terror and mass murder. The Communists evacuated the cities; marched masses of people into the countryside; and abolished money, the middle and professional classes, family life, holidays, and conveniences. They killed people with ties to the cities and the old regime, people who looked suspicious (such as individuals who wore glasses and had soft hands), and non-Communists (the "new" people). The Khmer Rouge strictly forbade sexual love and conjugal affection, a terrifying echo of George Orwell's *Nineteen Eighty-four* (1949).

Ngor vividly describes the practices of this Communist society in Cambodia. The people were organized in huge work gangs and often worked eighteen hours a day. They were surrounded by loudspeakers blaring propaganda and were terrorized in the name of "Angka," the all-knowing organization. While hundreds of thousands of Cambodians died, the invisible Communist elite lived in bourgeois comfort. They were city-bred intellectuals intent on creating an anticity, anti-intellectual revolution. Ngor provides an excellent portrait of Pol Pot, the Communist dictator. Pol Pot came from a well-to-do family with ties to the royal palace. He became a monk, failed in an engineering school, and then went to Paris, where he studied Marxism. He hoped to transform Cambodia into a self-sufficient Communist nation, as Stalin had done with the Soviet Union and Mao Tse-tung with China. Pol Pot and his inner circle were extreme nationalists and racists who sought to create not only a classless, homogeneous society but also a pure Cambodian people purged of Vietnamese, Buddhist, and Muslim elements. Temples were destroyed, and Buddhist monks and members of Muslim communities were killed. As in the Nazi Holocaust, the killers were represented by a variety of idealists, jobholders, opportunists, and sadists. Brainwashed children and teenagers were often used as spies and killers. At one camp, Tuol Sleng, twenty thousand political prisoners were killed and detailed records of tortures and confessions were kept. Routinized killing became both a tactic of terror and an end in itself.

The Communist overseers knew nothing about farming or industrial construction. "The country was ruled by the ignorant," says Ngor. The motto of the Khmer Rouge, "Blood avenges blood," was put into horrible practice: From 1975 to 1979, starvation, mass murder, and unbearable suffering claimed the lives of two million out of seven million Cambodians. Only nine out of forty-one of Ngor's immediate family survived.

Ngor and others have inevitably compared the genocide in Cambodia with the Nazi extermination of the Jews, the standard against which new instances of mind-boggling evil are measured. While Cambodia clearly suffered the largest ideologically inspired slaughter since 1945, most historians would characterize the Khmer Rouge reign of terror as "autogenocide." The Cambodian murders were localized and not primarily motivated by racial considerations, for most of the victims of the Khmer Rouge were Khmers themselves who were killed in the name of building a Communist utopia.

Ngor and his family were swept into the vortex of this event, and his narrative is extremely painful to read. Ngor was put in a labor battalion where he dug canals, planted rice, and hauled fertilizer. He suffered malaria, dysentery, and constant malnutrition. He retaliated by stealing food for himself and for others, by outwitting his guards, and by remaining in control of his emotions and his dignity. He was tortured three times because he was suspected of being a doctor: One of his fingers was chopped off, he was hung over a slow fire for four days, and he was subjected to a nerve-shattering water torture. His luck, endurance, and his will to go on for the sake of his wife enabled him to survive. Ngor repeatedly forewarns the reader to expect harrowing tales of torture and human depravity. There are scenes that describe the disemboweling of pregnant women by the professional torturers of the Khmer Rouge, and the slow hanging of others to strike terror into the population.

These scenes were omitted by the producers of *The Killing Fields* for fear of offending Western audiences. At one point, Ngor's life was spared when he flattered his guards by telling them that they possessed the power of life and death.

The most heartbreaking episode in the entire book is the death in childbirth of Ngor's devoted wife. Chang My Huoy had nursed Ngor back to life after his tortures, but Ngor, the trained obstetrician, was powerless to save the life of his malnourished and exhausted wife. Her last words to him were, "Take care of yourself, sweet." Like other survivors of massive traumas, Ngor suffers from survivor guilt. He shows that despite the overwhelming record of human cruelty and depravity, many Cambodians retained their humanity. A woman saved Ngor's life by giving him food. Even a few officials and guards were capable of an occasional kindness. The Khmer Rouge were able to kill the body, but not always the spirit.

In 1979, Ngor and his fellow Cambodians were liberated by the North Vietnamese, whom the Khmer Rouge had foolishly turned against. Ngor rescued his niece and adopted her as his daughter. He then met John Crowley, a sympathetic and helpful American official of a refugee agency. In 1980, Haing Ngor arrived in Los Angeles to start a new life.

He was chosen to audition for the film *The Killing Fields*, which told the true story of an American correspondent's search for Dith Pran, a Cambodian journalist who had saved his life from the Khmer Rouge. Ngor identified with Dith Pran and relived his own experiences as he made the film; he found a constructive outlet for his anger. *The Killing Fields* called the attention of the American public to the genocide in Cambodia, and Ngor won an Academy Award for best supporting actor. He maintains, however, that his best acting performance was before he left Cambodia, for the price was survival itself. Ngor is now a versatile actor and works with Cambodian refugee organizations. Yet his wounds will never heal. "I will never be forgiven by my memories," he concludes.

Cambodia itself remains occupied by North Vietnam. Rival factions continue to struggle, as Cambodia continues to be a political pawn of China and the Soviet Union. Many thousands of Cambodian refugees lead a marginal existence on the Thai border. Some life has returned to Phnom Penh, but most of the leaders of the Khmer Rouge have gone unpunished, and the Cambodian people remain in a state of shock over the past and uncertainty about the future. Ngor's riveting account is a reminder that twentieth century fanaticism, genocide, and mass murder remain an ever-present threat to our existence.

Leon Stein

Sources for Further Study

Chicago Tribune. January 17, 1988, XIV, p. 1.

The Christian Science Monitor. March 31, 1988, p. 1.

Library Journal. CXIII, February 1, 1988, p. 63.
Los Angeles Times Book Review. January 31, 1988, p. 3.
The New York Times Book Review. XCIII, February 21, 1988, p. 30.
Publishers Weekly. CCXXXII, December 18, 1987, p. 49.
The Washington Post Book World. XVIII, January 31, 1988, p. 6.

HANG-GLIDING FROM HELICON
New and Selected Poems, 1948-1988

Author: Daniel Hoffman (1923-   )
Publisher: Louisiana State University Press (Baton Rouge). 218 pp. $24.95
Type of work: Poetry

An impressive winnowing of poems from six earlier collections and forty-three new poems establish Hoffman as a major poet

Daniel Hoffman's *Hang-Gliding from Helicon: New and Selected Poems, 1948-1988* is a generous book and a personal book. It not only shows but also tells where the poet has been, what he has thought and done in his lifetime. It confronts the signs of age the poet observes, and it examines the shifts and changes he has undergone over a long career of teaching and writing. It allows the reader to trace the poet's ideas and to observe the development of his craft. Moreover, it reveals, particularly in the section called "Hang-Gliding from Helicon," who, among writers, have remained as influences. The book is a summing up of one man's achievement, and the summation should leave no doubt that Hoffman belongs among the major poets of his generation.

The book itself is elegantly, rather than sumptuously, designed and produced. It is a straightforward production and lacks introductory comment, notes, and diversions. The several sections are headed with the titles of the books from which the poems are drawn, followed by the years of the books' publication. For the most part, the poems are short. The book's final section, containing the forty-three new poems, is long enough to justify a separate book. It contains some of Hoffman's best work, and those poems bring to a satisfying conclusion this retrospective of the poet's life.

From the start of his career, Hoffman, like many an American writer, has combined scholarship and criticism with imaginative writing. Perhaps to a greater extent than most writers, he has identified with his region and has expended effort to represent and serve that region in his art. Hoffman's contribution to literary criticism, particularly the study of the relationship of myth to literature, has been impressive. Unfortunately, however, literary scholarship has tended to regard him as a better critic than poet, failing to see that the poems reflect the poet's sensitive awareness of myth and folklore as constituting the very stuff of poetry. Hoffman's previous collections of new poems, *The Center of Attention*, came out in 1974, followed by a book-length meditation on William Penn, the founder of Pennsylvania (*Brotherly Love*, 1981). All the while, he remained busy with critical works, such as *Others: Shock Troops of Stylistic Change* (1975) and *"Moonlight Dries No Mittens": Carl Sandburg Reconsidered* (1979). Adding those critical works to the earlier ones on Paul Bunyan, on Stephen Crane, on American fiction, on myth in the poetry of William Butler Yeats, Robert Graves, and Edwin Muir, and his much-celebrated *Poe Poe Poe Poe Poe Poe Poe* (1972), one discovers that Hoffman's titles in criticism exactly balance his titles in poetry—that is, if one counts the selected poems published in London in 1977 under the title *Able Was I Ere I Saw Elba: Selected Poems, 1954-1974*.

Hoffman's work, as represented by his published books (to say nothing of his editorial efforts and his contribution of occasional essays on poets and poetry), reveals a cohesive, almost perfectly integrated career. One suspects that Hoffman wished to call attention to that aspect of his poetry when he chose the classical example of the palindrome ("Able Was I Ere I Saw Elba") as the title for his first volume of selected poems. Just as one may read a palindrome backward or forward, so one may begin anywhere in reading Hoffman's poems and still observe the interplay of early, middle, and late ones. There are progressions, changes, but the central concerns remain remarkably consistent.

Nearly a quarter of the poems in *Hang-Gliding from Helicon* are unavailable elsewhere in book form, though all apparently have been published in magazines. In selecting poems from his earlier books, Hoffman has omitted any excerpt from *Brotherly Love*, doubtless recognizing that parts detached from long works do not represent the whole. He also chose to omit the title poem from his second collection, *A Little Geste and Other Poems* (1960), though some critics have regarded it as the most impressive poem in that book. "A Little Geste" is not only long but also a technical tour de force and, as such, would break the book's movement and divert the reader from what is essential. Hoffman's excision of poems and his generous offering of new poems permits a view, not of what is unusual in his work but of what is essential and enduring. Such a process necessarily takes on a valedictory quality.

Hoffman's title, *Hang-Gliding from Helicon*, announces that valedictory quality, for though a glider may soar as well as swoop, the nature of gliding demands that one go powerless into the air and let the breezes and the currents take one where they will. The mature poet, with six good books behind him, may be excused the belief that he no longer need aspire toward Helicon, home of the Muses, but may settle himself for the long glide down from those heady heights. It is an image of heroic acceptance—an act of cutting loose with nothing but the elements (and perhaps one's Muse) to bear one up.

Hoffman's title phrase occurs toward the end of a new poem, "Essay on Style," one of his most playful poems, in which he states that a persona "invoked the Abecedary of his affections." Thus begins an amusingly determined and alphabetically progressive series of alliterations, describing the writer's progress toward Helicon. The poem ends with a series of repetitions of the letter *H*, thus strengthening the suspicion that Hoffman is the poet. At the end, the poet has climbed "over ledges of syntactical terrain" and hacked "through thickets of thought" to reach his "headstrong Muse." Finally, with

> Her by his side, with
> Her blessing, he'll
> Hover, he'll swoop, and soar,
> Hang-gliding from Helicon, over the world.

The reader may recall that Hoffman's dedication of *Striking the Stones* (1968), a book which has much to say about poetry, read simply, "Again, Musebaby's," suggesting that the poems belonged to, or stemmed from, the Muse. "Essays on Style," then, besides being delightful, seems to summarize Hoffman's lifetime effort to say his say with the tools at his disposal—words adapted to the speech of his time but retaining the poet's form. In the middle of "Essays on Style," the poet asks, "What in these/ Days of disjunction endures?" The answer comes at once:

A
Diction to say
Desire, dawn, death, despair, descant,
Direct disclosures in dextrous dirges,
Devour, depart, dig, digress, discard and discord

He breaks in on his catalog of themes with what amounts to a panegyric, undercut by the colloquial:

—Doggone, it's a domain here a man can
Do or die in, go
Daft with the delicacy and the daring, the
Dazzle of dew in the darkness—let his

The quest for something which endures in these "days of disjunction" is central to Hoffman's poetry, and in all of his books, as in "Essays on Style," the poet's "doodlings" regularly "disclose new delights, for this dialect/ Defies desolation." From the start, Hoffman has been aware of the debased culture in which he lived. He set out to be a poet soon after returning from service in the air force during World War II, and thus participated in the postwar, postbomb anxiety and mechanized tedium of the late 1940's and the 1950's. When W. H. Auden, perhaps the single most gifted lyricist of the mid-twentieth century, selected Hoffman's *An Armada of Thirty Whales* for the Yale Series of Younger Poets Award in 1954, he wrote in a foreword that Hoffman, "while admitting the pains and tragedies of life, . . . can find joy in life and say so." He saw Hoffman's poems performing a central function of poetry and all art—"the preservation and renewal of natural piety toward every kind of created excellence." The older poet had also recognized his times as "days of disjunction," and spoke in the foreword of the difficulty of finding worthy themes, or even writing at all, in a "technological civilization."

Auden saw in Hoffman's work new possibilities for nature poetry and indicated that Hoffman had discovered verse forms appropriate for his age and for his poems of direct observation. Victims of the rhythms of the machine, most modern readers, Auden speculated, resist poetry because they associate "repeated pattern with all that is boring and disagreeable in their lives."

The resistance to poetry has persisted, and civilization has become enormously more technological than what Auden knew, but through it all Hoffman has continued to write his nature poems and his poems of affirmation, though in poems such as "Stop the Deathwish! Stop It! Stop!" he admits, wearily, that he spent the better part of his long youth "prenticed to arts for which there'll be small use/ in whatever work the future needs have done." Those arts, in addition to poetry, include Morse code and close observation of nature now defiled or simply paved over by progress.

To do justice to what endures in his work, Hoffman has omitted many fine poems, and he has reordered much of what remains. The thirty poems in his first book dwindle to thirteen, and the forty-one poems in *The City of Satisfactions* (1963) dwindle to but seventeen, significantly reordered to illuminate the mythic elements at work there.

Hoffman has divided his new poems in *Hang-Gliding from Helicon* into five sections, and, despite the third-person pronoun of the first poem's title, he strikes a personal and valedictory tone. The poem "Himself" denies the mirror's representation of the self. The "he" of the poem knows that somewhere in the house with him is a truer representation than what the mirror shows. There is, for example, "a youth he has outgrown," and the blessing given him "across the alien years" is that he may judge his actions by what that outworn youth would do. A third poem, called "A Stone," provides more than a whiff of mortality as the poet recognizes that he is moving toward a stone

> scored
> With parentheses, cupped hands
> Enclosing half an emptiness
> That awaits its filling-in.

Hoffman returns to a similar use of parentheses in section 2, at the end of a poem called "The Great American Novel," in which he says that he has spent most of his life gathering material. After a childhood recollection of learning to balance a new bicycle while his father sits at a collapsible table under a tree, Hoffman writes that no matter how often his father "harrows his pencil down the colums," the "total is always the same,/ The same parentheses always/ Signifying (Loss)." The poems are full of such recollections, often poignant with loss, sometimes equally poignant with a recalled joy—which one knows cannot recur. He imagines that most frequently seen spectacle, the ageing "Jogger," and then brilliantly turns the sad spectacle of a man running "in an event/ For which he hasn't trained" into a metaphysical truth:

> Somewhere under addenda
> Of belly and rump and jowl
>
> Strides the crisp youth and slender
> Who used to run a quick mile
>
> As if he were still the same
> Though what he ran toward became him.

The final word of this poem says it all: "His record is writ in flesh."

As the poet deteriorates, so apparently does nature suffer—and threaten. In "Crack!" the poet and his wife hear the crack—possibly caused by anything from sonic boom to bombs set by guerrillas—but, accustomed to such sounds, slip back to sleep while "deep below us, rigid rock/ Blocks the insensate seethe at the core." A poem with the all-too-familiar title "Slick" concludes in half a page with fish floating belly-up: "The earth is bleeding./ An ocean of salt/ Rubs in our wounds.

The fifth section opens with "Words"—a virtual leave-taking of poems. Several poems pay homage to writers such as Walt Whitman ("Crossing Walt Whitman Bridge"), Mark Twain ("Mark Twain, 1909"), Auden ("A Letter to W. H. Auden"), and Robert Graves ("Her Obedient Servant"). The book's last poem returns to the reflection of the first poem in the section. After asking the reader to consider that "the mind's a mirror of/ the world," Hoffman concludes "Reflections" by affirming the self:

> Our joy is truthful fallacy.
> Our final city will perfect
> its own impermanent reflection,
> this silver solipsism shining
> behind the mirror as before.

Leon V. Driskell

Source for Further Study

Library Journal. CXIII, May 15, 1988, p. 84.

HER OWN TERMS

Author: Judith Grossman (1937-   )
Publisher: Soho Press (New York). 277 pp. $16.95
Type of work: Novel
Time: The 1940's and 1950's
Locale: Oxford and London, England

A grim, compelling novel about the difficulties faced by a bright girl from a working-class family, who finds it as difficult to be accepted as a person at the University of Oxford as she did in her south London home environment

Principal characters:
IRENE TANNER, a brilliant young poet
HILDA TANNER, her mother
HEATHER TANNER, her older sister
ROGER, her lover, an Oxford student
STUART, her married lover
JOHN SINGLETON, an Oxford professor

It might be assumed that a bright young poet, who from childhood has been miserably alone in a working-class suburb of London, will find happiness when she wins a scholarship to the University of Oxford, where people are valued for their intelligence. Judith Grossman's first novel, *Her Own Terms*, demonstrates that for a woman in the rarefied atmosphere of an English university, acceptance does not come so easily. Certainly class and cultural handicaps can be surmounted at Oxford, but the very men who can overlook the lower-class backgrounds of other men will never forget the fact that a woman is a woman, however intelligent she may be. In this novel, the protagonist discovers that in the university world she must pay a price for companionship. The price is no less than her willingness to serve the men who dominate that world.

Appropriately, *Her Own Terms* begins with Irene Tanner's defiance of her sexuality: "I've never felt less like a woman—it's terribly exciting. This absolute *no*." After finishing her three years at Oxford, Irene is on a train en route to an abortionist in London. Because of her examinations, she has delayed the abortion until the fourth month of her pregnancy; because of her limited funds, she must risk a backroom abortionist. Her fear of death, however, is less than her fear of enslavement to men. Even when the personable Oxford professor John Singleton, whom she encounters on the train, warns her of the emotional results of an abortion and offers her a room and a job while she has her baby, Irene does not seriously reconsider her decision. With her new wisdom, she can see the hook beneath the bait. Although he certainly means to be kind to Irene, Singleton is noted for his womanizing while maintaining a comfortable married condition. If she depends once more on a lord of the universe, Irene knows that she will only postpone the attainment of independence. Thus, the first episode of the novel establishes the theme: an intelligent woman's difficulty in learning to live on "her own terms."

The frame of Grossman's novel is the abortion. In the initial scene on the train, Irene is presented with Singleton's alternative. Midway through the book, she visits the abortionist, who performs the painful procedure and assures her that she will lose the fetus in a period of hours. In the final chapter, Irene is back at Oxford among her women friends, who support her during the anxious hours when she waits for contractions and help her as she finally expels the fetus. At this point, Irene feels a pang which she had not anticipated: Looking at the dead fetus, she recognizes some similarities to her lover. As the book ends, Irene realizes that Singleton was right, that she will never forget what she has done, but that she too was right in making her decision, for she could not have trusted Singleton, or any other man, to value her rather than use her.

The passages which involve the abortion, the only passages which are set in the present, are brief in proportion to the total length of the book. It is this incident, however, which causes Irene to reevaluate her life. Significantly, the long section in which she recalls her childhood and her final escape to Oxford comes before she visits the abortionist. The second long section comes after the procedure. Thus, it is after the irreversible action has been taken and she is on her way back to her college that Irene relives her years at Oxford, as if by understanding what has been done to her there she can better endure the physical pain which is soon to come and the emotional pain which will last a lifetime.

In the section called "35 Agathon Way," for Irene's home address in a working-class area of London, the author traces her protagonist's development as a girl. Infatuated with her mother, Irene yearns for some demonstration of her mother's love, which in wartime seems as tightly rationed as everything else. In fact, her mother's nervousness and exhaustion are not surprising. With her husband in service, and periods of bombing alternating with periods of evacuation, Hilda Tanner has all she can do to deal with two squabbling girls and two babies. The fact that by nature Hilda is reserved and distant, however, leaves the affectionate Irene convinced that her mother does not love her, and her childhood becomes a desperate search for some way to merit the love for which she yearns. Affection from her father might have helped, but when he returns from the war, he is present only in body. Convinced that the best part of his life ended with the war, he is bored with the house full of females and annoyed by his one spoiled son.

With this model of an indifferent and loveless marriage before her, it is not surprising that Irene is attracted by the cultured life-style of her aunt, a teacher who lives a comfortable, celibate existence with a woman friend. It was Irene's grandmother, whose stoker husband was not above getting drunk and beating his family on Friday night, who had determined that her eldest daughter would rise above domestic servitude through becoming a teacher and a lady. Observing how much "Gran" admires her teacher daughter, Irene is probably drawn to academic accomplishments as much by hopes of pleasing her own mother as by the appeal of an easier life—one without baby diapers and economic desperation.

Despite much speculation about sex, the only sexual experience Irene has during her childhood is molestation by a filthy workman in a bombed house. The fact that she submits because she has been trained to be obedient suggests that the feminine pattern of behavior has already been established. At Oxford, she will again be docile when men assert themselves intellectually and sexually. Unfortunately, Irene does not clearly understand her own reactions until her three years at Oxford are nearly over.

The reason for Irene's blindness is that during her first lonely months at Oxford, she is preoccupied with her social and educational disabilities, not with the subtler discrimination against women. When at last she is invited to a meeting of poets, she is ecstatic. As a talented newcomer, she becomes a member of the inner circle, the only woman to be admitted. Only later, after the abortion, does she realize that she was never considered an equal. For example, Irene later learns that her men friends had openly discussed the question of assigning a man to her, assuming that every woman must be attached to someone. It was her poet friends who had settled upon Roger, an acquaintance who was persuaded to become involved with Irene in order to be included in the literary circle.

In his relationship with Irene, Roger is intellectually arrogant, equally scorning her logical skill and her field of study. Eventually, he becomes jealous and possessive, blaming his own flaws on defects in her character. By the time they become engaged, he has already begun to be unfaithful to her, while demanding that she see no one else while he studies in Berlin. His selfishness is later evident when he briefly visits her in England; for his own pleasure, he risks getting her pregnant, in lordly fashion reassuring her that there is no danger. He is wrong. By the time Irene discovers that she is indeed pregnant, she has enjoyed several months of freedom from his domination, enough time to realize that she no longer loves him and that he was never capable of loving her. Marriage, then, is out of the question, and until she meets John Singleton on the train, abortion seems the only possible option for Irene. At the end of her years at Oxford, however, Irene has at last learned to be wary of male domination, which so often seems to offer refuge to a woman who is lonely, insecure, or in trouble.

One of the difficulties in resisting male domination, Irene has discovered, is that like Roger most men can plausibly avoid taking the responsibility for their own misdeeds, explicitly or implicitly assigning any guilt to women. When Irene's father shows his first real interest in his brilliant daughter, flying to Oxford in order to transmit her mother's warning against unchastity, Irene is so moved that later, when he dies, she assumes guilt for the years when he neglected her. Similarly, when she meets a Cambridge University philosophy professor, Stuart, she is so impressed by his gentleness that she ignores the fact that he blames his new habit of infidelity on the influence of an earlier, supposedly predatory mistress. Stuart has used his logical powers to convince himself that he does not harm his girlfriends because he tells them how much he loves his wife, and that he does not harm his wife because he can successfully deceive her. It is hardly surprising that Irene rejects the offer made to her by another married professor, John Singleton. She has at last learned that men's sympathetic words to women provide no assurance of responsible action. Finally, she has realized that women cannot be dependent on the approval of their mothers or of any society of which they are a part, and least of all on the approval of men. The title suggests Irene's difficult new resolution, when at the end of the book she leaves Oxford to seek a happiness which she will define, a life on "her own terms."

Although some reviewers have criticized *Her Own Terms* for including abortion episodes that are grim and graphic and which, they argue, are unrelated to the rest of the novel, it is clear that those brief chapters in fact provide the necessary framework for the book. The abortion, which causes Irene such pain and grief, symbolizes the ultimate violence to a woman, violence which men have made necessary. In organizing her story, Grossman has begun *in medias res*, at a time when her protagonist's entire past is illuminated by the events of the present, and those events are all related to the termination of her pregnancy.

Her Own Terms is Grossman's first novel, so it remains to be seen what direction her work will take. Clearly she has demonstrated her ability to capture the nuances of speech and attitude, whether in working-class London or in Oxford, as well as the capacity to evaluate experience from the vantage point of her own maturity. Although she may have incorporated events from her own life into the story of Irene Tanner, she is consistently a separate authorial presence, discernible even through the first-person narration of her protagonist. This sometimes poignant, sometimes ironic distancing is evident at the end of the novel, when the author has her protagonist voice the buoyant innocence of youth: It takes only the warmth of sunlight on her face to persuade Irene that "the animal, at least, is intact. It's glad to have got away—it's hungry, and it wants to be happy."

Rosemary M. Canfield Reisman

Sources for Further Study

Booklist. LXXXIV, January 1, 1988, p. 749.
Chicago Tribune. February 7, 1988, XIV, p. 7.
Kirkus Reviews. LV, November 15, 1987, p. 1596.
Library Journal. CXIII, January, 1988, p. 98.
Los Angeles Times Book Review. February 7, 1988, p. 2.
The New York Times Book Review. XCIII, January 24, 1988, p. 1.
Publishers Weekly. CCXXXII, November 13, 1987, p. 60.
The Washington Post Book World. XVIII, January 3, 1988, p. 7.

A HISTORY OF PRIVATE LIFE
Volume II: Revelations of the Medieval World

Editor: Georges Duby (1919-)
First published: Histoire de la vie privée: De l'Europe féodale à la Renaissance, 1985
Translated from the French by Arthur Goldhammer
Publisher: Harvard University Press/Belknap Press (Cambridge, Massachusetts). Illustrated. 650 pp. $39.50
Type of work: Social history
Time: The eleventh century to the early sixteenth century
Locale: France and Italy

This history of private life focuses on the texture of everyday life, on living space, family structure, attitudes toward the body, and the more complex issue of the self-perception of the individual

A History of Private Life: Revelations of the Medieval World is the second volume in a series which began with *Histoire de la vie privée: De L'Empire romain à l'an mil* (1985; *A History of Private Life: From Pagan Rome to Byzantium*, 1987) and will continue through three additional volumes. This survey of the private life of past civilizations is one of the fruits of the new social history which began when the French historians Lucien Febvre and Marc Bloch founded *Annales: Économies, sociétés, civilisations* and Fernand Braudel began his influential studies of economic history as it was defined by everyday life. This new social history has aimed at exposing the past not from the perspective of sovereigns whose names frequently have been used to identify the periods of time in which they waged war and negotiated peace but from the perspective of the masses of men and women whose lives are more difficult to reconstruct.

The first volume, which focused on the ancient world of pagan Rome and Byzantium, had geographical centers that facilitated this project. In the second volume, the time frame is larger and the geographical boundaries are defined in large part by the expertise of the editors and contributors. The focus is upon France and Italy; feudal England is given a cursory architectural survey; medieval Spain is virtually ignored. The impact of the "infidels," the not yet fully assessed contribution of Arabic science and Islamic culture, is excluded from this inquiry. Breadth of vision is sacrificed in the interest of depth.

There are many justifications for adopting a tunnel vision of the medieval world. Regionalism is so predominant that the national boundaries which begin to define early modern history do not exist. It is important to recognize that this study is selective geographically and that even medieval Europe was not homogeneous. The portraits of private life which are sketched in this volume ignore kings, although they still obtrude because they are more likely to leave records. The segregation of women's quarters is described as a feature of some medieval castles. How prevalent was this segregation; was it a legacy of the ancient world; and if not, what caused it to develop? Were the boundaries of medieval Europe impervious to the influence of the powerful Turks who segregated their women? The Roman historian Cornelius

Tacitus describes Germanic women accompanying their men to the battlefield and banging pots to urge them into battle.

In his essay "Civilizing the Fortress: Eleventh to Thirteenth Century," Dominique Barthélemy cites two instances in which women's quarters are segregated. Barthélemy seems to intend these to be representative and so to serve as a corrective to earlier views that women came into their own during the Middle Ages. Even on such a basic issue as whether there were separate living quarters for women, the evidence is ambiguous. The reader is left without a clear sense of how much credence to give the "gynaeceum," a term coined by Danielle Régnier-Bohler, defined as "a group of women living together in an area set aside for the purpose." In a large household made up of many servants of both sexes, it makes perfect sense that unmarried men and women would have separate quarters and that unmarried women would be protected. It is startling, however, to discover that, except for two architectural cases cited in Barthélemy's essay, the generalizations about segregated women's quarters derive from fiction, "virtually the only source of information on this subject."

Ironically, the need for public order strongly affected the history of the development of private life. Georges Duby, the editor of this collection of essays, emphasizes that those who absorbed the authority once understood to be public and shared by free citizens became owners: "The master was lord over men, women, children, animals and belongings, just as he was lord over his oven, his stables, and his granaries." When serfs died, their property—livestock in the case of a man, clothing in the case of a woman—belonged to the lord. The lord arranged their marriages. Duby charts the gradual erosion among the poor of the distinction between slaves and free men until all poor men came to belong to the land as serfs. Those people who did not belong to the lord were still expected to swear allegiance to him. The position of the individual without power under feudalism is portrayed graphically and without sentimentality.

Leading questions are repeatedly posed about the relationships between men and women, but many of these are left unanswered. Duby asks:

> What about the "maids," the master's legitimate daughters? Were they offered as freely to knights-errant as fiction suggests in its depiction of the rites of hospitality? And were men roused from their sleep by insatiable females as often as the hagiographies allege?

The relationship between fiction and everyday life requires careful attention. In a world in which war and defense played such an important role, one might expect women to resemble the female soldiers of Sparta; instead, the medieval world produced the concept of courtly love in which the wife of the lord, the woman who embodied power, was an object of desire.

The explanation of courtly love offered in *A History of Private Life* is interesting but not likely to be conclusive. The lady of the lord is described as playing a civilizing role by charming unruly knights and so ensuring that order prevailed in the household:

> Undoubtedly the lord's wife was coveted, and the desire she inspired, sublimated into a sophisticated form of love, was used as a means of disciplining young knights. Stern taboos prevented the young knight from actually riding off with the lady. Yet occasionally she was taken by violence. The importance of rape in the romances obviously reflects reality. Sometimes of course the woman gave herself freely.

A History of Private Life offers no evidence for these conclusions concerning courtly love. Possibilities are mentioned and then reworded as factual conclusions. The comment that sometimes the ladies were abducted by the knights whom they trained in courtly manners leads to the undocumented conclusion, "The importance of rape in the romances obviously reflects reality."

Duby suggests that the *chansons de geste* and romances of the Middle Ages were written for young men, especially younger sons who had no hope of inheritance. It is not clear why the audience for the medieval romance is identified as masculine. Since courtly romances may have been read aloud in noble households, both men and women may have listened to these narratives concerning noble knights, fair ladies, and enchanters. Duby also interprets these courtly romances as offering their audience an escape from the frustrations of their private lives.

The romances themselves are discussed by Régnier-Bohler in "Imagining the Self." This essay takes a series of topics, such as "twins," "bathing and bleeding," and "nudity," and then discusses how they are handled in one or more medieval romances. Although she tells the reader that she is especially interested in the isolated or excluded individual who is later readmitted to the community, this issue does not seem to control the direction of the argument. In her discussion of enclosure, she observes that walls may offer protection but that they may also imprison. Then, she relates an argument from a thirteenth century text in which the author points out that Eve is enclosed because she is created from Adam's rib. After contrasting space without and within, she asks: "Judge you, then, if He did not show greater love to woman than to man, since He created man on the outside." Unfortunately, the source for this anecdote is not identified.

The discussion of "Tuscan Notables on the Eve of the Renaissance" by Charles de la Roncière focuses on many different levels of society under such categories as types of dwellings, position of the husband and father, wife and mother, the aged, family history, and domestic slaves. The legal structure endorsed the man as the head of the family. He is in charge not only of the property but also of the family members. A story related by the fourteenth century poet Franco Sacchetti is cited which supplies an analogue to William Shakespeare's *The Taming of the Shrew* (c. 1593-1594). The client of an innkeeper observed that his wife grumbled when asked to help her husband. When both his wife and the innkeeper died, the former client married the grumbling woman with the intention of subduing her and teaching her obedience. Beatings and insults seem to have produced the intended effect; the wife becomes properly subservient. From this story, Sacchetti draws the moral that the behavior of a wife depends upon the husband's strength of character.

In the last chapter, entitled "Toward Intimacy: The Fourteenth and Fifteenth

Centuries," Philippe Braunstein makes copious use of paintings to illustrate the intellectual developments he identifies as occurring in the late Middle Ages. His discussion of the handling of nudity is particularly interesting. In the earlier Middle Ages, male nudity was associated with madness and savagery, while female nudity was lascivious and shameful; captive women were degraded by conquerors who forced them to disrobe. Braunstein finds more humanity in Northern European painting after 1400, especially in paintings which conveyed the suffering of Christ. The next step was to depict Adam and Eve as fully individual and human figures. The panels of Jan van Eyck's *Mystical Lamb*, according to Braunstein, are the first portraits of Adam and Eve in which they appear as creatures of flesh and blood.

The relationship of the medieval world to the ancient world is not specifically addressed. In at least one Tuscan home, the master had copies of the works of Livy, Sallust, and Giovanni Villani's chronicle in his inventory. These works must have offered models for the writing of family history and chronicles. Nevertheless, the relationship between the Middle Ages and the culture which preceded it remains elusive.

This study of private life fruitfully raises a number of methodological problems that merit further discussion. For example, how should scholars handle the distinction between history and literature; it is simple enough if approached superficially but potentially is a complex topic. How much can be deduced from a study of the Domesday Book as opposed to the hagiographical accounts or the romances and chronicles that have survived? This book contributes significantly to the continuing discourse concerning historiography by raising questions and offering hypotheses that must be examined theoretically on their own grounds as well as in terms of their usefulness for the study of medieval civilization. Is it accurate, for example, to treat the organization of a religious community as analogous to the organization of a feudal lordship? Were there fundamental distinctions between secular and religious communities? To what degree were the communal households of the Middle Ages shaped by economic necessity? To what degree did social class determine the shape of the household, and how much mobility was there among different social classes? These and other such questions are raised by the methods used in what will undoubtedly become an influential study of the private life of the medieval world.

Jeanie R. Brink

Sources for Further Study

Booklist. LXXXIV, February 15, 1988, p. 958.
Kirkus Reviews. LVI, February 15, 1988, p. 274.
Library Journal. CXIII, March 1, 1988, p. 65.

Los Angeles Times Book Review. July 10, 1988, p. 11.
The New York Review of Books. XXXV, March, 17, 1988, p. 30.
The New York Times Book Review. XCIII, March 20, 1988, p. 24.
Publishers Weekly. CCXXXIII, February 5, 1988, p. 77.
The Times Educational Supplement. May 6, 1988, p. 19A.

HÖLDERLIN

Author: David Constantine (1944-)
Publisher: Oxford University Press (New York). 415 pp. $74.00
Type of work: Literary biography and criticism
Time: 1770-1843
Locale: Germany and France

A biography of a German Romantic who has taken an undisputed place among the greatest European poets

Principal personages:
FRIEDRICH HÖLDERLIN, a German Romantic poet
SUSETTE GONTARD, his lover, the wife of his employer
FRIEDRICH SCHILLER, a poet and dramatist who served for a time as his patron
JOHANN WOLFGANG VON GOETHE, a poet and dramatist who was impressed with his work

Known for his passionate evocations of ancient Greek heroes, myths, and values and remembered for his tragic madness during the last thirty-seven years of his life, Friedrich Hölderlin is a poet shrouded in remoteness and abstract language for most modern readers—German as well as English. Nevertheless, he has always exercised a great fascination for poets and serious readers because of his intense dedication to the art of language in philosophical fiction, poetic drama, and lyric verse in a variety of forms. He is an artist driven to pursue the secret of being, a truth that constantly eludes him but which he seems to believe may be captured by realizing the spirit of beauty through inspired recreations of Hellenic vision. This search for the "absent" endears him to those contemporary writers and literary theorists who have come to believe that literature's main purpose is to deal with the loss or absence of meaning generated by its own activity.

Whereas modernism is characterized by alienation and linguistic dispersion, Hölderlin's poetic search for meaning is centered in a strong religious belief that Spirit (what the Germans call *Geist*) can be recovered through a cultivation of what classical Greece had discovered to be essential to the perfection of human existence. To search for beauty in composure, balance, and a harmonious sense of oneness with the ultimately benign power of nature was the promise of Greek sensibility. The Good, in other words, was there for the having if only the self-destructive tendencies of mood and "benighted" temperament could be overcome. Hölderlin never really overcame his own benightedness, but this very failure to reach the Good that he always saw over the horizons of his poems lends his work a uniquely tragic air.

David Constantine speculates that the sense of loss in Hölderlin goes back to the coldness of his mother, who gave him little affection as a child and held back his patrimony when he matured. She wanted him to enter the church, but he had come to hate the dogma of his religious education. In his later youth, he kept his mother at a respectful distance. He fell in love with the beautiful wife of his employer, a businessman whose children he tutored. Susette Gontard gave him unbridled love and encouraged Hölderlin in the belief that in the enjoyment of their love he was actually bringing into perfection the promise of that higher Good his Hellenism had inspired. Susette herself became the inspiration for Diotima, the heroine of his novel *Hyperion oder der Eremit in Griechenland* (1797, 1799; *Hyperion: Or, The Hermit in Greece*, 1965), which he was seeing through several evolving versions. What she taught him was that life was finally greater than art. Paradoxically, this discovery strengthened his art, because it gave him a sense of limitations and enabled him to grasp the importance of accepting loss and imperfection as humanizing qualities—qualities without which a poet could not reach his audience.

The tension between perfection and imperfection keeps the poet human, but Hölderlin, deep down, felt that Spirit was endangered by this compromise. In his early years, this feeling could take the form of a strange prudishness. Before he became the lover of his employer's wife, he had tutored in another home, where he considered it his duty to discipline with great zeal his charge, the boy Fritz, whom he had caught masturbating. At the same time, he himself was involved in an affair with Wilhelmine Kirms, a guest in the house; she subsequently bore his child. This strange mixture of license and rigidity illustrates in Hölderlin's life what was also true of his art: He was always trying to save spirit from reality, but at the same time he understood that reality was the only reliable context for life and art. In later years he admitted that he had turned too completely from the ordinary in real life.

In the novel *Hyperion* and in his many great elegies and odes Hölderlin kept himself rooted to the ground of reality by fixing his eye strongly on two "objective" phenomena: politics and landscape. The hero in *Hyperion* is a Greek of Hölderlin's own time, a man like the poet charged with the promise of the French Revolution and determined to free his people from Ottoman tyranny. By rooting his hero's vision of freedom and beauty in the psychology and anxieties of the newly liberated consciousness of revolutionary Europe, Hölderlin gives flesh to his spirit and makes Hyperion a credible reincarnation of his mythical namesake.

Throughout his poetry, landscape is the great anchor of his "beautiful idealisms of moral excellence." The phrase comes from Percy Bysshe Shelley, and Shelley is the English poet with whom Hölderlin has the most in common. Shelley, however, dealt in diaphonous and insubstantial images of nature which, at their strongest, merely "stain the white radiance of eternity." Hölderlin looks at nature with as loving and detailed an eye as that of John Keats. Yet he leaves nature for spirit far more readily than does Keats; Hölderlin would never have settled "for a life of sensations rather than thoughts." Still, Hölderlin was able to flesh out the entire Greek world—its islands and sky, its plains and pastoral glens with their majestic ruins—with a powerful corporeal weight. Perhaps he was able to do so precisely because for all of its substance and contextualizing importance, the Greek landscape and seascape were themselves the product of his imagination. He had never been there. His rooms were covered with maps, and his grasp of Greek geography was as impressive as his mastery of elegy and ode and all the metrical intricacies of the ancient Greek poetic forms.

Just as Hölderlin knew that without the tension between the real and the ideal poetry would lose its movement and become static, he also knew that the modern world could never return to the Greek ideal even if his poetry could bring it back to life. Like Johann von Herder, who had influenced Johann von Goethe and Friedrich Schiller, the literary lions of Hölderlin's generation, Hölderlin believed in a form of cultural palingenesis, the idea that a universal value can be reborn in different modes at different times. The Greeks had achieved an idea of perfection that modern man could rediscover on his own terms. There was no choice. The terrible feelings of loss and alienation must be overcome. Hölderlin offered his poems, flooded with light and as sacred as a religious host. Constantine calls them the "poet's body."

Hölderlin has been made richly available to English readers in Michael Hamburger's translation, *Friedrich Hölderlin: Some Poems and Fragments*, first published in 1966 and reprinted in 1980. Constantine has performed an important service in supplementing Hamburger's fine translation. The present volume provides important biographical facts, places Hölderlin in his time, and also summarizes and comments on all Hölderlin's major works—long and short—thereby providing readers at all levels of literary sophistication with a very useful introduction. There is an excellent chronology, a reliable bibliography of secondary works, and a very practical section of English translations of all the German passages dealt with in the study itself.

Peter Brier

Source for Further Study

The Times Literary Supplement. October 7, 1988, p. 1106.

HOSPITAL OF THE TRANSFIGURATION

Author: Stanisław Lem (1921-   )
First published: Szpital przemienienia, in Poland, in 1957
Translated from the Polish by William Brand
Publisher: Harcourt Brace Jovanovich (New York). 207 pp. $17.95
Type of work: Novel
Time: 1939
Locale: Poland

Hoping but failing to evade the horrors of Nazi occupation, a young Polish doctor begins his career in a mental hospital just after Adolf Hitler's forces invade Poland

Principal characters:
STEFAN TRZYNIECKI, a young doctor who begins his career in a rural mental asylum
SEKUŁOWSKI, a poet, in hiding at the asylum
STANISŁAW "STASZEK" KRZECZOTEK, Stefan's fellow student, who brings him to the Hospital of the Transfiguration
"PAJPAK" PAJĄCZKOWSKI, the director of the asylum
NOSILEWSKA, a female doctor, with whom Staszek falls in love
ORYBALD KAUTERS, the staff neurosurgeon, a German citizen

Hospital of the Transfiguration is Stanisław Lem's first novel. He completed it in Kraków, Poland, in 1948; however, the book was not published until 1955, in a rewritten, state-approved version. The original title was *Szpital przemienienia*; it constitutes the first volume of the trilogy *Czas nieutracony* (time not lost, or time saved). Eventually, the original version appeared in Polish and in German. This is the first English translation.

In 1939, after German forces have overrun Poland, Stefan Trzyniecki, having just completed medical school, searches for his place in life. Amid the chaos of an occupied country and the encroaching terror of Nazi ideology, he tries to discover what he values and what he should do. At first he drifts; a series of coincidences brings him to a job he did not actively seek at Christo Transfigurato, a rural mental asylum near the town of his father's birth.

At the asylum, he gradually learns, through his relationships with major and minor characters, what his fundamental commitments are. These are expressed most succinctly in his dazed question, while he and a fellow doctor wander away from the asylum after Nazis have exterminated the patients and taken over the facility for an unspecified purpose: "How can they do such things and live?" In the asylum, Stefan has confirmed for himself in multiple ways the affirmation that life matters. Those who think otherwise are the truly mad. In one of the many philosophical conversations between Stefan and the hiding poet Sekułowski, the latter tells of a mad writer who "for one good metaphor" was willing to "annihilate a book and its author." Sekułowski says that this writer really believed in nothing. Believing in nothing, he was mad, missing the counterweight of ethical common sense that is necessary to mental balance.

Sekułowski's story helps define the madness of the Nazis who take and purge the asylum. Thiessdorff, the Nazi psychiatrist, explains: "Every nation is like an organism. Sometimes the body's sick cells have to be excised. This was such an excision." This insane metaphor stands in opposition to several metaphors Sekułowski presents in his conversations with Stefan. In one of these, the body is a flower garden in which tuberculosis bacteria are multiplying flowers. They succeed in overwhelming the garden's protective plants, the leukocytes, only to find that the garden then sinks away beneath them, so they too must die. Different metaphors produce opposing views of how human life may be valued. A metaphor that demands the destruction of human beings must ultimately be self-destructive. If, as in Thiessdorff's metaphor, the purpose is to separate the mentally healthy from the diseased, or the superior from the inferior, this purpose must eventually shatter on the rock of the realization that such definitions are arbitrary. Even the atheistic and cowardly Sekułowski values human life above all mere ideas; therefore, he appears more sane than his executioners, who shoot him out of simple disgust and blood lust, justified by a racist ideology.

The central portion of the novel presents Stefan's education in the value of human life. His main teachers are his experiences in the asylum and his conversations with Sekułowski. The asylum teaches him the relativity of mental illness and health.

Stefan needs only a short time in the hospital to see that there is very little difference between the staff and the patients. Untrained, often clumsy and cruel, the nursing staff tends to see the patients as problems rather than clients. One doctor speculates that asylums attract staff who are fascinated by abnormality. Stefan is sure of his own neurosis, and each doctor seems at least mildly abnormal to him. Stanisław "Staszek" Krzeczotek, the medical school friend who brings Stefan to the hospital, naïvely believes that they will be safe there from the Nazis and the effects of occupation. He is almost continuously partially debilitated by being hopelessly in love with someone. Nosilewska, the beautiful doctor whom Staszek yearns for, seems indifferent to anyone's love, though she proves most calmly effective in the crisis of the Nazi takeover. Orybald Kauters, the staff neurosurgeon, delays operating on a classic brain-tumor case so he can observe the complete course of the disease. He proves to be German-born and so moves comfortably from the Polish to the German administration of the hospital. Marglewski, another doctor, fills his spare time with research to show that genius and madness are virtually the same. He stages a demonstration to prove that recovering schizophrenics become nostalgic for the ecstatic states of their disease. Even though the presentation fails, he persists in believing that insanity may be more valuable than sanity.

Stefan encounters much evidence that what is conventionally defined as insanity looks remarkably like genius, the quality that most delights the mind. A young schizophrenic who never speaks sculpts a beautiful statue, *Strangling Angel*, that represents the mystery of death as eloquently as Sekułowski's poems. Several of the inmates have religious visions that beautify their lives. One drooling madman can perform instantaneous calculations of seven-digit numbers, because he has drawers in his head. Furthermore, the "cured" genius Sekułowski does not appear perfectly sane to Stefan. A poet and political writer, Sekułowski has come to the asylum for treatment of addiction, but he remains after his cure to hide from the Germans. His commentary on the asylum and the meaning of life provides a worldview that comes to seem reasonable to Stefan. Yet Sekułowski lacks the courage to live the ideas he believes and, in terror of the Nazis, betrays the hiding places of the patients the doctors have tried to protect from execution.

Only slight changes in circumstances could lead to exchanges of roles between staff and patients. Indeed, when the Nazis come, both Sekułowski and an alcoholic priest are made members of the staff to preserve them from execution. The fine and sometimes arbitrary line between doctor and patient illustrates another major aspect of Stefan's education in the asylum, the appreciation of mystery, a major theme in Lem's other fiction. Sekułowski articulates the mystery at the center of humanity and of the universe in a variety of ways, and Stefan's learning is reinforced by repeated experiences with patients, colleagues, acquaintances, and family.

For Stefan, Sekułowski becomes a spiritual father, taking the role Stefan's father and his uncles played in his youth. Sekułowski's ideas provide an outline of the worldview that pervades Lem's later work. To him, the universe is an utter mystery of fertility, generating energy and life so richly as to suggest some purpose behind it. Yet consciousness comes into being only to be annihilated. A human being is a miraculous accident so impressive as to suggest the violation of the laws of matter and energy. Yet the human body goes awry and destroys itself by the same laws. Writing poems is like stripping patches of paper off a wall to reveal intimations of a gorgeous and possibly meaningful pattern. Yet language sets painful and arbitrary limits on what one can say. A poet's function in the face of the Nazi madness is to suffer beautifully, yet Sekułowski betrays the helpless in his final terror.

The universe is a mystery. Though humanity is of the same substance with all matter, people understand virtually nothing about it. No meaningful pattern can be found in the cosmos, in part because human senses and mental faculties were not designed for that purpose. The meanings people claim to find are expressions of their wishes, such as Marglewski's desire to prove that insanity equals genius. Stefan's experiences with staff, patients, casual acquaintances, and his family all tend to confirm Sekułowski's view of the essential mystery of human existence.

Stefan also finds his fellow beings incomprehensible. His uncle and Sekułowski like to visit while they bathe. A few hours after his father has given deathbed advice, he eats vigorously and wishes Stefan a good trip back to the asylum. Staszek is an exciting conversationalist one moment and a morose, unsuccessful lover the next; he idolizes Sekułowski, yet quickly betrays him after the poet betrays the hiding patients. Woch, the operator of a nearby electrical substation whom Stefan meets on his frequent walks, is confiding and secretive by turns. The Nazis eventually link Woch with the Polish Resistance and execute him. Father Niezgloba has had alcoholism forced upon him by his ignorant parish and has suffered hallucinations. He witnesses the betrayals and executions at the hospital. He sees Dr. Kauters given permission to laugh at murder because he is a German, and he hears the devilish rationalizations of Thiessdorff, yet he continues to believe in a God who loves and cares for humanity.

Stefan experiences in his fellows the mystery Sekułowski describes as universal, a mystery that Nazi ideology vigorously denies in its claim to be able to distinguish perfectly between the superior and the inferior human being. For Stefan, as for all the wiser people he knows, the most significant aspect of this mystery is that humanity suffers without understanding why. When the Nazis execute the residents of Christo Transfigurato, they deny their brotherhood in suffering with the least of Christ's children; they deny the Christian metaphor that all people are of one body, with Christ as head. That metaphor, like Sekułowski's metaphor of the flower garden, points toward a saner ethical response. Stefan's father, a somewhat ridiculous failed inventor who often speaks in maxims, provides an ethical statement that seems to follow from this view of humanity's place in the universe: "Without tenderness it's worth nothing. And tenderness is so easy."

As Lem has said in an interview, the world is filled with misery and agony, some caused by the way things are and some caused by human cruelty. This novel illustrates this view that Lem shares with many modern novelists, and it offers the answer many of them offer. In the face of such suffering, the proper and practical response is to comfort one another, rather than to exterminate the sufferers in the vain hope of creating utopia. The novel ends with Stefan and Nosilewska, lost in the woods in the rain, bedding down in a farmer's shed. He finds that the papers she saved from Sekułowski are blank; he feels bankrupt, deprived of job, homeland, family, and fathers, both literal and spiritual. Nosilewska, who has suffered the same losses, comforts him: "The woman gave him pleasure, but not in the usual way. At every instant she controlled herself and she controlled him." When all else seems lost, when even tenderness is a bit hard, she succeeds, illustrating in this act the sum of Stefan's education.

Hospital of the Transfiguration is a strong first novel, humorous, whimsical, terrifying, and moving. It introduces many of the ideas that have persisted in Lem's work. Chief among these ideas is the opposition between a fascinating, beautiful, cruel universe and a human mind that is designed for species survival rather than for understanding the cosmos. Stefan's education at the asylum shows him this opposition even as the Nazis attempt to resolve it. They try to impose by murder a simple order upon the stubbornly complex universe, while Stefan learns the importance of believing in the value of human life, however this belief is achieved.

Terry Heller

Sources for Further Study

Booklist. LXXXV, November 1, 1988, p. 448.

Chicago Tribune. October 23, 1988, XIV, p. 7.

Kirkus Reviews. LVI, September 1, 1988, p. 1266.
Library Journal. CXIII, October 1, 1988, p. 101.
The New Republic. CXCIX, November 7, 1988, p. 39.
The New York Times Book Review. XCIII, October 30, 1988, p. 26.
Publishers Weekly. CCXXXIV, August 26, 1988, p. 76.
The Washington Post Book World. XVIII, October 30, 1988, p. 11.

THE IMMORTAL BARTFUSS

Author: Aharon Appelfeld (1932-)
First published: Bartfuss ben ha-almavet, 1985
Translated from the Hebrew by Jeffrey M. Green
Publisher: Weidenfeld & Nicolson (New York). 137 pp. $15.95
Type of work: Novel
Time: The 1970's
Locale: Primarily Israel, with flashbacks to Italy

An allegorical novel centering on a fifty-year-old Holocaust survivor who leads a brooding, restless, lonely life in modern-day Israel

Principal characters:
BARTFUSS, a secretive survivor of a German concentration camp who has migrated to Israel
ROSA, his embittered wife
BRIDGET, their retarded daughter
SCHMUGLER, a fellow survivor whom he befriends
THERESA, his former friend who rejects his overtures
SYLVIA, his former mistress who dies

Aharon Appelfeld is a survivor of the Holocaust whose writing is stamped by a melancholy sense of the doom he managed to elude. Born in Chernovtsy, Bukovina (then Rumanian, now within the Soviet Union), he was eight when the invading Germans sent him to a labor camp in 1940. There both of his parents died, but the boy managed in 1941 to escape into the inhospitable countryside, working as a shepherd and farm helper for three years, hiding his identity from hunters of Jews. In 1944 he became a field cook for the Soviet army. After the armistice he made his way to Italy with a small tide of refugees, and from there he migrated to what was then called Palestine. Appelfeld made a home on the outskirts of Jerusalem with his Argentine-born wife, two sons, and one daughter. His works are written in his adopted Hebrew, which, he has said in interviews, encourages a sparse, compact, elliptical style.

Appelfeld has published novels, story collections, and one book of essays. *The Immortal Bartfuss* is his sixth novel to be published in the United States. His best-known translated work is *Badenheim, 'ir nofesh* (1975; *Badenheim 1939*, 1980), literally "Badenheim, resort town" in Hebrew. Badenheim is a Jewish summer resort near Vienna, where visitors indulge themselves in rich food, idle conversation, and the usual vacation romances. The local sanitation department, however, begins to darken the communal climate by registering all vacationers and preparing their genealogies. The book's final paragraph grimly moves Badenheim's Jews to a freight train headed east while a Panglossian impresario continues to assert his faith in a rational and benevolent world.

In *Tor-ha-pela'ot* (1978; *The Age of Wonders*, 1981), the Holocaust again overtakes a group of bourgeois, assimilated, unwary Jews in an isolated Austrian town—and again Appelfeld makes no explicit reference to such historic events as Adolf Hitler's *Anschluss*, which annexed Austria to Germany. Indeed he refrains, here as in his other fiction, from any direct allusion to contemporaneous history. As in a Kafka text the overpowering ordeal descends inexplicably, irrationally, irresistibly. *The Age of Wonders* is a chillingly pessimistic study of Jewish self-denial, self-estrangement, and self-hatred, with secular Central European Jews denying their Judaic culture and despising their pious Eastern European brethren.

Kutonet veha-pasim (1983; *Tzili: The Story of a Life*, 1983) is a simpler tale than the first two, with the protagonist's wanderings an approximate outline of Appelfeld's own during and after World War II. Tzili is a slow-witted Eastern European girl who is abandoned by her impoverished Jewish family when they flee the Germans. Mistaken as the bastard daughter of a Gentile whore, she manages to survive excruciating hardships. Appelfeld here writes a bleak folktale depicting the endurance of the simpleton with animal strength as opposed to the destruction of self-conscious intellection.

In *Nesiga mislat* (1984; *The Retreat*, 1985), Appelfeld returns to the provincial Austria of the late 1930's. A middle-aged actress, Lotte Schloss, is dismissed by her theatrical company for being Jewish; she retreats to her daughter's home, only to find her Christian son-in-law hostile and her daughter docile to his wishes. What further refuge? Lotte heads for a place called The Retreat, an old mountaintop hotel near Vienna which invites aging Jews for lessons in adjusting to a Gentile society, promising the painless eradication of Jewish accents and traits. The novel concludes flatly and forebodingly, with the reader aware that European Jewry's encounter with tragic history is about to reach its apocalypse. A retreat, after all, is no escape.

To the Land of the Cattails (1986) is set in Appelfeld's native province of Bukovina, near the Ukraine. The coprotagonists are Toni, a beautiful but self-centered thirty-four-year-old Jewess, and her sensitive, adolescent son, Rudi. The divorced, promiscuous mother journeys eastward with her half-Gentile son to her rural homeland. Yet they never complete their return. They find Jews murdered and uprooted along way stations, with Toni's parents turning out to have mysteriously vanished. Rudi is separated from Toni, never to find her again. He innocently joins a cluster of Jews at a rural railroad station. They are waiting to be taken where all Jews in the region have been told to go—and where few will live to tell their tales. Again, Appelfeld's voice is muted, impassive, neutral rather than naturalistic: no congested, suffocating boxcars; no SS guards wielding whips; no electrified barbed wires; no gas chambers. Readers will bring their own awareness of modern history as nightmare to this as well as to Appelfeld's other fables.

With *The Immortal Bartfuss* Appelfeld abandons the milieu of a pre- and post-World War II Europe, except for brief reminiscences, and focuses on contemporary Israel. The central character survived the Holocaust and now resides in the seaport town of Jaffa. He is brooding, insular, self-isolated, and emotionally narcotized. At fifty, Bartfuss has one estranged married daughter, Paula; another, Bridget, who is retarded and lives at home; and an embittered wife, Rosa, whom he never loved and whom he cannot forgive for having survived the war by fornicating with peasants. For her part, Rosa cannot forgive him for having attempted to escape his responsibilities toward her and their daughters by leaving Italy after the war on an immigrant vessel. Somehow, she discovered his plan and managed to board the same boat. Thereafter she plays Medea, instilling venom in her daughters against their father.

Bartfuss sleeps in a room apart from his wife and impaired daughter, leaves the apartment at dawn, and returns close to midnight. He sits in cafés for hours at a time, incommunicative, solitary; alternatively, he wanders along the seashore for hours, again incommunicative and solitary. He has learned wariness, secretiveness, miserliness, has "developed a clipped language of refusal, protective syllables that were accompanied with a shrug of his left shoulder, all of which said, 'leave me alone.' "

Why is Bartfuss called "immortal"? Appelfeld hints that the epithet originated during the immediate postwar years, when Bartfuss belonged to a large smuggling ring in Italy and survived fifty bullets in his body, somehow escaping arrest. Now he makes a mysterious but apparently lucrative living as some sort of underworld trader who dispatches his business in a rapid outburst of transactions that consumes no more than fifteen minutes of his working day. So he has ample time to reflect and ruminate about his precarious past and detested present. Appelfeld summarized Bartfuss' behavior in an interview: He "has swallowed the Holocaust whole, and he walks about with it in all his limbs."

Nevertheless, Bartfuss' feelings, while atrophied, are by no means dead. In a café he sees Theresa, his close friend from concentration camp days, but she rejects his attempts to renew their intimacy: Memories frighten her; she can only live for the moment. An old confederate from Italy rebuffs Bartfuss' offer of a loan. When he wants to buy Bridget the gold-plated watch she covets, his daughter instead runs away from him, fearful of her mother's disapproval if she accepted her father's gift. Bartfuss is in an existential crisis: His burden of being is oppressively heavy.

Thirsty for fellowship, Bartfuss confides in another old confederate, Schmugler, only to have the latter dismiss his gesture; an angry Bartfuss pounds the man's face. He then buys an Omega watch for Bridget and renews the bonds of empathy with a former mistress, Sylvia. Sylvia, however, is soon taken ill and dies. Despairingly, Bartfuss asks Sylvia's former husband, "What have we Holocaust survivors done? Has our great experience changed us at all? . . . I expect . . . greatness of soul from people who underwent the Holocaust."

Bartfuss now knows what to do: He will overcome his inclination toward morbidity, withdrawal, and solitude. He will act generously, opening his soul, seeking out the people from whom he has kept his distance. In a grotesque yet pathetic scene he encounters Bridget, who tells him that she no longer fears him. He takes her to the seashore as in Italy he used to take mutely passive women for his sexual gratification. She clings to him, and when she twists her ankle in the sand he solicitously massages her leg. The full-breasted Bridget lies on her back with her eyes closed; Bartfuss feels his sexual impulses tested and wins a moral victory over such shamefully incestuous desires. The hapless Bridget, however, is then browbeaten by Rosa for having left home without permission.

Bartfuss soon meets Schmugler again and seeks his forgiveness for having hit him; they become friends, promising to meet regularly. He then chances upon another living ghost from his Italian past, Marian; Bartfuss was the only man who had treated her kindly without having sought her compliant sexual services in return. This mentally defective woman cannot recall Bartfuss, but he nevertheless insists on stuffing a bundle of bills in her pocket. Then he returns home, warmed by his good deed, and finally feels himself enveloped by the guiltless, worry-free full sleep against which he has fought for years.

Is Bartfuss a mythic character, a Wandering Jew even when settled—or, rather, unsettled—in Zion? Appelfeld's flat, understated, ambiguous tone offers this possible meaning. What cannot be doubted is that Bartfuss is a psychically scarred Holocaust survivor, victimized by one of history's most horrendous assaults, imbued with the folkloric deathlessness of the Jewish culture which has been besieged for many centuries, yet has managed to persist. At the end, remarkably, he has clearly crossed over from psychosis to fellowship. As Appelfeld comments, "He still hasn't lost his human face. That isn't a great deal, but it's something."

Aharon Appelfeld has earned perhaps a minor but surely a significant place in contemporary fiction. On one level his novels belong to the subgenre called Holocaust literature, as he focuses on the prelude or aftermath of a reality beyond a writer's imagination or direct expressiveness. Here he is in the company of Elie Wiesel, Jerzy Kosinski, and Primo Levi, and may be their aesthetic master with his resonantly disciplined prose and deeply disturbing images. On the plane of literary tradition his acknowledged ancestor is Franz Kafka, whom he has saluted for his objectively detached style, clarity of vision, ruminations on Jewish identity, and precise sense of the absurd. "Kafka's works," Appelfeld has informed the American author Philip Roth, "illuminated the narrow path which I tried to blaze for myself." The path may be narrow, but the furrow traced by Appelfeld's fiction will prove indelible in the world's literature.

Gerhard Brand

Sources for Further Study

Booklist. LXXXIV, January 1, 1988, p. 748.
Chicago Tribune. March 6, 1988, XIV, p. 6.
Kirkus Reviews. LV, December 1, 1987, p. 1634.
Library Journal. CXIII, January, 1988, p. 96.
London Review of Books. X, March 17, 1988, p. 14.
The New York Times Book Review. XCIII, February 28, 1988, p. 1.

The Observer. March 27, 1988, p. 42.
Publishers Weekly. CCXXXII, December 25, 1987, p. 63.
Time. CXXXI, February 22, 1988, p. 85.
The Times Literary Supplement. April 8, 1988, p. 383.

THE IMPERFECT PARADISE

Author: Linda Pastan (1932-)
Publisher: W. W. Norton (New York). 80 pp. $15.95
Type of work: Poetry

In elegiac poems, the poet tries to reconcile a desire for paradise with a desire to embrace our imperfect world

Linda Pastan has chosen two quotations as epigraphs for *The Imperfect Paradise*, and they pose, quite interestingly, one of the essential quandaries for the speaker in the poems which follow. The first quotation is from Stanley Kunitz: "We have all been expelled from the Garden, but the ones who suffer most in exile are those who are still permitted to dream of perfection." The second is by Wallace Stevens (from "The Poems of Our Climate"): "The imperfect is our paradise."

The speaker in Pastan's poems is definitely one of those who "suffer . . . in exile," as she wrestles with issues such as aging, mortality, loss, and the difficulties of married love. Nevertheless, she also celebrates the ordinary, the imperfect, in other poems in this volume. The tension that exists between the two positions espoused by the epigraphs is the fertile ground for Pastan's poems in *The Imperfect Paradise*.

The book's first section, "In the Rearview Mirror," opens with a poem that locates the human desire for permanence in works of art. In "Bird on Bough" the speaker begins with an epigraph about Chinese art that desribes the common image of a bird on a branch as "the bird-on-bough aspect of eternity." Playfully at first, the poet muses over the phrase: "Is it a cardinal on willow,/ or a dove on peach?" What begins, ostensibly, as a poem about Chinese art now turns to the speaker's desire for fixity in the midst of life's flux. Other than in art, that fixity is found only in the remembered past, "in the eternity/ that is childhood," where the speaker remembers, poignantly,

> the branch
> which would neither grow
> nor break
>
> and the solitary bird
> which would never
> fly away.

Section 1 introduces many of the themes of *The Imperfect Paradise*. "To a Daughter Leaving Home" vividly captures the moment of a child's independence, here dramatized in learning to ride a bicycle, and the mother's knowledge that the child is now lost to her. The mother speaks of her fear as the child pedals off, seeing her grow "smaller, more breakable/ with distance. . . ." The daughter, meanwhile, is oblivious to the mother's fear and sense of loss. Joyfully, the rider screams

with laughter,
the hair flapping
behind you like a
handkerchief waving
goodbye.

Images seen in a rearview mirror are images receding as the viewer moves away. Childhood, children, parents, and lovers are some of Pastan's subjects here. "Root Pruning," "After an Absence," and "Ceremony" confront the complexities of married love, another theme of the volume. "Root Pruning" starts with details of a daily walk and what at first appears to be the rather mundane subject of transplanting a holly bush. For Pastan, though, the mundane seldom remains simply that. The husband's action in the poem, of digging a shovel around the roots of the about-to-be-transplanted holly, takes on the significance of metaphor. The wife/speaker regrets that she was not "root pruned." Has the husband left? The wife feels that if she had "known some cutting edge" perhaps she "wouldn't feel now/ as if the ground had simply/ disappeared." The uncertainties of married love, its inevitable losses, are eloquently detailed by Pastan. In "After an Absence," the speaker likens married love to a terrain, "a garden in the desert/ where you stoop to drink, never knowing/ if your mouth will fill with water or sand."

"In the Rearview Mirror" closes the section to which it gives a name and, while focusing again on ordinary details, offers both an answer to the problem of a desire for permanence and a tone of hopefulness for the rest of the book. The speaker watches towns recede in the rearview mirror of a car, the towns "ceasing/ to exist the moment/ we pass." Imagination, though, is joined with memory as one solution to the human dilemma. The speaker fills the houses of the lost towns with people comforting one another in sleep and performing the minor rituals of life:

the Mother
whose hands have learned
the wisdom of kneading
touches the Father

The pun on "kneading" is especially apt.

The poem closes with its focus on the horizon, the sun about to come up "in an endless/ relay race of light." Whatever the speaker's destination, the place ahead is

half resurrected
from childhood and waiting
to be unwrapped like a withheld gift
from the white ribbon
of unwinding road.

Though "half resurrected" qualifies the optimism here, it diminishes it hardly at all.

Section 2, "Rereading *The Odyssey* in Middle Age," offers what is perhaps another answer to the poet's search for permanence. Previous "answers" have been art, memory, and imagination. Now she focuses on literature, specifically the linking of our lives with myth in order to find significance in daily actions and eventual (and inevitable) losses.

The section opens with "At the Loom," in which the speaker details Penelope's actions as she weaves. Penelope is both magician and artist, her hands "like silhouetted birds." She plays "like a harpist poised/ at the strings of an instrument/ whose chords are colors." What Penelope makes is a "slow accumulation." Surely her actions are meant to stand, in a sense, for what the speaker means to make out of minute, daily actions that seem meaningless but ultimately add up to some significance. Thus, Penelope weaves, "and patterns that seem/ random at first multiply/ into beauty." Ultimately what Penelope "makes" actually clothes the speaker, and she is comforted. More, perhaps we are all comforted: " . . . though the chilly stars/ go bone naked/ we are clothed."

The second section is a powerful one, using the backdrop of myth to highlight and deepen the poet's concerns. The title poem of the section again uses Penelope and her weaving to stimulate, this time, the poet's own musing. The speaker has always thought of the weaving as a shawl, though it was Laertes' shroud Penelope wove. The speaker recognizes her own misreading: "We make our myths from whole cloth anyway/ and make ouselves the heroines/ of others' imaginings." Recognizing this function of literature, the poet then moves into Penelope's mind, wondering what faithfulness means, wondering if Penelope's son Telemachus will find a shroud-weaver for himself. By night, Penelope unravels what she has made by day, to put off her suitors.

The section closes with "The Suitor," on a less than optimistic note. The poet recognizes here that each myth contains "a story/ that no one bothers to tell. Merely one of the crowd of Penelope-worshipers, the suitor of the poem never voices his desire and thus is never noticed by her. His passion and desire will "end badly"; he is only one of the many "in that unplumbed sea/ of wasted blood."

"Balancing Act," the book's third section, is indeed the center point, providing the middle ground between the two positions posed by the opening epigraphs. Ordinary life is described here, and celebrated to some extent, but these are the book's weakest poems, often not reaching the powerful metaphoric force of other poems in the book. "The Ordinary Weather of Summer" and "A Walk Before Breakfast," however, are exceptions to that statement. Both find, in the backdrop of sea and beach, significant room to speak of earlier Pastan themes.

In "The Ordinary Weather of Summer," for example, the speaker catalogs the woes of summer's heat: dogs panting, insects "at every window," and a couple quarreling. Mornings are cooler, the couple more amicable, and thus the cycle continues. Yet loss is not far from the surface. What the speaker sees is the inevitable end: "So we move another summer closer/ to our last summer together. . . ." The people are seen as fragile and helpless, like swimmers who walk up from the beach "shaking the water out of our blinded eyes."

It is in the book's fourth section, "The Descent," that Pastan's voice achieves its most powerful level. This section is the volume's true emotional center and *raison d'être*. The section opens with poems cataloging imaginary fears, but closes with a fear realized: the death of the speaker's mother. "Accidents," the opening poem, takes a hospital room as its setting, with the speaker recovering there after an accident. Other hospital visits have been in maternity wards, but this time there is no baby,

> only my own life swaddled
> in bandages
> and handed back to me
> like any new thing.

The speaker's brush with death has made her ever aware, however, of the world's dangers; there are other accidents out there "waiting to happen."

Most notable in the fourth section are "The Descent," "Family Tree," "The Deathwatch Beetle," and "Elegy." Pastan's plain, clear language is the perfect counterpart to the deep emotion faced in "The Descent," for example. The opening lines recall "To a Daughter Leaving Home," where the bicycle-rider pedals away. Now it is the mother who is disappearing:

> My mother grows smaller
> before my eyes, receding
> into the past tense slowly.
> It feels like an escalator down,
> she whispers, half asleep.

The speaker stands at the bedside, trying to become accustomed to her role as survivor. "Fear is using/ up the oxygen. I must/ get used to the change in the air. . . . " Where does the poet locate meaning? Perhaps pain can be used, paradoxically, to alleviate pain:

> how strange it is that beauty
> can become the ache
> in the bone that proves
> you are alive.

Pastan reaches for no easy answers here. The poet's touch at the end of "The Descent" is deft and delicate, and she faces it all with unsparing tenderness:

> it is hard to see where
> the descent will end,
> hard to believe
> it is death holding
> her elbow with such care,
> guiding her all the way down.

"Elegy," too, finds Pastan in rare voice. She never mentions her mother, simply describes the changed landscape after her death. Gravity, with all that word's resonance, is the poet's subject, and how things rise in spite of it. She understands their struggle in new ways, now:

> I know
> with what difficulty
> flowers
>
> must pull themselves
> all the way up
> their stems.

The poet has been dreaming, not of resurrections (again, no easy answers here) but "of the slow, sensual/ slide each night/ into sleep."

The mother's death provides an apt segue to the book's last section, "The Imperfect Paradise." Death is what prevents life on earth from being paradise, and death was also Adam and Eve's punishment for sinning in the original garden. Pastan now turns to Adam and Eve, especially Eve, and imagines their life after the Fall. Their original sin can sometimes be forgotten by them (in moments of love, and passion), even after being locked out of the garden:

> On a far tree
> faint as a moon
> cradled in branches
> an apple hangs.

In "Fruit of the Tree," the second poem of the final section, the poet recognizes the immensity of Adam and Eve's transgression, how it prefigures all man's later overreaching: "Eve would be the mother/ of Newton and Bohr." Pastan links nuclear physics to the fateful apple, and the poem ends ominously, with a stockpiled apple exploding and "releasing the smell/ of the whole/ dying year."

In *The Imperfect Paradise* Pastan attempts some formal poems. Section 4 ends with a pantoum ("Something About the Trees"), and the volume concludes with a sonnet sequence from which the book takes its title. They are six English sonnets: "Seasonal," "In the Garden," "Deep in These Woods," "Thief," "The Imperfect Paradise," and "Somewhere in the Euphrates." Unfortunately, these concluding poems are not Pastan at her best. The language seems stale and tired, lacking emotional intensity.

Ultimately, however, *The Imperfect Paradise* is an impressive book of poetry. Sections 1 and 4 are especially fine and show Pastan's plain language and clear sight paying off impressively. The poems about her mother's death are a tour de force of free verse and carefully modulated language and emotion.

Patricia Clark

Sources for Further Study

The Georgia Review. XLII, Summer, 1988, p. 407.
Library Journal. CXIII, May 15, 1988, p. 85.
The New York Times Book Review. XCIII, September 18, 1988, p. 42.

IN SEARCH OF J. D. SALINGER

Author: Ian Hamilton (1938-   )
Publisher: Random House (New York). 222 pp. $17.95
Type of work: Biography
Time: 1935-1965
Locale: New York, Pennsylvania, Ohio, Europe, and New Hampshire

An unauthorized biography of the celebrated but reclusive author of The Catcher in the Rye, *limited to the period between the subject's childhood and his withdrawal from the literary scene in 1965*

Principal personages:
J. D. SALINGER, an American novelist and writer of short stories
IAN HAMILTON, the author, a British-born biographer

The unauthorized biography is one of the strange subgenres to emerge in the late twentieth century, along with mystery novels in which fictional characters pursue real-life criminals, autobiographical journalism, and other hard-to-categorize works which suggest a sort of genre meltdown taking place in modern literature. It was formerly considered proper for a biographer to wait until his subject was at least on his deathbed, but things move faster these days, possibly as a subtle by-product of electronic technology. Furthermore, books about a living though refractory subject have proved to have an unexpected advantage over the biographies whose subject is comfortably embalmed: The cries of protest by the living subject can generate valuable publicity.

Special problems arise, however, when a subject, though world-famous, has been shunning the limelight for years. Jerome David Salinger actually turns and runs from interviewers. He is as elusive as the White Rabbit in *Alice's Adventures in Wonderland* (1865). Ian Hamilton, being British, may have thought that he understood standoffishness, but Salinger gives the word a whole new dimension. Whereas most American writers will do anything short of getting shot out of a cannon to sell their books, Salinger hides behind a six-and-a-half-foot fence at his New Hampshire retreat and outsells most of the competition. (*The Catcher in the Rye*, 1951, still sells about a quarter of a million copies a year and is read all over the world.) Salinger has often been accused of using a reverse ploy, attracting attention by seeming to shun it. If so, it is a ploy that no other writer has been willing to try.

Hamilton sometimes becomes an unintentionally comic figure in his own book, like a photographer running around with his head under a black cloth trying to snap a picture of a subject who refuses to hold still. Not only is Salinger personally unapproachable, but he also has set up what Hamilton calls a distant early warning network, so that any attempt to penetrate Salinger's world alerts friends, relatives, and acquaintances to be on guard.

In 1982, Hamilton published a biography of the New England poet Robert Lowell which received generally good reviews. On the strength of that success, he seems to have returned to the New World brimming with confidence not only as a biographer but also as an Englishman with a special understanding of Americans. There is something rather touching about his brisk, no-nonsense approach to the job of gathering material. He knew that *Time* magazine, with all of its resources, had been thwarted in an attempt to breach Salinger's defenses for a cover story that appeared in the September 15, 1961, issue, but Hamilton's attitude seems to have been that these were mere journalists, whereas he is a gentleman and a scholar, a professional biographer with all the social and intellectual advantages of an Oxford education. In addition to his personal qualifications, he was working under the aegis of the prestigious New York publishing firm of Random House.

The reader's sympathies are divided from the outset. On the one hand, he would like to indulge in the purely voyeuristic pleasure of snooping into Salinger's private affairs. He would particularly like to know why this celebrated author dropped out of public life and what, if anything, he is working on in his seclusion. On the other hand, Salinger is reminiscent of the last member of an endangered species, and the reader would like to see him left to roam free in the forest of his imagination. Hamilton himself says that his book is—or at least started out to be—a labor of love. He is one of the many people who discovered *The Catcher in the Rye* at an impressionable age and felt that it had been written especially for him. Salinger was one of those writers who, in Holden Caulfield's words, he would have liked to call up on the phone.

There is a certain sublime insensitivity about Hamilton that occasionally makes the reader wince. In 1984, he wrote to Salinger, telling him that he proposed to write a study of his life and work and requesting a personal interview "to set the record straight." He received a reply just as frigid as a knowledgeable American reader could have warned him to expect. Hamilton reports that Salinger's message was that

> he didn't suppose he could stop me writing a book about him, but he thought he ought to let me know—"for whatever little it may be worth"—that he had suffered so many intrusions on his privacy that he could endure no more of it—not "in a single lifetime."

Hamilton chose to consider the possibility that this was a sort of "come-on," and that "I can't stop you" could be interpreted to mean "Please go ahead." Besides, Hamilton candidly continues, "I had already accepted a commission for this book. I'd been paid (and I'd already spent) a fair amount of money." Later, as this unwelcome Boswell is beginning to understand the complexities of the task he has set himself, he says, "Somehow, in America, it was harder than ever to remember that this whole thing had started out as a rather stylish (as I saw it) literary game." It is sometimes not so difficult to understand why Salinger elected to surround himself with a six-and-a-half-foot fence.

Throughout his book, Hamilton maintains the fortitude of a door-to-door salesman who keeps getting doors slammed in his face. His best results in obtaining information came from mass mailings to people who had known Salinger before he became famous, including quite a few who had been enrolled in the same private schools Salinger is known to have attended. A number of former classmates sent back scraps of information which Hamilton pieced together to form a picture of a young man not too different from his most famous character, Holden Caulfield, a sensitive outsider always out of step with the rest of the world. Hamilton hints that Salinger had to be sent to a disciplinarian institution, Valley Forge Military Academy in Pennsylvania (the model for "Pencey" in *The Catcher in the Rye*), because he was too much to handle at home. Yet there is no proof that Salinger was ever an overt rebel or that he ever got into serious trouble. In fact, he seems to have had a talent for getting along with people he probably despised, a talent which saw him through his military service in World War II without much friction.

Salinger's way of rebelling seems always to have been through withdrawal, physical or mental. Many of the people who knew him never felt that they really knew him at all. Evidently, he has strong affinities with Holden Caulfield, with Seymour Glass, and with the lonely Sergeant X in "For Esmé, with Love and Squalor," his best and most revealing short story. His biographer takes considerable pains to show the autobiographical elements throughout Salinger's writings. Those who have read and cherished these published works probably understand him as well as he will allow himself to be understood in his lifetime. There is a strong probability, according to Hamilton, that upon Salinger's death, if not before, the fireplace will consume all of his unpublished manuscripts (including two complete novels), along with letters, notes, journals, and everything else. J. D. Salinger may remain one of the most mysterious literary figures of all time.

Hamilton was amazed at the ease with which he obtained access to many of Salinger's letters, the things biographers prize most. In one instance the British publishing house of Hamish Hamilton casually handed over thirty letters Salinger had sent to the head of the firm and to his chief editor between 1951 and 1960. If the unauthorized biography may be likened to the hostile takeover in the corporate world, however, then these letters may be likened to what Wall Streeters have nicknamed "the poison pill." The letters all but destroyed Hamilton's book. When Salinger was sent bound galleys of the original version, he replied through attorneys that he refused to allow his unpublished letters to be quoted. Random House fought him all the way to the Supreme Court, and lost. Hamilton had to cut thirty thousand words out of the book, which had been ready to go to press. He made other drastic changes to cover up the gaping wounds left by the excised material. He even changed the title from "J. D. Salinger: A Writing Life" to "In Search of J. D. Salinger," an admission that the White Rabbit had gotten away.

Hamilton's biography of Robert Lowell gives an indication of what he had in mind for his work on Salinger. *Robert Lowell: A Biography* (1982) is one of those fine, fat, definitive works printed on deckle-edged stock and replete with indented and italicized quotations from the subject's letters and personal papers. *In Search of J. D. Salinger* is only a shadow of what it might have been, a literary curiosity. Rarely if ever has a book undergone such a transformation between drawing board and launching pad—and it nearly did not get off the ground at all. In the process of writing it, Hamilton himself underwent a sea change. His genial Oxonian tea-and-crumpets manner of chapter 1 slowly gives way to a sort of wistful plaint. He had started his study as a labor of love but had found, as lovers have found before, that love cannot really conquer all and that it often ends in bitter feelings. He still admires the works of J. D. Salinger but is less enthusiastic about their author. It is easy to sympathize with Hamilton after all of his hard work, but at the same time it is hard to fault Salinger. He was not playing a "stylish literary game" or offering anything so gross as a "come-on"; he simply wanted to be left alone.

In lieu of turning out a definitive biography, Hamilton decided to try to make his book read like a novel, with the quest itself forming the plot. In this he may have been more successful than he intended. By some kind of Seymour-magic, Hamilton has become a character in a story by J. D. Salinger. Hamilton inadvertently paints himself as just the sort of person Seymour and Zooey and Franny would have hated and loved and probably forgiven—the well-intentioned, spiritually benighted, eternally compromising modern man, full of hopes and fears and terrible self-importance.

Bill Delaney

Sources for Further Study

Booklist. LXXXIV, May 15, 1988, p. 1554.
Boston Globe. May 29, 1988, p. B15.
Kirkus Reviews. LVI, April 15, 1988, p. 593.
Library Journal. CXIII, July, 1988, p. 81.
Los Angeles Times Book Review. June 12, 1988, p. 3.
National Review. XL, August 5, 1988, p. 48.
The New York Times Book Review. XCIII, June 5, 1988, p. 7.
Newsweek. CXI, May 23, 1988, p. 73.
Publishers Weekly. CCXXXIII, May 20, 1988, p. 80.
Time. CXXXI, May 23, 1988, p. 74.

IN THE AGE OF THE SMART MACHINE
The Future of Work and Power

Author: Shoshanna Zuboff (1951-   )
Publisher: Basic Books (New York). 468 pp. $19.95
Type of work: Sociology and social history

Shoshanna Zuboff examines the possibilities inherent in the technologization of the workplace, arguing that access to computer-based knowledge may empower white-collar workers, resulting in less hierarchical management structures

Shoshanna Zuboff's topic in this book is the advent of the new technology and the profound social changes which are coming with it. It is not simply a book discussing computers and how they will change people's lives, for it deals with the more general categories of information technology and shifting social relationships. The book's content in many respects will remind readers of *Future Shock* (1970), *The Third Wave* (1980), and other such works. Not a popularizer, however, Zuboff sets for herself, in her introduction, a task which is more similar to Fernand Braudel's approach in *The Structures of Everyday Life* (1982). This approach has strengths as well as weaknesses, but it is certainly a monumental effort.

The fact that Zuboff is writing an academic book is given away not only by the length of the book (468 pages) but also by her vocabulary and style. She uses rather specialized language, full of rare, hyphenated, and invented forms. Some examples are "intellective" (for mental or intellectual), "informate" (to enhance the gathering and interpretation of information), "acting-on" and "acting-with" (for object-oriented versus person-oriented behavior), and "de-skilling" (the loss of what were formerly human skills to automation). It is questionable whether these stylistic peculiarities are particularly helpful, though they lend a certain impression of precision to the writing and give the reader a sense that he or she is acquiring genuinely new information and thinking in new ways.

Zuboff has done a doctoral dissertation on the history of work, with particular focus on the industrial revolution. In this book she is trying to apply the insights gained in that study to the twentieth century revolution in information management. The problem is twofold. First, if what is happening is really new, then there is no dependable paradigm for understanding it. This problem is common to all futurologists. The second problem is that there is no guarantee that one stage in social evolution will mimic another one. For example, what sociological and cultural insights would have been gained by comparing the changes occurring in the industrial revolution with the changes which came with the abandonment of hunting and gathering for agricultural communities? There may be no other choice, but comparisons are nevertheless risky.

Blue-collar workers are the focus of the first chapters of Zuboff's work. She eloquently describes the automation of the factory workplace as the process of reducing skilled tasks to their machine-reproducible components and the empowering of those who are left in charge of the machines. These laborers-become-middle managers often find themselves in possession of information which can enhance both the process for which they have responsibility and their own jobs. Freed by automation from the definition of his or her task as the exertion and depletion of the body, the new blue-collar worker either finds meaning in the development of what Zuboff calls intellective skills or feels as if he or she is floundering in an unfamiliar world of mysterious data, data that are not amenable to dependable (that is, sentient) interpretation.

White-collar workers have had a slightly different response to the new technology than have their blue-collar counterparts. Zuboff begins by defining the essential difference between blue- and white-collar work as "acting-on" versus "acting-with." Executive skills have always been considered personal and intuitive, having generally to do with decisions taken alone or in connection with other people and factors not easily reduced to components, as was the work of artisans and laborers. Regardless of whether this was the case, executives in the late twentieth century have the power to keep their own jobs from being "de-skilled."

What has happened, however, is that the assistants to the executives have found their jobs converted: Clerks with major decision-making responsibilities have become secretaries, whose work has been reduced to those repetitive tasks which the executives, with the aid of technological advances, have increasingly been able to delegate. Thus, while blue-collar workers either lost their jobs or saw them converted from physical into mental tasks, white-collar workers saw their jobs stripped of their former responsibility and were given in their place those busy-work jobs in which the executive no longer had to be directly involved. To use Zuboff's language, the first stage of technological advance beyond the industrial revolution has informated work as well as automated it, a process that generally has worked out better for the blue-collar worker (if his or her job could be kept) than for the white-collar worker (whose job opportunities increased while the jobs required less skill and thus became less meaningful).

The next stage of automation and information may change all this again. Zuboff holds out the possibility that even for the white-collar worker automation could eventually informate as well. How does computer technology informate? By making what was formerly tacit, private, and usually fairly restricted knowledge explicit, public, and related to the whole (whatever it is), the new technology encourages people to collaborate when looking for solutions to problems. In other words, as intellective skills replace action-oriented ones, acting-on is replaced to a large degree by acting-with. In general, management has not become accustomed to this change and does not approve (since people talking with one another under the automated but not yet informated system usually were considered to be wasting time). Even so, this collaboration seems to be an emerging pattern of work in the age of computerization.

Zuboff emphasizes work in the first part of her book, while in the second and third parts she deals more specifically with the issue of power, though this approach ends up making the book somewhat repetitious. In her understanding, knowledge and power are really two sides of a coin; she proposes that information technology will inevitably put pressure on existing hierarchical and functional power structures. Pressure, however, is not the same thing as change, and present structures can be expected to resist any loss of their own power. Zuboff points out that those having power have always used whatever social mythology was current to justify their holding and keeping it. In the United States, social myths such as divine right, the Protestant work ethic, natural law, and social Darwinism have all been put to work in this way. Earlier in the twentieth century, however, scientific managerial principles became the paradigm by which managers understood and justified their positions. Exemplified by Frederick Taylor's approach to management, this new scientism went hand in hand with automation. It let a theoretical base for the process of the componential analysis of work and the replacement of humans by machines able to accomplish one or more of the components of the former task.

When managers use the new technology only to automate (that is, to replace workers) and keep information about the technology as well as information coming from the technology to themselves, they further centralize the decision-making process and enhance their own power. When they put this information into the hands of their subordinates, they dramatically improve the possibilities for "informating," that is, letting the workers learn more about their jobs and how to perform more effectively and efficiently. The latter route is often perceived as being dangerous, however, since then the boundaries of power are eroded and workers have to be trusted more. The technology itself allows for the two possibilities of centralization or customization, depending on how it is implemented. Given the chance to work with the data variables the computer can produce, the individual worker has the potential to optimize production creatively along many different paths. Management, on the other hand, can achieve standardization throughout a process by imposing guidelines, limiting training to monitoring levels, using the computers to monitor workers, or closing off possibilities for worker interaction with the machine-based information through hardware or software implementation.

Zuboff's closing section is the most interesting one, for it deals with the issues of new technology-based access to information and organizational structures. She shows how computerization can either lead to wider access to information at all levels or be used by managers to control their subordinates. Though both happen with regularity even in the same organization as it undergoes the process of conversion to information technology, she maintains that to some extent the tendency of the technologization itself puts pressure on organizational structures in an egalitarian direction. In other words, given knowledge power (computer data bases), people will start using it. If the computers are used to control them or if they are denied access to the information base, workers will find ways to sabotage the process by using the new equipment. Zuboff gives examples of workers who have hacked (that is, gained illegal access to the computers) for the purpose of thwarting management's computer-based control structure.

Zuboff then suggests a solution in the form of a learning division in every organization using the new technology. This division would be responsible for dissemination of knowledge (by means of a universal data base) throughout the organization for the purpose of optimizing each person's task, whether manager or laborer. The reason she puts so much stress on this idea of learning is that she is convinced that only in an informated environment will the new technology be put to its best use. As she puts it, "Learning is the new form of labor."

A different, but equally important point Zuboff makes in her last section has to do with organizational structures. She fears that hierarchical structures will not facilitate the exchange of information that is necessary to make the new technology and its users truly productive. Instead, she proposes an integrated horizontal structure of teams made up of specialists in different areas working on organizational tasks in a holistic way. Zuboff characterizes the relationships needed in the new working environment as "posthierarchical," which is not the same as saying that all workers are equal at every point. It means that the relationships of power are fluid, depending on the knowledge each person can bring to a common task. If this sounds utopian, it is also at the heart of Zuboff's thesis. Unless organizations can face the fact that the new technology potentially puts an incredible amount of knowledge power in the hands of even the lowliest worker and help him or her use that knowledge well, a tremendous opportunity will have been wasted. Worse yet, the technology will likely be used in other, more sinister ways to achieve higher degrees of control by managers, worsening relations between labor and management rather than erasing the boundaries between them.

One can only hope that Zuboff is right, especially in her optimism about the new technology itself driving the necessary changes to put the machines to their best use as well as to further human potential. Each technological advance has brought with it a host of new environmental and sociological problems, and it is hard to imagine that this time it will be any different. Still, Zuboff is generally sane and compelling at many points. Furthermore, in the end, the question is not whether change will come but how human beings will respond to it.

Robert A. Bascom

Sources for Further Study

Booklist. LXXXIV, May 1, 1988, p. 1465.

Choice. XXVI, September, 1988, p. 185.

Fortune. CXVII, June 6, 1988, p. 258.

Inc. X, September, 1988, p. 23.

Library Journal. CXIII, June 15, 1988, p. 51.

Los Angeles Times Book Review. May 8, 1988, p. 4.

The New York Times Book Review. XCIII, April 24, 1988, p. 1.

Publishers Weekly. CCXXXIII, April 8, 1988, p. 84.

The Wall Street Journal. May 23, 1988, p. 17.

INFINITE IN ALL DIRECTIONS
Gifford Lectures Given at Aberdeen, Scotland, April-November 1985

Author: Freeman J. Dyson (1923-)
Publisher: Harper & Row (New York). 321 pp. $19.95
Type of work: Science

A scientist's meditations on relationships between science and ethics in the technological development of the modern world

The Gifford Lectureships, according to the will of Adam Gifford (1820-1887), the Scottish judge whose bequest established them, are intended "for promoting, advancing, teaching, and diffusing the study of natural theology, in the widest sense of that term, in other words, the knowledge of God" and "of the foundations of ethics." Important philosophical works such as William James's *Varieties of Religious Experience* (1902), Alfred North Whitehead's *Process and Reality: An Essay in Cosmology* (1929), and Michael Polanyi's *Personal Knowledge: Towards a Post-Critical Philosophy* (1958), each of which was first presented in a Gifford Lecture series, show the broad range of material that can be included under Lord Gifford's stipulations.

Freeman J. Dyson's *Infinite in All Directions: Gifford Lectures Given at Aberdeen, Scotland, April-November 1985*, continues the Gifford tradition, although at a different level and with different intent. Dyson characterizes the Gifford Lectures as "an occasion for an elderly theologian or scientist to express in polished prose the sum total of his life's wisdom," and then declines to claim for himself any equality with his predecessors or propose any single, extensive argument. Instead, he offers a two-part series of essays on the theme "In Praise of Diversity," the general title of the Aberdeen lectures. The first part, "Life in the Universe," considers life as a scientific phenomenon; the second, "People and Machines," considers the ethical and political implications of modern technology.

Dyson's career has prepared him well to range over these vast regions. Since 1953, while a professor at the Institute for Advanced Study in Princeton, New Jersey, he has conducted research in theoretical physics and has served as an adviser and consultant to the United States Department of Defense and to the Arms Control and Disarmament Agency; he has also written and spoken widely about the peculiar dilemmas of the nuclear age and about the ethical problems and concerns of nuclear warfare strategies. The underlying optimism of his earlier books *Disturbing the Universe* (1979) and *Weapons and Hope* (1984) pervades the present text, clearly qualified, however, by a sense of the gravity and urgency of these ethical considerations.

In the first three essays of part 1, Dyson analyzes two kinds of scientific activity and their results. One kind attempts to reduce all phenomena to a single explanatory hypothesis; scientists of this kind, whom Dyson characterizes as "unifiers," have included such intellectual titans as Sir Isaac Newton, Charles Darwin, and Albert Einstein. The other kind, concerned with concrete solutions to pragmatic problems, recognize the complexity of the universe without attempting to dissolve it; these scientists, generally less well-known than the others, Dyson calls "diversifiers." One of these, the German physicist Emil Wiechert, speaking before a Prussian scientific society in 1896, gave Dyson both the principal concept of the first part and a phrase for the title of the book as a whole:

> So far as modern science is concerned, we have to abandon completely the idea that by going into the realm of the small we shall reach the ultimate foundations of the universe. I believe we can abandon this idea without any regret. The universe is infinite in all directions, not only above us in the large but also below us in the small. If we start from our human scale of existence and explore the content of the universe further and further, we finally arrive, both in the large and in the small, at misty distances where first our senses and then even our concepts fail us.

Throughout these chapters, Dyson explores the ways in which awareness of diversity enriches both the understanding of science and the conception of the human place in the cosmos.

While the dichotomy in scientific activity is neither strictly logical nor necessary, the history of post-Newtonian science and modern industry suggests its validity in practice, which Dyson demonstrates in the second and third chapters. These chapters examine particular instances of the dichotomy to show how the "diversifying" pole surprises investigators with clear but unexpected explanations of phenomena. In the second chapter, for example, Dyson reviews three "unifying" concepts: superstrings (a highly abstract, mathematical theory of the infinitesimally small elements of physical reality); black holes (collapsed stars of progressively smaller volume and larger mass); and the Oort Cloud of comets associated with the solar system. Each of these concepts has roots in abstract theory but ramifies into practical consequences, showing that the scientific imagination may predict, ahead of concrete evidence, coherent interactions of apparently unrelated phenomena; explanation based on such predictions is the main business of "unifying" science. In contrast, the fourth and last concern of the chapter, the life history of the monarch butterfly, presents the "diversifying" pole of scientific activity in the immediate, tangible, familiar but unanswered questions of the butterfly's development and migration. Progress in many sciences may eventually answer these questions, but now the butterfly represents, for Dyson, "living proof that nature's imagination is richer than our own."

In the last three chapters of part 1, Dyson discusses questions that link him more nearly to the Gifford tradition: How did life begin and how will it end? In dealing with the first, however, he announces that he is concerned with a scientific answer because the available data (and hypotheses drawn from them) do not permit more philosophical or theological speculation. Giving careful credit to their sources, Dyson reviews scientific theories of the origin of life, dividing them into "unifying" and "diversifying" concepts. In one of the latter, the "double-origin" theory that he examines most specifically, the life processes of metabolism and replication are conceived of as separately rather than simultaneously established in nature, much as computer hardware and software are intricately linked but logically separable. Additional evidence suggests that statistical processes of chemical change ("genetic drift") introduce an important random force in evolution. Dyson thus argues that not one process but at least two (natural selection and genetic drift) account for the evolution of life in all of its complex diversity. In the fifth chapter, he shows how this complexity can be interpreted through simpler, mathematical models of physical and chemical processes. Finally, true to his theme, he shows that these models recognize the "qualitative features of life" that he considers to be essential: "looseness of structure and tolerance of errors."

When Dyson turns to consider the end of life, however, the frontier between science and theology is obscured. In the sixth chapter, he reviews how biology's longstanding lack of interest in cosmology (theories of the origin and dissolution of the physical universe) has been replaced by new commonalities between biologists and cosmologists, who now together consider the end of life in the triumph of entropy, a central doctrine of modern physical theory. To answer this remote but gripping concern, Dyson admits that he must "give up immediately any pretence of being scientifically respectable." His vision is, at this moment, an act of faith rather than a verifiable hypothesis: Given the diversity and complexity achieved so far, is it not possible that the further evolution of life—which "resides in organization rather than in substance"—will include mental activity so etherealized that it will not only survive but flourish in the utter cold? Even if new theories of particle physics are proven so as to show that matter is finally (at however distant a moment) transient, must that necessarily mean that dissolution of life? Can there not instead be some further and higher evolution beyond the physical as we understand it? Dyson again uses mathematical modeling to conclude that there is hope: "No matter how far we go into the future, there will always be new things happening, new information coming in, new worlds to explore, a constantly expanding domain of life, consciousness and memory."

The move from part 1 to part 2, "People and Machines," is radical. Where the first part took the whole of creation as its field, the second is narrowly focused upon the history of modern technology and its likely developments in the next century. So great and sudden a shift seems to be a fatal discontinuity only so long as a tacit proviso is ignored: Dyson's faith in the "constantly expanding domain of life" is justified only if humankind resolves the immediate, local problems of living with technology. The cosmic diversity outlined in part 1 as a fact of nature is held up in part 2 as a goal to be emulated in human affairs, so that those essential "qualitative features of life"—"looseness of structure and tolerance of errors"—are recognized and preserved in political, ethical, and technological structures.

The first four chapters of part 2 deal with technology as applied to economic needs, including the presumed eventual necessity for exploration and colonization of other planets. Conscious of a pedigree that includes both science and science fiction, Dyson is careful to show that the technological pathway he traces reaches not only out toward space but also into the cell and back to the great age of exploration on this planet: All these investigations and the fruit they bear are part of a fundamentally human motive and desire. Interplanetary "space butterflies," the genetically engineered descendants of the monarch in part 1, are presented as equally likely (although surprising and unconventional) products of a technology that will also produce more efficient, less expensive nuclear power stations and sophisticated refrigeration systems based on ice ponds. Although at times vectors of development seem fanciful or unlikely, Dyson's proposals are always informed by a clear sense of the central obstacle, not technological but intellectual, which is the inability to provide for diversity and error within any human enterprise.

The next five chapters deal with weapons technology and its consequences. This general subject, about which Dyson has written and spoken at length elsewhere, he here considers under several topical headings that he labels as "fashionable"—nuclear winter, the unification of Germany, and the Reagan Administration's Strategic Defense Initiative ("Star Wars"). As before, the keynote of the section, struck in chapter 11, "The Balance of Power," is diversity. An acute historical analysis of the political balance of power shows that the alternatives are either to move toward one-world government ("unifying") or toward nonnuclear national sovereignty ("diversifying") as global political structures. Backing his conclusion are detailed, specific critiques of the "unifying" alternatives that, according to Dyson, are likely to lead to global catastrophe. In chapter 15, considering the possibility of nuclear winter, Dyson argues that the radical defect in present approaches to nuclear disarmament stems from inattention to the two elements required for a valid resolution:

> If a political arrangement is to be durable, it must pay attention both to technical facts and to ethical principles. Technology without morality is barbarous; morality without technology is impotent. . . . The case for the feasibility of abolishing nuclear weapons would be stronger if we treated them with less respect. The hope of successful abolition becomes more realistic if it is understood that nuclear weapons are absurd rather than omnipotent.

Dyson concludes his survey with two chapters that look to the technology of the twenty-first century, identifying three areas of revolutionary change: genetic engineering, artificial intelligence (the development of computer hardware and software that will be able to "think" rather than merely "compute"), and space science. At the remote frontier of speculation, he entertains the possibility of the "most momentous choice" the human species faces: whether "to remain one species united by a common bodily shape as well as by a common history, or to let ourselves diversify as the other species of plants and animals will diversify." Although Dyson seems happy not to have the responsibility for the decision, the rest of the book resounds with the choice he would make.

Taken as a whole, the book shows both the defects and the virtues of its genesis as a lecture series. Too often, for example, the theme of "diversity" annexes so wide a variety of subjects that nothing in reality or fantasy is excluded from consideration. Furthermore, as the bibliographical notes show, single chapters often comprise blocks of materials originally composed for other audiences and at different dates between 1978 and 1987, then welded together for Gifford presentation, and finally revised for publication. Such extensive revision may sharpen the focus of ethical reflection, but it sometimes leads to odd discontinuities in the book's formal and logical development, as the two-part division acknowledges by implication.

On the other hand, however, the very range of ideas expressed, their affiliations with and similarities to the different concerns of apparently remote fields, and the usually clear definition of subject matter within individual chapters allow a reader either to follow the theme in all of its variations, or simply to read selectively on those issues and subjects of immediate interest. In these positive ways, then, *Infinite in All Directions* is literate, highly readable, sophisticated and thought-provoking evidence of the author's claims in praise of diversity.

Dale B. Billingsley

Sources for Further Study

Books in Canada. XVII, May, 1988, p. 6.
Natural History. XCVII, June, 1988, p. 30.
Nature. XXXIII, April 21, 1988, p. 748.
The New York Times Book Review. XCIII, July 24, 1988, p. 24.
Time. CXXXI, March 21, 1988, p. 75.
U.S. News and World Report. CIV, April 18, 1988, p. 72.
The Washington Post Book World. XVIII, April 17, 1988, p. 5.

THE INNER ROOM

Author: James Merrill (1926-   )
Publisher: Alfred A. Knopf (New York). 95 pp. $16.95
Type of work: Poetry

In this volume James Merrill includes various examples of his finely crafted short poems, several long poems, and a set of prose poems dealing with Japanese images, the prose interspersed with subtle rhymed haiku and a verse play

James Merrill, whose craft has frequently been noted, does not disappoint his readers in *The Inner Room*. In this book he uses a number of quatrains with an *abba* rhyme; his skill somehow reminds one of a lapidary's, with each word set as if it were a jewel. In the sequence "For a Bestiary," the first poem, "Carp," provides an excellent example. He begins with a clichéd action, feeding bread to the fish, which leads him to the literary cliché of "bread on the waters." This is quickly transformed into "literary crusts," a "half fiction" for the shiny fish in the water. Then he asks:

> Banked in its grate of reeds—
> An underwater fire,
> How lit?—might prove desire
> Itself the fast that feeds.

The poem ends with the writer imagining the fish frozen in the pond in winter and a skater gliding on the ice above them, writing "(Ah, loop and curlicue/ Of letters we once knew)/ *Here sleep the appetites*." The images are brilliant, the pattern of six syllables per line (with seven in the first three lines of the second stanza) are perfectly suited to the subject, and the subject is explored in a manner as sleek and smooth as the fish themselves.

The four long poems in the volume include "Morning Glory" and "A Room at the Heart of Things" in the first section and "Walks in Rome" and "Losing the Marbles" in the fifth and final one. Merrill, word-enchanted, plays with the various meanings of words and their parts in a number of his poems, but "Losing the Marbles" may be among his best examples of wordplay. He begins with the Elgin Marbles and ancient Greece and ends with the effects of light on children's marbles, which he has loosed between the slats of a deck where the light transforms them into works of art also. His technique is formidable; the third section is a condensation of section 5, using only a few of the words, or parts of the words that are also themselves words, the whole making not only sense but lyrical poetry as well.

Merrill uses a number of different poetic forms with ease. "Dead Center" is a villanelle; "Parnassians" is an Italian sonnet; several poems, including one of the bits in "Eight Bits" and "Processional," the final poem in the book, contain anagrams; "David's Watercolor" is written in Sapphic stanzas; and "Hindu Illumination" uses rimas dissolutas. Other aspects of his technique are equally dazzling. His rhymes are inobtrusive and innovative: planetarium/drum; interlaced/waste; shot/apricot. He often uses slant rhyme, and when he does not use rhyme directly, he usually sets up a careful repetition of assonance and consonance. For example, in "Cornwall" the first stanza uses eight *e* sounds. The second stanza is dominated by four *u* sounds, and the third stanza has seven *o* sounds. The fourth stanza utilizes a combination of the previous sounds, three *e*'s and four *o*'s, in addition to two *a*'s and three *i*'s. The fifth stanza relies primarily on the *e* sounds—eight of them—and the following stanza contains four *o* sounds (three of them in key words) and four *e* sounds (all of them in key words). This dextrous use of sounds adds greatly to the musicality of his verse.

Although these poetic devices serve him well in this book and in his other books, Merrill is not content with the forms he has already mastered. In this volume he experiments with the prose poem. "Prose for Departure" marks both a departure from old forms to new and Merrill's departure to another country and another culture (Japan). Merrill's signature is firmly upon these works; interspersed in the prose, but most often at the end, is a rhymed haiku, delicate and subtle—but not weak. The form is appropriate for the geographical place and doubly appropriate in that Merrill's work echoes Basho's travel journals. "Afternoons at the Noh" and the final poem, "In the Shop" are perhaps the best in this section, although the ending of "Strategies" is artfully accomplished, blending landscape, myth, and the poet:

> If every trip is an incarnation in miniature, let this be the one in which to arrange myself like flowers. Aim at composure like the target a Zen archer sees through shut eyes. Close my borders to foreign devils. Take for model a cone of snow with fire in its bowels.

Some critics see Merrill's mythological poem "The Book of Ephraim," written after he had read William Butler Yeats's *A Vision* (1925), as his major accomplishment. *A Vision*, however, is generally used as a source to explain Yeats's other work rather than a central work in itself. That may very well be the fate of "The Book of Ephraim" as well. Merrill, living in the cynical last half of the twentieth century, could not write a straightforward myth, so throughout this long poem, which was first published in *Divine Comedies* (1976) and later with its sequel, *Mirabell: Books of Number* (1978), and the final book of the trilogy, *Scripts for the Pageant* (1980), as well as *The Changing Light at Sandover* (1982), is replete with undercutting irony and wit. These long poems bear close study for the illumination they shed on previous poems and especially on later ones. Although Merrill's irony and wit do not always sit easily on myth's shoulders, these are important works, and their importance becomes even more apparent with the appearance in this volume of his one-act verse play "The Image Maker."

The three works in *The Changing Light at Sandover* explored, among other subjects, the nature of God and modern man's lack of religious faith. These two major themes are treated again in this play, but on a more simple and profound level.

The chief character in this play is a santero, a saint-carver in a Caribbean village.

This carver (clearly allied to Aristotle's "maker" as well as to the Christian concept of God) practices Santeria, a Latin American religion that combines concepts of Yoruba lore from West African religions, brought to the New World by slaves, with the Catholicism their masters imposed on them. The other characters are the carver's mother (whose voice is heard offstage but whom the audience never sees), the santero's niece, and the effigies in the workshop, which come to life when the carver goes on an errand for his sick and demanding mother. Merrill, who has always been fascinated by opposites within similarities, found the *santos* of this religion especially appealing because of their doubleness. He had learned about voodoo from his friend Maya Deren (a dancer and the founder of the Creative Film Foundation) that these figures, although outwardly Christian saints, also represented an *orisha*, a pagan deity which combines a natural force and a human concern. The santero has the power to create these puppets and to shape their saint's features and costumes, but inside they belong to the Yoruba god, who is chaotic and incorrigible. In the play the santero is called away from his hut by the voice of the damaged Saint Barbara, who is imitating the mother's voice. While he is gone, the *santos* come to life, and their wild and evil selves prevail. Francisco kills the pet dove, and the power of Chango, the evil god, working through Barbara, ignites a wall calendar, thus destroying all the holy days. When the santero returns, he proceeds to clean up the remnants of the fire, throws out the dead bird, and then appeases Chango with cigar smoke and a ceremony. After all this is finished, he begins again on the repair of Barbara.

The doubleness of the puppets is equaled by the doubleness and sometimes tripleness of every other character in the play. The old mother is herself, naturally, but also complaining humankind, as well as the epitome of selfishness. The young niece is innocence and superstition. The santero is carver and poet (and God). When the *santo* Miguel, in his evil self, claims that

> I am the generator.
> By reason's lamp or fever's flickering ray
> I make the Image Maker.
> Whatever god is magnified by men,
> I, I stare through their glass until
> He does my will!

This passage continues the concept from "The Book of Ephraim" that humans are naturally god-making creatures. Most likely the santero is also a manifestation of Merrill himself. Although the santero works in a medium different from Merrill's, there are obvious correspondences. In the beginning of the play the santero, describing his method, says that "it's never easy!"—that he must carefully select his materials and make his plans, but he never knows exactly how the finished product will turn out:

> At last the figure is begun.
> And never mind how well

I know my saint, I'm in for a surprise
Or two before I'm done—
A crafty smile, a new, hard-pressed
Look in the eyes . . .

Thus, the artist is also a discoverer. One of the things that the artist discovers along the way is that the product shapes the maker as much as the maker shapes it, a truism that Merrill has acknowledged, saying of his poetry, "It created me."

Merrill, who has won numerous prizes, including two National Book awards, the Bollingen Prize in Poetry, and the Pulitzer Prize, has written another prize-winning book, regardless of whether any prize is ever awarded it. The reader will award the prize—for mastery of technique that is complex and formidable, and for the even greater character and discipline that it takes to dismiss technique in order to write simply and clearly about a profound subject.

Ann Struthers

Sources for Further Study

Booklist. LXXXV, October 1, 1988, p. 214.
Library Journal. CXIII, November 15, 1988, p. 75.
Publishers Weekly. CCXXXIV, October 21, 1988, p. 52.

INTO MY OWN
The English Years of Robert Frost, 1912-1915

Author: John Evangelist Walsh (1927-)
Publisher: Grove Press (New York). 286 pages. $19.95
Type of work: Literary biography
Time: 1912-1915
Locale: Beaconsfield, Ledington, and Ryton, England

In this biographical study, John Evangelist Walsh demonstrates how important were the two and a half years that Robert Frost and his family spent in England from 1912 to 1915 in terms of establishing his reputation as an American poet

Principal personages:
ROBERT FROST, an American poet
ELEANOR FROST, his wife
LESLEY,
IRMA,
CAROL, and
MARJORIE FROST, their children
EZRA POUND, an American poet and critic
EDWARD THOMAS,
WILFRID GIBSON, and
LASCELLES ABERCROMBIE, English poets

At the age of thirty-eight, Robert Frost was a schoolteacher and an unsuccessful poultry farmer, with a wife and four young children to support. For almost twenty years, he had been writing poems and trying to publish them without much success in small magazines and local newspapers, subsisting for much of that time on the income from a small farm in Derry, New Hampshire, and a modest annuity left to him by his grandfather. The Derry farm had been willed to Frost by his grandfather on the condition that he farm it for at least ten years. In 1911, after more than a decade of hard work, the farm was his to keep or sell. That winter, on the threshold of middle age, restless and dissatisfied with his life, Frost made a daring decision. He would take his family and a briefcase full of unpublished poems and try to publish them in England. In August, 1912, the Frosts sailed from Boston to Glasgow on the USS *Parisian*; they arrived by train in London ready to embark on their adventure.

Scholars have always recognized that these years, from 1912 to 1915, were absolutely crucial for Frost's career as a poet, but the English years have never before received the kind of careful and sympathetic treatment they are afforded in John Evangelist Walsh's important biographical study, *Into My Own: The English Years of Robert Frost*. Frost had the misfortune to choose an unsympathetic biographer in Lawrance Thompson, whose three-volume biography makes the poet out to be a monster of selfishness, vindictiveness, and jealousy, building his literary reputation at the expense of his wife and children. Scholars have debated the accuracy of Thompson's portrait and his friends and kin have objected to the misrepresentation, but the impressions left by Thompson's marshaling of voluminous (however biased) evidence have done their work. Rather than the shrewd, genial New England philosopher-poet, Frost began to be seen as an unscrupulous egotist and manipulator of others. Later, revisionist scholars have worked to undo the mischief of the Thompson biography. Beginning with William Pritchard's *Frost: A Literary Life Reconsidered* (1984), a fairer and more impartial biographical portrait began to emerge. Nowhere is this scholarship more important than with Frost's English years. Walsh's *Into My Own* presents an objective and carefully documented account of Frost's experiences in Beaconsfield and later in Dymock, where Frost worked to find an English publisher for his poems and established important friendships with a number of influential writers and critics, among them Ezra Pound, F. S. Flint, T. E. Hulme, Wilfrid Gibson, and Edward Thomas.

The Frost whom Walsh portrays is a kind and considerate father and husband, devoted to his family and eager to share with them the once-in-a-lifetime adventure of living abroad, made possible by the sale of the Derry farm and by his grandfather's annuity. Frost comes across as a mature and seasoned writer, certain of his talent and ability and eager to find a publisher for the accumulated poems written during his Derry years. That he finally found a publisher in David Nutt of London was sheer luck. The manuscript of *A Boy's Will* (1913) was accepted by Nutt's widow as a vanity item under very unfavorable terms, and Frost immediately set out to promote his book in London literary circles. A chance introduction to Pound in the fall of 1912 led to Pound's offer to review *A Boy's Will* in *Poetry* and *The Smart Set*. In Beaconsfield, Frost was living close enough to London to meet with other writers, and being naturally gregarious, he soon struck up literary friendships that helped him to formulate his theories of prosody and encouraged him to move beyond conventional lyric poetry to the more daring, colloquial, blank-verse dramatic monologues and dialogues that would appear in *North of Boston* (1914). Frost was canny enough to sense the risks of Pound's patronage, and he soon detached himself from Pound and instead cultivated friendships among Georgian poets such as Gibson, Lascelles Abercrombie, and W. H. Davies.

Frost's relationship with Pound is particularly problematic. His break with Pound in the summer of 1913, after a friendship of four months, has led some critics to charge Frost with ingratitude or worse, but both men had strong personalities, and Pound was difficult to get along with. Frost was first introduced to Pound through a mutual friend, the poet F. S. Flint, when Pound was serving as a corresponding editor for *Poetry* magazine. Pound was trying to find new American talent and was eager to meet Frost. With Pound's calling card in his hand, Frost sought him out in his Kensington flat in March, 1913, and was met by a brusque, flamboyant figure with bushy red hair, in a dressing gown, who promptly asked why Frost had taken so long to come around. He then demanded to see a copy of *A Boy's Will*, and when Frost confessed that he had not brought one, Pound announced that they would go immediately to the publisher to get one.

At the Nutt office, Pound snatched the single copy out of Frost's hand, never realizing that Frost had not yet seen a copy of his poems. Pound kept the volume, offering to review it for *Poetry*; when the review appeared in May, Frost was appalled at Pound's carelessness and inaccuracy. Not only did Pound rework some of Frost's lines according to his own Imagist principles but he also hinted that Frost's verse showed naïveté and unsophistication, calling it "folk poetry." Frost was offended by the tone of the review, and he was also put off by Pound's rude behavior in several subsequent meetings that spring, as well as by Pound's insistence that he write free verse or else lose Pound's patronage. The final break came that summer, when Frost discovered that Pound had sent a manuscript copy of "The Death of the Hired Man" to *The Smart Set* instead of to *Poetry*, as Frost had requested. When his manuscript was finally returned, Frost decided that he had had enough of that "incredible ass," as he bluntly referred to Pound. Many years later, however, in 1957, Frost would prove instrumental in securing Pound's release from St. Elizabeths Hospital in Washington, D.C., where Pound had been confined for treason since the end of World War II.

Perhaps the most important friendship that Frost made was with the Welsh poet Edward Thomas in 1913. Thomas, then thirty-six, had been working as a biographer, book reviewer, and journalist for more than a decade since his graduation from the University of Oxford, struggling to support his wife and three children and, like Frost, growing increasingly discontented with his lot. Frost instinctively recognized his friend's latent poetic gifts in the paragraphs of Thomas' nature book *In Pursuit of Spring* (1914). Artistically, the crucial period in their relationship occurred during the spring of 1914, when Thomas and his son paid a visit to the Frosts in Dymock during a bicycling trip through Wales. Other friends of Thomas had glimpsed the potential poet lurking beneath the frustrated journalist, but it took the soothing effect of Frost's praise and encouragement to get Thomas to believe in himself as a poet. By the fall of 1914, Thomas was writing verse, and in turn his perceptive reviews of *North of Boston* helped win for Frost an English audience for his unconventional dramatic verse. Reading Frost had also helped to awaken in Thomas a latent sense of his own potential as a poet, of the possibilities of making a transition from prose to quiet, unpretentious blank-verse nature poetry, in a style similar to that of Frost. Hence, in a December 15, 1914, letter to Frost, Thomas speaks of his American friend as "the only begetter" of his newly written verse. During the six months after that, Thomas wrote almost one hundred poems, many of them among his most important works, before he decided to enlist in 1915. Thomas had been planning to emigrate with his family to New Hampshire and settle near Frost, but the outbreak of World War I awakened in him a sense of his patriotic responsibility to his own country and he joined the Artists' Rifles, later transferring to the Royal Artillery. He died in combat in France in 1917.

During the brief period of their friendship, Frost and Thomas encouraged and inspired each other's work. Their walks in the country found their way into at least two of Frost's later poems, "Iris at Night" and "The Road Not Taken," with its oblique tonal references to Thomas' indecisiveness. Frost also wrote a fine posthumous tribute to Thomas in his sonnet "A Soldier." On Thomas' part, his lyric poem "Aspens" may well have been inspired by Frost's "The Sound of Trees," and may in turn have suggested Frost's later "Tree at My Window." Frost also encouraged Thomas to balance his nature poetry with the sound of the human voice, these "speaking tones" being evident in Thomas' fine poems "Man and Dog," "The Gypsy," and "Wind and Mist."

What is less certain is how much poetry Frost actually wrote during the period from September, 1912, to February, 1916, and how much he had brought with him to England from his earlier Derry years. Walsh claims in his introduction that during the two years Frost spent in England "he wrote and published much of the poetry on which his rank and reputation are at last to rest." To be sure, these were important years in terms of Frost's early critical recognition, but in fact he published only the first two of his nine volumes of poetry in England, and the bulk of this verse was probably written before 1912. These years were most important for Frost in terms of his maturation and self-assurance as an artist, for he needed the support and encouragement of other writers and critics after the prolonged isolation of the Derry years. What Frost gained in England was more important than writing time: a publisher, an audience for his work, a renewed sense of his artistic worth and originality, and an awareness of his distinctive Yankee colloquial voice.

After *North of Boston* was published and favorably reviewed, the volume was noticed by Mrs. Henry Holt, wife of the New York publisher, who wrote an appreciative letter to Frost in August, 1914, and who persuaded her husband's firm to inquire about the American rights to Frost's poetry. Holt bought the unbound sheets of *North of Boston*, issuing a small American edition and agreeing to publish Frost's future volumes. With that assurance, Frost decided that he and his family could finally afford to return to the United States. By the fall of 1914, they were all feeling homesick for New England. Frost wanted to postpone his departure from England, but the German threat of unrestricted submarine warfare made it necessary for them to book passage as soon as possible. On February 13, 1915, the Frosts boarded the *St. Paul* in Liverpool; they arrived in Boston nine days later, after a stormy passage. Awaiting them in Boston was a favorable review of *North of Boston* by Amy Lowell in *The New Republic* and a check for forty dollars from Frost's publisher for "The Death of a Hired Man." Frost's American reputation was secured two months later, with an article in *The Atlantic Monthly* by English critic Edward Garnett, arranged as a favor by Thomas.

Frost had left the United States in 1912 as a virtually unknown poet and returned in 1915 to be hailed as one of America's major new poetic voices. His gamble had paid off. Like so many other American writers, he had to go abroad in order to be recognized at home, but unlike the other modernists, Pound and T. S. Eliot in particular, he would not build his reputation as an expatriate poet but would henceforth remain close to his New England roots, becoming in time the first poet in residence at Amherst College and later at the University of Michigan, and helping to found the Breadloaf Writer's School in Middlebury, Vermont. As Walsh so ably demonstrates, Frost truly came into his own as a poet during his English years.

Andrew J. Angyal

Sources for Further Study

The Atlantic. CCLXIII, January, 1989, p. 120.
Booklist. LXXXV, November 1, 1988, p. 445.
Kirkus Reviews. LVI, September 15, 1988, p. 1395.
The New York Times. CXXXVIII, November 15, 1988, p. C21.
Publishers Weekly. CCXXXIV, October 21, 1988, p. 42.

THE INVENTION OF HEBREW PROSE
Modern Fiction and the Language of Realism

Author: Robert Alter (1935-)
Publisher: University of Washington Press (Seattle). 122 pp. $15.00
Type of work: Literary criticism

Through close examination of modern secular texts, Robert Alter traces the emergence of Hebrew as a living and evolving literary language

The survival of Hebrew as a spoken language, let alone its development within a modern secular literature, is a miracle second only to the survival of Judaism itself. Like Judaism, Hebrew has withstood all manner of attempts to eliminate it. The most obvious pressures on Hebrew were external and historical, beginning as early as the Babylonian Captivity (597 B.C.) and the Diaspora which followed it; they continued through the Roman annexation of Palestine and the relentless intolerance of medieval Christianity. Edicts of toleration, issued periodically in various Central and Eastern European countries from the fifteenth to the eighteenth centuries, were usually pragmatic, inspired by business rather than moral considerations. They did little to ameliorate the prejudice which contracted the development of Hebrew and did nothing to stop the pogroms of czarist Russia. By the late nineteenth century, except in a few isolated communities in Eastern Europe and Palestine, Hebrew as a spoken language had almost ceased to exist—and this nearly half a century before German Nazism nearly succeeded in exterminating the Jewish people themselves.

Less obvious causes for Hebrew's near disappearance as a living language came, paradoxically, from within the Jewish community. Yiddish, derived from medieval High German with borrowings from Hebrew, Russian, Polish, and English, was the language of the *shtetlach* (villages, settlements) in which most ethnic Eastern European Jews lived. Though often written in Hebrew characters, Yiddish is a language quite distinct from Hebrew; the Jewish agrarian peasants among whom Yiddish originated tended to view Hebrew as a privileged tongue, to be reserved for sacred literature. The rabbinic establishment was loath to remove facility in reading and writing Hebrew as one of the few distinguishing characteristics of class. New vocabulary was unnecessary, since its locutions were scriptural, and evolution of the language became static, since the *midrashim* (commentaries) relied upon formula. An unhappy consequence of this closure was that the teaching of Hebrew became appallingly inept, particularly in nineteenth century Eastern Europe. Boys were taught to read the few passages from the Torah which were necessary for bar mitzvah, and girls were not taught at all.

It is against this background that Robert Alter, a professor of Hebrew and comparative literature at the University of California at Berkeley, begins his engrossing study of Hebrew's emergence as a vernacular language which sprang up within a century, despite powerful historical forces opposing it. What makes Alter's study so valuable is that the history it treats and the individuals who effectively saved Hebrew as a modern living language are so little known outside the circle of those who can read it. Hebrew resists translation into the idiom of other languages, as Alter amply demonstrates, and the historical climate of the first half of the twentieth century was hardly conducive to attempts at such translation. Astounding as it seems, no substantive anthology of Hebrew poetry was readily available to English readers until the publication of T. Carmi's *The Penguin Book of Hebrew Verse* (1981). Were it not for translations published in the modern state of Israel, most Hebrew prose writers would likewise be unavailable to English readers.

Alter combines the approach he used in two earlier books, *The Art of Biblical Narrative* (1981) and *The Art of Biblical Poetry* (1985), with a chronological arrangement of authors. Though this attention to chronology demonstrates that most Hebrew writers developed in their own milieu the realism which characterized most nineteenth century European writing, the concomitant element in Alter's analysis—isolation and dissection of representative paragraphs from the works of these writers—illustrates the degree to which each was bound to sacred tradition. Thus, Alter succeeds in showing the unique position of Hebrew as an ancient language which continues to evolve. His work is concerned as much with the Hebrew language as with those who wrote in it.

It is not surprising that the earliest Hebrew secular prose tends to be stiff and didactic. Hebrew writers of the late nineteenth century were struggling to use a tool which for at least two thousand years had had no active use outside the *midrashim*. Consequently, the first Hebrew work which could be called a novel, Avraham Mapu's *'Ahavat Tsiyon* (1853; the love of Zion), is essentially a patchwork of biblical fragments forced into a setting contemporary with the age of Isaiah. The result bears certain resemblances to the contemporary movement to revive the appreciation of Latin by translating familiar Victorian classics into that language; witness, for example, Clive Harcourt Carruthers' *Alicia in Terra Mirabili* (1964), his translation of Lewis Carroll's *Alice's Adventures in Wonderland* (1865). Both Mapu and Carruthers faced nearly insurmountable vocabulary problems, Carruthers having to deal with Carroll's solecisms and Mapu with the fear of committing them in a sacred language.

Sacred origins notwithstanding, modern Hebrew prose moved parallel to European realism, though it never abandoned the past. Shalom Yakov Abramowitz's *Ha'avot vehabanim* (1868; fathers and sons) is a good example. The title comes straight from the novel of Ivan Turgenev, though Abramowitz's work was so ungainly, even in its revised form, that Abramowitz turned to Yiddish for the next eighteen years of his career, producing a celebrated series of satiric novels under the pseudonym "Mendele the Bookseller."

What remains striking about Abramowitz's Hebrew novel is the degree to which it assumes familiarity with biblical prose. Analogies are meant to clarify through comparison, though Abramowitz derives his almost exclusively from classical sources. A phrase from a Yom Kippur prayer or quotations from the Hebrew Bible are unlikely to clarify their secular contexts, except for those already familiar with the sacred originals. The audience who could appreciate Abramowitz's rich allusions was thus limited. Alter's commentary reveals the natural ease with which Abramowitz applied his education in classical Hebrew to the novels he wrote.

Subsequent writers, such as Haim Nahman Bialik, were able to use Hebrew more gracefully in a modern context. Bialik considered himself the Hebrew Mendele, and wrote that he considered Mendele the creator of the modern Hebrew *nusakh* (chanting or musical mode), though it is probably more accurate to say that Bialik himself propagated the Hebrew *nusakh* through his translations from the Yiddish of Mendele's *Sefer haqabtsanim* (1910; the book of beggars). Alter examines paragraphs from Mendele's later works, written when Abramowitz finally returned to Hebrew after his success in Yiddish.

Prospects for literary Hebrew were more promising at the beginning of the twentieth century. Bialik, Saul Tchernichovsky, Yakov Steinberg, and Zalman Schneour were its poets, though Hebrew prose remained derivative; it resembled that of Anton Chekhov and Fyodor Dostoevski with biblical underpinnings. The question at this stage was not whether Hebrew prose would be produced, but whether what would be produced would be worthy of the language. A primary concern among many was that the two strata of the classical language, biblical and rabbinic, should not be intermingled in modern contexts. This was a charge leveled at Uri Nissan Gnessin and Yosef Haim Brenner. These two writers overcame the solecisms and awkwardness of their mentor, Micha Yosef Berdichevsky.

Gnessin's prose, particularly, moves beyond the formalism of the *nusakh* writers. Though it retains the norms of rabbinic grammar, its style has elements which recall Dostoevski, Chekhov, and perhaps even Émile Zola. It emphasizes experience rather than linguistic formulation, and Alter illustrates this in his analysis of several paragraphs drawn from Gnessin's relatively small output of short stories and his single novella, *Hatsidah* (1905; to the side). Gnessin's influence on Central and Eastern European literature was more profound than that of many of his contemporaries; he was translated earlier and more widely. Though Alter does not note it, Gnessin's facile use of flashbacks and flash-forwards, even within a single paragraph, seem to find their counterpart in Franz Kafka's German. Alter's comparison of Gnessin's prose to that of Joseph Conrad is, however, more insightful, since Gnessin maintains a flexible narrative line which never becomes expressionist. His real contribution to Hebrew is the ease with which he moves from recent past to past completed, then back to present, this in a language whose tenses have relatively few distinctions between degrees of fulfilled and frequentative (continuing) time.

Strange as it may seem, none of the Hebrew writers considered above had any active involvement with the emerging Zionist movement. Perhaps they were simply too preoccupied with modifying the language to accommodate their needs; still, no literature begins with a political enlightenment. Almost all literary traditions spring from mythic or religious origins, and Hebrew's ancient origins especially assured that this would hold true in the works of its first modern writers. Yet modern Hebrew literature evolved very quickly, and Hebrew, not Yiddish, was considered the Jewish national language from Zionism's beginnings. Hebrew, like Latin among

Roman Catholics, united a people which was actually multicultural.

By 1910, many Hebrew writers were emigrating from Europe to Palestine; one of these was Shmuel Yosef Czaczkes, who after his arrival there would change his surname to Agnon. Though he originally emigrated in 1907, he returned to Europe and was caught in Germany at the start of World War I. He made the best of his forced residence; when he finally returned to Palestine, he was a published author of considerable reputation. Agnon is a traditionalist, best known for his short fiction. Perhaps Agnon's greatest contribution to modern Hebrew fiction was his ability to produce realistic prose before the language itself had developed a vernacular.

The life of David Fogel, as Alter briefly sketches it, is a paradigm of European Jewish experience in the early twentieth century. Fogel was born in the Ukraine in 1891. At nineteen, he wandered through various Eastern European cities, was arrested as an alien in Vienna at the start of World War I, and spent two and a half years in prison. Unlike Agnon, Fogel could find no patron, and after the war he suffered with recurring tuberculosis and a loveless marriage. In late 1929, he immigrated to Palestine, but returned to Europe only four months later, apparently unable to cope with the harsh reality of pioneer life. Though he began as a poet, Fogel is best known for his prose: a novella titled *Beit marpei'* (1927; sanitarium) and psychological novels, *Hayei nisu'im* (1929-1930; married life) and *Nokhaḥ hayam* (1932; facing the sea). Nothing is known of his life after 1944, only that he was interned by the Nazis and sent to Germany, never to be seen again.

Fogel's writing could best be described as post-Impressionist. This emerges clearly in his use of synesthesia and in the sensuality of his imagery. There is a conspicuous absence of Jewish reference in his novels. It is impossible to say whether Fogel had read D. H. Lawrence's works, but there is no doubt that he uses Lawrentian themes, such as awareness of individual sexuality and the war between sense and intellect, in his own prose.

Alter concludes his study by considering the degree to which Hebrew prose is mimetic (imitative of reality) when compared with realistic works of other literatures. By considering a wide variety of authors, as different as Mark Twain and Norman Mailer, he demonstrates, much as does Erich Auerbach in his classic study *Mimesis: Dargestellte Wirklichkeit in der Abendländischen Literatur* (1946; *Mimesis: The Representation of Reality in Western Literature*, 1953), that literature intensifies the reality of the period in which it is set. Alter attributes Hebrew's remarkably swift evolution toward realism to the absence of inherited stylistic models, the lack of such models, he suggests, impelled creation of a literary vernacular before the development of modern Hebrew as a spoken language. In the wake of Israel's founding, Hebrew prose will likely become less derivative of European models but no less imitative of its own distinctive culture, which is itself a blending of old and new.

Robert J. Forman

Source for Further Study

The Christian Century. CV, October 12, 1988, p. 907.

THE INVENTION OF MEMORY
A New View of the Brain

Author: Israel Rosenfield (1939-)
Publisher: Basic Books (New York). 229 pp. $18.95
Type of work: Psychology

Rosenfield attacks two widely held assumptions about the brain, permanent memory and localization of function, arguing in favor of a theory known as Neural Darwinism

Though the mysterious inner workings of the mind have long been a source of fascination and investigation, two theories about how the brain works have for the most part never been challenged. The first is that memories exist in a permanent storage file in the brain. Much like a computer that holds all the data programmed into it, the mind, it is believed, holds a record of everything it has ever experienced. Wilder Penfield's experiments in the 1930's seemed to confirm this, when electrical stimulation of certain areas in his patients' brains triggered memories of long-forgotten incidents. The second assumption is that brain function is localized—that is, certain brain activities can be traced to occur in specific areas of the brain. This idea was advanced by the dramatic brain research conducted by European scientists in the late nineteenth century, most notably by Paul Broca, who discovered in 1861 that a loss of speech could be correlated with the existence of a small lesion on the left side of the brain. Belief in permanent memory and localization of function has continued to form the basis for much of the brain research conducted in the twentieth century. In *The Invention of Memory: A New View of the Brain*, however, Israel Rosenfield argues that these two long-held assumptions may simply be wrong. As his subtitle suggests, he offers a new theory about how the brain works, basing his views on a careful reexamination of past research, in many cases arguing for different conclusions from the same set of data, and synthesizing that information with more recent neurobiological discoveries.

Rosenfield favors a theory known as "Neural Darwinism," first proposed by Gerald Edelman, winner of the 1972 Nobel Prize for Medicine or Physiology. According to this theory, memory is not a fixed record, but an ever-renewing re-creation, based on the stimulation and subsequent interaction of selected nerve networks, or "maps," in the brain. A present stimulus, usually linked to an emotion, activates a past connection of nerve cells, and these interact with one another on the basis of a fluid system of categorization. The "shapes" of the neuron maps are continually altered by experience. Since it must adapt to a constantly changing world, the mind, Rosenfield argues, cannot afford to operate from a rigid filing system of stored information. Its survival depends upon the constant interaction of past experience with present environment; a category that was useful yesterday may no longer be useful today. Only the fittest neuronal connections—the ones that help the organism cope, the ones that are strengthened through useful repetition will survive; hence the "Darwinism" among the neurons.

Rosenfield builds his case for Neural Darwinism by first dismantling the theories of permanent memory and localization of function. Aside from the fact that neurobiologists have never been able to explain exactly how and where permanent memories are stored, at the theoretical level inconsistency and paradox abound. For example, if memories are a fixed record, why is it that, as Sigmund Freud noted, memory is often fragmentary and inexact? If a memory is fixed and filed, why does it come out in a slightly or sometimes radically different way each time it is recalled? The same question could be posed to the nineteenth century localizationists, who believed in word and symbol centers in the brain where fixed records of words and images were stored and that damage to these centers would inhibit a patient's ability to recall words and symbols. Ask someone to draw several five-pointed stars in a row; rather than producing several identical images (presumably from his stored image of such a star), he will probably make stars that are all slightly different from one another. If the brain were merely copying a fixed image, why are all the drawings not identical replicas? Further, the idea that the brain "knows" a horse when it sees one because it has a stored image of a horse on file offers no explanation for how the brain copes the first time it sees an elephant. The localizationist view that perception depends upon recall of a stored image, contends Rosenfield, leads to the absurd conclusion that "the world is knowable . . . only if it is already known."

For Rosenfield, these paradoxes point the way toward the importance of context in both recall and perception, something he believes the earlier researchers overlooked. In 1891, Jules Dejerine's work with brain-damaged patients who were unable to recognize words or multidigit numbers confirmed his belief in the existence of specialized memory centers in the brain. Dejerine concluded that either his patients had suffered damage to the memory centers where words were stored or there was some disconnection between the center for visual images and the center for making sense of those symbols as language. Yet that these patients were able to recognize some letters or some single-digit numbers leads Rosenfield to a different conclusion. If a man can recognize *5* but not *564*, it does not necessarily mean that the visual record of *564* has been damaged while the one for *5* has not. Rather, Rosenfield argues, it indicates an inability to make sense of context. The meaning of a multidigit number depends on where each number is placed, its context. The symbol for *5* will have one meaning when it appears in the phrase "5 pencils" and quite another when it is followed by *64*, as in the multidigit *564*. In this way words are like multidigit numbers; the meaning of an *l* changes according to its context, as in "talk" and "lake." Interestingly, notes Rosenfield, the common phenomenon of brain-damaged patients losing their ability to construct sentences but still being able to utter obscenities is another evidence for the importance of context, since obscenities as exclamations are often context-independent. What the brain-damaged patients are really manifesting, says Rosenfield, is not a damaged symbol center but an inability to organize and reorganize stimuli in useful ways. The earlier researchers were simply looking in the wrong direction. It is not recall of a stored image that holds the key to the brain's functioning, but the brain's procedures for making sense of present context as well as its procedures for learning from experience. A pioneer in this new approach to the brain is the English scientist David Marr, who, according to Rosenfield, between 1970 and 1980 "reformulated the fundamental questions that studies of brain function must answer." Though Marr does not fully abandon localizationism, by using computer models to examine the procedures of perception he does show that it is possible for the brain to recognize shapes—independent of any fixed memory system.

According to Rosenfield, looking at the brain's procedures represents a more productive course than studying its supposed centers of stored information. One of the most compelling procedures for Rosenfield is the brain's ability to use past experience to derive new and unexpected insights, to come up with new categories and new generalizations. It is this capacity that is indeed the hallmark of human civilization, man's ability to advance continually—through brain work—beyond his former place. Failure to account for the ability to invent new generalizations and categories from new sets of stimuli, according to Rosenfield, is the flaw in much current research, including James McClelland and David Rumelhart's work with PDP (parallel distributed processor) models. While McClelland and Rumelhart's computer simulations attempt to demonstrate how a child learns to construct the past tense from present-tense verbs, eventually distinguishing regular from irregular forms, they do not show how a child develops the very idea of present and past, establishing a new category and context where the words will make sense.

Rosenfield likes Neural Darwinism because it resolves many of the difficulties inherent in earlier research. There is no one vast memory library where incoming information is filed according to some a priori Dewey decimal system. Rather, there are numerous fragments of remembered information, maps of neurons, capable of interacting with one another and recombining in new and useful ways, allowing for different meanings to emerge in different contexts. These maps, or neuronal groups, are located in different parts of the brain. Which neuronal groups are communicating with one another at any one time determines how the information is categorized. Sounds, for example, can be classified as music, noise, or speech, or as a way of locating things in space—depending on the present context, past experience, or the needs of the moment. The sounds of a Bach concerto coming from an apartment window may be music to someone walking by, an annoying noise to a sleeping neighbor, or a sign that someone is home to a visiting friend. The same sound can mean all these things and more to the same person at different times. That much twentieth century avant-garde music includes sounds that used to be considered simply "noise" demonstrates how the capacity for recategorization can work on a mass cultural level.

The interacting-maps theory also explains the common phenomenon of hearing an old song and having it trigger an entire set of associations from another time and place. Rosenfield shows how author Marcel Proust intuitively understood Neural Darwinism in his recognition of the power of a present sensation in eliciting memories. Proust also recognized that memory is often "impure": The present and past, or several different pasts, will often blend together—something the interacting-maps theory explains. It also provides a physiological explanation for the phenomenon noted by philosopher Henri Bergson, that "an effort, an emotion, can bring suddenly to consciousness words believed definitely lost." Bergson's conclusion in 1911 that "the brain's function is to choose from the past, to diminish it, to simplify it, to utilize it, but not to preserve it" sounds like a remarkable forerunner to the theory of Neural Darwinism.

Neural Darwinism also offers an explanation for dreams: The Neuronal maps, released from the organizing influence of present environment, combine in new, often-nonlogical ways. The fluidity of memory fragments in dream—how a third-grade teacher can appear in one's college classroom, or how one character can combine several features belonging to other people ("it was my brother but not my brother")—supports the view that neuronal groups never represent any specific item, person, or event, and that information is not permanently filed in the brain under a fixed system of categorization.

Thus, past experience becomes important, present context becomes important, and the tremendous diversity in human thought is explained. The capacity for uniqueness is inherent in the very procedures by which the brain makes sense of its world. Twins may share many genetic and even environmental similarities, but their mental lives will never be identical. Their perceptions of the world will always be to some degree unique creations; their memories, even of shared events, will become part of an ongoing imaginative process. As Rosenfield writes, "Humanism never had a better defense."

Rosenfield's book does not represent an attempt to convey ground-breaking discoveries he has made in the laboratory; his achievement is purely intellectual. If the body of brain research were itself likened to a brain, with all of its studies and theories likened to neuronal maps, then Rosenfield performs with them the kind of mental procedure that he most admires: the generation of new ideas, a reformulation of the past, yielding a new combination of information. Not all Rosenfield's arguments are airtight. His attack against localization of function does not address all the evidence in this theory's favor; nor is it entirely clear why Neural Darwinism cannot coexist with the view that some functions are performed by particular areas of the brain. His views are certainly stimulating, and the best judgment of their validity will no doubt come from further research.

Though Rosenfield clearly intends his book for the lay reader, he draws his ideas from much research that is no doubt unfamiliar to this audience, making it difficult for the reader either to agree wholeheartedly with or intelligently to dispute his findings. Though carefully stated, his arguments are often so intricate that they are difficult to follow. Yet for the reader who struggles through the difficult passages, the rewards include many bright new insights into the workings of the mind. For many, the greatest reward in reading this book will be simply an increased admiration, even awe, for the remarkable human brain.

Dana Gerhardt

Sources for Further Study

Booklist. LXXXIV, March 15, 1988, p. 1212.
Kirkus Reviews. LVI, February 15, 1988, p. 268.
Library Journal. CXIII, April 15, 1988, p. 85.
Los Angeles Times. June 3, 1988, V, p. 10.
Nature. CCCXXXIII, June 23, 1988, p. 713.
The New York Times Book Review. XCIII, May 22, 1988, p. 37.
Psychology Today. XXII, May, 1988, p. 68.
Publishers Weekly. CCXXXIII, February 19, 1988, p. 67.

JACK OF DIAMONDS
And Other Stories

Author: Elizabeth Spencer (1921-)
Publisher: Viking Press (New York). 184 pp. $15.95
Type of work: Short stories
Time: The 1950's to the 1980's
Locale: Canada, the United States, and Italy

A collection of five short stories exploring the themes which are characteristic of Elizabeth Spencer's fiction, particularly those of transience, of alienation, and of community

Born and educated in Mississippi, Elizabeth Spencer later lived in Italy, married an Englishman, and settled permanently in Montreal. Her work reflects the breadth of her experience. Although her first three novels were set in her native state, the Jamesian short novel for which she is best known, *The Light in the Piazza* (1960), and the work that succeeded it, *Knights and Dragons* (1965), were both stories of American women in Italy, while *The Snare* (1972) took place in New Orleans. Even though Spencer returned to Mississippi for the setting of *The Salt Line* (1984), it was the coastal region, and thus a very different environment from that of those earlier novels set in the inland part of the state.

The short stories for which Spencer is so highly praised are as varied in setting as her novels. Those collected in *The Stories of Elizabeth Spencer* (1981), which represent three decades of work, range from Mississippi, Louisiana, and Tennessee to New York, Rome, and Montreal. As Eudora Welty points out in her foreword to that volume, however, it is almost inevitable for Southern writers to be fascinated with relationships and with the problems of individual identity which inevitably arise from those relationships. It might be added that Southern writers are also very much aware of the past as a factor that affects relationships and influences the sense of personal identity. Although she no longer lives in the South, and although many of her stories are set outside of it, Spencer's themes are those so familiar in Southern literature, the themes of William Faulkner, of Flannery O'Connor, of Welty, and of the writers who are still emerging in the ongoing Southern Renaissance.

Like her earlier works, the five stories in *Jack of Diamonds: And Other Stories*, though varied in setting, deal with the dominant themes of Southern literature. The two longest stories are also the most complex. Both "The Cousins" and "The Business Venture" are set in small towns in the Deep South, where certain families have lived for generations. Their complexity arises from the size of the society: Because a larger number of characters are intimately involved with one another, their pattern of relationships is particularly complicated. The other stories, "Jean-Pierre" and "The Skater," set in Montreal, and "Jack of Diamonds," which takes place in New York City and in a Lake George weekend home, are more limited in cast, reflecting the fact that, for better or for worse, in an urban area, the central family unit is usually more isolated.

In the title story of the book, for example, when Rosalind Jennings lost her mother, there was no community of kinfolk and lifelong friends to give her a sense of security. She had only her father, Nat Jennings, and the memory of her dead mother. At the beginning of the story, Rosalind returns to the family's weekend place for the first time since her mother's death. At first, it seems that Rosalind is about to break out of her isolation. The permanent residents are happy to see her again and sympathetic about her loss; some weekenders her own age, whom she knew slightly in her childhood, welcome Rosalind into their activities; and a brilliant local boy pays special attention to her. She can look forward to the arrival of her father and her new stepmother, Eva Jennings, who she must admit is kind and considerate. Above all, as long as she can return to Lake George, Rosalind can feel close to her mother, whose presence permeates every room, whose taste is reflected in every one of the furnishings she chose for the place that she so loved.

Unfortunately, there is to be no real community for Rosalind. The adolescent brother and sister plan only to use her, and the permanent residents, including the family of the boy she likes so much, will always shut her out from real intimacy. During her stay at Lake George, Rosalind also realizes that her father himself is as two-faced as a playing card. It was her anger at his deceit that sent Rosalind's mother fleeing from the summer place the day she met her death in an auto accident. When Rosalind learns that Nat has betrayed her as casually as he betrayed her mother and that he is selling the place which is all Rosalind has of the past, she realizes that she is now completely alone.

In "The Skater," Sara Mangham is a mother bereft by the loss of her children, who have grown up and left her. Neither her comfortable marriage to Ted Mangham, a lawyer, nor an interesting love affair with Karl Darcas, a television producer, can fill the emptiness in her heart. With no children to mother, Sara feels quite alone. Then she meets her husband's intense young client, Goss McIvor, an orphan who is being deprived of his inheritance. Because he is so alone, Sara finds joy in taking the role of his mother. For him, unhesitatingly she risks the career of her husband and the affluence that career provides; for him she uses, angers, and loses her lover. What makes it all worthwhile, aside from her success at protecting his inheritance, is that for a time she has once again known her own identity. In the maternal relationship, Sara is fulfilled; as a wife or as a mistress she can never feel complete.

In "Jean-Pierre," Spencer focuses on the relationship between two people who abandon their own communities in order to marry. The story is seen through the eyes of an English-speaking Montreal woman who surprises herself by falling in love with Jean-Pierre Courtois. To the protests of her family, she answers only that married or not married, she knows that she belongs to him. The test of her attachment comes in early June, when he mysteriously disappears, evidently to return to his own people. At the end of the story, he has returned, knowing, as she knows, that however little they comprehend each other, they have a relationship that will endure permanently.

"The Cousins," too, ends with an affirmation of permanence, after a period of distancing and doubt. The story begins with a widow's pilgrimage to Italy, to see a cousin for the first time in thirty years. During their college years, five young people who had grown up together in the same small Alabama town, where their parents were all related, had decided to take a summer trip through Europe. On the trip, the complex emotional relationships among them, relationships which reached back into childhood, became even more complicated. They were no longer brothers and sisters. Indeed, Ella came to realize that she was in love with two of her cousins—Ben, an English major, and Eric Mason, a law student. When an illness separated them and Ella found herself alone with Eric, the two cousins became physically involved. Then came a letter informing Eric that he had been dropped from law school; the affair broke up, and Eric spent the next thirty years in Italy. Ben blamed Ella. At the end of the story, however, she discovers that although the rest of the cousins have gone their separate ways, the bond between her cousin Eric and herself has survived time and distance.

If a common background and common ideas can provide the basis for social stability and deeper understanding between individuals, sometimes such a comfortable similarity can deteriorate into a stultifying conformity. The set of young married people to which Eileen Waybridge and her husband, Charlie Waybridge, belong in "The Business Venture" has rejected the moral values of previous generations and substituted a self-indulgent hedonism. Although Eileen thinks wistfully that she would like Charlie to keep his marriage vows, she has had to accept his easy adulteries, even with the other women in their social group. If times have changed, however, the attitude toward blacks has not, and when Nelle Townshend, a member of the group, takes a black partner in her cleaning business, she risks social ostracism and financial loss; he risks his life. It is ironic that although the group of like-minded young people can easily abandon the deepest moral values of their forebears, they cannot respond to what is merely a new business equality between the races; they will not support or protect the one member of their set who exemplifies positive social change.

Throughout Spencer's collection, the theme of transience is closely related to the themes of community and alienation. Both in "Jean-Pierre" and in "The Cousins," a relationship must prove itself over a period of time; both stories begin with community, move to isolation and alienation, and finally establish new relationships between old lovers. In "The Skater," a new relationship is established to replace the family situation lost to time; yet one suspects that it will finally be impermanent and that Sara's old isolation will return. At the end of "Jack of Diamonds" and "The Business Venture," however, it is clear that the community of loyalty and love that appeared to exist is merely an illusion. Nelle Townshend's old friends are willing to destroy her future; Rosalind Jennings' father and stepmother are planning to eliminate the memory of her childhood and her mother—in a sense, to erase the past as if it had never existed.

As Welty has pointed out, Spencer writes as a Southerner. Because Spencer grew up in a traditional community, where the past was always present, she is conscious of the problems and the possibilities which have always fascinated Southern writers. Wherever her characters live, whatever their situations, they are viewed as people moving through time, attempting to find profound and reliable relationships without losing their own identities in the process. This collection indicates the variety that is possible in the skillful handling of such elemental themes.

Rosemary M. Canfield Reisman

Sources for Further Study

America. CLIX, October 1, 1988, p. 202.
Booklist. LXXXIV, June 15, 1988, p. 1709.
Chicago Tribune. August 24, 1988, V, p. 3.
Kirkus Reviews. LVI, June 1, 1988, p. 787.
Library Journal. CXIII, July, 1988, p. 96.
Los Angeles Times. September 16, 1988, V, p. 10.
The New York Times Book Review. XCIII, September 4, 1988, p. 6.
Publishers Weekly. CCXXXIII, June 3, 1988, p. 70.
Time. CXXXII, August 15, 1988, p. 64.
USA Today. August 24, 1988, p. D4.

JANE AUSTEN
Her Life

Author: Park Honan (1928-)
First published: 1987, in Great Britain
Publisher: St. Martin's Press/A Thomas Dunne Book (New York). Illustrated. 452 pp. $24.95
Type of work: Literary biography
Time: 1775-1817
Locale: Southern England

This biography of Jane Austen uses previously unknown or unpublished material to set her firmly in the contexts of her age, class, and society

Principal personages:
JANE AUSTEN, a novelist
GEORGE AUSTEN, her father, a clergyman
CASSANDRA LEIGH AUSTEN, her mother
CASSANDRA AUSTEN, her sister
JAMES AUSTEN, her brother, a clergyman
EDWARD AUSTEN KNIGHT, her brother, adopted heir of a wealthy landowner
HENRY AUSTEN, her brother, a banker and later clergyman
FRANCIS AUSTEN, her brother, a naval officer
CHARLES AUSTEN, her brother, a naval officer
JANE PERROT, her aunt

The standard view of Jane Austen, fostered to some extent by the novelist's own remarks, is of a reserved and restricted writer, working on a consciously small scale and deliberately unaffected by major events of the time. She refused all suggestions that she should venture on abstract or political themes, and once wrote that the true subject of her fiction was "three or four families in an English country village." The great events of her life—the American Revolution, the French Revolution, the war with Napoleon Bonaparte—are all on the face of it ignored in her novels. She has been accused accordingly of a kind of triviality, or lack of interest, and in the late twentieth century of too easy an acceptance of the inferior status of women.

Park Honan's biography sets out to counteract this view. It begins by pointing out how many contacts with the world of great events Austen had, and how close to her they were. Her brother Francis, for example, only a year older than she, went into the Royal Navy, was known to and liked by Lord Horatio Nelson himself, and ended his days as admiral of the fleet. In the course of an eventful career, Francis missed the Battle of Trafalgar in 1805 only because his ship was sent in for provisioning shortly before the French and Spanish fleets came out to challenge the Royal Navy; nevertheless, he saw a considerable amount of action and took on rather strange and peculiar commissions for the East India Company. Honan acquits Sir Francis (as he later became) of the charge of openly encouraging opium addiction, though opium in the end provided a large part of the East India Company's profits, but he did engage in undercover activities, he transported bullion for the company on navy warships, and his name appeared in connection with unexplained deaths. His career reminds one more of the fiction of C. S. Forester or John Buchan than of Jane Austen. He and his sister were devoted to each other, however, and they remained in continual touch. There is no doubt that, if only at second hand, Jane Austen was acquainted with battle, trade, the realities of war, discipline, and life at sea. At one point in one of her novels, it becomes clear to the reader that she knew what sodomy was—a practice very familiar on navy warships, if also at that time a capital crime, for which her brother had seen men hanged. One of her less delicate heroines, discussing admirals, remarks on "Rears and Vices"—rear admiral and vice admiral are designated ranks—but then asks to be excused of any thought of punning. Nevertheless, the pun is there, and meant to be understood. The novelist therefore knew more of irregular sexuality than people have often supposed.

Other aspects of life to which she was exposed include the trial of Warren Hastings, one of her family's connections, in which the great nabob was at length acquitted, and also the barely credible cruelties and involutions of English law at that time. In 1799, the novelist's aunt, Jane Perrot, went to buy a card of lace at a milliner's shop, paid for it, and walked out. She was then challenged by the shopkeepers, and an extra card of lace was discovered in her possession. Had she stolen it? Her counsel, Honan shows, thought that she had—a serious matter, for all thefts of more than the value of twelve pence were at that time hanging offenses in England. In reality, if elderly and respectable Aunt Jane had been convicted, she would probably have been sent to the penal colony in Australia (a fate she would not have survived). As it was, she was kept in prison for seven months, till the case came to trial, and then was acquitted—the shop assistant had made mistakes in wrapping parcels before. It is inconceivable that this matter was not a subject for great concern and discussion within the Austen circle. Not much further in the background loom cases such as that of a more remote family connection, who was appointed to a colonial governorship by George III and took up the post, only to find that the insane king had not recorded the appointment. The man was eventually forced to repay all of his salary and expenses at compound interest to the treasury, with potentially ruinous effect on at least one of Jane's brothers. One fact which does come out with great force in Honan's book is the deep insecurity of even middle-class life in Georgian England. Men were killed in war; men and women could be ruined, imprisoned, hanged; both sexes were likely to die of disease, falls from horses, or household accidents with shocking frequency and suddenness.

Are these matters reflected in Jane Austen's fiction, as one would expect them to be? Superficially, this is not the case. The new light which Honan casts, however, makes it possible to see unexpected shadows in the novels. It may appear an accident, or a comic device, to have the Bennet family in *Pride and Prejudice* (1813) hopelessly vulnerable as a result of an entailed estate—which means that the family estate has to go to a man, though Mr. Bennet has had the ill luck only to have five daughters, who will therefore on his death (like Aunt Jane Perrot) find themselves suddenly removed from comfort and transported, if not to Australia, at best to poverty and the uncertain charity of remote relations. Yet entailed estates were common knowledge to the Austen family, who both benefited and lost from them. The novelist herself faced a difficult position on the death of her father, though she, with her mother and sister, had the good luck to have loving and well-off brothers, who rallied round and saw that their female relatives were placed in security. Still, the brothers did not all react in the same way. There may be a real basis for the scene in *Sense and Sensibility* (1811) in which a rich brother slowly whittles down his obligations to mother and sisters, egged on by his greedy wife, till a handsome lump sum has become an "occasional present" of food—a present, one is meant to believe, which will even then rarely if ever eventuate.

One may well conclude, then, that Austen's true subject was not merely "the feminine heart" or the tangles of class distinctions in country villages but included money, self-preservation, the inequality of the sexes, and the balance between the dictates of propriety and those of survival. In Honan's view, her apparently light-hearted tone is a sign not of triviality but of courage. The novelist was not unaware of the issues of revolution, war, and slavery, but she chose instead to show how these were translated into the lives of her own sex and class—as translated they certainly were.

A further issue which Honan brings into focus is the accusation that though her novels invariably center on courtship and marriage, this is a subject about which Austen herself knew nothing at first hand. She remained unmarried all of her life. Hostile impressions of her recorded later—but prompted, Honan shows, by internal family tensions not unconnected with money and status—present her as a stiff and sexless martinet. She could be seen as someone who knew nothing about men and little about marriage. Against this, Honan delves into the issue of the novelist's love affairs, of which there seem to have been at least three. Early in life, a young male relative was actually sent away by his family because it was believed that he was heading for marriage with Jane, something that would have been unsuitable both because she had no money and because he was expected to restore the family fortunes—which he did, becoming Lord Chief Justice of Ireland long after his first sweetheart was dead. Later, Jane seems to have been pursued in a summer romance by a young man now unidentifiable; this relationship was broken, as so often happened in those days, by his sudden and premature death. Finally, family tradition now makes it certain that Jane was proposed to by another relative, Harris Bigg-Wither, and to have accepted him, on December 2, 1802—only to withdraw from the engagement the following morning. The tradition of Austen as a fearful and inexperienced spinster might make this seem a decision born of mere timidity. In fact, as Honan makes clear in an extremely interesting chapter, it is most likely that money once more played a decisive part. The match would have been extremely advantageous for Jane and for her immediate family. Most likely she accepted out of prudence and then honorably withdrew on realizing her motives. Once more, the truth makes Austen seem more realistic, more sensible, and braver than the previously accepted image.

The question remains as to how far the genesis, and the achievement, of the works of fiction are illuminated by biography. Briefly, one may say that family experience interpreted in its broadest sense provides many hints for the close interweaving of personal and financial motives, of male arrangements and female accommodations, so characteristic of Jane Austen's fiction. Entails, West Indian sugar plantations, bereavements, and embarrassing flirtations all played their part in the life of the Austen family, and they reappear as central motifs in her novels. It is true that at no point can one turn an Austen novel into a *roman à clef* and say that this or that real incident is the key to a particular novel—but then the novelist would be held in less esteem if that were true. At many points, however, one can say that an incident in a novel is the sort of thing which generated genuine conflict, genuine turmoil, in life. Possibly the two greatest reactions to the contrasts which Honan draws are, first, to admire the sense and balance with which Austen played down, in fiction, the often-heartbreaking scenes of reality, and, second, to admire the quiet courage of her own life, far removed from the heroic scenes of her brothers in appearance but requiring at least comparable fortitude in fact.

As for the achievement of the novels, it is now clear how deeply one can analyze them in terms of class awareness—even native English critics of modern times have failed, through lack of information, to see how exactly Austen places her characters on or across critical social borderlines—and how well they respond even to such apparently anachronistic modes of criticism as feminism or discourse analysis. Feminism of a sort is not hard to find in Austen's background: She had at least one close relative whose French husband was guillotined during the Revolution but who responded by living the rest of her life in cheerful, slightly shocking, independence. Nor are feminist sentiments absent from Jane Austen's reading. Nevertheless, although she is still often criticized for appearing to yield dominance to male characters, it is frequently instructive to note the real structure of the male/female conversations she depicts: dominated to all appearance by male monologues, in fact craftily steered and managed by female interjections. One may say finally that few pages are as comic as those in which Honan counterpoises the reality of the novels against the pompous, patronizing, imperceptive reviews of so many male contemporary critics. Behind this, it is pleasant to see the author slowly making her way on talent, being increasingly lionized by at first disbelieving admirers, and all the time quietly keeping her own accounts of profit and loss. In her lifetime, she made, Honan shows, less than seven hundred pounds through her work as an author: little enough, in modern eyes, but intensely satisfying to the author herself.

Honan's book gives every reader new material with which to approach the novels. It is jammed with detail—on family trees, on the reading and writing of Jane's Oxford-student brothers, on the careers of her family, on the graft and corruption of wartime society, on the very scythes with which the London parks were mowed. The book reminds the reader that past societies, "flattened" as they are by the effects of time, were as complex and confusing as any modern one and that an understanding of them is dependent on both the genius of novelists and the indefatigable industry of biographers.

T. A. Shippey

Sources for Further Study

Booklist. LXXXIV, February 15, 1988, p. 966.
Kirkus Reviews. LVI, January 1, 1988, p. 39.
Library Journal. CXIII, March 1, 1988, p. 67.
London Review of Books. X, January 21, 1988, p. 18.
Los Angeles Times Book Review. February 21, 1988, p. 5.
The New York Times Book Review. XCIII, February 28, 1988, p. 15.
Newsweek. CXI, March 14, 1988, p. 58B.
The Observer. November 22, 1987, p. 24.
Publishers Weekly. CCXXXII, January 8, 1988, p. 67.
The Sunday Times. January 17, 1988, p. G13.
The Times Literary Supplement. November 6, 1987, p. 1216.

JEAN STAFFORD

Author: David Roberts (1943-)
Publisher: Little, Brown (Boston). Illustrated. 494 pp. $24.95
Type of work: Biography
Time: The mid-twentieth century
Locale: Boulder, Colorado; Germany; and New York City

A well-shaped treatment of an American writer's life, less satisfying as a study of her art

Principal personages:
JEAN STAFFORD, a writer of fiction whose career was sadly aborted twenty years before her death
JOHN STAFFORD, her father, a failed writer
ROBERT HIGHTOWER, her first male confidant
ROBERT LOWELL, her first husband, a great poet
OLIVER JENSON, her second husband
A. J. LEIBLING, her third husband, a writer of short stories

Jean Stafford is best remembered today as a writer of short stories. *The Collected Stories of Jean Stafford* (1969) won a Pulitzer Prize, several of her stories have received O. Henry awards, and her short fiction has been frequently anthologized. Yet she had the ambition to become a great novelist, writing several unpublished novels before her twenty-sixth year and completing three that were published: *Boston Adventure* (1944), *The Mountain Lion* (1947), and *The Catherine Wheel* (1952). In the last twenty years of her life, Stafford published little fiction but wrote some first-rate journalism; even as her health deteriorated drastically, she was promising to deliver to publishers the great novel she seemed incapable of completing.

David Roberts speaks with affection of Stafford's work in his preface—indeed, it seems to have been his reason for undertaking a biography. Yet his actual discussion of Stafford's work is minimal. He cites a few passages from each of the novels to give the flavor of her style. He is an objective critic, acknowledging his subject's strengths and weaknesses, but there is not enough in his description of the artist to excite interest in her work. Even more surprising is his stinting of Stafford's short stories, which are considered her main contribution to American literature. Roberts identifies a list of the best ones, but it is not at all clear what makes Stafford a distinctive short-story writer or how she compares with her contemporaries.

Like most biographers, Roberts mines Stafford's fiction (published and unpublished) for clues about her personality and background. He is scrupulous in his efforts to separate fiction from fact, admitting several times that he cannot be sure that events in the fiction are to be taken as biography. Occasionally he is tiresome in his fretting over whether a certain event actually happened. He quotes from many of her letters which conclusively demonstrate how capable she was of exaggerating and lying about the actual events of her life, but he does not spend enough time considering how all Stafford's fiction represented the imaginative truth of her life.

Roberts is at his best in narrating the drama of Stafford's life. If her work is not illuminated by his biography, the structure of her career is brilliantly established. Stafford's father was a failed writer. Most of what he wrote was not published. His Western stories and novels were poorly conceived, and later in life he became something of a crank as he wrote and rewrote his treatise on the national debt. He had lost his wealth in stock-market speculation and spent his life trying to prove that it was the system, not his irresponsibility and bad luck, that was to blame.

Before John Stafford lost his money and before it was apparent that his writing career would never succeed, he served as a figure of some solace and inspiration for his youngest daughter, Jean. Although her older brother and two sisters never seem to have realized it, she was always the outsider—teased by them and made to feel inadequate. To them the family seemed happy, especially in the early days when they still had money. Jean, however, was a serious, highly intelligent, imaginative child who found little to interest her in an unintellectual mother and less than sympathetic siblings. Stafford needed her share of love, felt close to her father and brother at times, but in the end felt bitter about her isolation. She had a mind that quickly found fault with her pedestrian surroundings and with other minds that were conventional and stolid.

Without ever quite making it explicit, Roberts demonstrates Stafford's extreme alienation. She would eventually find soulmates in a few young men and women who wanted to be writers, but even their company proved less than satisfying for a perfectionist whose correspondence was as well drafted as her fiction. She excelled in college, but doing well in courses meant almost nothing to her. By her early twenties she was writing autobiographical novels and traveling to Germany for postgraduate study. School, however, was just a way of biding her time until she found a style mature enough to match her imaginative insights.

Stafford was in Germany in 1936, a time when Nazi control over Germany was already complete. She had little interest in politics. In fact, Roberts doubts that she understood the monstrousness of Adolf Hitler's attacks on the Jews. Her life was so inward that she proved incapable of absorbing a culture so different from her own. She was not a very sympathetic person—a fact Roberts skips over rather quickly. There is some evidence that she was a bigot, but Roberts never faces this unpleasant side of Stafford squarely.

Stafford seems to have contracted either gonorrhea or syphilis during her stay in Germany. Because Roberts' evidence is ambiguous, he can only speculate that her mixed feelings about sex stemmed from having caught the disease. She may have been dismissed from a teaching job at Stephens College in Columbia, Missouri, because of the results of a Wassermann test. She also claimed to friends that she never actually slept with her first husband, the poet Robert Lowell. What does seem clear is that for Stafford intercourse was fraught with frightening consequences—a feeling she communicated to her lifelong friend, Robert Hightower. In many ways, he was her most intimate male friend. Even though she seems to have been sexually attracted to him (after an initial standoffish period), they went to bed only once.

Hightower found their intercourse unsatisfying, and Roberts presents much evidence to suggest that Stafford was trying to preserve an intimacy with Hightower that may have depended on their not becoming lovers. Roberts dwells on this aspect of Stafford's life because her fiction is so chary of dealing with the sexual issues which are the staple of so many modern writers.

Stafford's great tormented love was Lowell. Roberts presents Stafford's years with Lowell with great forbearance. Lowell was a literary genius, but he was also something of a monster. As Roberts suggests, Lowell had great insight into human feelings but lacked the fundamental quality of empathy for people in his own life. He scarcely seemed bothered by a car accident, probably caused by his drunkenness, in which Stafford was severely injured. Her nose required several operations, and her teeth were damaged. The nose would be a source of pain throughout her life, as she went through several operations to improve her appearance and her breathing. There is nothing to indicate that Lowell understood Stafford's agony. On the contrary, in one of their arguments he hit her so hard that he broke the already damaged nose.

It was Lowell's imaginative intensity, his haunting brilliance, that kept Stafford by his side. Eventually, he left her for another woman, and they were divorced. For many years, however, she clung to their time together—even annotating one of his books of verse to show the biographical sources of most of his lines. Stafford lived by words. For her, style was paramount. She would often read Marcel Proust as a warm-up for her own day's composition. Her first published novel is an elaborate imitation of the styles of Proust and Henry James.

Roberts attributes much of the decline of Stafford's literary powers to her illnesses. By her mid-twenties, she was a heavy drinker and smoker. She developed heart and respiratory problems. The only way she could stop her compulsive drinking was to have herself committed to New York Hospital. She was well-known to the staff there by the mid-1960's, and by the end of her life she had made more than thirty visits there. Hospital stays were, in fact, a kind of sabbatical for Stafford, who was never really comfortable on her own.

Stafford tried psychotherapy, but Oliver Jenson (her second husband) may have been correct in observing that the last thing she should have done was dwell on the pain of her past. He was a man who infuriated Stafford by counseling her to forget her grievances and to live more fully in the present. He was right in the sense that there is abundant evidence to indicate she lived almost entirely in her own mind. She rarely went out and had no hobbies, no real interests outside herself. When she did entertain, it was to gather celebrities around her. She was a remarkable storyteller, as precise orally as she was on paper. Indeed, friends who heard Stafford tell a story several times noted how faithful she was to the version she had obviously worked out with great care.

Much of Stafford's third marriage to A. J. Liebling—best known for his stories and articles in *The New Yorker*—was happy. He adored her writing, pampered her, took her on trips, and made her feel that she was the center of his life. Yet the marriage began to weaken when it became clear that the couple really had very little in common. It was also distressing for Stafford to watch the obese Liebling's physical and literary powers begin to fade. They had had a good time living in their Long Island home, but they now found themselves together as two writers who had largely used up their literary capital.

When Liebling died, Stafford was at a loss. She was a figure of considerable social prominence in the Hamptons, where Dick Cavett, Alger Hiss, and an assortment of cultural figures became a part of her circle. Alone in her Long Island home, however, she had to breathe through an oxygen mask several hours a day and depend on her housekeeper and a young couple who had a house behind hers.

It is a tribute to Roberts' insight into his subject that his account of the last gruesome days of Stafford's life makes compelling reading. The logic of his biography is to show how the very interiority of Stafford's vision led to her last isolated days. She suffered a stroke that prevented her from speaking, from employing the rich verbal style she had spent so many years perfecting. In this case, the pattern of the subject's life has handed the biographer a novelistic conclusion. To put it another way, Roberts has shown a writer's sensitivity in dramatizing the way Stafford's stroke brought an end to a literary talent that had been slowly extinguishing itself for more than twenty years.

Carl Rollyson

Sources for Further Study

The American Scholar. LVII, Summer, 1988, p. 373.
The Atlantic. CCLXII, September, 1988, p. 98.
Booklist. LXXXIV, June 1, 1988, p. 1638.
Kirkus Reviews. LVI, June 1, 1988, p. 814.
Library Journal. CXIII, June 15, 1988, p. 61.
Los Angeles Times Book Review. August 14, 1988, p. 1.
The New York Times Book Review. XCIII, August 28, 1988, p. 3.
Newsweek. CXII, August 22, 1988, p. 66.
Publishers Weekly. CCXXXIII, June 24, 1988, p. 98.
Time. CXXXII, September 19, 1988, p. 95.
The Times Literary Supplement. August 19, 1988, p. 900.

J. G. FRAZER
His Life and Work

Author: Robert Ackerman (1935-   )
Publisher: Cambridge University Press (New York). Illustrated. 348 pp. $39.50
Type of work: Biography
Time: 1854-1941
Locale: Cambridge, England

Robert Ackerman's scholarly biography of the renowned British anthropologist and classicist Sir James George Frazer treats with impressive detail the growth of anthropology as a science recognized by the great universities and provides a clear outline of Frazer's theories as developed in his works

Principal personages:
SIR JAMES GEORGE FRAZER, a British anthropologist and classicist
ELIZABETH "LILLY" DE BOYS GROVE FRAZER, his wife and tireless champion of his works

It would be difficult to find a modern anthropologist, archaeologist, classicist, or religionist who has not encountered and been influenced by the enormous body of works written by Sir James George Frazer. His 1898 translation and commentary of Pausanias' *Periēgēsis tēs Hellados* (c. A.D. 150; *Description of Greece*) which fills six thick quarto-sized volumes bound in characteristic forest green, and his magnum opus which ensured recognition of comparative anthropology as a scholarly discipline, *The Golden Bough: A Study in Magic and Religion* (1890), the third edition of which fills eleven quarto volumes not counting its full-volume general index, remain essentials in every university library and continue to be reprinted. Bookstores, even those catering primarily to popular taste, stock Theodor H. Gaster's one-volume abridgment *The New Golden Bough* (1959) in inexpensive paperback format. Were Frazer to have written nothing else, these two works would have assured his reputation; nevertheless, he did write more, much more, everything from translations and commentaries of the second century A.D. mythographer Apollodorus and *Fasti* (before A.D. 8; English translation, 1929) of the Roman poet Ovid to editions of the eighteenth century essayist Joseph Addison and the poet William Cowper. In short (if one can apply that word even indirectly to Frazer, who never wrote anything that was not compendious), Frazer's mark on intellectual history is indelible and profound.

With Frazer's greatness duly noted, one must also remark that to a large extent his popularity has always resided with educated general readers rather than scholars and specialists. Since World War II especially, but even in the last years of Frazer's life, anthropologists have turned to psychology to explain similarities in the rituals of geographically distant cultures, and French structuralists such as Claude Lévi-Strauss have come to the fore. Even among classicists (Frazer's own formal training was in Greek and Latin), Frazer's Victorian translations annd digressive commentaries often elicit smiles.

Why, then, did Robert Ackerman write a life of Frazer? There are several good answers to this question. First, before Ackerman's treatment, no scholarly outline on the development of Frazer's thought existed. Robert Angus Downie's *James George Frazer: The Portrait of a Scholar* (1940) is a well-intentioned appreciation written by Frazer's former secretary. It was written under a commission by Lady Frazer with the stipulation that not even a hint of criticism appear. Ackerman's work properly sets Frazer's scholarship in its historical context, notes where it has become outmoded, and indicates the new directions comparative anthropology, archaeology, and classical studies have taken in these areas since Frazer's death. Second, unlike Downie's book, Ackerman's deals relatively little with Frazer's private life, his nonacademic concerns, or external facts not directly relating to Frazer's work. Ackerman's is a scholarly biography which therefore logically deals with Frazer's scholarship. He considers each of Frazer's works, from the early article "Totemism" (1885), written originally for the *Encyclopaedia Britannica* (and which along with another article, "Taboo," influenced Sigmund Freud) to the masterful four-volume *Totemism and Exogamy* (1910). More important, Ackerman discusses, in reference to the latter work, the scholarly influences and broadened knowledge which allowed Frazer to develop a more than one-thousand-page work from a slim early volume of only eighty-seven pages.

As one might guess, Ackerman's biography does not pander to readers who desire to discover little-known or possibly sordid details of Frazer's private life. He appropriately skirts the contemporary taste for psychological hypothesis and neatly distills the massive body of Frazer's thought into an amazingly short volume. Ackerman's is a study that will be read with most profit by those already acquainted with Frazer's works. Its greatest virtue is that it logically relates the disparate areas in which Frazer wrote and demonstrates clearly the progress of his scholarship.

The pattern it outlines is impressive. Though Ackerman eschews the sensational, he notes the important influence on Frazer's work of two individuals: William Robertson Smith, his early University of Cambridge mentor, and Frazer's wife, Lilly, whom he met and married in his middle years. Smith's *Lectures on the Religion of the Semites* (1889) was the first book to apply comparative evolutionary anthropological methods to Semitic religion. The difficulties inherent in this can be appreciated only when one realizes the paucity of secondary material upon which he could draw. It was Smith, Frazer's colleague at Trinity College, Cambridge, who first interested his younger friend in the infant science of anthropology and in the comparative approach Frazer would use with such élan in *The Golden Bough.* At the very least, the two formed a deep emotional attachment, to the extent that Frazer continually remolded Smith's ideas to suit his own developing scholarship, even long after Smith had died. Smith became an editor of the *Encyclopaedia Britannica*, the still-remarkable edition of 1884-1886 which gathered essays by the finest British scholars of the day, and it was he who convinced his classicist junior colleague that he could write in anthropology. Until that time, Frazer had seen himself as a conventional classicist; his only writings were an essay on the growth of Plato's theory of the ideal (unpublished until 1930) and a school edition of the Roman historian Sallust (1884). Smith's comparative approach clearly influenced Frazer's work on Pausanias, who until the publication of Frazer's translation and commentary had been considered an obscure and unreliable ancient geographer.

Lilly met Frazer only eight months after Smith's death. Her first husband had been the British master mariner Charles Baylee Grove. After Grove's death, she found herself in England with two teenage children (Lilly Mary and Charles Grenville) but without much money. Lilly was intelligent and quick-witted, however, and decided to earn her living by writing. Her quick marriage to Frazer probably sprang from mutual need, but it grew into deep love. By all accounts, Lilly was formidable in all matters, particularly so in business affairs, and she often made canny publishing suggestions to George Macmillan, founder of the firm which published all Frazer's major works. The most colorful passages of Ackerman's book deal with Lilly's possessive devotion to her husband; she literally did not leave his side when he worked. It was through her efforts that Frazer's works received almost immediate French translation, thereby allowing them to circulate simultaneously in two scholarly languages. She herself was an accomplished linguist as well as an author and translator of fiction and stories for children. It is a romantic curiosity that she died the very same day and less than five hours after her husband, on May 7, 1941.

Frazer's great contribution, one that can never be challenged even if modern anthropological methods prove certain specifics wrong, is his application of Smith's comparative method. The technique can be discerned in virtually all Frazer's works, though perhaps nowhere is it more attenuated (or dubious) than in *The Golden Bough*, his work on the priest-king motif in folklore. Starting beside Lake Nemi (in central Italy) with a priest of Diana's grove circling a sacred oak tree in an attempt to thwart the man who would kill him and assume his place, it proceeds in nine subsequent volumes of text to analyze vegetation rituals worldwide as they existed in every culture and at every time. The problem, obvious to Frazer's academic contemporaries, is that the specifics of many vegetation rituals can only be surmised. Even so, the mere compilation is impressive, even in the age of the computer. The popular appeal of *The Golden Bough* is its magnificent romance, present in its very title, which refers to Vergil's *Aeneid* (c. 29-19 B.C.): the branch Aeneas must pluck to assure his entrance to the Underworld. That Frazer carries this analogy successfully to volume 11, on the Norse god Balder, is doubtful; even he does not insist on a firm connection in his preface to the third edition. *The Golden Bough* still has, nevertheless, a popular appeal which goes right to the heart of the imaginative reader.

Ackerman explores quite successfully one of the pervasive elements in Frazer's works: his distaste for all religion. Though born to a devout Scottish Anglican family (the same religious background as that of his beloved mentor Smith), Frazer rejected Christianity from his earliest Trinity College years. Ackerman duly notes the obvious delight Frazer takes in tying elements of the Christian Crucifixion and Eucharist to primitive fertility myths, and how Frazer is able to see elements of

Babylonian religion in the Jewish festival of Purim. Persuasively, Ackerman suggests that Frazer wrote *Folk-Lore in the Old Testament* (1918) as an attempt to honor Smith and to debunk living religion simultaneously. There is no doubt that Frazer was hostile toward religion, particularly Christianity; his correspondence is filled with such references, and he once refused a potentially lucrative guest lectureship in part because of the institution's religious affiliation.

What Ackerman only hints at, yet what was just as important in the shaping of Frazer's ideas, is the contribution of Victorian England. Frazer's view of folklore relies inevitably on the great individual, the dominant personality who shapes the thought of a community, then is successfully challenged and replaced by a younger, more vital person. This view implicitly denies the worth of the collective, the group who remain merely unimaginative followers. Easily, it seems, one might read Frazer not only against the works of Charles Darwin (whom Ackerman does several times mention) but also against the way Great Britain saw its own role in the late nineteenth century and at least until World War I.

Students of Frazer's works know that their author rarely retracted any of his printed ideas; he simply added a footnote in the subsequent edition. That so many of his works appear in multiple editions is testimony to his enormous popularity. Though he would receive numerous honorary degrees—most notably from the University of Oxford (1899) and the Sorbonne (1921)—a knighthood (1914), and other important recognitions, his own institution, the University of Cambridge, never granted him a professorship. Even sympathetic junior colleagues such as John Roscoe and R. R. Marett came to challenge his ideas. Yet, just as Frazer's notion of the supplanted priest-king continues to influence his society after his death, the works of Frazer continue to inspire each new generation of anthropologists, archaeologists, and classicists to find its own Golden Bough.

Robert J. Forman

Sources for Further Study

Choice. XXV, July, 1988, p. 1728.
Listener. CXIX, January 21, 1988, p. 22.
The New Republic. CXCVIII, April 18, 1988, p. 40.
The New York Times Book Review. XCIII, March 6, 1988, p. 16.
The Observer. January 17, 1988, p. 24.
The Times Literary Supplement. February 5, 1988, p. 131.

JOHN CHEEVER
A Biography

Author: Scott Donaldson (1928-)
Publisher: Random House (New York). Illustrated. 416 pp. $22.50
Type of work: Literary biography
Time: 1912-1982
Locale: The eastern United States

Scott Donaldson investigates, fully and for the first time, the life of an author who for most of his sixty-year career successfully managed to preempt biographical inquiry by fashioning a background for himself much as he fashioned the stories and novels that indeed were what he rather disingenuously claimed they were not: "crypto-autobiographical"

Principal personages:
JOHN CHEEVER, an American novelist and short-story writer
MARY WINTERNITZ CHEEVER, his wife
SUSAN CHEEVER, their daughter
MALCOLM COWLEY, his friend and literary adviser
WILLIAM MAXWELL, fiction editor at *The New Yorker*
JOHN UPDIKE, Cheever's friend and colleague
HOPE LANGE, an actress with whom Cheever had a long-lasting affair

The last of the twenty-five photographs reproduced in *John Cheever: A Biography* is by far the most interesting. Taken in August, 1979, it shows Cheever walking across a field, alone, carrying in his left hand the MacDowell medal he had been awarded just a short time before. He is seen from the back and side, facing the sun and about to stride out of the camera's field of vision. Clad in a dark suit and photographed in black and white against a field of dark stubble and a distant stand of even darker trees, he appears as a figure easily overlooked, at the point of vanishing altogether. The photograph seems to sum up all too well the life Cheever led, as that life has now for the first time been fully told by Scott Donaldson. His Cheever is, on the one hand, the author of novels and short fiction that "tell us more about people in the American middle class during that half century [1930-1980] than any other writer's work has done or can do." His Cheever is also, however, the man whose triumph came only at the very end of his life. "Hurt in childhood, he grew up divided against himself. A battle raged inside him between light and dark, celebration and sorrow, love and hate." Looking back at the photograph after reading Donaldson's compelling work, one is immediately struck by the troubling mixture of loneliness and stoic independence, of determination and pain, on Cheever's averted face.

To read *John Cheever* is an illumination, to acclaim it a pleasure—an all too rare pleasure, given the tendentiousness of so many biographies, the clutter of superfluous detail in some, and the redundancy of still others. Generous, honest, forthright, exhaustive, yet humble, it differs from Susan Cheever's memoir *Home Before Dark* (1984) in a number of important ways. It is less personal than what Cheever's daughter wrote, but also longer, far more detailed and extensive, far less shocking in its revelations, but far more balanced in its judgments, and, thankfully, entirely free of that undercurrent of pain that gave the daughter's most intimate revelations a certain edge of resentment. Donaldson's book also proves to be easier to follow in its treatment of Cheever's life: twenty-two chapters, chronologically arranged, most dealing with periods of no more than from one to four years. The four pages of acknowledgments and thirty-seven of notes attest the depth and range of Donaldson's research.

Donaldson does not attempt to alter the basic pattern of Cheever's life. What he does is to flesh out the pattern, adding facts, correcting errors, and challenging, in a number of cases demystifying, the legends for which Cheever himself was largely responsible. William Maxwell, Cheever's former editor at *The New Yorker* magazine, once called him a "story-making machine," and Cheever did not try to limit his capacity for invention to his fiction writing. Intensely private, remarkably inventive, and desirous of approval, Cheever has proven a less than trustworthy guide to his personal and family history. As a result, he is an especially fit as well as especially difficult subject for biographical study. Excepting Susan Cheever, Donaldson is Cheever's first biographer. Others have discussed his life, but always briefly, and invariably trusting Cheever's own account of the facts. In discussing his background, Cheever not only tended to embellish the facts, but indeed often provided multiple versions of the same incident. Although he cannot always sort out fact from fabrication, Donaldson's research enables him to reach the one inevitable conclusion which managed to elude previous critics. Whether, for example, Cheever's father owned a shoe factory, as Cheever liked to claim, or was a shoe salesman, as available records show, "hardly matters, except that it mattered to John Cheever." This and the numerous other conclusions Donaldson draws are always fair-minded, well-reasoned, and illuminating.

Even better, though, than these efforts to distinguish fact from fiction are the sections devoted to those periods of Cheever's life about which extraordinarily little has been known, the 1930's in particular: the time he spent in Boston with his older brother Fred, his move to New York immediately after, and the short time he spent in Washington, D.C. About the only gap Donaldson fails to fill in is the summer of 1931, which Cheever and his brother spent in Europe.

Fiction, Cheever was fond of saying, is not crypto-autobiography; it is instead the most exalted form of human communication. Yet reading his fiction in the light of Donaldson's biography makes clear that it is both: exalted and crypto-autobiographical. Much to his credit, however, Donaldson chooses not to plunder the novels and stories for what biographical parallels he can use. Instead, he is content to point out the general ways in which the literature illustrates the life, discerning general yet illuminating patterns rather than specific correspondences. He generally keeps his literary judgments to himself and never makes the mistake of actually confusing the fiction with autobiography. (In *Home Before Dark*, excerpts from the drafts of stories and novels that Cheever wrote in his journal are presented as if autobiographical disclosures; only readers familiar with the fiction will catch on to what Susan Cheever is doing.)

Donaldson provides a number of useful plot summaries of less familiar works, helpful overviews of the critical response to each of Cheever's novels and collections of stories, and a wealth of actual sources for certain characters and situations from the fiction (but, again, never so as even to suggest that the fiction can be reduced to a series of such sources and correspondences). He makes one especially useful point in discussing a major difference between the fiction and the life: In his writing, Cheever tended to find ways of resolving those filial, marital, and sexual crises that he was unable to resolve adequately in his own life. If there is a fault in Donaldson's treatment of the fiction, it is that except for his look at *Bullet Park* (1969), he fails to discuss or even consider the compositional process and history of any of Cheever's works. Since his is a biographical rather than a genetic study, the omission is understandable and mentioned here only because Donaldson does discuss the compositional history of this one novel. If the one, why not the others?

In *John Cheever*, as in his three previous biographical studies—*Poet in America: Winfield Townley Scott* (1972), *By Force of Will: The Life and Art of Ernest Hemingway* (1977), and *Fool for Love: F. Scott Fitzgerald* (1983)—Donaldson lays considerable but not undue emphasis on the writer's relationship with his parents. "The most unfortunate legacy" that Cheever received from his weak, unsuccessful father and his industrious, dominant mother was "the conviction that he was not loved." One measure of the dissatisfaction Cheever felt over his upbringing was his unwillingness to return to his native Quincy. Another is the insecurity that he continued to feel throughout his entire lifetime and that caused him to search out substitute homes: at the Yaddo colony, where he did some of his best writing, and in suburbia, where, ironically enough, Cheever's uncertain financial and professional status served less to alleviate than to exacerbate the insecurity he experienced as a child. Without ever once falling into the trap of Freudian reductivism, Donaldson draws a compelling portrait of a haunted man whose life was all too much of a piece.

Yet Cheever does not emerge from these pages as a victim. His decision to leave his brother Fred and make a career for himself in New York as a writer of fiction during the worst years of the Depression evidences the extent of his courage, determination, and Emersonian self-reliance. His steadfastness in the face of adversity becomes especially apparent in Donaldson's brief but telling handling of the relationship between Cheever the writer of short stories and Cheever the novelist. The usual view is that Cheever was a writer of short stories who tried to make the leap to the more demanding form of the novel (unsuccessfully, as his densest reviewers like to repeat). Although Donaldson clearly finds the stories more interesting than the novels, he persuasively argues that Cheever did not graduate from story to novel but instead was forced to abandon his early efforts at novel writing in order to keep himself fed and to establish his reputation as a writer of fiction (long or short). Short stories did not prove the way to wealth or success. His first collection earned for him a $250 advance and just $140 in additional royalties. Publishers were reluctant to invest in collections of stories, and reviewers often proved less than accepting of the collections that did appear. Concerning the critical response to *The Enormous Radio and Other Stories* (1953), for example, Donaldson writes, "In effect, Cheever laid ten years of his best work on the line . . . and was largely rebuked for the effort." Pegged as a writer of supposedly formulaic short stories, Cheever and his fragile ego continued to take a beating.

Cheever's marital situation offered little relief, and he often sought from others what his wife Mary, like his parents earlier, either could not or would not give him. Even in the 1930's, he seemed intent on securing surrogate parents for himself: brother Ben and then Malcolm Cowley, who accepted his first story, "Expelled," for publication in *The New Republic*; Hazel Hawthorne in Boston and Elizabeth Ames at Yaddo. As David Hays, a psychiatrist who treated Cheever in 1966, has concluded, Cheever wanted Mary to care for him, but because he saw her as not only the nurturing but also the "neglectful" mother, he turned to others for love and comfort. When it was clear that she did care for him, he felt dependent and so rebelled, again by having affairs. Donaldson makes note of Cheever's many amorous affairs, both hetero- and homosexual, drawing conclusions but not casting judgments and never indulging in voyeuristic exposé. Concerning Cheever's homosexuality, Donaldson proves especially discerning. He notes that Cheever "stayed in the closet and made his confessions in the fiction, where most readers chose to ignore them." He further notes that it is now possible to see "that homosexuality formed a central element in Cheever's fiction throughout his career," but one whose potential explosiveness Cheever used comic hyperbole to defuse. Finally, he plausibly claims that for Cheever homosexual feelings "were only tolerable within the context of a conventional family life."

If there is a weakness in *John Cheever*, it is in the handling of Cheever's later years. Donaldson provides a detailed account of the turmoil of Cheever's alcoholic period, of his triumph first over alcoholism and then over obscurity and adverse criticism with the publication of *Falconer* in 1977, of the financial security and fame that immediately followed, from the publication of the retrospective *The Collected Stories of John Cheever* (1978) to the honorary degree from Harvard University, the Pulitzer Prize, National Book Critics Circle award, and Howells Medal in 1979, and the National Medal for Literature bestowed just two months before his death on June 18, 1982, the same year he received a $500,000 advance from Alfred A. Knopf for his next two books. The accounting adds a certain poignancy to Cheever's story—of personal victories finally won and rewards belatedly bestowed. Oddly, what these pages fail to convey is what *Home Before Dark* provides in its treatment of this same period: the sense of disorientation and attacks of "otherness" that Cheever, ever the spiritual nomad, continued to experience. In his efforts to clarify the affirmation of Cheever's later years, Donaldson had to neglect this aspect to a certain degree. If this is a mistake in judgment, it is one of the very few he makes.

As for the question Donaldson raises at the very end of this biography, whether Cheever's reputation will eventually equal that of the writer he most resembles, F. Scott Fitzgerald, the answer is assuredly yes. As T. Coraghessan Boyle has pointed out, Cheever's art is truly inimitable in ways that the work of contemporary American fiction's most often imitated writer, Donald Barthelme, assuredly is not. Cheever's reputation will undoubtedly continue to grow, and with it the importance and usefulness of Donaldson's biography.

Robert A. Morace

Sources for Further Study

The Atlantic. CCLXII, August, 1988, p. 80.
Booklist. LXXXIV, May 15, 1988, p. 1554.
Kirkus Reviews. LVI, May 15, 1988, p. 737.
Library Journal. CXIII, July, 1988, p. 80.
Los Angeles Times Book Review. July 17, 1988, p. 1.
The New York Times Book Review. XCIII, July 10, 1988, p. 1.
Publishers Weekly. CCXXXIII, May 20, 1988, p. 72.
Time. CXXXI, June 27, 1988, p. 59.

KATHERINE MANSFIELD
A Secret Life

Author: Claire Tomalin (1933-)
Publisher: Alfred A. Knopf (New York). Illustrated. 292 pp. $22.95
Type of work: Literary biography
Time: 1888-1923
Locale: New Zealand, England, and Europe

A highly readable biography of Katherine Mansfield, stressing her secretive life of sexual freedom and her influence on D. H. Lawrence and Virginia Woolf

Principal personages:
KATHERINE MANSFIELD BEAUCHAMP, the short-story writer, the subject of the book
HAROLD and
ANNIE BEAUCHAMP, her parents
IDA CONSTANCE BAKER, her lifelong, devoted friend
GARNET TROWELL, the father of her stillborn child
GEORGE BOWDEN, her first husband
JOHN MIDDLETON MURRY, her second husband, the editor of the *Athenaeum*
D. H. LAWRENCE, the novelist, a sometime friend and neighbor of the Murrys
FRIEDA LAWRENCE, his wife
VIRGINIA WOOLF, the novelist, a rival of Katherine Mansfield
LADY OTTOLINE MORRELL, a patron of the arts and a Bloomsbury hostess
A. R. ORAGE, the editor of *New Age* magazine

Katherine Mansfield lived only thirty-four years and in that short time produced but a modest body of work, mostly short fiction. Normally, such circumstances would almost guarantee obscurity, since very few fiction writers have been able to establish reputations without at least one significant novel. (Edgar Allan Poe and Anton Chekhov are among Mansfield's few peers in this regard.) This being the case, it is particularly remarkable that Claire Tomalin is the third biographer in a decade to chronicle the short, tragic life of Katherine Mansfield. Jeffrey Meyers' *Katherine Mansfield* (1978) and Antony Alpers' definitive *The Life of Katherine Mansfield* (1980) would seem to leave little room for fresh information or insights. What can Tomalin claim to provide as justification for yet another biography?

To her credit, Tomalin faces this question on the opening pages of her study and offers as justification her reinterpretations of certain key events: Mansfield's sexual experimentation, which led to gonorrhea in 1909; her being blackmailed in 1920 by the same man who gave her this disease; and her influence on D. H. Lawrence and Virginia Woolf. Above all, in Tomalin's words, "It could even be said that her story hinges on a single physical fact. By becoming pregnant during the first months of her passionately sought freedom in London, she set in motion a sequence of events which ran to her death fourteen years later. . . ." In addition, Tomalin is the first woman to analyze objectively Mansfield's life and work. If Tomalin's biography does not offer startling new revelations, the shift in emphasis her book provides is reason enough to commend it to anyone familiar with Meyers' or Alpers' works, and the lively and frank manner of her reporting are more than sufficient to recommend it to new readers. This is, in short, a fine if somewhat limited piece of work.

Katherine Mansfield Beauchamp was born in 1888, the third daughter of Harold Beauchamp, a successful New Zealand banker whose life was sufficiently interesting and accomplished to warrant its own autobiography. Mansfield's mother was a typical woman of her time and class, determined to rear her daugthers as suitable wives and social ornaments. From the start, the chubby, bookish Mansfield was a rebel and outsider; eventually, she was written out of her mother's will. After a series of schools in Wellington, Mansfield and her sisters were allowed to attend Queen's College in Harley Street, London, from 1903 to 1906. Queen's was unusually progressive for its time, stressing individualism, academic achievement, and self-motivation rather than the usual stifling regimen of an English girls' boarding school. Here Mansfield met Ida Constance Baker, her devoted, almost slavish, friend, whom she alternately loved and mistreated for the rest of her life. This friendship and these years in London were crucial to Mansfield's development, for they helped to form her intellectually, artistically, and psychologically, particularly by fostering an inability to remain for long in one place.

After the freedom and glamour of London and Queen's, Wellington appeared provincial and dull. Mansfield tried to immerse herself in the local artistic life, but finally in 1908 she was able to secure a modest allowance of one hundred pounds a year and her father's permission to return to London. Edwardian London was awash with anti-Victorianism, and Mansfield quickly caught the spirit of emancipation. When a brief affair left her pregnant with Garnet Trowell's child, she hastily and duplicitously married George Bowden, whom she promptly left. The following year, Mrs. Beauchamp came from New Zealand to accompany Mansfield to Europe, where she miscarried. Shortly thereafter, she met Polish refugee Floryan Sobieniowski, who introduced her to Chekhov and swept her off her feet. Both actions were disastrous: The affair left Mansfield with gonorrhea, from which she suffered for the rest of her life, and from Chekhov she plagiarized her first successful short story, "The Child," for which Sobieniowski was later able to blackmail her. (Wisely, Tomalin places the details of this event and its discovery in an appendix, where they are available to those who want them but do not interrupt the narrative for those who do not.) Disillusioned with Sobieniowski, Mansfield briefly reunited with Bowden, who introduced her to A. R. Orage, editor of the avant-garde and politically radical *New Age*. Orage published a number of Mansfield's early fiction, at the same time helping her to streamline her prose and shape her stories. Her best early story, "A Birthday," was published under his tutelage, but unfortunately Mansfield failed to follow this lead and produced instead a series of works that Tomalin dismisses as "wasted energy."

Mansfield's association with *New Age* eventually led to a meeting with John

Middleton Murry, then at Cambridge and editor of *Rhythm*, who, in Tomalin's words, "was to play a crucial, and largely unfortunate, role in her life." Almost from the beginning, their relationship was ambivalent and strained by Murry's inability to love and Mansfield's contradictory need for independence and devotion. Their life together (they met in 1911, married in 1918) was characterized by long periods of separation punctuated by moments of bliss. Partly from poverty (at least at first), partly because of Mansfield's declining health, and partly because of her restless spirit, they were constantly on the move, from flats in London to cottages in the country to various addresses in Europe. Murry's loyalty was increasingly toward editing, first with *Rhythm*, then in 1919 with *Athenaeum*, which provided a generous salary, while Mansfield worked fitfully at fiction, devotedly at letter writing.

This peripatetic life and Murry's connections eventually brought Mansfield into the important literary circles of the day. From 1913 until 1916, the Murrys were very close to D. H. Lawrence, with Mansfield providing at least some material for the character of Gudrun in *Women in Love* (1920). Lawrence's temper and the Murrys' increasingly friendly relations with Lady Ottoline Morrell and the Bloomsbury group brought their friendship to a stormy close, though not before Mansfield had probably contracted tuberculosis from Lawrence. Meanwhile, Mansfield was forming an uneasy friendship and rivalry with Virginia Woolf, whose Hogarth Press published "Prelude" in 1918. It is probable that Mansfield suggested the basis for Woolf's first important short story, "Kew Gardens," thus precipitating an important change in Woolf's artistic development. Along the way she was courted by Bertrand Russell, entertained at Garsington, and maintained by the faithful but unappreciated services of Ida Baker.

The last five years of Mansfield's life form a sometimes tragic, sometimes pathetic record of illness and suffering. Unable to accept good medical advice, Mansfield pursued an almost suicidal course of various treatments for tuberculosis, apparently unaware until almost the end that she was also suffering from gonorrhea. If she had heeded sound advice, she might have lived; sadly, her last years provide from one point of view a morality tale whose theme is the awful price to be paid for personal license. That she produced some of her best work during this time is at once heroic and infuriating. What might she have written had she lived another ten or even five years?

Tomalin's handling of the complex life of Katherine Mansfield and her relations with her family, friends, and lovers is masterful. The narrative proceeds at a swift though stately pace, and her assessment of Mansfield as a woman is sympathetic, but balanced by frank assessments of her weaknesses and failures. At one point the biographer remarks candidly, "Katherine was a liar all her life." The book's subtitle, *A Secret Life*, is somewhat misleading, as it conjures up images of unrevealed sins and indiscretions. A more accurate term than "secret" would be "secretive," for Tomalin is particularly revealing in discussing Mansfield's need for masquerade, drama, and duplicity. Though she inspired desire in her lovers, jealousy in Virginia Woolf, and devotion in Ida Baker, Mansfield was often manipulative and duplicitous. She deserved better than she received from the self-centered and unreliable Murry, but in turn she often treated him shabbily while conversely idealizing his lukewarm affections. One of the great strengths of this biography, apart from the intrinsic interest of its narrative, is Tomalin's prose style—as swift and secure and economical as a bird in flight. Equally gratifying, she delves deeply into the contradictions of Mansfield's complex personality without resorting to murky psychologizing.

Having said all this, one still puts down Tomalin's book wondering whether Katherine Mansfield's interest to later generations is literary or biographical. Would she have received so much attention from critics and biographers had she lived a quiet life writing short stories? Or does her literary reputation rest at least in part on her associations with Lawrence and the Bloomsbury group, her friendships with the likes of Bertrand Russell and Aldous Huxley, her marriage to John Middleton Murry? Tomalin does not address such questions, and her brief and general analyses of Mansfield's stories do not provide much help to the reader. Tomalin's strength as a critic is her ability to make sharp, telling judgments about the general nature and quality of Mansfield's accomplishments, but these provide only a vague idea of Mansfield's literary accomplishments. Moreover, apart from linking "The Garden Party" to an event in her youth in New Zealand and tracing in outline the character of Murry as he appears in some of Mansfield's later stories, the author makes little attempt to relate the biography to the fiction. For readers seeking "pure" biography, this will seem an advantage; those wanting to connect the artist to her works will have to turn elsewhere or make the comparison themselves.

Tomalin's book is a fine example of the biographer's art. It is concise, well written, and clearly organized around central insights that shape and control but do not distort the life they elucidate. Occasionally, the reader longs for more detail, as for example in the brief treatment of Mansfield's flirtation with Mark Gertler. The episode is much clearer in Alpers' version. Thus, Tomalin's biography supplements but does not replace Antony Alpers'. Curious readers will want to consult both, Alpers for his wealth of detail, Tomalin for her sensitive and probing portrayal of a gifted, flawed, and fascinating artist.

Dean Baldwin

Sources for Further Study

The Atlantic. CCLXI, May, 1988, p. 94.
Booklist. LXXXIV, March 15, 1988, p. 1216.
Kirkus Reviews. LVI, January 15, 1988, p. 114.
London Review of Books. IX, November 26, 1987, p. 24.
New Statesman. CXIV, October 30, 1987, p. 29.
The New York Review of Books. XXXV, March 17, 1988, p. 28.

The New York Times Book Review. XCIII, May 15, 1988, p. 15.
Publishers Weekly. CCXXXIII, February 5, 1988, p. 77.
The Times Literary Supplement. January 8, 1988, p. 27.
The Washington Post Book World. XVIII, March 27, 1988, p. 4.

KHUBILAI KHAN
His Life and Times

Author: Morris Rossabi (1941-)
Publisher: University of California Press (Berkeley). Illustrated. 322 pp. $25.00
Type of work: Historical biography
Time: 1215-1294
Locale: Mongolia, China, and other Asian areas

A biographical portrait of Khubilai Khan with an emphasis on the period in which he lived

Principal personages:
KHUBILAI KHAN, a Mongol ruler, the founder of the Yüan Dynasty of China
ARIGH BOKE, his younger brother, who challenged him for the position of Great Khan
CHINGGIS KHAN, a Mongol ruler, his grandfather
MARCO POLO, a Venetian merchant and explorer who spent seventeen years in his service

In the English-speaking world, Samuel Taylor Coleridge's poem "Kubla Khan" has immortalized the founder of the Mongol Dynasty:

In Xanadu did Kubla Khan
A stately pleasure dome decree:
Where Alph, the sacred river, ran
Through caverns measureless to man
Down to a sunless sea.

Coleridge aside, Khubilai Khan was a significant historical figure. Among his accomplishments were the conquest of Southern China, the establishment of a "foreign" dynasty over all China, the forging of cultural and economic links with Europe, promotion of the arts and literacy, promotion of trade through the use of paper money, and improvements in transport and communications. Perhaps his most significant achievement, however, was his own evolution from pastoral nomadic ruler to administrator of an empire. It is this development that Morris Rossabi chronicles in *Khubilai Khan: His Life and Times*.

Rossabi's approach to his subject is basically topical, although chronological order is also a consideration. An initial chapter introduces the early Mongols and their traditions and places them in the context of the world of the twelfth and thirteenth centuries.

Having set the historical stage, Rossabi introduces Khubilai and discusses his early life, including his relationship with his mother and her family. Traditionally, the Mongol power structure required the lesser khans and the Great Khan to prove repeatedly their military and political abilities, and none was beyond challenge by another; succession was not automatic and almost never secure, as the continual rivalry between Khubilai and his younger brother Arigh Boke illustrates.

This conflict is discussed in a chapter chronicling Khubilai's struggles to maintain his position as Great Khan after his election in May of 1260. In this period Khubilai continued the Mongol tradition of expansion, moving his forces into Southern China in an effort (eventually successful) to subjugate the Southern Sung Dynasty and place all China under Mongol rule. Meanwhile, Khubilai succeeded in having the Korean king acknowledge fealty to him and placed a resident commissioner in Korea. With the aid of the Koreans, Khubilai launched his first attempt at subjugating the Japanese—which became his first failure at conquest, a sore point to which he would return.

Having secured his position for the time being against both foreign and domestic challenges, Khubilai began to concentrate on administrative and other matters relating to governing a diverse empire. Rossabi's fifth chapter chronicles Khubilai's activities as Emperor of China. A significant portion of his attention was given to economic problems and the launching of public works programs. One particularly far-reaching accomplishment was Khubilai's improvement of the transportation system. He promoted the building of roads throughout the empire; at the same time, he established a network of postal stations that greatly improved communications. "By the end of Khubilai's reign," Rossobi observes,

> China had more than 1,400 postal stations, which had at their disposal about 50,000 horses, 8,400 oxen, 6,700 mules, 4,000 carts, almost 6,000 boats, over 200 dogs, and 1,150 sheep. The individual stations varied considerably, but they all had hostels for visitors, kitchens, a main hall, enclosures for animals, and storehouses for grain. Under ideal conditions, the rider-messengers at the postal stations could cover 250 miles a day to deliver significant news, a remarkably efficient mail service for the thirteenth, or any other, century.

In this period Khubilai also recruited something of an international cadre of advisers in all areas of government. He drew from Chinese Confucians, Persian Muslims, Tibetan Buddhists, and European Christians. For a Mongol, Khubilai was remarkably tolerant; indeed, it could be said that domains under his rule enjoyed a greater degree of religious freedom than any other area in Asia or Europe at that time.

At the same time, Khubilai was extending his knowledge of the domains under his rule, believing that he "had a responsibility to promote the cultural expressions of diverse lands and ethnic groups." This commitment was balanced, however, by a universalist vision. In this respect Khubilai's approach is best illustrated in his choice of a written script to be used in the administration of his domain. Rather than choose the Chinese ideographs or the Monogolian script, he chose to create a new official script that would "help unify his realm and assert his claim to universal rule." To head this project, he designated the Tibetan lama 'Phags-pa. The lama developed an alphabet, based upon Tibetan, which was square in shape—hence the name "Square Script." As Rossabi notes, this choice showed Khubilai's concern for "universality":

> It emphasized and was derived from the colloquial version of the Mongol language, it blended well with Khubilai's endeavor to encourage the employment of the colloquial in writing—

> even, for example, the use of coloquial Chinese for official government documents in China. In short, the 'Phags-pa alphabet appeared ideally suited to transcribe the languages, those with alphabets and those with characters, in Khubilai's domain, to serve as a universal script, and to contribute to the unification of the frequently antagonistic peoples under Mongol rule.

The development of this script and the growth of printed texts under Khubilai "offered more access to books and initiated the rise in literacy characteristic of the Ming and Ch'ing dynasties"—the successors to the Mongol Yüan Dynasty established by Khubilai.

In spite of these and other achievements, Khubilai's administration of the empire began to suffer as his attentions turned elsewhere. In chapter 7, Rossabi details "mismanagement and the Chinese response." The formulation of policies for financing and administrating the empire had been placed largely in the hands of Muslim experts. Their real and perceived excesses caused difficulties in the Chinese areas, especially after the conquest and integration of the Southern Sung empire in 1279. In the 1280's also came the loss of Khubilai's most experienced advisers, making him more dependent on the non-Chinese and causing more tensions. This period marked the beginning of Khubilai's decline.

The last chapter of the book chronicles this period of decline, during which Khubilai became increasingly concerned with conquest of the Japanese and other Asian peoples. Personal troubles such as the deaths of his wife and favorite son caused him to seek solace in drink and food. As a result he grew obese and suffered from ailments associated with alcoholism. At the same time, he began to lose interest in the details of governing the empire, removing himself from domestic affairs and concentrating on "foreign adventures." This fact was noticed by several Mongol khans, who made strong challenges to Khubilai's rule in this period. Despite such threats, he managed to arrange for his grandson's "proper, orderly, and unchallenged succession to the throne." Still, infighting continued, leading to the collapse of the Yüan Dynasty in 1368, less than seventy-five years after Khubilai's death.

Rossabi's biography of Khubilai Khan is a first-rate work of scholarship, revealing a mastery of primary sources. Throughout, Rossabi points out the bias in the sources used as he compares various accounts of the same event. This is historical writing as it should be—identifying diverse interpretations and guiding the reader through the chaff to the heart of the matter. Rossabi's style is simple, direct, and readable. While some knowledge of world history during the twelfth and thirteenth centuries would be helpful, the general reader should have no trouble understanding the work, which offers a wealth of information about the period.

Steven A. McCarver

Sources for Further Study

Boston Globe. May 29, 1988, p. 15.

Kirkus Reviews. LVI, March 15, 1988, p. 439.

Library Journal. CXIII, April 15, 1988, p. 79.
The New Republic. CXCVIII, April 18, 1988, p. 46.
The New York Times Book Review. XCIII, September 11, 1988, p. 27.
San Francisco Review of Books. XII, Spring, 1988, p. 40.
The Times Literary Supplement. August 5, 1988, p. 849.

THE KING OF CHILDREN
A Biography of Janusz Korczak

Author: Betty Jean Lifton (1926-)
Publisher: Farrar, Straus & Giroux (New York). Illustrated. 404 pp. $22.50
Type of work: Biography
Time: 1878-1942
Locale: Warsaw, Poland

A sensitive biography of Janusz Korczak, and an analysis of his educational theories, his works, and his world

Principal personages:
JANUSZ KORCZAK (HENRYK GOLDSZMIT), the Polish educator
STEFANIA (STEFA) WILCZYNSKA, a partner at his orphanage
MARYNA ROGOWSKA FALSKA, the founder of a Warsaw orphanage managed on his principles

Betty Jean Lifton has written about children a number of times; however, the subject of Janusz Korczak was new to her, as it will be to most American readers. After hearing about him from a European friend, she began to investigate his life and works. The result is a highly detailed portrait of a very unusual man who defended the rights and welfare of the child despite the ignorance, apathy, intolerance, and war that marked his era.

Janusz Korczak was born Henryk Goldszmit in 1878 to middle-class Jewish parents in Warsaw. Lifton writes movingly about how young Henryk was not allowed to play with the rough children in the neighborhood and, therefore, had to create his own world in the drawing room to which he was confined. His early years were also marked by the increasing madness of his father. After his father was institutionalized, he had to become the man of the house. The result of these circumstances was that Henryk lost his childhood; he never had the freedom and innocence of the child. In an attempt to recover that lost childhood, he spent the rest of his life caring for children and living in their world.

Young Goldszmit went to medical school in Warsaw and was writing at the same time. He had decided to become a doctor rather than a full-time writer because "medicine is deeds" and literature only words. His first important work was *Dziecko salonu* (1906; the child in the drawing room). The book tells the story of a child who has "lost his soul" in conforming to his parents' wishes. When he becomes an adult, he rebels and enters the larger world of experience among all classes of people; this choice finally leads him to discover his vocation as a writer. The book clearly reflects Goldszmit's own experiences; he, too, was in the process of winning his independence from an overbearing mother by becoming an author as well as a doctor. He chose pediatrics for his specialty. As he was completing a residency, Goldszmit was conscripted into the Russian army during the Russo-Japanese War.

When Goldszmit returned from the war in 1906, he found that he was famous as Janusz Korczak, the pen name he had chosen for *Dziecko salonu*. He put into practice his theories about children in his pediatric work and in his administration of a summer camp. At camp, Korczak (as he was now known) found that the children resisted the programs and instruction he presented to them; he learned that it was essential to have order and discipline so that children might benefit from any instruction. He acknowledged his naïve views and set about finding ways to correct the situation. After establishing discipline, he set up a children's court and a newspaper, hoping that the children would govern themselves.

In 1910, Korczak gave up his lucrative private medical practice to become the director of an orphanage for Jewish children. He participated in the planning of the facility and the methods that would be used to educate the children. He went to a number of countries to investigate orphanages and how they dealt with the children; while in England, he came to a dramatic decision. He decided not to have a child of his own but to dedicate his life to "uphold the child and defend his rights." This decision was the result of his own experiences as a deprived child with an irresponsible parent; moreover, Korczak was an eternal child and considered that he could love all the children with whom he came in contact better than one of his own.

The orphanage opened in 1912, and Korczak began to create the Children's Republic of which he had dreamed. Children were to govern themselves, to have their own court and newspaper, and even to decide which of the teachers should be retained or dismissed. Korczak had some difficulties with members of the Jewish community, who thought that the orphanage was "too Polish" because Korczak had not limited the school to Jewish orphans. Korczak was a Jew but also a patriotic Pole, and he tried to overcome sectarian differences between the groups in Poland. Furthermore, in Korczak's view a child had no divisive nationality or religion but automatically belonged to the world of children.

Korczak's experiment in a workable community at the orphanage was interrupted by World War I. Once more, he was forced to serve in the Russian army. He did, however, make some use of this enforced tour by writing *Jak Kochać dziecko* (1920-1921; how to love a child). The book declares that it is first necessary to see the child "as a separate being with the inalienable right to grow into the person he was meant to be." He was one of the first to see the child as having a separate identity rather than being a small adult.

After the war, Korczak returned to the orphanage, but he had met two women who were to be very important in his life. The first, Stefania Wilczynska (who later insisted on being called Madame Stefa), was a partner who shared Korczak's philosophy and dedication to the child. She was to remain with him until the end. Lifton suggests that she may have loved Korczak, but their relationship remained a working one, and she finally came to see him as another child she needed to nurture. The other woman, the wealthy Maryna Falska, established an orphanage in Warsaw on Korczak's principles. Korczak visited and helped in running this orphanage as well as the one he founded. There were some differences of opinion between him and Falska, however, and they would sever their relationship later in the crisis of Nazi occupation.

The period between the two wars was the happiest of Korczak's life. The orphanage became famous, and his ideas on children were beginning to be accepted. He also wrote his greatest book during this period, *Król Maciuś Pierwszy* (1923; *Matthew, the Young King*, 1928, best known as *King Matt the First*). King Matt is a child-king who thinks that children can rule more wisely than adults. They and King Matt lack the necessary experience, however, and the kingdom is invaded and conquered. The book, which has been described as "the eternal tragedy of every noble reformer," comments ironically on Korczak's attempts at reform, especially his desire to create a children's republic. One of Korczak's endearing qualities is his ability to see clearly and at the same time make light of his own most cherished ideals.

Lifton devotes a number of chapters to describing the fully functioning orphanage under Korczak. He did not provide the children with vocational education, since he believed that in the short time they were with him they should receive a "moral education." He attempted to guide the children to discover and enforce their own system of justice. Children would sue one another for offenses and thereby regulate their behavior; if an offender acted in an antisocial manner, he faced expulsion from the orphanage. Korczak's guiding presence and his rewards and compromises helped the system succeed. He established a close relationship with the children and told them stories and played with them as well as ministering to their needs. He later did an inventory and found that only a very few of his wards ended up badly. Most became responsible citizens, and a few even became teachers in the orphanage.

The happy period began to end with the political turmoil of the 1930's; some members of the staff became Communists, and right-wing Polish groups began to complain that Polish children should not be in an institution run by a Jew. Hitler was coming to power, and the anti-Semitic Fascist ideology increasingly dominated public life. Wilczynska, who took care of most of the practical matters in the orphanage, visited Palestine at the urging of a former pupil. She began to see life there as safer and more fulfilling than the one she had known so well in Warsaw. Even Korczak visited Palestine and talked about taking up residence there. He was getting old and had many health problems, and he no longer was a bold educational reformer but someone trying to preserve what had been accomplished.

When World War II began in 1939, Poland became the first nation to fall victim to the Nazis. The orphanage and its leader were threatened by the German occupation forces, the Polish collaborators, and right-wing anti-Semites. Korczak had to go about begging and cajoling in order to get scarce food and fuel to keep the orphanage going. At one point, he was arrested for refusing to wear the yellow armband the Nazis required of Jews. It was a difficult time, but Korczak did his best to preserve the mood and aim of the orphanage, even though the number of orphans had swelled from 100 to 150 and finally 180.

The Nazis then decided to isolate and restrict the Jews to the Warsaw ghetto. The orphanage was, however, outside the boundary line, so Korczak exchanged buildings with a Polish high school within the ghetto. The difficulty of supplying food for all the children increased, but Korczak managed to keep things going by appealing to the Jewish Council. Wilczynska had an opportunity to emigrate to Palestine but decided that her place was with the children and Korczak. Korczak also rejected an offer to leave; he knew that the children needed him more than ever at this time. He also refused to hide the Jewish children outside the ghetto. He imagined their fear if they had to be hidden in dark closets and decided that it was best for him and his children to remain where they were.

Korczak was becoming emaciated, eating only what he needed to survive. The demands of the Nazis for men and material increased, and the ghetto was being stripped of whatever was of value. All smugglers were executed, and death squads assassinated a large number of people on the Nazis' list. Yet Korczak did not abandon his children. He tried his best to give some aid also to the thousands of orphans wandering the streets of the ghetto; he could do little and most perished, but he tried to alleviate their suffering.

In 1942, Nazi soldiers appeared at the orphanage and ordered all Jews into the street. Korczak and Wilczynska did their best to keep the children calm; he carried a child on his shoulder and took another by the hand. Some witnesses have said that they saw a Nazi officer hand Korczak a white slip signifying permission to return home, but he refused to leave his children. He joined them in their journey to the death camp at Treblinka. Korczak, Wilczynska, and all the children perished there; there are no surviving witnesses to report when or how. He remained faithful to the vow he had made earlier in his life and lived and died with his children.

Drawing on her interviews with men and women who knew Korczak and on the Warsaw ghetto journal that Korczak wrote and hid, Lifton has constructed a compelling tale of a rare human being. Korczak had an insight into the world of children that was uncanny. He became more alive and animated when he met or talked to a child. Moreover, he never wavered in his defense of the child as an entity and of the children under his care. His decision to remain with the orphanage children was only the final confirmation of a lifetime of commitment to all children.

James Sullivan

Sources for Further Study

Chicago Tribune. May 1, 1988, XIV, p. 1.
Choice. XXVI, September, 1988, p. 177.
Kirkus Reviews. LVI, February 15, 1988, p. 264.
Library Journal. CXIII, August, 1988, p. 157.
Los Angeles Times Book Review. May 22, 1988, p. 12.

The New Republic. CXCVIII, June 6, 1988, p. 44.
The New York Review of Books. XXXV, September 29, 1988, p. 7.
The New York Times Book Review. XCIII, July 31, 1988, p. 16.
Publishers Weekly. CCXXXIII, February 12, 1988, p. 75.
The Washington Post Book World. XVIII, June 19, 1988, p. 14.

THE KING OF THE FIELDS

Author: Isaac Bashevis Singer (1904-)
Translated from the Yiddish by the author
Publisher: Farrar, Straus & Giroux (New York). 244 pp. $18.95
Type of work: Historical novel
Time: The Middle Ages
Locale: Poland

This disturbing novel, set in an ancient Poland filled with lust and violence, raises philosophical questions about the nature of man and his world

Principal characters:
CYBULA, the aging leader of the Lesniks
LASKA, his daughter, the wife of Krol Rudy
KORA, his mistress
YAGODA, Kora's daughter, his wife
KROL RUDY, the red-haired leader of a band of Poles
NOSEK, a Polish *knieze* (knight)
BEN DOSA, a Jewish shoemaker from Babylon
KOSOKA, the mistress first of Cybula, then of Krol Rudy; later Ben Dosa's wife
KROL YODLA, the leader of another band of Poles

In *The King of the Fields* Isaac Bashevis Singer returns to territory familiar to his readers. Set in ancient, rural Poland, it is highly reminiscent of *Der Knekht* (1961; *The Slave*, 1962). Once again, a Jew, Ben Dosa, torn from his homeland, becomes the servant of violent Gentiles. Once more, a non-Jewish woman, Kosoka, falls in love with him, and he initially resists her advances. Finally, he recognizes that she is attracted not only to him but also to his religion, and he recognizes his own love for her. Together they flee, she converts to Judaism, and they marry.

Also typical of Singer's work are the demons and spirits who seem to rule the characters' lives. Many of the Lesniks, a hunter-gatherer tribe, believe in the power of Baba Yaga and make blood sacrifices to her. They regard the invading Poles as sacrilegious for their attempts to cultivate the ground, since plowing and sowing desecrate Mother Earth. Some Lesniks view the Polish leader, Krol Rudy, as a *smok*, "part man, part snake, part devil," who commands other spirits and deceives people. Cybula, the Lesnik leader, worships a variety of nature gods, though he regards Shmiercz, lord of death, as the most powerful deity.

In this primitive world, carnality and violence abound. Both Krol Rudy and Cybula rape the twelve-year-old Yagoda as soon as they meet her. Kora, Yagoda's mother, sleeps with everyone in the camp. Later she successfully plots the death of the Poles, who have killed and raped many of the Lesniks. She attempts to sacrifice Kosoka to Baba Yaga, and she dies by the hand of her own daughter. These elements, though more pronounced than in Singer's previous works, will come as no surprise.

In a number of ways, however, *The King of the Fields* differs, not always successfully, from the author's earlier fiction. His best works have in a sense been quasi-historical, quasi-imaginative re-creations of the past. *Sotan in Goray* (1935; *Satan in Goray*, 1955) and *The Slave* explore seventeenth century Polish and Jewish life in the wake of the Chmielnicki massacres (1648-1649). *Die Familie Muskat* (1950; *The Family Moskat*, 1950) and *Neshome Ekspeditsyes* (1974; *Shosha*, 1978) consider the early twentieth century Jewish community in Warsaw. *The King of the Fields* remains in Poland but moves back well before these other novels, into an era that is curiously indeterminate. The Lesniks are an illiterate people just emerged from their nomadic state. The Poles are little more advanced; they, too, are illiterate and barbaric, but they rely on agriculture and have a more clearly defined social structure. Such details suggest the pre-Christian era, but Singer also refers to followers of Jesus praying in Roman catacombs, thus hinting at early imperial Rome. Cybula and Nosek visit Miasto, a medieval walled city, where they meet Ben Dosa, who comes from post-Talmudic Babylon; later, a Catholic bishop comes to convert the Poles (c. A.D. 900). Laska, a Lesnik, even speaks a bit of Yiddish. German neighbors are called *Niemcies*, which is in fact the ancient Polish name for them. Singer even gives the correct derivation of the word as meaning unintelligible. Polish knights he calls *kniezes*, though actually the *knez* served as head of the village. The Lesniks apparently have even less historical authenticity, seemingly a fictional tribe taking its name from Leszko, grandfather of the first Polish king, Mieszko I, who in turn may be the source of the bishop Mieczyslaw, another apparently ahistorical character.

In *The Slave* Singer suggests that, in the words of T. S. Eliot, "time present and time past/ Are both perhaps present in time future,/ And time future contained in time past." In that novel the widower Jacob, about to cross the Vistula, reflects on his biblical namesake.

> His name was Jacob also; he too had lost a beloved wife . . . among strangers. . . . Like the Biblical Jacob, he was crossing the river, bearing only a staff, pursued by another Esau. . . . Perhaps four thousand years would again pass; somewhere, at another river, another Jacob would walk mourning another Rachel. Or who knew, perhaps it was always the same Jacob and the same Rachel.

All time, then, is eternally present. The earlier novel conveyed this view in a coherent narrative. There the peasants seemed prehistoric; here they actually are. The effect in the present work is disorienting and raises the question whether the chaos in the novel is intentional or inadvertent. Is the novel a conscious depiction of Singer's worldview or an unconscious representation of the author's mind?

Also unusual for Singer is the role of the Jewish character, who appears only midway through the book and remains peripheral to the action. In a novel devoid of attractive figures, he proves more appealing than most, but even he is flawed. His treatment of Kosoka is harsh, and while he rejects her largely because he wants to remain loyal to his wife in Babylon, at the end of the novel he marries her anyway.

The most fascinating personality is Cybula, for only he seeks to understand his world. Ben Dosa never doubts, whether he is spurning Kosoka or wedding her, serving the Poles and Lesniks or fleeing them. Nosek, too, despite his real wisdom, believes that he is all-knowing, though he easily falls prey to the merchants of Miasto. Virtually all the others in the work seek only sensual gratification. When Laska tells her father that her husband, Krol Rudy, has died, her grief seems to derive solely from the loss of a sexual partner. As she says, "Tatele, I need a man." Neither Ben Dosa nor Bishop Mieczyslaw can teach the Poles and Lesniks, who remain attached to their brutal paganism. When the bishop recounts the parable of the wise and foolish virgins, the only lesson Krol Rudy derives is that "the bridegroom was left with only five virgins . . . ? Well, it's better than nothing!"

Only Cybula appreciates the beauty and wonder of the universe. Much as he hates the Poles and their new ways, he finds their wheat field strangely lovely. He persuades the Lesniks to abandon their plans to destroy the crops and kill the newcomers, and despite having been reared as a hunter he begins to question this way of life. "Why did a stag or even a hare deserve to be killed?" he wonders, and he realizes that "those who plowed and sowed harmed no one." He works hard to learn the written language Ben Dosa teaches, and he asks about the origin of evil. When Kora imprisons Kosoka in a pigsty, Cybula rescues her. He recognizes that beneath their differences, Jew and Catholic worship the same God, revere the same Bible. As Ben Dosa observes, Cybula seems a likely disciple, the typical Singer God-seeker who ponders the eternal questions and thus undergoes spiritual regeneration. One expects him to become a vegetarian, a nonviolent peace-lover, perhaps even a Jew. Ultimately, though, he rejects the God he seems so close to finding. "There is only one god, and he is all there is—the god of death, Shmiercz," he tells Ben Dosa. Deciding that man lacks free will in a universe ruled by malign forces, he leads Yagoda to the top of a mountain, where they will apparently commit suicide.

Singer's vision has grown progressively darker. In *The Slave* Jacob and Wanda/Sarah are revered as saints after a seeming miracle. In *Sonim de Geshichte fun a Liebe* (1966; *Enemies: A Love Story*, 1972) the God-deniers are destroyed, but those who accept Him are saved. *Shosha* ends more ambiguously, as Aaron Greidinger and Haiml Chentshiner wait for an answer to the eternal questions. Even in that work, though, from death comes regeneration. Aaron, like Cybula, sees the suffering of animals; unlike Cybula, Aaron becomes a vegetarian. Haiml loses his first wife in the Holocaust, but he creates a new life for himself in Israel. Aaron and Haiml remain in the dark, but they still believe that an answer exists to the riddle of the universe and that they may yet find that answer.

Ben Dosa in *The King of the Fields* claims that "the true God is the God of life," but the thrust of the novel does not support such a vision. Poles kill Lesniks, Lesniks kill Poles, other Poles come to supplant the Lesniks once more. Cybula, Krol Rudy, and Krol Yodla succeed one another as king of the fields. At the very moment that Kosoka prepares to begin a new life with Ben Dosa, the glass of wine slips from her hand, an omen that she will "die in childbirth." Yagoda is pregnant with Cybula's baby, but Cybula comments on the last page of the novel that "nothing will come of it." Laska's child is sick; Cybula predicts that the boy will die, but if he lives his fate will be no better. In a form of the ancient fertility rite, Yagoda kills her mother, but instead of regeneration there follows only apparent suicide.

Throughout his career Singer has been accused of pessimism. His earlier works suggested that such criticism was misguided; *The King of the Fields* indicates that it was merely premature.

Joseph Rosenblum

Sources for Further Study

Booklist. LXXXIV, June 1, 1988, p. 1626.
Chicago Tribune. November 6, 1988, XIV, p. 5.
Kirkus Reviews. LVI, August 15, 1988, p. 1188.
Library Journal. CXIII, July, 1988, p. 96.
The New York Times Book Review. XCIII, October 16, 1988, p. 12.
Publishers Weekly. CCXXXIV, September 2, 1988, p. 86.
Time. CXXXII, October 31, 1988, p. 88.
USA Today. October 21, 1988, p. D4.
The Washington Post Book World. XVIII, October 23, 1988, p. 3.

KRAZY KAT
A Novel in Five Panels

Author: Jay Cantor (1948-   )
Publisher: Alfred A. Knopf (New York). Illustrated. 250 pp. $16.95
Type of work: Novel
Time: The 1980's
Locale: The United States

A novel that is at once a parody and a pastiche in which author Jay Cantor mixes and matches forms at least as well as he does a host of social themes

Principal characters:
KAT, the novel's feline heroine, who metamorphoses from comic-strip character to nightclub performer
IGNATZ MOUSE, the rodent who tries to get Kat to work again; later her accompanist in her nightclub act
THE PRODUCER, a maker of films and backer of other entertainments, including Kat's act

In *The Death of Che Guevara* (1983), Jay Cantor mixed fact and fiction, history and imagination to create a deeply meditative first novel. In *Krazy Kat: A Novel in Five Panels* he attempts to fashion another equally inventive literary hybrid, a comic-strip novel. "Shall we give 'em a new one today?" asks the Kat in a panel from the original strip used on the novel's title page. "Have you got a new one?" replies the Kat's beloved nemesis, Ignatz Mouse. Cantor certainly does, for in conception if not entirely in execution, his comic-strip novel is brilliant. What if Krazy Kat, Ignatz Mouse, and other of the strip's regular characters (Offissa Bull Pup, Joe Stork, Mrs. Mice) walked—or perhaps awoke—into the nuclear age? What if the strip ended in 1944 not because of the death of its creator, George Herriman, but because the explosion of the first atomic bomb at Alamogordo that same year left Krazy too depressed to work? What if the bricks hurled by the Mouse at the ever-loving, ever-innocent Kat escalated into bombs, as well as contemporary bricks of racism and sexism—in short, anything that does what an atom bomb or a cartoon does: make people into shadows, the round into the flat?

The novel's structure is as simple as that of a comic strip. Sandwiched between a prefatory Thornton Wilderish "Our Town" and two appended songs by Ignatz Mouse are the novel's five "panels," or chapters. "The Gadget" depicts the cause and consequence of the Kat's malaise: the bomb which she at first mistakes for another sign of, or vehicle for, the Mouse's love. The Kat cannot work in the age of nuclear anxiety; the Mouse's task is to show her that she must, and much of the novel's humor derives from his cartoonish efforts to cure her of her dis-ease. When the letters he writes under the nom de plume of an admiring, coaxing J. Robert Oppenheimer fail, the Mouse turns to other, more dramatic means. The novel's second panel, "The Talking Cure," written in the form of the Mouse's self-justifying,

Freudian-slip-laden letters to Offissa Bull Pup, concerns his efforts to use psychoanalysis to make the Kat well by making her "round." His goal is not, however, simply to restore her to what she was before but to transform her and the comic-strip form into something new as well: "America *needs* a truly *democratic* high art. America needs the round comic strip!" "The Talking Cure" is so wonderfully and pointedly funny because psychoanalysis, particularly in its most popular manifestations, so readily lends itself to satire, for it frequently misses the point by emphasizing reductive deterministic causes and allegorical correspondences. (What makes the brick hurt, the correspondence-school psychoanalyst Mouse tells the Kat, is her fear of intimacy.)

When "The Talking Cure" fails, which is to say when the panel ends, "The Talking Pictures" begins. Like the Mouse, the Producer is an exploitative male whose power to exploit derives in large measure from the willingness of others to conform to his image of them. His first "bomb" is his decision to make a Krazy Kat film in which all the parts will be played by humans (the fate of Popeye, Superman, Wonderwoman, and Steve Canyon), and the second is his plan for spinoffs: television shows, brick-shaped lunch boxes, and the like. Eventually, however, the Producer abandons his plans when he discovers that Kat and the others do not own their own rights. *"Hearst still owns you! And he won't sell!* Not at a price a sane man can afford!"

Twice defeated, the Mouse turns in "The Possessed" to armed revolution. The chapter title reminds the reader of Fyodor Dostoevski's great work about political revolution, while the radical organization which the Mouse founds, COMISALAD-ONE (Comic Strip Artists Liberation Army, Division One), cartoonishly echoes the Symbionese Liberation Army, with Kat playing the part of hostage, à la Patty Hearst. Taking "*Death to the Fascist Copyright Holders Who Suck the Brains of Avant-Garde Artists*" as their motto, Mouse and his COMISALAD colleagues advocate radical art, politics, and sex. Their words come to nothing, however, as the Producer and his SWAT team use yet another modern medium, television, to trick the group into believing that the revolution has already begun.

As the group is taken, Kat's "consciousness flickered," and the form this consciousness takes is outlined in the last and longest of the novel's five panels. In "Venus in Furs," the Kat's comic-strip näiveté continues to give way to the malaise of uncertainty, as she worries about her sexual, social, and racial roles. At one point, she takes time from the dissertation she is writing on Jasper Johns to have an adulterous affair with a famous art historian, who, she says, makes her feel three-dimensional, and at another she plays masochist to the Mouse's Sade, perversely quoting the line, "To bow and to bend is our delight," from the old Shaker hymn "Simple Gifts," which forms an important if understated motif throughout the novel.

"One year later" Kat and Mouse have their virtue and perseverance (respectively) rewarded when they make the leap from art history and pop psychoanalysis to the art of entertainment. As an article in the trade paper *Variety* explains,

> It looks like the man whom the Hearst Corporation calls simply the Producer has the making of another of his multimedia hits in Kat Higgs Bosun and her piano player, Ignatz. Their combination of torch numbers, original specialty items, and between-times blue George-and-Gracie-like chatter, are already wow on the club, concert hall, and college circuit.

Ignatz, always contentious, finds the Producer's plans distasteful, but he is even more critical of the highbrow critic whose approving essay on their act the Mouse dismisses as condescending and self-serving. Kat (now Kate) discerns something deeper: a genuine appreciation of their simple art. As she explains in defense of the critic (and of Cantor's cartoon novel as well), "It's a complicated business nowadays to produce *real* simplicity." Kat had earlier tried to explain the art of Jasper Johns along similar lines. His paintings, she said, aspire to innocence and flatness, to being nothing more and nothing less than what they are. Yet Kat herself is not entirely satisfied by her apologia. The modern arts, she feels, do lack something essential: real pain, real compassion, real pleasure—in sum, "all the good things she felt when Ignatz played and she sang some standard." Whereas the high arts seek to surprise and shock, the low arts attempt something quite different but perhaps no less difficult and certainly no less important: "just to master a sorrow, improvise a pleasure." The question is whether the two can, or even should, be combined in the postwar nuclear age, when innocence is out and anxiety and suspicion are in, a time when "less suddenly seemed like lots, and next to nothing was best of all." Cantor clearly wants much more, an art more than minimalist, one which is uniform yet various, simple yet inventive, entertaining yet provoking, näive yet postmodern. What he wants is *Krazy Kat*, a kind of avant-garde pop art in which one may detect irony in Kat's reference to the "great works by Count Tolstoy and Duke Ellington." Kat's simple affirmations can no longer be thought sufficient; yet when she decides to abandon dissertation for singing, art history for art, in order "to show her true soul before an audience, to sing, to give pleasure," it is as Kate rather than as Kat, as the possessor of a new kind of awareness which allows her to revitalize the old forms for a new and more troubling age without surrendering to that age.

Early in the novel, Kat seems to find evidence of such a surrender in contemporary comic-strip cats such as Garfield and Heathcliff that she judges too "round," and "servile," which is to say too humanly and obsessively self-conscious. Cantor's own obsessive self-consciousness fully evidences itself throughout the novel, particularly in its range of intertextual reference which extends from brief allusions to parodies of entire literary and subliterary forms. There is even a voice that sounds suspiciously like the one D. H. Lawrence adopts in his brilliant but eccentric *Studies in Classic American Literature* (1923): "America wants its popular culture to be a prelapsarian playpen, sex-hunger without teeth. America hates its soul-making geniuses. You are too small—too *spiritually* small." Cantor's attitude toward popular culture seems to be at once reverential and critical. He likes the simplicity and näiveté of the Krazy Kat strip, even as he recognizes it as a technical and ideological anachronism. Yet he appears skeptical of the virtues of the merely modern (or postmodern), which tends to be too detached and exploitative in its efforts to be innovative and up-to-date, even as he recognizes that Herriman's strip was itself a work of aesthetic innovation.

Its inventiveness and transformative power make *Krazy Kat* a truly remarkable fiction. Yet Cantor places a burden on this comic-strip novel that it cannot quite bear. In a telephone interview with Barth Healey of *The New York Times Book Review*, Cantor has said that Kate "discovers that if she wants power, she must act for herself. We are not talking about sexual power, but the power to build her own artistic career. We would like sexuality to be about love but often it is about power. She has to explore her need and desire for power first." Here, and in the novel, Cantor does to Kat what Mouse does when he forces her to submit to his talking cure: He hits her with a kind of verbal brick. Like its title character, the novel begins to reel under the weight of too many contemporary burdens: sexism, racism, terrorism, psychoanalysis, class conflict, being and nothingness, the uses and abuses of television and film, the fate of the novel, the threat of nuclear extinction. Especially grating is the preemptive strike Cantor launches against any reader who may object to this thematic and topical overkill. Such readers, the novel implies, seek to limit the novelist's freedom, from the perspective of either the highbrow academic critic or the lowbrow consumer.

Although *Krazy Kat* is not an entirely successful novel in terms of what it achieves, it is nevertheless remarkable for what it risks. It risks, for example, being as flat and dimensionless as the comic strip. It makes "roundness" (the Mouse's buzzword) a problem that the characters only begin to master as the novel develops. Cantor captures all the flatness of character and speech as well as of time and place, all the monologic and monochromatic quality of the comic strip, in a work that is neither strip nor (conventional) novel but a hybrid form in which each keeps the other alive by transforming it into something new through a process of endless metamorphosis and temporary reconciliation. Just as remarkable is the confusion of realms. His comic-strip characters want to become real (round), but in doing so they often become merely more cartoonish and absurd. Their striving for roundness helps to make plain just how flat and cartoonish modern man has become and how like a comic strip his life now seems. If in *Krazy Kat* Cantor does not succeed quite as well as Robert Coover does in his similarly inventive but more energetically written postmodern political satire, "The Cat in the Hat for President" (1968), he has written a work which seeks to continue the tradition of the novel by extending its range and daring.

Robert A. Morace

Sources for Further Study

Booklist. LXXXIV, January 15, 1988, p. 827.

Boston Review. XIII, February, 1988, p. 30.

Choice. XXV, May, 1988, p. 1398.
Kirkus Reviews. LV, December 1, 1987, p. 1636.
Library Journal. CXIII, January, 1988, p. 97.
Los Angeles Times Book Review. January 10, 1988, p. 3.
The Nation. CCXLVI, May 14, 1988, p. 682.
The New York Times. CXXXVII, January 6, 1988, p. 19.
The New York Times Book Review. XCIII, January 24, 1988, p. 1.
Newsweek. CXI, February 29, 1988, p. 68.
Publishers Weekly. CCXXXII, December 11, 1987, p. 47.
The Village Voice. XXXIII, February 2, 1988, p. 64.
The Washington Post. January 11, 1988, p. B2.

LANGUAGE IN LITERATURE

Author: Roman Jakobson (1896-1982)
Edited by Krystyna Pomorska and Stephen Rudy
Publisher: Harvard University Press (Cambridge, Massachusetts). 592 pp. $25.00
Type of work: Linguistics and literary criticism

This volume collects many of Roman Jakobson's most important essays from his early association with the Russian Formalists, through his seminal work in the Prague School, and up to his later writings on language and literature during his more than forty years of residence in the United States

If by no other measure than sheer longevity and productivity, Roman Jakobson would have to be counted among the most significant figures in literary study of the twentieth century. A precocious student of languages as a youth, he was among the founders of the Moscow Linguistic Circle in 1915 and a supporter of its St. Petersburg counterpart, the Society for the Study of Poetic Language (OPOJAZ), established the following year. A decade later, he would be among the originators of a similar group in Prague. Ferociously learned, possessed of prodigious energy, and above all single-mindedly committed to the project of establishing methodologically sound bases for the study of literature, Jakobson labored tirelessly from his teens to his death at age eighty-six to discover the secrets of literary language and codify them into principles that could stand the test of science.

Why literature? Jakobson's training in Oriental languages might well have led to a distinguished career in linguistics, and indeed, his contributions to certain branches of that discipline (notably phonology) are far from negligible. As a teenager Jakobson circulated among the literary and artistic avant-garde of prerevolutionary Russia. It was in this milieu that his tastes and, one might also say, his convictions were largely formed. To comprehend Jakobson's long career, remarkable despite the range of topics and disciplines on which he wrote and for its unwavering commitment to a limited number of guiding principles, one should bear in mind his formation by the aesthetic practice of high modernism that dominated the cultural scene in the twilight of the Romanov dynasty and remained vital through the early years following the Bolshevik Revolution.

The opening three essays in *Language in Literature* illustrate the young Jakobson's frank partisanship for the avant-garde. Assessing contemporary movements such as Dadaism and Futurism, he throws down the gauntlet most directly in a short, polemical piece written in 1921, "On Realism in Art." It ends with the following tart sarcasm that sets the agenda, if not necessarily the tone, for virtually all of his major work to follow:

> A term once used in American slang to denote a socially inept person was "turkey." There are probably "turkeys" in Turkey, and there are doubtless men named Harry who are blessed with great amounts of hair. But we should not jump to conclusions concerning the social aptitudes of the Turks or the hairiness of men named Harry. This "commandment" is self-evident to the point of imbecility, yet those who speak of artistic realism continually sin against it.

In perhaps his most famous essay, "Linguistics and Poetics," the matter is put more technically, but the underlying idea is the same: "Poeticalness is not a supplementation of discourse with rhetorical adornment but a total reevaluation of the discourse and of all its components whatsoever." In another place, Jakobson writes:

> Poeticity is present when the word is felt as a word and not a mere representation of the object being named or an outburst of emotion, when words and their composition, their meaning, their external and inner form, acquire a weight and value of their own instead of referring indifferently to reality.

All these formulations confirm that from his youth in Moscow through his maturity in interwar Prague and into old age in the United States, Jakobson never significantly wavered from the Formalist creed.

The complications, indeed the impasse, encountered by the early Formalists when they attempted to account for the evolutionary potential in literature—the manifest tendency for styles and techniques to alter from one epoch to another—were glimpsed early by Jakobson. His and Yury Tynyanov's 1928 theses, "Problems in the Study of Language and Literature," focus on the difficulties with admirable clarity and economy. Merely to recognize a problem, however, is not yet to solve it. What remains after all the brilliance and the erudition that marked Jakobson's entire career is a set of problems which he saw at an early point but never overcame. Why was this so?

Two passages from the Jakobson-Tynyanov theses establish the fundamental problematic. On the one hand:

> The history of literature (art), being simultaneous with other historical series, is characterized, as is each of these series, by a complex network of specific structural laws. Without an elucidation of these laws, it is impossible to establish in a scientific manner the correlation between the literary series and other historical series.

This statement establishes the basis of what is elsewhere called "the autonomy of the aesthetic function." At the same time:

> A disclosure of the immanent laws of the history of literature (and language) allows us to determine the character of each specific change in literary (and linguistic) systems. . . . The question of a specific choice of path, or at least of the dominant, can be solved only through an analysis of the correlation between the literary series and other historical series.

Another way of stating Jakobson's point is to say that literary history, or the literary series, is only relatively autonomous in relation to the sociohistorical conditions that surround and motivate it. As he would assert unequivocally elsewhere, apropos both the Russian Formalists and the Prague Structuralists:

> Neither Tynjanov nor Mukařovský nor Šklovskij nor I have ever proclaimed the self-sufficiency of art. What we have been trying to show is that art is an integral part of the social structure, a component that interacts with all the others and is itself mutable since both the domain of art and its relationship to the other constituents of the social structure are in constant dialectical flux.

This assertion, however, leaves open precisely the question that Jakobson and his coworkers thrust to the forefront of theoretical poetics: To wit, what is the position of literary (or more generally, aesthetic) practice within the overall structure of society? Jakobson's insistence on a hierarchy of functions in works of art goes begging when it comes time for him to theorize the place of art in society. The best he can offer is an admission that some such theory will be necessary if historical poetics is to realize its full potential. That particular tomorrow never came.

Thus it is that Jakobson's mature work tends to split into two quite distinct types of inquiry. He is probably most famous for his theoretical pieces in linguistics, poetics, and semiotics, represented here by "Linguistics and Poetics," "Poetry of Grammar and Grammar of Poetry," and "On the Relation Between Visual and Auditory Signs," among others. Nevertheless, these texts, however justly praised, would remain comparatively empty statements of principle, absent the concrete analyses of poetic texts instanced in essays such as those on Charles Baudelaire's "Les Chats," William Shakespeare's sonnet 129, and William Butler Yeats's "Sorrow of Love." These latter examples illustrate the power of Jakobson's method and thus substantiate the claims made about language and literature in the more familiar programmatic texts.

There is another side to Jakobson's work that is also represented in *Language in Literature*, and nowhere more poignantly than in the long eulogy to the friend of his youth, the Russian poet Vladimir Mayakovsky. "On a Generation That Squandered Its Poets" is arguably Jakobson's finest performance. It gives the lie to the charge often lodged against theoreticians of literature that they are incapable of evaluating and sensitively responding to literary art, that their coldly technical procedures leave the life of literature drained in the laboratory of method. No one can read this account of Mayakovsky's life and art and fail to register the passion of its author. Nor is it possible to resist the tactful and pertinent deployment of biographical facts that Jakobson brings to bear on his reading of major poetic themes. On his account, the life and art of Mayakovsky were so intimately intertwined as to be indistinguishable, a point he takes over from Mayakovsky himself:

> And it was Majakovskij who wrote that even a poet's style of dress, even his intimate conversations with his wife, should be determined by the whole of his poetic production. He understood very well the close connection between poetry and life.

This very principle allows Jakobson to make the audacious judgment, against the philistine outcries of official Soviet culture which could make no sense of Mayakovsky's suicide, that the very logic of his poetic career made the poet's taking his own life, if not inevitable, then all too comprehensible.

"On a Generation That Squandered Its Poets" does not stop there, however, with a persuasive explanation of the poetic and personal trajectory of a single poet. The essay ends on an even more somber note:

> As for the future, it doesn't belong to us either. In a few decades we shall be cruelly labeled as products of the past millennium. All we had were compelling songs of the future; and suddenly

> these songs are no longer part of the dynamic of history, but have been transformed into historico-literary facts. When singers have been killed and their song has been dragged into a museum and pinned to the wall of the past, the generation they represent is even more desolate, orphaned, and lost—impoverished in the most real sense of the word.

One cannot help but read these lines against the larger historical drama that was unfolding as they were written in 1931. Jakobson's essay not only eulogizes Mayakovsky and the others of his generation who died young, it also protests the falling of that long darkness over all of Soviet culture that had become plain with the consolidation of the Stalinist regime at the close of the 1920's, a time which marked the end of, among other things, the freedom of the Formalists to publish. Jakobson's work must be read as more than merely a shrewd and illuminating assessment of a particular poetic oeuvre. It is as well, and perhaps more powerfully, a bold intervention in the cultural politics of the period. Its force derives less from any method Jakobson may have adopted than from its patent resistance to the coercive forces that sought to silence him and his cohorts forever.

The final essay in this collection would seem to confirm one's sense of Jakobson as the arch Formalist. Its subject is the semiotic crossover or translation between visual and poetic structures. The three examples cited are William Blake, Henri Rousseau, and Paul Klee. Analyses of texts by the first and last adhere to largely technical matters of poetic form, but when Jakobson discusses Rousseau's famous painting *The Dream* and the poem which Rousseau insisted accompany its exhibition, something else intervenes. His description of the similar structures in poem and painting, their comparable symmetries, is entirely persuasive. At the same time, one recognizes that the real force of his reading derives less from the precision of the method than from its psychological acumen, which is grounded in Guillaume Apollinaire's famous paper, "Le Douanier." There, one finds the warrant for interpreting painting and poem together: Rousseau's confession that his early love, Yadwigha, had inspired the painting. Jakobson was too practiced an interpreter to ignore this detail altogether, although he was also too shrewd a theoretician to let the biographical fact govern the interpretation without justifying it by structural analysis of both texts. If there is a lesson here, it surely is that, despite the methodological limitations manifested in Formalism and Structuralism, the practice of formal analysis can be as supple, as illuminating, and as original as any less rigorous or technical hermeneutic procedure. Jakobson's science of literature remains as much a dream today as it did in his youth. Any advance in that direction, however, will undoubtedly have to reckon with the prescientific achievements he himself attained. The inadequacy of Jakobsonian theory should not blind the reader to the gains realized in his critical practice.

Michael Sprinker

Sources for Further Study

Kirkus Reviews. LV, September 15, 1987, p. 1370.
Library Journal. November 1, 1987, p. 112.

THE LAST LION
Winston Spencer Churchill, Alone, 1932-1940

Author: William Manchester (1922-   )
Publisher: Little, Brown (Boston). Illustrated. 756 pp. $24.95
Type of work: Historical biography
Time: 1932-1940
Locale: England and the Continent

A moving biography of the life of Winston Churchill that dramatically presents his relationships with the powerful people and events leading to World War II, during the years of his exclusion from a leadership role in the British government

Principal personages:
WINSTON SPENCER CHURCHILL, the controversial, world-renowned British statesman
CLEMENTINE CHURCHILL, his independent but supportive wife
RAMSEY MACDONALD, Prime Minister of England, 1924-1935
STANLEY BALDWIN, Prime Minister of England, 1935-1937, but actually the dominant power in the government from 1931 to 1937
NEVILLE CHAMBERLAIN, Prime Minister of England, 1937-1940
ADOLF HITLER, Führer of the Third Reich (Nazi Germany), 1934-1945
SIR ROBERT "VAN" VANSITTART, the permanent undersecretary of the British Foreign Office
FREDERICK A. "THE PROF" LINDEMANN, a close friend of Churchill and his adviser on scientific matters
DUNCAN SANDYS, Member of Parliament, Churchill's son-in-law and strong supporter
GEOFFREY DAWSON, the editor of *The Times*, Churchill's implacable foe
LORD HALIFAX, Foreign Secretary under Chamberlain
SIR NEVILLE HENDERSON, Britain's ambassador to Nazi Germany

The Last Lion: Winston Spencer Churchill, Alone, 1932-1940 is a powerful biography of one of the great leaders of the twentieth century. It is also so rich in detail about the people, forces, and events of Winston Churchill's time that William Manchester finds it necessary to emphasize to the reader that the "work is a biography, not a history." Churchill is presented in all of his impulsiveness, callousness, and obstinacy, but his vision, rhetorical effectiveness, adherence to principle, and power to inspire and lead also emerge, revealing an authentically great man.

This is the second volume in a projected three-volume biography. It acquaints the reader with Churchill's life at Chartwell, his country estate, and moves with Churchill to the public stage of the British Parliament, where he attempts to resist the forces moving toward the annihilation of civilization in Europe and England.

Manchester's facts are drawn from extensive research, using primary historical and biographical sources. These include taped interviews, manuscript collections, and various archives and published collections of British, French, German, American, Polish, Italian, Czechoslovakian, and Russian documents. The sources are extensively but unobtrusively documented; the text is supplemented by useful maps and a rich selection of photographs. Manchester's thoroughness and objective, balanced presentation give great credibility to the work, while the sheer force of his narrative makes the book more gripping than most novels.

Manchester portrays Churchill as one of the world's truly great leaders despite his flaws: "England's most singular statesman, a brilliant, domineering, intuitive, inconsiderate, self-centered, emotional, generous, ruthless, visionary, megalomaniacal, and heroic genius who inspires fear, devotion, rage, and admiration among his peers." Churchill's interests included history, literature, bricklaying, painting, military science, hunting, philosophy, landscaping, architecture, and government.

Manchester devotes the first section of the work to presenting Churchill's typical activities at Chartwell. Churchill emerges as an unusual, colorful character. He rose at 8:00 A.M., bathed, and returned to bed for breakfast, depending totally on servants to help carry out these routine tasks. He spent the rest of the morning with the newspapers and his mail. He had guests for lunch and dinner and was an avid conversationalist who talked much more than he listened. In the afternoon, he fed his goldfish, took a siesta, and painted. If he was working on a particular project, such as a fence or wall, he might lay bricks for a while. From 11:00 P.M. until between 2:00 A.M. and 4:00 A.M., he worked at his profession of writing, assisted by his secretaries, who took dictation and typed the drafts.

Manchester's selection of details effectively reveal Churchill's character. He presents Churchill as struggling to get dressed for lunch, assisted by servants, and always arriving late as a result of consistently underestimating the amount of time he needed to do everything. He describes Churchill's drinking Scotch all day and brandy or champagne at meals, but pacing his drinking so as to avoid drunkenness. Manchester reveals how Churchill wrote and rehearsed his speeches and used a written text in delivering them, yet was able to make them sound spontaneous. The animal sounds with which the Churchill family members greeted one another and the exotic *petits noms* they used reveal that they were not like the usual upper-class British family.

The complexity of Churchill's character is evident in his views toward war. Generally regarded as a militarist, Churchill is shown to have had anything but a simplistic view of war. He argued that the "hazards and discomforts of war . . . strengthen a young man's character," and it is evident that as a youth he regarded war as magnificent. Yet even as a young man he had written, "War, disguise it as you may, is but a dirty, shoddy business, which only a fool would play at." After World War I, he wrote, "War, which was cruel and magnificent, has become cruel and squalid."

Manchester describes a large underground network of informants on which Churchill relied during the 1930's. These informants kept him abreast of England's lack of military preparedness and developments in Nazi Germany and elsewhere in Europe. Many of these informants in the military and government service took substantial risks by giving Churchill what was often top-secret information, but they did it from a concern for England's safety. At one point, Manchester criticizes

"Churchill's carelessness in shielding such informants," although no example of this alleged carelessness is given.

Throughout, Manchester is objective in presenting Churchill's flaws. He shows Churchill's typical British upper-class disregard for servants. He observes that Churchill treated his staff as servants and was very hot-tempered in dealing with them. He points out that though Churchill had a prodigious memory, he did not remember his employees' names. Manchester also shows the statesman's pettiness on some matters, his arrogance, and his ingratitude toward those who helped him.

Serious as some of Churchill's flaws were, they pale in comparison with his strengths and positive accomplishments. As Manchester says, "The man who stood against Nazi Germany when his peers ridiculed him—and who later refused to quit when those around him believed England's cause lost, thereby saving Western civilization—is surely entitled to a few warts."

Manchester presents Churchill's public life in vivid detail. A senior statesman who had been a minister in six cabinets, Churchill was a powerful debater in Parliament and a man of enormous international prestige. In contrast, his prestige within England during the 1930's was low. Most of his colleagues in Parliament viewed him as having great intellect and will but as lacking sound judgment.

Manchester shows Churchill to have been outstandingly courageous, with enormous insight into world events. His courage during World War II has been often noted, but Manchester highlights an often-overlooked example of that courage in the way Churchill unwaveringly warned against the growing threat of Nazi aggression. The mood of the nation was overwhelmingly pacifist, and no one wanted to hear Churchill's warnings. The leaders of the government, who had embraced a policy of appeasement, ostracized Churchill politically.

Churchill's insight into world events grew out of an in-depth knowledge of events and an almost intuitive recognition of their significance. He recognized Adolf Hitler as an enemy of freedom before Hitler had risen to power. Through his informants, Churchill had as much information at his disposal as any minister of the government, and he eloquently used the information to attempt to persuade the government to change course and to alert the public to the growing threat.

During Churchill's political exile, and later, when he had regained political power, he stood by his convictions with or without support and, frequently, without regard to their implication for the achievement of his personal ambitions. Manchester cites contemporaries who began to see in Churchill someone whom England needed. As Brian Gardner writes, "For someone who was meant to be an adventurer, his warnings had been going on a remarkably long time, and with strange consistency, determination, and integrity."

Something of Churchill's character can be seen in his action toward Prime Minister Neville Chamberlain after Churchill became First Lord of the Admiralty. Despite his disagreement with Chamberlain's policies, Churchill considered that, as a member of the cabinet, he could not speak against Chamberlain in public. When Chamberlain came under heavy attack in Parliament for his failed policies, Churchill defended Chamberlain in debate, although to do so probably did not advance his own chances of becoming prime minister.

Manchester deals with Churchill's family and family relationships in much less detail than his public life. The glimpses he does give, however, are revealing. Manchester describes a strong, caring relationship between Winston and his wife, Clementine; he notes serious conflicts between Winston and his son Randolph. He also describes conflicts with Sarah over her insistence on going into show business and on marrying someone of whom Winston and Clementine disapproved. No conflicts are shown in Winston's relationship with Diana and Mary. Churchill seems to have been indulgent with all of his children, especially Sarah.

Manchester's discussion of Churchill as a writer is particularly revealing. Churchill earned a good living by professional writing, but this work did not make him rich; yet Churchill lived as though he were rich. Manchester's description of Churchill's attempts to stay ahead of his creditors during a major financial setback in 1938 is poignant. His necessity to meet deadlines increased an already prodigious output. He wrote from one to five thousand words per day. During the 1930's, Churchill's writings were turned out in such volume and at such speed that their literary quality is not as high as that of his greatest writings. Nevertheless, according to Manchester, "his was the most persuasive rhetoric in England." Churchill's writings, including books, articles, and syndicated columns, were widely read throughout England and in numerous other countries.

The breadth and scope of this volume of *The Last Lion* is monumental. While keeping his focus on Churchill, Manchester dramatically describes events in Europe leading to World War II. He makes vivid the pacifist mood of England and France, whose populations wished to avoid war at almost any cost. Their leaders thought that they could prevent war if they acceded to Hitler's demands. Manchester exposes these leaders for placing party politics and the pacifist mood of the public above their nations' safety. He shows them as clinging adamantly to a policy of appeasement and makes clear that this policy aided Hitler in his rapid development of a terrifying military power in Nazi Germany.

Early in 1939, however, public opinion began turning toward Churchill and toward militancy. While showing the change in the public attitude in Britain, Manchester shows the constancy of Hitler's attitude. Although Hitler hated all Englishmen, Churchill was the only one he feared.

This is a truly remarkable work. Characters are portrayed in all their complexity; the forces and events of the period leading toward the cataclysm of World War II are forcefully delineated. Within this milieu, Churchill emerges as eccentric, a man with limitations, but one of history's authentically great leaders. He is revealed as withstanding enormous personal and political troubles. He is also shown as one who could see beyond the horizon, who held fast to his vision, and who attempted to prepare his nation for a rising storm. When that storm broke, he inspired his countrymen to rise above their fears. Manchester says, "Despite his high birth he had an almost mystical faith in the power of the ordinary Englishman to survive, to endure, and, in the end, to prevail." Churchill idealized them, as Isaiah Berlin says, "with such intensity that in the end they approached his ideal and began to see themselves as he saw them."

Manchester portrays Winston Churchill as a powerful, memorable character. *The Last Lion* represents a remarkable aid to understanding him; its subject, treatment, mode of presentation, and style combine to make it a major addition to biographical literature.

Kenneth E. Walker

Sources for Further Study

Booklist. LXXXV, October 15, 1988, p. 361.
Boston Globe. October 23, 1988, p. 101.
Kirkus Reviews. LVI, September 1, 1988, p. 1305.
Library Journal. CXIII, November 1, 1988, p. 93.
Los Angeles Daily Journal. November 25, 1988, p. 5.
Los Angeles Times Book Review. December 11, 1988, p. 6.
The New York Times Book Review. XCIII, November 27, 1988, p. 16.
Newsweek. CXII, December 12, 1988, p. 77.
Time. CXXXII, October 31, 1988, p. 87.
The Washington Post Book World. XVIII, October 16, 1988, p. 1.

LETOURNEAU'S USED AUTO PARTS

Author: Carolyn Chute (1947-   )
Publisher: Ticknor & Fields (New York). 244 pp. $16.95
Type of work: Novel
Time: The 1980's
Locale: The fictional community of Egypt, in southern Maine

Hard times and encroaching yuppiedom threaten the collection of waifs housed in trailers and shacks near the junkyard of benevolent despot Big Lucien Letourneau

Principal characters:
BIG LUCIEN LETOURNEAU, a Franco-American wheeler-dealer with a talent for romance and a reputed heart of gold
MAXINE LETOURNEAU, his big, mean former wife
E. BLACKSTONE "EARL" BABBIDGE, a junkyard worker and born-again Christian
LILLIAN GREENLAW, his second wife
JUNE MARIE GREENLAW, the daughter of Big Lucien and Lillian, lover of Earl Babbidge, and second wife of Crowe Bovey
CROWE BOVEY, a worker in Big Lucien's junkyard and a gun freak

The world of *Letourneau's Used Auto Parts* is rich in personalities and tribal history but poor in worldly goods. Carolyn Chute returns to the small town of *The Beans of Egypt, Maine* (1985), a first novel which won enthusiastic reviews for its no-nonsense depiction of rural poverty. *Letourneau's Used Auto Parts* paints another populous clan perched on the edge of society. Egypt is not in the "Down East" part of Maine, with its coastal fishing villages. Chute's Maine is inland, near Portland. The Letourneaus belong to the large Franco-American population of southwestern Maine. Several generations removed from Quebec, their ties to the old language and ways are tenuous. The Letourneaus, like Chute's Bean family, have their roots in an area slated for a suburban boom. The arrival of new people—yuppies and out-of-staters—was the final factor in the breakdown of one central character in *The Beans of Egypt, Maine*. The Letourneaus face the same problem.

Big Lucien Letourneau is a power in Egypt, a family patriarch and owner of a junkyard which employs a significant number of the townspeople. He expands his family circle with hard luck cases housed in Miracle City, a backyard trailer camp. Though Big Lucien is the reigning divinity in this world, the novel shows him indirectly, around the corner or out of town, visible only by reflection. Other people interpret his wishes or follow his orders. His voice, with its French accent, can be heard, but Big Lucien himself remains invisible, enigmatic to the reader. Everyone looks for or at Big Lucien; the reader forms an impression of him through the vision of others.

At times it seems that everyone in Egypt belongs to Big Lucien. They are his family, his workers, his tenants. A heart of gold and a rumored fortune earn for him the name "Big Mister Pluto." Yet times are hard. Before Chute drops her readers on the streets of Portland, it is not Pluto's wealth that Big Lucien has come to personify but his role as the ancient king of Hell.

Letourneau's Used Auto Parts opens within feeling distance of hellfire. Crowe Bovey, one of Big Lucien's mechanics, returns from three days with a girlfriend to find his family dead in a fire. With his family and home goes Crowe's hold on independent life. His is the first and most dramatic slide into the circle of Big Lucien's charity the reader witnesses, but Miracle City is already peopled with sad cases. The town zoning officer is their attendant demon, eternally prowling Letourneau land in search of trailers or "camps" which have not been "grandfathered" into semilegitimacy. In a closing scene, the officer is burned in effigy as revenge. He represents the interests of a town too concerned with the interests of affluent newcomers to worry about the natives. The code officer and his employers are men who wear tan double-knit polyester suits, in sharp contrast with the horny-handed men in Letourneau's Used Auto Parts work shirts.

The Letourneau home is a rambling pile just back of the junk yard. Here live Big Lucien's old mother, Mémère (Gramma) Poulin, his sisters, the "tantes" (aunts), headed by the redoubtable worker Flavie, and a floating collection of informal wives and their children. Except for the eternal former wife Maxine, Big Lucien's wives are temporary. Each has her particular personality and temporal slot, but they disappear, one by one, without a trace or an explanation. The Letourneaus favor evening chats out on the porch and warm cake served by the tantes. The young wives brood over their babies while Flavie runs the house.

Big Lucien's dark eyes are one secret of his magic. He passes them down to all of his children, along with a lower lip that thickens in times of doubt. To be seen by Big Lucien, to live in his eyes, is a precious charm that somehow draws women to him. Big, mean Maxine will do anything to feel herself in his eyes. Strange women drive up from Boston to draw his wonderful eyes. No one but the zoning officer can resist him. Even his mechanics continue to work long after they receive their last paychecks, past the point when they lose their homes and wind up in the rundown trailers and temporary shacks of Miracle City.

Potato companies or "the mill" employ the women of Egypt and wring them dry in exchange for a regular paycheck. Letourneau's junkyard maims and defeats men without even paying them. All the male workers are identified by their shirts, at first marked with each man's first name, as well as the name of the junkyard. By the novel's end, shirts are worn interchangeably, and new men wear shirts abandoned by others. One worker loses his front teeth in an accident at the yard, but such injuries are commonplace and go unwept in the macho atmosphere. Another worker kills himself out in the yard, but work goes on just the same.

Under the shadow of Big Lucien's patriarchy are other family groups. Armand Letourneau and his son Severin, Babbidge and his ten icy-eyed children, and the bereft Bovey are all dependent on Big Lucien for employment. Except for Armand, they all wind up housed by him too. Babbidge is the most like Big Lucien in his masculine power, a potency which manifests itself in the persistence of his image in his children. All the Babbidge babies and grandbabies share his eyes and square-shouldered physique. In other local families, children are shaped by the mother.

Armand's wife, a full-blooded Passamaquoddy Indian, produces a son, Severin, who looks exactly like her. Severin in turn is dominated by his wife, Gussie Crocker. Gussie's family is a matriarchy; her father is submerged in the human wave of pink-haired children produced by his pink-haired wife, August. They too join Big Lucien's tribe when they lose their home to the bank.

In *The Beans of Egypt, Maine*, Chute explored the lives of the ever-increasing Bean family and the slide of Earlene Pomerleau from the material comfort of her childhood to marriage and poverty with Beal Bean. Narrative voice changed with succeeding episodes of the book. Earlene spoke in the first person. In *Letourneau's Used Auto Parts*, however, there is no first-person narrator. No single character holds the central position in the general fall into hard times. Even the children are devalued; a few have names, but most are anonymous. The Babbidge household has three Jennifers. Letourneau babies are satellites to their parents, around whom they orbit in mute adoration. It seems natural when Junie Greenlaw leaves the Babbidge home to live in the Letourneau house, though Big Lucien was known to her only through reputation in her childhood. His children are naturally her own "real" siblings, and she bonds to them.

Chute's men are gods to their women, their patriarchal sway unchallenged. Yet it is the possession of the women that defines their divinity. Are there gods without worshippers? What is Earl Babbidge without his harem? Bovey reestablishes his hold on life by marrying Babbidge's pregnant stepdaughter. "Finders keepers losers weepers," he gloats over her watermelon of a belly. These gods are in twilight, and there is little hope for the children they beget. As a girl, Junie Greenlaw plans to stay single, triumph in business, drive sporty cars. At the novel's end, she is dependent upon Big Lucien, married to Bovey, and in labor. One of Big Lucien's daughters is in college, dresses in style, and has a college boyfriend, yet as she studies sociology, she is living in a milieu well designed to destroy her plans. Much time is spent observing her brothers, Norman and Little Lucien, who choose the unstable, dangerous life of woodsmen over the alienation of formal schooling. Would the success of an independent woman destroy the Letourneau pantheon?

Plot is not the strongest element of *Letourneau's Used Auto Parts*. The characterization of the Letourneau tribe and their neighbors and the detailed descriptions of their lives and the objects around them are the areas in which Chute excels. The reader learns the brand name of their cigarettes, how they dress, their tattoos, what cars they drive, and what is painted on their pickup trucks. The men are labeled by their work shirts and the company emblems on their trucks. They wear jeans burned with battery acid and worn white. The reader goes into their homes, smells the smells, and sees what they eat and how. These details are all telling factors in characterization. One knows that Lillian Greenlaw Babbidge has lost hope in her romantic vision when she changes her style of clothing and hairdo. Having been a youthful twin of her daughter, dressed in the same styles, her frizzy hair tied back with bright scarves, Lillian changes to wearing old-lady waves and hand-me-downs from the minister's wife.

The desperation of Chute's men takes violent forms. In *The Beans of Egypt, Maine*, the woodsman Reuben Bean is jailed after a violent rampage, beginning with the wanton slaughter of deer and ending with a vicious attack on the game warden. His nephew, Beal Bean, ends his life in a hail of bullets, attacking a yuppie neighbor's many-windowed home. In *Letourneau's Used Auto Parts*, Bovey shoots small animals and piles them in the back of his pickup truck. Big Lucien orders his men to kill Babbidge's neglected watch dogs. Big Lucien himself is the victim of violent seizures and headaches that make him shriek with pain, and he is prone to drunken rampages that end in jail. When he plows snow, he destroys the children's swing set, rocks the house, and blocks his family inside. Babbidge beats his children and impregnates his stepdaughter.

Chute's women cope, care for the childen, and pick up their men when their trucks break down or they get out of jail. Their love is inarticulate, unromantic, an embrace of natural necessity. Tough old Maxine is without romantic illusions, yet she lives permanently in Big Lucien's orbit. Lillian announces the death of her love of Babbidge, yet she sticks with him. The Letourneaus are not noble savages. They are often foolish, stupid, and repulsive in their habits, but there is no question they are concretely realistic reminders of the richness and complications of life. Things do not improve, yet most of them pick up their kids and keep living.

Chute makes no bones about the rooting in reality of her characters and the events of their lives. In interviews given at the time of publication of *The Beans of Egypt, Maine*, she talked frankly about her own life and experience of poverty. She dropped out of school to get married at sixteen. Divorced and a mother, she worked a series of marginal jobs. Remarried to a man both illiterate and unemployed, she lost a baby boy because of inadequate medical care. Her first novel grew out of the void after his death. She wrote to bring life into the world, and to her astonishment her novel was an enormous success. Now her extended family enjoys a measure of financial security.

Chute's story has an impact on the public reception of her work, but it can definitely stand alone. It is powerful fiction, evocative of a world most readers will know only from the perspective of the Letourneaus' yuppie neighbors. Chute's first novel was dedicated to her dead son. The second bears on its flyleaf the observation that "It is only the superhuman who can rise to Compassion." The reader of *Letourneau's Used Auto Parts* will be compromised by entry into Miracle City. The last scene of the novel gives a direct view of Big Lucien, on his release from jail in Portland. He is no Plutonic divinity, but a small, ordinary man with thinning hair and stooped shoulders, welcomed by Maxine and a small grandson. One might meet him on the street tomorrow. Chute has given her readers a chance to recognize him, and themselves.

Anne W. Sienkewicz

Sources for Further Study

Booklist. LXXXIV, April 15, 1988, p. 1369.
Kirkus Reviews. LVI, April 1, 1988, p. 473.
Library Journal. CXIII, June 15, 1988, p. 67.
Los Angeles Times Book Review. June 5, 1988, p. 3.
The Nation. CCXLVII, July 2, 1988, p. 29.
The New Republic. CXCIX, July 11, 1988, p. 40.
The New York Times Book Review. XCIII, July 31, 1988, p. 9.
Newsweek. CXI, June 13, 1988, p. 79.
Publishers Weekly. CCXXXIII, April 29, 1988, p. 63.
Time. CXXXI, June 20, 1988, p. E6.

THE LETTER LEFT TO ME

Author: Joseph McElroy (1930-   )
Publisher: Alfred A. Knopf (New York). 152 pp. $16.95
Type of work: Novel
Time: The mid to late 1940's
Locale: Brooklyn Heights, New York, and the campus of a small college in a rural area

An adolescent's attempt to understand the letter left to him by his father develops into a brilliantly executed narrative investigation into the ways in which meaning is not so much communicated as improvised

Principal characters:
THE SON, the narrator and principal character
THE FATHER, the writer of the letter which the son receives three or four days after the father's death
THE MOTHER, who hands her son the letter
POP, the father's stepfather
THE DEAN, an administrator at the son's college

That Joseph McElroy grew up in the Brooklyn Heights section of New York; that he could see the Brooklyn Bridge from the window of his parents' apartment; that his father attended Boys' High School and later (on a scholarship) Harvard University, where he majored in chemistry, and later still went into business, attracted by the chance of making the kind of money his own parents never had; that the father, "somewhat puritanical and a high achiever," died when his son was fifteen, leaving the boy to feel then and later very much in his father's shadow—all these facts are worth mentioning in a review of *The Letter Left to Me* because they figure so prominently not only in the life of the novel's author but also in the life of its anonymous protagonist. McElroy has used details from his own life in his fiction before, but never quite so fully and specifically as he does in this, his seventh novel. Together his works form what McElroy has called "a cryptoautobiography," but to approach *The Letter Left to Me* as if it were merely an autobiographical novel is to make a fundamental mistake. The novel deserves, even demands, to be read the way the hero of another McElroy novel, *Hind's Kidnap* (1969), says a Dürer woodcut should be viewed: as a remarkably complex surface whose depth of referential meaning is illusory and beside the point, the point being the intricacy of the design. McElroy's art is therefore not so much referential as it is proof that "to write" is, as Roland Barthes has claimed, an intransitive verb. Even the adolescent protagonist of *The Letter Left to Me* seems to intuit and, to a degree, to accept Barthes's point, writing "sometimes lines and lines in my diary called forth *by* my diary, with its too small pages." He writes to fill the blankness with his self-begetting words, yet to fill is not enough; even as he writes, he feels constrained, as if the writing needs to spill off the page.

On the one hand the novel invites being read in terms of "life"—the author's and the nameless boy's—as an autobiographical novel or a work of psychological realism. On the other hand, the novel resists this kind of reductive reading insofar as

McElroy uses narrative not to tell a story but to explore a metaphor. Instead of depicting characters and analyzing their motivations, he writes a prose that is elliptical, discontinuous, and achingly abstract, but also incantatory and surprisingly compelling. Instead of psychological depth, McElroy gives his reader a densely packed verbal surface which resists easy comprehension yet sustains interest by teasing the reader with its own relational complexities. His sentences rarely if ever explain or even describe. They are instead always and only starting points along a labyrinthine and endless way. The indefiniteness of his writing goes well beyond that of Henry James (whose dialogue McElroy seems to parody toward the end of *The Letter Left to Me*); the sentence "Life is scarcely to be believed and we have to do something about it" nicely illustrates the novel's drift. Yet even as he disrupts the story line, submerging it under the complexities of the novel's surface texture, McElroy lures the reader on, not with a mystery to be solved but instead with the very idea of mystery itself.

The novel begins by calling attention to its own syntactical complexity, a sign—or paradigm—of things to come: "The woman holding, then handing over the letter to this poised, dumbfounded fifteen-year-old: is the letter also hers?" The letter in question is "the letter left to me," the letter left to—or for—the son who narrates the novel (in the present tense) but who here refers to himself in the third person, as the reader soon comes to learn. It is interesting and perhaps significant that he repeats this clandestine self-description just a few pages later, but in slightly altered form, becoming now "the dumbfounded, poised fifteen-year-old" and so suggesting not only a distinction but a difference too, though a difference of decidedly uncertain meaning. Here and elsewhere, whatever occurs later in the novel—which is to say, whatever is narrated later—serves less to clarify earlier events as to complicate them. The letter, for example, is dated February 22 (Washington's Birthday), but the year (the son and reader only later learn) is three years prior to the mother's handing the letter to the son in the novel's opening scene, or sentence. To speak of the letter is, however, a bit misleading, for the letter is plural. It exists less as an object to be held and read than as a sign to be interpreted or, like a good postmodernist fiction, a machine for generating interpretations. Considered allegorically rather than semiotically, the letter is a token that the father still lives, in a manner of speaking; proof that he is indeed dead (something the boy cannot quite bring himself to believe); a subject for family discussions (from which the boy is strangely excluded); a treasure (the boy's), a "real" message truly meant; a souvenir; a story (the father's), replete with "proper" ending; and the answer to the boy's question, "What have I without him here?" Instead of providing an answer, the letter evokes additional questions. Whose letter is it?—the son's, the father's, or maybe the mother's? Was the letter written *to* the son or *for* the son? Does it imply separation or solidarity? Is it gift or curse? If it is, as the son says, a "belonging"—"my letter"—does it also serve as a way of belonging, of being part of something larger than oneself?

What has really become of his father? To remember the father is to keep him alive by reconstructing him in words and images (memories). The novel complicates this rather simple point by having the boy wonder whether his father lives *in* the letter or in what the son makes *of* the letter. The former implies the authority of the letter and its author, the boy's father; the latter suggests the autonomy of the reader and the act of reading (a position similar to the one advanced by semioticians and reader-response critics). The son's efforts to read the letter, to know what it and its author mean, lead him well beyond the letter's margins to a reconstruction of its author's, his father's life. "I'm building," the boy notes, "but backwards naturally." The word choice here is especially apropos. The son does not in fact reconstruct, he builds, and what he builds is not natural but artificial: art. He does not discover meaning; he makes it, and what he makes is a version, a facsimile, of the original—or, to be as precise as the novel, a facsimile of what passes for the original. In *The Letter Left to Me*, originals are conspicuously absent. Counterfeits, on the other hand, abound. The father has died, as has his father before him, and at an even age—ten rather than fifteen. More important, the letter which the mother hands to the son is not what the reader and narrator first assume it to be. It is not what the father actually wrote; it is instead a two-page typewritten version of an original manuscript, now lost. That the father always wrote in longhand raises the question of who may have (type)written this seemingly very private piece of correspondence. This typescript of the original handwritten manuscript is later "handsomely printed" by the father's stepfather ("Pop") and in this, now its third, form is sent to one hundred new recipients, who naïvely equate their text with "the letter sent to me." To complicate matters further, McElroy allows his (and the boy's) reader to gain access to the contents of the letter slowly and only partially, when the son chooses to include brief excerpts (usually quoted but sometimes paraphrased) in the course of his narration. Because the boy's quoting of the letter is not only partial and selective but also random and repetitive, the decidedly mediated version which the reader assembles during the course of his reading of the novel remains fragmentary and therefore dependent on his willingness to accept this incompleteness (and all it implies) and to regard the letter that figures so prominently in the title of the novel not as the key to unlocking the novel's mysterious meaning but instead as mere pretext, or, rather, as pre-text. "What *could* you really say about it?" the boy wonders. Has his father "closed the subject"? Has he uttered (that is, written) the proverbial last word, or the first?

"I grasp that there's another way to see all this." Indeed, there are many ways, for *The Letter Left to Me* proceeds chiefly by multiplying its own interpretive possibilities rather than by adding linearly to its submerged and decidedly minimalist plot. The letter is not an object to be possessed and preserved but an event of uncertain meaning to which meanings attach themselves. The letter printed by Pop and then a few years later again reproduced and distributed by the college dean to each of the two or three hundred members of the boy's freshman class evokes responses from each of its recipients. Each response involves a reading of the letter and in turn becomes part of the son's perpetual rereading. Each response, whether actually known to the boy or only imagined by him, becomes part of his increasingly comprehensive yet also increasingly fragmentary metareading of the endlessly metamorphosing original. Here, as in his six earlier novels, McElroy creates "ambiguities from excess . . . in order to [have the character and the reader] have at least a chance of finding the key to it all." The excess of information—of multiplying readings and not quite synonymous repetitions—does not result in the paranoid plots of Thomas Pynchon but in a strange sense of abundance and even hope. Yet the hopefulness is not without its own dangers. One, already mentioned, is the desire to accept a partial reading of the letter and all it suggests as complete and final, as the last word. Another involves allowing the "reading" of what is in effect an existential or self-referential metaphor, the letter, to become an obsession, the means for imposing order on abundance. The partialness of all readings and all metaphors and all metaphoric texts (which are always pre-texts) is what the novel dramatizes. Seen in this context, the question that one of the son's college classmates asks, whether the letter was written before or after the father's death, seems insightful rather than silly, for in a very real sense the letter is only written when it is read, when the reader becomes the writer and the son the father.

What saves the son from becoming engulfed by his own partial readings or those of others is his acute awareness of his verbal environment. He knows that his words are the words of others and that theirs are the words of others still. In this respect, he especially resembles (or echoes) his maker, McElroy, who has noted his own desire "to bust loose in order to hold fast to a self that might get lost in blandness and closet imitation." The boy shares McElroy's anxiety of influence. Fearing that his words may merely be echoes, and feeling both grateful for and "overmatched" by his father's letter, he develops strategies to distance himself from all that is not clearly his own. His extensive use of the "he/she said" tag and his placing quotation marks around individual phrases are the two most notable. These strategies do not so much assign authorship as undermine it by calling attention to the used-upness of everyday speech.

> His letter had these familiar *phrases*: "Try to take my word for it—I earnestly wish you to be a better man than I am."
>
> This was my father, whom I missed. For what? . . . For his face and body, his wit. And *because he was my father*—the answer a grownup would familiarly give a child.

The son's recognition of what Fredric Jameson has called "the prison house of language" and his parallel search for his own words and linguistic identity lead him in two directions: ahead to the linguistic freedom for which he yearns and back to the very source of all language.

"Dumbfounded," then, in a double sense—puzzled and speechless—the son finds himself where so many of McElroy's characters do: "between." They are inhabitants less of physical reality than of "middle states" and "neutral neighborhoods": detached, observant, passive, indecisive, but yearning. The son seeks not only recognition—both as "himself" and as his father's son—but obscurity as well

(he exists in the shadow of the father and of language). More important, he does not "speak" because he does not "know" (his guide, his father, is both literally and metaphorically dead), but his "not knowing" proves not to be the negative state, or absence, he first assumes it to be. "You could go upon what you were yet to know." Knowledge, or truth, is not an either/or matter, either you have it or you do not, but both together because "things are blessedly incomplete" and entirely "interdependent." Truth is not an absolute; it is a process, a matter of fluid relationships.

"Shot through with things unsaid," the son feels the need to speak in order to fill the void, not with speech that pretends to the kind of authority he associates with the father but that is instead tentative and self-aware. "The letter my father had left for me was words. I saw this soon after I received it, yet saw it gradually." The letter is not an explanation but a question, not a meaning but a texture, dense and difficult yet richly rewarding. "I like books," McElroy has said, "that try to push the reader into a strange state of mind in which everything has to be relearned." *The Letter Left to Me* does just that. It teaches the reader how to read and how the process of disruption and disintegration can be reversed and the individual, in this case the son reintegrated into life and speech. At novel's end, boy (son) meets girl (Nina, from a nearby college) and says to her what he has not said to anyone else, except perhaps the reader. "I felt naïve but had spoken." Just as importantly, he seems determined to say more, to speak himself into the as yet unspoken and unwritten future. Even as his words project him forward, however, they drive him back to his origin, to his father and "the letter left to me," and less obviously to another father, this one of the postmodern novel, for one hears in the son's concluding words—"The letter is everywhere and I can't answer for it. I'll answer the letter. I can't. But I will"—the echo of Samuel Beckett's grimly comic line, "You must go on, I can't go on, I'll go on." Ending on this note of qualified hopefulness—or qualified hopelessness—McElroy pays homage to the very forces of constraint and possibility against which and also toward which both son and author must struggle and aspire. On the basis of *The Letter Left to Me*, McElroy's shortest but in some ways best novel, the chances for success are quite good.

Robert A. Morace

Sources for Further Study

Booklist. LXXXV, October 15, 1988, p. 364.

Kirkus Reviews. LVI, August 15, 1988, p. 1184.

Library Journal. CXIII, November 1, 1988, p. 109.

The New Republic. CXCIX, October 17, 1988, p. 46.

The New York Times Book Review. XCIII, October 9, 1988, p. 7.

Publishers Weekly. CCXXXIV, August 26, 1988, p. 77.

The Washington Post Book World. XVIII, October 30, 1988, p. 5.

LETTERS AND DRAWINGS OF BRUNO SCHULZ
With Selected Prose

Author: Bruno Schulz (1892-1942)
Translated from the Polish by Walter Arndt with Victoria Nelson
Edited, with an introduction, by Jerzy Ficowski
Publisher: Harper & Row (New York). Illustrated. 256 pp. $25.00
Type of work: Letters, reviews, and narrative prose
Time: 1921-1941
Locale: Primarily Drohobycz, Poland

The drawings, letters, reviews, and prose narratives collected here provide a fascinating glimpse into Schulz's chief obsessions and a startling reaffirmation of his genius

A once-powerful nation that has been overrun, several times partitioned out of existence, and, during World War II, very nearly erased from the face of the earth altogether—its schools closed, its language forbidden, its culture destroyed, its capital razed, its population systematically murdered—Poland has learned to guard its history jealously, seeking to recover and preserve its past in order to perpetuate the essence of its own fragile being. Not surprisingly, the Romantic strain is especially strong in Polish life, in its arts (Adam Mickiewicz and Frédéric Chopin, for example) as well as its politics (Lech Walesa and Father Jerzy Popieluszko). It takes the form of a noble if often doomed idealism that cannot be separated from the sense of devotion to the past, to a figurative as well as literal remembering. Such devotion, such painstaking reconstruction of the past, helps to explain the intensity and persistence of Jerzy Ficowski's efforts to track down, edit, and publish the works of Bruno Schulz, yet another of those Polish writers who have largely been overlooked outside Eastern Europe. Hailed in 1933 by Stanisław Witkiewicz as a truly major Polish writer, Schulz published only two collections of short fiction, *Sklepy cynamonowe* (1933; *The Street of Crocodiles*, 1963; also as *Cinnamon Shops*) and *Sanatorium pod klepsydrą* (1937; *The Sanatorium Under the Sign of the Hourglass* 1978), before being murdered by a Nazi in 1942 in the streets of Drohobycz, the provincial town in which he had spent his entire life.

Summarily shot for being outside the Jewish ghetto, he was left in the street until, under cover of darkness, friends removed his body to the Jewish cemetery for burial; after the war, no one could remember which grave was his. His literary remains fared no better, scattered and for the most part destroyed during the Nazi occupation. *Letters and Drawings of Bruno Schulz: With Selected Prose* is therefore necessarily a slender volume as well as an immense labor of love, an act of deep devotion. Its substance is similarly deep, far deeper than its slender size seems to suggest. Ficowski includes a generous selection of Schulz's drawings, nearly all Schulz's surviving letters, a number of his reviews and essays, and, perhaps best of all, three previously untranslated and uncollected prose narratives that are as good as, maybe better than, any of the works in the two published collections and that again make clear that when dealing with Schulz's imaginative writing, traditional designations such as "short story" prove woefully inadequate. The loss of nearly all

Schulz's letters written before the publication of his first book, *Cinnamon Shops*, is especially regrettable, for as Schulz himself explains in a later letter, it was into his correspondence that he put all of his early literary energy, having no other outlet. In fact, it was a correspondent, Debora Vogel, who encouraged Schulz to pursue the narrative possibilities of the long literary postscripts he began appending to his letters. Unfortunately, none of his letters to Vogel survives, nor do those he wrote to Witkiewicz, Witold Gombrowicz, Thomas Mann, his patroness Zofia Nałkowska, or his fiancée, Józefina Szelińska.

These omissions would normally make one wary of making any sweeping claims about Schulz's life and aesthetics, but, extensive as the omissions are and disheartening as it surely is not to have the early letter versions of the *Cinnamon Shops* stories, such claims can be made, for Schulz's life and art remained remarkably consistent—as consistent, it seems, as his outward existence was uneventful. He spent nearly all of his adult life teaching drawing and crafts in the local high school. It was work he chose yet came to despise as soon as he realized that teaching was not the profession he had hoped it would be but instead a form of manual labor that did not permit him time to devote himself to the drawing in which he was trained and to which his artistic sensibility was far better suited. "Every day I leave that scene brutalized and soiled inside, filled with distaste for myself and so violently drained of energy that several hours are not enough to restore it." Dissatisfaction drove Schulz to consider his options. One was to take a leave of absence, but this course required his applying for a government grant. When, after much delay and even greater anxiety on Schulz's part, the grant was approved, Schulz wrote a letter of thanks to the ministry's section chief that evidences precisely the kind of self-abasement that characterizes the male figures in Schulz's sadomasochistic drawings. The grant did not solve Schulz's problems; only death or the imagination to which he longed to devote himself could do that. By April, 1936, he saw that the grant was running out, and with it the time to write and draw, and so he once again had to contemplate his impossible financial situation—low pay combined with burdensome family responsibilities, all complicated by the threat of staff cutbacks and chronic ill health. There is something so overwhelming yet, in a way, trivial, about Schulz's predicament (and his response to it) as to be almost comical, as if he were condemned to suffer the endless frustrations and pratfalls typical of silent film comedy or of the fiction of Franz Kafka which Schulz admired so much.

The letters provide less a record of Schulz's outward life than of his psychological obsessions. "Morbidly shy" and suffering from a monumental inferiority complex, Schulz used writing, especially letter writing, the way other, less inwardly turned individuals use social contacts. He sought from his correspondents the validation and encouragement of his talent that he did not and could not get in his native Drohobycz. The need was desperate enough that in at least one case, his extensive correspondence with Zenow Waśniewski, Schulz actually appears to have been unable to break off a correspondence he seems unwilling to continue (or, rather, to have Waśniewski continue). Similarly, he could contemplate and even crave leaving

Drohobycz for Lwów or Warsaw (providing someone else would find him work and accommodations), but he never did leave the town that was the source of his flights of imagination and the chief obstacle to his achieving wider recognition. Possessor of a startlingly original imagination, he lacked self-discipline and was appallingly, even pathologically indecisive. To a degree, Schulz's psychological makeup, as well as his self-criticism, seems to have been conditioned by his reading of Sigmund Freud. In a letter to Stefan Szuman, he confides his "truest and profoundest" dream, from age seven; he cuts off his penis with a knife and then must face not only the horror of his act but knowledge that it is irrevocable and that the guilt and punishment are eternal. The most terrifying feature of the dream may well be the form that punishment takes: The child is confined in a glass retort and subject to the disapproving stares of all who pass by. Given such a dream, Schulz had good reason to want to stay in Drohobycz—that is to say, he had good psychological reasons not to cut himself off irrevocably from his small, provincial world—and equally good reason to turn away from others and inward toward the imagination.

Schulz's withdrawal is further characterized by an obsessive desire for purity (or, alternately, a fear of contamination), which may be read as a desire to be self-contained, utterly self-sufficient. The feeling of being "brutalized and soiled" by his contact with his students and colleagues (quoted above) evidences this obsession quite directly; it is more subtly present in the revulsion he experiences upon seeing his work parodied (even if involuntarily) or in reading that he has been linked with Gombrowicz (whose fiction Schulz greatly admired). Schulz is surely right to distinguish between his own highly interiorized stories and Gombrowicz's far more sociologically oriented work, but his act implies a certain compulsion, an obsessive need to establish his own territory, to ensure its purity, and to exert an absolute control over it. All this is perversely (but in Schulz's case also consistently) coupled with an equally obsessive desire to undervalue himself and his works (including the paintings and drawings he sold for far less than they were worth). This obsession leads to an impasse, to his inability to write or draw at all, and the reason for this failure, Schulz often points out, is Schulz himself. By a pscyhological sleight of wits, Schulz the Romantic transforms himself into a Polish Kafka, railing against the fate he claims to deserve.

In the letters, self-criticism often slips into self-loathing, and self-loathing in turn into self-defense. Someone's failure to reply to a letter often led Schulz to ask if he had perhaps disappointed his correspondent in some way but then to berate that person for remaining silent, to demand that the other not only write but write frequently, and to write despite the fact that Schulz would not do the same. He felt similarly ambivalent about his writing—protective yet doubtful. Uncertain about its merit, he needed others to validate its worth for him—and to validate his own worth as well, though he was sure, some of the time at least, that what a life, his or anyone's, invariably added up to was zero. Schulz was, however, not so much manic-depressive as aesthetic-depressive. His life was divided into bouts of work separated by long periods of depression—or, to put it in a slightly different way, long periods of reality (in Schulz's mind the two were very nearly synonymous). Work—writing and drawing—was his happiness and sole salvation, the one sure remedy for the malaise of prosaic everyday existence. Work was also what he could only rarely bring himself to do, largely because his fear of being controlled in any way caused him to attempt to exert absolute control over the conditions in which he was able or willing to work. The preconditions he set for himself were impossible and intolerable: absolute quiet and therefore absolute isolation. Such dedication borders on absurdity and leads one to wonder whether anyone has ever led a more Kafkaesque life than Schulz, the man responsible for introducing Kafka to Polish readers. Not only did Schulz lead such a life, but he also led it so originally, as if by some strange time warp he was Kafka's precursor and the model for Gregor Samsa, Joseph K., and all the other Schulz-like characters in Kafka's "pseudo-realistic" stories and novels. The Kafkaesque Schulz would not leave Drohobycz to be with his fiancée in Warsaw, but he would frequently write to friends in that city about their failure to attend to her needs, particularly her desire for companionship. As he exclaimed in a letter to Romana Halpern, Józefina was not only his salvation but the very basis of his continued existence as a writer and artist. "By her love she has redeemed me, who was nearly lost and marooned in a remote no-man's-land, a barren underworld of fantasy. She brought me back to life and the earthly realm. . . . I must have Józefina's . . . closeness and connection with me assured in order even to function. That is the zero level from which I rise on the scale of fantasy." She redeems him from fantasy in order that he can return to it, but not in actuality, for what Schulz describes here is not what he has but what he has lost: Realizing the hopelessness of their situation, Józefina has just broken off their engagement.

The imagination that was Schulz's truest reality and only real salvation (and torment) derived its strength from the depth of loneliness and insecurity that compelled him to devise an alternative to the drabness of the modern commercial world that had already infected Drohobycz and, too, from the childhood that Schulz sought not so much to return to as create in all the illusory vividness of a dream. He rejected the spiritually flattened world of reality and realism, and he chose in their place legend and myth. "The legend is the organ by which greatness is apprehended," whereas "psychology implies the mediocrity of the average, faith in uniformity, the gray commonwealth of the ant. . . . The laws of greatness cannot be reconciled with the modalities of daily thought." Neither can Schulz's fiction be reconciled with "the modalities of daily thought." In his work conventional realism is not a transparent means but a point of departure that leads in two directions: up toward a pure, nearly metaphysical, utterly abstract, and wondrously dense lyricism, and down (or rather in) toward the "matrix" of all words and all reality in what Schulz calls myth.

The writer's task, then, is not to represent the world but to transform and redeem it, as Schulz does so brilliantly in story after story and perhaps most strangely and evocatively in the prose narrative "The Republic of Dreams," which begins:

> Here on the Warsaw pavement in these days of tumult, heat and dazzle I retreat in my mind to the remote city of my dreams, I let my vision rise to command that low, sprawling, polymorphic countryside. . . . How to express this in words? Where other towns developed into economies, evolved into statistics, quantified themselves—ours regressed into essence. . . . Here events are not ephemeral surface phantoms; they have roots sunk into the deep of things and penetrate the essence. Here decisions take place every moment, laying down precedents once and for all. Everything that happens here happens once and is irrevocable. This is why such weightiness, such heavy emphasis, such sadness inheres in what takes place.

Schulz's language is as excessive, as opulent, as extravagant, as hallucinatory as that of Gabriel Garćia Márquez. It does not mirror; it makes. It quite literally creates a world, at once primal and transcendental. Nevertheless, it may have been the literally creative aspect of his writing that led Schulz to doubt and despair—to question whether anything at all existed beyond words. "I need a friend," one letter begins;

> I need the closeness of a kindred spirit. I long for some outside confirmation of the inner world whose existence I postulate. To cling to it by sheer faith alone, to lug it along with me in spite of everything, is a toil and torment of Atlas. Sometimes it seems to me, even with all the strain of heaving, that I have nothing on my shoulders. I'd like to drop that weight onto someone else's shoulders for a while, straighten the crook in my neck and take a look at what I've been carrying.

Shortly before his death, Schulz had the opportunity to leave Drohobycz (ironically, for Warsaw), and he entrusted all of his papers (including correspondence) to a Catholic living outside the ghetto. Schulz never did leave, and his papers never have been found. Thanks, however, to the efforts of his indefatigable editor, Ficowski, and to the excellent translation prepared by Walter Arndt and Victoria Nelson, more of this remarkable writer's work has become available to English-language readers, who will have the opportunity to dwell not on the pathology and torment of Schulz's life and mind but instead on Schulz's genius for transforming the tragicomedy that was his life into what is unquestionably among the strangest and finest fiction of the twentieth or any other century.

Robert A. Morace

Sources for Further Study

Kirkus Reviews. LVI, September 1, 1988, p. 1390.
Library Journal. CXIII, November 1, 1988, p. 96.
The New Republic. CC, January 2, 1989, p. 28.
The New York Times Book Review. XCIII, October 30, 1988, p. 3.
Publishers Weekly. CCXXXIV, September 2, 1988, p. 91.
The Washington Post Book World. XVIII, December 18, 1988, p. 4.

THE LETTERS OF EDITH WHARTON

Author: Edith Wharton (1862-1937)
Edited, with an introduction, by R. W. B. Lewis and Nancy Lewis
Publisher: Charles Scribner's Sons (New York). Illustrated. 654 pp. $29.95
Type of work: Letters
Time: 1874-1937
Locale: The United States, England, the Continent, and Africa

A selection of some four hundred letters from one of America's great novelists

In spite of the unfair yet abiding assessment of Edith Wharton as a second-rate Henry James, she occupies a unique position in the history of American literature. She is what James himself might have called "the real thing," a bluestocking artist whose novel *The House of Mirth* (1905) alone would place her in the first ranks of the best American writers.

Wharton was an indefatigable correspondent, writing as many as six letters a day for long periods of her life. It is no surprise to find that more than four thousand of her letters are extant and available for study. R. W. B. Lewis and Nancy Lewis have made a judicious selection of nearly four hundred for this collection. In addition to her daily letters, she wrote some forty books—fiction, poetry, travel articles, a book on gardening, one on house decoration, her autobiography—plus translations, forewords, introductions and short stories. After she began her professional life—and she attacked her chosen métier with great professionalism—she published, with only one or two exceptions, a book every year between 1897 and her death in 1937. She accomplished this despite great personal upheavals, the self-imposed rigors of wartime charity work, a hectic social life, and a breathtaking whirl of travel and study.

Edith Newbold Jones was born during the Civil War in 1862. Her family, the Rhinelander Joneses, were part of old New York, part of the mercantile aristocracy which based its wealth on extensive real-estate holdings. She married Teddy Wharton, a charming ne'er-do-well, in 1885. In 1901, they began construction of The Mount in Lenox, Massachusetts, a house and garden into which she poured her unflagging zeal for and her considerable knowledge of architecture, decoration, and landscaping. Eventually, The Mount was sold during a marital contretemps. After years of coping with Teddy Wharton's increasingly severe bouts of mania and depression, she was divorced from him and spent the rest of her life in Europe, an émigré from a life she loathed, a society she rejected, and a country for which she had a curiously ambiguous contempt. She describes herself in one of her letters to Sara Norton as "out of sympathy" with everything in America: "One's friends are delightful; but *we* are none of us Americans, we don't think or feel as the Americans do, we are the wretched exotics produced in a European glass-house, the most déplacé and useless class on earth!"

Throughout her life Wharton wrote letters—to friends, to acquaintances, to her publishers and agents, and to her family. To those left behind in the United States, she is chatty, sometimes fulsome, always inquisitive about other friends and acquaintances. Her sister-in-law, Mary Cadwalader Jones, became a sort of long-distance amanuensis who handled her American affairs and even corrected proofs of her writings. She had, however, another sort of family to whom she wrote some of the most spirited and interesting letters in this collection. These were the cherished and never neglected *Unsereiners*, as Bernard Berenson dubbed them: those on whom she could count to share her enthusiasms, both personal and literary, and those who would understand implicitly these epistolary conversations which spoke not only to the intellect but to the heart and soul as well.

An autodidact, Wharton had the lifelong habit of reading voraciously, a custom which endeared her mightily to those of her friends who shared her love of knowledge and which at first mystified and then alienated entirely her sporty husband. Berenson and she sent each other books regularly, and in their heady communications, one may discern a sort of literary one-upmanship. From the legends of the Edda to the correspondence of Friedrich von Schiller, they explored a variety of fields, and their comments on books and writers, on philosophy, science, and ideas read like notes from an erudite competition. Their exchange of ideas seems effortless and casual, yet at the same time serious and challenging. These are people for whom the expansion of the mind is such a vital commitment that life is unthinkable without the stimulation of books.

Wharton's letters to the I Tatti family—B. B., as he was known by his intimates; the often-ill, estimable Mary, his wife; his secretary-cum-paramour Nicky Mariano—are at once affectionate and solicitous, provocative in their descriptions of her daily life and travels, and gently but firmly critical when necessary. In one amusing passage concerning a trip they made to Germany together, she recounts to Mary B. B.'s consternation when she faked an inability to distinguish Claude Lorrain from Nicolas Poussin, and, again, when she tried to teach her worldly yet naïve companion the fine art of successful motoring in Eastern Europe. In another letter, she suggests tactfully how Mary can improve the manuscript of her life of Bernard.

Others of these letters reveal that she could be ruthlessly frank in her criticism. Whether friend, foe, or acquaintance, she pulled no punches when it was a question of bad writing. To Sinclair Lewis, who dedicated *Babbitt* (1922) to her, she writes of her objections to his style:

> I've only begun to say what I wanted, but the rest must be talked—except for one suggestion, which I venture to make now, & that is, that in your next book, you should use slang in dialogue more sparingly. I believe the real art in this respect is to use just enough to *colour* your dialogue, not so much that in a few years it will be almost incomprehensible. It gives more relief to your characters, I'm sure, than to take down their jargon word for word.—

Even those for whom she had special affection were not spared if she believed that they had misused the language. When W. Morton Fullerton sought her opinion of his manuscript, she returned a thoughtful criticism of his style in which she implored him to "adopt a franker idiom." Urging him to read Ralph Waldo Emerson and Matthew Arnold, among others, to refrain from "scientific-politico-economic charabia," to leave France and its Gallicisms behind, she makes specific suggestions for improving his work: "Drop 30 percent of your Latinisms ('engendering a divergency' & so on), mow down every old cliché, uproot all the dragging circumlocutions, compress, diversify, clarify, vivify. . . ."

This letter, however, is atypical of those to Fullerton. The correspondent for London's *The Times* in Paris when Wharton first met him (or so he said), Fullerton was the occasion for the clear, unequivocal evidence in these letters that she was not the cold, passionless figure so often described by her literary critics. Her letters to Fullerton, the discovery of which is in itself an intriguing tale not yet fully told, are testament to her capacity for physical love. Fullerton, apparently, was something of a roué, a man who entangled himself amorously with both sexes. He was a half-hearted rake, however, a man who did not know how to end an affair, or who did not want to, once he had initiated it. Wharton's letters leave no doubt that she succumbed quite willingly to his sexual charms. Her early correspondence with him is girlish, as coquettish as she ever gets, yet ever mindful of her own worth. Having "hoarded" her emotional life, she fears spending it on one who has bartered lavishly with his own:

> And I'm so afraid that the treasures I long to unpack for you, that have come to me in magic ships from enchanted islands, are only, to you, the old familiar red calico and beads of the clever trader, who has had dealings in every latitude, & knows just what to carry in the hold to please the simple native—I'm so afraid of this, that often & often I stuff my shining treasures back into their box, lest I should see you smiling at them!

She does not shun the challenge of putting the erotically charged nature of their early relationship into words. He cannot come into a room without her feeling "a ripple of flame" all over her body; his touch expands her beating heart, and his embrace turns her words into "throbbing pulses" and her thoughts into a "great golden blur."

Too soon, however, her letters almost plead for his attention, for a reciprocity of feeling she never seems to have enjoyed: "At present, in the whole universe I see but one thing, am conscious of but one thing, you, and our love for each other." Eventually, she becomes querulous, demanding, and finally bitter: "You write to me like a lover, you treat me like a casual acquaintance." These later letters are no billets-doux; they are often painful to read, so naked is the desire of their author to find some grounds on which to understand this vacillating man. That their relationship changed is abundantly clear, yet even in her later, businesslike letters to Fullerton, Wharton occasionally reminds him of how she loved him and of the pain that he has caused her. Finally, with masterful understatement, the editors include a letter from her secretary rather peremptorily asking Fullerton to come and clear his books from Wharton's apartment.

The long, descriptive accounts of her travels to North Africa, throughout France,

Italy, Spain, and Germany, disclose a love of the road that, were she not so rooted by this time in her homes in France, could be attributed to the wanderlust of a wealthy, slightly eccentric gadfly. Travel to her was a necessity; she was one of the first modern tourists, availing herself immediately of the automobile for her tireless peregrinations in search of beauty. With her chauffeur and her slightly dazed companions, she explored even the least accessible towns. Her friends were the beneficiaries of her rapidly written impressions and her love of detail.

The recipients of these letters were an impressive group indeed. In addition to the forementioned, they included André Gide, Paul Bourget, Kenneth Clark, Theodore Roosevelt, Charles Eliot Norton, and Henry James, although only a few of her letters to him survive. The ones that are included here are chronicles of Wharton's trips to the front during World War I. They read like dispatches from a colorful, talented war reporter, and show that she practiced in her letters one of the theories she propounded for her fiction. For each of her battlefield adventures, she captures an "illuminating incident" that most clearly expresses the situation, for James. These "big summing-up impressions" of the horrors and danger of war arise from an accumulation of carefully rendered minutiae—how she traveled, with whom, the color of the Meuse, the difficulties finding accommodations, the mud-spattered, weary soldiers. She makes vivid her "sense of being in the very gates of Hell."

The editors have also included letters to her publishers in which she deals with the problems of getting her works into print. Wharton was a demanding author, one who did not fear telling Scribner's just how much she loathed a title page or how much she resented their lack of sufficient publicity for her works. In one instance, she even threatens to sue an editor who attempted to reduce her commission. These are letters from a writer well aware of her popular appeal and one who is anxious that she not be shortchanged or underestimated.

Many of the letters are similar in their descriptions of her social routine. She was a much sought-after guest and an equally popular hostess, and, consequently, she often resorts to making lists of the people she has seen, the houses she has visited, and the guests she has entertained. For all of their monotony and faint suggestion of self-congratulation, these letters represent an important history of life on a scale that would be hard to duplicate. She was fêted by some of the wealthiest and most influential men and women of the period, and lived through and recorded some of the epochal events of the late nineteenth and early twentieth centuries. For example, she writes to her friend Sara Norton, in 1909, of seeing the first "aeroplane" ever to "cross a great city." Little did she know that Wilbur Wright himself was in that plane—a fact noted by the editors with their usual punctiliousness.

This collection will serve as a companion piece to Lewis' Pulitzer Prize-winning biography of Wharton. In the editors' introductions (which aroused some controversy in *The Times Literary Supplement*), notes, and appendices, the story of her life is again recorded, but it is in the letters themselves that the subject makes herself known as a strong-willed, driven, passionate woman—a woman of great talent, remarkable strength, and hidden kindness.

To Berenson, appropriately enough the man who espoused connoisseurship as a method of study, she writes,

> Oh, bless you again & again: especially for "What is true of life is true of art: its ultimate aim is ecstasy," & what follows. It coincided so thrillingly with the "aesthetic" of my own métier that I've so long yearned to write that I could hug you—& myself.

With these words, in fact throughout these extraordinary letters, Edith Wharton, one of the great novelists of manners in English, reveals that she pursued life as relentlessly as she did art.

William U. Eiland

Sources for Further Study

Booklist. LXXXIV, May 1, 1988, p. 1473.
Commentary. LXXXVI, September, 1988, p. 64.
Kirkus Reviews. LVI, May 15, 1988, p. 744.
Library Journal. CXIII, June 1, 1988, p. 114.
National Review. XL, September 16, 1988, p. 51.
The New Republic. CXCIX, August 29, 1988, p. 40.
The New York Times. July 31, 1988, p. C23.
Publishers Weekly. CCXXXIII, May 27, 1988, p. 48.
Time. CXXXII, July 25, 1988, p. 80.
The Times Literary Supplement. November 25, 1988, p. 1301.
The Washington Post Book World. XVIII, July 24, 1988, p. 3.

THE LETTERS OF JOHN CHEEVER

Author: John Cheever (1912-1982)
Edited, with an introduction, by Benjamin Cheever
Publisher: Simon & Schuster (New York). Illustrated. 397 pp. $19.95
Type of work: Letters
Time: 1933-1982
Locale: New York and Europe

John Cheever's letters reveal much about this important American novelist and short-story writer, but the collection also tells the story of the editor-son searching for his father and surprising himself with his discoveries

The primary justification for a volume of letters such as the present one is that it sheds some light—however oblique—on the writer and the writer's work. That the present collection of letters most certainly does. Through the course of these letters, readers can watch John Cheever the writer emerge, as his style develops and his fame grows. The writer who would win the National Book Award for his first novel, *The Wapshot Chronicle* (1957), is here in that year, complaining that it has taken him twenty years to get a novel published. The short-story writer who would cap his career with a Pulitzer Prize for *The Collected Stories of John Cheever* in 1978 is also here, reaping the rewards for half a century of work—and still complaining about his competition.

Yet there is a second book here as well, a hidden text, as it were: a book about a son's search for his father, and his discovery of the real man through the letters he is editing. In Benjamin Cheever's introduction to this volume ("The Man I Thought I Knew"), in his notes that become longer as the volume proceeds, and in his insertion of selected entries from his father's journal toward the end of the book, the son reveals his attempts to find and come to grips with his real father. It is not an easy journey, but it is a fascinating, almost voyeuristic one for admirers of Cheever. Benjamin Cheever slowly uncovers "a man of massive and fundamental contradictions," an alcoholic and bisexual father whom he still, in the end, loves, and with whom, through this very work, he is finally able to make his peace.

As Benjamin Cheever admits early in his introduction to the volume, this is not a collection of letters in the conventional sense. "His correspondence will not provide a concrete explanation of his life or his fiction, but it should shed light on both. It has for me." Readers learn much about the writer through Cheever's letters. He was a prolific correspondent, sometimes writing thirty letters a week, to a great range of friends, including a number of writers who are, like Cheever, important in the development of modern American literature—the editor and critic Malcolm Cowley, for example, and the novelist and journalist Josephine Herbst, two of Cheever's steadiest correspondents over the years.

Readers witness the difficulties Cheever had especially at the beginning, to establish himself as a writer—to make enough money to *be* a writer. ("When you have no money you live, at least," he wrote in 1935, "in continual anxiety.") Readers share his experiences as he first sells a story to *The New Yorker* in 1935 (he would publish 120 stories in the magazine in the following decades) and as he visits to the Yaddo writers colony. During World War II, he is stuck in the stateside army for three years, almost in a cocoon, but even here he is able to write (and to publish his first collection of short stories, *The Way Some People Live*, 1943). After the war, Cheever's success grows, as he establishes himself, first as a short-story writer and later as a novelist. In 1953 he publishes *The Enormous Radio and Other Stories*; *Time* magazine does a cover story on him in 1964, following *The Wapshot Scandal*; in 1977, with the publication of his novel *Falconer*, he is on the cover of *Newsweek*. Through all these events, the reader observes Cheever's reaction to his growing fame and fortune, to his increasing reputation among readers and critics alike.

There are two gaps in this story. Cheever seems almost reticent about how he works, and consequently there is little on his actual writing practices. This is the writer who, in an apartment house in New York in the 1940's, as his son tells us,

> would put on his suit in the morning and take the elevator down with the other men heading out to work, but he wouldn't get off at the first floor. He'd go on down to the basement and to a maid's room. . . . Here he'd take off his suit, hang it up, and type in his underwear.

There is even less on the world around him. Cheever seems to go through history without a nod of acknowledgment. "I seem to miss the Big Things, the Big Shapes," he confesses in a 1953 letter; "I miss them in this letter." Instead, as with most correspondents, there is more on domestic matters: chatty letters about children growing up and moving away; apartments rented in New York, houses bought in its suburbs; travel to Rome, to the Soviet Union; teaching stints at Sing Sing, at Iowa; problems with the marriage, with drinking, with himself.

What is also here is an abundance of fascinating detail about a writer's life. Readers hear all Cheever's complaints about, and problems with, editors, agents, publishers, all of his "disappointment and bewilderment," as his son notes, with his profession. Yet they also share his insights into the writing process itself. Fiction is "an exercise of memory that was imperfectly understood," he writes enigmatically late in his career. He understands the false ecstasy writers sometimes feel, as he notes to Herbst in 1952:

> To each of them comes a month, sometimes a year, when they feel that at last they have hit the purest spring of creativity. What rapture! What transports! With their eyes inflamed and their pants unbuttoned, they come out of the basement or the coat closet at dusk, convinced that they have the world by the tail. It does not really matter that the manuscripts they leave behind them will be nothing but a sore and a humiliation to their descendents.

Cheever also recognizes early in his career why the novel may not be appropriate for the modern age. The form

> was created largely by and for the growth and decline of a middle-class that men of my generation are strangers to. Our lives have not been sustained or constant or ordered. Our characters don't die in bed. The powerful sense of passed and passing time that seems to be the one defin-

able and commendable quality of the novel is not our property. Our lives are not long and well-told stories.

This is a remarkable analysis of the novel, by someone who struggled with the form for some decades.

At the same time, there is significant insight into contemporary literature, some perceptive comments about its creators—and not a little backbiting. Cheever's split personality is most dramatically revealed in relation to John Updike. "I think his magnanimity specious and his work seems motivated by covetousness, exhibitionism and a stony heart," Cheever writes in 1965. On the other hand, he can be wonderfully gracious: Regarding *Rabbit Is Rich* (1981), he writes to Updike, "I think it is the most important American novel I have read in many years." John Irving, Cheever mocks, "has always struck me as having been saddened by the discovery that to have been the captain of the Exeter Wrestling Team was a fleeting honor." On the other hand, "Whenever I win any sort of prize," he writes to Saul Bellow near the end of his life, "I always take out . . . a yellowed newspaper copy of your beautiful Nobel [Prize] speech and crib from this."

Cheever's stories and novels are marked by closely observed details, by the concrete ways in which the writer captures social mores and fashions, and his letters convey these qualities as well. Cheever has a sharp and self-effacing wit, a vivid and comic way of describing people and places. Ben's mother has taught him patty-cake too soon, the father points out in 1949, "and now when he's asked to wave goodbye he flails his arms around in the air, wets his pants and slaps himself on the stomach." Much later, he remarks that one of his dogs had gotten so nearsighted "that while he insists upon my throwing tennis balls for him he then insists that I put on my glasses and go and find the ball." There is often a wonderful wisdom behind the wit: "I've told my own sons that when they find me lacking they can continue to love me and find other men who will wear underwear, pitch no-hitters and invent the telephone."

The advice has apparently worked—in spite of Cheever. When he died, his son writes in the first lines of the introductory essay, "I tried to start his lungs again by blowing air through his lips." This volume is, in some way, a final parting, and through it Ben Cheever comes to grips with his father, as both man and writer. He does not excuse or blame him, but he tries to explain his father's alcoholism, his infidelities (he had a long affair with the actress Hope Lange), and other family tragedies.

His relationship with his father was never an easy one. Ben is my "favorite" child, Cheever writes in 1965; however, in a hospital after his heart attack in 1973, when Ben will not get him a drink or a cigarette, Cheever says, "You've always been a disappointment as a son." In perhaps the unkindest slap of all, in his final alcoholic collapse, Cheever withholds his phone number from Benjamin.

The son's greatest discovery is John Cheever's bisexuality. "Looking back at my father's life, and at his writing," Ben admits, "it must seem difficult to believe that I didn't know about his bisexuality, but I didn't even suspect." In this volume, as Cheever's homosexuality becomes more active and graphic in his later letters, Benjamin comments more and more, explaining and questioning, even quoting entries from his father's journals. It is the son's attempt to come to grips with the father, much as his sister Susan did in 1984, in her autobiographical *Home Before Dark*.

If there is a problem with the volume, it is in this editing. Perhaps because Benjamin Cheever does not fully understand how the two stories are intertwined, he is not able to explain his own editing sufficiently. The book is divided into chapters of Cheever's epistolary life: "The 1930's: Starting Out," for example, is the first, twenty-five page chapter, "War and Marriage" the second. (There is also a wealth of wonderful photographs accompanying the text.) But Benjamin Cheever does not explain his own methods as editor: why, for example, he uses his father's journals so selectively, why he reproduces some letters and not others, or his rationale for his own way (often useful) of adding notes to the letters.

In spite of this editorial weakness, *The Letters of John Cheever* is an intriguing book and a fascinating revelation of Cheever as writer and as a man. Benjamin Cheever finally wants his father to be remembered for his "joy and the talent he had for passing that joy on to the people around him."

> The man who comes alive again in these letters is more complete than the man I thought I knew and knew I loved. . . . He is intensely himself, and he gives the world a blessed wholeness that I always felt in his company, and that I sorely miss.

In a letter to Herbst in 1959, John Cheever remarked that he was pleased to learn that she was saving his letters, "although I always throw the damned things away myself. Yesterday's roses, yesterday's kisses, yesterday's snows." Here is Benjamin Cheever's final kiss to his father.

David Peck

Sources for Further Study

Booklist. LXXXV, December 1, 1988, p. 435.
Boston Globe. November 20, 1988, p. 110.
Chicago Tribune. November 27, 1988, XIV, p. 6.
Kirkus Reviews. LVI, October 15, 1988, p. 1501.
Library Journal. CXIII, December, 1988, p. 100.
The Nation. CCXLVII, December 5, 1988, p. 606.
The New York Times Book Review. XCIII, December 18, 1988, p. 12.
Publishers Weekly. CCXXXIV, October 28, 1988, p. 68.
Time. CXXXII, November 28, 1988, p. 98.
The Washington Post Book World. XVIII, November 27, 1988, p. 1.

LETTERS OF MARSHALL McLUHAN

Author: (Herbert) Marshall McLuhan (1911-1980)
First published: 1987, in Canada
Selected and edited by Matie Molinaro, Corinne McLuhan, and William Toye
Publisher: Oxford University Press (Toronto, Canada). Illustrated. 562 pp. $30.00
Type of work: Letters
Time: 1911-1980
Locale: Principally Canada, England, and the United States

This work presents the only collection of letters by Marshall McLuhan, media philosopher and critic of the 1960's and 1970's and to date one of the most important and controversial analysts of the media

Principal personages:
MARSHALL McLUHAN, media critic and analyst
ELSIE McLUHAN, his mother
MAURICE McLUHAN, his brother
WALTER ONG, a Jesuit priest, scholar, and one-time student of McLuhan
WYNDHAM LEWIS, a British painter and author
EZRA POUND, an influential American poet
PIERRE ELLIOTT TRUDEAU, Prime Minister of Canada, 1968-1979; 1980-1984

One of the seminal insights of Marshall McLuhan was that the media, through their presentations, created a new and different sort of reality. In the 1960's and 1970's, there were few names more widely found in the media, coupled with both praise and blame, than that of McLuhan. Since his death, however, his name has faded from public—and media—consciousness. Informed of this fact, McLuhan would undoubtedly have cited it as further evidence of the correctness of his insights.

It must be said at the outset that reading these letters will not help much in explaining the phenomenon that came to be called "McLuhanism." Nor are these letters particularly interesting; McLuhan is not to be numbered among the notable letter writers of the English language. The reasons for this are not far to seek; McLuhan is too earnest and too much the teacher to allow for that ease of manner and polish of style which mark the best letter writers.

There was perhaps some confusion in the purposes of the three editors when compiling this work. From 100,000 pages of letters, Corinne McLuhan, Marshall McLuhan's wife, and Matie Molinaro, his literary agent, selected some fifteen hundred letters which they believed would constitute an autobiography of McLuhan; they saw it as a tribute to him. Needing a professional editor, they selected William Toye, editorial director of Oxford University Press in Canada, who reduced the selection to about 450 letters, a manageable single volume. In addition to the biographical, Toye's purposes included demonstrating McLuhan's intellectual development and interests and presenting his ideas, with their clarifications and elaborations. The editors chose to include letters to famous and important people, even though such letters may have little intrinsic interest. All the chronological introductions and notes in the text are by Toye, and Molinaro contributes a brief preface.

Such a collection of letters, then, presents several questions. While a counsel of perfection would wish for the whole of the correspondence, that was clearly impossible. It would, however, have been interesting to know whether the proportion of letters to various correspondents as seen in the text are in fact borne out by the whole of the collection. If the development and refining of McLuhan's ideas is to be important, it might have been useful occasionally to have seen the other side of the corespondence, that is, the discussion of ideas.

McLuhan was born in 1911 in Edmonton, Alberta. He received a B.A. from the University of Manitoba in 1933 and an M.A. in 1934; he was awarded a postgraduate scholarship to study at Cambridge University, from which he received a B.A. in 1936. During 1936-1937, he taught at the University of Wisconsin, and he became a Catholic in 1937. From 1937 to 1944, he taught in the English department at St. Louis University, except for 1939-1940 when he studied at Cambridge for the Ph.D. degree, which he received in 1943. McLuhan married Corinne Lewis in 1939. From 1944 to 1946, he taught at Assumption College in Windsor, Ontario, and from 1946 until his death, he was on the staff of St. Michael's College of the University of Toronto. It was here that he conducted his career as critic of society and interpreter of the electronic age. McLuhan died on New Year's Day, 1980.

The collection of letters is arranged chronologically, with each of the three sections prefaced by a useful brief biographical sketch of the years covered. The first section spans the period from 1911 to 1936, though the letters begin only in 1931. In this section of some forty letters, all but a few are to his mother or his immediate family. McLuhan is seen here as already much interested in literature, devoted to his mother, rather self-consciously "adult," and a bit of a prig. His brother Maurice was only two years his junior, but McLuhan addresses him from the stance of a rather pompous, successful uncle, explaining how to succeed intellectually and morally in life. The most interesting of the letters are those from England.

In the second group of letters, from 1936 to 1946, about twenty-five are to his mother, but the section is highlighted by a series of letters to British painter and writer Wyndham Lewis, at that time living in Canada. The letters are rather entertaining, as McLuhan attempts to arrange a visit by Lewis to St. Louis for speaking engagements and portrait commissions. Lewis was always short of money, and McLuhan's efforts to aid him certainly passed the boundaries of the routine.

The third group of letters, from 1946 to 1979, is clearly the most important and the most extensive, comprising about 350 of the total of some 450 letters in the collection; there are only five letters to his mother here. The letters of this section are more relaxed, and, as McLuhan grows older, his style becomes less rigorous and more free, even to the point of occasionally dashing off ideas as they occur to him. Ironically, his own prose style sometimes assumes the characteristics of the electronic media with which he became so concerned.

It is difficult in a brief account to summarize McLuhan's main ideas on the media, but several of the themes and characteristics of his discussions can usefully be mentioned. As far as his discussions of media are concerned (this is by far the dominant subject of his letters), it must be said that these letters are not any clearer about McLuhan's ideas and insights than his published works. McLuhan was frequently criticized in his heyday as a proponent of the electronic age and a prophet of the death of the book. In fact, as many letters clearly show, McLuhan disliked intensely what he saw the media doing to humanity and to culture; he maintained repeatedly that he was not judging or promoting any particular view of the media but was simply trying to make his generation aware of what the media were doing to the human race. Although he deplored what was happening, he believed that humankind had to understand what was occurring in order to combat the change and to save those elements most human. In some of his later letters, McLuhan can become a bit querulous about what he sees as failures to understand what he has been trying to say.

The letters also reveal McLuhan's continuing intellectual life. He reads widely, frequently reporting on the books he has read. He finds new insights in all sorts of books, from chemistry to sociology to literature. McLuhan never ceased to think and was always willing to alter his theories and insights, adding to his store of ideas. As his circle of correspondents widened, so too did his reading and his perspective. While McLuhan began as a literary critic (generally in the vein of the New Criticism), he became a social critic, approaching the changes and trends in society mainly through his insights into the electronic media.

The letters of this period also reveal McLuhan's industriousness: He lectures, writes, travels, and consults. He was much on the go, juggling many projects, following up lines of investigation that occurred to him through his reading and that were suggested to him by his correspondents. One of the rather sad topics which recurs throughout the letters is that of the book he is writing, or the paper which he is going to publish, and which never appear or are completed. It is clear that, to a certain extent, his career as media guru overwhelmed his natural scholarly bent.

McLuhan often connects his approach to the media as deriving from his study of Symbolist art and poetry. There are several excellent examples in his letters of his fondness for grabbing an insight or an idea and trying to make a variety of elements fit into it. One example is the distinction between the terms "figure" and "ground" as they are originally used in painting. Another would be his concern for the five traditional divisions of rhetoric—which he asserts to be the organizing principle of works as diverse as James Joyce's *Finnegans Wake* (1939), T. S. Eliot's *Four Quartets* (1943), Adam Smith's *An Inquiry into the Nature and Cause of the Wealth of Nations* (1776), Niccolò Machiavelli's *Il principe* (1532; *The Prince*, 1560), the plays of the Renaissance, and Saint Augustine's *De doctrina Christiana* (books 1-3, 396-397, book 4, 426; *On Christian Instruction*). In the latter years of his life, McLuhan was much taken with the growing biological and psychological awareness of the two hemispheres of the brain.

His interest in these and other ideas verifies his capacity for learning and growth; McLuhan was the farthest thing from a man of one idea. It also speaks for his enthusiasm—for helping a friend such as Lewis, for investigating a new idea, for attempting to educate a public that he believed did not understand the world they were taking for granted. He was possessed of an enthusiasm which he never lost, and the letters make this clear. Half-prepared he may have been sometimes, half-understanding of the implications of his own insights he may have been sometimes, but he was always eager and concerned to grow in understanding and to transmit that understanding.

While McLuhan gave to a generation such concepts, now taken for common currency, as the global village, the information explosion, and, most famously, the medium as message, his work had its deepest roots in much older sources. The letters of all three periods of his life make it clear that his view of the world and of his place in it springs first from a traditional humanism. Letter after letter speaks of his concern for youth, for "the kids." His concerns are not merely intellectual but also moral, though he is far from being a moralist in the usual sense of that term. The second important root of his analysis of media, society, and popular culture was his Catholicism, which not only inspired his missionary zeal but also shaped his personal point of view. He calls Christians who kneel before the new electric environment "misguided" and the electronic media a "Luciferan product," a "mock-up of the mystical body" of Christ. At bottom, as these letters make clear, Marshall McLuhan was far from being the prophet of a new age or the destroyer of the old.

Gordon N. Bergquist

Sources for Further Study

Books in Canada. XVII, April, 1988, p. 31.
The Christian Science Monitor. April 6, 1988, p. 19.
The Guardian. CXXXVIII, March 20, 1988, p. 28.
Library Journal. CXIII, May 1, 1988, p. 74.
London Review of Books. X, March 17, 1988, p. 3.
Macleans. C, December 21, 1987, p. 54.
Manchester Guardian Weekly. CXXXVIII, March 20, 1988, p. 28.
The New Republic. CXCIX, July 18, 1988, p. 35.
The Observer. March 6, 1988, p. 42.
Saturday Night. CIII, May, 1988, p. 59.
Spectator. CCLX, March 12, 1988, p. 34.
The Times Literary Supplement. May 6, 1988, p. 493.

THE LETTERS OF T. S. ELIOT
Volume I, 1898-1922

Author: T. S. Eliot (1888-1965)
Edited with an introduction by Valerie Eliot
Publisher: Harcourt Brace Jovanovich (New York). Illustrated. 639 pp. $29.95
Type of work: Letters
Time: 1898-1922
Locale: England and the United States

A definitive collection of letters drawn from public and private sources and edited by the great poet's widow

Principal personages:
T. S. ELIOT, an Anglo-American poet
VIVIENNE ELIOT, his first wife
CHARLOTTE ELIOT, his mother
HENRY WARE ELIOT, his brother
EZRA POUND, a fellow poet
BERTRAND RUSSELL, his good friend, a great philosopher
CONRAD AIKEN, his friend, a fellow poet
RICHARD ALDINGTON, his close friend, an English writer
RICHARD COBDEN-SANDERSON, his close associate, a publisher
ELEANOR HINKLEY, his cousin
JOHN QUINN, an American attorney and art patron who helped support his work
SYDNEY SCHIFF, an Englishman who befriended and supported him

Although there have been several biographies of T. S. Eliot in recent years, these works were undertaken without complete access to this large collection of letters, some of which have become available only since the late 1970's. Before he died, Eliot gave his consent to such a collection, which claims to include all of his significant extant correspondence up to the age of thirty-four.

In spite of its seeming sanction by Eliot, his widow admits in her introduction that he burned many personal and family letters. Eliot did not wish a biography of himself written, and there are aspects of his life—especially his first marriage—on which he refused to comment at much length, and which still remain a matter for considerable speculation. Yet he also admitted that most letter writers had some hope that their correspondence would survive. Certainly Eliot's letters are well worth reading for their insights into both the rational and emotional sides of his life and work.

It has always been a matter of enormous importance that Eliot decided to live in England. His native land, the United States, made him uncomfortable. It was rude and unfinished, and he craved a setting that was more sophisticated and refined, though not—he hastened to add in one of his letters—necessarily more profound or intelligent. Rawboned, industrialized America put him off—as did the cruder sort of American visitor, such as the writer Maxwell Bodenheim, "an odd American Jew . . . a vagrant poet," who thought that he could thrive in London as easily as he had done in the United States. Eliot recognized his intelligence while calling him "pathetic" and "foolish," and pointed out that the English needed much cultivating. How could Bodenheim, with "only a common school education and no university degree, with no money, no connections, and no social polish or experience," think that he could succeed?

The comments on Bodenheim are revealing of Eliot as both a man and a poet. Eliot took all manner of care to please his English hosts. He reveled in knowing how to behave as English as the English. He married an Englishwoman, worked in an English bank, and prided himself on having more influence over the English than any American writer, with the possible exception of Henry James. Although Eliot's letters are full of his complaints about being a foreigner, of never feeling quite at home, he never seriously considered returning to the United States. He loved his mother dearly and sometimes wrote to her at weekly intervals, yet he went through a period of more than six years without visiting her in St. Louis. To be sure, he was strapped for money during this period and fiercely dedicated to his writing and bank job, but it is also the case that he measured his success by English standards.

In the earliest letters in this volume, there are wonderful glimpses of Eliot the student of philosophy, debating whether he should return to the United States to obtain his doctorate. He had written a thesis, but university life (in England and the United States) appalled him. Professors could stimulate him with historical and philosophical questions, but they were of no use to a young man bent on becoming a modern poet, who needed the stimulation of irreverent and revolutionary personalities such as Ezra Pound. Even Bertrand Russell, who had first met Eliot in his student days at Harvard University, admits in a letter included in this volume that he did not see the significance of Eliot's verse for many years. Eliot's ambition was to live in London and to be judged by the literary lights of that great city.

Eliot had confidence enough to turn his back on America and to abandon his graduate studies. By 1915, he had written his great poem "The Love Song of J. Alfred Prufrock" and many other deft verses that had already assured his place as the premier young poet of his time. Yet he suffered crises of confidence. As a man, he was only half formed, excessively polite and wary of letting down his guard with anyone. Writing from Oxford to Conrad Aiken, his college chum, on December 31, 1914, Eliot expresses the feelings of a man who has not quite found himself:

> I should not mind being in London, to work at the British Museum. How much more self-conscious one is in a big city! . . . Just at present this is an inconvenience, for I have been going through one of those nervous sexual attacks which I suffer from when alone in a city.

The young Eliot felt that he somehow had to take charge, to prove himself to his father and family, to take on responsibilities that would define his adulthood. On June 26, 1915, he married Vivienne Haigh-Wood in a very private ceremony. For the first few weeks he seemed deliriously happy, writing to his mother and other members of the family about his plans to stay in England, to make his way as a poet and literary man. There was still some talk of his finishing a degree at Harvard, but he soon saw to it that the English marriage made his establishment in England an apparently sensible alternative.

Almost immediately, however, Vivienne began to suffer from various maladies—most of which were attributed to her nerves or which were exacerbated by her mental anguish. Eliot's letters are filled with references to her illnesses, to trouble with her teeth, her eyes, her stomach, her head (terrible migraines)—not to mention more ordinary sicknesses such as influenza. Vivienne could be immobilized for days, even weeks. She was quite aware of how debilitating her various illnesses were on her husband, who was also prone to nervous breakdowns and collapses. Never a prolific writer, Eliot often contented himself with one, two, or three poems a year, supplemented by his exquisitely articulate literary criticism. As one of his letters indicates, he made his lack of literary industry into a virtue, for he was quite aware that the publication of an Eliot poem was regarded as an event. The only problem was that each poem had to be a perfect representative of its kind in order to excite anticipation for the next one.

In the massive correspondence that Eliot carried on, he is nearly always the gentleman-entrepreneur, calculating precisely how he will get on in the literary world. He had Pound working diligently for him. Eliot was the sort of proud yet deserving young chap that inspired distinguished elders such as Bertrand Russell to write to Eliot's father, assuring him that his son was destined for greatness. Vivienne, on occasion, would do the same, petitioning others for help on behalf of her genius husband. Judging by her letters, she had a lively, keen intelligence and grieved over the anxiety her health caused him.

Although Eliot did not like to have to ask for money, he accepted it willingly and graciously from his family. He was pleased to be a success as a banker, to put his mind to matters of international finance, and did not see the hours he devoted to commerce as taking away from his writing. On the contrary, his job gave him a valued independence from literary journals and cliques. To his correspondents, he relates a few of the details of his banking days with gusto and pride.

Yet the poet could never quite get into the clear. His life with Vivienne, as she put it herself in a letter, seemed "a long scramble and *effort*." After the first years of the marriage, there are hints in the letters (particularly in hers) that their existence was a trial he found hard to bear. At one point, he had to take a three-month leave of absence from his bank in order to settle his badly frayed nerves.

What is perhaps most impressive about his letters is the consistency of Eliot's civility, whether he is dealing with personal, social, family, or literary matters. He had a code by which he lived, a code that might seem artificial to some, but which meant everything to him. The very act of writing a letter, his style implies, is a kind of courtesy. His letter to Herbert Read on June 2, 1921, gives the flavor of his gentlemanly correspondence:

> My dear Read,
>
> I am humiliated, after such a long silence, to be writing to you on a purely practical subject—

> but circumstances all this winter and spring—a great deal of anxious illness, not my own—have been very unfavourable to the correspondence I had hoped for.

In part, Eliot's deference to his English correspondents sprang from his consciousness of being a foreigner and his tireless effort never to give offense to anyone who might be of service to him. Yet the poet's manners surely go deeper than that. They are the very essence of a writer whose learned and magisterial poems are about civilization. World War I distressed him greatly, yet it is hard to specify exactly why (he says remarkably little about the war itself), unless it is realized that for him war meant the destruction of civilization. For Eliot, it was not enough to be intelligent or even to be a genius unless human brilliance was put to the test of society. Human beings had to develop selves that got along with and cultivated one another. Thus, even a simple piece of business correspondence from Eliot is certain to be correct in its form of address and content.

If Eliot was correct and polite, he could also be whimsical and amusing. Some letters contain drafts of poems, and a few have drawings. Valerie Eliot annotates the letters, so that her husband's references to certain events or circumstances are clear. The problem with these letters—as with any collection of letters—is that there is no narrative, no shaping of a life other than the shape individual letters bring to it. Consequently, there is a certain repetitiveness in the letters, and the reading of them is somewhat disrupted if the footnotes and the biographical chronology are consulted. On the other hand, the repetitiveness is sometimes helpful, because Eliot's version of events can be checked against the versions of his correspondents, some of whose letters are wisely included.

Two useful indexes and many photographs taken of Eliot in childhood, adolescence, and early adulthood help to make this volume a comprehensive introduction to his life and career.

Carl Rollyson

Sources for Further Study

Booklist. LXXXV, November 15, 1988, p. 532.

Chicago Tribune. September 25, 1988, XIV, p. 1.

The Christian Science Monitor. September 28, 1988, p. 19.

Interview. XVIII, December, 1988, p. 141.

Los Angeles Times. October 6, 1988, V, p. 1.

The Nation. CCXLVII, December 5, 1988, p. 593.

The New Republic. CXCIX, December 12, 1988, p. 28.

The New York Review of Books. XXXV, November 10, 1988, p. 3.

The New York Times Book Review. XCIII, October 16, 1988, p. 1.

The Times Literary Supplement. September 23, 1988, p. 1037.

LETTERS TO OLGA
June, 1979-September, 1982

Author: Václav Havel (1936-)
First published: Briefe an Olga: Identität und Existenz—Betrachtungen aus dem Gefängnis, 1984, in West Germany
Translated from the Czech by Paul Wilson
Publisher: Alfred A. Knopf (New York). 397 pp. $25.00
Type of work: Letters
Time: June, 1979, to September, 1982
Locale: Czechoslovakia

A philosophical investigation in the form of letters, written in prison by the Czech playwright and human-rights activist Václav Havel

The publication of literary correspondence is a growth industry. Massive multi-volume collections, one-volume selections, and volumes which present both sides of the correspondence between two writers are appearing in ever-increasing numbers. Most of these volumes (the ongoing Cambridge edition of the letters of Joseph Conrad is a good example) are consulted primarly for biographical material and for the light they shed on the development of the writer's work; a few, such as the letters of D. H. Lawrence and George Bernard Shaw, are absorbing performances in their own right. Whether mundane or dazzling, however, most collections of letters are miscellanies to be mined by the scholar or browsed in by the general reader; they are not books with an overarching form, intended to be read straight through.

There are exceptions to this rule. Notable examples include Viktor Shklovsky's *Zoo, ili Pisma ne o liubvi* (1923; *Zoo, or Letters Not About Love*, 1971) and Andrei Sinyavsky's *Golos iz khora* (1973; *A Voice from the Chorus*, 1976), both of which have affinities with the book under review. Shklovsky's book consists largely of letters which he wrote to Elsa Triolet, a young woman with whom he had fallen in love during his sojourn among the Russian émigrés in Berlin, while the text of Sinyavsky's book was extracted from letters which he wrote to his wife from a Soviet labor camp. Both writers produced books with a unity and conscious design quite foreign to the average collection of letters.

Like *A Voice from the Chorus*, Václav Havel's *Letters to Olga: June, 1979-September, 1982* was written in prison. In 1979, Havel was convicted of "subversion" against the Czech government and was sentenced to four and a half years of hard labor. Havel's trial culminated several years of increasingly intense harrassment by Czech authorities as a result of his participation in the human-rights organization Charter 77 and its offshoot, the Committee to Defend the Unjustly Prosecuted (or VONS, the Czech acronym by which it was known). He served more than three years of his sentence; his early release can be attributed in part to his ill health (the authorities were fearful that he might die in prison) and in part to the fact that his imprisonment became a cause célèbre in the international literary community.

Between June 4, 1979, shortly after his arrest, and September 4, 1982, about four months before his release, Havel wrote to his wife Olga more than 150 letters, a few of which were confiscated by the censor and thus never reached her. Following his release, 125 of these letters were collected in a samizdat volume under the title *Dopisy Olze (červen 1979-září 1982)*. The book was first formally published in an abridged German translation, in 1984; a Czech edition followed in 1985, issued by an émigré publisher in Canada. The English translation, by Paul Wilson, deletes two letters and makes occasional cuts; it is, Wilson says, about one-sixth shorter than the Czech edition. Like many books published by Alfred A. Knopf, it is a beautifully made volume.

That Havel should have had to spend years in prison was both absurd and predictable. He was born into a wealthy and influential family. In the late 1940's, however, when the Communists nationalized the Czech economy, his parents were stripped of their wealth, and the once-privileged youth found himself discriminated against as a class enemy. Nevertheless, while working at a chemical factory he was able to complete his secondary education at night school, later studying at the Prague Academy of the Arts. Following compulsory military service, he joined a Prague theater group, gaining experience in every aspect of dramatic production, from lighting and props to playwriting.

Havel's first major play, *Zahradní slavnost* (1963; *The Garden Party*, 1969), and its successor, *Vyrozumění* (1965; *The Memorandum*, 1967), his most widely produced work, established his international reputation. Both of these plays center on bureaucracies, microcosms of society at large; both explore the ways in which language, instead of revealing reality, can be imposed on it as a self-contained system. While reflecting the influence of the Theater of the Absurd, Havel's early plays lack the nihilism which characterizes that movement. In their exuberance of invention they epitomize the Czech renaissance of the 1960's.

Only in a society as Kafkaesque as the bureaucracies of his plays could Havel have even become a dissident. As some of his later, more autobiographical plays make clear, he views his role with a mixture of irony and understatement. Of himself and his fellow human-rights activists, he has said that there was no conscious decision to become dissidents. "We just happened to. We don't know how. And we started landing in jails—we also don't know how. We just did some things that seemed the decent things to do." Self-deprecation aside, Havel was in fact well aware of the risk entailed by his actions—and was aware too that, like many of his fellow artists (Milan Kundera, Joseph Škvorecký, and Miloš Forman, to name some of the most prominent émigrés), he could leave Czechoslovakia. A stubborn sense of responsibility, deeper than his irony and diffidence, deeper even than his instinct for self-preservation, compelled him to stay; inevitably, he found himself in prison.

During his imprisonment (he served time at three different locations), Havel suffered from a variety of physical ailments, including severe hemorrhoids that eventually required surgery. The prison authorities harassed and taunted him, hoping to break his spirit. He was allowed to write one four-page letter a week to his wife; no other writing—no diary, no playwriting—was permitted. In those circumstances, the weekly letters to Olga became extremely important to Havel. As he recalled after his release, "The letters gave me a chance to develop a new way of looking at myself and examining my attitudes to the fundamental things in life. I became more and more wrapped up in them, I depended on them to the point where almost nothing else mattered."

Readers who come to these letters having known Havel through his plays will be surprised by what they find. Havel writes very little here about the theater or about literature in any form (though he frequently refers to philosophers); there are a handful of penetrating passages in which he discusses his work and that of other playwrights, but no extended analysis. Perhaps more surprising is the absence of the humor that animates works such as *The Memorandum*. It is true that, to a degree impossible to calculate, the content of Havel's letters reflects the strict and sometimes arbitrary censorship imposed by the prison authorities. "Humor was banned," Havel recalls, but that explanation is not entirely convincing, for it seems unlikely that much of his characteristic humor would be recognized as such by the authorities. Perhaps he believed that his preoccupations while in prison did not lend themselves to humor. *Letters to Olga* is a philosophical investigation conducted by a man who was stripped to essentials.

There is a tendency to think of philosophy as a specialized professional activity—whatever it is that academic philosophers do—as if the most vital philosophical questions did not grow out of perennial human needs and conflicts and desires. When Havel writes that his purpose is "to inquire after the nature of Being," he uses language that most "civilians" (that is, nonphilosophers) would be hesitant to claim. In prison, he was beyond worrying about embarrassing himself. For his own sake, he sought "to reconsider things—originally, authentically, from the beginning."

That ambition is the source of this book's great appeal. As he examines his experience, asking himself what it means to be human, Havel seeks both understanding and a practical code for living; alongside his philosophizing there are many reminders of everyday life. Havel's letters challenge the reader to undertake a similar quest for essentials.

At the same time, however, Havel's determination to assess his experience of the world "originally, authentically, from the beginning" leads him into an inescapable bind. On the one hand, he wishes to detach himself from any dogmatic interpretation of experience; thus, while he greatly respects Christianity (indeed, his analysis of the human condition is translatable, almost point-by-point, into Christian terms), he rejects belief in it and all other religions as such. On the other hand, however, he is faced with the impossibility of a naked confrontation with experience, free of any inherited presuppositions and terminology. As a result, he adopts the distinctive language of phenomenology, especially as influenced by Martin Heidegger. Thus, instead of God, Havel speaks of "the 'absolute horizon' of Being." Instead of Original Sin, he speaks of humankind's "thrownness into the world" and its consequence: "the longing to step beyond all our concrete horizons and thus to touch again the lost fullness of Being."

Readers for whom human life is reducible to purely materialistic terms will dismiss this as mumbo-jumbo, indistinguishable from religious formulations. Yet will readers who are searching for something more be satisfied with Havel's injunction to heed "the voice of Being"? Probably not.

John Wilson

Sources for Further Study

Booklist. LXXXIV, March 1, 1988, p. 1090.
Kirkus Reviews. LVI, January 15, 1988, p. 103.
Library Journal. CXIII, March 1, 1988, p. 67.
Los Angeles Times Book Review. April 3, 1988, p. 3.
Maclean's. CI, May 16, 1988, p. 57.
The New York Review of Books. XXXV, December 22, 1988, p. 36.
The New York Times Book Review. XCIII, May 8, 1988, p. 10.
Publishers Weekly. CCXXXIII, January 22, 1988, p. 93.
Washington Monthly. XX, October, 1988, p. 57.
World Literature Today. LIX, Autumn, 1985, p. 621.

LIBRA

Author: Don DeLillo (1936-   )
Publisher: Viking Penguin (New York). 456 pp. $19.95
Type of work: Novel
Time: the 1950's to the early 1960's
Locale: The United States, the Soviet Union, and Japan

A fictionalized account of the Kennedy assassination that focuses on the life of Lee Harvey Oswald and his role within a conspiracy to kill the president

Principal characters:
LEE HARVEY OSWALD, a loner and misfit
MARINA OSWALD, his Russian-born wife
MARGUERITE OSWALD, his mother
JACK RUBY, a Dallas strip club owner
WALTER "WIN" EVERETT, JR., a teacher and an agent with the Central Intelligence Agency (CIA)
LAURENCE "LARRY" PARMENTER, a CIA agent
T. J. MACKEY, a maverick CIA agent and trainer of anti-Castro Cuban exiles
DAVID FERRIE, a onetime pilot with ties to the CIA
NICHOLAS BRANCH, a retired senior analyst for the CIA, commissioned to write an in-house account of the assassination

The assassination of John F. Kennedy was an event that continues to grip the hearts and minds of those who remember it. In the years since Kennedy's death in 1963, the persistent rumors of a conspiracy behind his murder have grown in scope and apparent likelihood. Twenty-five years after the assassination, polls indicated that—despite the findings of the Warren Commission—the majority of the American people no longer believed that Lee Harvey Oswald acted alone. The Mafia, the Central Intelligence Agency (CIA), Fidel Castro, and Texas oil men all came in for their share of close scrutiny in the case, while books and articles by assassination theorists kept the mystery surrounding the president's death very much in the public eye.

With *Libra*, novelist Don DeLillo explores the event which marked the true beginning of the 1960's and has so dominated the American psyche, seeking insights into American society in a fictionalized account of the assassination. His focus is not Kennedy but Oswald, the loner and misfit whose subsequent murder by Jack Ruby, two days after the shooting, sealed forever a crucial link to the truth behind the case. Making no claim to be anything other than "a work of imagination," as DeLillo terms it in his author's note, *Libra* invents characters and even deliberately departs from the factual record on occasion. DeLillo delves deeply into Oswald's thoughts and feelings as he moves through his life toward the moment when his path will intersect, fatally, with Kennedy's. DeLillo's objective is not the formulation of a new conspiracy theory but rather a meditation on the larger significance of an interweaving of seemingly unrelated events which will culminate in a national tragedy.

The format DeLillo chooses for his story consists of three narrative lines, one chronicling Oswald's life, another tracing the development of a convoluted plot against the president, formulated by rogue CIA agents, and the third describing the long, obsessive investigation of the case by Nicholas Branch, a retired CIA agent assigned to write a secret report on the assassination for the agency. Although the most predictable approach would have been to use Branch as a framing device, with the rest of the story growing out of his discoveries, DeLillo uses him instead as a jumping-off point, a lone representative of all conspiracy theorists and of the American people as well, shut in his tiny room awash in a sea of fragmented information, minutiae, and half-truths. Branch provides the book's overview, its sense of historical perspective, as well as its follow-up on the lives of those involved in the conspiracy, most of whom have since died under questionable circumstances. Branch's despair at the volumes of often-conflicting information he has accumulated echoes the frustration of a nation stunned and disillusioned by the clouded facts surrounding a key moment in its history.

The book's two remaining narrative lines are told from multiple points of view. The development of the assassination plot, in particular, shifts from character to character as it grows and twists toward its bloody conclusion. The climate that gives rise to the conspiracy is the mood of anger and disappointment among those CIA agents most directly involved in the disastrous Bay of Pigs invasion, Kennedy's failed attempt to overthrow Fidel Castro. The conspiracy is not sanctioned by the CIA as a whole but is instead the plan of several agents working independently on a scheme to override what they view as Kennedy's new, conciliatory attitude toward the Cuban leader.

In its initial phase, the plan calls for an assassination attempt which will fail. As devised by Walter "Win" Everett, Jr., a disgraced agent relegated to teaching in a Texas women's college, the plot turns on the idea not of killing Kennedy but of laying a trail of evidence which will focus blame for an unsuccessful attempt on Castro, thus leading to a new hard line against the Cuban Communist regime. Everett devises an imaginary assassin whose trail will lead to Castro's door—a shadowy figure who becomes redundant when the conspirators discover Lee Harvey Oswald, a man who could be their fictional assassin come to life. Everett's plan is given a deadly twist, however, by T. J. Mackey, a freewheeling, maverick agent with ties to anti-Castro Cuban refugees, who decides that an attempt is not enough—Kennedy must die in the shooting.

It is *Libra*'s third narrative line that forms the heart of DeLillo's story. In his masterful reconstruction of Oswald's life he creates a complex and troubling portrait of a lifelong misfit that has a startling ring of truth, despite its fictional underpinnings. DeLillo's psychological depiction of Oswald incorporates the odd, disjointed facts that are actually known about his life—his military service, his defection to the Soviet Union and subsequent return with a Russian wife, his attempt on the life of General Edwin Walker—and provides a framework for them within the larger context of Oswald as a troubled man seeking a place in history to compensate for the place he has not won in society. The book's title is a reference to Oswald's astrological sign, which is symbolized by a scale—a fact which leads one of the characters to describe him as a personality suspended in a delicate balance, one which could tip either way.

Oswald's portion of the story is told primarily from three points of view: his own, his mother's, and his wife Marina's. As a boy, he lives with his thrice-married mother, Marguerite, in a series of shabby apartments. With few friends of his own, he is bullied by other boys and begins to withdraw, causing a social worker to report that "he feels almost as if there is a veil between him and other people through which they cannot reach him, but he prefers this veil to remain intact." As a teenager, he discovers Marxism and embraces it with all the exuberance of youth and the special fervor of an outsider who has at last found a means of turning his separateness into a badge of superiority.

Oswald enlists in the United States Marine Corps, spends time in a brutal military prison, and, following his discharge, defects to the Soviet Union. Convinced that here at last he will find acceptance and admiration, he is devastated to find himself still an outsider. Returning to the United States with his Russian wife and baby daughter, he is questioned by intelligence officials and begins a string of low-paying jobs until he is at last recruited by both the CIA and the Federal Bureau of Investigation (FBI) as an informer. While living in New Orleans, he reencounters David Ferrie, a pilot and gun dealer on the fringes of the intelligence community whom he had known as a teenager. It will be Ferrie who first obliquely suggests to him the possibility of assassinating the president.

For DeLillo, Oswald is the enigma, the blank page, at the center of the Kennedy assassination, and he proceeds to fill in that page with a blending of fact and fiction that brings the figure of Lee Harvey Oswald to life. Yet DeLillo does not stop with the physical details and circumstances of Oswald's life; he goes on to offer a compelling, speculative look inside the man's mind as well. It is here that the book's fictional account takes on a particularly chilling tone of authenticity. Through Oswald's inner ramblings and secret thoughts, his growing delusions of grandeur and paranoia, the reader sees his progress toward becoming a real-life version of the imaginary assassin created by Win Everett and his fellow conspirators. In the book's latter chapters, Oswald sees himself more and more as a key figure in history, drawing comparisons between himself and Kennedy, searching for hidden messages in the pages of left-wing journals and pamphlets, and finally coming to believe that everything around him is in some way connected to what he sees as his special purpose on earth.

What makes this portrait so convincing is the shock of recognition it inspires. There are subtle connections and similarities between the Oswald of *Libra* and several other infamous figures in the late twentieth century—among them John Hinckley, Ronald Reagan's would-be assassin; Arthur Bremer, who wounded Alabama governor George Wallace; and Mark David Chapman, the man who shot John Lennon. Like all three of these men, DeLillo's Oswald is an isolated and increasingly disturbed misfit. With Hinckley, he shares a conviction that an act of political violence will win for him importance and respect, while the diary he keeps and his earlier attempt on the life of General Walker link him with Bremer, whose own diary revealed alternate plans to assassinate several political figures rather than a specific hatred of Wallace. Oswald's growing sense of identification with Kennedy mirrors Chapman's obsession with Lennon, and his reflection near the end of the book—"He thought the only end to isolation was to reach the point where he was no longer separated from the true struggles that went on around him. The name we give this point is history"—echoes Chapman's unsettling comment on the Beatles, "They changed history . . . and I changed them." In an era that has been marked by the tragic actions of several disturbed loners, DeLillo's Oswald comes, finally, to represent them all.

DeLillo also expertly develops his story's supporting players. The CIA agents and hangers-on emerge vividly to play their parts in history: Win Everett, a devoted husband and father seeking a means of retaking Cuba and regaining his importance within the agency at the same time; T. J. Mackey, a renegade agent, running his own operations outside the agency's dictates and far more ruthless than Everett in his objectives; David Ferrie, a bald pilot grounded for his dalliances with young men, a fringe player never aware of the full scope of the plot. The two most important women in Oswald's life are sketched in with similar clarity: Marguerite Oswald, an outspoken woman rambling on defensively in an effort to make sense of her son's action, and Marina, the confused, unhappy wife watching the quiet young man she married disappear into a haggard, abusive killer. Also sharply portrayed is Jack Ruby, the seedy nightclub owner whose motives for murdering Oswald are a mixture of genuine grief and his quest for a much-needed loan from the Mafia, promised to him if Oswald is silenced. DeLillo has a keen ear for dialogue, and the exaggerations and heightened reality of his characters' speech patterns are a key factor in the reader's understanding of them as individuals.

Libra builds inexorably toward that day in Dallas when Oswald does indeed take his place in history, and DeLillo's description of the assassination itself is exceptionally powerful. Told from multiple points of view by Oswald, the CIA's back-up assassins (one of whose shots actually kills Kennedy), numerous bystanders, a motorcycle policeman, a secret service agent, and John Connally's wife, Nellie, these passages capture the full horror and confusion of those moments which have remained frozen in the nation's collective memory.

DeLillo is searching in *Libra* not for the truth connecting the mass of physical evidence surrounding the Kennedy assassination but rather for the human truth which underlies the event. Abandoning a strict adherence to the facts of the case, he explores instead the human elements that come into play in the realms of power, politics, social alienation, clandestine operations, and political murder. What emerges from his efforts is, as he states in his author's note, "a way of thinking about the assassination without being constrained by half-facts or overwhelmed by possibilities, by the tide of speculation that widens with the years."

Janet E. Lorenz

Sources for Further Study

Booklist. LXXXIV, June 1, 1988, p. 1625.
Chicago Tribune. July 31, 1988, XIV, p. 1.
Gentleman's Quarterly. LVIII, August, 1988, p. 111.
Kirkus Reviews. LVI, June 15, 1988, p. 843.
Library Journal. CXIII, July, 1988, p. 91.
Los Angeles Times Book Review. July 31, 1988, p. 3.
Maclean's. CI, August 29, 1988, p. 50.
The New York Review of Books. XXXV, August 18, 1988, p. 6.
The New York Times Book Review. XCIII, July 24, 1988, p. 1.
Newsweek. CXII, August 15, 1988, p. 59.
Publishers Weekly. CCXXXIV, July 1, 1988, p. 66.
Time. CXXXII, August 1, 1988, p. 65.